THE ENCYCLOPEDIA OF

INTERNATIONAL ORGANIZED CRIME

THE ENCYCLOPEDIA OF
INTERNATIONAL ORGANIZED CRIME

Carlo DeVito

☑®
Facts On File, Inc.

The Encyclopedia of International Organized Crime

Copyright © 2005 by Carlo DeVito

Facts On File, Inc.
132 West 31st Street
New York NY 10001

Library of Congress Cataloging-in-Publication Data

DeVito, Carlo.
The encyclopedia of international organized crime / Carlo DeVito.
p. cm.
ISBN 0-8160-4848-7 (HC : alk. paper)
1. Organized crime—Encyclopedias. 2. Transnational crime—Encyclopedias. 3. Gangs—Encyclopedias.
4. Criminals—Biography. I. Title.
HV6441.D48 2004
364.1'06'03—dc22   2003024724

Special thanks to Gary Francoeur and David Amoruso
And to Dominique, Dawson, and Dylan DeVito

—————————————————————

Contents

Foreword

As a reporter, columnist, and author who has written extensively about organized crime for more than three decades, my primary beat has been what is referred to by the Federal Bureau of Investigation (FBI) as "traditional organized crime." In official court documents, the FBI identifies the organization as La Cosa Nostra (LCN). Most Americans know it as the Mafia—the long-entrenched network of Italian-American criminals that has been personified in recent years on television in the award-winning HBO series, *The Sopranos,* and in movie classics such as *The Godfather* and *Goodfellas.*

In New York, where I have been based throughout my career, and elsewhere, I have also reported about other ethnic organized crime groups, including some that have worked hand in glove with the mob. These include gangsters whose lineage was Russian, Asian, Irish, Cuban, and African American. I have also written about Colombian, Mexican, and Dominican drug dealers, as well as other ethnic gangs with no alliances with the Mafia, such as the Jamaican Posse and the BTK, a violent Vietnamese gang.

In 1997, I traveled to Hong Kong and interviewed a "semi-retired" 53-year-old member of one of 15 triad societies based in the former British colony that was returned to China the following year. The veteran gangster described how he drank wine mixed with blood of chickens whose necks were broken during a four-hour-long induction ceremony four decades earlier, when he was 14. I learned that triad rules and structures were similar to those of the LCN. The boss, called a dragon head, was a "438." The number-two man, the mob equivalent of an underboss, was an incense master, or 443. The lowest inducted member, a blue lantern, or 49, is the equivalent of a mob soldier.

Five years earlier, the *New York Daily News* sent me to Palermo, Sicily, to cover the escalating violence by the Sicilian Mafia, which included the executions of fierce anti-Mafia prosecutors Giovanni Falcone and Pietro Borsellino. While there, I reported and wrote about then-fugitive Mafia boss of Corleone, Salvatore Riina, who was later captured and convicted of masterminding the bombing deaths of both men, and about Rosario Mule, the Mafia boss of Camporeale, a tiny town about six miles from Palermo from which my maternal grandparents emigrated 100 years ago.

But as this book reveals, during my career I have barely scratched the surface of organized crime activity throughout the world. In *The Encyclopedia of International Organized Crime,* you will learn about a variety of players, from Terry Adams—the John Gotti of London—who heads the Clerkenwell Crime Syndicate in the United Kingdom, to the Almighty Latin King Nation, a loosely connected network of Hispanic gangsters that began as a gang of Puerto Rican hoodlums in Chicago and now has chapters in Arizona, California, Connecticut, Florida, Ohio, Massachusetts, Michigan, Minnesota, New York, Puerto Rico, Texas, and Wisconsin. You will discover that the Heaven and Earth Society, a patriotic organization that began in Fujian Province in the 17th century evolved to form the original triad societies and that Chinese, Japanese, Russian, and Vietnamese organized gangs operate in Australia.

In this tome the author describes how Neapolitan women Maria Licciardi and Rosetta "Ice Eyes" Cutolo came to lead powerful Camorra families in Italy and informs you about the Bandidos, a Houston motorcycle gang that formed in 1966 and now has chapters in Louisiana, Mississippi, Arkansas, New Mexico, Washington, Colorado, and South

Dakota. Along the way, you'll also learn about terrorist groups in India and Pakistan, the 18th Street Gang in Los Angeles, and Jaime Herrera-Nevares, the patriarch of a huge criminal syndicate that ran a "farm-to-the-arm" heroin operation from Durango, Mexico, to Chicago, as well as about the Inagawa-kai, reputedly the largest gang in Tokyo, with more than 8,000 gang members.

As you might expect, there is much infighting and violence among many of the crime groups. But as author Carlo DeVito points out, organized crime groups often enjoy working relationships with others to their mutual benefit. In New York, for example, former Harlem heroin kingpin Leroy Barnes bought his junk from suppliers with the Lucchese family, while gangsters from the former Soviet Union had working relations with the Genovese crime family. In Montreal, the Hells Angels, the Mafia, and the Irish West End Gang formed a "consortium" to regulate the drug trade in their city.

DeVito has included sections on the two United States federal investigative agencies that are at the forefront of the battle against organized crime, the FBI and the Drug Enforcement Administration (DEA). He also profiles several American and Sicilian Mafia families, many North American motorcycle gangs, and several notorious prison gangs, including the Aryan Brotherhood and the Nazi Low Riders—white racist organizations that got their start in California prisons—and the Ñeta—a Hispanic prison gang that began in the Río Piedras prison in Puerto Rico. He also has a section on the *vory v zakone,* or "thieves in law," a Russian organized group with roots in the prison system of the former Soviet Union.

It is impossible to learn everything there is to know about all facets of organized crime in this first crime book by DeVito, but *The Encyclopedia of International Organized Crime* will give you a wealth of knowledge about a wide range of diverse, dangerous organized criminal groups as well as the different schemes and scams they use to finance their way in their never-ending battles with the various law enforcement agencies that challenge them around the world.

—Mafia expert Jerry Capeci writes a weekly column about organized crime for the *New York Sun* that also appears online at http://www.ganglandnews. com. He is author of *The Complete Idiot's Guide to the Mafia* and *Wiseguys Say the Darndest Things.* He has coauthored three books on the mob: *Murder Machine, Mob Star: The Story of John Gotti,* and *Gotti: Rise & Fall.*

Introduction

To many people today, especially in the United States, the Mafia is synonymous with organized crime. The Mafia frequently has been glorified, lionized, and otherwise mythologized through legions of books, movies, documentaries and television series. To many readers of popular crime novels and nonfiction, a gangland of other types of criminals certainly does not exist.

A number of converging forces have altered the criminal landscape tremendously in the United States and around the world. Certainly one of them has been the U.S. government. With crackdowns by the DEA, the FBI, and the U.S. attorney general's office, by way of the RICO statutes, the traditional Mafia, as it is known, has been severely crippled. Many of the top capos are either in jail or facing sentencing.

Another problem is the makeup of new immigrants. In the past, the Mafia usually drew heavily on the waves of poor and uneducated Italian immigrants, some of whom could be recruited to fill its ranks. It also drew on poor second-generation families of other ethnic backgrounds. However, very few second- and third-generation descendants of immigrants seek membership in nefarious organizations. Between upwardly mobile second- and third-generation Italian families and the dwindling number of immigrants upon which the Mafia traditionally counted for recruitment, the Mafia has had problems filling its ranks.

Within the criminal world, the most powerful of new immigrants are the Asians and Russians. These criminals are now vying for power in our nation's cities. The Chinese have the triads and the tongs, the Japanese have the notorious Yakuza, and the Russians have the Russian Mafiya. Other groups include South and Central Americans and Caribbeans. These groups are ruthless and are pressing the Mafia for territory and money. Crime is not what it used to be.

However, these are not new organizations. These are groups that have been terrorizing law-abiding citizens in other countries around the world. Southeast Asia has the triads. China, Hong Kong, and Taiwan have the tong. Japan has the Yakuza. The Caribbean has the Jamaican posse groups. Russia has its Mafiya. The Latin Americans have the cartels. These organizations, bands of ruthless outlaws, are at work all around the world.

What is meant by organized crime? The Interpol definition, adopted by the General Assembly of the member countries of Interpol in 1998, is as follows:

Any enterprise or group of persons engaged in a continuing illegal activity which has as its primary purpose the generation of profits irrespective of national boundaries. The OC Branch is dealing with identified criminal organizations. It centralizes, evaluates and analyses information on internationally operating criminal organizations and their activities. It conducts projects of special interest.

The biggest criminal organizations include the triads, the tongs, the Yakuza, Russian organized groups from the territory of the former Soviet Union, the Italian Mafia, the South American cartels, outlaw motorcycle gangs, and so on. Their main criminal activities are racketeering, fraud, car theft, robbery, armed assault, drug dealing, trafficking in weapons and radioactive material, trafficking in human beings and exploitation through prostitution, alien smuggling, smuggling of precious and antique goods, extortion for protection money, gambling, embezzling from industries and financial institutions up to infiltration and control of private and commercial banks, and controlling of black markets.

Entries A-Z

ACUNA, Arturo   *See* OPERATION FOXHUNT.

ADAMS, Patrick

Patrick Adams is possibly one of the most violent organized-crime figures in British organized-crime history. He was particularly adept at using high speed motorcycles in his very dramatic and highly creative mob hits.

Adams, on almost all business dealings, defers to the family's ring leader, Terry Adams; however, Adams has been known to take things into his own hands, such as his dealings with Mad Frankie Frazier and his son, David. The 1991 shooting of Mad Frankie Frazier shortly after his release from prison was seen as Adams's handiwork. While Frazier survived the assassination attempt, he has refused to discuss the incident openly with the press. According to http://geocities.com/OrganizedCrimeSyndicates, "Patrick later turned his knife on Frazier's son David after a drug deal soured. This run-in left David holding a portion of his ear as a warning not to cross the Adamses again. Many other criminals have not been so lucky as the Adamses are suspected of ordering at least 25 murders over a 3 year period."

See also: ADAMS, TERRY; ADAMS, TOMMY; CLERKEN-WELL CRIME SYNDICATE.

ADAMS, Terry

According to http://geocities.com/OrganizedCrime Syndicates, "The brains behind the Clerkenwell Crime Syndicate, a vast criminal conspiracy, is 48-year-old Terry Adams, a man so secretive" that public photos of him are extremely scarce. Terry Adams is easily the most powerful and charismatic British gangster since the Kray twins. He is athletically built, with silver, shoulder-length hair, and stands an impressive 6′1″.

Terry Adams is the undisputed leader of the Clerkenwell Crime Syndicate, known simply as The Firm. Former associates and surviving ex-employees have described him as a Machiavellian ruler who exercises control through both cunning and violent force if necessary to establish his unquestioned authority. The British press has noted his love of antiques, fine drink, and fancy cars (his favorites being custom-built Cadillacs and Bentleys).

Adams and his family shun the press as much as possible. Photo ops are strictly forbidden, and even mention in text is said to be abhorrent to the elusive prince of the British underworld. Even legendary Brit gangsters—especially one of the most famous, Mad Frankie Frazier, long known for his willingness to expound on any subject—refuses to discuss The Firm with the press. Frazier suffered a gunshot wound to the head after being released from jail, and his son David lost a piece of his ear after some dealings with the Adamses allegedly ran afoul. According to http://geocities.com/OrganizedCrimeSyndicates, "Terry Adams is thought of as a star by his minions, who all stand as he enters a room. The immaculately attired hood favors long black coats and white frilly shirts. In the London underworld, he is the closest thing to John Gotti."

See also: ADAMS, PATRICK; ADAMS, TOMMY; CLERKENWELL CRIME SYNDICATE.

ADAMS, Tommy

Tommy Adams is alleged to be the financier for the Clerkenwell Crime Syndicate run by his brother Terry Adams. He is also the most well known of the three Adams brothers. In 1985, Tommy, a favorite Fleet Street mention, survived a highly publicized trial, being acquitted of laundering the proceeds of a gold-bullion heist.

According to http://geocities.com/OrganizedCrime Syndicates, "Tommy is presently serving a 7 year jail term for masterminding a large hash-smuggling ring. Tommy secured an $80 million credit line with Columbian cartels and made important contacts with the yardie gangs through an underling. Tommy is 3 years into his sentence and is sure to return to the gang's fold upon his release."

See also: ADAMS, PATRICK; ADAMS, TERRY; CLERKENWELL CRIME SYNDICATE.

AGCA, Mehmet Ali

Mehmet Ali Agca is a Turkish terrorist who shot Pope John Paul II on May 13, 1981, in an assassination attempt. Originally Agca claimed to be a member of the Popular Front for the Liberation of Palestine and later confessed to being a part of a Bulgarian/KGB plot to kill the pope due to his support of Poland's Solidarity movement. Both were found to be untrue.

It has since been discovered that in 1981, a contract was issued by one of Turkish godfather Abuzer Ugurlu's "chief lieutenants on the life of Pope John Paul II. Ugurlu reportedly authorized the payment of 1.7 million U.S. dollars for the murder of the pontiff," reported http://geocities.com/Organized CrimeSyndicates. Agca was sentenced to life imprisonment in Italy but was pardoned by president Carlo Azeglio Ciampi in June 2000.

Agca returned to Turkey, where he was imprisoned for the murder of a newspaper editor. In 1979 Mehmet murdered the chief editor of the *Milliyet*, Abdi Ipekci. When Agca was arrested, the police discovered a false passport in the name of Mehmet Oezbey that belonged to Abdullah Catli. On May 13, 1981, insiders mentioned Abdullah Catli in connection with the assault against the pope. He is currently in a Turkish prison.

See also: BASAK, HUSEYIN; CATLI, ABDULLAH; DONMEZ, OSMAN; KILIC, DUNDAR; OZBIZERDIK, ONUR; UGURLU, ABUZER.

AGLIERI, Pietro (a.k.a. U Signurinu; the Little Gentleman)

With the capture of Corleone clan chieftain Giovanni Brusca, Pietro Aglieri ascended to the top of one of Italy's most feared and noted crime clans. His taking control of the reins of power capped an unusually fast climb to the top of Italian organized crime. Aglieri had made a name for himself by killing Salvatore Riina, one of Italy's most notorious crime figures and a huge rival of the Corleone clan. This accomplishment catapulted Aglieri's name to the top of the ranks.

"Thirty six years old at the time of his coronation, Aglieri was three years younger than his predecessor," wrote http://geocities.com/OrganizedCrime Syndicates. "In spite of his youth and misleading nickname (the Little Gentleman), Aglieri was every bit as violent as the rest of the Corleone bosses before him. Aglieri's reign proved to be one of the shortest on record as Italian authorities captured him at a farmhouse outside of Palermo in June of 1997."

AGRON, Evsei (a.k.a. the Little Don)

Evsei Agron arrived at Kennedy Airport in the United States on October 8, 1975, one of 5,200 Soviet Jews who fled Russia and came to the United States that year. Many of these Jewish immigrants were tough Russian gangsters who were deported by the KGB. When he arrived, Agron had already served seven years in a Russian work camp for murder. When released from that prison, he left as a full-fledged member of the vor brotherhood (sort of the Russian version of the Italian "made guy"). Before coming to the United States. Agron already had some experience with the free Western world. When he first left Russia in 1971, he went to Hamburg, Germany, where he ran a huge prostitution and gambling operation. In Brighton Beach, New York, the people knew who he was when he arrived: His reputation and his being part of the vor brotherhood made Agron the most feared man in Brighton Beach, and if there were any nonbelievers, he intended to change their minds.

Agron did not attract much attention at first. He had an office inside the El Caribe Country Club, from which he ran a ruthless organization that by 1980 extorted from the Russian community tens of thousands of dollars a week. Agron's group bled money from all Russians, from doctors and lawyers to store owners. One time Agron threatened to kill a Russian's daughter on her wedding day if her father did not pay $15,000 immediately. People always paid; they knew what would happen if they refused—one of Agron's henchmen would pay them a visit, and Agron's men had the same reputation as Agron himself.

Two, the Nayfeld brothers, were gangsters who came from Gomel, Russia. One brother, Benjamin, was a former member of the Russian Olympic weight-lifting team. One time he killed a Jewish man in the presence of a crowd of law-abiding Russians in a parking lot in Brighton Beach: Benjamin grabbed him with one hand, lifted him up in the air, and stabbed a knife through his heart with the other. The victim was said to have insulted Benjamin's girlfriend. At the trial 18 people testified that Benjamin was correct when he said he had been attacked by the victim; he walked out a free man. His brother, Boris, was even more terrifying. Many Russians say that his eyes are completely white, a sign that he has no soul and is possessed by the devil.

These were just two of Agron's employees, and of these three the Russians still hated Agron the most. Agron was known to carry an electric cattleprod with which to torture his victims. In contrast with most Russian vor members, Agron found being feared more important than being respected.

One night in 1980 Agron was walking through Coney Island when someone shot him in the stomach. He was brought to Coney Island Hospital where he was guarded by an ex-policeman who had been hired by the Genovese family, because by the 1980s Agron was connected to them. When the police asked Agron if he knew who shot him, he answered, "Yes." The cop then asked him to identify the perpetrator so that they could arrest the accused. Agron answered, "No, I'll take care of it."

Many people wanted to see Agron dead, people he had ripped off in the past or maybe someone in his organization who was ambitious. Whatever the reason and whoever was behind the hit, Agron resumed

his life as if nothing had happened. His men went back to the streets and ran rampant—truck hijacking became a favorite criminal activity. Agron even bought himself a Russian newspaper company to provide the Brighton Beach Russians with the daily news. Now they would read what he wanted them to read. By this time Agron was reaching the top of his game, his position among his group of ruthless Russian mobsters was unquestioned, and he had even expanded to six other major U.S. cities.

Agron was supported by two very powerful allies: the Genovese family and Ronald Greenwald, a Jewish rabbi who was active in politics. In return for their friendship, the Italians received Russian manpower and expanded their operation to the Russian neighborhoods. The friendship with the Italians was very important for Agron: The Italians had an enormous army of soldiers and the political connections to get criminals out of trouble. But even though they made much money together, there was friction between the Russian gangsters and the Italian mobsters. Most of the Italians lived modestly and would try not to attract attention, while the Russians on the other hand loved the attention and loved to show their wealth. The Russians did not have the same codes as the Italians: Italians do not kill civilians, not even the family members of mobsters who have erred against the mob, but the Russians do not have this rule.

By the mid-1980s Agron was doing bigger heists and making more money than ever before, but even with Agron as a sort of godfather, the Russian groups in his neighborhood were still running wild and out of control. Despite his power in Brighton Beach, Agron still could be killed at any moment because there was just no structure and control. In January 1984 while he was walking toward his front door, Agron was shot again. A hit man shot him twice, once in the face and once in the neck, both from close range. Agron was brought to Coney Island Hospital for a second time and survived, but his face would be damaged for the rest of his lifetime, and it would look as if he was smiling a perpetual, weird grin. Again he told the police that he would handle business himself.

Agron had a few ideas about who might be behind the attack. The prime suspect was Boris Goldberg, an Israeli ex-army officer from Russia. Goldberg ran a group of criminals along with David "Napoleon" Shuster, a criminal mastermind. The Goldberg group had enormous firepower stashed away safely. Among the weapons were guns with silencers, boxes of grenades, and plastic explosives with detonators. The group sold cocaine to street dealers. Goldberg was married to the daughter of Bob Guccione, the owner of *Penthouse* magazine.

Because of their criminal interests it was inevitable that Agron and Goldberg would meet. One of the things that had caused friction between the two had been extortion territories. They had several meetings discussing which area would belong to whom, but every time things went wrong. After the botched hit on Agron in May 1984, Agron himself called Goldberg for a sitdown at Agron's country club. When Goldberg and a trusted soldier arrived, they were welcomed by 50 silent, heavily armed Russians who sat at a round table. After a heated discussion in which Agron asked Goldberg if he was behind the hit, things began to get out of hand. Agron did not believe Goldberg and wanted to kill him, Goldberg then said: "If you want trouble, . . . I'm ready." Agron told one of his henchmen to look outside and see if Goldberg was bluffing; he wasn't. The parking lot in front of the country club was filled with armed men running around. Agron decided to leave it at that, and the sitdown ended without bloodshed. Agron believed that he had located his attacker and felt safe. The perpetrator now knew not to try again. Agron forgot, however, that Goldberg was not the only enemy who wanted him dead.

On May 4, 1985, Agron was preparing himself to go out on the town and relax in a Turkish bathhouse in Manhattan, and while doing so, Agron felt he could also discuss some business. He dressed and stepped outside his apartment. At 8:35 in the morning Agron pressed the elevator button. Out of nowhere, a man wearing sunglasses stepped out of the shadows and shot Agron in the head twice close range. Agron fell to the floor and, at the age of 53, "the Little Don" died. Agron was probably the first Russian godfather who set up an organization in the United States. He would not be the last.

See also: GENOVESE CRIME FAMILY; RUSSIAN MAFIYA.

Reference

David Amoruso. "Evsei Agron." Gangsters Incorporated. Available online. URL: http://gangstersinc.tripod.com/ Agron.html. Downloaded on July 19, 2004.

—*D.A.*

AGUECI, Alberto G. and Vito

Alberto G. "the Baker" Agueci and Vito Agueci were Canadian mobsters who operated in upstate New York under the auspices of vicious Buffalo crime boss Stefano Magaddino. The two were arrested in July 1961 on a narcotics violation. They had worked for Magaddino with the understanding that he would provide protection against other mobsters and help in dealing with police. After the arrest, Magaddino refused to help the Agueci brothers, forcing Alberto's wife to sell the family's house to pay bills and bail bonds.

After his release from prison, Alberto Agueci went to Magaddino's house and threatened to kill him. Magaddino later sent two enforcers after Agueci to teach him and those watching a lesson. Agueci's mutilated body was found in November of that same year.

"While [he was] still alive, over thirty pounds of flesh had been cut from his body, his jaw broken, and half his teeth kicked or knocked out," wrote Thomas L. Jones in *The Dying of the Light: The Joseph Valachi Story*. "A blowtorch had been applied to his face, blinding him, and he had been tied to a tree with barbed wire before his genitals had been hacked off and stuffed into his mouth."

While Vito Agueci had sworn revenge on Magaddino, he was convicted and was sentenced to many years in prison where he befriended, for a short period, an American mobster named Joseph Valachi.

See also: BARGARELLA, LEOLUCA; BRUSCA, GIOVANNI; CORLEONE CLAN; FALCONE, GIOVANNI; PALAZZOLO, GIUSEPPE; PROVENZANO, BERNARDO; RIINA, SALVATORE; SPERA, BENEDETTO.

References

http://geocities.com/OrganizedCrimeSyndicates.
Thomas L. Jones. "The Dying of the Light: The Joseph Valachi Story." 2003 Courtroom Television Network LLC. Available online. URL: http://www.CrimeLibrary. com. Downloaded on July 30, 2004.

AIUPPA, Joseph (a.k.a. Joey Doves)

Joseph Aiuppa was connected to John Dillinger and the Alvin Karpis gangs in the 1930s. He was also a gunman in the Al Capone mob. He was associated with gambling activities and allegedly ran prostitution along the strip in Cicero, Illinois. He attended school until third grade. He was convicted in 1960 for failing to register as a dealer in gambling devices, receiving a sentence of one year and one day. He owned and/or operated several lounges or clubs in the Cicero area and was a partner in a company that built and distributed slot machines. He was known as an avid hunter and was arrested in 1962 for having approximately 500 doves in his possession on his return from a hunting trip to Kansas. The legal limit was 24 game birds. In 1971 he became a mob boss, and he was convicted in 1985 for skimming profits from Las Vegas casinos. He died in jail at age 89.

See also: ANDRIACCHI, JOSEPH; CARLISI, SAMUEL; DIFRONZO, JOHN; LAPIETRA, ANGELO; LOMBARDO, JOSEPH; MARCELLO, JAMES.

ALMIGHTY Latin King Nation (ALKN)

The Almighty Latin King Nation (ALKN) was created in Chicago during the 1940s in an attempt to overcome racism and prejudice. The founders wanted members to rise above the racism and to create an organization of "kings" equipped to fight off injustice and thereby better themselves and their communities. Ironically, most of its members were already incarcerated for serious offenses. Inevitably, the ALKN became one of Chicago's largest and most violent street gangs. All members had to have a Latin bloodline: Most members were Puerto Rican, but they soon extended membership to other ethnic groups (Spanish, Caribbean, Latvian, Italian, Portuguese, and South American). The Latin Kings membership remains mostly Hispanic.

In terms of symbolism and tattoos, the ALKN tend to use crowns. Many of the crowns used may be set with five jewels to represent Love, Respect, Sacrifice, Honor, and Obedience. On graffiti and tattoos, the crown may be accompanied by the initials *LK* and some form of inflammatory symbolism aimed at opposing gangs, for example, "pitch forks down" as an insult directed at the Folks alliance. Documents and graffiti may include a lion standing on its haunches and wearing a crown. Formal documents, such as the charter, may include a coat of arms containing two crowned lions flanking a crowned battle shield, emblazoned with a cross, as well as a variety of inscriptions. Although not common, lions have also been observed on tattoos.

A former Latin Kings gang member testifies about organized crime at a hearing in Trenton, New Jersey. (AP)

The Chicago Police Department estimates that more than 25,000 Latin King members reside in their city. The gang also has organized chapters in Arizona, California, Connecticut, Florida, Ohio, Massachusetts, Michigan, Minnesota, New York, Puerto Rico, Texas, and Wisconsin.

When compared to most street gangs, the Latin Kings are generally more structured and organized. The gang's rules are strictly enforced, and the gang has a written constitution. They have the all-for-one mentality with the motto "Once a King, Always a King." Those who break the rules are punished by their fellow gang members. These violations may be suspension from the gang, membership termination, physical assault, or death. This is one of the few gangs that accepts females. Members celebrate January 6 as "King's Holy Day" and the first week in March as "King's Week."

Reference

Know Gangs. "Almighty Latin King Nation." Available online. URL: http://www.knowgangs.com/gang_resources/latin_kings/alkn_001.htm. Downloaded on July 19, 2004.

AMEZCUA-CONTRERAS, Jesús

The Amezcua-Contreras brothers, operating out of Guadalajara, Mexico, are said to head a methamphetamine production and trafficking organization of global dimensions. Jesús Amezcua heads the operation with support from his brothers Adán and Luis.

ANDRIACCHI, Joseph (a.k.a. Joe the Builder)

Joseph "Joe the Builder" Andriacchi was a longtime lieutenant in the Chicago organized-crime syndicate known as the Outfit. An upper-echelon member, at 69 years of age, he is one of a triumvirate of current leaders who allegedly runs that organization, along with John "No Nose" DiFronzo and Joseph "Joey the Clown" Lombardo.

See also: AIUPPA, JOSEPH; CARLISI, SAMUEL; DIFRONZO, JOHN; LAPIETRA, ANGELO; LOMBARDO, JOSEPH.

ANSARI, Aftab

Aftab Ansari is an associate of Dawood Ibrahim. Ansari, a former resident of Lalapur in Varanasi, India, has worked with Pakistan-based terrorist groups to execute operations for Ibrahim. Ansari is credited with the attack on the United States Consulate in Kolkata. Ansari was in Delhi's Tihar jail, where he was being charged with a minimum of eight different criminal offenses, but he obtained bail and fled the country immediately.

While in jail, he met Asif Raza Khan, an explosives trafficker for the Student Islamic Movement of India, who has proven to be an excellent ally. In early 2001, Ansari and Khan began to work together, Khan providing Ansari with arms and strongmen in return for a piece of the profits from some kidnapping operations. Some of the profits eventually found their way to Mohammad Atta, one of the hijackers involved in the September 11, 2001, attack on the World Trade Center in New York City.

See also: BAKSH, NOOR; GOGA, IRFAN; IBRAHIM, DAWOOD; RAJAN, CHHOTA; SHAKEEL, CHHOTA; SINGH, SANJAY.

Reference

Praveen Swami. "Disappearing Act." *Frontline* 19, no. 3 (February 2, 2002). Available online. URL: http://www.flonnet.com/fl1903/19030300.htm. Accessed on November 24, 2004.

ARELLANO FÉLIX, Benjamín

Brother to Francisco and Ramón Arellano Félix, all of whom shared responsibilities in running the Tijuana Organization, based in Tijuana, Mexico, Benjamín Arellano Félix was indicted on May 2, 1989, in San Diego on charges of operating a continuing criminal enterprise that involved the importation and distribution of cocaine. Arellano Félix is frequently seen in Mexico, never having been arrested on these charges.

Francisco, Benjamín, and Ramón Arellano Félix, the three brothers who headed the Tijuana drug cartel based in Mexico. (AP)

The Tijuana cartel was among the most violent of the Mexican organizations and has been connected by Mexican officials to the violent death of Cardinal Juan Jesús Posadas-Ocampo, who was killed in the crossfire of rival drug gangs at the Guadalajara Airport in 1993. During 1994 this group was engaged in a turf battle over methamphetamine territory in San Diego. Twenty-six homicides were committed during one summer as rival groups battled over trafficking regions.

See also: ARELLANO FÉLIX, FRANCISCO; ARELLANO FÉLIX, RAMÓN; TIJUANA ORGANIZATION.

Reference

Thomas A. Constantine. "Drug Interdiction and Other Matters Related to the National Drug Control Policy." Hearing before the Subcommittee on Coast Guard and Maritime Transportation of the Committee on Transportation and Infrastructure, House of Representatives, 104th Congress, 2nd Session, September 12, 1996. Joint Hearing with Senate Caucus on International Narcotics Control. Washington, D.C.: U.S. Government Printing Office, 1997, 104–169.

ARELLANO FÉLIX, Francisco

Brother of Benjamín and Ramón Arellano Félix, all of whom shared responsibilities in heading up the Tijuana Organization, a drug cartel based in Tijuana, Mexico. Francisco Rafael Arellano Félix, his brother, was indicted in San Diego in 1980 for possession and conspiracy to possess cocaine. He has not been arrested.

See also: ARELLANO FÉLIX, BENJAMÍN; ARELLANO FÉLIX, RAMÓN; TIJUANA ORGANIZATION.

ARELLANO FÉLIX, Ramón

Brother to Benjamín and Francisco Arellano Félix, all of whom shared responsibilities in heading up the Tijuana Organization, a drug cartel based in Tijuana, Mexico.

See also: ARELLANO FÉLIX, BENJAMÍN; ARELLANO FÉLIX, FRANCISCO; TIJUANA ORGANIZATION.

ARYAN Brotherhood

Aryan Brotherhood originated in California's San Quentin Prison in the 1960s and has since spread to other prisons throughout the United States. Affiliated with the paramilitary hate group Aryan Nations, Aryan Brotherhood reportedly engages in extortion, drug operations, and violence in correctional facilities; many members bear the identifying tattoo of a swastika and the Nazi SS lightning bolt. Aryan Nations also publishes *The Way,* a newsletter for prisoners.

The 1987 inaugural issue of that publication described its purpose as being "to provide a good source of Bible study into the Israel Identity message and its related histories and politics for convicts, while also providing news and happenings of concern to our chained brothers and sisters."

BROTHERHOOD OF HATE

Aryan Brotherhood is not known to be as systematically organized as other prison gangs (such as the Bloods, Crips, or the Mexican Mafia), but its reputation for violence is well documented. In April 1997 John Stojetz, an Aryan Brotherhood leader at an Ohio prison, was convicted of murdering a 17-year-old black prisoner. In October 1994 Donald Riley, a member of the brotherhood, was sentenced to life in prison for the murder in Houston of a black marine who had recently returned from service in the Persian Gulf War. Moreover, of the eight inmates murdered by fellow prisoners at the Pelican Bay State Prison in California since 1996, six have been linked to an internal war within Aryan Brotherhood. A local prosecutor characterized the situation at the prison as a "reign of terror." In Pelican Bay's Security Housing Unit, there are reported to be as many as 50 inmates who are members of the group.

In the 1980s, Aryan Brotherhood members challenged a Missouri prison's ban on inmates receiving literature from Aryan Nations and similar groups. The courts upheld the ban.

The Missouri inmates were also members of a "Christian Identity" organization, the Church of Jesus Christ Christian. Members of the Identity movement claim that Anglo-Saxons, not Jews, are the biblical chosen people, that nonwhites are "mud people" on the level of animals, and that Jews are the "children of Satan."

Other racist groups have emerged from behind bars as well. One of the men charged with the 1998 murder of James Byrd Jr. (Byrd, an African American, had his throat cut and was dragged $2\frac{1}{2}$ miles by a pickup truck in a brutal Jasper, Texas, hate crime), reportedly has a Klan tattoo depicting the lynching of a black man and another that reads *C.K.A.,* which stands for

Confederate Knights of America. C.K.A. is a small white supremacist prison gang in Texas penitentiaries.

Like Aryan Brotherhood, the white supremacist gang Nazi Low Riders (NLR) originated inside the California prison system but also has active members beyond penitentiary walls. Serving a prison term appears to be a requirement for membership. The gang is controlled by the "seniors," all of whom have been NLR members for at least five years and are voted in by other seniors. Only seniors can induct new members, and they are responsible for educating the members they recruit. There is reason to believe that Aryan Brotherhood aligned itself with NLR in the late 1970s or early 1980s when the California Department of Corrections began to crack down on Aryan Brotherhood members; many of them ended up isolated from the rest of the prison population because of their gang ties. NLR remained a separate gang but helped promote Aryan Brotherhood's interests within the prison system.

Like Aryan Brotherhood, NLR rallies its members around standard racist propaganda and rhetoric that bolster "white pride" while blaming Jews, blacks, and other groups for most of the problems in America. Still, their activity is not limited to race baiting: NLR members reportedly seek to dominate a significant portion of the prison drug trade and other criminal activity within the white penitentiary population. Outside prisons, NLR members are involved in drug trafficking (especially methamphetamine, or speed) and have been responsible for a number of attacks on blacks.

ARYAN BROTHERHOOD AND *THE TURNER DIARIES*
HATE CRIME IN JASPER, TEXAS

The brutal and apparently racially motivated murder in Jasper, Texas, of James Byrd Jr., an African American, made headlines in June 1998.

Two of the three men charged with the murder claimed membership in the Aryan Brotherhood. During the drive on back country roads with Byrd's body chained to the back of their pickup truck, one of the suspects reportedly said, "We're starting *The Turner Diaries* early." *The Turner Diaries* is a self-published novel in which blacks and Jews are targeted for murder by white supremacists.

THE TURNER DIARIES

The Turner Diaries was written in 1978 by William Pierce, head of the National Alliance, one of the largest and most organized neo-Nazi groups in the United States.

The novel has become a Bible for right-wing extremists. It calls for the violent overthrow of the federal government and the systematic killing of Jews and nonwhites.

Pierce's book has reportedly inspired a number of people who were connected to vicious crimes, including Timothy McVeigh, who was convicted of bombing the Alfred P. Murrah Federal Building in Oklahoma City.

Reprinted by permission of the Anti-Defamation League.

ARYAN Nations

Headquartered near Hayden Lake, Idaho, Aryan Nations is a paramilitary hate group founded in the mid-1970s by Rev. Richard Girnt Butler, now 78 years old. It was formed around Butler's Church of Jesus Christ Christian, one of several hundred churches affiliated with Identity, a pseudo-theological hate movement. Identity doctrine maintains that Anglo-Saxons, not Jews, are the biblical chosen people, that nonwhites are "mud people" on the level of animals, and that Jews are "children of Satan." The group has a following of several hundred.

Aryan Nations members militantly advocate anti-Semitism and the establishment of a white racist state. Although primarily an Identity group, Butler's Aryan Nations reflects a Nazi-like philosophy; Butler himself has praised Hitler. During the 1980s, several of Butler's followers joined members of the neo-Nazi National Alliance and some KKK splinter groups to form a secret organization called the Silent Brotherhood, also known as the Order, which planned to overthrow the U.S. government. To raise money for their planned revolution, members of the Order engaged in a crime spree involving murder, counterfeiting, bank robberies, and armored car holdups. The group's activities ended with the death of its founder and leader, Robert J. Matthews, in a shootout with federal agents in December 1984, and the incarceration of many of its members.

As noted, anti-Semitism is a basic tenet of the Aryan Nations ideology. Dennis Hilligoss, the group's state coordinator in Oregon, recently said, "The Jew is like a destroying virus that attacks our racial body to destroy our Aryan culture and purity of our race."

Richard Butler, founder of the Aryan Nations sect, salutes with other members of the neo-Nazi group at an Aryan Nations rally. (AP)

In 1996, Aryan Nations published a "Declaration of Independence" for the Aryan race on its Web site. This declaration states that "all people are created equally subject to the eternal laws of nature. . . . [s]uch is now the necessity which impels them [Aryans] to alter their form of government. The history of the present Zionist Occupied Government of the United States of America is a history of repeated injuries and usurpations [sic], all having a direct object—the establishment of an absolute tyranny over these states; moreover throughout the entire world. . . . We, therefore, the representatives of the Aryan people, in council, appealing to the supreme God of our folk for the rectitude of intentions . . . solemnly publish and declare that the Aryan people in America, are, and of rights ought to be, a free and independent nation; that they are absolved from all allegiance to the United States of America, and that all political connection between them and the federal government thereof, is and ought to be, totally dissolved; and that as a free and independent nation they have full power to levy war, conclude peace, contract alliances, establish commerce, and perform all other acts which independent nations may of right do." The declaration concludes, "WE MUST SECURE THE EXISTENCE OF OUR PEOPLE AND A FUTURE FOR WHITE CHILDREN."

To aid in recruitment efforts, Aryan Nations hosts many racist activities during its summer festivals of hate at Hayden Lake, called the World Congress of Aryan Nations. At these conferences, Butler's organization has offered courses in urban terrorism and guerrilla warfare. Numerous extremists have addressed Aryan Nations gatherings. John Trochmann, a featured speaker at the 1990 congress, later became the leader of the Militia of Montana.

Since 1979, Aryan Nations has been engaged in prison outreach. This is an important aspect of the Aryan Nations' agenda, given that so many members of the Order and Aryan Nations are serving long prison sentences. Aryan Nations corresponds on an ongoing basis with prison inmates through letters and its periodicals. In 1987, Aryan Nations began to publish a "prison outreach newsletter" called *The Way,* which has facilitated recruitment and connections between Aryan nations and its offspring, Aryan Brotherhood, a network of prison gang members.

With Richard Butler's failing health and increasing inability to assert himself as a viable leader, the Aryan Nations' Ohio chapter appears to be positioning itself as a possible new headquarters for the group. On February 16, 1997, the Church of Jesus Christ Christian, an Aryan Nations "church" in New Vienna, Ohio, and the Knights of the Ku Klux Klan organized a rally at the state capital in Columbus, Ohio, to protest Black History Month. The existence of the group in the area was publicized in the wake of a shootout in nearby Wilmington, Ohio, a day prior to the rally between two brothers with ties to the Aryan Nations and police officers. The two may have been on their way to attend the rally. In late 1997, members held rallies in several Ohio cities and distributed antiblack and anti-Semitic fliers throughout northern Kentucky and southwestern Ohio. One of the fliers specifically targeted local rabbis and synagogues in Dayton, Ohio. In November, about 100 Aryan Nations supporters attended a fundraiser, hosted by the Ohio chapter.

In September 1997, Ohio's Aryan Nations leader, Harold Ray Redfeairn, was sentenced to six months in prison for carrying a concealed weapon.

FURTHER BACKGROUND

Butler has called Hayden Lake—an otherwise peaceful community—the "international headquarters of the White race." In the 1990s, though, Butler's organization suffered from internal difficulties, with several of its members leaving to form new groups. Carl Franklin, chief of staff for Aryan Nations, left in 1993 as a result of disagreements with Butler, who had previously named him his successor. Wayne Jones, security chief at the Aryan compound since the late 1980s, departed along with Franklin. They and two other members moved to western Montana to form their own white supremacist group called the Church of Jesus Christ Christian of Montana.

Following these departures, two more key members, Charles and Betty Tate, left to join Kirk Lyons, their son-in-law, a North Carolina–based lawyer who has defended right-wing extremists and has called himself an active sympathizer with their causes. In addition, a one-time Aryan Nations official, Floyd Cochran, has quit the group and renounced anti-Semitism and racism.

The growing leadership crisis became even more apparent at the annual Aryan Nations World Congress held at the group's compound on July 21–23, 1995. Attendance was approximately 125. About 25 of these were skinheads, including a contingent from a Utah-based skinhead gang called the Army of Israel. A fistfight broke out over charges that the wife of staff leader Tim Bishop was stealing money from the organization. The fracas contributed to Bishop's decision to resign his post and quit the compound for Kansas, where he once was Ku Klux Klan Grand Dragon. Adding to the leadership crisis is the apparent decline of Butler's health, coupled with his wife's death in December 1995.

Aryan Nations has been mentioned prominently in connection with one of the incidents that militia groups cite as evidence of a government conspiracy against citizenry—the 1992 Randy Weaver confrontation in Idaho. Weaver, a white separatist who had reportedly visited the Aryan Nations compound in the past, resisted an effort by federal agents to arrest him at his remote cabin for alleged weapons violations. Weaver's wife and son were killed during the ensuing standoff, along with a deputy U.S. marshal. During the siege, groups of Aryan Nations supporters, in addition to skinheads and other neo-Nazis, rallied in support of Weaver near his cabin.

The Aryan Nations has for years hosted youth gatherings in its rural Idaho compound. These events, usually held in April to coincide with Hitler's birthday, have attracted numerous skinheads.

The post of successor to Butler remains vacant. It is believed, however, that Louis Beam, who has been touted in the past as Butler's heir apparent, may step in to fill the void. Beam, who was David Duke's Texas KKK Grand Dragon in the 1970s, has served as the Aryan Nations' ambassador-at-large. He purchased property on the northern Idaho panhandle not far from the Aryan Nations headquarters at Hayden Lake. He attended a gun-rights rally whose sponsoring group, reports the *Spokane Spokesman-Review,* included militia members and sympathizers, and he attended a recent Aryan Nations World Congress. Moreover, he has written in support of "leaderless resistance," a strategy that calls for the formation of autonomous cells organized around ideology, not leaders, so as to be better able to carry out actions against perceived enemies with reduced risk of infiltration.

In addition, Beam delivered a rousing speech at the Aryan Nations 1995 World Congress that bolstered his standing as the number-one possibility to succeed Butler.

Reprinted by permission of the Anti-Defamation League.

Reference

Bill Morlin. "'Lone Wolves' Line Up." *Spokane Spokesman Review,* September 10, 2000.

ASKOLAR, Sunil

Sunil Askolar started out as a young gofer for famed alleged Indian Mafia dons Suresh Manchekar and Guru Satam, providing tea and cigarettes for the notorious dons. When the two dons ended their joint operations, he followed Manchekar. He quickly became a favorite and was passed up the line over more experienced men due to Manchekar's doting.

Askolar proved a solid henchman. His first assassination attempt of renowned mobster (and former mentor) Chintya Zaukar failed in 1992, but his second try the following year succeeded. This and a series of other successes in 1993 and 1994 earned him a reputation that moved him further up in the organization.

Askolar and other mobsters were forced underground by strong police crackdowns, but Askolar proved relentless. Askolar and a known associate, Bala Pawar, were killed on the Eastern Express Highway near Mulund on October 3, 1998.

See also: BAKSH, NOOR; GOGA, IRFAN; IBRAHIM, DAWOOD; MANCHEKAR, SURESH; RAJAN, CHHOTA; SATAM, GURU; SHAKEEL, CHHOTA; SINGH, SANJAY.

Reference

J. Dey. "Askolar: From Errand Boy to Thane Terror." *The Indian Express,* September 10, 2001.

ATOBRAH Gang

The Metropolitan Police's Serious and Organized Crime Group took one of London's biggest drugs rings, which was processing millions of pounds worth of cocaine into crack cocaine and was using an eight-year-old girl as a runner, out of circulation.

The last two defendants in the case, Delroy Abrahams and Sandra Lyndsey, were sentenced on January 7, 2003, to 12 years and five years respectively for their part in the conspiracy.

On November 1, 2002, Middlesex Guildhall Crown Court ordered that assets with a total value of £4,595,000, representing the profit believed to be gained by the gang members, be forfeited, that the ringleader Rebecca Atobrah, age 49, of 34 Mountbatten Close, Gypsy Hill, be sentenced to 18 years at Middlesex Guildhall Crown Court, and that an asset confiscation order to the value of £2,940,000 be made against her. She had pleaded guilty to conspiracy to supply crack cocaine on February 27, 2002.

Joseph Dartey, age 48, of 110b Chichelle Road, NW2, Atobrah's trusted lieutenant, pleaded guilty to the conspiracy on January 25, 2002, and was sentenced to 14 years and an asset confiscation order to the value of £500,000.

Their distributors: Patrick Reid, age 59, of 36 Greenwood Terrace, Harlesden NW10, who pleaded guilty to the conspiracy on April 23, 2002, was sentenced to 12 years and an asset confiscation order to the value of £500,000; and Michael Dewer, age 38, of West Hill, Wembley NW10, who pleaded guilty to the conspiracy on April 19, 2002, was sentenced to seven years and an asset confiscation order to the value of £85,000.

Emile Beckford, age 42, of 1a Whitefriars Avenue, Harrow, who pleaded guilty to the conspiracy on April 19, 2002, was sentenced to 10 years and an asset confiscation order to the value of £350,000; and Delroy Abrahams, age 36, of 170b Hannover Road, NW10, the gang's main dealer, pleaded guilty to the conspiracy on August 2, 2002, and was sentenced on January 7, 2002, to 12 years.

Delroy's girlfriend Sandra Lyndsey, 40, who was convicted of the conspiracy at Wood Green Crown Court on May 14, 2002, was sentenced on January 7, 2003, to five years.

Officers from SO7 Serious and Organised Crime Command arrested the suspects in a series of dawn raids across London on February 19, 2001. The arrests were the result of a long-term, covert operation, during which the suspects were under surveillance for 18 months.

The cocaine being distributed by the gang originated in Colombia, from where Atrobah arranged to have it brought into London via the United States and

Europe. The drugs were then passed to Abrahams for distribution in the northwest London area, particularly the Stonebridge Park Estate area of Harlesden.

When it reached London, the cocaine was processed into crack cocaine by Atobrah and Dartey. It was assessed that between 100 and 200 kilograms of cocaine, worth between £3 million and £6 million was distributed by the gang.

Atobrah converted much of her profits into vehicles and real estate in Ghana. Two brand-new Landrover Freelander vehicles and a large quantity of furniture were seized from a freight container in Ghana by detectives from SO7(2). All the property has been forfeited to the Ghanaian authorities.

At one stage Abrahams was using an eight-year-old girl to carry drugs and money between vehicles and houses.

Another of the co-conspirators, Solomon Nubour, 52, from Wealdstone, was sentenced to 12 years imprisonment in January 2001 for possession with intent to supply after he was arrested in possession of 2.5 kilograms of crack cocaine. He was Atobrah's trusted lieutenant until his arrest. An asset confiscation order to the value of £220,000 was also made against him.

Detective Chief Superintendent John Coles, head of the Met's Serious and Organised Crime Group (SO7), said: "In February last year, we successfully thwarted one of the biggest operations responsible for the large scale importation and distribution of crack cocaine in London. The operation has been especially successful because we have dismantled a crack distribution network from the top down. The sentences reflect this and are an important sign of the Met's commitment and determination to fight drug and firearms crime in London. We are unrelenting in our efforts to tackle those people who turn to crime and finance their illegal lifestyle by selling and importing drugs . . . By taking the main players out of the equation and putting them and their networks behind bars in these types of operations—we should see a real slow-down in terms of drug related crime. This operation has effectively cut off one of the capital's main crack cocaine supplies at its source."

Reference
Metropolitan Police (Scotland Yard). "Last Two Crack Gang Members Sentenced." *Bulletin 2003/0010.* January 8, 2003.

AUSTRALIA and Organized Crime
Most organized crime in Australia goes through Asian crime syndicates, mostly from more established Chinese gangs, Japanese gangs, and more recently Russian and Vietnamese gangs. Russian organized crime has attracted a great deal of media interest since the breakup of the Soviet Union. However, it seems there is little evidence that it has established any significant Australian presence so far.

CHINESE ORGANIZED CRIME IN AUSTRALIA
The attention of Australian law-enforcement agencies has focused on Chinese organized criminal activity in relation to a wide range of matters, including drug importation and distribution, illegal gambling, illegal prostitution, extortion, immigration malpractice, and money laundering. A relatively new area in which the Chinese are believed to be prominent is sophisticated credit-card fraud.

CHINESE DRUG-TRAFFICKING ACTIVITIES
In terms of what might be termed *mainstream* importation of heroin to meet Australian market demand, the principal source region (in terms of regularity of supply) is Southeast Asia. This statement is not intended to diminish the importance and threat from other regions; a significant amount of heroin is known to be sourced from Southwest Asia and the Middle East (even though seizure results indicate that these areas are responsible for 5 to 10 percent of overall supply, some enforcement authorities estimate that the real order of magnitude is much higher than this).

Australian law enforcement agencies believe that ethnic Chinese have been for many years, and still are, the major organizers of heroin imports into Australia. A 1988 media report cited the National Crime Authority's Chinese liaison officer as saying that the Chinese had been linked to every major seizure of heroin in the previous two financial years, totalling 63 kilograms, and that an estimated 96 percent of those cargoes seized had been triad-related.

TRIAD SOCIETIES AND CHINESE ORGANIZED CRIME
Within Australia, it is apparent that several triad societies do exist. As in Hong Kong, they provide a local pool of contacts for criminal ventures. Moreover, Australian residents who were triad members in Hong Kong or other foreign countries have immediate access to a range of colleagues overseas who may

be prepared to assist with criminal activities. There have been claims that certain triad groups in Australia have operated as organizations when establishing gambling and protection rackets, but it is also possible that the criminals concerned were using a triad's name for their own benefit and were acting outside the organization.

JAPANESE ORGANIZED CRIME IN AUSTRALIA

The upsurge in Yakuza violence comes at a time when all the gangsters' traditional lines of income have been falling. Loan-sharking, gambling, drugs, and brothels have all suffered steep falls in business. Speculative golf clubs and property developments, in which gangsters invested heavily, have collapsed. So have other money-laundering operations and investments in the stock market. Credit lines, once easy to obtain from banks and brokers, are no longer available. Furthermore after a series of scandals that linked top politicians and businessmen with Yakuza deals and helped bring down the Japanese government, companies have been trying to clean up and sever connections with the underworld.

There have been many warnings from police sources since at least the mid-1980s that Australia is, or risks becoming, a target for Yakuza groups. There have also, since the mid-1980s, been many claims of Yakuza activities in Australia. Although earlier visits were recorded, it was from about the mid-1980s that visits to Australia by alleged or admitted Yakuza members began to attract the attention of law-enforcement agencies and the media. It seems there are no accurate statistics on the number of Yakuza visitors, although a media report stated in 1994 that "the Australian police are now identifying known Yakuza members arriving in Australia at a rate of about 40 a year." This of course leaves open the number of visits by Yakuza members who were not identified as such. Since the Japanese crackdown on the Yakuza, many gang members are reported to have abandoned their distinctive dress, hairstyles, and mannerisms. This would make them more difficult to detect at the customs barrier.

Intelligence investigations reveal that there are presently business practices of coercion among local Japanese businessmen involved in the tourist industry, for example, tour operators conveying Japanese tourists to particular Japanese souvenir shops and, in turn, receiving commission. In fact some souvenir shop owners have approached the guides for their cooperation.

Several Japanese Yakuza members and gang leaders have been identified as having visited Australia. A number of Yakuza members were detected violating immigration laws, mainly through failing to declare their past criminal records when applying for visas. In cooperation with the Department of Immigration, Local Government and Ethnic Affairs, AFP officers "supervised" their departure from Australia.

On March 21, 1994, the *Australian Financial Review* reported, "Japan's organized crime syndicates are moving into Australian industry, and targeting legitimate companies as a crackdown on the gangs at home sends them looking for new opportunities abroad."

The Federal Police have recently opened five separate and substantial investigations into Yakuza investment and crime in Australia. Four of these involve attempts to either invest in or extort money from legitimate businesses and business people operating in Australia.

According to Australian government reports, there are indications that a Japanese syndicate is attempting to buy into an established Australian export industry to provide the conduit and cover for a major international drug transshipment route. Japanese gangs have also moved to enter the construction industry in Australia, including sophisticated efforts to extort information about bidding for particular projects.

The absence of a large, geographically concentrated, Japanese community in Australia makes it less easy for Yakuza to prey on Japanese in the way that Vietnamese and Chinese criminals have been said to prey on their (larger) respective ethnic communities in Australia. In addition, the close interest taken in Yakuza visitors by Australian law-enforcement agencies and the attendant media publicity may have discouraged visiting Yakuza from seeing Australia as anything more than a holiday destination.

VIETNAMESE GANGS IN AUSTRALIA

During the last dozen years there has been concern expressed about the growth in Australia of organized criminal activity by Vietnamese, with media attention focusing initially on "crime gangs." Media sources sighted increasingly heavily armed Vietnamese gang members who were moving into drugs and gambling, establishing links with Australian crime figures, and becoming involved in standover rackets in their own community. Police believed that most groups were mainly involved in crimes against their own community including murder, extortion, robbery, and petty drug dealing, with standover and extortion being the most common.

Vietnamese gangs are known to be highly mobile. Vietnamese gang members often travel interstate, perpetrating a variety of criminal acts in a short period of time. Such gangs utilize contacts in various U.S. cities which were made in refugee camps in Southeast Asia.

Vietnamese crime groups are generally considered to be less organized but more violent than ethnic Chinese organized crime groups. Some groups, such as the New York–based BTK (Born to Kill) Gang, are well structured with a definite leadership hierarchy. Other gangs are very unstructured and constantly changing in affiliation. Vietnamese nationals of Chinese descent (sometimes called "Viet-ching") often play an important role as members of Vietnamese gangs or as links between Vietnamese and Chinese crime groups.

Vietnamese crime groups are involved in a wide range of criminal activities. Witnesses have identified the major areas of Vietnamese-related criminal activity as extortion, fraud, auto theft, terrorism (political and criminal), high-technology theft, gambling, prostitution, narcotics trafficking, and home-invasion robberies.

During the past 10 years a number of Vietnamese criminal groups have come to law-enforcement attention in Australia. In some states these groups have come to play a prominent role in the organization of criminal activity. Their field of operations has included distributing heroin, organizing extortion and illegal gambling operations, and undertaking armed robberies of both businesses and private homes.

At the same time it has become apparent that a number of these Vietnamese groups are organizing heroin shipments, either independently of or in association with established Chinese heroin trafficking operations. An increasing amount of heroin coming to Australia appears to have been transshipped through Vietnam.

DRUG-TRAFFICKING ACTIVITIES

Vietnamese syndicates appear to be willing to become involved at all levels of the heroin trade from street dealing to importing. They are also willing to purchase from Chinese importers and to wholesale to other groups, such as Romanian and Lebanese dealers. The heroin that the Vietnamese import themselves is believed to come via Vietnam, which is apparently experiencing both increased production of opium (the drug from which heroin is produced) and increased transit of heroin produced elsewhere in the region. Vietnamese syndicates are thought to have been responsible for only a small amount—perhaps 5 percent—of the total heroin importation into Australia in recent years. Intelligence and seizures have indicated that the Vietnamese importers deal in smaller quantities than their Chinese counterparts, although this may be starting to change.

Until recently, the quantities seized indicated that each shipment by Vietnamese gangs was relatively small—under a kilogram. However, a shipment of 14 kilograms of heroin that arrived in a shipping container through the port of Melbourne was seized in November 1994. This shipment was apparently imported by a Vietnamese group.

This network, formed around the dominant 5T Gang, was engaged in securing a large market with Cabramatta as its center, by supplying high-quality Southeast Asian heroin (from 65 to 75 percent pure) for the same price that lower purity heroin was sold for elsewhere (a cap of 0.03 grams cost $40–$50 on the street). This attracted addicts and dealers far and wide. By organizing its own importations of heroin (typically impregnated in fabric, or carried by couriers returning from Vietnam), the network was able to reduce greatly its reliance (and its overheads) on the Chinese criminals who supply the greater proportion of the market. The 5T Gang also cut out the middlemen, and sold directly to the street.

See also: BORYOKUDAN; INAGAWA-KAI; SUMIYOSHI-KAI; YAMAGUCHI-GUMI.

Reference

Parliamentary Joint Committee on the National Crime Authority. *Asian Organised Crime in Australia, A Discussion Paper by the Parliamentary Joint Committee on National Crime Authority: Australia and Organized Crime.*

BADALAMANTI, Gaetano

Gaetano Badalamanti was the top boss of the Ciucull Mafia of Palermo, Sicily. He is known as a *mammas-antissma,* or top boss, and became internationally famous in April 1984 as the mastermind of "The Pizza Connection." He helped broker the connection with the Bonanno family to create the ring that became so successful. He was eventually arrested and sentenced to prison with hundreds of others involved in the ring.

BAKSH, Noor

"Noor Baksh was a Pakistani national and had managed to cross over into India through Nepal," Police Chief M. C. Dwivedi told the media after Baksh was apprehended by Indian police. Baksh had confessed to being involved in the murderous attack on alleged Mumbai mobster Chhota Rajan in Bangkok in September 2000. Baksh was alleged to be a member of a rival gang led by Dawood Ibrahim.

"Noor Baksh has admitted that he was assigned to keep a watch outside Rohit Verma's house while Dawood's other henchmen went inside to target Chota Rajan," Dwivedi told Sharat Pradhan of the India Abroad News Service on October 6, 2000. The arrest was made after a wild shoot-out by the Special Task Force (STF) of India.

See also: ANSARI, AFTAB; GOGA, IRFAN; IBRAHIM, DAWOOD; RAJAN, CHHOTA; SHAKEEL, CHHOTA; SINGH, SANJAY.

Reference
Sharat Pradhan. "Gangster Confesses to Attack on Alleged Mumbai Mobster Chhota Rajan." India Abroad News Service. October 6, 2000.

BANDIDOS

This outlaw motorcycle club was formed in 1966 in Houston by Donald Eugene Chambers to control drug trafficking and prostitution in Texas after seeing a TV commercial with the Frito Bandido trademark mascot raising hell to sell potato chips. Chambers called his gang the Bandidos and adopted the fat, machete- and pistol-wielding cartoon cowboy as the club's colors.

The Bandidos, also called the Bandido Nation, are the fastest-growing outlaw motorcycle gang in the United States, with about 30 chapters and 500 members. It even has an Australian chapter, acquired with much bloodletting. The club is concentrated in Texas and extends into Louisiana, Mississippi, Arkansas, New Mexico, Colorado, South Dakota, and Washington State. The Bandidos are run by a mother chapter made up of a president, four regional vice presidents, and regional and local chapter officers.

The Bandidos are involved in drug trafficking, prostitution, contract murder, fencing, extortion, stealing and running weapons, welfare and bank fraud, and arson. The bikers make most of their

Members of the Bandidos motorcycle gang ride to the funeral of one of their own. (AP)

dos-controlled towns. They also own a nightclub together in Oklahoma City. The clubs consider themselves brother organizations and wear each other's tattoos.

See also: MOTORCYCLE GANGS.

BANDIDOS/ROCK Machine

The Rock Machine motorcycle gang was formed in Canada in the mid-1980s by the Cazzetta brothers, Salvatore and Giovanni. The founding members with the Cazzettas were Paul "Sasquatch" Porter, Renaud Jomphe, André Sauvageau, Gilles Lambert, Martin Bourget, Richard Lagacé, Serge Pinel, and Johnny Plescio. Rather than wear colors, which made identification by police too easy, members chose to wear unique gold rings with an eagle's head engraving.

The organization expanded and, by the early 1990s, held a significant portion of Quebec's lucrative drug trade. This angered the city's foremost biker gang, the infamous Hells Angels, who demanded a slice of the pie. But the Rock Machine, along with other independent drug gangs, refused to back down. The gang murdered Hells Angels sympathizer Pierre Daoust on July 13, 1994, and thus began Canada's most brutal gang war ever.

Despite the murders, the Rock Machine endured. The Rock Machine became an official biker gang on June 2, 1999, revealing its colors at a Bandidos celebration in New Mexico. The group expanded into Ontario, creating three more chapters, and also established a puppet club, the Palmers, that is active in both Montreal and Quebec City.

After numerous meetings, the Rock Machine became probationary Bandidos on December 1, 2000; on the exact date one year later, they became official Bandidos club members. The club has expanded its influence and has established several puppet gangs throughout the province. Their war with the Hells Angels, which has resulted in the death of more than 150 people, rages on in the streets of Quebec. The Rock Machine/Bandidos organization was crippled in June 2002 when police arrested more than 60 of the gang's members and associates in a series of raids across Quebec and Ontario. The raids jailed every full member of the gang in Quebec.

See also: CAZZETTA, GIOVANNI; CAZZETTA, SALVATORE; MOTORCYCLE GANGS.

money manufacturing and selling methamphetamine. Club members and associates who are pilots smuggle drugs and guns across the border and state lines.

A nomad chapter takes care of Bandidos security, counterintelligence, and internal discipline. The chapter is made up of charter members who have been with the club for more than five years. The elite group does not live in one area, although many of its members gravitate to Lubbock, Texas. The chapter compiles files on police forces and other outlaw motorcycle gangs whom they consider enemies.

The Bandidos's alliance with the Outlaws Motorcycle gang began in 1978 in an effort to expand their drug network. The Outlaws provide the Bandidos with cocaine that they buy from Colombian and Cuban suppliers. Both clubs socialize in Bandi-

Reference
Gary Francoeur. "Bandidos/Rock Machine." Wiseguy-
Wally. Available online. URL: http://www.geocities.com/
wiseguywally/RockMachine.html. Downloaded on July
19, 2004.

—G.F.

BANK of Credit and Commerce International (a.k.a. Bank of Crooks and Criminals International)

In summer 1991, the Bank of England took the unprecedented step of shutting down one of the world's largest banks, the Bank of Credit and Commerce International (BCCI). Soon afterward, the district attorney of Manhattan, Robert Morgenthau, handed down criminal indictments against top officials of the bank. Soon, the popular media were filled with tales of drug-money laundering, bankrolling of Middle East terrorists, underwriting of Saddam Hussein's quest for a nuclear bomb, and so on. BCCI was linked to some of the Persian Gulf's wealthiest sheiks and was described as a secret slush fund for the Central Intelligence Agency (CIA). *Time* magazine even quoted CIA head Robert Gates, referring to BCCI as the "Bank of Crooks and Criminals International."

Two rather critical facts, however, were invariably left out of the story—even during the lengthy soap-opera trial of former BCCI attorney Robert Altman.

The first fact was the extraordinarily close alliance between BCCI and some of Britain's most powerful financial houses and aristocratic families.

The second fact was that BCCI was created and then built up as a "world class" bank primarily to manage the covert funds that poured into the secret war in Afghanistan. Hardly any mention was made of the fact that BCCI was in the middle of the Afghan effort—serving as the de facto central bank for a multibillion-dollar Golden Crescent illegal arms-for-drugs trade that mushroomed during 1979–90.

When the last of the Red army troops pulled out of Kabul in February 1989, the massive British-devised and American-led covert-action program in support of the Afghan mujahideen began to wind down. BCCI lost its raison d'être, and went the way of the 1960s-era Investors Overseas Service (IOS), and the Vietnam War-era Nugen Hand Bank of Australia: The money was siphoned out, a diversionary scandal was manufactured, and its doors were shut.

During the decade of the Afghan War, BCCI's assets had grown from an initial capitalization in 1972 of $2.5 million to $4 billion in 1980 to an astounding $23 billion at the point that the Bank of England moved to shut it down. The bulk of the $23 billion disappeared and to this day is still unaccounted for.

A BRITISH "CROWN JEWEL"

During its meteoric rise in the 1980s BCCI was anything but a "Third World bank." Nominally founded in 1972 by Pakistani banker Agha Hasan Abedi, it was initially capitalized by the British Sheik Zayed of Abu Dhabi, incorporated in Luxembourg, and conducted all of its real business in London. True, Abedi was closely allied with the Pakistani military, especially with Gen. Mohammed Zia ul-Haq, who took power in 1977; and BCCI was used as a laundromat for the billions of dollars a year generated by the hundreds of heroin laboratories in Pakistan's North West Frontier Province (NWFP) that processed Afghani opium and smuggled it onto the world market. Likewise, BCCI was the central bank for the British and American arms flows to the Afghan mujahideen.

BCCI became a "crown jewel" in the British offshore hot-money system because of its ties to the city of London.

In 1976, BCCI established a Swiss base of operations by purchasing 85 percent of Banque de Commerce et Placements (BCP) of Geneva. The remaining 15 percent was retained by the original owner, Thesarus Continental Securities Corp., a wholly owned subsidiary of Union Bank of Switzerland (UBS). Under BCCI control, BCP was managed by Alfred Hartmann, a former senior official of UBS. Hartmann eventually became chief financial officer for BCCI Holding and was the person most accountable for the "lost" $23 billion. While serving as BCCI's "man in Switzerland," Hartmann was always operating on behalf of the Rothschild family. Hartmann was president of Rothschild Bank AG of Zurich, was vice-chairman of NY-Intermaritime Bank of Geneva (run by Mossad operative Bruce Rappaport), and was a member of the board of directors of the elite N.M. Rothschild and Sons in London.

BCCI's Swiss, London, and Caribbean branches were an essential part of the cash pipeline for the Bush-led "parallel government" of the 1980s. According to congressional testimony, Lt. Col. Oliver North and British arms dealer Leslie Aspin opened up four joint bank accounts in BCCI's Paris branch, and when the Colombian Medellín Cartel put $10 million into the Bush covert war chest, the funds were conduited through one of Bruce Rappaport's Swiss accounts. When Syrian guns-and-dope trafficker Mansur al-Kassar arranged to sell $42 million in arms to Iran on behalf of the Bush-North effort, he and Leslie Aspin funneled the profits through BCCI's Cayman Islands branch.

Former Senate investigator Jack Blum summed up the BCCI case in 1991 testimony before a congressional committee: "This bank was a product of the Afghan War and people very close to the mujahideen have said that many Pakistani military officials who were deeply involved in assisting and supporting the Afghan rebel movement were stealing our foreign assistance money and using BCCI to hide the money they stole; to market American weapons that were to be delivered that they stole; and to market and manage funds that came from the selling of heroin that was apparently engineered by one of the mujahideen groups."

Reprinted with permission of *Executive Intelligence Review*. Originally published as "The Real Story of the BCCI" by Bill Engdahl and Jeffrey Steinberg, October 13, 1995.

Reference

Bill Engdahl and Jerry Steinberg. "The Real Story of the BCCI." *Executive Intelligence Review*. October 13, 1995. Reprinted with permission of *Executive Intelligence Review*.

BARGARELLA, Leoluca

Leoluca Bargarella was one of the most violent and brutal killers in the history of the Italian Mafia. He gained a strong foothold in the Italian underworld of crime by befriending his brother-in-law, Salvatore "Toto" Riina. Then, with Riina's capture on January 15, 1993, Leoluca was installed as the replacement for the so-called boss of bosses. "Bargarella was a wanted figure long before his ascension to the top of the Corleonese operation due to his planning of the murder of Boris Giuliano, 'dogged police head from Palermo,' in July of 1979," reports http://geocities.com/OrganizedCrimeSyndicates. "Word of his rise in the criminal world led many underworld watchers to believe the Corleone clan would continue its murderous reign, quite possibly turning the level of violence up to previously unmatched proportions."

Such unchecked drive for power, such disregard for the formalities of modern civilization, repulsed a country rife with colorful Mafia figures. His street operations were immediately pressured by Italian authorities, who quickly set up a campaign of revenge and defeat for the Sicilian hoodlum. Italian authorities were not deterred, and Bargarella was captured in just two years, ending his greedy and depraved spree. In June 1995 he was sentenced to life imprisonment.

See also: AGLIERI, PIETRO; BRUSCA, GIOVANNI; CORLEONE CLAN; FALCONE, GIOVANNI; PALAZZOLO, GIUSEPPE; PROVENZANO, BERNARDO; RIINA, SALVATORE; SPERA, BENEDETTO.

BARNES, Leroy (a.k.a. Mr. Untouchable; the King of Harlem)

Leroy "Mr. Untouchable" Barnes was a legendary drug dealer and crime boss in Harlem who was the John Gotti of his day, according to famed crime writer Jerry Capeci. Barnes was a well-known drug dealer, and yet he survived numerous trials. The name "Mr. Untouchable" was given to him by the *New York Times* who featured him on the cover of their Sunday magazine. All the while he was dealing drugs, Barnes was also a deacon of a popular Harlem church that was famed for giving out turkeys to needy families on Thanksgiving and toys to less-fortunate children on Christmas.

"He was acquitted three times of drug, murder, and bribery charges in three trials in Manhattan and The Bronx," wrote Capeci in March 1999. Barnes was one of the biggest distributors of heroin in New York City. His biggest supplier, Matthew Madonna, a man he met in an upstate prison in the late 1950s, smuggled the product into the United States. The two had a system that the police never cracked, which involved switching a series of cars parked in municipal parking lots; the cars were filled with either cash or drugs. The two would switch keys, identify locations, and then go their separate ways.

In February 1975, Madonna was arrested for drug trafficking, but Barnes found a new supplier and continued to operate very successfully. At this point, he was as well known as any Mafia boss in the City. He wore fancy clothes, dined at expensive restaurants, was often photographed out on the town, and drove a Citroen-Maserati. He was called The King of Harlem and was known to carry as much as $100,000 in cash.

After surviving a charge of income tax evasion by the Internal Revenue Service (Barnes paid $250,000 in income taxes based on "miscellaneous income"), in 1977 Barnes was finally arrested. So great was Barnes's reputation, that the federal judge presiding over the trial ordered the first-ever anonymous jury. He was found guilty and sentenced to 20 years to life without parole. He served most of sentence at the maximum security prison in Marion, Ill.

Until 1981, Barnes continued to be involved in his former operations until they began to break down. Soon, he found out that his former partners were cheating him out of profits and having affairs with his wife and former girlfriends. It was also reported that they were doing drugs in front of Barnes's two small daughters. Incensed, Barnes decided to cooperate with federal and state authorities.

In the ensuing months, Barnes told the authorities about his involvement and helped set up his wife, girlfriend and partners, as well as more than 50 other drug dealers and other associates. He was rewarded for his efforts by being moved to a more hospitable prison situation in Otisville, N.Y. He worked with many high-ranking law-enforcement officials.

After 21 years behind bars and serving at the behest of the authorities for most of those years, Barnes was released in August 1998 and relocated under the Federal Witness Protection Program.

Reference

Jerry Capeci. "Barnes Free at Last." *New York Daily News,* March 15, 1999.

BARRANQUILLA Cartel

This cartel's operation was centered in Barranquilla, Colombia. Barranquilla was the jumping-off point for drug traffickers out of Colombia in the 1980s and was the city used by the Medellín cartel at the height of its power.

The Medellín cartel used Southern Air cargo planes to transport their product. Southern Air was a U.S. government–sponsored operation helping prodemocratic insurgents in Nicaragua.

"The deal called for U.S. planes to deliver guns to the cartel which, in turn, 'put cocaine aboard the planes and the cocaine was taken to United States military base[s],' [Allan Raul] Rudd [a Colombian drug trafficker] said. 'The guns were delivered and sold to the contras in Nicaragua by the cartel.'"

"Federal informant Wanda Palacio testified that she was with Medellín bosses when they oversaw the loading of cocaine aboard Southern Air Transport planes at Barranquilla, Colombia, in 1983 and October 1985," wrote *San Jose Mercury News* reporter Gary Webb in his book, *Dark Alliance.* "In October 1986, after a contra supply plane crashed in Nicaragua, Palacio identified its dead co-pilot, Wallace 'Buzz' Sawyer, as one of the Southern Air pilots on the October 1985 cocaine flight. Sawyer's logs, recovered from the crash, later confirmed that he had flown a Southern Air plane into Barranquilla in early October 1985."

Eventually, when subsequent pressures were put on the Medellín cartel, the Barranquilla group who organized the planes, the fields, and security were also put out of business.

Reference

Consortium News. "Two New Contra-Coke Books." *The Consortium for Independent Journalism* (July 9, 1998).

BASAK, Huseyin

A huge mover and shaker in the illicit empire of Dundar Kilic, Huseyin Basak is seen as a power broker within the organization. His big claim to fame was planning the execution of Nihat Akgun, a high-ranking mobster and good friend of Kilic's rival mob boss Alaatin Cakici. Eventually he was arrested and imprisoned on a charge of attempted murder; however, while incarcerated in a minimum security prison, Basak escaped. He secretly fled "to Istanbul where he partnered with several prominent businessmen," according to http://geocities.com/Organized CrimeSyndicates.

See also: DONMEZ, OSMAN; KILIC, DUNDAR; OZBIZ-ERDIK, ONUR; UGURLU, ABUZER.

Reference

Organized Crime Syndicates. "Godfathers Are Growing Fewer." Turkish Probe issue 361, *Turkish Daily News.* Available online. URL: http://geocities.com/Organized CrimeSyndicates. Posted on December 12, 1999.

BATTLE, José Miguel (a.k.a. El Padrino)

Battle, who fled his native Cuba after Fidel Castro's revolution, was born in 1929. José Miguel Battle is the alleged leader of the Cuban-American syndicate known as The Corporation, the largest Hispanic crime syndicate in the United States. According to authorities, Battle controls numbers rackets from New York to Florida.

Battle moved to the Miami, Florida, area from New Jersey in the 1980s. The President's Commission on Organized Crime in 1985 estimated The Corporation's annual profits from New York at $45 million. Authorities believe that the main portion of Battle's wealth comes from the numbers racket called *bolita* that is popular in Hispanic neighborhoods and from other gambling operations located in New York-area storefronts. Battle owns a 30-acre ranch. In 1986 Battle listed as one of Dade County's wealthiest men with a net worth of $175 million.

Battle was said to have ordered the deaths of at least 20 people. He pleaded guilty to a murder charge in 1977, was arrested for a passport violation in 1997 (for which he was eventually convicted), and in a raid on his home Battle was also found to be in possession of a shotgun. This was a violation of his parole from the 1977 conviction. The 68-year Battle was convicted a second time in 1997 for the gun charge. He was placed in the government's custody at Jackson Memorial Hospital, where he was undergoing treatment for kidney disease.

See also: CORPORATION, THE.

BAYBASIN Clan

An alert from Interpol–Germany (October 26, 1993) indicated that the Baybasin family was conducting an extensive heroin-trafficking operation between Turkey, Germany, the Netherlands, Italy, and Spain and "laundering" sizable sums of money in Europe. The head of the clan is Hussein Baybasin, born in Lice in 1956, who was picked up in Istanbul in 1976 while in possession of 11 kilos of heroin and then again in Great Britain in 1984 with 6 kilos of the same drug, for which he was sentenced to 12 years in prison. The clan also includes Mehmet Emin Baybasin, born in Lice in 1942, Hussein's uncle, who in February 1994 was sought in Turkey in connection with a "laboratory" in the village of Yagmurlu, not far from Lice; here the police found 67 kilos of heroin. Nedim Baybasin, born in Lice in 1965, Hussein's cousin and Mehmet Emin's son, was at the scene. Nedim was arrested in Germany on June 13, 1984, (along with Mehmet Serif Baybasin, born in Lice in 1944) with 32 kilos of heroin and was subsequently sentenced to 13 years in prison. Mehmet Emin and Mehmet Serif have close ties with Kurdish separatists, and the latter is known to German police as a Partiya Karkaren

Kurdistan (PKK), or Kurdistan Workers' Party, arms trafficker. All told, there are a dozen or so Baybasin brothers, cousins, uncles, and so on with records in several European countries and whose similar exploits could fill a book.

See also: DEMIR CLAN; KAYA CLAN; KITAY CLAN; KONUKLU-AY CLAN; KURDISH CRIMINAL CLANS AND THE PKK; SAKIK CLAN; SENAR CLAN.

Reference

Department for the Study of the Contemporary Criminal Menace. "Two Typical 'Degenerate Guerilla Groups': The Liberation Tigers of Emil Eelam and the Kurdistan Worker's Party." *Notes and Etudes* ("Terrorism and Political Violence" special) 32 (June 1996). Available online. URL: http://www.drmcc.org/docs/ne32.pdf. Accessed on December 16, 2004.

BEAULIEU, Georges (a.k.a. Bo-Boy)

Georges Beaulieu, called Bo-Boy, was born in the early 1950s and became the president of the Gitans biker gang at a young age, although the Commission d'Enquete sur le Crime Organisé (CECO) claimed that Jacques Boudou was the real, unofficial leader of the band.

When the Gitans became Hells Angels, Beaulieu remained the group's boss. His leadership played an important role in developing the Sherbrooke chapter into a structured and highly influential organization.

Members of the Sherbrooke chapter are suspected by police of having been involved in the March 24, 1985, slaughter of five members of the North chapter. The men were gunned down at the gang's Lennoxville clubhouse. Days before, Beaulieu had been seen purchasing a shipment of sleeping bags at a sports store. The sleeping bags were placed over the dead North chapter members before they were dropped into the St. Lawrence River.

Beaulieu, accompanied by Gilles Lachance and Luc Michaud of the Montreal chapter and Ronald McDonald of the Halifax chapter, flew to Vancouver three days after the slaughter to explain the murders to the members of the Hells Angels British Columbia chapters.

A few weeks later, on April 17, Beaulieu, Charles "Cash" Filteau, Jean-Yves "Boule" Tremblay, Guy "Mouski" Rodrigue, Louis "Bidou" Brochu, and Gerry "Le Chat" Coulombe traveled to Paris to celebrate the Paris chapter's fourth anniversary and to tell them what happened to the North chapter.

After the bodies were fished out of the river and police began to make arrests, Beaulieu went into hiding. He was arrested in a telephone booth in Amsterdam on April 4, 1988, while he was talking with a member of the club's Quebec chapter. He was extradited back to Canada where he pleaded guilty to five murders and was jailed.

Beaulieu was arrested in Acapulco, Mexico, on April 3, 2001, along with Hells Angels Jacques Rodrigue and Guy Dubé, reputed kingpin Claude Faber, and associates Richard Lock, Jacques Benoit, Alain Saint-Gelais, and Mario Bonce. The eight men were deemed "undesirables" and shipped back to Canada. Dubé was arrested upon their arrival and charged with drug trafficking and conspiring to traffic in drugs.

See also: HELLS ANGELS.

Reference

Gary Francouer. "Georges 'Bo-Boy' Beaulieu." Wiseguy-Wally. Available online. URL: http://www.geocities.com/wiseguywally/GeorgesBeaulieu.html. Downloaded on July 19, 2004.

—*G.F.*

BEIGELMAN, Vladimir

Vladimir Beigelman was reputed to be a major cocaine trafficker with ties to both the Cali Cartel and La Cosa Nostra. Part of the Russian Mafiya, Beigelman was shot to death by two unknown males who fired four shots into his head, neck, and back as he exited a van in Queens, New York, on December 2, 1993. Witnesses told police that the shooters appeared to be Hispanic. Beigelman may have been blamed for losing a large shipment of cocaine.

See also: RUSSIAN MAFIYA.

Reference

New Jersey State Commission of Investigation, New York Organized Crime Task Force, New York State Commission of Investigation, Pennsylvania Crime Commission, with Rutgers University. "The Tri-State Joint Soviet-Émigré Organized Crime Project," 1992. Available online. URL: http://www.state.nj.us/sci/pdf/russian.pdf. Accessed on November 24, 2004.

BELZIL, Yvon

Yvon Belzil was born in Trois-Pistoles, Quebec, and moved to Montreal at a young age. He had a reputation for carrying a loaded gun at all times. He also was not afraid to use it.

Belzil met Claude Dubois in the 1960s, and the two became fast friends. They allegedly soon set up a successful fencing operation together, an operation that made them each $300–$400 a week. The Dubois brothers and Belzil would rise to the top of Montreal's underworld during the next 10 years.

In 1966 Belzil and Claude Dubois opened the Clé d'Or strip club together. During one of many raids police found more than 50 tissues filled with sperm. When the government shut down the bar four years later, Belzil and Dubois lost a major money maker. They were each making about $800 a week from the club.

The two, along with Claude Jodoin, opened the La Grande, a gay night club on Saint-Catherine Street, in May 1972. Belzil made about $500 a week from the club until it was closed in 1981.

Around this time, Richard Désormiers, Frank Cotroni's brother-in-law, began to make trouble in Dubois Gang–controlled bars. After a year of this, Claude Dubois had enough and decided to have Désormiers killed. The contract was given to Belzil, Claude Dubeau, and Donald Lavoie.

On July 22, 1973, Lavoie and Dubeau walked into the Mon Pays bar and shot Désormiers and Jacques-André Bourassa, the manager, several times. As this was going on inside, Belzil stole Désormiers's Cadillac from the parking lot.

After Belzil appeared before the Commission d'Enquete sur le Crime Organisé (CECO), he, his girlfriend, Claude Dubois and his wife, and Claude Jodoin took a two-week vacation to Haiti. They liked the island so much that Belzil and Dubois decided to return and buy a hotel there, but before they could do that, they were deported on a request from Montreal police.

According to Claude Jodoin, a gang member who later turned informant, Belzil began to plot to eliminate Claude Dubois and replace him in the late '70s. After he unsuccessfully tried to turn Adrien and Jean-Paul Dubois against their brother, Belzil opened an escort service in close proximity to an agency controlled by Claude Dubois. He even hired Raymond Duclos, a criminal who testified against Dubois for the CECO, to work in the establishment. This was a veritable slap in the face to Dubois.

The Dubois brothers ordered Belzil to close his escort agency's doors. Belzil was furious and, one afternoon in a gang hangout, according to Jodoin, he jumped a gang member known as Petit Louis and pummeled him helplessly. Claude and Jean-Paul Dubois quickly broke up the fight, and Claude flung Belzil against a wall and leveled him with a powerful uppercut. Belzil got up and left, threatening to get even with the brothers.

A meeting was arranged for the next day to try to iron things but, because of increased police pressure, Belzil panicked and left Montreal that night for his hometown, Trois-Pistoles. From there, he and associate Raymond Duclos went to Abitibi, where they stayed on a farm while they waited for the heat to die down back in the city.

Belzil returned to Montreal in October 1980 and asked Claude Jodoin to set up a meeting with Claude Dubois. The two met and agreed to put their differences aside.

When Donald Lavoie turned police informant, Belzil allegedly came up with several plots to silence him. One idea was to blow up him and his police escorts with a bazooka as they arrived at the courthouse. Belzil also suggested that his wife and children be kidnapped and, if despite this, Lavoie still agreed to take the stand against them, they would be tortured and murdered.

Lavoie's incriminating information came back to haunt Belzil on April 8, 1982. Police officers raided his Saint-Leonard house and arrested him. Claude Dubois was also picked up at his home in Écho Lake. They were charged with the murders of Richard Désormiers and Jacques-André Bourassa. Claude Dubeau, who was already behind bars, was also charged with the murders.

Lavoie and Claude Jodoin testified against their former associates. The three were found guilty on November 12, 1983, and were sentenced to life imprisonment. The Quebec Court of Appeals reduced their sentences to 10 years in 1989 because, they decided, Jacques-André Bourassa's murder had not been premeditated. Belzil was released from prison in the early 1990s.

See also: DUBOIS GANG; LAVOIE, DONALD.

Reference

Gary Francoeur. "Yvon Belzil." WiseguyWally. Available online. URL: http://www.geocities.com/wiseguywally/ YvonBelzil.html. Downloaded on July 19, 2004.

—G.F.

BERGER, Claude (a.k.a. Burger)

Claude "Burger" Berger was born on May 8, 1949, and grew up in Sherbrooke, Quebec, Canada. He began to associate with bikers as a teenager and, as he became older, he earned the respect of the city's criminal element. He was soon a full-patch member of the Gitans biker gang, and in 1984, when the club was absorbed by the Hells Angels, Berger became a member of the notorious motorcycle gang.

Besides being a hardcore biker, Berger has another passion: music. He held the position of third trumpet with the Quebec Symphony Orchestra for more than 10 years before he was replaced in April 1998. He is also a part of the Rock BB Blues, a popular Sherbrooke band, and taught music part time at the local college for more than 20 years.

Police raided a bar owned by Berger and Hells Angel Gilles Dumas in 1995 and seized illegal video poker machines, cocaine and marijuana, and a shotgun. Four people were arrested in the bust, but no charges were levied against the two owners. Surprisingly, and to public outrage, Berger and Dumas would receive a $71,000 municipal grant for renovations on the bar two years later.

Berger was charged with illegal possession of a firearm on April 22, 1997, after police raided a bar. Officers said they saw him fleeing the bar and trying to hide a gun. He was arrested but later acquitted of the charge.

Police arrested Berger at his house next door to the Hells Angels' Lennoxville clubhouse on November 5, 1998, and charged him with producing and conspiring to produce marijuana and of nine counts of living off the profits of crime. Twenty-one others, including Gilles Dumas and Marc Bordage, members of the Hells Angels Quebec chapter, were also picked up and charged with crimes ranging from drug trafficking to attempted murder. Berger was released two weeks later, after he posted bail. Police seized more than $3 million in drugs, $45 million in counterfeit U.S. currency, six guns, two stolen vehicles, and a seaplane believed to have been used to transport drugs.

Berger's problems with the law continued. A motorist unknowingly parked his car in Berger's space in front of the Hells Angels' clubhouse on September 18, 2001. When the civilian returned to his car, he was confronted by a man, who told him that he was not allowed to park there. The motorist was then escorted into the clubhouse where, he claimed, Berger complained that he had been issued a parking ticket because the man had taken his spot. Berger and three other bikers then allegedly surrounded the man and forced him to sign a $50 check to cover the cost of the ticket. The victim's son quickly alerted police, who arrested Berger. He appeared before a judge the next day and was released on $1,000 bail.

In early 2002, Berger and three other Hells Angels, according to organized crime expert Guy Ouellette, retired in good standing from the Sherbrooke chapter.

See also: HELLS ANGELS (CANADA).

Reference
Gary Francoeur. "Claude 'Burger' Berger." Wiseguy Wally. Available online. URL: http://www.geocities.com/wiseguywally/ClaudeBerger.html. Downloaded on July 19, 2004.

—*G.F.*

BERNAL-MADRIGAL, Alejandro

Alejandro Bernal-Madrigal (a.k.a. Juvenal) was a Bogotá-based transportation coordinator for top Mexico- and Colombia-based traffickers. He was responsible for multiton shipments of cocaine from Colombia to Mexico for onward transport to the United States. Juvenal also transported large amounts of drug money to Mexico.

Bernal was born in Pereira. He came from a middle-class family. Bernal returned to Colombia in 1995 after he served a three-year sentence for cocaine possession in Mexico. At that point, many of the major and older cocaine cartels, such as Cali and Medellín, had been or were in the midst of being dismantled. Bernal was part of the new breed of cartel manager who lived a middle-class businessman's life and who employed legitimate professionals, using them to tap into top-flight technology. He used cell phones and laptop computers and the Internet to schedule his business dealings. Bernal shipped into Mexico, thereby reducing his risk of confiscation and loss of money due to stepped up border security. He also thought this would inoculate him from prosecution in the United States.

He had worked for the Medellín cartel and later ran the Bogotá cartel after the arrest of Justo Pastor Perafan. He was arrested in October 1999 by Colombian authorities and remains in jail.

See also: BOGOTÁ CARTEL; MEDELLÍN CARTEL; PERAFAN, JUSTO PASTOR.

Reference
Thomas Constantine. "Drug Interdiction and Other Matters Related to the National Drug Control Policy." Hearing before the Subcommittee on Coast Guard and Maritime Transportation of the Committee on Transportation and Infrastructure, House of Representatives, 104th Congress, 2nd Session, September 12, 1996. Joint Hearing with Senate Caucus on International Narcotics Control. Washington, D.C.: U.S. Government Printing Office, 1997, 104–169.

BIG Circle Boys (a.k.a. Big Circle Gang; Dai Huen Jai)

The Big Circle Gang, which is sometimes referred to as a "Mainland-based triad," is a relatively new group that initially consisted primarily of former Red Army guards placed in Chinese concentration or prison camps. On Red China government maps, these camps were identified with big red circles; thus, the name. Whether they escaped or were expelled from China is under debate, but they left China for Hong Kong. Big Circle Gang members are particularly violent, specializing in armed robberies of jewelry stores in Hong Kong as well as in heroin trafficking. The Big Circle Gang is not technically a triad, but most Big Circle Gang members are also members of various triad societies. Johnny Kon, a former Big Circle associate and convicted heroin smuggler, testified that he helped organize a group of Big Circle Gang members into a tightly organized and disciplined group known as the Flaming Eagles; this group expanded from jewelry store robberies in Hong Kong to a worldwide heroin-distribution network. All of Kon's Big Circle associates were also members of other triads.

See also: FLAMING EAGLES; KON, JOHNNY.

Reference
Parliamentary Joint Committee on the National Crime Authority. *Asian Organized Crime in Australia, A Discussion Paper by the Parliamentary Joint Committee on National Crime Authority: Australia and Organized Crime.*

BIGGS, Ronald

Ronald Biggs was one of the members of the group that pulled off the Great Train Robbery in England. He was the brains behind the 11-member gang that robbed the London-to-Glasgow post train in 1963.

The operation was a success: The group took home more than $4 million, and it made the members celebrities.

Biggs was apprehended but later escaped from Wandsworth Prison in London in 1965. He then ran off to France. In Paris, Biggs received plastic surgery to change his appearance and slowly made his way toward Australia, where his wife and three sons joined him. Understanding that Scotland Yard detectives were on to him, Biggs ran off to Brazil, telling his wife that he would phone. He did not. He arrived in Brazil in 1971. Scotland Yard discovered his whereabouts in 1974, but it was too late. Biggs was the father of a young son, Michael, and Brazil, which now considered him a citizen, refused to extradite him.

Biggs has protested to anyone who would listen that he has not lived off the money from the robbery, but that it dwindled long ago. He is not allowed to work in Brazil, where he lives in Rio de Janeiro, charges for interviews, and charges tourists to have a beer with him and to receive a T-shirt reading: "I was in Brazil and found Ronnie Biggs . . . really."

By 2001, Brazil did in fact hand Biggs over: At the age of 68 years old, he stood in court for eight minutes and then resumed the sentence of 30 years, for which he had only served 15 months.

BIG Swords   See TRIADS.

BING Kong Tong

The Bing Kong Tong was a powerful tong group in San Francisco's Chinatown in the 1920s. The Hop Sing and Suey Sing tongs had ganged up against the powerful Bing Kong Tong Society, resulting in one of the most violent Asian crime episodes in American history. The killings were considered both cruel as well as violent, and the body count quickly rose. Colorful Santa Rosa prosecutor Wallace Ware represented the D.A.s office when the tong war erupted in San Francisco. The Bing Kong Tong's influence ranged throughout the Asian communities of the West Coast and southwestern states as well. Four members of the Bing Kong Tong were tried and convicted of a major murder in Kingman, Arizona, in the 1920s as well.

The Bing Kong Tong Society (a.k.a. Association; Free Masons) remains a solid trade union today and has been little linked with organized crime for some time by law-enforcement authorities.

See also: HOP SING TONG; TONGS.

BLACK Gangster Disciples (BGDs)

In the mid-1990s a federal task force was formed to investigate the Black Gangster Disciples' (BGDs) involvement in several murders and drug sales. The government found that the gang was making more than $100 million a year in illegal drug sales. Several high-ranking members were convicted and are serving life sentences. The gang has made several attempts to legitimize their image. Some members dropped the "B" and began to call themselves Gangster Disciples, or GDs.

In the 1990s the Gangster Disciples entered politics through the formation of the "Growth and Development" movement. Gangster Disciples began to blanket the city of Chicago, attempting to register voters from the inner city. They then "encouraged" the newly registered voters to vote for candidates loyal to their cause. While incarcerated, the Black Gangster Disciples will unite with allied gangs under the guise of the Brothers of Struggle (BOS). The gang continues to be involved in large-scale drug trafficking, murders, and white-collar crime.

The Black Gangster Disciple Nation was formed on the south side of Chicago in the late 1960s by David Barksdale, leader of the Gonzanto Disciples, and Larry Hoover, leader of the Supreme Disciples. The two groups united to form the Black Gangster Disciple Nation (BGDN). David Barksdale became the leader of BGDN, and Hoover became his second in command. Barksdale died in 1972, and Hoover took over the leadership position. After Barksdale's death, Jerome Freeman, who was loyal to Barksdale and never wanted the two groups to unite in the first place, established a parallel leadership position to Hoover. As a result of this split, two distinct groups emerged within the BGDN. Freeman formed a street gang that calls itself Black Disciples, or BDs, while Hoover renamed his gang the Black Gangster Disciples, or BGDs. These two gangs have at times been bitter rivals. The Black Disciples have remained relatively small in numbers and have not branched out as have the BGDs.

The BGDs use the six-pointed star, (the Star of David) as their symbol, which represents life, loyalty, understanding, knowledge, wisdom, and love. They also use the upward-crossed pitchforks and a heart with wings. Tattoos utilized by the BGDs include a devil's tail and a top hat with a staff—the top of the staff has a pitchfork with the numbers three, six, zero, and at the bottom is an upside-down cross. Oakland Raiders clothing is common, and they often carry white, light grey, or black bandannas.

The BGDs are present throughout the United States. Their leaders are located in Chicago, and they have a strong presence in most Midwest cities. The BGDs is one of the country's largest criminal organizations.

Reference

Know Gangs. "Black Gangster Disciples." Available online. URL: http://www.knowgangs.com/gang_resources/black_gangster_disciples/bgd_001.htm. Downloaded on July 19, 2004.

BLACK Guerrilla Family (BGF)

The Black Guerrilla Family, or BGF, was founded in 1966 by former Black Panther George Jackson. Originally, the BGF was called the Black Family or the Black Vanguard and are associated with the "Black Mafia." Some BGF members were formerly associated with the Black Liberation Army, the Symbionese Liberation Army, and the Weatherman underground organization. The BGF is the most "politically" oriented of the major prison gangs. It was formed as a Marxist/Maoist/Leninist revolutionary organization with specific goals to eradicate racism, to struggle to maintain dignity in prison, and to overthrow the U.S. government.

All members must be black. Though small in number, the BGF has a very strict death oath that requires a life pledge of loyalty to the gang. Prospective members must be nominated by an existing member. BGF commonly uses different versions of a dragon surrounding a prison tower and holding a correctional officer in its clutches. Members will also use a crossed rifle and machete or the letters *BGF*.

The BGF has members nationwide in both state and federal prisons. The gang is strongly organized on both the East and West Coasts. Although the BGF experienced a decline in membership and strength in the '90s, it has recently reorganized and gained sub-

stantial power and growth due to its alignment with the 415s, the Crips, the Bloods, and the Black Gangster Disciples. Several members of the Crips and the Bloods have recently been found with documentation from "Dove Life" (Crips) and "Blood Line" (Bloods). Both groups are believed to have working alliances with the BGF under these aliases. Members of the 415 gang and the BGF have been found with documentation suggesting membership in a group called the Firm. The Firm is believed to be a working alliance between the 415 and BGF gangs. The BGF is currently experiencing internal conflict between old and new membership in federal custody. Younger members have created a new version of the gang known as the New Man/New Woman, or the Northern Structure of the BGF.

Members of the newly formed Northern Structure believe that old BGF members are no longer concentrating on the correct group mission and are becoming extinct. The Northern Structure membership believes that the alliances between the BGF, the Crips, the Bloods, and the 415s will result in the Crips continuing to support the old BGF members, or Southern Structure, and the Bloods and the 415s siding with the Northern Structure. Current intelligence suggests that state BGF members continue to support the old BGF membership within federal custody. The BGF has also created what appears to be a political and paramilitary subgroup known as the New Afrikan Revolutionary Nation, or NARN. This group's purpose is to gather and analyze data to enhance BGF security practices and education.

Reference

Know Gangs. "Black Guerrilla Family." Available online. URL: http://www.knowgangs.com/gang_resources/black_guerrilla_family/bgf_001.htm. Downloaded on July 19, 2004.

BLACK Panther Party

The Black Panther Party, originally called the Black Panther Party for Self-Defense, was an American black revolutionary party founded in 1966 in Oakland, California, by Huey Newton and Bobby Seale. Seale was the party's national chairman, and Newton was the defense minister. The original aim of the group was to take a militaristic stance to protect African Americans living in ghettos across the country from acts of police brutality. They also insisted that since African Americans did not enjoy equal protection under the law they should be exempted from the draft, and the party demanded reparations for past injustices in the age of slavery. There were splinter groups in California, Chicago, New York, Baltimore, and many other cities, eventually counting more than 2,000 members at its height.

However, the group eventually turned Marxist and made an enemy of the Federal Bureau of Investigation. This came about by several neighborhood riots, which the FBI insisted were fueled by the Black Panthers. Also, their new, especially militant stance, which included the carrying of firearms (Huey Newton was known to walk the street armed with an M-1 carbine), made them a target.

Tension finally boiled over in the late 1960s and early 1970s in Los Angeles, San Francisco, Chicago, and New York. Newton was jailed for the murder of a patrolman, served his sentence, and was then murdered by a young drug dealer in 1987. Bobby Seale went on trial as part of the Chicago 8. During the trial he was bound and gagged in a chair in the courtroom. He was eventually jailed. He later became a minor celebrity chef, selling barbecue sauce and cookbooks.

The Panthers started off with good intentions but were infiltrated by those who would use the altruistic organization as a cover for their nefarious activities, eventually tainting the entire group. The Black Panthers eventually dissolved sometime in the 1980s.

BLACK P-Stone Nation (BPS)

The Black P-Stone Nation is a street gang that has operated in Chicago since the early 1960s. This group was originally known as the Grass-roots Independent Voters of Illinois. During the 1960s, under the lead of Jeff Fort, they became known as the Blackstone Rangers. After Fort assumed control he applied for and received federal inner-city grants for his organization, claiming that they would put the money to use for the education of inner-city children and the expansion of jobs. In 1969 Fort received an invitation to President Nixon's inauguration. At the same time Fort consolidated approximately 50 South Side Chicago (Woodlawn District) street gangs into a supreme power, namely the Black P-Stone Nation. The money Fort received from the federal government was utilized by this group for the purchase of weapons and drugs to strengthen his hold on the gang. In the early 1970s Fort was discovered misappropriating the government funds, convicted, and sent to prison. The Black P-Stone Nation is a multiracial, multigender gang. Common identifiers include the five-point star, pyramids with 21 blocks (symbolizing the original 21 members), an eye, the initials BPS, and other People Nation symbols (another gang with which they are aligned).

It is estimated the BPS has more than 20,000 members in the Chicago area. The gang has factions throughout the Midwest and the East Coast.

Reference

Know Gangs. "Black P-Stone Nation." Available online. URL: http://www.knowgangs.com/gangresources/black_p_stone/blackpstonenation_001.htm. Downloaded on July 19, 2004.

BLACK Tuna Gang

In 1979 a joint Drug Enforcement Administration/Federal Bureau of Investigation task force in Miami immobilized the Black Tuna Gang, a major marijuana smuggling ring responsible for bringing 500 tons of marijuana into the United States during a 16-month period.

The Black Tuna Gang derived its name from the radio code name for a mysterious Colombian sugar grower and drug dealer, Raul Davila-Jimeno, who was the major supplier of the organization. Many of the gang members wore solid-gold medallions bearing a black-tuna emblem. The medallions served as a talisman and a symbol of their membership in this smuggling group. With the assistance of this small private army, Davila, who called himself a sugar, coffee, and petroleum exporter, virtually ruled Santa Marta, Colombia, where the majority of Colombian marijuana was grown. It was a highly organized ring, with gang members maintaining security and eavesdropping on radio frequencies used by police and U.S. Customs officials.

The Black Tuna Gang operated, at least briefly, from a suite in Miami Beach's Fontainebleau Hotel and arranged bulk deliveries to a moored houseboat. They were affiliated with the vice-president of a prestigious Fort Lauderdale yacht brokerage and were thus able to obtain specialized boats that could carry tons of marijuana without sitting suspiciously low in the water. The contraband was transported in these modified boats and unloaded at a series of waterfront "stash houses" in posh neighborhoods.

The Black Tuna Gang ran an elaborate operation, complete with electronically equipped trucks that were used to maintain contact with the freighters and to monitor law enforcement channels. They were also creative: As a signal that they were ready to proceed with a drug deal, the smugglers sent Davila a box of disposable diapers. This meant, "The baby is ready; send the mother."

Ultimately, partners in a Miami used-car agency were indicted as the masterminds of the Black Tuna Gang, which federal prosecutors called the "biggest and slickest" gang yet uncovered. It was the meticulous work of a DEA/FBI probe of Florida banks called Operation Banco, which began in 1977, that led investigators to the auto dealers and ultimately resulted in the downfall of the Black Tuna Gang. Operation Banco traced the group's drug profits through South Florida banks until members of the Black Tuna Gang made a large cash deposit in Miami Beach Bank. This case was notable as the first combined investigation by the DEA and the FBI on drug profits behind the marijuana trade.

Reference

U.S. Drug Enforcement Administration, U.S. Department of Justice. "A Tradition of Excellence, DEA History 1985–1990." Available online. URL: http://www.dea.gov/pubs/history/index.html. Downloaded on July 28, 2004.

BLASS, Richard (a.k.a. the Cat)

Richard "the Cat" Blass was born in 1945 in the Rosemont sector of Montreal. He would earn his well-deserved nickname because of his ability to escape death. Like a cat, he seemed to have nine lives.

From a young age, Blass earned a reputation for violence. After he lost a boxing match to amateur boxer Michel Gouin, Blass attacked him with a knife. He was arrested and pleaded guilty to assault. He spent a day in jail.

The more Blass became involved in crime, the more he began to hate the mob. The Italians had a complete lock on Montreal's rackets in the 1960s. Blass grew tired of having only their scraps and, with a small band of loyal followers, led a revolt against

them. He especially held grudges against Frank Cotroni and the Di Maulo brothers, Jos and Vincenzo, who all began to receive death threats on their telephones.

On May 7, 1968, Blass and Robert Allard, his right-hand man, planned to ambush Frank Cotroni outside his home. A police officer saw them cruising the streets and gave chase. They managed to lose the cop car but abandoned their plot for the night.

Frustrated that his plot against Cotroni had failed, Blass and his gang turned their anger against the first Italian they could find. Giuseppe Colizza, a 20-year-old with no criminal ties, was shot five times in the head on May 27, 1968.

Then it was Francesco Grado's turn. Grado, a reputed loanshark, was found dead inside his car on Rousselot Street. He had been riddled with bullets.

On June 9, another innocent was violently ambushed by Blass's gang. Giuseppe DiMarco, a law-abiding citizen with no prior arrests, was shot several times as he sat in his automobile. He survived but was left paralyzed.

Then the Mafia struck back. Blass was drinking in a bar on August 24, 1968, when two assassins entered the establishment. Blass saw the pending danger and dashed from the bar. He scurried down the street as the hit men gave chase, firing at their target. Blass lost them in a crowd.

Blass barely escaped death a couple of weeks later when the motel at which he was staying, Le Manoir de Plaisance in Saint-Hyppolyte, burned down. Two men and a woman died in the fire, but Blass got out in time. A coroner concluded that the fire had been set intentionally.

He was a marked man. Less than a month later, in October 1968, a third murder attempt took place. Blass and an associate, Claude Ménard, drove into a Saint-Michel garage when they were ambushed by gunmen. Ménard probably saved their lives by smashing the car through the door and speeding down the street. Blass was taken to the emergency room of the Jean-Talon Hospital where he was treated for his three gunshot wounds, one in the head and two in the back. He survived and, in an action that earned him a lot of respect in Montreal's underworld, refused to identify his attackers. But he did vow revenge.

Two months after being released from the hospital, in January 1969, Blass was arrested after a botched bank robbery in Sherbrooke in which he fired at police as he fled through the streets of the city. He was sentenced to four consecutive 10-year prison terms.

On October 16, 1969, as Blass and other prisoners were being transported from Bordeaux prison to the courthouse, Blass and eight fellow inmates overwhelmed the guards and escaped. After a brief manhunt, all the cons were captured. Blass was apprehended after an anonymous caller gave police the address of the apartment where the fugitive was hiding with his wife.

Blass made another prison break on October 23, 1974. In an organized escape, Blass smashed the glass that separated visitors from prisoners and, a female visitor provided Blass and four others with firearms. They forced their way outside and fled.

Once again a fugitive, Blass set his sights on vengeance. He walked into the Gargantua Tavern in Montreal on October 30 and shot to death Raymond Laurin and Roger Lévesque. The two men had been his partners in the 1970 Sherbrooke bank robbery, and Blass had been bitter that they had not been jailed.

Blass returned to the Gargantua Tavern on January 21, 1975, with another hoodlum to kill the witnesses to the murders of Laurin and Lévesque. In a deplorable act, the men locked 10 men and three women in a storage closet, blocked the door with a jukebox, and set fire to the building. All 13 people died horribly.

Police finally tracked Blass down three days later, on January 23. He and 28-year-old Lucienne Smith had taken refuge in a chalet in Val David in the Laurentians. Police surrounded the cottage and demanded that he give up. The Cat refused. Two policemen busted down the door at 4:30 A.M. on January 24 and exchanged gunfire with the fugitive. Blass was hit 23 times and died. He was only 28.

Reference

Gary Francoeur. "Richard 'Le Chat' Blass." Wiseguy-Wally. Available online. URL: http://www.geocities.com/wiseguywally/RichardBlass.html. Downloaded on July 19, 2004.

—G.F.

BLOODS and Crips

An understanding of these rival Los Angeles–based street gangs, their characteristics, and illegal activi-

ties will enhance one's abilities to easily recognize the potential risks of these gang members both in the street and in our correctional facilities.

HISTORY

The Crips and the Bloods began as violent, local, predominantly black and Hispanic street gangs in southern Los Angeles, California, in 1969. Active and highly successful in the drug trade, members of both groups are now being discovered in numerous other cities and states where they are attempting to control the local drug trade. Membership is predominantly male, but both gangs also have female members.

There are several beliefs as to how the Crips name came about. A popular one is that *Crips* is derived from a horror movie entitled *Tales of the Crypt.* An original Crips gang member relates that the term began due to an original member being handicapped. Since he was a cripple, they shortened this term to *Crip,* and the name was used in his honor. A recent and more plausible story has the term *Crips* developing from the fact that members were looking for the hardest and toughest thing imaginable; thus they came up with Superman and the only thing that could hurt him was kryptonite—this was shortened to *Crip.*

In reaction, other gangs formed to provide protection against the Crips. These became known as the Bloods. The first known Bloods gang was formed by individuals from Piru Street in Compton, California. Compton gangs affiliated with the Bloods were called Pirus. These rivalries made gang warfare more prevalent and became a focal point of gang activity. Firearms were used with regularity, and drive-by shootings produced a dramatic increase in assaults and homicides.

Because the Crips and the Bloods are now aligning with the Folk and the Peoples Nations out of Chicago, they closely follow the Chicago philosophies. Chicago-based or -influenced gangs display an all-for-one, one-for-all mentality with complete devotion to their set and nation. Most codes of conduct require lifetime allegiance to the group. The groups have a strict set of laws that result in violations for breaking these rules. Inner disciplinary punishments are issued by the leaders of the group for violating the set rules. They range from performing menial tasks to physical assault for a set time period to death. The philosophies vary somewhat depending upon the set and location.

SYMBOLS/IDENTIFIERS

The Crips adopted the color blue for their clothing to set them apart from other gang members. Also, the Crips began to use the word *Cuzz,* short for "cousin," in greetings to identify each other.

The Bloods adopted the color red and began to use the term *Bloods* to identify each other.

Within Crips sets, blue continues to be the dominant color. However, other dark colors such as black, brown, and purple may also be blended to identify certain sets.

Bloods sets still use red as the dominant color in most cases. However, other colors may be used if they are significant to the gang name, such as Lime Street Pirus.

The primary personal accessories that identify gang affiliations are hats, handkerchiefs, shoelaces, and belts.

Most gang members are identified by a nickname or street name. Often, members will not know each other by their legal names. A nickname is important because it can give insights into a member's psychological perspective of himself or herself, an indication of his/her physical description, and can aid in identification based on graffiti.

The first letter of the real name and a gang term often will be used for a nickname. Examples are C-Bone or T-Loc. These terms are intended to express a hardness or madness to non-gang-members. Many members will tattoo their moniker on their body.

Both Crips and Bloods have their own rules for speaking or writing to their "homeboys," another name for a gang member.

Some common rules exist, such as Crips do not use the letter *B;* Bloods will not use the letter *C* and will replace it with a *B.* For example, *cigarette* would become *bigarette.*

Communications may take different forms, and authorities must recognize these identifiers if they are to deal with gangs successfully. Clothing, guns, jewelry, hand signals, and tattoos are all forms of communication to gang members.

Graffiti is used by gang members to communicate territorial limits and to broadcast warnings or publicize a challenge to other street gangs. Challenges are made by one gang putting their graffiti on another's territory. This can be considered a killing offense by the gangs. Also, simply crossing out other gang's graffiti may lead to serious retaliation. Graffiti is an

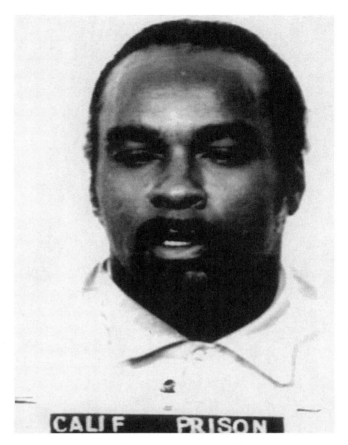

Stanley "Tookie" Williams, cofounder of the Crips (AP/California Department of Corrections)

effective way to keep track of gang rosters, geographic locations, and gang violence.

ENEMIES/RIVALS AND THEIR ALLIES

Crips and Bloods sets are rivals, and since Crips and Bloods are affiliated with Folk and Peoples Nations respectively, they are then rivals of all Folk or People sets and subsets.

Traditionally, Folk Nation–aligned sets and Peoples Nation–aligned sets are rivals. In addition, various other national and local street gangs develop as rivals, allies, and/or initiate alliances. Under each of these alliances there are literally hundreds of individual sets or gangs. These alliances and rivalries are constantly changing and need to be reviewed frequently.

For the Crips, allies are any gang that considers the Bloods an enemy and vice versa for the Bloods.

ORGANIZATION STRUCTURE

Authorities have discovered a centralized leadership in the New York and New England regions, whereas

Crips members display their signs. (AP)

on the West Coast neither the Crips nor the Bloods has centralized leadership. Instead, they are fragmented gangs that can be arranged into larger group affiliations generally based on their geographic area. This fragmentation makes these gangs more difficult for law enforcement to track and identify. The Crips and the Bloods do have an alliance with the Chicago-based gangs that make up the Folk and the Peoples Nations respectively.

Individual gangs are referred to as "sets." These sets, particularly the Crips sets, often form affiliations (group sets) within a geographic area. For example, Compton Crips (as many as 20 individual sets); Hoover Crips (about 10 individual sets); East Coast Crips (many sets). Set groupings are also based on the particular city where they may be located; for example, Compton Crips, LA Crips, San Diego

Crips. Areas and neighborhoods were soon identified as either Crips or Bloods territory. Presently there are about 200 known Crips gangs and 70 Bloods gangs in Los Angeles.

There are generally four types of individuals associated with street gangs. The "hard-cores" are exactly that. They talk, act, dress, and commit criminal acts as gang members. "Associates" will identify with gang members in their neighborhood but seldom involve themselves deeply with gang activity. Dope suppliers would be an example of an associate. "Peripherals" are those outside the gang who identify with the gang for protection or for favors. This group mainly consists of women. They are used to carry drugs or guns for members in return for money or drugs, though all-female gangs have also emerged. The last type is the "Gonna-Be." Gonna-

Be's are people who claim to be gang members in an attempt to influence people in areas outside the control of the gang. Gonna-Be's usually are not gang members but assume some characteristics such as wearing a particular gang color. These people are the recruitment pool for the gangs' new members. These Gonna-Be's can be more dangerous than the members themselves.

Most gang members range from eight to 35 years of age. The members ages eight to 18 appear to be the most violent. This is the period of time when new members are trying to prove themselves to older gang members and raise their status within the group.

Within gangs usually three groupings will appear: "Old Gangsters," or OGs, who are likely to be the originators of the set; "Gangsters," who are the hard-core members; and "BGs" (baby gangsters) or "TGs" (tiny gangsters), who are the younger child and juvenile members. The older members who have earned their reputations will often control younger members; for this reason they are referred to as "Shot Callers."

RECRUITMENT/INITIATION

Recruitment by these gangs is required by their bylaws and is usually pursued in a very aggressive and persistent manner. Recruitment often involves memorization of alliance and set history, organization, and mythical symbolism referred to as "knowledge." This knowledge, where it is copied, is often written and passed around by members/prospective members. The writings are often coded or cryptic, using a specific alphabet.

Initiation into these groups is accomplished by proving your loyalty to the gang, that you will give your life to the gang and that you love the gang. This is accomplished by ordering the prospect to commit crime, physically assaulting the prospect, having the prospect play Russian roulette or otherwise risk life for the group.

The most common form of initiation is described by members as "walking the line." The prospect is instructed to walk between two lines of group members, with his/her hands behind them, while the members beat and kick him/her, the objective being to get to the end of the gauntlet standing. Once the individual's knees touch the ground, he/she must repeat the process.

DISRUPTIVE BEHAVIOR THREAT IN SCHOOLS AND PRISONS

Authorities have observed that many of the behaviors listed within this section have also been observed by educators and school resource officers within the educational systems of the country, regardless of the location or in public and private schools. This includes large-city, urban, and rural schools.

When gang members are enrolled in schools or put into the general prison population, serious problems have developed. Teachers, students, and corrections officers are attacked with increasing frequency. Non-gang prisoners are often raped, assaulted, or killed by gang members in their efforts to establish turf or deal drugs inside the institutions. In schools, violent activities often occur in the vicinity of school grounds. At schools with gang populations, special screening and searches will often produce narcotics or weapons. Checking graffiti inside the school or prison oftentimes will indicate a potential "hit" on another student, a teacher, an inmate, or an officer.

As prison populations become more saturated with gang members, officials will need to watch for emerging prison gangs, such as the Death Row Crips (DRC) and the United Blood Nation (UBN), or the Cop Killas (CK). Although these gangs have only surfaced in isolated areas, there will be a natural growth inside the prisons as more members are sentenced.

BLOODS

The New York City Department of Correction in conjunction with information from the New England region intelligence brief had identified that these gang members are predominately black; however, the Bloods have accepted other ethnic groups into the gang. Hispanics, whites, Greeks, and Chinese members have been identified. In New York City jails, approximately 9 percent of the Bloods are Hispanic. These individuals engage in activities such as drug sales, robberies, car thefts, extortions, rapes, and murders.

To gain acceptance to the gang, individuals must "blood-in." This means they must spill someone's blood or have their own blood spilled. There are various ways to blood-in (fights, slashing, assaults against law-enforcement personnel, rapes, robberies, group sex for women initiates), but blood should be spilled. Bloods trace their history to

Chicago and Los Angeles, where open territorial fights are commonplace.

In New York City and the New England area, the Bloods have demonstrated a propensity for violent attacks against unknowing victims. Usually, victims are slashed across the face with little or no warning of the attack. Bloods have been identified in areas throughout New York City, in Brooklyn's 77th precinct (Crown Heights), Queens's 100th precinct (Far Rockaway), and Manhattan's 28th precinct (11th Street); in Bridgeport, East Lyme, Norwich, and New London, Connecticut; and in Providence, Rhode Island.

In New York City and New England jails, the Bloods have developed a reputation as a vicious gang, known especially for brutal stabbings and slashings throughout the Department of Corrections. The Bloods (approximately 500) have grown in number to where they now outnumber both the Latin Kings (approximately 350) and the Ñetas (approximately 350).

Bloods refers to the United Blood Nation, which in New York City jails encompasses these Blood sets: Nine Trey Gangsta Bloods (NTG); Miller Gangsta Bloods (MGB); Young Bloods; Valentine Bloods (VB); Mad Dog Bloods (MDB); One Eight Trey Bloods (183); Mad Stone Bloods (MSB); Gangsta Killer Bloods (GKB); Five Nine Brims (5–9 Brims); Sex Money Murder Bloods; and Blood Stone Villains (BSV).

Bloods can be identified by their tattoos: two burned dots over a single burned dot. This represents a dog's paw, and Bloods refer to themselves as "dogs." Additionally, Bloods wear the color red or clothing identified with the Chicago Bulls basketball team.

Besides their tattoos and clothing, the Bloods display signs and speak in codes. One such sign is to curl the thumb and index finger until they meet to from a circle. The three remaining fingers are extended straight out. This hand is then placed against the stomach area, palm of the hand face down with thumb and index finger touching the stomach (solar plexus area). Next, the hand is moved in a circular motion, turning the palm of the hand face up, touching the pinkie finger and the wrist to the midstomach area. As this process is completed, a Blood will say "031," which translates to "I have love for you, Blood." The Bloods change their codes on a regular basis and generally revert from new codes to old. Some codes are changed in their entirety.

B-L-O-O-D stands for: *Blood Love Overcomes Our Depressions.*

The Bloods organizational structure is:

- First Superior (this is the leader). Functions to oversee the set and act as the disciplinary officer.

- Second Superior. Functions to assist and advise the First Superior and carry out the First Superior's duties in his absence.

- Minister of Defense. Functions to provide strategies and information to the First Superior for the operations of the set.

- Minister of Information. Provides information concerning the set and its enemies.

- Head of Security. Provides weapons and discipline to all members of the set.

- Commanding Officer. Dictates orders as specified by the Superior.

- Captain. Disseminates orders among the Lieutenants.

- Head Lieutenant. Assists and advises the Captain, and carries out the Captain's duties in his absence.

- Lieutenant. Ensures that the Principal Soldiers carry out orders as issued by the Captain.

- Principal Soldier. Complies with orders from Lieutenants and keeps banging (fighting the enemy) at all times.

In general, every Blood's function is to keep banging at all times. No Blood is better than the next. Each Blood is a soldier, putting in "work" (fighting), maintaining the superiority of all Bloods over their enemies.

Each set follows this structure, with an individual identified for each position. Because there are many different sets, the Blood leadership in the streets of New York is not strong. Different boroughs or areas are under different sets. In the jails, leadership is strong; however, individuals do attempt to form new sets so that they can assume leadership. This is frowned on by the existing sets.

The Bloods' concepts of war are:

- Always listen before you talk, look before you walk, and observe before you stalk.

- In war, you must follow the commands of the higher rank, who is designated such because they are more if not better informed than you.

- Never make important decisions while angry because an intemperate nature can cause one to run into a brick wall. Allow time to rationalize.
- What is pain to a warrior is but a privilege; pain and handling pain are measures of a warrior, for to know victory is to know defeat.
- The injuries that you inflict on the enemy should be considered such a vicious act of terrorism that the damage inflicted causes the enemy never to consider revenge.
- Never allow the enemy to live in your midst because one day he may rise up to repay you for the mistake.
- One must be a fox to recognize a trap, and a lion to fight and intimidate the enemy.
- The best defense is oftentimes a good offense.
- There is no greater sin in war than ignorance.
- War has no room for diplomacy; war is outright vicious.
- Beware those around you who shout out the most, yet find time to talk during conflict. These individuals will reason with the enemy.
- In war, strive for rendering the enemy harmless, disrupting the enemy's alliances, and attacking before you are attacked.
- Silence and observation are major weapons in defense.
- During war or peace, never allow your priorities to be misguided.

Bloods have a view of themselves as gangsters, and as such many have taken gang names of organized-crime members: Capone, Nitti, Baby Face Nelson, Gambino, Scarface.

Reference
Southeastern Connecticut Gang Activities Group (SEGAG). "Bloods and Crips." Available online. URL: http:// www.segag.org. Downloaded on July 19, 2004.

BLOUIN, Martin (a.k.a. Blue)
Martin "Blue" Blouin was born on March 31, 1965, and became a member of the Rock Machine biker gang's Quebec chapter in the early 1990s. At that time Blouin had already been before the courts on 10 different occasions.

Police arrested Blouin, Fred Faucher, André Sauvageau, Normand Baker, and Guy Langlois in a Boucherville hotel on July 14, 1994. Police seized two pistols, three radio-detonated bombs, and 12 pounds of dynamite and charged the five Rock Machine members with conspiring to murder members of the Evil Ones biker club, a Hells Angels puppet gang.

Blouin pleaded guilty on charges of murder conspiracy and possession of firearms and explosives and, on February 3, 1995, was sentenced to 30 months in prison.

The Rock Machine member got tired of sitting in a jail cell and broke out in September 1997. He wasn't on the streets long: Police picked him up less than a week later. He posed no resistance when agents raided his Lac-Frontière hotel room.

On September 6, 2001, while on parole, Blouin was pulled over by police as he drove along Lafleche Street in Baie-Comeau. Inside his automobile, officers found a loaded 9-millimeter gun and a knife.

See also: HELLS ANGELS.

Reference
Gary Francoeur. "Martin 'Blue' Blouin." Wiseguy-Wally. Available online. URL: http://www.geocities.com/wiseguywally/MartinBlouin.html. Downloaded on July 19, 2004.

—G.F.

BLUE Lanterns
An aspiring member of a Chinese triad but not officially a member of a triad, until the prospective recruit is admitted to the gang.
See also: TRIADS.

BOGOTÁ Cartel
This cartel, set up in Bogotá, Colombia, was run for many years by Justo Pastor Perafan. From 1988 to 1997 the cartel under Perafan shipped more than 30 tons of drugs into the United States; more drugs were shipped into Western Europe. Like his contemporary, Escobar, Perafan lived a violent and flashy lifestyle. Perafan was later indicted by both the U.S. and Colombia governments. He lived as a fugitive in Venezuela but was eventually captured in 1996 and later stood trial and was sentenced to no more than 30 years in a Federal Court in New York.

The cartel led a smaller, second life under Alejandro Bernal-Madrigal. Bernal led a quieter life, that of a middle-class businessman. He used encrypted satellite telephones, laptops, and the Internet to run his business. He was apprehended in October 1999 and remains in jail. That was effectively the end of the Bogota Cartel.

See also: BERNAL-MADRIGAL, ALEJANDRO; PERAFAN, JUSTO PASTOR.

BONANNO Crime Family

The Bonanno crime family has had a rough time: Their members were caught selling drugs, and they were infiltrated by the famous Donnie Brasco (real name: Joseph Pistone), an undercover Federal Bureau of Investigation agent who helped decimate the Bonanno crime family. But they are making a comeback.

There are presently about 150 members in the family. The family's first Don was Joe Bonanno. The Bonannos' primary sources of income include narcotics trafficking, home-video pornography, pizza parlors, and espresso cafés.

The present reputed boss is Joseph Massino, 57 years old, currently part owner of the famed Casablanca Restaurant in Queens. According to authorities, he is currently the only New York Mafia boss not serving time. His principal source of legitimate income, authorities say, is King Caterers, a Long Island business that provides food to street vendors. Massino's underboss is Salvatore A. Vitale, Massino's brother-in-law.

See also: COLOMBO CRIME FAMILY; COMMISSION, THE; GAMBINO CRIME FAMILY; GENOVESE CRIME FAMILY; LUCCHESE CRIME FAMILY.

Reference

David Amoruso. "Bonanno Crime Family." Gangsters Incorporated. Available online. URL: http://gangstersinc. tripod.com/Bon.html. Downloaded on July 19, 2004.

—*D.A.*

BORN to Kill (a.k.a. BTK)

Born to Kill, also known by its anagram BTK, is a well-known, vicious Asian-American street gang, made up of Vietnamese refugees. The gang first appeared in the Chinatown section of New York City in the 1980s and quickly became infamous for vicious and random acts of brutality perpetrated on the merchants and citizens of Chinatown, under the leadership of psychopath David Thai. Their flashy dress, outrageous violence, and brutal methods made them a high-profile target for local, state, and federal police authorities.

BORYOKUDAN

Japanese crime groups are referred to by the Japanese National Police Agency as the *boryokudan,* which means "the violent ones." *Boryokudan* has replaced the historical label of *Yakuza,* a slang term which Japanese gang members gave themselves to depict an underdog image.

The official membership of Boryokudan groups in Japan is estimated to be 88,300, but there may be as many as 10 times that number of other criminal associates. The Boryokudan wield enormous influence in Japan and have penetrated many aspects of Japanese life, reaping substantial illegitimate profits and investing in many legitimate businesses. Boryokudan have become increasingly active internationally, particularly in global money-laundering operations and narcotics trafficking. The Japanese National Police estimate Boryokudan earnings worldwide to total $10 billion annually, a third of which comes from drug-trafficking activities.

The roots of the Boryokudan can be traced to the early 17th century when there existed a lower class of independent samurai warriors. These legendary figures have been the subject of many Japanese stories and as bandit heroes can be likened to Robin Hood.

Boryokudan origins can be traced to two other groups that evolved during the 18th and 19th centuries—street peddlers and gambling gangs. The street peddlers were organized into gangs with complex organizational structures that emphasized total loyalty. The gambling gangs were known as bakuto. Tattooing, which until recently was widely popular among Boryokudan members, and finger cutting (the practice of cutting off a joint of the little finger as an indication of remorse when an assigned task was not performed) began with the bakuto, which also maintained some degree of secrecy within each group.

In the 20th century, expansion of boryokudan activities corresponded with the growth of the Japanese economy. Boryokudan entered into a variety of businesses, most notably construction and transportation. Recently there have been numerous publicly reported incidents revealing the Boryokudan's involvement in public corruption that has also involved major figures in industry and finance.

During the past three decades, the Boryokudan have become immersed in real-estate development, company racketeering, and large-scale loansharking. Much of their business activity is facilitated through extortion, and Boryokudan leaders have often used strong-arm tactics in business transactions of all sizes.

The success of Japanese criminal groups on the domestic front has been facilitated by their being allowed to operate in the open. Boryokudan have functioned largely as public corporations, maintaining offices that display their group logo, and even carrying business cards that identify their gang.

The Boryokudan, until recently, submitted membership lists to the National Police Agency (NPA). While the Japanese police have recently used the substantial intelligence base generated by these lists to expand anti-Boryokudan efforts, a significant number of Japanese police officers have traditionally held some degree of respect for the gangsters. Breaking with past acceptance of Boryokudan, on March 1, 1992, the Japanese government began enforcement of a new "Boryokudan Countermeasures Law." The Japanese government has also promulgated new money-laundering statutes to go into effect at the end of l992.

During the last three decades, Japanese organized crime has expanded overseas. While Japanese crime groups have been active in Korea since the end of World War II, Boryokudan prostitution operations in Korea greatly expanded in the 1970s. During that decade, the Boryokudan became deeply involved in the international sex trade. Boryokudan-controlled prostitution, pornography, and "sex tour" operations stretched to Taiwan, the Philippines, and Thailand and later to South America, Europe, and the United States. Boryokudan members have recruited American women from Hawaii and the West Coast into prostitution in Japan.

Boryokudan operations in the United States during recent years have included gun running, drug trafficking, gambling, extortion, immigration fraud, securities violations, and money laundering.

Boryokudan gangs currently play a primary role in bringing crystal methamphetamine, also known as "ice," into Hawaii, where it is now regarded by law-enforcement officials as the number-one drug problem.

Japanese criminal figures routinely visit Las Vegas and to a lesser extent Atlantic City on gambling junkets. Additionally, Boryokudan members have been tied to illegal gambling operations in the United States.

Boryokudan members have kept a low profile in extortion operations in the United States. Although Boryokudan corporate extortionists, known as *sekoiya*, made appearances at corporate board meetings of such companies as BankAmerica and Chase Manhattan Bank in the early 1980s, these "visits" were of little consequence. No recent attempts to strong-arm blue-chip American firms have been documented. Street-level extortion of businesses by Boryokudan has been reported in Hawaii and southern California in recent years, but such activity has been minimal compared to the high level of Boryokudan extortion operations in Japan.

Currently, U.S. law-enforcement concern about Japanese crime groups is primarily focused on money laundering. Numerous instances exist where U.S. properties were purchased by individuals with alleged Boryokudan ties. U.S. law-enforcement authorities are convinced that substantial sums of money are still being successfully laundered in the United States.

The three largest Boryokudan groups are the Yamaguchi-gumi, the Inagawa-kai, and the Sumiyoshi-kai, which between them accounted in 1992 for about half the total membership. The Yamaguchi-gumi, headquartered in Kobe, is by far the largest group having (in 1992) 944 affiliate gangs and 26,200 Yakuza under its command. These gangs had been able to expand through tribute payments from their affiliate gangs, without direct involvement in the affiliates' illegal activities. In addition, most illegal activity in these gangs is not directed from the top. In some respects the way the gangs operate on a day-to-day basis resembles a pyramided franchise structure. Subordinates make regular payments to the person ranking above them. In exchange, they are allowed to use the name of the organization to provide the necessary fear and intimidation to support their own independently organized criminal activities. However, the whole gang is capable of operating as a single unit, controlled from the top, if necessary—in response to attacks on one of its members, for example. The higher levels also have the ability to mediate turf disputes between competing subunits of the gang.

A 1994 media report states that many Yakuza groups have tried to bypass the countermeasures law by reincorporating themselves as industrial, political, and even religious groups. The Yamaguchi-gumi has apparently reestablished part of its organization as the National League to Purify the Land, a nonprofit charity ostensibly dedicated to stamping out drug abuse. The Sumiyoshi-kai, the second largest gang, has become Hori Enterprises. The Inagawa-kai, the third largest, is now Inagawa Industries. Some Yakuza members, however, have apparently become increasingly violent in Japan since 1992.

See also: INAGAWA-KAI; SUMIYOSHI-KAI; YAMAGUCHI-GUMI.

Reference

Parliamentary Joint Committee on the National Crime Authority. *Asian Organised Crime in Australia, A Discussion Paper by the Parliamentary Joint Committee on National Crime Authority: Australia and Organized Crime.*

BOUCHARD, Conrad

Conrad Bouchard started in the Montreal underworld by singing Italian opera melodies in Mafia-owned nightclubs. He befriended mobsters and was soon working alongside Peter "the Russian" Stepanoff and Giuseppe "Pep" Cotroni in drug trafficking, armed robberies and fencing stolen bonds. The organization's second-in-command, Luigi Greco, took a liking to Bouchard and decided to "school" him in the life. Bouchard wasn't very well liked by all underworld figures, but his relationship to Greco make him untouchable. He even bought a house next door to the chieftain, and they spent a lot of time together. In June 1959 police tracked Bouchard, accompanying Giuseppe Cotroni and René Robert, on a trip to New York City to meet with drug traffickers.

The singer-turned-gangster ran into serious legal problems in the late 1960s. He was linked to two frauds in 1966. A Quebec City branch of the Provincial Bank reported a loss of $110,000, and the Canadian Acceptance Corporation in Montreal was taken for $269,000. Bouchard was also charged in a $723,000 armed robbery at a Laval bank, north of Montreal, and for receiving a share of the profits from another bank robbery. He was convicted on the crimes and received a 30-month prison sentence.

Bouchard was again arrested in June 1969 and charged with conspiring to manufacture and distribute hundreds of thousands of counterfeit six-cent stamps. Things became even worse for him when, while out on bail, he was implicated in a sophisticated million-dollar scam involving a bank and two firms. With all of his legal expenses, Bouchard sank deeper into drug trafficking, but police tracked all of his movements and took notes as he met with known traffickers. Narcotics Squad officers burst into Bouchard's hotel room on January 15, 1972, and arrested him. He tried desperately to hide an address book in his waistband but it was confiscated. He was charged with conspiring to import heroin and drug possession. Luigi Greco, Bouchard's mentor and underboss of the organization, died in a chemical fire in his pizzeria in 1972. Bouchard was devastated by the unfortunate news and paid his respects to his teacher by singing Schubert's "Ave Maria" at the ceremony. Police kept the pressure on Conrad Bouchard, and an agent managed to infiltrate his narcotics network. Even more harmful evidence was gathered against the mobster, and in 1974 Bouchard was seen as beyond rehabilitation and was sentenced to life imprisonment. He died of cancer in 1995.

Reference

Gary Francoeur. "Conrad Bouchard." WiseguyWally. Available online. URL: http://www.geocities.com/wiseguywally/ConradBouchard.html. Downloaded on July 19, 2004.

—G.F.

BOUCHER, Maurice (a.k.a. Mom)

Maurice Boucher, known to his criminal cohorts as "Mom," was born on June 21, 1953. He was raised in the Hochelaga-Maisonneuve section of Montreal and at a very young age became fascinated with the criminals in his neighborhood. He admired the thick wads of cash they carried and the respect they received.

Boucher first got in trouble with the law in 1973 at the age of 19. He was arrested for stealing $200 but managed to avoid jail time. He wasn't so fortunate in 1976, though, when he received a 40-month jail sentence for armed robbery. He would serve 23 more months in 1984 for armed sexual aggression.

Boucher and Salvatore Cazzetta were members of the SS motorcycle gang until its dissolution in 1984. Cazzetta, along with his younger brother Giovanni, went on to form the formidable Rock Machine biker club. Boucher, on the other hand, approached the world's most renowned motorcycle gang, the Hells Angels.

The Hells Angels bestowed on Boucher his colors on May 1, 1987, days after Martin Huneault, president of a gang, the Death Riders, was shot to death in a Laval bar. The murder allowed the Hells Angels to control drug trafficking in Laval and the lower Laurentians. It also paved Boucher's way to the top of Quebec's deadly biker underworld.

Boucher avoided the spotlight and, by the early 1990s, had risen to become the president of the Hells Angels Montreal chapter. He also ran the Montreal-based Rockers motorcycle gang, and it was rumored he received $500 for every kilo of cocaine sold in the French Canadian city.

But that still wasn't enough for the monopolistic Boucher. He wanted a piece of the Rock Machine's downtown Montreal drug profits. The Rock Machine refused and an onslaught commenced.

Boucher was on his way to Sherbrooke on March 24, 1995, when police officers stopped him on suspicion of having hashish. An unregistered 9-millimeter pistol was found tucked in his belt. "Mom" pleaded guilty to two firearm charges and was sentenced to six months in prison. He was released after serving almost four months of his sentence.

Boucher, along with eight other influential members, formed the Hells Angels Nomads chapter on June 24, 1995. The new faction, with Boucher as its undisputed leader, had two goals before them: taking over Ontario's lucrative drug market and eliminating the rival Rock Machine.

While still on parole for firearm possession, Boucher was overheard on a wiretapped telephone advising Hells Angels sympathizer Steven Bertrand to assault someone with a baseball bat. Police issued an arrest warrant for his arrest, and Boucher turned himself in at 5:30 P.M. on October 25, 1995. The judge ruled that the prosecution had not proved that Boucher was a threat to society, so "Mom" was liberated.

But police knew that Boucher was key to the Hells Angels' Quebec operations and arrested him again on December 19, 1997. He was charged with ordering the murders of two prison guards. Diane Lavigne was gunned down in her automobile as she drove home after her shift at Montreal's Bordeaux prison, and Pierre Rondeau was murdered while at the wheel of a prison transport bus.

Security was severe in the courtroom, and everyone entering was examined and videotaped.

Stéphane Gagné, who admitted to participating in the slayings on Boucher's orders, testified against the feared Hells Angels leader. But the defense hammered away at his credibility to such an extent that the jury ruled that Gagné had none.

The world was stunned on November 27, 1998, when the jury pronounced Boucher innocent of all charges. Friends applauded as he swaggered out of the courtroom. Boucher, accompanied by bodyguards, spent his first night of freedom at Montreal's Molson Centre, where he watched boxer Davey Hilton defeat Stéphane Ouellet in a surprising upset. The 18,000 fight fans in the building welcomed Boucher and gave him a standing ovation.

Boucher met with Rock Machine leader Frederic "Fred" Faucher at the Bleu Marin restaurant in Montreal on October 8, 2000, to negotiate a peace agreement between the two gangs. A reporter from the French tabloid *Allo Police* was invited to the dinner and took a picture of the two men shaking hands. But the peace did not even last two months, and when the Rock Machine became probationary Bandidos on December 1, 2000, the killings picked up once more.

The Hells Angels leader's legal problems continued to plague him. He was arrested again on October 10, 2000, after Quebec's Court of Appeal dismissed Boucher's 1998 acquittal of killing two prison guards and agreed to a new trail. Boucher was apprehended by police while leaving a restaurant.

Boucher was placed in an isolated cell at Tanguay's Women Prison. Contact with the general population was prohibited. The unit contained two televisions, a radio, a Walkman, a Nintendo entertainment system, a washer and a dryer.

On March 28, 2001, as part of Opération Printemps 2001, Boucher learned from his jail cell that he would be charged with 13 additional murders as well as drug trafficking and gangsterism charges.

Boucher's second trial on charges of ordering the murders of prison guards Diane Lavigne and Pierre Rondeau began in March 2002. He was also charged with the attempted murder of Robert Corriveau, a guard who was injured in the same attack that killed Rondeau. The prosecution's main witness was once again Stéphane "Godasse" Gagné. He testified that he, along with bikers Paul "Fon Fon" Fontaine and Andre "Toots" Tousignant, were ordered to kill the guards by Boucher himself. Defense lawyers tried to undermine Gagne's credibility by describing him as a "hit man" and a "liar." The jury began its deliberation on April 25, 2002. Eleven days later, they reached a verdict: guilty. Boucher was sentenced to life in a federal penitentiary without the possibility of parole for 25 years. The decision was shocking, as many had long seen the Hells Angels as untouchable.

See also: HELLS ANGELS.

Reference

Gary Francoeur. "Maurice 'Mom' Boucher." Wiseguy-Wally. Available online. URL: http://www.geocities.com/wiseguywally/MauriceBoucher.html. Downloaded on July 19, 2004.

—G.F.

BOUT, Victor

Victor Anatoliyevich Bout was born on January 13, 1967, in Dushanbe, Tajikistan. Not much is known about his early life, but at one point he joined the military and after training began to work at a Russian military base in Vitebsk as a navigator. After a few years he expanded his duties and trained commando troops of the Russian air force. In 1991 Bout graduated from Moscow's Military Institute for foreign languages and could speak six languages fluently; he now expanded his duties in the military and became a translator for the Russian army in Angola, Africa. However, in that same year, 1991, the military base where Bout was working was disbanded as a result of the collapse of the Soviet Union. Bout and his fellow officers were out of a job, but they were well trained, had access to all the equipment they needed, and, more important, had all the international contacts. So it was that Bout started Transavia Export Cargo Company, which in 1993 helped supply the Belgian peacekeeping forces in Somalia, Africa. But that was not the only work Bout's company did: Once his company had been set up, Bout made contacts with an Afghani group called the Northern Alliance and was selling them large amounts of weapons. In fact, from 1992 until 1995 Bout supplied several Afghani groups with tons of ammunition and weapons. With the money he made from these deals, allegedly $50 million, Bout expanded his empire.

In March 1995 Bout started a company in the Belgian city Oostende (Ostend), named Trans Aviation Network Group. The company had difficulty from the start when their main customer, the Afghani Northern Alliance, was pushed out of power by the Taliban. In May 1995 a plane filled with weapons and ammunition destined for the Northern Alliance was intercepted in Afghanistan by the Taliban. The crew was held captive until August 16, 1996, when they managed to escape. Not long after, Bout had a new customer, the Taliban. It was not his first contact with the Taliban: He had sold them weapons before but not in the large shipments he sent them now. Business was good; Bout enjoyed his life in Ostend, Belgium: He bought a mansion and had several expensive cars; in Moscow he bought an apartment in one of the more exclusive neighborhoods. But life in Belgium did not stay sweet for long. In 1997 Belgian newspapers published reports about Bout's shady operation, and when Belgian authorities began to look into his business, Bout moved to the United Arab Emirates.

His United Arab Emirates company was also founded in 1995 and, based first in Sharjah and later in 2001 in Ajman, would be his main base of operations. The UAE was a perfect place for a man like Bout: It was a major financial center and a crossroad for East and West trade, and with its bank secrecy laws and free trade zones, it was paradise on earth for any arms dealer. From his base in Sharjah, Bout ran his empire, which by 1995 also included Africa. In 1995 Bout founded Air Cess in Liberia, the beginning of Bout's grip on weapons supplying in Africa. Bout did not care who he supplied with weapons or for what cause as long as people he supplied paid the dollars. U.S. and UN officials say that Bout airlifted thousands of assault rifles and grenade and missile launchers and millions of ammunition rounds into Africa. Clients of Bout's companies include Angola, Cameroon, Central African Republic, Democratic Republic of Congo, Equatorial Guinea, Kenya, Liberia, Libya, Congo-Brazzaville, Rwanda, Sierra Leone, South Africa, Sudan, Swaziland, and Uganda.

Most of the weapons that arrived in Africa came from Bulgaria, to which Bout had made frequent trips between 1995 and 2000. In 2000 Bout was seen visiting six weapons factories there. Between July 1997 and September 1998 Bout organized 38 flights, with weapons shipments worth an estimated $14 million, to African nations. In the summer of 2000, four of Bout's planes landed in Liberia with weapons on board. Among the shipments were helicopters, armored vehicles, antiaircraft guns, and automatic rifles. By now, of course, law enforcement was beginning to understand Bout's place in the world of arms dealing and decided to take him down, something that would be more difficult than thought at first.

By the time the world took notice of Bout, he was safely in his home in Sharjah in the United Arab Emirates and had made the political connections and money that made him almost untouchable. On top of that, the law enforcement units did not even have any proof. Bout's empire was a maze of people, companies, planes, and routes. It was impossible to check where and when Bout's planes flew and which planes belonged to him. Bout kept moving himself and his companies around and had nothing registered in his own name. When they finally had the evidence to charge him, Bout was protected by highly placed UAE royalty and officials such as Sultan Hamad Said Nassir al Suwaidi, advisor to the ruler of Sharjah, who apparently also co-owned one of Bout's companies. Authorities wanted him, but when he seemed too far out of reach, the interest to catch him died down, as did the intensity with which he was hunted. But then came September 11, 2001, which changed everyone's priorities.

On September 11, 2001, al-Qaeda terrorists attacked New York and the entire free world. Al-Qaeda was very close to the extreme muslims of the Afghani Taliban, a group that was supplied with weapons by Bout. So it was that after September 11 Bout became a top priority for the United States. Old evidence was pulled from the shelves, and new evidence was collected. It looked like Bout's time was up. His name was everywhere, in newspapers and on television; everyone knew of Victor Bout's arms-dealing empire, but no one knew where Bout was or how to catch him. By now the United States and Interpol were looking everywhere but couldn't find him; the United Arab Emirates were hesitant to cooperate but eventually caved in, although one can only guess if they really did, and even if they did, Bout was always safe in his homeland, Russia, where corrupt officials knew how to hide a man like Bout. Russia was asked by the United States and Interpol to deliver Bout; at the height of the tension Moscow decided to give a press conference in which they said that Bout was not in Russia. It turned out to be an enormous blunder because at exactly the same time as the Moscow press conference, Bout was giving his own conference at a Moscow radio station, Ekho Moskvy, in a live interview in which he claimed his innocence and told that he "was just a businessman." Victor Bout is still on the run and still in freedom; the status of his arms-dealing empire is unknown at this moment, but with all the money and connections he has made in the past, Bout does not really need to continue that business.

Reference

David Amoruso. "Victor Bout." Gangsters Incorporated. Available online. URL: http://gangstersinc.tripod.com/VictorBout.html. Downloaded on July 19, 2004.

—D.A.

BOWMAN, Harry Joseph (a.k.a. Taco)

As president of the international Outlaws Motorcycle Club, Bowman allegedly was involved in a number of violent acts. Reputedly, Bowman led the Outlaws' operations in more than 30 cities in the United States and some 20 chapters in at least four other countries. The Outlaws have chapters in Florida, Illinois, Wisconsin, Tennessee, North Carolina, Ohio, Indiana, Georgia, New York, Pennsylvania, Massachusetts, Kentucky, and Michigan, as well as in Canada. Overseas, the Outlaws have established chapters in Australia, France, and Norway. Bowman has strong ties to Michigan.

He was accused of murdering two Outlaws members, Arthur Allen Vincent in Ormond Beach, Florida, in 1982, and Donald Fogg in Indiana in 1995. He was also indicted for the murder of Raymond Chaffin, president of a rival motorcycle club, the Warlocks, in Edgewater, Florida, in 1991.

Bowman, known by the nickname Taco, was also charged with the 1994 bombings of rival motorcycle clubhouses—the Warlocks' clubhouse in Orlando, Florida, and the Hell's Henchmen clubhouse in Cook County, Illinois.

At the age of 49, Bowman was wanted by the FBI for numerous crimes that include murder, attempted murder, narcotics distribution, bombings, extortion, robbery, and firearms violation. Bowman was considered an armed and extremely dangerous individual. A reward of $50,000 had been offered for information directly leading to his arrest.

Bowman disappeared after being charged in August 1997 in an indictment obtained by the U.S. Attorney's Office for the Middle District of Florida. At the time of his disappearance, Bowman was a resident of Grosse Pointe Farms, Michigan.

He was arrested June 8, 1999, by FBI agents and Sterling Heights, Michigan, police officers at a residence in suburban Detroit. FBI negotiators spoke to

Bowman on the phone, and he knew that the house was surrounded. He was arrested without incident.

Director Louis Freeh said, "The capture of Harry Joseph Bowman shows again the importance of the public's cooperation with law enforcement in the search for fugitives. A tip from the public led directly to Bowman's arrest. The successful conclusion to the search also demonstrates the enormous value of close working relationships between the FBI and local law enforcement agencies. In this instance, the initiative and work of the Sterling Heights Police Department were outstanding."

See also: OUTLAWS MOTORCYCLE CLUB.

Reference

U.S. Department of Justice, Federal Bureau of Investigation. "Press Release, June 8, 1999." Available online. URL: http://www.fbi.gov/pressrel/pressrel99/bowman. htm. Accessed on November 24, 2004.

BOYD Gang

Dashing, daring, and flamboyant, Edwin Alonzo Boyd and his gang burst onto the front pages of Toronto newspapers due to a series of well-executed bank robberies and two breakouts from Toronto's infamous Don Jail. Boyd's swashbuckling style of hopping bank counters and lightning-fast stickups electrified Toronto residents. Although his gang's reign as Canada's most notorious crooks was relatively short—a mere 10 months—their escapades were the stuff that legends are made of. These men were local heroes until two of the members shot down two detectives in cold blood, killing one. The gang consisted of four members, Edwin Boyd, Willie Jackson, Lennie Jackson, and Steve Suchan. The two Jacksons were not related.

Boyd robbed his first bank in September 1949. He plastered his face with makeup and stuffed his cheeks with cotton to disguise his appearance and escaped with the loot, even though the bank manager emptied his revolver at the fleeing robber. Boyd decided to see just how well his disguise had worked, so a day or two later, bold as brass, he walked into the same bank and changed a $20 bill with the teller he had robbed. He was not recognized, so he decided to hone his skills and become a full-time bank robber.

Boyd continued robbing banks, sometimes with his former jail guard partner, Howard Gault, sometimes solo. His solo efforts were not always successful. At one stickup the bank manager grabbed a gun from a desk drawer and popped off a few rounds at Boyd who returned fire. He had no choice but to turn tail and run but this time without the loot. Another time, Boyd was chased in his stolen car by a bank employee, just barely escaping.

Finally his luck ran out. On his last attempt with Gault, everything went wrong, and even though Boyd got away, Gault did not. Gault broke down under police questioning and spilled the beans. Soon the two of them were comfortably behind the iron bars of the Don Jail.

During this time there was another gang pulling bank jobs in and around the city. They were more violent and carried heavy arms, including a submachine gun. They sometimes clubbed a bank employee over the head or fired their guns into the wall to get their point across. Two of the members of this gang were Steve Suchan (real name Valent Lesso) and Lennie Jackson. Suchan avoided capture, but Jackson wasn't so lucky.

Steve Suchan was a multitalented musician and probably the least likely bank robber in the history of Toronto. However, when he discovered that he could not make a decent living as a violinist, he traded his violin in for a handgun at a pawnshop.

Jackson had had an accident while trying to hop a freight train sometime earlier and now walked on a wooden foot. He had been working at a local bar where many of Toronto's more successful crooks hung out. He liked the cars these guys drove, and he liked the large amounts of cash they spread around even better. It did not take Jackson long to make a career change and throw in with them. But, unfortunately for Jackson, he had been picked up by the police with some incriminating evidence and was lodged in the Don Jail when Boyd arrived.

Boyd ended up in the same area as Jackson, and soon the two were comparing notes. Not long after this, another career criminal came into the cellblock. Born just across the Don River in the tough Toronto neighborhood of Cabbagetown, Willie Jackson had a long history of violent robberies on his résumé. Willie Jackson was a joker and a prankster and quickly became friends with the other two. He was also awaiting transfer to Kingston Penitentiary to serve seven years for robbery with violence.

Not only did Lennie Jackson's wooden foot help him to walk upright, but it also came in handy to hide such things as hacksaw blades. So Lennie Jackson whipped out the blades, and the three proceeded to saw the bars from the window leading outside. On November 4, 1951, the three slid through the opening and dropped to the prisoner's exercise yard below. Using some bedsheets that they had tied together, they then lassoed the top of the surrounding wall and climbed to freedom.

Steve Suchan had arranged a safe house in Cabbagetown that they could reach quickly and organize themselves. Later, Lennie Jackson and his girlfriend, Ann Roberts, took off for Montreal with Suchan close behind. Boyd and Willie Jackson landed at Steve Suchan's parent's house in the west end.

Realizing they would need money to keep in hiding for a while, they robbed a nearby bank. A couple of weeks later they pulled off the biggest holdup in Toronto's history. After splitting up the money, Lennie Jackson and Suchan headed back to Montreal to lay low. Boyd and Willie Jackson hid out at Suchan's parent's home.

Steve Suchan's father came up with a great idea: He had a little hiding spot in the wall where the boys could safely stash their money. The next morning the old man was gone, and so was most of the loot. The whole gang then headed down to Montreal to hide out with wives and girlfriends in tow. Willie Jackson got busted for carrying a gun and was soon returned to Toronto, where he received an additional two years for escaping custody. The rest of the gang also came back to Toronto but under their own steam.

On March 6, 1952, Detectives Edmund Tong and Roy Perry pulled over a black Mercury Monarch automobile. It is unlikely that Tong knew that the car contained Suchan and Lennie Jackson, or he would have had his revolver at the ready. As Tong approached the suspect vehicle, he was gunned down and fell to the ground in a heap. The weapons were then aimed at the police car, which still held Perry, and they peppered the cruiser with bullets. Although Perry was wounded in the arm, he was very lucky to escape with his life. Tong died several days later but not before naming his killer, Suchan.

The manhunt was on, and this time it would be relentless. Suchan and Lennie Jackson made it back to Montreal unscathed. Even though he had nothing to do with the shooting, Boyd felt the heat. His picture was once again plastered all over every Toronto newspaper. Up until this time, Boyd and his wife could at least leave their house and attend a movie after dark, but now they had to stay completely out of sight.

Meanwhile, in Montreal the next day, the police were in Suchan's apartment waiting for him to return home. As he entered his place, he was told by police to freeze; he reached for his gun and was shot down before he could unholster it. A few days later, due to a neighbors tip, the police moved in on Lennie Jackson's apartment. The second arrest did not go as easily, and a lengthy shootout ensued. Finally, with dozens of tear-gas bombs burning his eyes and lungs, Lennie Jackson came out with a few bullet holes in him. The two survived their wounds and would soon be returned to Toronto.

Now Boyd was the only gang member left to be captured. Detective Dolph Payne had kept Boyd's brother under surveillance and discovered that he had rented a flat on Heath Street but had not moved in yet. He secured a key to the backdoor from the owner. Payne then watched Boyd move into the flat from a neighbor's house. Wanting to avoid a shootout, he waited until he was sure everyone was asleep. At the crack of dawn the police crept inside the house and captured Boyd and his wife while they were still in bed. Boyd's brother, who was sleeping in another room, was also apprehended—no shootouts, no struggle, not even a whimper.

Boyd was once again a resident of the Don Jail, and much to his delight the other three gang members soon showed up. Incredibly, the powers that be at the Don herded the four of them together into the otherwise empty deathrow cellblock.

Soon they had a piece of metal, a file, and more hacksaw blades smuggled in to them. By eyeballing the guard's keys, they were able to file the metal piece down to something that resembled a key, but it actually worked. Now they could let themselves out of their cells for a half hour or so while all the guards were supervising the transfer of prisoners to Toronto's City Hall courthouse. It took several days to saw through the bars, but finally they were ready.

Just before dawn on September 8, 1952, the four slipped out through the bars onto a wall that was conveniently located just outside the window. But to their horror, a cop was stationed at the base of the wall. They lay on top of the wall for a few minutes watching the cop and wondering what to do next. Suddenly, the officer walked across the laneway and knocked on a backdoor at the Riverdale hospital; as the door opened, he entered. It did not take them long to drop to the ground and disappear down the hill into the wilds of the Don Valley, which ran next to the jail.

Once again a huge manhunt ensued. The reward for information leading to the gang's capture hit $26,000, causing hundreds of phone calls and letters to the police. Most of these leads proved false.

They holed up in an old barn near Yonge and Sheppard. One at a time they would leave the barn to scrounge up clothes and food. Rumor has it that Boyd actually spent a night with his wife on one of his excursions. But they tended to be a bit lax while hiding out here and were spotted many times. Most people thought they were just hoboes seeking shelter, but some became suspicious and called police.

On September 16, 1952, police closed in on the barn and surprised the gang. They were apprehended without incident and finally returned to the familiar old Don Jail. They would never escape jail again.

Edwin Alonzo Boyd was found guilty of bank robbery and various other crimes; he received several concurrent life sentences. He was released on parole in 1966. He assumed a new legal identity and moved to western Canada.

Willie Jackson received a total of 31 years, which included the time that he had already been given in his previous convictions. He was also paroled in 1966.

Both Lennie Jackson and Steve Suchan were sentenced to death by hanging for the murder of Detective Edmund Tong.

Various other nonmembers of the gang with connections to the criminals received jail time for crimes ranging from harboring a criminal to armed robbery.

Justice was swift and sure. On December 16, 1952, Lennie Jackson and Steve Suchan were led from their cells to the gallows at the Don Jail. At 12:14 A.M. the hangman released the trap door, and the duo fell through on the end of a hangman's rope. They were officially pronounced dead at 1:00 A.M.

Reference

http://www.geocities.com/Hollywood/Club/7400/boyd-gang.html.

BRONSHTEIN, Antuan

Russian émigré Antuan Bronshtein was an enforcer for numerous Russian mob interests. He shot Jerome Slobotkin to death near Slobotkin's Philadelphia home on February 19, 1991. In 1988, Slobotkin had testified against Nicodemo Scarfo and other Scarfo associates.

Bronshtein also murdered Alexander Gutman. Bronshtein shot Gutman to death execution-style with a Northeast Philadelphia resident on January 11, 1994, at the Gutman's Philadelphia jewelry store. *See also:* RUSSIAN MAFIYA.

Reference

New Jersey State Commission of Investigation, New York Organized Crime Task Force, New York State Commission of Investigation, Pennsylvania Crime Commission, with Rutgers University. "The Tri-State Joint Soviet-Émigré Organized Crime Project." Available online. URL: http://www.state.nj.us/sci/pdf/russian.pdf. Accessed on November 24, 2004.

BROTHERHOOD

Primarily located in the towns of Groton, Ledyard, Mystic, New London and in the correctional facilities in Connecticut, recent information has noted the presence of the Brotherhood in other New England states as well. The gang is a spin off of the Chicago-based Folk Nation group Brotherhood of the Struggle/Black Gangster Disciples.

Membership is primarily blacks and black Hispanic males. The Brotherhood has an established hierarchy and a chain of command.

Folk Nation gang members use symbols and identifying apparel on the right side of their bodies, such as the six-pointed Star of David or a six-pointed crown, a heart, or a flame or torch. Brotherhood members identify each other by means of "colors," white beads, worn on the neck or on their wrists. Brotherhood members also can be identified by wearing black and white beads. Members who are on the ministers of security team wear a white band on the ring finger.

Other means of identifying Brotherhood members are graffiti which comes in the form of arms crossed in front to show the "X" mark and tattoos which are similar to their graffiti. Members also greet each other by shaking hands, with thumbs facing upward.

The gang maintains alliances with the Young Black Youth, Brotherhood of the Struggle, Latin Kings, Pump Nation, and Ñeta. While imprisoned, members may identify with the BOS. Rivals include 20 Luv, Los Solidos, and ECB.

The Brotherhood's main businesses include drugs, assaults, intimidation, extortion, and murder.

The Brotherhood adhere to a set of 15 rules and regulations, "qualifications and positional functions" of ranking members, and a formal pledge and oath that all members of the Brotherhood take upon entering the Brotherhood.

They also adhere to a Code for "Penalties and Infractions," which include penalties and fines for violations.

The Brotherhood has a reputation for violence such as assaults, extortion, attempted murder and murder of rival gang members, civilians, and inmates for refusing membership or disrespecting their gang. Incidents of assaults and intimidation toward white inmates and civilians have been reported.

Funds are generally derived from extortion of weaker inmates, students, and civilians or from receipts from illegal drug activity.

The established hierarchy is as follows: president, vice president, generals of security, "MOST"—ministers of security team, lieutenants, representatives, secretary of communication, secretary spokesman of roots, investigators, and treasurer. This group originated with three military dependents who had been affiliated with the Black Gangster Disciples set in the region of the Great Lakes naval base, located near Chicago, Illinois.

Reference

Southeastern Connecticut Gang Activities Group (SEGAG). "Brotherhood." Available online. URL: http://www. segag.org. Downloaded on July 19, 2004.

BROTHERHOOD of the Struggle

The Brotherhood of the Struggle was formed in the State of Illinois Prison System in the '60s and is a spin off of the Black Gangster Disciple Nation from Chicago. The New England region Brotherhood was founded on the streets of Bridgeport, Stamford, and Norwalk, Connecticut, in the mid- to late '80s. There are also reports of Brotherhood members in the cities of Danbury and Waterbury.

Primarily black males, the Brotherhood has an established hierarchy and a chain of command as follows: president, vice president, generals of security, lieutenants, representatives, secretary of communication, secretary, spokesman of roots, investigators, and treasury. There are currently 15 bylaws that the members follow, along with a pledge and an oath that all members take upon entering the gang.

White beads worn on the neck or wrist and white bands on the hands, and at times black/white beads, are the gang's colors. Members of the Brotherhood display the Star of David, the initials *BE,* and at times display their belts open and turned to the right.

They have alliances with Folk Nation, Gangster Disciples, Latin Kings, Pump Nation, Ñeta, Nation, and at times the BOWS. Rival gangs include 20 Luv, Los Solidos, Black Gangster Disciples, and ECB. Their criminal activities include narcotics, weapons, extortion, assaults, and intimidation.

Members of the Brotherhood have exhibited violence both inside correctional facilities and on the streets. Violence includes assaults on staff, inmates, and gang members who do not conduct themselves in a manner in accordance with gang rules. Brotherhood members have also assaulted inmates who refuse to join their gang.

The main source of income for the Brotherhood is funds derived from drug trade and extortion.

The Brotherhood is organized with rank structure to include president, vice president, generals of security, lieutenants, representatives, secretary of communications, secretary, spokesman of roots, investigators, and treasury.

Members are known to possess weapons and utilize semi- and fully automatic weapons on the street. They carry and use these weapons to protect their drug turf and trade. Inside facilities, Brotherhood members have been found to be in possession of shanks. They protect other members with their member of security team (MOST). These members stand posts in dining halls, recreation areas, and housing units to protect other Brotherhood members from attacks by rival gang members. The Brotherhood also has peace treaties with the Latin Kings, Pump Nation, and Ñeta. Intelligence from our facilities has indicated that on at least two occasions the Brotherhood has honored this treaty by backing these gangs when they engaged rival gangs in disturbances.

HISTORY

The Brotherhood of the Struggle was formed in the State of Illinois Prison System in the '60s and is a spin off of the "Black Gangster Disciple Nation" from Chicago. In Chicago the B.O.S. and the B.G.D. are seen as nearly synonymous.

The members of the New England gang known as the B.O.S. consider and refer to each other as "Gangsters." The B.O.S. and the Nation gangs sometimes use the initials *B.O.S.* in graffiti in reference to the Brotherhood of the Struggle, incarcerated Brotherhood members who are currently in struggle with the correctional system. The Brotherhood is also referred to at times as The Brotherhood of Roots, as is evidenced by their graffiti.

Members of the Brotherhood are predominantly black and male and are known to walk with their belt buckles open and turned to the right, wear their right pants leg rolled up, or have a handkerchief tied around their right arm or leg.

In the late '60s and the early '70s, several gangs in the Chicago area formed a nation of gangs in response to the emergence of gangs in the area. The leader and founder of the Black Gangster Disciple Nation (BGDN), was David "King David" Barksdale, who was wounded in an ambush in 1969 and died of kidney failure in 1974. The Brotherhood of the Struggle is a direct spin off of the BGDN.

The Star of David, a six-pointed star, was adopted by the gang in his honor and is displayed by members of the Brotherhood on the streets as well as in facilities. In addition, Brotherhood members display white beads, a white bracelet on their wrists, and a white band or ring on their fingers.

The Brotherhood has been involved in narcotics trafficking; violent incidents including brutal assaults on staff, inmates, and citizens in the community; and extortion. Intimidation, recruiting, and weapons possessions have also been reported.

BYLAWS
The Brotherhood adhere to a set of 15 rules and regulations, qualifications and positional functions of ranking members, and a formal pledge and an oath that all members of the Brotherhood take on entering the Brotherhood.

They also adhere to a code for penalties and infraction, which include penalties and fines for violations.

Reference
Southeastern Connecticut Gang Activities Group (SEGAG). "Brotherhood of the Struggle." Available online. URL: http://www.segag.org. Downloaded on July 19, 2004.

BRUINSMA, Klaas (a.k.a. De Dominee)
Klaas Bruinsma would become known as the first Dutch godfather. His organization would be the first organized and extremely violent group in Holland. He was feared throughout the land and banned from or wanted by most countries for his role in numerous drugs shipments. He made millions shipping thousands of kilograms of drugs through Europe. But like many other criminals, Bruinsma too would fall. Klaas Bruinsma was born on October 6, 1953, in Amsterdam, Holland, into a wealthy world: His father was the chief executive officer of a major Dutch beverage factory and had made a small fortune by the time his son was born. Klaas's father Ton Bruinsma was a complicated man: He had been married twice before marrying the woman who would give birth to his four children, Klaas included. But the marriage did not last, and the woman left them and returned to her native England. After this third divorce Ton Bruinsma started a love relation with his maid Fokje. Fokje eventually became the mother for the four children, raising them and being there at difficult moments. Klaas especially loved her very much. In 1964 the family moved to Blaricum and took residence in a villa there. Klaas's father Ton wanted to harden his kids for the future and had his own thoughts on how to achieve this. Every Sunday night he would have the children clean out thousands of bottles from the factory. He kept telling his kids to toughen up and not show fear. Klaas, in whom Ton saw most of himself, was the focus of the toughening up. He would order the boy to get on his bike and get packages far away when both knew the package would be delivered the next day. "It'll make him tough" was Ton's answer. Ton took Klaas out sailing when the local population came out in scores, warning them to not go out, but they would go out sailing in the middle of a storm, and Klaas loved it. In his teens Klaas left a good school, where he was often absent, and went to a lower educational school. Here he came into contact with hashish, which he started to use, and dealing among fellow students. On September 4, 1970, at age 16, Klaas was arrested for the first time. He came off with a warning.

As time moved on Klaas left home and moved in with his grandmother. He went to a new school in Amsterdam and he continued his hashish business. In 1974 Klaas was expelled for truancy. He rented an apartment in Amsterdam and decided to devote himself fully to the drug trade. Via his dealer Thea Moear, he supplied drugs (marijuana and hashish) to several coffeeshops and cafés. Bruinsma and Moear eventually started to work together, eventually becoming partners. In 1976 Bruinsma was arrested while making a drug deal for 100 kilograms of hashish. He was sentenced to six months in prison, of which three months was probation. When he got out, police thought Bruinsma had learned his lesson since they did not hear anything from him anymore. But Bruinsma had changed identities and was now called Frans van Arkel. He was more active than ever before. After Thea Moear left her husband, Hugo Ferrol, taking with her most of their drug business, she joined up with Bruinsma. Together they started the Organization that would live on to this day.

Until this moment the Dutch underworld had been a relatively friendly place, but from this point it began a descent into darkness. Early in 1978 Bruinsma and Moear added two new members to the organization—Etienne Urka (born in Paramaribo, Suriname) and a promising kick-boxer named Andre Brilleman. Bruinsma and Moear also bought two buildings in Amsterdam, together worth around 300,000 guilders ($150,000), fixed them up, and added security. They also opened several coffeeshops.

In late 1979 Bruinsma was arrested for being the mastermind behind a shipment of 1,500 kilos of hashish from Pakistan to Holland. He was sentenced to 18 months in prison but 12 months, being released in late 1980. Right away he continued expanding his organization. The offices were made ready: One floor was turned into a training ground for the bodyguards and enforcers, and another floor was turned into a room where meetings could take place. Bruinsma also added a bodyguard/driver, Geurt Roos, to his personal staff. Bruinsma also expanded his customer list. He now supplied drugs to Germany, Belgium, France, Scandinavian countries, and England. Bruinsma's client in England was Roy Adkins. As Bruinsma's illegal empire was growing, he also started setting up legitimate fronts and constructing buildings so that he could launder all his dirty money. By 1983 Bruinsma had proven to be a relatively good boss. His bodyguards and enforcers had participated in several violent incidents and hits, and Bruinsma was winning both the business competition with Hugo Ferrol as well as the violent street fights necessary to the business's survival. But even after all this, Bruinsma was still considered a rich mama's boy by the Amsterdam underworld. Some even thought that not Bruinsma but Thea Moear ran everything, which was not true. With this rich-boy reputation Bruinsma was still a target for takeover by certain criminals. Things would change very

quickly when Bruinsma proved his toughness in a shootout with four other criminals at the house of one of his former soldiers. The soldier in question was Pietje Pieterse, who was greatly upset at Bruinsma because he felt he was underpaid. As a result Pietje stole two stashes filled with 600 kilograms of Bruinsma's hashish.

Pietje invited Bruinsma to his house. He told Bruinsma that he had backup upstairs from three known tough guys in case Bruinsma attempted anything funny. He then told Bruinsma about the stolen merchandise. In the argument that followed, Bruinsma shot Pieterse in the hip. Immediately the three enforcers came downstairs. Bruinsma fired a warning shot in the air, but the first enforcer came toward him. Bruinsma fired again, and the man fell to the floor. Then another assailant fired three shots at Bruinsma, all hitting him and sending him down. One of the men held Bruinsma in a choke hold. Bruinsma yelled: "No police. No police. Call an ambulance." After a further struggle, that was exactly what happened. The guys who were able to flee did so; the others were left in their own blood. With medics, detectives, one dead body, and Pieterse wounded, a shot-to-bits Bruinsma said to Pieterse before he was carried of by the medics: "Jesus Christ Piet, how come you always have such a mess in your home?"

At the trial a few months later on January 31, 1984, Bruinsma was sentenced to five years in prison, though the sentence was later lowered. The thugs involved in the shootout were all put on Bruinsma's death list. One of them was strangled twice in prison while awaiting sentencing, and after the trial he fled to the United States. Years later Bruinsma's penalty was reduced to payment of $600,000. The two would meet once more on a toney shopping street in Amsterdam. Seeing him eye to eye for the first time since the incident, Bruinsma clapped his hands and within seconds he was surrounded by bodyguards, "See this guy, boys? Remember this face, because this is the guy who has to pay." Pieterse fled Holland for Switzerland, and his death sentence would be reduced to a sentence that left him confined to a wheelchair. On December 19, 1984, Dutch courts sentenced Bruinsma to three years in prison, two years less than initially sentenced. While in prison Bruinsma got a visit from his father Ton. He cried at seeing his son in this situation, and Klaas later said it was a sign of how weak he had become. On April 30 of that year, a few months after his visit to his son, Ton Bruinsma died at age 63. When Bruinsma was released from prison, he decided that as a professional criminal it would be better to check into a hotel instead of having a steady home. Bruinsma and his bodyguards at first spent a lot of time in the Okura Hotel. Bruinsma was known to come down into the lobby, barefooted, wearing only his robe. The eight to 10 bodyguards who surrounded him were dressed in designer suits and talked through walkie-talkies. When the hotel asked him to tone down his flashy displays, he left. After checking out of the Okura, Bruinsma made the prestigious Amsterdam Amstel Hotel his home. He would stay in the suite next to the royal suite that was for foreign kings or presidents; when such personages came to town, Bruinsma went elsewhere so as to avoid unpleasant episodes between the dozens of bodyguards and security checks. Bruinsma also beefed up his security. At this stage of his career Bruinsma could not leave Holland: He was banned from the United States, and other nations had asked for his arrest. Bruinsma also reorganized his staff: His underboss Thea Moear was demoted, and her place was taken over by Etienne Urka. He also structured his divisions: The drugs section was headed by Roy Adkins. He then put in place a staff that would exclusively handle all the laundering of drug proceeds. He established an enforcement division, made up of hit men who either took the contract or passed it on down the ladder. A public-relations division was also organized to keep the Organization out of the spotlight and handle media relations when the Organization received negative press. He also added the gambling division (slot and game machines) headed by Sam Klepper (who later died) and his right hand, John Mieremet.

With everything in place Bruinsma made his power felt. From prison, Bruinsma had ordered a hit on his former soldier kickboxer Andre Brilleman after he found out that Brilleman had stolen from him. Brilleman was found in a steel drum filled with cement, his face shot at close range. Later it was found that Brilleman was lured to a secure house where he was hit unconscious by six men waving baseball bats. Then they took him to an abandoned warehouse where he regained consciousness. They cut off his genitals and used a saw to cut off his legs all while he was still alive. They then put him in the steel drum and filled it up with cement and dumped it in the river. After this Bruinsma had total loyalty from many underworld members on the street. By the late 1980s he had totally isolated himself from the dirty work. His Organization had grown to a full time staff of 200. He was the main drug supplier in Europe and made millions upon millions. Everything went superbly, and Bruinsma started to think about retirement. But before his retirement Bruinsma wanted to make one last big shipment. The shipment in question was 45,000 kilograms of hashish, worth an estimated 400 million guilders (about $250 million). The deal was set in place and as Bruinsma waited, he became more and more paranoid. His people took it for what it was, a big shipment and lots of money; who wouldn't be a bit paranoid? The shipment got through and was brought to a warehouse where it was kept until it would be further distributed. It looked as though Bruinsma would get his retirement. But on Saturday February 24, 1990, police found the stashed drugs. The entire heap of 45,000 kilograms was burned by law enforcement. No one was arrested. After this Bruinsma started to blame people and fine employees when they made mistakes. Roy Adkins was fined, eventually leading to a violent argument between Adkins and Bruinsma. They had a shootout in Yab Yum, a high-class Amsterdam brothel.

Bruinsma was upset. He had been counting on the money from the now lost shipment. He declared war on the entire Amsterdam underworld and decreed that every coffeeshop in Amsterdam was to use his slot machines. If they refused, as one policeman put it, "He'd send by some Yugoslavians with Uzis." He also made his move for the red-light district. Bruinsma's descent into paranoia and drug addiction included shooting up bars and assaulting prostitutes who happened to look at him funny. This kind of behavior made more enemies, which he did not need, and he soon lost support among his own troops. Bruinsma started to attract attention from the Dutch internal revenue service and investigative commissions. Bruinsma knew his end was coming, but he did not seem to care. Bruinsma himself had now become a big risk for the Organization.

In September 1990 Roy Adkins was shot gangland style while he was having a drink in a bar. Although most underworld sources surmised that Bruinsma was behind it, the murder was never officially solved. Mixed up in cocaine and paranoia, Bruinsma's position was taken over more and more by Etienne Urka. Urka commanded the respect of the troops and was running most of the day-to-day operations. With law enforcement focusing all their powers on Bruinsma, and with the added pressures applied by rival underworld organizations, it was decided that it was best to have someone take Bruinsma off the Organization's hands. Bruinsma was blind to his own demise. On the night of June 27, 1991, Bruinsma was having fun at a bar at the Amsterdam Hilton Hotel. Inside he was talking with several underworld figures, as well as Martijn Hoogland, a vicious hit man and former policeman who was working with a group of Yugoslavians. The leader of this group had been whacked by Bruinsma. In the conversation Bruinsma told Hoogland, "I'll eat you too." The conversation continued until 4 A.M. in the morning. At that point a drunk and coked up Bruinsma tried to get to his taxi when some of the guys he had been talking to told him they would give him a lift.

Walking toward a group that contained Hoogland, Bruinsma was overheard yelling, "Have a little respect will ya', Who do you think I am?" followed by: "Don't expect me to be frightened because you're an ex cop." Then shots were heard. Bruinsma, hit in the chest, from 50 centimeters fell on his back, arms spread across the ground. A second shot was fired from close range under his chin. A third shot was fired from close range behind his right ear. At age 37 Klaas Bruinsma, the first Dutch godfather, was dead.

Reference

David Amoruso. "Klaas Bruinsma." Gangsters Incorporated. Available online. URL: http://gangstersinc.tripod.com/KlaasBruinsma. Downloaded on July 19, 2004.

—D.A.

BRUSCA, Giovanni (a.k.a. U Verru)

Known even by his Sicilian mobster colleagues as an especially vicious and violent sociopath, Brusca was a veteran soldier and follower in the Corleone clan during the reign of Luciano Liggio and Salvatore Riina. Brusca ruled by violence and bloodshed, even within his inner circle. "Known as 'the pig,' Brusca was a physically unimpressive figure, short and squat with beady eyes. His reign was marked by a rash of murders, bombings, and kidnappings which sparked outrage worldwide. In his most notorious act of butchery, Brusca personally tortured and strangled the 11-year-old son of a Mafia informant before dis-carding the evidence in a vat of acid," according to http://geocities.com/OrganizedCrimeSyndicates.

Italian authorities were closing in on Brusca when he ordered the murder of Italian prosecutor Giovanni Falcone near Palermo in 1992. Italy and the world were outraged by this defiant act, and Brusca went into hiding. In absentia, he was sentenced to life in prison. In June 1996, Brusca, "the pig," was captured and began to serve his life sentence. Despite his tough, violent, and antisocial behavior, Brusca eventually turned informant once behind bars.

BUTEAU, Yves (a.k.a. Le Boss)

Yves "Le Boss" Buteau would play a major role in establishing the Hells Angels as a major force in Montreal and across Canada. He started off as a member of the Montreal-based Popeyes biker gang. By the mid-1970s, he was president. On August 14, 1976, at the age of 25, Buteau was among the many arrested at a hotel in Saint-Andre-Avellion when almost 50 Popeyes entered and trashed the place.

The Popeyes, Montreal's strongest biker club, became Canada's first Hells Angels chapter on December 5, 1977. Hells Angels legend Sonny Barger himself awarded Buteau his colors and respected him so much that he was the only Canadian authorized to use the title of "Hells Angels International."

According to Yves "Apache" Trudeau, a Hells Angel who later turned informant, Buteau, Jean-Pierre "Matt le Crosseur" Mathieu and he were responsible for the deaths of Outlaw Daniel Mclean and his girlfriend Carmen Piché. The three bikers planted a bomb on the Outlaw's bike in Verdun on May 9, 1979, and detonated it while the 30-year-old and his girlfriend were on the bike.

As president, Buteau established contacts with many biker gangs across the country. These clubs eventually became Canada's other Hells Angels chapters. He supplied drugs to the Gitans and Atomes in Sherbrooke and expanded the club's drug networks.

Intelligent and calm, Buteau changed his gang from a group of beer-swigging brawlers into an organized criminal empire. He wanted members to be clean shaven, keep lower profiles, and avoid hassles. In spring 1982, at a meeting of Quebec Hells Angels, he prohibited the use of cocaine by members under penalty of death.

Gino Goudreau, a small-time drug dealer who later became a member of the Outlaws, ended

Buteau's reign on September 8, 1983. Buteau had spent the night at Le Petit Bourg bar with fellow Hells Angel René Lamoureux and Satan's Choice member Guy "Frenchy" Gilbert. When the group exited the bar, Goudreau opened fire. Two bullets tore into the Hells Angels president's chest, killing him. He had no time to pull the gun that was tucked into his belt. Gilbert, struck in the stomach, also died. Lamoureux was hit twice but survived.

More than 2,000 people gathered around a Sorel church on September 12, 1983, to watch Buteau's funeral. One hundred fifty gang members from across Canada, the United States, and England attended and rode from Sorel to Drummondville in a show of homage for the dead biker leader.

See also: HELLS ANGELS.

Reference

Gary Francoeur. "Yves 'Le Boss' Buteau." Wiseguy-Wally. Available online. URL: http://www.geocities.com/wiseguywally/YvesButeau.html. Downloaded on July 19, 2004.

—*G.F.*

CAICEDO-TASCON, Giovanni

Giovanni Caicedo-Tascon is an established cocaine trafficker who was connected to the North Valle and Cali cartels. According to Thomas A. Constantine, administrator, DEA, speaking in a statement before the Senate Foreign Relations Committee, Subcommittee on the Western Hemisphere, Peace Corps, Narcotics, and Terrorism, on February 26, 1998, "His organization runs cocaine laboratories in Colombia and transports multiton quantities of cocaine for distribution in the United States. Caicedo-Tascon's organization is particularly active in the New York City area."

See also: CALI CARTEL; NORTHERN VALLE ORGANIZATION.

Reference

Thomas A. Constantine. "Statement before the Senate Foreign Relations Committee, Subcommittee on the Western Hemisphere, Peace Corps, Narcotics, and Terrorism Regarding International Organized Crime Syndicates and Their Impact on the United States." 1998 Congressional Hearings, U.S. Congress, February 26, 1998.

CAKICI, Alaatin

Arrested in August 1998, Alaatin Cakici was one of the most powerful Mafia dons in the history of Turkish organized crime. According to some reports, his power and reach led all the way into the Turkish government and the Turkish secret service. Cakici had risen in the world of crime by making money through extortion, heroin smuggling, and assassination to the highest position in the ranks of his country's illegal world of violence and ill-gotten gains.

Cakici was a dashing, athletic, and talented criminal youth who took a big step up in the Turkish underworld when he married the famed Dundar Kilic's daughter, Ugur. According to http://geocities. com/OrganizedCrimeSyndicates, "Alaatin reportedly ordered the murder of his estranged wife when she began speaking of his business dealings freely. There were also rumors that she may have carried on an affair during their union. Whatever the cause, Ugur was cut down in a hail of bullets by a man who once served as her husband's chauffeur. Witnessing the entire incident was Ugur's then twelve-year-old son Onur."

Cakici had arrived. He was now a most wanted fugitive by Interpol. In August 1998 French authorities apprehended him and held him due to his Interpol red notice. In December of that year, he was returned to Turkey, where he faced a total of 384 years in prison. However, fate smiled on the notorious mafioso. The Turkish government had just suffered a public-relations nightmare with regard to the Susurluk case, including an embarrassing parade of officials who were ostracized in the press and the courts for links to Abdullah Catli. Many government officials did not want to see another batch of scandal-ridden government officials. Cakici played it up for all that it was worth.

"Will Cakici, who was deported from France on December 13, now shed light on the underworld contacts of Turkish politicians? 'If I talk,' he said immediately after he was arrested in France, 'there will be an earthquake in Turkey.'" reported Gerd Hoehler in the *Frankfurter Rundschau* (December 26, 1999). "He claimed to have telephoned 'at least ten times' with former Turkish prime minister, now deputy premier, Mesut Yilmaz. 'Woe betide us if he spills the beans,'" wrote the mass-circulation Turkish daily *Sabah*. Cakici received a laughable eight years' imprisonment.

While the official courts were kind to Cakici, the underworld court of opinion went against him. With his court troubles behind him, Cakici went to Usak prison. But there, the local illegal empire was run by the Ergin brothers. In prison, Cakici faced a new threat. "Unhappy with the presence of the well-known mobster in their midst, the Ergin boys quickly rallied their troops and declared war on the imprisoned godfather. On the outside, Cakici's brother Gencay and several close associates were shot by upstart members of his former father-in-law's organization. The shooter in the attempt on Gencay was later identified as sixteen-year-old Onur Ozbizerdik, the son of Ugur Kilic," reported http://geocities.com/OrganizedCrimeSyndicates.

Alaatin Cakici is still in prison and is still alive, and he still has people in Turkey who are out to kill him.

See also: BASAK, HUSEYIN; DONMEZ, OSMAN; KILIC, DUNDAR; OSBIZERDIK, ONUR; UGURLU, ABUZER.

References

Radikal's Ismet Berkan. "Why Yilmaz Keeps Quiet." *Turkish Daily News,* August 27, 1988; Jon Hemming, "Turkish Mafia Suspects Capture Rekindles Scandal." Press Agency Ozgurluk, August 23, 1998; Hikmet Cetinkaya, "Columnist Raps Mafia Politician." *Cumhuriyet,* media ties, http://geocities.com/OrganizedCrimesSyndicates. Posted on October 15, 1998.

CALI Cartel

Up through the early 1990s the Medellín cartel had dominated the drug trade, but its reign of relentless public terror against the Colombian government had driven Colombian authorities to serious action that led to the cartel's ultimate defeat. By the early 1990s, the Medellín drug lords were either killed or incarcerated. Having observed the fate of the brutal and violent Medellín cartel, the Cali leaders passed themselves off as law-abiding businessmen, investing in their country's future, earning public respect, and taking economic control of the Cali region. Because they operated in a less violent manner, the government did not aggressively pursue them, thereby allowing the Cali Mafia leaders to operate and grow in wealth and power with virtual impunity.

In the global arena, the cartels expanded their markets to Europe. After the fall of the Soviet Union in 1990, they quickly moved into Eastern Europe, taking advantage of the political and economic chaos by using these newly created democracies as the "back door" to transit their cocaine to Western Europe. For example, in 1992 large loads of cocaine were seized in Czechoslovakia, Poland, and Hungary. In 1993 Russian authorities seized 1.1 tons of cocaine hidden in cans of corned beef hash. This shipment originated in Cali, Colombia, and was destined for the Netherlands via St. Petersburg, Russia.

In post–cold war Europe, without border controls and an eastern border sealed against communism, international businesses and world governments were threatened by the drug cartels from Colombia.

In the early 1990s the Drug Enforcement Administration (DEA) estimated that they collectively produced and exported from Colombia between 500 and 800 tons of cocaine a year. The organizations were structured and operated much like major international corporations. They had enormous financial resources, with which they could afford to buy the best legal minds, the most sophisticated technology, and the most skilled financial experts.

Among the major Cali drug lords, the Rodríguez Orejuela brothers—Gilberto and his younger brother, Miguel—were known as the transportation specialists who moved cocaine out of Colombia into the United States and other countries. Gilberto was responsible for the strategic, long-term planning of the organization. Miguel was the hands-on manager who ran the day-to-day operations. José Santa Cruz Londono was responsible for establishing distribution cells in the United States.

These Cali leaders ran an incredibly sophisticated, highly structured drug-trafficking organization that was tightly controlled by its leaders in Cali. Each day, details of loads and money shipments were electronically dictated to heads of cocaine cells operating within the United States. The Cali drug lords knew the how, when, and where of every cocaine shipment, down to the markings on the packages. The Cali bosses set production targets for the cocaine they sold and were intimately involved in every phase of the business—production, transportation, financing, and communications.

Each organization had its own hierarchy of leaders, its own distribution networks, and customers in nations around the world. The operations were divided into separate cells. Each cell was run by a cell director—always a Colombian national—who reported directly to the drug lords in Colombia. These organizations were truly international operations run with efficiency and geared for huge profits. The massive scale of their trafficking operations dwarfed law-enforcement efforts in Colombia, in the United States, and in the transit nations between them.

"The Cali traffickers employed transporters from Mexico to ship cocaine into the United States and, in so doing, cemented the partnership between the Cali traffickers and their Mexican counterparts. More recently, the organized Colombian traffickers began to pay drug traffickers in Mexico in kilos of cocaine, in lieu of cash," said Harold D. Wankel, chief of operations, Drug Enforcement Administration, before the House Judiciary Committee on July 31, 1996.

"The assassination of Manuel de Dios, a prominent journalist in New York was ordered by Cali chieftain José Santa Cruz Londono in March of 1992," said Thomas A. Constantine, a DEA administrator before the Senate Caucus on International Narcotics Control and the House Subcommittee on Coast Guard and Maritime Transportation. John Mena, the architect of the de Dios murder, pleaded guilty and admitted being responsible for three additional contract killings on behalf of the Cali cartel.

"During the late 1980s the Cali group assumed greater and greater power as their predecessors from the Medellín cartel self-destructed. Where the Medellín cartel was brash and publicly violent in their activities, the criminals, who ran their organization from Cali, labored behind the pretense of legitimacy, by posing as businessmen carrying out their professional obligations. The Cali leaders—the Rodríguez Orejuela brothers, José Santa Cruz Londono, Helmer "Pacho" Herrera Buitrago—amassed fortunes and ran their multibillion dollar cocaine businesses from

Millions of dollars seized at a Cali drug cartel house in Cali, Colombia (AP)

high-rises and ranches in Colombia. Miguel Rodríguez-Orejuela and his associates comprised what was, until then, the most powerful international organized crime group in history. They employed 727 aircraft to ferry drugs to Mexico, from where they were smuggled into the United States, and then return to Colombia with the money from U.S. drug sales. Using landing areas in Mexico, they were able to evade U.S. law enforcement officials and make important alliances with transportation and distribution experts in Mexico," said Thomas A. Constantine, a DEA administrator, in a statement before the Senate Foreign Relations Committee, on February 26, 1998.

"With intense law enforcement pressure focused on the Cali leadership by the brave men and women in the Colombian National Police during 1995 and 1996, all of the top leadership of the Cali syndicate are either in jail or dead," Mr. Constantine went on to say. "The fine work done by General Serrano and other CNP officers is a testament to the commitment and dedication of Colombia's law enforcement officials in the face of great personal danger and a government whose leadership is riddled with drug corruption."

See also: CAICEDO-TASCON, GIOVANNI.

CAMARENA, Enrique

Perhaps no single event had a more significant impact on the Drug Enforcement Administration (DEA) than the abduction and murder of Special Agent Enrique Camarena in Mexico in 1985. His murder led to the most comprehensive homicide investigation ever undertaken by the DEA, which ultimately uncovered corruption and complicity by numerous Mexican officials.

Known as "Kiki" to his friends, Special Agent Camarena had a reputation for believing that the actions of each and every individual made a difference in the drug war. He was assigned to the DEA's Guadalajara Resident Office in Mexico and was working to identify drug-trafficking kingpins when he left his office to meet his wife for lunch on February 7, 1985. A late-model car pulled up beside Camarena, and four men grabbed him, threw him into the back of the car, and sped off. Hours later, Alfredo Zavala Avelar, a Mexican Agriculture Department pilot working with antidrug authorities, was also abducted.

Immediately after Mrs. Camarena reported her husband missing, the DEA Guadalajara Resident Office made every effort to locate him. After determining that Special Agent Camarena's disappearance had no innocent explanation, Resident Agent in Charge James Kuykendall promptly notified his superiors and attempted to enlist the support of the Mexican police. Meanwhile, special agents assigned to the Guadalajara Resident Office began to query confidential informants and police contacts for information about the whereabouts of Special Agent Camarena. Mexico Country Attache Edward Heath then requested assistance from U.S. Ambassador Gavin, who called the Mexican attorney general and requested his assistance in resolving the disappearance of the special agent. Next, all DEA domestic special agents (SAs) and country attaches in Latin America were notified of the agent's disappearance and were requested to query all sources knowledgeable about Mexican trafficking organizations for any intelligence that might lead to his rescue. DEA headquarters then quickly established a special group to coordinate the investigation, and 25 special agents were sent to Guadalajara to assist in the search for Special Agent Camarena. Administrator Lawn comforted Geneva Camarena, widow of the missing agent.

Throughout February 1985 the DEA continued its efforts to locate Camarena. Witnesses were interviewed, and numerous leads were followed. Searches were made of several residences and ranches in Mexico. Based on the information that was developed, the DEA requested the Mexican Federal Judicial Police (MFJP) to consider Rafael Caro-Quintero, Miguel Félix Gallardo, and Ernesto Fonseca-Carrillo as suspects in the kidnapping. All three were notorious narcotics traffickers based in Guadalajara and were believed to have the resources and motive to commit such an act.

On February 9, 1985, Rafael Caro-Quintero was confronted by MFJP officers at the Guadalajara airport as he was preparing to leave on a private jet with several of his associates. After an armed standoff, the Mexican officer in charge, an MFJP comandante, spoke privately with Caro-Quintero and then allowed him and his associates to depart.

Subsequently, a local farm worker discovered two bodies in a field adjacent to a busy road about 1 kilometer from a ranch in Michoacan, Mexico. The bodies, which apparently had been dumped there, were identified as those of Special Agent Camarena and Captain Zavala. Soil samples taken from the two bodies by FBI special agents in Mexico proved the bodies had previously been buried elsewhere and then moved. On March 7 and 8, 1985, a U.S. pathologist and forensic team analyzed the discovery site and performed an autopsy. The pathologist's findings made positive identifications and indicated that death in both cases was due to blunt force injuries to the head.

On March 8, 1985, Agent Camarena's body was returned to the United States for burial. For the DEA and the American public, the 1985 torture and murder of Agent Camarena marked a turning point in the war on drugs. His violent death brought the American public face-to-face with the vicious brutality of drug trafficking.

See also: CARO-QUINTERO, RAFAEL; FÉLIX GALLARDO, MIGUEL.

Reference

U.S. Drug Enforcement Administration, U.S. Department of Justice. "A Tradition of Excellence, DEA History 1985–1990." Available online. URL: http://www.dea.gov/pubs/history/index.html. Downloaded on July 28, 2004.

CARBONE, Paul Bonaventure

Paul Bonaventure Carbone and his organized crime associate François Spirito were among the first modern gangsters in France. Located in Marseilles, Spirito and fellow organized-crime associate Paul Carbone set the standard for the French Mafia dons of later years. Originally, Spirito and Carbone worked closely with Marseilles city officials to help organize fascist shock troops, to help the French fascist movement of the 1930s. Rounding up hordes of local ne'er-do-wells, Spirito and Carbone sold their violence and mayhem for a price to the fascist and local leaders when communist demonstrations were taking place.

Carbone operated brothels in Cairo and Marseilles and was a gunrunner during the Spanish Civil War. During World War II, Carbone and Spirito were collaborationists with the German occupying forces, having had tight connections with the fascist movement in France years before.

During the war, Spirito and Carbone informed on a band of French Resistance fighters who had killed a number of German and French collaborationists who were running things in Marseilles. Carbone died shortly thereafter when a train he was riding in bound for Marseilles was blown up by the French Resistance.

See also: CORSICAN MAFIA; FRENCH CONNECTION, THE; SPIRITO, FRANÇOIS.

CARLISI, Samuel (a.k.a. Sam Wings)

Sammy was the driver of Joey Aiuppa, former Chicago Outfit boss. Sammy received his nickname in the 1970s because he flew around the country as a mob courier. He often represented Joseph Ferriola, another high-ranking outfit capo, who suffered from cancer. He allegedly killed Ferriola's underbosses Michael and Tony Spilotro.

Sammy was well known for racketeering, loan sharking, and arson as well as several illegal gambling businesses in the Chicago area and the west suburbs. He was sentenced to prison where he died in 1997. Little Jimmy Marcello was his chauffeur and henchman.

See also: AIUPPA, JOSEPH; ANDRIACCHI, JOSEPH; DIFRONZO, JOHN; LAPIETRA, ANGELO; LOMBARDO, JOSEPH; MARCELLO, JAMES.

CARO-QUINTERO, Miguel Angel

"In spite of the tremendous heat put on the group's founder Rafael Caro-Quintero after the 1985 mur-der of Drug Enforcement Administration (DEA) officer Enrique Camarena, it was business as usual under the direction of Miguel Angel Caro-Quintero," reported http://geocities.com/OrganizedCrimeSyndicates. "A dozen years younger than his brother, Miguel was one of three remaining brothers of El Greñas appointed to oversee the continued operation of the Sonora cartel. Miguel soon established dominance over his brothers Jorge and Genaro and rose to the pinnacle of the group's operations."

Miguel Angel was the head of the Caro-Quintero organization noted for smuggling large quantities of marijuana, heroin, and cocaine from Mexico into the United States, and has become involved in the production and manufacturing of methamphetamine. Miguel is a DEA fugitive based on two federal indictments issued in 1988 and 1993 in the District Court for the District of Colorado, and two issued in 1994 in the District Court for the District of Arizona.

Miguel renewed the time-tested program of political payments which led to better protection and huge economic successes. By the early 1980s, the gang was a major exporter of sinsemilla, shipping nearly four tons of it per day across the border at their highest point.

According to DEA testimony on October 27, 1997, "After receiving bribes, a federal judge in Hermosillo, Mexico, dismissed charges against Miguel Caro-Quintero in 1992, and since that time, he has operated freely within Mexico." He instantly became the subject of numerous U.S. indictments and also the subject of provisional arrest warrants in Mexico issued in the United States. A request for the extradition of Miguel and Rafael Caro-Quintero was forwarded to the government of Mexico by the United States."

"The state department offered a reward of $2,000,000 for any information leading to his arrest and conviction. Like his brother, Miguel was captured on December 20, 2001, due to the intense pressure put on the Mexican government by the U.S. government," reported http://geocities.com/OrganizedCrimeSyndicates. "Miguel currently in custody in Mexico faces extradition to the United States to face trial for his involvement in the importation of sinsemilla into Arizona and Colorado."

See also: CARO-QUINTERO, RAFAEL; SONORA-GUADALAJARA CARTEL.

CARO-QUINTERO, Rafael (a.k.a. El Greñas)

According to the Drug Enforcement Administration (DEA) report on Extradictable Drug Traffickers (September 1999), "Rafael Caro-Quintero began his smuggling career in the mid-1970s under the leadership of Miguel Angel Felix-Gallardo. By the 1980s, Caro-Quintero had risen quickly in stature within the organization; he was active in cultivating cannabis throughout Mexico and smuggling marijuana, heroin, and cocaine from Mexico into the United States."

"Rafael expanded his family's network influence by offering an expensive high grade of seedless cannabis at a wholesale price. At the time, sinsemilla sold for $2,500 a pound in the United States. The popularity of the product made Rafael one of the most powerful traffickers in all of Mexico. . . . For protection, Caro-Quintero ensured uninterrupted delivery of his goods by doling out huge payments to the Mexican Federal Judicial Police and the Federal Bureau of Social and Political Investigations," reported http://geocities.com/OrganizedCrimeSyndicates.

It has been alleged by several sources, including former DEA agents, that the Caro-Quintero smuggling ring was a well-known contra supporter and that part of their proceeds went to and some of their protection came from the Central Intelligence Agency (CIA), which was deeply intertwined in a covert war in Central America.

With all of his power, money, and influence, Caro-Quintero remained overconfident. Against the advice of other cartel leaders, he ordered the abduction and murder of U.S. DEA agent Enrique Camarena on February 7, 1985. Today information exists that while Caro-Quintero definitely gave the order for Camarena to be killed, he also may have had a silent partner in clandestine U.S. operations—partners who felt that Camarena was going to blow the lid off the CIA's involvement with well-known international drug smugglers. However, the U.S. State Department demanded an immediate crackdown. "The Caro-Quintero web of protection soon dissolved and the boss was forced to flee. The search for El Greñas ended when a joint task force of Mexican and American DEA agents found Caro-Quintero living in Costa Rica in a half-million-dollar villa paid for by notorious Colombian kingpin Pablo Escobar."

Caro-Quintero pled guilty to a host of other charges, which included the smuggling of arms, forced human labor and slavery, and bribing public officials. Rafael Caro-Quintero was sentenced to a prison term of 34 years on September 24, 1988. Rafael was then 36 years old. He passed control of the Sonora cartel onto his younger brother Miguel Angel.

According to the DEA, on April 29, 1987, a Central District of California grand jury returned an indictment charging Rafael Caro-Quintero with Continuing Criminal Enterprise (CCE), narcotics and firearms violations, Travel Act conspiracy, and false-statement violations. On July 14, 1988, a District of Arizona grand jury indicted Rafael Caro-Quintero for CCE, bribery, and narcotics violations. On July 30, 1991, a Central District of California grand jury returned an indictment charging Rafael Caro-Quintero with racketeering charges, kidnapping and murder of a federal agent, aiding and abetting, and accessory after the fact. In January 1997, a U.S. provisional arrest warrant request was issued to the government of Mexico for the purpose of extraditing Caro-Quintero. Rafael remains a fugitive from justice in the United States.

See also: CARO-QUINTERO, MIGUEL ANGEL; SONORA-GUADALAJARA CARTEL.

CARRILLO FUENTES, Amado

Amado Carrillo Fuentes was the head of the Juárez Organization. His was a Mexican-based organization whose renown was based on his ability to transport drugs into the United States by air for Colombian drug traffickers. He was known as the Lord of the Skies. He was heavily pursued by U.S. and Mexican authorities. So heavily pressured was Carrillo Fuentes by law enforcement that he eventually sought cosmetic surgery to alter his appearance. It did not work, and he was killed in 1997.

See also: JUÁREZ CARTEL.

CARROLL, David (a.k.a. Wolf)

David Carroll, who would earn the nickname "Wolf," was born in Halifax in 1952. He joined up with the 13th Tribe biker club, an organization that controlled much of the drug market in Halifax and instilled fear in the locals.

In the early 1980s the 13th Tribe came to the attention of the Hells Angels. The Angels were impressed with how the 13th Tribe took care of business, and on December 5, 1984, after a yearlong prospecting period, the club officially became the Hells Angels Halifax chapter.

According to law enforcement, the Halifax chapter played a part in the 1985 slaughter of five members of the Hells Angels North Chapter in Lennoxville. Police arrested Carroll, along with Halifax members Randall "Blondie" Mersereau, Patrick "Frenchy" Guernier, and John Christansen. They were brought to Sherbrooke to stand trial on charges of first-degree murder. The bikers were later acquitted.

Although Carroll was exonerated of murder, he, Mersereau, and Guernier were convicted of living off the proceeds of prostitution on May 30, 1986. All received one-year prison sentences.

According to police, Wolf spent the late 1980s and early 1990s expanding his activities and increasing his influence. On June 24, 1995, he left the Halifax chapter for the Quebec-based Nomads, a gang that consisted of elite members, and allegedly took over much of the drug trafficking in the Laurentians.

Carroll was among the more than 100 Hells Angels members and associates accused in Operation Printemps 2001. He avoided arrest, however, and remains in hiding. He faces murder and gangsterism charges.

See also: HELLS ANGELS.

Reference

Gary Francoeur. "David 'Wolf' Carroll." Wiseguy-Wally. Available online. URL: http://www.geocities.com/wiseguywally/DavidCarroll.html. Downloaded on July 19, 2004.

—G.F.

CASTELLANO, Paul (a.k.a. Big Paul)

Paul Castellano was born Constantino Paul Castellano in Brooklyn on June 26, 1915. His parents were both from Sicily and had immigrated to the United States to give their children a better life. Castellano's father was a butcher, and he also controlled a small gambling operation. Castellano was the youngest of three children and the only boy. He dropped out of school in the eighth grade, became a meat cutter with his dad, and also helped him out with the gambling operation. Being involved in gambling and bookmaking, Castellano was bound to come into contact with heavier crimes, and at the age of 19 he did. Together with two friends, Castellano was involved in an armed robbery. His two

friends managed to escape, but Castellano was not that lucky. He was arrested and convicted and spent three months in prison without naming his two friends. Once he got out, he was celebrated as a hero. He had done the right thing and had proven that he was a stand-up guy.

After this brush with the law, Castellano kept a very low profile. In 1937 he married the sister-in-law of Carlo Gambino; this marriage would almost guarantee Castellano mob glory. In 1957 Castellano was on his way to the Apalachin meeting, a sign of his and, more important, Carlo Gambino's rise to the top. It should have been Castellano's finest moment to date, but it turned out to be a disaster, earning him his second brush with the law and his second prison term. When called to testify about Apalachin before a New York grand jury, he again remained silent and was found guilty of contempt. He was sentenced to five years in prison, of which he served seven months. On his release, back in Brooklyn, his stature had again grown. He had earned respect and again showed that he was a stand-up guy. Pretty soon things were back to normal, Castellano was back in business with his meat company

Mobster Paul Castellano (AP)

55

called Blue Ribbon Meats. A very successful meat wholesale company that, thanks to mob influence, was only doing better and better. Castellano was living the good life.

As Carlo Gambino's health worsened, it became clear he needed to appoint a successor. For Carlo it went between his underboss Neil Dellacroce and Paul Castellano. Carlo chose Castellano and in doing so sealed Castellano's fate and broke the Gambino family into two factions. When Gambino died at his Long Island home in 1975, a meeting took place where Gambino's decision was discussed. The result of the meeting was that Castellano would be boss, and no one would step up. Dellacroce honored Gambino's choice and was happy to stay on as underboss. Castellano was now the most powerful Mafia boss in the United States. Castellano's reign was a quiet one. Castellano was not flashy and lived very far away from the daily grind of the streets. He lived in a mansion in Todt Hill, Staten Island. The mansion was valued at $3.5 million and had the nickname "The White House." At his mansion Castellano was isolated and ran his criminal empire, away from his family's soldiers and away from the tough streets. He lost touch with the streets and the basic rules. He started to see himself more as a businessman than as a boss of a crime family. Because Castellano was up in his White House all day, the soldiers on the street started to lose respect for him. They were on the street trying to make the dollars, and he was up in his house and never showed respect. With a faction already unhappy with Castellano from the beginning, things only got worse.

On February 25, 1985, the five bosses of the five families were all indicted in the famous Commission Case. As boss of the Gambino crime organization, Castellano, of course, was indicted, but for Castellano the indictments were doubly bad news. The indictments had wiretapped evidence coming from a bug in Castellano's mansion. The bug did Castellano no good. Legally they were incriminating, and on the streets, to the soldiers, he now really looked like a mark. The rebel faction was stirring things up again, but they were still held back by underboss Neil Dellacroce. However when Dellacroce died, Castellano's position seemed very weak. The rebel faction was led by John Gotti, who never liked Castellano and who had always wanted Dellacroce to follow in Gambino's footsteps. Gotti was held back by Dellacroce, but now with Dellacroce dead, nothing could stop

him. Gotti began to gain support within the Gambino family to whack Castellano. When Castellano did not attend Dellacroce's wake, Gotti had no problem with support. Plans were made, a hit team assembled, and on December 16, 1985, Paul Castellano, along with his newly appointed underboss Tommy Bilotti, was gunned down in front of Sparks Steak House. Castellano's reign had ended in a way typical for most mobsters: He died a violent death.

See also: D'ARCO, ALPHONSE; GAMBINO, CARLO; GOTTI, JOHN; GRAVANO, SALVATORE.

Reference

David Amoruso. "Paul Castellano," Gangsters Incorporated. Available online. URL: http://gangstersinc.tripod.com/Paul.html. Downloaded on July 19, 2004.

—D.A.

CATLI, Abdullah

"It was a luxurious Mercedes-Benz. There were four passengers in it. One was a Kurd. The other three were Turks. One of the three was a woman. One of the other two a fugitive. The last person was the president of a police academy in Istanbul," reported the American Kurdish Information Network on November 12, 1996. The people in this car created the greatest governmental crisis in 20th-century Turkey.

In the same car were Gonca Us, a Turkish beauty queen with ties to the Turkish mob, and "Sedat Bucak, a member of the Turkish parliament and the head of Bucak tribe in Turkish-controlled Kurdistan. He is a darling of the Turks for declaring a war on rebel Kurds. His forces control the Siverek Valley between the cities of Diyarbakir and Urfa. Huseyin Kocadag, the president of Eroge Police Academy, was also the former deputy Chief of Police for Istanbul, Turkey. His name is closely linked with the creation of the counterinsurgency group called Special Teams. A crack civilian unit operating in Kurdistan, these 'Contra Guerrillas' specialize in inflicting death and suffering on unsuspecting Kurds."

On Sunday, November 3, 1996, a truck hit the car they were driving in Susurluk, a town in western Turkey. "A lurid glimpse of this underbelly of the Turkish state opened suddenly on November 3, 1996, when a Mercedes-Benz overturned in a traffic accident," wrote Ertugrul Kurkcu in *Covert Action Quarterly* number 61. "But what raised eyebrows was the seemingly incongruous presence of . . .

Convicted international drug smuggler and fascist gang leader Abdullah Catli (right) with two Turkish police officials (AP/Hurriyet)

Abdullah Catli. . . . Police had supposedly been hunting Catli, a convicted international drug smuggler since 1978, for his part in the killing of scores of left-wing activists. At that time, Catli had been head of the 'Gray Wolves,' the youth arm of the neofascist MHP (National Action Party)." Also on Catli was the coveted green Turkish passport, "one that is usually issued to senior civil servants, obviating the need for visa requirements. In the trunk, there was an arsenal: guns, silencers and ammunition," reported the American Kurdish Information Network.

Abdullah Catli had been the chairman of the Gray Wolves in Ankara since 1977. In the late 1970s, the fascist Gray Wolves gang murdered five people and wounded 14 in a café in Ankara; on March 24, 1978, the Gray Wolves murdered the state prosecutor Dagan Oz in Ankara; Catli ordered the murder of seven members of the Turkish Workers Party on October 9, 1978; and in 1979, the chief editor of the *Milliyet,* Abdi Ipekci, was murdered by Mehmet Agca. When Agca was arrested, the police discovered

a false passport in the name of Mehmet Oezbey, belonging to Abdullah Catli. On May 13, 1981, insiders mentioned Abdullah Catli in connection with the assault against the pope. Interpol issued an international warrant for the arrest of Abdullah Catli. Using the name of Mehmet Oezbey, Catli commanded the official Turkish contraguerrilla in the massacres in the '80s against the Armenian organization ASALA. After the failed coup against Aliyev in Azerbaijan, Aliyev named those responsible. One of the names he prominently dropped was that of Abdullah Catli. Despite his international Interpol warrant and proven involvement in drug trafficking, Abdullah Catli received a diplomatic passport, a police passport, and a gun permit.

Also, despite his avowed nationalist political claims, Catli was knee-deep in the drug-smuggling world. It is now clear that Catli used nationalistic speeches and propaganda to recruit an army of grotesque thugs who marauded the Turkish countryside. He also used this army to travel international drug routes to transport heroin from Turkey to Italy. It is now known that Catli was a well-known associate of Abuzer Ugurlu.

Catli's death in the car with these other individuals created huge national and international headlines that would reverberate throughout the world for the rest of that decade. Catli's death was the trigger necessary to enlist the cooperation of the Turkish police and government on a level that had never before been seen in that country's history. For all his violence and crimes, Catli's death was a far greater blow to his cause and his fellow underworld kingpins than he, or anyone else, could ever have imagined. As in Italy, many citizens had always assumed some complicity between local police and international drug kingpins: It had been so for decades in that country. But to know that the drug gangs were so intricately interwoven with the upper echelons of the national government and that these mafiosos were so brazen as to be seen in public with officials was a shock to the public. Again, as in Italy and the death of its two crime-fighting judges, the outcry was deafening. The incident opened huge gashes in the government, and several ministers were videotaped leaving their offices in handcuffs. The resulting investigation was called the Susurluk scandal, named for the small town where the accident took place.

See also: BASAK, HUSEYIN; DONMEZ, OSMAN; KILIC, DUNDAR; OZBIZERDIK, ONUR; UGURLU, ABUZER.

CAZZETTA, Giovanni

Giovanni Cazzetta, Salvatore Cazzetta's younger brother, was born in the mid-1950s. He grew up on the mean streets of Saint-Henri and joined the Outlaws motorcycle gang at a young age.

He remained an Outlaw until 1984 when he quit the club to form the Rock Machine biker gang with his brother. They recruited some of the best talent around and formed alliances with the Italian Mafia, the West End Gang, and the Dubois Gang. Giovanni Cazzetta held the position of second-in-command. Only his brother Salvatore had more sway.

Police found Giovanni in possession of three kilograms of cocaine in April 1992. Facing a lengthy and costly trial, the biker—who speaks Italian, English, and French—pleaded guilty in the spring of 1993 and was sentenced to four years in prison.

In May 1997 a police informer, posing as a front for a wealthy Calgary businessman looking to import 15 kilograms of cocaine to Alberta, tried to set up a drug transaction with the Cazzettas, but the Rock Machine leader did not have such a large amount. Instead, he set up a meeting with Richard Matticks, a reputed senior member of the West End Gang. The three men sat in a restaurant on May 14, 1997, and Matticks agreed to sell the informer eight kilograms of cocaine at $39,000 each.

Police rented an apartment on Saint-Urbain Street for the transaction and equipped it with hidden microphones and cameras. Matticks sent henchmen Frank Bonneville and Donald Waite to deliver the cocaine and pick up the $312,000 owed him. Montreal's Carcajou antigang task force burst into the apartment, arrested both men, and seized the drugs.

The agents then obtained a warrant for Cazzetta and Matticks, explaining to a judge that the two men had been directly involved in the drug deal. Giovanni, who lived in Chateauguay, was arrested in Montreal; Matticks was apprehended at his house in Lachine. Neither man was armed or put up resistance. Cazzetta and the three West End gangsters were charged with trafficking in narcotics and conspiring to traffic in narcotics.

Matticks, Bonneville, and Waite pleaded guilty on June 17, 1997, and were sentenced to three, four, and two years, respectively. Cazzetta, who was still on parole from his 1993 drug conviction, chose to fight the charges and went to trial. He was sentenced to nine years on April 14, 1998.

While incarcerated, Cazzetta was found guilty of money laundering. He received five more years, to be run concurrently with his nine-year sentence, and the government seized much of gang leader's assets, including his engraved Rock Machine gold ring, a 1994 Jeep Cherokee, a 1959 Corvette, and a 1992 Lexus.

See also: BANDIDOS/ROCK MACHINE.

Reference

Gary Francoeur. "Giovanni Cazzetta." WiseguyWally. Available online. URL: http://www.geocities.com/wiseguywally/ GiovanniCazzetta.html. Downloaded on July 19, 2004.

—G.F.

CAZZETTA, Salvatore

Salvatore Cazzetta was born in 1954 and grew up on the tough streets of Saint-Henri, Montreal. When his SS biker gang dissolved into the Hells Angels in

1984, Cazzetta decided to go on his own way. He knew about the Hells Angels and wanted no part of an organization that flaunted its membership so openly.

Along with his younger brother Giovanni, he hoped to create a new breed of bikers. Their organization would be like any other biker gang but without patches. This meant much less public notoriety and police pressure. In its place, members would wear special gold rings to identify themselves. This gang was called the Rock Machine.

The brothers built up their network and, by the early 1990s, the Rock Machine had 10 members in Montreal and had opened a branch in Quebec City. More than 100 others supposedly worked for them, distributing millions of dollars worth of drugs.

Cazzetta was a shrewd businessman, driven to succeed, and he understood that the best way to survive and prosper in the underworld was to acquire contacts. He developed working relationships with Montreal's Italian Mafia, the West End Gang, and the French-Canadian Dubois gang.

But all good things must come to an end. Cazzetta, who now owned a house in l'Épiphanie worth more than $2 million, was accused of importing cocaine from the United States. Paul Larue, a Canadian narcotics trafficker who had been convicted in Florida, became an informer and explained to the Drug Enforcement Administration (DEA) Cazzetta's supposed involvement in the plot.

Cazzetta went into hiding, but he was finally apprehended on May 8, 1994, in Fort Erie, Ontario. He was eventually extradited to the United States, where he pleaded guilty to drug-trafficking charges. He was sentenced in late June 1999 to 12 years in prison.

See also: BANDIDOS/ROCK MACHINE.

Reference

Gary Francoeur. "Salvatore Cazzetta." WiseguyWally. Available online. URL: http://www.geocities.com/wiseguywally/SalvatoreCazzetta.html. Downloaded on July 19, 2004.

—G.F.

CELIK, Oral

On May 5, 2000, the Anadolu News Agency reported, "Oral Celik, one of the defendants of the Abdi Ipekci murder case, was put in prison for threatening a textile industrialist with a gun. Celik could not pay the 500 million Lira bail and was put in Ulucanlar prison." If it proved anything, it proved that the once-elusive and once-proud Celik had truly fallen on hard times.

"Oral Celik, who is connected with many incidents, including the attempted assassination of the pope," stated the *Turkish Daily News* on January 24, 1997. "Oral Celik returned to Turkey after spending many years abroad as a fugitive following the assassination attempt on the pope and was released from jail recently after being acquitted of killing journalist Abdi Ipekci and a teacher in Malatya. As well as being a close friend of Abdullah Catli, Oral Celik is known as the mastermind behind many international scandals and of the ultranationalist Mafia." He was also a murderous assassin employed in numerous killings who killed for political beliefs as well as for money. It is thought that Celik is also linked to Abuzer Ugurlu through his closeness with Catli.

Celik was implicated in the attempt on the pope's life. While many believed he had intimate knowledge of the conspiracy, he was able to escape conviction in a Turkish court of law and was released. He was also a key witness before the Susurluk Commission, the body that was formed immediately after the car accident that brought to light the linkage between national ministers and the Turkish Mafia.

See also: BASAK, HUSEYIN; CATLI, ABDULLAH; DONMEZ, OSMAN; KILIC, DUNDAR; OZBIZERDIK, ONUR; UGURLU, ABUZER.

CHAN, Wing Young (a.k.a. Big Head)

In New York City, Wing Young Chan was the longtime *dailo dai*, or "Big Brother," of the On Leong Tong. A Chinese immigrant, Chan was the head of the On Leong Merchant's Association and originally started out as a dishwasher. "Chan held court at the popular 400-seat Harmony Palace on Mott Street, which was famous in Chinatown for the best dim sum and the most beautiful Chinese pop singers in New York City," according to organized-crime expert Mark C. Gribben. Chan was indicted in a federal court in New York for taking part in several murders, as well as involving the On Leong Tong in drug trafficking and distribution, as well as trafficking in human beings, bringing in illegal aliens, as well as supplying On Leong Tong–run brothels with sex slaves from mainland China.

See also: GHOST SHADOWS; ON LEONG TONG.

Reference

Mark C. Gribben. "Moon Festival Shakedown." Reprinted by permission.

—M.G.

CHARRON, Alain

Alain Charron was born in Trois-Pistoles, Quebec, in 1948. He moved to Montreal and became associated with the Dubois brothers, who began to make a name for themselves in the late 1960s. Over the years, he would become especially close to Adrien, the youngest of the nine Dubois brothers, and Donald Lavoie, who the media once described as Charron's "blood brother."

Police raided Charron's Notre Dame Street apartment on October 4, 1974, and seized an assortment of firearms, some ski masks, and handcuffs. They arrested Charron, Maurice Dubois, Roland Dubois, René Dubois, and Réal Lévesque but released them later that night for lack of proof.

Charron and Donald Lavoie were charged with the murders of Henry Fernandez and Linda Maiore. Fernandez had supposedly tipped off police about the arsenal at Charron's apartment. The two were acquitted of the crime.

During the winter of 1978, according to Donald Lavoie, he and Charron murdered Jean Carreau in a chalet in Lac Beauport. Accompanied by Jean Tremblay and Claude Marcoux, Charron and Lavoie wanted to eliminate Carreau so that they could replace him for a planned armed robbery at the University of Laval. The victim's bones were later found in the woods by a jogger and his dog.

When Lavoie turned government informant in 1980, Charron retreated to a Laurentian Cottage, near Claude Dubois's home. He also began to act as Dubois's bodyguard.

On January 17, 1981, Charron and his girlfriend, along with Claude Dubois and his wife, decided to get away from the stress they were facing because of Lavoie's defection and left for the United States. Armed with false identification, as they were not allowed to leave the country, they arrived at the Ogdensbury, New York, border, where immigration officers discovered Dubois's and his wife's real identification papers. The two were held for a few hours and returned to Canada. Charron and his girlfriend were able to enter and two days later, thanks to the help of two of the gang's soldiers, Dubois and his wife gained entry into the United States. The four of them vacationed in Florida for three weeks before returning to Montreal.

Lavoie revealed to authorities in January 1982 that Charron was responsible for the murder of Jean Carreau. Charron learned of the news and went into hiding.

In February 1982 a suitcase containing 50 pounds of hashish was sent from Charron in Miami to Schenectady, New York, where it was supposed to be smuggled into Canada for sale, but the suitcase was lost in the mail, and Charron traveled to New York to help locate it. It was eventually found, but not before the drug had deteriorated.

Charron was arrested in West Palm Beach, Florida, in May 1983 as he arrived for a doctor's appointment. He had been changing location and identities every three months as a precautionary measure. His extradition to Canada was approved four months later, and he was formally charged with Carreau's murder on November 9, 1983.

The trial began in June 1985. During the trial, Judge Jean-Luc Dutil refused to allow Charron's lawyer to ask informant Donald Lavoie a question. The defense challenged the judge's decision, but the Supreme Court of Canada finally dismissed their appeal in 1990. The trial continued, and Charron was eventually acquitted.

In autumn 1992, Charron was among 19 people arrested in Baleine, Nova Scotia, and charged with importing 53 tons of hashish. They were found in possession of 27 tons, with a value of $365 million. Two fishing boats were seized in the bust.

In January 1993, while Charron was out on bail, American authorities discovered 50 kilograms of cocaine hidden in a secret compartment of a Cadillac that had been rented out to him. The drug had been shipped from South America to Buffalo and was arranged to be smuggled across the border into Canada.

Charron was arrested as he exited an airplane in Nassau, Bahamas, where he intended to spend a few days in the sun, on February 17, 1996. The United States charged him with the Buffalo seizure 10 days later.

Things only became worse for Charron. His name again came up in March 1996 in connection to a popular tavern in Saint-Sauveur. The bar was among seven locations raided by the Royal Canadian Mounted Police (RCMP) in the Laurentians, the Eastern Townships, and Montreal. Charron's home in Val-Morin was also among those raided. Police seized $20,000 in cash, computer systems, a coin collection valued at $20,000, more than 100 boxes of documents, and a 1946 Bentley. Police explained that the raids were carried out to determine whether Charron and his associates could be charged with living off the profits of narcotics trafficking.

Charron asked the Bahamas government to be given status of habeas corpus, but the country's Supreme Court authorized Charron's extradition to the United States on March 17, 1998. His lawyers appealed the court's decision but were unsuccessful. Charron was sentenced to serve eight years in prison in June 2001. In 2002 he was transferred to the Sainte-Anne-des-Plaines penitentiary in Quebec to finish serving his sentence for cocaine trafficking while charges were still pending from his 1992 bust for importing hashish. In March 2003 Charron was sentenced to five years in prison and fined $150,000 for his role in the hashish importation scheme.

See also: DUBOIS GANG; LAVOIE, DONALD.

Reference

Gary Francoeur. "Alain Charron." WiseguyWally. Available online. URL: http://www.geocities.com/wiseguywally/AlainCharron.html. Downloaded on July 19, 2004.

—*G.F.*

CLERKENWELL Crime Syndicate (a.k.a. Clerkendel Crime Firm)

Since the early 1980s, the Clerkenwell Crime Syndicate has been the most powerful criminal group in Britain. According to http://www.ProbertEncyclopaedia.com, "The Adams family are a major London crime gang specialising in drugs and extortion. The gang have a reputation for hiring Afro-Caribbeans to carry out the murder of informants and competitors. In July 1991 Frankie Fraser, former enforcer for the Richardson gang, was shot at point-blank range as he left Turnmill's Nite Club in Clerkenwell, London, on orders from the Adams family. The Adams family are known to regularly bribe a quantity of Metropolitan Police officers." The Adamses have also been involved in the theft of gold bullion and securities fraud schemes as well.

The ring is run by Terry Adams, unquestionably the brains behind the syndicate. Patrick Adams, the Clerkenwell Crime Firm's enforcer, is known for his brutality and violence. Tommy Adams is the Adams family financier, securing lines of credit with various illicit organizations, especially with South American cartels.

See also: ADAMS, PATRICK; ADAMS, TERRY; ADAMS, TOMMY.

COCAINE and Crack

Cocaine, in both powdered and crack forms, permeates the United States. Colombian drug-trafficking organizations continue to control coca cultivation and cocaine production, most of which occurs in Colombia. Colombian organizations and their surrogates control transportation through the Caribbean corridor, while Mexican drug-trafficking organizations control the movement of cocaine through Mexico and across the Southwest border. An established system of transportation hubs and distribution centers allows Mexican and Colombian organizations to manage the flow of cocaine to markets throughout the United States. Inside the United States, Mexican organizations dominate transportation and wholesale distribution in the West and the Midwest, while Colombian organizations, although still involved, appear to be ceding some responsibility for transportation and wholesale distribution to other groups, particularly Dominicans, in the eastern United States. Although Mexican and Dominican organizations dominate among identifiable groups at the retail distribution level, independent dealers—including African Americans, Caucasians, and Hispanics—appear to be the norm. The production and availability of crack is directly linked to the availability of cocaine powder. Both production and distribution continue to be associated with street gangs.

ASSESSMENT OF THE THREAT TO THE UNITED STATES

Cocaine remains a major problem throughout the country. Availability and demand for both continue to be high. Information provided to the National Drug Intelligence Center (NDIC) by federal, state, and local agencies and organizations indicates that the transportation, distribution, abuse, and criminal activity related to powdered and crack cocaine continue to constitute the greatest drug threat to the United States.

Of the 412 state and local agencies responding to the National Drug Threat Survey, 109 rate cocaine as

Kilos of cocaine and weapons seized from an alleged crack cocaine lab in Westchester, Florida, southwest of Miami (AP)

one of the greatest drug threats in their areas. More than 280 agencies in every state, the District of Columbia, Guam, and the Northern Marianas consider the cocaine problem in their area stable but at high levels. Only 80 agencies note an increase in the cocaine problem, and 20 say that the problem is decreasing.

Although cocaine trafficking, abuse, and related criminal activity span the nation, the cocaine problem is greater in certain regions of the country: New England, New York/New Jersey, Mid-Atlantic, Southeast, and Florida/Caribbean. Cocaine has been surpassed by methamphetamine in most of the western and midwestern states, but it is still considered a major threat by law enforcement in metropolitan areas throughout the country and along the Southwest border.

Crack is a major problem in urban areas. Of those metropolitan police departments identifying crack as a problem, most considered it the greatest threat. The ready availability of cocaine and the movement of street gangs beyond traditional areas of operation have led to the spread of crack to many suburban and rural areas. Law-enforcement agencies in many areas report that crack abuse and distribution are having a serious negative impact on society, leading to violence and other criminal activities, principally by street gangs.

Of the 113 agencies that identify a specific correlation between drugs and violent crime, 67 note a correlation between cocaine and crack trafficking and violent crime. Of those agencies, 53 emphasize the relationship between crack and violent crime—more than for any other drug. Agencies highlight gang-related violence, particularly turf wars, as a primary effect of crack trafficking.

DEMAND

Interagency estimates place annual demand for cocaine in the United States at approximately 300 metric tons, or 35 percent of estimated annual potential production and about 50 percent of estimated worldwide demand. Overall, cocaine use has remained relatively stable for the past five years, with the estimated number of hardcore users ranging from 3.3 million to 3.6 million each year.

National studies indicate relative overall stability in the use of powdered cocaine, or cocaine hydrochloride. In 1999, cocaine was the second most-commonly used illegal drug (after marijuana) in the United States. National Household Survey on Drug Abuse (NHSDA) data for 1999 indicate that approximately 25 million individuals of age 12 or older reported lifetime cocaine use, approximately 4 million reported past-year use, and 1.5 million reported current use. The prevalence of cocaine use varied considerably across age groups: Lifetime use was highest among 26 to 34 year olds, but rates of past-year and current use were higher among young adults of age 18 to 25.

COCAINE ADMISSIONS, 1993–1998
(Number and Percent Distribution)

Year	Nonsmoked	Smoked (Crack)	Total	Percentage of All Drugs
1998	63,002	170,491	233,493	14.9
1997	60,405	169,724	230,129	15.0
1996	66,777	190,143	256,920	16.0
1995	69,421	202,865	272,286	16.6
1994	76,322	217,344	293,666	18.0
1993	75,860	201,216	277,076	17.5

Source: U.S. Department of Health and Human Services, Substance Abuse and Mental Health Services Administration (SAMHSA), Treatment Episode Data Set, 1998.

The most recent information available from the Treatment Episode Data Set (TEDS), a survey of national admissions to substance abuse treatment services, shows that cocaine accounted for nearly 15 percent of all admissions to publicly funded treatment facilities in 1998 (see table above). Of those cocaine

Joseph Keefe, chief of operations for the Drug Enforcement Administration (DEA), speaks at a January 2002 news conference, announcing the breakup of a money-laundering network catering to Colombian drug organizations. U.S. and Colombian law enforcement officials arrested 37 people and seized $8 million and hundreds of pounds of cocaine. (AP)

COCAINE ADMISSIONS BY SEX/RACE/AGE

	Nonsmoked	Smoked (Crack)
Total Admissions	63,002	170,491
Sex		
Male	65.8%	58.1%
Female	34.2%	41.9%
Total	100.0%	100.0%
Race		
White	49.5%	33.1%
Black	34.6%	59.3%
Hispanic	13.4%	5.6%
Other	2.5%	1.9%
Total	100.0%	100.0%
Average Age at Admission	32.8	34.4

Source: U.S. Department of Health and Human Services, Substance Abuse and Mental Health Services Administration, Treatment Episode Data Set, 1998.

PERCENT OF EIGHTH, TENTH, AND TWELFTH GRADERS REPORTING LIFETIME, PAST-YEAR, AND CURRENT COCAINE USE

	Lifetime			Past-Year			Current		
	8th	10th	12th	8th	10th	12th	8th	10th	12th
1999	4.7	7.7	9.8	2.7	4.9	6.2	1.3	1.8	2.6
1998	4.6	7.2	9.3	3.1	4.7	5.7	1.4	2.1	2.4
1997	4.4	7.1	8.7	2.8	4.7	5.5	1.1	2.0	2.3
1996	4.5	6.5	7.1	3.0	4.2	4.9	1.3	1.7	2.0
1995	4.2	5.0	6.0	2.6	3.5	4.0	1.2	1.7	1.8
1994	3.6	4.3	5.9	2.1	2.8	3.6	1.0	1.2	1.5
1993	2.9	3.6	6.1	1.7	2.1	3.3	0.7	0.9	1.3
1992	2.9	3.3	6.1	1.5	1.9	3.1	0.7	0.7	1.3

Source: U.S. Department of Health and Human Services, National Institute on Drug Abuse, Monitoring the Future Study, 1999.

admissions, 27 percent were for powdered (non-smoked) cocaine. According to TEDS data, the typical powdered cocaine user who was admitted to publicly funded treatment is white, male, and 32 years of age (see table above left).

Findings from the Arrestee Drug Abuse Monitoring (ADAM) Program continue to show that cocaine is the drug most frequently detected among arrestees, but the percentage of arrestees testing positive for cocaine has decreased at many sites. Data from the Drug Abuse Warning Network (DAWN), which include both powdered and crack cocaine, show cocaine to be the drug most frequently mentioned in hospital emergency department episodes, accounting for 30 percent of all episodes in 1999. Total cocaine mentions have remained relatively stable for the past five years.

Across the 42 metropolitan areas surveyed by DAWN, cocaine remained the drug most frequently mentioned by medical examiners in 1998. Although medical-examiner mentions of cocaine were relatively stable overall, seven cities reported large increases in 1998, while four reported large decreases.

The use of crack, unlike powdered cocaine, has varied considerably during the past five years. Estimates of the number of current crack users in the United States have ranged from 650,000 in 1996 to 413,000 in 1999, but there are no estimates of the level of demand for crack. Data from the NHSDA for 1999 indicate that almost 6 million individuals age 12 or older reported lifetime crack use, while approximately 1 million reported crack use in the past year, and about 413,000 reported current use.

Although cocaine and crack accounted for only 15 percent of admissions to publicly funded treatment facilities in 1998, most—73 percent—were for treatments for crack. TEDS data indicate that the typical crack user who is admitted to publicly funded treatment is black, male, and 34 years of age. Almost 42 percent of admissions to publicly funded treatment for crack abuse were female, compared with 34 percent of admissions for powdered cocaine. More than 40 percent of admissions to publicly funded treatment for crack use smoked on a daily basis; of admissions for powdered cocaine use, less than 29 percent used it daily.

PRODUCTION

Coca is cultivated primarily in Colombia; the country accounts for an estimated 67 percent of the powdered cocaine available for worldwide consumption. Peru and Bolivia, which account for 21 and 12 percent, respectively, are the only other significant source countries. The conversion of cocaine to crack

PERCENT OF PAST-YEAR COCAINE USE

School Year	Junior High	Senior High	12th Grade	Total (6–12)
1999–2000	2.2	5.3	7.1	3.7
1998–1999	2.7	6.1	8.0	4.7
1997–1998	2.8	6.0	7.9	4.6
1996–1997	3.0	5.9	7.0	4.5
1995–1996	2.7	5.6	7.1	4.3
1994–1995	1.9	4.5	5.3	3.3

Source: Parents' Resource Institute on Drug Education Survey, 1999–2000.
Note: Data is for cocaine and crack combined.

occurs almost exclusively at the retail level in the area in which the crack is to be distributed.

Coca cultivation estimates support potential production of 765 metric tons of 100 percent pure cocaine in 1999. Seizures of cocaine bound for the United States indicate that bulk wholesale shipments actually average 80 to 90 percent purity. Of the 587 metric tons of cocaine detected to be departing South America in 1999, 512 were believed to be destined for the United States. Of this amount, 76 metric tons were seized in transit, and another 56 metric tons were seized at the U.S. border.

TRANSPORTATION

Federal, state, and local law-enforcement information indicates the existence of a well-coordinated, integrated logistics system that spans the United States, allowing major Mexican and Colombian drug-trafficking organizations to manage the flow of cocaine to markets throughout the country. These organizations control the movement of cocaine from source countries to the United States through various points of entry, through and among transportation hubs in the Southwest and Southeast regions, and from distribution centers to markets throughout the nation.

TRANSPORTATION TO THE UNITED STATES

Interagency analysis of cocaine shipments detected from South America to the United States in 1999 shows a modest change from 1998 in the use of the primary transportation corridors (Mexico–Central America, Caribbean, and direct to continental United States). Midyear data for 2000 indicate greater use of Mexico and illustrate the fluidity of cocaine trafficking and the flexibility of the organizations that control it. In 1999, Mexico remained the primary conduit for cocaine destined for the United States, accounting for 54 percent of detected movement (59 percent in 1998). However, midyear data for 2000 indicate that approximately 66 percent of cocaine bound for the United States transited Mexico. In 1999, the Caribbean Corridor accounted for 43 percent of all detected shipments (30 percent in 1998), and Haiti and Puerto Rico remained the primary destinations for cocaine shipments through the Caribbean Corridor. Midyear data for 2000 show a reduction in the use of the Caribbean Corridor, particularly Haiti and Puerto Rico, to 33 percent of detected movement, but shipments to Jamaica

appear to have increased. In 1999, transit directly to the continental United States accounted for only 3 percent of detected shipments (11 percent in 1998).

Mexican and Colombian drug-trafficking organizations continue to control most cocaine transportation to the United States. Mexican organizations control the transit of cocaine across the Southwest border primarily at ports of entry (POEs) by vehicles (commercial trucks, privately owned vehicles, buses, and taxis) and by couriers on foot. Mexican organizations also use private vehicles, couriers, pack animals, and private aircraft to cross the border between POEs. Colombian organizations, in cooperation with Dominican, Jamaican, Bahamian, and Haitian groups, control the transportation of cocaine in the Caribbean. Containerized cargo, airdrops, go-fast boats, fishing vessels, and coastal freighters are used to move cocaine among the Caribbean islands and to the United States.

TRANSPORTATION WITHIN THE UNITED STATES

Law-enforcement information indicates that Mexican organizations dominate cocaine transportation in the United States, particularly in the Pacific, West Central, Southwest, Great Lakes, and Southeast regions. A number of agencies in the Mid-Atlantic Region also note Mexican involvement in cocaine transportation. However, many agencies throughout the country, especially in suburban and rural jurisdictions, state that local independent dealers, mainly Caucasians, are almost as prominent as Mexican organizations. Colombian organizations continue to be involved, particularly in the eastern United States, but have begun to depend more heavily on Caribbean groups—primarily Dominican, Haitian (especially in Florida), and Jamaican—to move cocaine. Organized gangs, including outlaw motorcycle gangs (OMGs) and street gangs, appear to be more prominent in transporting cocaine than was previously believed.

Responses to the National Drug Threat Survey and domestic seizure information provided by the El Paso Intelligence Center (EPIC) document the redundancy and interconnectivity of the logistics system through which drug-trafficking organizations manage the flow of cocaine to U.S. markets. This system enables traffickers to direct supply among transportation hubs and distribution centers, to supply multiple markets through alternate routes, and probably to supplement cocaine supplies in areas experiencing shortages as a result of seizures and other law-enforcement activity.

TRANSPORTATION HUBS

The principal transportation hubs in the United States are Los Angeles, Central Arizona (Tucson and Phoenix), El Paso, Houston, Miami, and Puerto Rico. Mexican organizations control the movement of cocaine to transportation hubs through smuggling corridors in the Southwest region. They also control the movement of cocaine from transportation hubs in the Southwest to the distribution centers of Atlanta, Chicago, Dallas, New York, and Philadelphia, as well as to markets throughout the country. Colombian organizations control the flow of cocaine into and through Miami and Puerto Rico as well as the flow of some cocaine into Houston, supplying organizations throughout the eastern United States and in the Great Lakes Region.

Los Angeles: The primary source of cocaine to the Los Angeles area is Mexico, via southern California (San Diego) and El Paso, Texas. The Los Angeles High Intensity Drug Trafficking Area (HIDTA) states that Mexican drug-trafficking organizations are now sending smaller shipments of cocaine to Los Angeles simultaneously to reduce losses from the seizure of large shipments. From Los Angeles, Mexican organizations supply cocaine to other Mexican organizations in Chicago and Detroit and to Dominican and possibly Colombian organizations in New York. Los Angeles–based Mexican organizations also supply cocaine to associates in cities north of Los Angeles along Interstate 5. Past seizures indicate some maritime transport to Los Angeles from Colombia, but available information does not indicate to what extent. The continued presence of Colombian organizations suggests that they may control some shipments directly to Los Angeles and probably control shipments to associated Colombian organizations in Oakland, San Francisco, Seattle, and other locations on the U.S. West Coast. The Los Angeles Field Division of the Drug Enforcement Administration (DEA) notes that Peruvian groups are attempting to establish cocaine routes to Los Angeles independent of Colombian or Mexican organizations.

Transportation hub: A city or area that is the intended primary destination of drugs and from which one or more distribution centers are supplied. Transportation hubs usually function as distribution centers as well.

Distribution center: A city that supplies drugs to local markets in and out of state.

Transshipment point: A city or area in which drugs are temporarily stored with the ultimate intent being transportation to another location for distribution.

Central Arizona: Mexican organizations operating from Tucson and Phoenix control cocaine transportation from Mexico directly into Arizona. From Arizona, they manage the movement of cocaine to Atlanta, Chicago, Cleveland, Los Angeles, Minneapolis, and New York, as well as to several cities between Arizona and the Great Lakes Region.

El Paso: Mexican organizations based in El Paso control the flow of cocaine into El Paso through several entry points in the El Paso metropolitan area and along the border between Columbus, New Mexico, and Del Rio, Texas. In addition to supplying cocaine to Los Angeles, El Paso-based Mexican organizations supply associates—primarily Mexican—in Chicago, Denver, New York, and Philadelphia.

Houston: Mexican and Colombian organizations manage cocaine transportation into and through Houston, which is supplied overland from Mexico via border entry points between Del Rio and Brownsville and by sea. McAllen, Texas, in particular, is a major transshipment point. The DEA Houston Field Division notes a high volume of cocaine shipped through McAllen in tractor trailers en route primarily to Houston but also to Dallas, Chicago, New York, and other areas to the north and the east. Maritime shipments of cocaine directly from Colombia and the Caribbean to Houston probably constitute a majority of the Colombian market share in Houston. From Houston, the cocaine is shipped to associated African-American, Colombian, Dominican, and Mexican organizations in Atlanta, Chicago, New York City, Rochester (N.Y.), and Tampa.

Miami: Miami is one of the most important transportation hubs in the eastern United States. Colombian organizations control the flow of cocaine into Miami primarily from the Caribbean, but, according to the Tampa Police Department, Tampa is also a source of some of the cocaine transported to the Miami area. The Miami Police Department reports that New York City is the primary destination for cocaine shipped out of Miami. Additional information from law-enforcement agencies indicates a significant increase in cocaine smuggling aboard Haitian coastal freighters.

Puerto Rico: Colombian organizations and their Caribbean associates control cocaine transportation from the northern coasts of Colombia and Venezuela either directly to Puerto Rico or indirectly through the Dominican Republic, Haiti, Trinidad and Tobago, St. Croix, St. Martin/Sint Maarten, and St. Thomas. Traffickers smuggle multihundred-kilogram shipments of cocaine directly to Puerto Rico using a variety of air and maritime methods including commercial and cargo aircraft, go-fast vessels, and containerized cargo. There is a significant lack of information, however, regarding the use of containerized cargo. Traffickers also employ a combination of go-fast vessels, cruise ships, ferries, fishing boats, private yachts, and motherships to "island hop" cocaine to Puerto Rico. There are indications that, because of increased detection and monitoring activity near Haiti and the Dominican Republic, airdrops in the waters east of Puerto Rico may be increasing. From Puerto Rico, traffickers use commercial flights, air cargo, containerized cargo, private watercraft, and cruise ships to move cocaine to associates in New York, Miami, Orlando, Philadelphia, and Newark.

Jacksonville and Tampa, Florida: These cities are noteworthy sources of cocaine to other cities in the United States, but there is insufficient information to classify either as a transportation hub or distribution center. Colombian organizations transport cocaine directly to both cities. Jacksonville appears to lack the widespread influence of the major distribution centers, but criminal organizations in Jacksonville supply cocaine to associates in north Florida,

Georgia, New York, and Illinois. The FBI Jacksonville Field Division notes a marked increase in cocaine smuggling through the Port of Jacksonville. Tampa appears to have less influence than even Jacksonville as a distribution center but may supplement cocaine supplies at transportation hubs. Colombian and Central American organizations in Tampa supply and are supplied by associates in Houston and Miami.

DISTRIBUTION

Mexican organizations continue to dominate wholesale cocaine distribution, particularly in the Pacific, Southwest, West Central, Great Lakes, and Southeast regions. However, information from law-enforcement agencies indicates that Mexican organizations are establishing operations and gaining market share in the eastern United States, especially in New York and Philadelphia. Colombian organizations continue to dominate wholesale distribution in the eastern United States but apparently have ceded responsibility for some wholesale distribution to Dominican and Jamaican associates throughout the New England, New York/New Jersey, and Florida/Caribbean regions. Colombian wholesale distribution organizations also dominate the larger market areas of the Mid-Atlantic. According to responses to the National Drug Threat Survey, local independent dealers, particularly Caucasians, are almost as prominent in wholesale cocaine distribution as Mexican organizations—especially in suburban and rural areas. Survey responses also indicate that although Mexican organizations maintain a presence in retail distribution, they surrender dominance to local independent dealers

Wholesale: The level of distribution at which drugs are purchased directly from a source of supply or importer and sold, normally, to midlevel distributors in pound, kilogram, or multiunit quantities.

Midlevel: The level of distribution at which drugs are purchased directly from wholesale distributors in pound, kilogram, or multiunit quantities and sold in smaller quantities to other midlevel distributors or to retail distributors.

Retail: The level of distribution at which drugs are sold directly to users.

(including Caucasians, African Americans, and Hispanics) and street gangs.

Local independent dealers and street gangs continue to dominate crack distribution, almost all of which occurs at the retail level. Federal, state, and local law-enforcement agencies report that crack distributors prefer to move cocaine and convert it to crack locally to avoid the more severe penalties associated with trafficking crack. Almost 300 of the 412 state and local agencies responding to the National Drug Threat Survey identify crack as a problem in their areas, of which almost 80 percent state that crack conversion occurs locally. Local independent dealers, African-American groups, and street gangs are identified as prominently involved in converting cocaine to crack. Several agencies also note the involvement of Mexican, Caucasian, and Dominican groups in crack conversion and distribution.

Crack distribution patterns mirror those of cocaine: Street gangs and local independent dealers control crack distribution to associates in and out of state. Of 412 respondents to the National Drug Threat Survey, 270 agencies identify local independent dealers, and 190 identify street gangs as the dominant crack distributors in their areas. The next most frequently mentioned are Caucasians, identified by 122 different agencies, and Mexicans, mentioned by only 49.

DISTRIBUTION CENTERS

In addition to using the transportation hubs for wholesale distribution, Mexican and Colombian criminal organizations use several other U.S. cities as distribution centers, supplying wholesale quantities of cocaine to organizations in and out of state. Among the distribution centers, the most prominent in terms of regional influence and importance are New York, Chicago, Dallas, Atlanta, Detroit, and Philadelphia. Other probable distribution centers are Columbus, Ohio; St. Louis, Missouri; Minneapolis and St. Paul, Minnesota; Seattle, Washington; and Denver, Colorado. Information from law enforcement agencies and the EPIC indicates a high volume of cocaine movement to these cities, but there is insufficient information to determine their importance as distribution centers.

New York: Cocaine-trafficking organizations in New York City, one of the largest cocaine markets in the country, are supplied by virtually every available means of transportation: by sea via containerized cargo, by land from the Southwest border and from the Southeast region, by air (especially couriers), and by various parcel services. Mexican and Colombian organizations in Los Angeles, El Paso, Houston, Miami, and Jacksonville control most cocaine shipments to New York, but according to the New York City Police Department, Asian, Dominican, and Jamaican groups are also involved. Colombian and Dominican organizations control the majority of wholesale and midlevel cocaine distribution within New York, but there are indications that Mexican organizations are gaining influence. According to the New York Police Department, local independent dealers (Caucasians and African Americans) and street gangs, as well as Asian, Central American, and Italian organized-crime groups also are involved in wholesale distribution. New York-based Colombian, Dominican, and Jamaican organizations supply cocaine to markets in some of the most populous areas of the United States. The influence of New York City as a distribution center extends throughout the New England, New York/New Jersey, and Mid-Atlantic Regions and reaches into the Southeast and Great Lakes regions.

Chicago: Mexican and Colombian organizations coordinate the flow of cocaine from Los Angeles, Central Arizona, El Paso, and Houston to associated Mexican and Colombian organizations in Chicago. Responses to the National Drug Threat Survey indicate some movement of cocaine from Jacksonville, Florida, through Roanoke, Virginia, to Chicago. Mexican organizations dominate wholesale and midlevel distribution in Chicago, but the Chicago Police Department identifies Colombian and street-gang involvement in wholesale distribution as well. At the retail level, Mexican organizations also dominate distribution, but street gangs, local independent dealers—Caucasians, African Americans, and Hispanics—are heavily involved. From Chicago, Mexican organizations coordinate distribution to markets throughout the Great Lakes region and into limited areas of the Southeast and West Central regions.

Dallas: The primary sources of cocaine to the Dallas metropolitan area are El Paso and Houston, but some cocaine apparently is shipped directly from points between Brownsville and El Paso. Within Dallas, Mexican organizations control the majority of wholesale and midlevel cocaine distribution, but the Dallas Police Department also identifies the involvement of street gangs and Colombian, Central American, and Caribbean groups. Mexican organizations, street gangs, local independent dealers (particularly Caucasians), and Asian groups are all involved in retail distribution. The influence of Dallas as a regional distribution center extends throughout north and east Texas, overlapping that of El Paso and Houston, and reaches into Arkansas, Kansas, Louisiana, Mississippi, and Oklahoma. The Dallas Police Department notes an increase in cocaine transshipment through Dallas during the past few years.

Atlanta: The Atlanta Police Department identifies Miami, Brownsville, Texas, and Savannah, Georgia, as the primary sources of cocaine to the area, but the Jacksonville and Houston Police Departments also identify Atlanta as a destination for cocaine that leaves their jurisdictions. The large number of cocaine sources to Atlanta and the high volume of cocaine transiting those source areas suggest that the volume of cocaine transported to Atlanta is correspondingly high. According to the Atlanta Police Department, Mexican organizations, local independent dealers, and street gangs dominate cocaine distribution at the wholesale level. At the retail level, street gangs, local independent dealers, and Caucasians, as well as Colombian, Jamaican, and Mexican groups, are all involved. Atlanta's influence as a distribution center appears to be limited to the Southeast region, particularly Alabama, Georgia, North Carolina, South Carolina, and Tennessee, but it includes many of the more populous cities in those states.

Detroit: According to the DEA Detroit Field Division, organizations in Chicago, Miami, New York, Los Angeles, and Texas supply cocaine to organizations in Detroit. Within Detroit, Colombian, Mexican, and Jamaican organizations, as well as Caucasians, are involved in wholesale and midlevel cocaine distribution. According to the Detroit Police Department, street gangs and local independent dealers dominate retail distribution. Detroit's influence as a regional distri-

bution center overlaps that of Chicago but is more limited in extent. Detroit-based organizations manage cocaine distribution throughout Michigan and to markets in Indiana, Iowa, Kentucky, Ohio, western Pennsylvania, and West Virginia.

Philadelphia: Mexican and Colombian organizations in El Paso, Miami, and New York supply wholesale cocaine distribution groups operating in Philadelphia. These groups include Dominican and Colombian organizations, street gangs, and local independent dealers including African Americans, Asians, and Caucasians. But Caribbean groups—particularly Dominicans with connections to other Dominican groups in New York City—dominate wholesale and midlevel cocaine distribution. According to the Philadelphia Police Department, Dominican groups, street gangs, Caucasians, and OMGs are all involved in cocaine distribution at the retail level. Philadelphia-based organizations, particularly Dominicans, distribute cocaine to groups throughout Pennsylvania and in Delaware, Maryland, Massachusetts, Virginia, and Washington, D.C.

Other probable distribution centers include Columbus, Ohio; St. Louis, Missouri; Minneapolis and St. Paul, Minnesota; Seattle, Washington; and Denver, Colorado. Drug-trafficking organizations in these cities distribute locally and to groups and independent dealers in surrounding states. The influence of these cities, however, does not appear to match that of the distribution centers noted above. According to information provided by police departments and sheriff's offices in each of these cities, locally based Mexican organizations with ties to Mexican organizations along the Southwest border are heavily involved in cocaine transportation and distribution. In Columbus, Dominican and Jamaican organizations with connections to New York and Florida dominate cocaine distribution. In the Minneapolis and St. Paul areas, the dominant cocaine distributors are local street gangs with ties to gangs in Chicago, and Mexican groups with connections to Mexican organizations in Arizona, California, and Texas. Mexican, Colombian, and Central American groups dominate cocaine distribution in Seattle. Although drug-trafficking organizations in each of these cities clearly maintain connections to other organizations and independent dealers in and out of state, more information is needed to characterize wholesale and retail distribution patterns in these areas.

PROJECTIONS

Almost all national indicators point to continued overall stability in cocaine and crack availability and abuse but at high levels. Despite indications of overall stability, some changes in the cocaine and crack situation could pose challenges for drug-control efforts in the near future.

Reference

"Cocaine and Crack." *National Drug Intelligence Center, National Drug Threat Assessment 2001—The Domestic Perspectives, October 2000.*

COLOMBO Crime Family

The Colombo crime family are controlled by father and son Persico; however, due to a family war, they also are weakened. Current estimates place membership at 100. The family's first don was Joseph Profaci.

The family's primary activities include narcotics, gambling, loan-sharking, cigarette smuggling, pornography, counterfeiting, hijacking, bankruptcy fraud, and more. Despite the small size of the Colombo family, it maintains an impressive presence in a wide variety of criminal activities.

Current boss is Carmine "the Snake" Persico, who is currently serving 139 years for murder and racketeering. His son, Alphonse "Allie Boy" Persico, who is currently serving an 18-month sentence issued in February 2000 for illegal gun possession in Miami, has reputedly taken over, but his grip is weak. The current acting boss is Joel "Joe Waverly" Cacace.

The Colombo crime family was founded by Joseph Profaci, a close friend of Joseph Bonanno, boss of the Bonanno crime family. As the 20th century wound down, Persico's son Alphonse was annointed family boss, but by the time the new millennium rolled around, Alphonse was cooling his heels in federal prison, and former underboss William (Wild Bill) Cutolo was missing and believed dead. Successor underboss John (Jackie) DeRoss was awaiting trial for racketeering with Alphonse Persico. Being boss of the Colombo family is not as appealing as it once was. Many of its

members are jailed, the internal war created great and lasting mistrust, and the loss of significant income from major labor racketeering has crippled the organization.

See also: BONANNO CRIME FAMILY; COMMISSION, THE; GAMBINO CRIME FAMILY; GENOVESE CRIME FAMILY; LUCCHESE CRIME FAMILY.

Reference

David Amoruso. "Colombo Crime Family." Gangsters Incorporated. Available online. URL: http://gangstersinc. tripod.com/Col.html. Downloaded on July 19, 2004.

—D.A.

COMMISSION, The

The Commission is a ruling body composed of the top figures from the five families of New York, including the Bonnano, Columbo, Gambino, Genovese, and Lucchese families. At times when the Commission has actually met, more organized-crime groups have been invited to attend.

The Commission was set up by the heads of the five families as a way in which they could adjudicate differences between families and come to an understanding on a variety of disputes without having to result in violence. In this way, the five families waged war on other groups, as well as organized most effectively their nefarious activities.

See also: BONANNO CRIME FAMILY; COLOMBO CRIME FAMILY; GAMBINO CRIME FAMILY; GENOVESE CRIME FAMILY; LUCCHESE CRIME FAMILY.

Reference

David Amoruso. "The Commission." Gangsters Incorporated. Available online. URL: http://gangstersinc.tripod. com/thecommission.html. Downloaded on July 19, 2004.

—D.A.

COP Killas

The Cop Killas are a racially mixed gang located throughout the United States. The gang also includes female gang members, also known as Lady Killas. It is believed that this group is the enforcement arm of the Imperial Blood Brothers United Nation.

The gang identifies itself by wearing the colors blue and black. A string of beads indicates the rank of the individual member. The killers wear all black beads, while probationary members wear blue beads. All other members wear six black beads and six blue beads. Popular emblems that also identify the gang members include a cracked police badge and Calvin Klein clothing. The current Cop Killa handshake is currently unknown.

The Cop Killas have alliances or partial alliances with different gangs in more than 47 states. Known alliances are with the Imperial Blood Brothers United Nation and other antiestablishment black militias. Other loose alliances include Ñeta, Brotherhood, La Familia (N.Y.), Vice Lords (Ohio), Latin Kings (N.Y.), Pump Nation, and 20 Love.

Cop Killas rivals include the All Mighty Latin Kings and Queens Nation and Charter Nation, as well as the Crips, and of course all law enforcement officers.

The Cop Killas received the blessing of the Blood Brothers in winter 1996. As a result of that blessing, the Cop Killas have become the enforcement arm for Blood Brothers, a.k.a. Blood Brothers United Nation or Imperial Blood Brothers United Nation in Connecticut, creating one of the largest gangs to be in one single area with more than 2,000 members to date (825 BB, and 1,235 CK). On March 6 1996, the CK reached 21 states with active recruiting continuing.

Members of Cop Killas are known to use physical violence, firearms, and motor vehicles for assault, intimidation, and homicide. Their money comes from specialized front businesses operated by Imperial Blood Brothers United Nation to fund the organization.

Cop Killas have a highly organized and formalized rank structure that includes one Elder, Executive Staff, Security, Secretary of Communications, Region Commanders, Chapter leaders with each Chapter leader reporting to their region's Commander.

It has recently come to the attention of law enforcement officials that this group has largely been consumed by the Bloods and other gangs. While some members may still count themselves as Cop Killas, authorities have stopped following the gang as a single group or organization.

Reference

Southeastern Connecticut Gang Activities Group (SEGAG). "Cop Killas." Available online. URL: http://www.segag. org. Downloaded on July 19, 2004.

CORLEONE Clan

Easily the most powerful Sicilian Mafia clan in Italy's long history of such organized-crime groups, the Corleone clan has become known for its powerful and ruthless bosses as well as its well-funded and powerful allies. Former bosses include such infamous leaders as Dr. Michele Navarra, Luciano Liggio, and Salvatore Riina.

See also: AGLIERI, PIETRO; BARGARELLA, LEOLUCA; BRUSCA, GIOVANNI; FALCONE, GIOVANNI; PALAZ-ZOLO, GIUSEPPE; PROVENZANO, BERNARDO; RIINA, SALVATORE; SPERA, BENEDETTO.

CORNELL, George

George Cornell was a member of the Richardson Gang and was a boyhood friend of the Kray twins. Richardson and Ronny Kray, in adulthood, could not stomach the sight of each other. Because of his boyhood association with the Krays, the Richardsons used him as a point man in conversations with the Krays.

Two major factors led to Cornell's death. First, he happened to be the only gangland personality to emerge from a shooting that took place in a bar named Mr. Smith and the Witchdoctor, where the Kray's cousin Dickie Hart was murdered. Second, it was reported that Cornell had allegedly insulted Ron.

In 1965, at a public house known as The Windows, Ronnie Kray calmly walked into the bar with an associate, drew a gun, and shot Cornell in the forehead, killing him instantly, and then calmly walked out of the restaurant as if he were a paying customer. Kray was arrested, but none of the witnesses would identify him as the shooter, and he was released.

See also: FRASER, FRANK; KRAY TWINS; MCVITE, JACK; RICHARDSON, CHARLIE; RICHARDSON, EDDIE; RICHARDSON GANG.

CORPORAN, Pedro

According to William Norman Grigg in the *New American* magazine, a New York Drug Enforcement Task Force (NYDETF) memo written on February 9, 1994, stated, "Corporan now enjoys a 'cult hero' status within the Dominican community in Washington Heights. On the surface, Corporan is a local business owner and author of several 'anti-drug' editorials published in the *El Diario* newspaper. In addition, Corporan has been the most vocal supporter and right-hand man to Dr. Jose Francisco Peña-Gomez, who is running for President in the Dominican Republic. . . ."

The NYDETF alleged that he used the alias Pedro Cabrera and that he had been arrested twice for carrying a gun, and had "delivered one million dollars . . . to an undercover detective in Group T-12 for deposit into an 'Operation Pisces' account." Because of the international scope of the operations, the NYDETF could only do so much to pursue Corporan. Corporan was funneling some of the profits from his drug operations back to Peña-Gomez, whose presidential bid was being backed by the Clinton administration.

Rafael "Fiquito" Vásquez, a confederate of Corporan, identified Corporan as a "heavy" drug dealer in New York City in 1997. Corporan fled the country that year but was never charged with any crimes.

See also: JHERI-CURL GANG; OPERATION PISCES.

Reference

Grigg, William Norman. "Smuggler's Dues." *New American.* 13, no. 9 (April 28, 1997).

CORPORATION, The

The Corporation is believed to be the single largest Hispanic crime syndicate in the United States. Headed by José Miguel Battle, a former Cuban citizen, The Corporation stretches from the New York metropolitan area to the tip of Florida. The power of this violent crime operation comes from running numbers, extortion, and numerous other illegal activities.

See also: BATTLE, JOSÉ MIGUEL.

CORROZO, Nicholas

Nicholas Corrozo was named as the head of the Gambino crime family, when John Gotti, who was running the family from behind bars, was forced to abdicate. However, while the "Dapper Don's" reign was showy and somewhat resilient, Corrozo's stay at the top was short. Corrozo was arrested in Miami as he emerged from the ocean. He was charged with conspiracy to commit murder, arson, loansharking, and extortion.

See also: GOTTI, JOHN.

COTRONI, Francesco

Francesco "Frank" Cotroni, the fifth of six children, was born in Montreal in 1931. He followed his older brother Vic into a life of crime and, by the late '50s, was a high-ranking member of the Montreal Mafia. Unlike his older Calabrian-born brothers, Frank felt more at ease speaking in French and English than Italian. He married a French woman, Pauline Désormiers, and had six children. He was known on the streets of Montreal in all three languages: "The Big Guy," "Il Cice," and "Le Gros." Cotroni was first arrested in September 1960 with Jos Di Maulo and Michel "The Penguin" Di Paolo for possession of deadly weapons. He was carrying a gun that fired armor-piercing bullets. Two months later, while out on bail, Frank was again arrested after leading 30 family enforcers into Montreal's Chez Paree nightclub and trashing the place. Thirty thousand dollars in damages were caused, and he was once again behind bars.

Frank Cotroni and several of his soldiers were charged in the late '60s with conspiring to dig a tunnel under Trans-Island Street in northwestern Montreal, into the vaults of a City and District Savings Bank of Montreal branch. But the plot was uncovered by police before the tunnel could be completed, and the loot, which would have been almost $6 million, was never pilfered. Although several of his men were found guilty, Cotroni was acquitted of all charges.

On February 1, 1971, while on vacation in Mexico, he was stopped and imprisoned by police, following a complaint by an Acapulco jeweler concerning jewelry worth $2,080 which had been purchased on a stolen credit card. The whole ordeal turned out to be a misunderstanding, but Cotroni had to spend 12 days behind bars before the mess was cleared up.

In 1972, Cotroni was once again back in court. Dionysos Chionsis, a Greek immigrant, told police that three men had demanded $250 a week for "protection." One of the extortionists had allegedly said that they worked for Frank Cotroni, but the case fell apart when, on his second day of testimony, the scared restaurant owner suddenly came down with amnesia. The charges against Cotroni were dropped.

Problems continued to plague Cotroni. He was arrested on drug-trafficking charges on November 8, 1974, as he met with his brother Vic. The case was brought before the Supreme Court of Canada, and he was extradited to the United States to stand trial.

The state's main witness, Sicilian drug-trafficker Giuseppe "Pino" Catania convinced the jury of Cotroni's guilt, and Cotroni was sentenced to 15 years in prison and a fine of $20,000. Cotroni was paroled on April 25, 1979, after serving one-third of his prison sentence and immediately returned to Montreal and continued his criminal empire. He managed to keep a low profile for a few years but, once again, Frank ran into trouble with law enforcement. He was arrested on August 30, 1983, in a Saint-Leonard restaurant after a federal grand jury in New Haven, Connecticut, indicted him on conspiring to distribute heroin.

Vic Cotroni, Frank's older brother and godfather of the Montreal crime family, died of cancer on September 19, 1984. Frank, who was being held at the Parthenais prison in Montreal while fighting extradition, requested a humanitarian leave to attend the funeral but was refused. Réal Simard, who oversaw Frank's activities in Toronto, was arrested for murder and decided to testify against his boss. Simard told police of his role in the murder of a north-end drug dealer who had been badmouthing Cotroni. Giuseppe Montegano was shot four times in the head in June 1981 at a private club owned by Cotroni's son, Francesco. On December 8, 1987, Cotroni pleaded guilty and was sentenced to eight years in prison for manslaughter. His son Francesco and two associates also pleaded guilty in the plot. About the same time, Cotroni was convicted to a six-year term for the conspiracy case in Connecticut. As he served time for those two crimes, Cotroni held an interview with a reporter in the prison yard. "The Big Guy" denounced his life of crime and, as he smoked an expensive cigar and watched a prison softball game, assured the world that he was going straight. Cotroni, his son Francesco, and 22 others were nabbed on April 17, 1996, in a massive joint drug ring between the Italian Mafia and another criminal gang. Police claimed the network was responsible for importing hundreds, if not thousands, of kilograms of cocaine into the country. Cotroni, who allegedly ran the ring with Daniel Serero, was once again behind bars, this time for a seven-year sentence. While behind bars, the Calabrian mob boss received bad news on May 19, 1999: His son Paolo was shot to death in the driveway of his Repentigny home. In what police believe was a retaliation, 69-year-old Vincent Melia was shot in the face in a bar just before Paolo's funeral service was about to begin. On October 30, 2001, Cotroni,

at the age of 70, having spent almost 30 of these years behind bars, was paroled from a minimum-security prison in Laval. He had served two-thirds of his term, and police promised to keep a close eye on him. Frank Cotroni died of brain cancer in his Montreal home on August 17, 2004.

Reference

Gary Francoeur. "Francesco 'Frank' Cotroni." Wiseguy-Wally. Available online. URL: http://www.geocities.com/wiseguywally/FrancescoCotroni.html. Downloaded on July 19, 2004.

—G.F.

COTRONI, Francesco, Jr.

Francesco Cotroni Jr., the fourth of Frank Cotroni's six children, was born in 1960. He followed in his father's legendary footsteps and became involved in a life of crime. In April 1981 an argument erupted between Francesco and Giuseppe Montegano, a small-time drug trafficker, supposedly over a cocaine transaction. The two argued at the Agrigento social club, a bar owned by Francesco, over the drug's quality. Frank Cotroni Sr. heard of the incident and dispatched hit man Réal Simard to investigate the conflict. Simard met with both men to hear their sides of the story. Francesco explained that the drug that he had bought from Montegano was of poor quality. Montegano claimed that the young Cotroni had returned the cocaine, claiming that it was not good, but he had cut it first. Simard relayed the information to Frank Sr., and the Calabrian handed down his decision: Montegano had to be eliminated.

Montegano was invited to Francesco's bar on June 14, 1981 under the pretext that he would be paid the drug money owed him. Réal Simard, Francesco Rao, and Daniel Arena concocted a plot to abduct him and kill him elsewhere, but Montegano became suspicious and a struggle ensued. Simard produced a gun and shot him twice in the head. After Réal Simard was arrested in Toronto for the murder of Mario Héroux and the attempted murder of Robert Hétu on November 30, 1983 and sentenced to life in prison, he chose to become an informant and provided police with devastating evidence against Frank Cotroni and his underlings, including details on the Montegano slaying. Early October 10, 1986, police put operation "Si-Co," for Simard-Cotroni, into action and raided several homes and arrested multiple suspects. Francesco was apprehended at his home in Anjou. His father Frank and associates Daniel Arena and Francesco Raso were also nabbed. All were charged with the first-degree murder of Giuseppe Montegano. Francesco was freed on $100,000 bail under the conditions that he live with his sister Rosina and maintain his employment at Ital-Video Poker on Jean–Talon Street. Their trial was set for January 5, 1988, but the defendants shocked everyone by pleading guilty to manslaughter charges a month before the trial was to begin. The judge allowed Francesco to spend the Christmas holidays with his family before sentencing him to three years on January 15, 1988. Frank Sr. received eight years, Raso got five years, and Arena was sentenced to seven years in prison.

Francesco married Milena Di Maulo, the daughter of high-ranking mobster Jos Di Maulo, in summer 1991. The event was held at the Marie-Riene-du-Monde cathedral in downtown Montreal and was attended by some of the top members of the Mafia, the West End Gang, and the Dubois Clan. The couple would have two children together, but their marriage would end in divorce in late 2000.

Since his release from prison, Francesco was in charge of his father's drug network. He traveled to Colombia in February 1995 and met with Gilberto Rodriguez-Orejuela and Miguel Rodriguez Orejuela, the reputed heads of the Cali cartel. Francesco was also seen meeting major drug traffickers at the Villa Sorrento Hotel in Mexico, which is co-owned by his father. He would run the network until Frank Sr. was released from jail on September 28, 1995. On April 17, 1996. Francesco and his father were among 24 arrested in a joint RCMP-MUC operation against members of the Italian Mafia and another Montreal gang. The Cotronis had allied themselves with Daniel Serero, a major drug trafficker, to import large shipments of drugs. One hundred seventy kilograms of cocaine were seized in the bust. When Francesco was picked up, police found a bomb-making manual in his home. Francesco's lawyer Martin Tremblay attempted to convince the jury that his client had played a secondary role in the drug-importation network. They did not buy it and sentenced him to eight years in prison. His father received a seven-year sentence. In March 2000, Francesco was moved to a transition house because of his good behavior behind bars. A few months later he went up for parole. He told officials that his "father has always done every-

thing so that my brothers, my sister, and I go straight." He also denied being a part of a criminal organization: "I am not part of any clan. I know a lot of people, including Vito Rizzuto, but I am not part of any gang." His parole was denied. Seven months later, in October, Francesco's parole came through. His father was paroled shortly after.

Reference

Gary Francoeur. "Francesco Cotroni Jr." Wiseguy-Wally. Available online. URL: http://www.geocities.com/wiseguywally/FrancescoCotroniJr.html. Downloaded on July 19, 2004.

—*G.F.*

COTRONI, Giuseppe

Giuseppe "Pep" Cotroni, Vic's younger brother, was born on February 22, 1920, in Calabria, Italy. When he was only four, the family emigrated to Montreal's Italian section. He made his name mainly as a specialist in armed robbery and fencing stolen goods. By 1937, Pep, as he was often called, had been charged eight times for such offenses. In 1949, Cotroni was jailed for receiving stolen bonds. He was released from St. Vincent de Paul prison in April 1953 after serving almost four years. Jail did not alter Cotroni's view on crime though, and in the autumn of 1954, the Royal Canadian Mounted Police (RCMP) learned that he now partnered Lucien Rivard in heroin trafficking. Drugs would be imported by Corsican traffickers and smuggled to American customers by the Montreal organization. Pep's older brother, Vic, and Luigi Greco were supposedly his principal financial backers in the drug business and received a cut of the proceeds.

Cotroni traveled to Paris on March 14, 1957, and was followed by agents of the French central office for narcotics. They tailed him to the Le Français bar, but Pep must have sensed that something was wrong and left after a brief moment. Minutes later, police noticed Corsican drug trafficker Jean-Baptiste Croce entering the bar.

On November 14, 1957, Pep Cotroni and Luigi Greco represented Montreal at the infamous Apalachin Mafia conference. The meeting was interrupted when a New York State police trooper noticed a large number of black limousines in the area. Sixty men were arrested as they tried to flee, but almost as many, including the two Montrealers, escaped.

Cotroni, accompanied by Luigi Greco and some employees of the Bonfire Restaurant, vacationed at his cottage in Sainte-Adele, north of Montreal, one weekend. At about 5 P.M. the group sat down and drank from a bottle of anisette. Cotroni, Gaston Savard, and Ernest Costello began to feel harsh pains in their stomachs and legs and were taken to the hospital for treatment. Cotroni and Savard, who had only taken sips, survived but Costello, who had drank his entire glass, died of poisoning. Police discovered that the cottage's window had been forced open and that the anisette had been spiked with the deadly poison strychnine. Cotroni and Greco both declared that they had no enemies, and no one was ever arrested for the act.

In 1959, the U.S. Bureau of Narcotics targeted Cotroni's heroin network. Agent Patrick Biase, playing the role of Dave Costa, accompanied drug-courier-turned-informant Eddie Smith to Montreal to meet the mobster. Cotroni, with his right-hand man René Robert, met with Smith and Biase and agreed to sell them two kilograms of heroin for $7,000 each. Other deals were made and, when the investigation concluded, Cotroni and Robert were arrested on narcotics-trafficking charges.

In November 1959, Pep Cotroni, at age 39, was sentenced to 10 years in prison and fined $88,000. René Robert, 31, received an eight-year sentence. He was given another seven years in jail to be served consecutively on May 18, 1960, for a stolen-bonds conviction. The bonds had been taken during a $3,750,000 robbery from the Brockville Trust & Savings company in 1958. The robbery, according to police, had been the act of one of Cotroni's main lieutenants, Peter "the Russian" Stepanoff. Giuseppe Cotroni was liberated from prison in April 1971. He returned to his criminal activities and continued to accumulate an impressive fortune through narcotics trafficking and his various legitimate interests. Pep successfully avoided further prosecution until his death of natural causes in September 1979.

Reference

Gary Francoeur. "Giuseppe 'Pep' Cotroni." WiseguyWally. Available online. URL: http://www.geocities.com/wiseguywally/GiuseppeCotroni.html. Downloaded on July 19, 2004.

—G.F.

COTRONI, Paolo

Paolo "Paul" Cotroni, the second of Frank Cotroni's five sons, was born in the mid-1950s. He followed in his father's footsteps and continued the family's legacy.

According to police, Paolo Cotroni ran a lucrative narcotics network that sold drugs out of mob-controlled nightclubs and bars. He was also known to have established strong connections with the Hells Angels and two of their puppet clubs, the Rockers and the Death Riders.

Cotroni was arrested on August 30, 1990, after police found a stolen 26-foot boat, worth $125,000, in the backyard of his Repentigny home. The boat, *Fountain Fever,* had been one of two vessels pilfered from the Can-Am company on August 21.

He spent the night in prison and appeared the next day before judge Michel Hétu at the Joliette courthouse. He was charged with stealing and fencing the boat. He would be found guilty and fined $15,000.

Cotroni's name headlines again in 1992 when police connected him to a fire that burned down the Oscar Nightclub in Saint-Leonard. The establishment had been the target of several incidents since Paolo's girlfriend, Michele Veilleux, had been fired. Cotroni was never charged with any crime connected to the fire.

On August 23, 1998, after returning home from dinner at his younger brother Jimmy's house, Cotroni was ambushed by two men as he got out of his car. He was shot six times, including twice in the head. A concerned neighbor pursued the attackers, but they got into a car where an accomplice waited and sped away.

He was taken to the Sacré-Coeur Hospital in Cartierville, where he was placed on life support. The entire Cotroni family was present except Paolo's father Frank and his brother Francesco Jr., who were both behind bars for cocaine trafficking. On August 25, two days after the attack, the family made the painful decision to remove Paolo from life support. The official time of death was 1:40 P.M.

On the morning of Paolo's funeral, August 28, 1998, a masked assassin strolled into a Montreal espresso bar and fired a round from a 12-gauge shotgun into the face of 69-year-old Vincenzo Melia. The victim was taken to a hospital, and he survived.

Reference

Gary Francoeur. "Paolo 'Paul' Cotroni." WiseguyWally. Available online. URL: http://www.geocities.com/wiseguywally/PaoloCotroni.html. Downloaded on July 19, 2004.

—G.F.

COTRONI, Vincenzo

Vincenzo "the Egg" Cotroni was born in 1911 in Calabria, Italy, and in 1924, at age 14, immigrated with his family to Montreal. The family lived in a small shabby apartment near the corner of Ontario and Saint-Timothée Streets. Rather than attend school, he worked briefly as a carpenter and then as a professional wrestler under the name Vic Vincent.

But Cotroni found his true calling as a criminal—a path his brothers Giuseppe and Frank would also follow—and by the age of 20 had accumulated a lengthy record of minor offenses. The charges included theft, possession of counterfeit money, illegal sale of alcohol, assault, and battery.

The Egg, as he was sometimes called, was also charged with the rape of Maria Bresciano, but the charges were dropped, and the alleged victim became Cotroni's wife. She would stay loyally by his side until her death.

While he was already an extremely successful and politically connected individual in Montreal's underworld, Cotroni's biggest opportunity came when Carmine Galante, an influential member of the New York–based Bonanno crime family, arrived in Montreal in 1953. The Brooklyn gangster, nicknamed "Lilo," planned to make Montreal a pivotal location in the importation of narcotics from overseas for distribution in New York City and across America. Galante also demanded a "street tax" from gambling houses, nightclubs, after-hours lounges, prostitutes, and illegal abortionists.

Cotroni became a close associate to the feared Bonanno mobster and would eventually become godfather to one of Galante's children. When Salvatore "Little Sal" Giglio, the Bonanno gangster who was responsible for the Bonanno family's interests in Canada, was deported after police found 240 illegal Cuban cigars and 880 American cigarettes on him that had not been declared, Cotroni was bestowed the important position.

In the 1960s, the Montreal godfather, who never learned to read or write, was riding high and enjoying life. He owned a limousine, a duplex in Rosemont, and a brand-new home in Lavaltrie. The house featured marvelous marble floors, an enormous conference room, a walk-in industrial-size refrigerator, a built-in movie screen, six bathrooms, and expensive crystal chandeliers. Cotroni also donated large sums of money to Montreal churches and charities and was the father of two children; a daughter with his wife Maria and a son with his French-Canadian mistress.

Cotroni liked to keep a low profile and did not appreciate it when *Maclean's,* a popular Canadian magazine, referred to him as the "godfather" of Montreal in one of their articles. Cotroni, with lawyer Jean-Paul Sainte-Marie, sued the magazine for $1.25 million in damages. The judge concluded that Cotroni's reputation was "tainted" and only awarded him an insulting $2—one dollar for the English version of *Maclean's* and another for the French version. When the 1970s rolled around, Cotroni had crept even further into the shadows and had transferred the day-to-day activities of the family to his apprentice, the hot-headed Paolo Violi. Cotroni's role became more that of an advisor to the younger Calabrian.

In 1974, Cotroni was subpoenaed to stand before the Quebec Police Commission's inquiry into organized crime. He was sent to jail for one year on a contempt charge because his testimony, the Commission concluded, was "deliberately incomprehensible; rambling, vague, and nebulous." His lawyer eventually won a reversal but only after Cotroni had spent several months behind bars.

On April 30, 1974, Cotroni and Violi were overheard on a police wiretap threatening Hamilton mob boss Johnny "Pops" Papalia. Papalia had used the two Montreal mobsters' names in a $300,000 extortion plot without notifying or cutting them in on the score. The two men summoned him to a meeting and demanded $150,000. Papalia argued that he only received $40,000, and Cotroni responded "Let's hope because, eh, we'll kill you." The three men were sentenced to six years in prison, but Cotroni and Violi had their convictions overturned on appeal.

On January 22, 1978, Paolo Violi, Cotroni's heir to the throne, was gunned down by the family's Sicilian faction, led by Nicolo Rizzuto. Cotroni remained sheltered in his Lavaltrie home for weeks after the slaying. The godfather had most likely at least approved the hit on Violi.

Vincenzo Cotroni, the old-fashioned Mafia don who built a powerful criminal organization and accumulated a fortune, died of cancer on September 19, 1984. He was 74. His funeral featured floral arrangements on 23 cars and a 17-piece brass band. It rained as his coffin was lowered into the ground, and many mourned the passing of the city's most legendary "man of respect."

Reference

Gary Francoeur. "Vic 'The Egg' Cotroni." WiseguyWally. Available online. URL: http://www.geocities.com/wiseguywally/VicCotroni.html. Downloaded on July 19, 2004.

—G.F.

COULOMBE, Gerry (a.k.a. the Cat)

Gerry "the Cat" Coulombe was born in 1955 and began his criminal career as a member of the Missles motorcycle gang, based in the Saguenay-Lac-Saint-Jean area, just north of Quebec City. The gang was primarily active in drug trafficking and prostitution and known for its extremely vicious actions. The Missles waged war against other local biker gangs—El Conquatcheros, the Lacmas, and the Hondix—and several members would eventually go on to bigger and better things. Luc "Sam" Michaud, Jean-Yves "Boule" Tremblay, Jocelyn "Le Prof" Girard, and Marcel "Polpon" Blackburn would all become Hells Angels.

By the early 1980s Coulombe moved to Montreal and joined the SS biker gang, where he became associated with Maurice "Mom" Boucher and Salvatore Cazzetta. With him, The Cat brought along his extensive criminal record, which included convictions for drug trafficking, contempt of court, violation of parole, theft of car batteries, and assault.

The SS disbanded in 1984 and Coulombe, like several Missles before him, became associated with the Hells Angels Montreal chapter. By 1985 he was a prospect with the club. On March 23, 1985, Coulombe said he picked up firearms from Hells Angels Robert "Tiny" Richard, Denis "Pas Fiable" Houle, and Jacques "La Pelle" Pelletier and delivered them to the Lennoxville clubhouse. The next morning, he stood guard outside the building as five members of the North chapter were slaughtered within.

Days after the murders, Coulombe and Normand "Biff" Hamel, on Réjean "Zig-Zag" Lessard's orders, rented two large trucks and emptied the North Chapter's Laval clubhouse and the dead Angels' apartments.

On June 26, 1985, Coulombe was told that he would receive his colors and be initiated into the club the next day. He called Hells Angels Gaétan "Gaet" Proulx and Jean-Paul "Donat" Ramsay, both of whom he was close to, but neither knew anything about it. Coulombe began to worry that he might be next on the hit list.

The very next day, the Sûreté du Québec SWAT team, armed with submachine guns, crashed into the prospect's room as he slept. He was taken into custody, and when police questioned him, Coulombe broke down and became an informant against the Hells Angels.

With the information provided by Coulombe, and later Yves "Apache" Trudeau and Gilles "Le Nez" Lachance, 17 Hells Angels were charged with first-degree murder on October 2, 1985. Gerry Coulombe testified against his former comrades and is living under a new identity somewhere in Canada.

See also: HELLS ANGELS.

Reference

Gary Francoeur. "Gerry 'Le Chat' Coulombe." Wiseguy-Wally. Available online. URL: http://www.geocities.com/wiseguywally/GerryCoulombe.html. Downloaded on July 19, 2004.

—G.F.

CRACK: The Crack Epidemic of the 1980s

In the early 1980s the majority of cocaine being shipped to the United States was coming through the Bahamas. Soon there was a huge glut of cocaine powder in these islands, which caused the price to drop by as much as 80 percent. Faced with dropping prices for their illegal product, drug dealers made a shrewd marketing decision to convert the powder to "crack," a smokeable form of cocaine. It was cheap, simple to produce, ready to use, and highly profitable for dealers to develop. As early as 1981, reports of crack appeared in Los Angeles, San Diego, Houston, and the Caribbean.

At this time, powder cocaine was available on the street at an average of 55 percent purity for $100 per gram, and crack was sold at average purity levels of more than 80 percent for the same price. In some major cities, such as New York, Detroit, and Philadelphia, one dosage unit of crack could be obtained for as little as $2.50. Never before had any form of cocaine been available at such low prices and at such high purity. More important, from a marketing standpoint, was that it produced an instant high and that addicted its users in a very short time. Eventually, Caribbean immigrants taught young people in

Miami how to produce crack, and they in turn went into business in the United States.

With the influx of traffickers and cocaine, South Florida had become a principal area for the "conversion laboratories," used to convert cocaine base into cocaine hydrochloride, the form in which cocaine is sold. The majority of these labs were found in South Florida, but they also appeared in other parts of the country, indicating the expansion of Colombian trafficking.

For example, in 1985, four conversion laboratories were seized in New York State, four in California, two in Virginia, and one each in North Carolina and Arizona. One year later, 23 more conversion labs were seized in the United States.

The first crack house had been discovered in Miami in 1982. However, this form of cocaine was not fully appreciated as a major threat because it was primarily being consumed by middle-class users who were not associated with cocaine addicts. In fact, crack was initially considered a purely Miami phenomenon until it became a serious problem in New York City, where it first appeared in December 1983. In the New York City area, it was estimated that more than three-fourths of the early crack consumers were white professionals or middle-class youngsters from Long Island, suburban New Jersey, or largely upper-class Westchester County. However, partly because crack sold for as little as $5 a rock, it ultimately spread to less-affluent neighborhoods.

The crack epidemic dramatically increased the numbers of Americans addicted to cocaine. In 1985, the number of people who admitted using cocaine on a routine basis increased from 4.2 million to 5.8 million, according to the Department of Health and Human Service's National Household Survey. Likewise, cocaine-related hospital emergencies continued to increase nationwide during 1985 and 1986. According to DAWN (Drug Abuse Warning Network) statistics, in 1985, cocaine-related hospital emergencies rose by 12 percent from 23,500 to 26,300; in 1986, they increased 110 percent from 26,300 to 55,200. Between 1984 and 1987, cocaine incidents increased fourfold.

By this time, the Medellín cartel was at the height of its power and controlled cocaine trafficking from the conversion and packaging process in Colombia, to the transportation of cocaine to the United States, as well as to the first level of wholesale distribution in U.S. communities. While the Medellín cartel had established a foothold in U.S. communities, its rival, the Cali Mafia, began to dominate markets in the northeastern United States. The Cali Mafia was less visible, less violent, and more businesslike than the Medellín cartel. Operating through a system of cells, where members were insulated from one another, the Cali Mafia steadily began to establish far-reaching networks that eventually ensured that they would dominate the cocaine trade well into the 1990s.

By early 1986 crack had a stranglehold on the ghettos of New York City and was dominated by traffickers and dealers from the Dominican Republic. Crack distribution and abuse exploded in 1986 and by year-end was available in 28 states and the District of Colombia. According to the 1985–86 National Narcotics Intelligence Consumers Committee Report, crack was available in Atlanta, Boston, Detroit, Kansas City, Miami, New York City, Newark, San Francisco, Seattle, St. Louis, Dallas, Denver, Minneapolis, and Phoenix.

Approximately 5,000 pounds of cocaine, valued at $250 million, were seized in Chicago in July 1987. The cocaine was smuggled in 130 banana boxes. Pictured in front of the seized cocaine are, left to right, Chicago ASAC John T. Peoples; Police Superintendent Fred Rice; Attorney General Edwin Meese III; Chicago SAC Philip V. Fisher, and ASAC Garfield Hammonds, Jr.

By 1987 crack was reported to be available in the District of Colombia and all but four U.S. states. Crack was abundantly available in at least 19 cities in 13 states: Texas (Dallas), Oklahoma (Tulsa, Oklahoma City), Michigan (Detroit), California (Los Angeles, Riverside, Santa Barbara), Florida (Miami, Ft. Lauderdale, Tampa), New York (New York City), Oregon (Portland), Washington (Seattle), Missouri (Kansas City), Minnesota (Minneapolis), Colorado (Denver), Nevada (Las Vegas), and Maryland (Hagerstown, Salisbury). By 1988, crack had replaced heroin as the greatest problem in Detroit, and it was available in Los Angeles in multikilogram quantities.

Meanwhile, wholesale and retail prices for cocaine had declined, while purity levels for kilogram amounts of the drug had remained at 90 percent or higher. Street-level gram purity rose from 25 percent in 1981 to 55 percent in 1987 to 70 percent in 1988. By the late 1980s, more than 10,000 gang members were dealing drugs in some 50 cities from Baltimore to Seattle. The crack trade had created a violent subworld, and crack-related murders in many large cities were skyrocketing. For example, a 1988 study by the Bureau of Justice Statistics found that in New York City, crack use was tied to 32 percent of all homicides and 60 percent of drug-related homicides. On a daily basis, the evening news reported the violence of drive-by shootings and crack users trying to obtain money for their next hit. Smokeable crack appealed to a new group of users, especially women, because it did not have the stigma associated with needles or heroin, and because it was smoked, many mistakenly equated crack with marijuana. As a result, a generation of addicted children were born to—and frequently abandoned by—crack-using mothers. By the late 1980s about one out of every 10 newborns in the United States (375,000 per year) had been exposed in the womb to one or more illicit drug.

In October 1986 Attorney General Edwin Meese explained the U.S. anticrack strategy: "The most effective long-term way to reduce crack trafficking is to reduce the amount of cocaine entering this country. The federal government's main priorities against cocaine are reducing production in source countries, interdicting shipments entering the United States, and disrupting major trafficking rings." Thus, the Drug Enforcement Agency (DEA) attacked the major trafficking organizations, primarily the Medellín and Cali cartels, which were producing cocaine and smuggling it into the United States. To help accomplish this, the Anti-Drug Abuse Act of 1986 allocated $8 million for domestic cocaine enforcement. A portion of this budget was used to establish DEA Crack Teams. Each of these teams consisted of two DEA special agents who assisted state and local law-enforcement agencies in the investigation of large-scale violators and interstate trafficking networks.

The agents either worked with existing DEA-funded state and local task forces or with local law-enforcement agencies that had established their own special crack groups. In addition, DEA Crack Teams were also deployed to states experiencing extensive crack problems. Examples included Arizona, which was vulnerable to a rapid influx of crack dealers from Los Angeles street groups, and Louisiana, where traffickers from Haiti were dealing to migrant workers in rural areas. Another significant source of support for the Crack Teams was the Comprehensive Crime Control Act of 1984 that provided for asset-forfeiture sharing with state and local law-enforcement agencies.

The Anti-Drug Abuse Act of 1986 later provided $44 million to the Bureau of Justice Assistance (BJA)

grant program for urban law-enforcement agencies, and $1.5 million was made available for the establishment of five Crack Task Forces, which were established in Los Angeles, Houston, Minneapolis, Denver, and Detroit. The DEA assisted these task forces through mutual sharing of information on crack-trafficking organizations and by attending periodic meetings of the task forces. By the late 1980s the DEA's domestic crack-cocaine-enforcement activities were conducted through three multiagency initiatives: DEA Crack Teams, Department of Justice's BJA Crack Task Forces, and State and Local Task Forces. Additionally, the DEA supported 40 state and local task forces and 11 shared-funding task forces that investigated midlevel and street narcotics violators. Cocaine investigations dominated DEA enforcement activities, as cocaine arrests accounted for nearly 65 percent of the DEA's total arrests in 1988. Simultaneously, DEA seizures substantially increased. The DEA had seized only 200 kilograms of cocaine in 1977; but the number of seizures jumped to 60,000 kilograms by 1988.

See also: COCAINE AND CRACK.

Reference

U.S. Drug Enforcement Administration, U.S. Department of Justice. "A Tradition of Excellence, DEA History 1985–1990." Available online. URL: http://www.dea. gov/pubs/history/index. html. Downloaded on July 28, 2004.

CRIPS *See* BLOODS AND CRIPS.

CULIACÁN

What Cali and Medellín are to Colombia's narcotics traffickers, called "narcotraffickers," Sinaloa is to the drug lords of Mexico, and Culiacán is its largest city. Nestled between the Pacific Ocean and the Sierra Madre in Mexico's northwest, this drug-rich Mexican state is just a two-day drive from the U.S. border. Sinaloa, says former Mexican Federal Police Commander Guillermo González Calderoni, "is the cradle of the biggest traffickers Mexico has ever known."

For decades Sinaloa has been Mexico's breadbasket. Its fertile fields have produced huge crops of soybeans and sesame seeds—and vast amounts of marijuana and heroin destined for U.S. markets. Sinaloa's poor *campesinos* have made it big, growing and selling these narcotics and networking their way from the foothills of the Sierra Madre to become major players in Mexico's drug cartels:

Ernesto "Don Neto" Fonseca, Miguel Angel Félix Gallardo, Rafael Caro-Quintero, Guero Palma, Amado Carrillo Fuentes, Ismael "El Mayo" Zambada, Joaquín "El Chapo" Guzmán, Manuel Salcido Uzeta a.k.a. El Cochiloco, and the Arellano Félix brothers.

They are Mexico's most infamous narcotraffickers, and they all have made Culiacán, Sinaloa's state capital, their hometown.

These drug lords live in luxury homes in the hills of Culiacán, a city of 600,000 that seems prosperous and modern compared to the rural villages that dominate Sinaloa. The drug business is so ingrained in Culiacán that its souvenir shops sell items with emblems commemorating the outlaw culture: marijuana-leaf belts, machine-gun buckles, embroideries of airplanes like those used for smuggling. There is even a patron saint of drug smuggling—the legendary *bandito* Jesús Malverde, whose image is seen dangling from the chain necklaces of many young Culiacán men.

Malverde's chapel in downtown Culiacán is a glass brick building just across the street from the government palace. On the day that a production crew from PBS's *Frontline* visited, a string-and-horn band played Mexican ballad songs—*corridos*—glorifying Mexican traffickers and the miracles of their patron saint, Jesús Malverde. It was unclear who hired the band until a late-model gold Ford pick-up pulled up and three men emerged, one wearing shiny snakeskin cowboy boots and carrying a giant wreath of flowers. He placed it inside the chapel at the foot of Malverde's image. Onlookers and local journalists told *Frontline* that this was a prosperous narcotrafficker giving thanks for a good harvest and a successful run north.

His tribute joined dozens of others; the chapel walls are crowded with plaques bearing the names of known trafficking families or pictures of men and their trucks, all paying tribute for "safe passage from Sinaloa to Sacramento" and other journeys north.

According to legend, Jesús Malverde was a thief who robbed the rich to give to the poor. He was hanged in 1909 by Sinaloa's governor, but the legend of this bandit's defiance and style of justice was passed along through *corridos* which helped turn him into a people's saint. A wedding party, for example, pulled up outside the chapel. The bride in her white dress entered the inner sanctuary to kneel before the glossy plaster bust of Malverde. Soon after, a short, graying matron purchased a necklace containing his image, whispering quietly in prayer.

According to the Drug Enforcement Administration (DEA), Malverde's believers, who usually come and go in pickup trucks, have carried his image as far as Florida, Texas, and California, and although belief in Malverde is a mixture of Catholicism and animism, the local diocese says the Malverde chapel is an embarrassment. "Nobody has become a saint robbing and killing; he was a *bandito*," laments Father Antonio Ramirez.

Many trace Sinaloa's first narcotics crop—opium—to the numerous Chinese settlers who arrived in the last half of the 19th century. "It was a good agricultural place for it, and generation after generation the people just did it; they perfected it," explains Edward Heath, former country attaché for the DEA in Mexico. But large-scale production of opium did not start until the 1940s and World War II. Japan gained control of the Asian opium supply, and the U.S. military needed morphine for its soldiers. So the United States turned to Mexico for help. "We were concerned that our supply of opium or morphine would be cut off because the world was at war. So we needed a supply close by. But that was one of those black box things. Who knows when it happened, who did it, and why," says Edward Heath. During this period of a government-tolerated opium trade, many Sinaloans made their fortune. "Everybody was growing it; it was institutional. Some government officials bought the harvest from the farmers to export themselves. There were even soldiers up in the hills caring for the plants," explains Dr. Ley Dominguez, a 77-year-old lifelong resident of Mocorito, one of Sinaloa's most notorious opium regions. After Japan's defeat, however, the United States no longer needed Sinaloa's inferior strain of opium. But many farmers continued to produce opium and heroin; operations became more clandestine, and a smuggling network was set up.

In the mid-1980s Sinaloa's marijuana and heroin smugglers turned to a new product: cocaine. Colombia's drug traffickers were finding it increasingly difficult to bring cocaine into the United States through south Florida, so they began to look for alternate routes and found willing partners in Mexico's smugglers.

The relationship lasted a few years until the Mexicans tired of just smuggling cocaine for a fee and began to demand payment in cocaine. The Mexicans soon set up their own distribution networks in the United States and greatly increased their profits and power. "From that moment on, the power of corruption definitely increased," said Guillermo González Calderoni. "The organizations became much richer, much more powerful, with much more control. Now it wasn't one million or two million, it was 15, 20, 30, 40 million dollars that they could make off a single payment."

So the gangsters from Culiacán became world-famous kingpins of complex criminal enterprises, many resembling multinational corporations in structure.

"They're not the common criminal that you're going to see with a golden tooth, black shirt and a white tie with a .45, just standing in a corner. They're not like that anymore. They have another type of thinking. They work with computers, with the best technicians in every field. They have the best chemists in the world. The best lawyers. The best architects. They have the best of the best," said Juan Ponce Edmondson of Interpol.

Since the 1940s, competition in Sinaloa for the huge, easy profits of the drug business has been violent and pervasive. A neighborhood within Culiacán was called at an early stage "a new Chicago with gangsters in huarache sandals" because of frequent gun battles. In the 1970s, the violence forced the Mexican military to launch Operation Condor, which flooded streets and countryside with soldiers. Face-offs between traffickers and the military were brutal, and eventually gang leaders relocated to other areas of Mexico—Guadalajara, Mexicali, or Tijuana—where they were unknown and safe. But the tradition continues.

Today, local newspapers cover an average of two drug-related murders a day. Young men drive Sinaloa's highways and streets in new trucks and sport-utility vehicles. They are seen at honky-tonk bars wearing snakeskin boots, cowboy hats, gaudy silk shirts with jeans and gold necklaces, sporting AK-47s or marijuana-leaf medallions. Some are very young. But a 15- or 16-year-old boy in Sinaloa "is already a bully, a gunman, a man," says former police commander Guillermo González Calderoni. "They [the traffickers] were made there. And that is where they are being made every day."

Reference

Jake Bergman. "Culiacán: The Place Mexico's Drug Kingpins Call Home." *Frontline*. Available online. URL: http://www.pbs.org/wgbh/pages/frontline/show/drugs/business/place.html. Posted on October 9, 2000.
Copyright PBS *Frontline* 1998. Reprinted by permission.

CUTOLO, Rosetta (a.k.a. Ice Eyes)

With the crackdown by the Italian government on organized crime that put countless of members and bosses behind bars, and with the bloody wars that decimated the clans and families, the role of women in the mob began to change. With most qualified men in prison, dead, or too young, women slowly placed themselves in the seats of power of the Camorra. One of the first women to do so was Rosetta "Ice Eyes" Cutolo. Cutolo followed in the footsteps of her brother Raffaele, who was imprisoned. Rosetta became known for her ruthlessness and great leadership qualities. Under her leadership income from extortion and the drug trade increased to record heights. When she eventually was arrested she was convicted only for associating or having contact with the Mafia. She was acquitted nine times of murder.

Reference

David Amoruso. "Rosetta Cutolo." Gangsters Incorporated. Available online. URL: http://gangstersinc.tripod.com/cutolo.html. Downloaded on July 19, 2004.

—D.A.

DAI Huen Jai   *See* BIG CIRCLE BOYS.

D'ARCO, Alphonse (a.k.a. Little Al)

Alphonse "Little Al" D'Arco was born July 28, 1932, in Brooklyn, New York. As early as D'Arco could remember, he congregated with people who were either associates, members, or even bosses of the Mafia. As he grew up in Brooklyn he made visits to bosses of all the five families in New York. Pretty soon Little Al knew that this was the life for him: He too wanted to become a wiseguy, a made guy; he too wanted to belong to a family.

To become a member D'Arco first had to become an associate of one of the five New York families, and so he did; he became an associate of the Lucchese crime family. As an associate D'Arco stood at the bottom of the food chain and could only do his best and hope that one day he would become a made guy. During his years as an associate D'Arco had spent some time in prison in the 1960s. It wasn't until 1982, at the age of 50, that Alphonse D'Arco became a made guy in the Lucchese crime family under boss Anthony "Tony Ducks" Corallo. He was assigned to the crew of capo Paul Vario (made famous worldwide by the movie *Goodfellas,* in which Vario was played by Paul Sorvino).

After finally becoming a made guy, D'Arco did not have much time to enjoy it; in 1983 he was arrested for dealing heroin and was sent to prison until 1986.

When he was released, things started to move fast for Little Al. In 1988 D'Arco was appointed capo of Paul Vario's crew (after Vario died) by Vic Amuso, who had succeeded Anthony Corallo as acting boss after the former had been imprisoned. D'Arco had waited years to become a made member, and now he was one. In 1990 D'Arco's boss Vic Amuso and his underboss Anthony "Gaspipe" Casso fled following a federal indictment. In 1991 Amuso appointed D'Arco acting boss of the Lucchese crime family to run day-to-day operations of the crime organization while they were gone. Now D'Arco was at his highest level: He controlled one of the five families. In his 30 years of involvement with the Lucchese crime family, D'Arco had learned all there was to know on how to run the business. The Lucchese family made money through a variety of illegal activities including gambling, loan-sharking, and dealing in stolen property. Now D'Arco oversaw all of that and also had to keep the real powers who were on the lam happy and content somehow. This proved more difficult than anything.

Amuso and Casso became increasingly paranoid. They ordered mobster after mobster whacked because they thought they had either flipped or would flip. Casso was extremely difficult to manage, as D'Arco recalled, since Casso kept asking about money matters. As a result of Casso's badgering, D'Arco started to keep records of money coming in and would send them to Casso. He would also keep some copies himself. In 1991 D'Arco received word from Amuso that he should whack Lucchese capo Pete Chiodo. Chiodo had fallen out of favor with Amuso when he pleaded guilty in the same case for which Amuso was now on the lam. Amuso feared that Chiodo would flip and so told D'Arco to take care of it. D'Arco tried. He even had his son on the hit team, but the venture failed. Chiodo survived and immediately called for the FBI. He had some stories to tell. When Amuso was finally arrested, D'Arco thought he might get some easy time; he was wrong. While in prison Amuso started to think about D'Arco and his time as acting boss and decided that he was not happy with him. Amuso decided that D'Arco was to rule the streets as part of a four-man ruling commission made up of Steven Crea, Frank Lastorino, and Sal Avellino. D'Arco felt uneasy with these new changes. When at meetings he saw how Amuso was trying to avoid him, D'Arco became unsure of his future in the Mafia, but D'Arco decided to keep going with it. It was the life he had chosen.

On September 18, 1991, however when he attended a meeting at the Kimberley Hotel in New York, he was sure that it was not the stress. The meeting D'Arco attended went on into the early hours of the morning. D'Arco had no worries until Michael DeSantis arrived. He noticed that DeSantis was wearing what looked like a bulletproof vest underneath his shirt, and he also saw a bulge on his hip that looked exactly like a gun. At this point D'Arco excused himself and ran. At home D'Arco packed his bags and drove his wife and his children to a hideout on Long Island. On September 21, he went to the FBI and decided to become a cooperating witness.

In his mob career D'Arco had been part of or committed 10 murders and also admitted to drug dealing and labor racketeering. At one trial D'Arco was asked by the prosecuting counsel if it was worth it, D'Arco answered: "No. I'm sixty-five years old. What has it gotten me? Nothing, absolutely nothing. Yes, I have my wife and I have my son. But I was the one who got my son into the Mafia. And what did I accomplish by doing that? My son is a drug dealer! No, I've got nothing to show for it. What a waste of my life."

See also: CASTELLANO, PAUL; GAMBINO, CARLO; GOTTI, JOHN; GRAVANO, SALVATORE.

Reference
David Amoruso. "Alphonse D'Arco." Gangsters Incorporated. Available online. URL: http://gangstersinc.tripod.com/Darco.html. Downloaded on July 19, 2004.

—D.A.

DASTI, Frank

Frank Dasti was born in 1914 and would become one of the most loyal followers of the Cotroni brothers in Montreal. He rose through the ranks alongside such men as Vincenzo Soccio, Diodato Mastracchio, and Jimmy Orlando and became one of Montreal's most respected underworld figures. Along with fellow mobsters Romeo Bucci, Peter Adamo, and William Obront, Dasti owned shares in the Béret Bleu Club. He also ran the Victoria Sporting Club, the organization's biggest gambling joint and, in 1955, Dasti was listed by the U.S. Bureau of Narcotics as being a close collaborator of Giuseppe "Pep" Cotroni and Lucien Rivard. Police tracked Dasti to the Park Sheraton Hotel in New York City on May 9, 1969, where he was seen meeting with Guido "The Bull" Penosi, a reputed drug trafficker with links to the Gambino crime family. He returned to the Big Apple three months later, on August 13, where he met with Paolo Gambino, a brother of mob boss Carlo Gambino. The next day, Dasti met with mobsters Guido Penosi and Steve Panepinto.

Dasti's movements were closely tracked by police, and in 1970 they heard him discussing drug deals on wiretapped telephones. They learned that Dasti, along with Angelo Lanzo and an unidentified member of the organization, were about to complete a transaction for 12 kilograms of heroin with New York wiseguys. The deal would have brought them $144,000 but it kept being delayed because of constant police pressure. At about this time Dasti was overheard berating associate Joseph Horvath in a telephone conversation after Horvath had exaggerated the weight of heroin he had sold to New York mobsters. "If a man weighs 150 pounds," Dasti explained, "you shouldn't say he weighs 180 pounds." Horvath knew better than to respond, and he accepted the reproach. Dasti was back in New York on September 19, 1971. Police noticed his presence at the funeral of mobster James "Jimmy Doyle" Pulmeri. Pulmeri, part of the Lucchese crime family, had been murdered three days earlier. Police arrested Lucien "the Cat" Madere, Dasti's drug courier, and American wiseguy Paul Oddo as the two were making a narcotics transaction at the Park Sheraton Hotel in New York. Ten kilograms of heroin were discovered inside Madere's car. Medere was sentenced to six years in prison, and Oddo received 10 years. Dasti avoided arrest.

Life was good for Dasti, and the money kept rolling in. He opened up the Pizzeria Tower restaurant on Décarie Boulevard, which quickly became a popular gathering place for members of the Mafia. It also became the target of intense police surveillance. Dasti was arrested in the lobby of the Park Lane Hotel in New York City on December 19, 1972, and was charged with trafficking in narcotics. He was released on bail on June 1, 1973, after Judge James A. Coolahan agreed to reduce his bail from $250,000 to $100,000. His wife and his nephew, René Di Fruscia, put up the money; since his arrest the two had worked with loyal associate Joe Horvath to raise the required amount from Montreal's underworld figures. Anthony Del Vecchio testified against Dasti, and on October 11, 1974, Dasti was convicted on three counts and was sentenced to 20 years in prison; he was also fined $20,000. Things were not finished though. Just three weeks later, on November 8, Dasti was indicted with Frank Cotroni, Guido Orsini, Paul Oddo, Jorge Asaf y Bala, and Claudio Martinez on drug-trafficking charges. Sicilian drug trafficker Giuseppe "Pino" Catania testified against the group, and on March 24, 1974, Dasti was given 15 additional years. Dasti, who had loyally served the Cotroni brothers for 40 years, was paroled in the early 1980s. He died a few years later.

Reference

Gary Francoeur. "Frank Dasti." WiseguyWally. Available online. URL: http://www.geocities.com/wiseguywally/FrankDasti.html. Downloaded on July 19, 2004.

—G.F.

DAVID, Christian

An international French assassin and heroin smuggler, David was involved in the French Connection group that was smuggling opium from Turkey into Marseilles and smuggling out heroin. He claims to have been offered a contract by Corsican Mafia bigshot Antoine Guerini to assassinate President John F. Kennedy. David was also a sometime employee of the Central Intelligence Agency (CIA).

He was eventually convicted of smuggling opium through Latin America and extradited back to France for a murder of a French policeman that he committed in his youth during his Marseilles years.

References

Salvador Astucia. *Opium Lords: Israel, the Golden Triangle, and the Kennedy Assassination.* Gaithersburg, Md.: Dsharpwriter, 2002.

Salvador Astucia. "Opium Lords: Israel, the Golden Triangle, and the Kennedy Assassination." Available online. URL: http://www.jfkmontreal.com/toch.htm. Downloaded on July 19, 2004.

DAVILA-JIMENO, Raul   See BLACK TUNA GANG.

DEFRIES, C. Eugene

The case of C. Eugene DeFries, former president, and four other former officers of the Marine Engineers Beneficial Association, the largest maritime union in the United States, represents the first successful prosecution of an entire governing body of a union for racketeering, as well as the first prosecution of a nationwide election fraud scheme carried out by union officials.

Reference

Janet Reno. "1995 Annual Report of the Attorney General of the United States." U.S. Department of Justice. Available online. URL: http://www.usdoj.gov/ag/annualreports/ar95/toc.htm. Downloaded on July 29, 2004.

DEMEO, Roy

Legendary Gambino family hit man Roy DeMeo was once the most feared man in the mob. Federal authorities have estimated that he killed nearly 200 people. He was easily one of the most brutal killers the Mafia had ever seen. DeMeo was a top hit man for New York's Gambino family and was devoted to his work. His was inventive and efficient, owing to what might be called his "assembly-line" methods.

According to Carl Sifakis's *The Mafia Encyclopedia,* a former associate of DeMeo explained, "When the person would walk in, somebody would shoot him in the head with a silencer, somebody would wrap a towel around his head to stop the blood, and somebody would stab him in the heart to stop the blood from pumping.

"They would then drag him into the bathroom, put him in the shower, bleed him, pull him out, put him on a pool liner in the living room, take him apart, and package him." Indeed, DeMeo's victims never came out in one piece and were often hacked to small bits to facilitate the disposal process.

Once a butcher's apprentice in his youth, DeMeo demanded that things be done his way and taught his crew how to take a body apart bit by bit. He also showed them the finer point of putting the head into a trash compactor to further diminish the possibility of the victim being identified. For these purposes, DeMeo kept a special "clubhouse," a bar-turned-slaughter-house where the hits could be carried out to DeMeo's exact specifications. When no one was being murdered, DeMeo's crew liked to invite their girls over for dates, just as they would in any other clubhouse.

At first, DeMeo's efficiency and enthusiasm were thought to be assets to the Gambinos. He became one of Paul Castellano and Nino Gaggi's most trusted hit men and was given the most sensitive jobs. When Gaggi was tried on racketeering charges, DeMeo stepped in and assassinated three government witnesses. He also carried out personal killings for Castellano, including the murder of Castellano's son-in-law.

Most of DeMeo's victims were mobsters, including members of his own crew, but he would kill anyone who got in his way. If DeMeo even suspected someone of being an informer, that person disappeared for good.

Soon it became clear that DeMeo and his crew were running rampant, murdering for profit, for revenge, and even for plain old kicks. Federal authorities began to investigate the DeMeo crew by the early 1980s, and Castellano, knowing that the trail would lead from DeMeo to Gaggi to himself, tried to get DeMeo to tone down his operations. But no one could slow down Roy DeMeo. Instead, he became even more erratic. DeMeo was in it for pleasure by that point, and he liked to tell people about it.

Castellano called DeMeo in for a meeting, but DeMeo never showed. Shortly thereafter, a bug in Castellano's home revealed that he was making attempts to put a contract out on DeMeo, but he could find no takers. DeMeo was too widely feared; even John Gotti decided to pass on the contract.

Sifakis reports that Castellano finally said to Gaggi, "Take care of him, Nino." Gaggi was the only man DeMeo still trusted and the only man who could get close to him. Business was taken care of,

and on January 10, 1983, DeMeo's body was found in the trunk of his car.

References

Jerry Capeci and Gene Mustain. *Murder Machine.* New York: E.P. Dutton, 1992.

Carl Sifakis. *The Mafia Encyclopedia.* 2d ed. New York: Facts On File, 1999.

—D.A.

DEMERS, Marcel (a.k.a. Le Maire, The Mayor)

Marcel Demers, known as "Le Maire" (the Mayor), was born on March 10, 1957. He is a founding member of the Rock Machine's Quebec City chapter and the gang's former president.

As one of the club's most influential members, Demers became a prime target for the rival Hells Angels. On November 14, 1996, a masked man fired at least five bullets at Demers as he got out of his car outside a corner store in a Quebec City suburb. The attacker escaped in a car.

"The Mayor" was almost gunned down a second time on June 5, 1999. He was struck several times in the back and left arm as he drove his car down a street in the Quebec City suburb of Beauport. Despite his injuries, he managed to drive himself to Enfant Jesus Hospital and walk to the emergency department. Two Hells Angels associates were arrested for the attack.

On October 15, 2000, Demers and Rock Machine leader Fred Faucher were expelled from the Le Bristo Plus bar on Saint-Jean Street in Quebec City. The owner called the police because he did not want them in his establishment.

Two hundred twenty-five police officers were kept busy on December 6, 2000, as they tracked and arrested 16 Rock Machine members and associates on drug-trafficking charges. The ring, run by Demers and Quebec City chapter president Fred Faucher, distributed 2 kilograms of cocaine a month and generated almost $5 million in profits annually, police said.

Demers, pleaded guilty to 17 counts of drug trafficking and was sentenced to nine years in prison.

See also: BANDIDOS.

Reference

Gary Francoeur. "Marcel 'Le Maire' Demers." Wiseguy-Wally. Available online. URL: http://www.geocities.com/wiseguywally/MarcelDemers.html. Downloaded on July 19, 2004.

—G.F.

DEMIR Clan

In January 1993 police in Offenbach, Germany, dismantled a network headed by Abdulkudusi Demir. He confessed to having paid DM250,000 a year (approximately FF800,000) to a PKK (Partiya Karkaren Kurdistan, or Kurdistan Workers' Party) fundraiser to be able to sell drugs. In October 1994 the German weekly *Focus* exposed the Demir clan as one of the major heroin traffickers in Germany. According to that publication, the Demirs controlled a hotel chain in Istanbul, as well as garages and electronic appliance stores.

See also: BAYBASIN CLAN; KAYA CLAN; KITAY CLAN; KONUKLU-AY CLAN; KURDISH CRIMINAL CLANS AND THE PKK; SAKIK CLAN; SENAR CLAN.

Reference

Center for the Study of Contemporary Criminal Menace. "Criminal Kurdish Clans and the PKK." DRMCC. Available online. URL: http://www.drmcc.org/html/archives/ne/ne33/ne357.html. Downloaded on July 19, 2004.

DENARO, Matteo Messina (a.k.a. U Siccu)

Currently the second most powerful Sicilian don not in captivity, Matteo inherited the mantle previously occupied by his father, the late Francesco Messina. Matteo is a don who loves video games, beautiful women, designer suits with silk ties, and Rolex watches. He favors brand new Porsches and frequents the most popular nightspots. To his reserved table comes an endless stream of Cristal champagne.

Matteo has been forced to reduce his public profile as he is among the most wanted criminals in Italy. Legitimately, Matteo is the owner of a sand-and-gravel company, but his most lucrative profits are made as a member of the underworld.

Matteo began his criminal career well more than a decade ago under the direction of Bernardo Provenzano. Provenzano who referred to Matteo as "the playboy," used the young hood as a hit man and an enforcer. After the arrest of Toto Riina, Provenzano elevated the young criminal's status as one of his trusted advisors. "*U siccu*" (the thin one) is poised to take charge if he is not captured first.

See also: MAZARA DEL VALLO.

DESANTIS, Vincenzo (a.k.a. Jimmy-Rent-a-Gun)

Vincenzo DeSantis, also known as "Jimmy Rent-a-Gun," got his start in the 1960s, working for Montreal mob boss Paolo Violi and as a bartender at Violi's Reggio Bar.

When Violi wanted soldiers Tony Vanelli and Moreno Gallo to plead guilty to the killing of Angelo Facchino to avoid what he felt would be a lengthy and very public trial, he sent Rent-a-Gun DeSantis to pass the message. Both complied and pleaded guilty. Vanelli received four years, and Gallo was sentenced to life.

DeSantis was among the reputed mobsters that the Quebec Police Commission's inquiry into organized crime, Commission d'Enquête sur le Crime Organisé (CECO), called before them in the 1970s. Wearing a flashy purple velvet suit and green-and-black shoes, he refused to testify because he claimed that the commission "discriminates against the Italians and we French Canadians." Judge Jean Dutil did not buy it and sentenced DeSantis to one year in prison for contempt.

He was again in the news, this time with Paolo Cotroni, after the December 17, 1992 arson of the Oscar nightclub in Saint-Leonard. Cotroni's girlfriend had been fired and, on the night of the fire, DeSantis was reportedly seen in the club until closing time, around 3:45 or 4:00 A.M. Both DeSantis and Cotroni insisted that they had nothing to do with the incident. Neither was charged.

DeSantis has since avoided both law enforcement and the media and remains one of Cotroni's most trusted associates. He is among several underworld figures, including Raynald Desjardins, who had once claimed to be an employee of Expotronique, a Saint-Leonard company owned by Frank Cotroni's oldest son, Nicodemo.

Reference

Gary Francoeur. "Vincenzo 'Rent-A-Gun' DeSantis." WiseguyWally. Available online. URL: http://www.geocities.com/wiseguywally/VincenzoDeSantis.html. Downloaded on July 19, 2004.

—*G.F.*

DESJARDINS, André (a.k.a. Dédé)

André "Dédé" Desjardins was born in 1931 and grew up around the south-central part of Montreal. During the years he became one of the city's most successful loan sharks and, because of his involvement in Quebec unions, earned the label of the "King of Construction." He also developed close ties with some of Montreal's toughest thugs, including members of the Montreal Mafia and the Hells Angels.

He began his construction career when he was only 14 years old, working as an apprentice plumber, but that did not stop him from using other methods to make money. He was first arrested in 1949 and would be convicted of robbery on three other occasions.

From the Café Évangéline, Desjardins built up a considerable client for his loan-sharking business. He became so successful that he began to supply money to other criminals so that they could begin to lend out money on their own. Among his friends were Eugene Lafort, Gérald Fontaine, father of Hells Angel Paul "Fon Fon" Fontaine, and members of the Devils Disciples motorcycle gang.

After joining Local 144 of the United Association of Plumbers and Pipefitters in 1957, Desjardins quickly rose through the syndicate's ranks. In 1974, while he served as the union's president, he was accused of inciting violence when $30 million worth of damage was carried out during a fight between members of the Quebec Federation of Labourers and the Confederation of National Trade Unions at the construction site of the LG2 James Bay hydroelectric project.

The next year Desjardins appeared before the Cliche Commission, which was investigating violent crimes in the construction industry. He was accused of using extortion tactics to have vacation checks paid early for workers on strike. Desjardins handed in his resignation in 1976, after the commission confirmed his connections to organized crime. Even after this, according to authorities, he continued to exercise a certain amount of influence with the smaller Quebec unions.

At about this time, he opened several legitimate businesses, usually in other people's names, including two jewelry shops, a furniture store, a restaurant in Laval, and a 25-room motel in the Dominican Republic, where he spent much of his time.

Desjardins made headlines again in the early 1980s. He was arrested once on a charge of robbing car tires and, with union executive Raynald Bertrand, of conspiring to incite union members to refuse work. He was acquitted both times.

In July 1983 the United States government processed a request with Canadian authorities for Desjardins's extradition to Florida in connection with William Obront's $50-million-a-year drug ring that brought millions of phony quaaludes into the United States. The network was responsible for 70 percent of the quaalude market in the country, and Desjardins's name came up as a possible supplier. To the surprise of the public, Desjardins was never picked up by police.

Desjardins was gunned down on April 27, 2000, after eating breakfast at Shawn's restaurant on Metropolitan Boulevard in Saint-Leonard. He was walking toward his sport-utility vehicle when he was shot several times. A semiautomatic firearm equipped with a silencer was found near the body. Investigators had spotted him having lunch with Maurice "Mom" Boucher, chief of the Hells Angels Nomads chapter, the day before.

Reference

Gary Francoeur. "André 'Dédé Desjardins." Wiseguy-Wally. Available online. URL: http://www.geocities.com/wiseguywally/AndreDesjardins.html. Downloaded on July 19, 2004.

—G.F.

DESTEFANO, Sam (a.k.a. Mad Sam)

"Mad Sam" is not well known to the outside world, but one of his "students" is: Tony "the Ant" Spilotro. DeStefano taught Spilotro everything he knew about murder and torture, and he knew a lot about that subject. DeStefano grew up in southern Illinois and moved to Chicago when he was a teenager. He officially began his criminal career in 1927 when at age 18 he was convicted of rape. Later he received convictions for assault with a deadly weapon, bank robbery, extortion, and possession of counterfeit stamps.

After a while DeStefano became involved with Sam "Momo" Giancana's West Side 42 Gang, a gang that was made up of an assortment of vicious thugs and bootleggers. By the 1960s DeStefano had moved up the ranks, going from petty hoodlum to a major force in Chicago's loan-sharking and drug-trafficking rackets. Along with his brother Mario Anthony, DeStefano succeeded in bringing to Chicago what has become known as "the juice loan": a loan-sharking operation in which violence is used to force payments from debtors.

Even though most of the 42 Gang became top mobsters in the Chicago operation, DeStefano never climbed the ranks. He was too unstable for any top position in the Chicago Mafia, but they still had use for him, especially notorious mob bosses Sam "Momo" Giancana and Paul "the Waiter" Ricca.

DeStefano became known as a stone-cold executioner and a peerless loan collector. He collected a variety of instruments of torture in his basement, but his favorite tool was the ice pick. DeStefano used ice picks to stab his victims in the throat, testicles, and torso, either to squeeze payments out of them or as foreplay to murder.

Mad Sam was one of the most deranged, sick, notorious, and feared hit men in the history of the Chicago Mafia. Sam DeStefano lived in a nice far-west-side suburb of Chicago with his wife and three children. He looked everything like the normal family man, but that was because people could not look in his basement. Sam DeStefano's basement was where he turned into Mad Sam and tortured and killed his victims. It was soundproof and had all the torture tools that a hit man could need. One of DeStefano's victims was Artie Adler, a local restaurant owner who had been late on juice payments. One week, Adler could not pay and was brought to Sam's basement. Sam went to work with the ice pick, and Adler had a heart attack. The body was dumped into a sewer near North Sayre and Harlem on the far west side, and there it stayed, in the frozen winter waters of the sewer, until the spring thaw. The Department of Sanitation received a call in the spring about a backed up sewer and that's when Adler's perfectly preserved corpse was discovered.

Not all of Sam's victims went out of the basement dead. Some like Peter Cappelletti were just humiliated and tortured. One time Cappelletti tried to run off with $25,000.00 he owed Sam. Cappelletti was caught and brought to Mario DeStefano's restaurant in Cicero. The poor guy was stripped naked and handcuffed to a boiling radiator, where he was beaten and tortured by Sam for three full days. On the night of the third day DeStefano phoned Cappelletti's family and invited them all to a luxurious dinner at the restaurant in the man's honor. That Saturday Cappelletti's whole family turned up at Mario's place and received a multicourse Italian dinner. The guest of honor was not there at the table, but DeStefano assured the family that he would be joining them soon. Once the meal was finished, the naked and severely burned man was brought in front of his family and thrown at the feet of his mother. According to different stories, DeStefano forced Cappelletti's family to urinate on him or did it himself in front of them. He let Cappelletti live, after Cappel-letti promised to make things right, and made him an example to others who thought they could steal from him.

When Sam Giancana ordered the hit of Sam DeStefano's younger brother Michael, Sam carried out the hit with no second thoughts. When questioned about the 1955 murder, DeStefano refused to answer any questions and instead giggled uncontrollably. When investigators tried repeating their questions, DeStefano only laughed harder. Perhaps more strange was DeStefano's behavior after the execution. Michael DeStefano was a drug addict, a fact that seemed to hurt his remorseless brother to no end. After completing the murder with Mario Anthony DeStefano's assistance, Sam DeStefano took great pains to cleanse his brother's corpse to remove any traces of the drugs before abandoning the body in the trunk of a car.

Then there was the hit of Leo Foreman. Leo Foreman led a double life: He was a legitimate real estate agent on the one hand and a mob juice loan collector on the other. Foreman collected juice for DeStefano. One day in November 1963, DeStefano paid a visit to Foreman's real estate offices and started an argument. The quarrel ended with Foreman throwing DeStefano out. Foreman was later lured to the Cicero home of Sam's brother Mario DeStefano by Tony Spilotro and Chuckie Crimaldi. Foreman went because he was told that Sam wanted to kiss and make up for the ealier argument. Once in the house Leo Foreman was coaxed into the basement where he was grabbed and tied up by Spilotro, Mario DeStefano, and Crimaldi. The three then proceeded to beat Foreman to soften him up a bit before Sam DeStefano got there. Foreman was beaten on his knees with a hammer and also beaten about the head, ribs, and crotch. Sam applied his normal technique with his ice pick, stabbing Leo 20 times. They tortured Foreman so that it would hurt but not kill him. When Foreman had been sufficiently wounded, a pajama-clad DeStefano glided from a nearby bedroom, laughing at the wounded man. According to Crimaldi, who later turned government witness, DeStefano screamed and giggled as he admonished Foreman, saying, "I told you I'd get you. Greed got you killed!" Foreman pleaded for his life as DeStefano shot him repeatedly in the buttocks. DeStefano and his crew watched Foreman bleed and whimper for a while before torturing him to death with a butcher knife. Far from letting a death spoil their party, DeStefano and the boys then took turns excising chunks of flesh from Foreman's arms.

Eventually the madness of Mad Sam became too great, and he fell out of favor. When Sam DeStefano was called to testify in court, he would often demand to speak through a bullhorn. He often acted as his own attorney, and his courtroom antics included appearing in pajamas, arriving on a stretcher, and ranting longwindedly in an attempt to discredit investigators by accusing them of colluding with Joseph Stalin. In 1972, the FBI won Chuckie Crimaldi. Tony Spilotro and the DeStefano brothers, Mario and Sam, were indicted for the murder of Leo Foreman on the evidence given by Crimaldi. The three of them were incarcerated pending trial, which was set for May 1973. At the pretrial, Sam DeStefano made a circus of the proceedings, acting as his own attorney. Sam began to alienate the judge and the jury. Making the trial such a high-profile media event was an obvious mistake. It would be very hard to influence the judge and the jury with bribes or other forms of corruption if the trial was front-page news, so Mario and Spilotro devised a plan to keep Sam quiet for good.

Mario and Tony went to Sam telling him that they had located the safe house where Chuckie Crimaldi was being held by the authorities. Sam was ecstatic. What fun he would have exacting revenge on Crimaldi, the stool pigeon. Mario and Tony told Sam that the guards covering Crimaldi had been bribed to turn their backs that Saturday and that the three of them could whack Chuckie there and then. It was all set. Saturday came, and Sam was out in his garage at his home. Mario came up the driveway, followed closely by Tony Spilotro. With the three within a few feet of each other, Mario stepped aside and Spilotro pulled out a double-barreled shotgun that he had been hiding. Spilotro fired both barrels in quick succession: The first shot removed Mad Sam's arm, and the second hit him with full force in the chest. Sam was dead before he hit the ground. On April 14, 1973, "Mad Sam" was no longer, but his skills were passed on to Tony "The Ant" Spilotro (who was acquitted in the Foreman murder trial) who would use them whenever he needed to in a long and gruesome career.

See also: SPILOTRO, ANTHONY.

Reference

David Amoruso. "Sam DeStefano." Gangsters Incorporated. Available online. URL: http://gangstersinc.tripod.com/destefano.html. Downloaded on July 19, 2004.

—D.A.

DIABLOS

An outlaw motorcycle gang known for violence, the Diablos have chapters in many cities and have chapters from California to the northeastern United States. The Escondido Diablos, located in Escondido, California, were prohibited by court order from wearing their gang colors as they were in a war with another local Westside Gang. In little more than a year, both gangs were linked to five homicides, five attempted homicides, 91 cases of vandalism, 56 assaults, and eight robberies.

On September 24, 1998, member Raymond "Stoney" Stone confessed to murdering Michael D'Amato (a member of Wallingford, Connecticut's, James Gang) in 1992. He was sentenced to 20 years. He and seven other Diablos members were also charged with various other offenses.

Nationwide, the Diablos are known for drug trafficking and transportation, as well as theft, extortion, and other illegal activities.

DIFRONZO, John (a.k.a. No Nose)

A former crew chief and enforcer for the Outfit in Chicago, Illinois, John "No Nose" DiFronzo was known to dabble in extortion, loan-sharking, and other illegal activities. He is currently one of the leaders of the Outfit, along with Joseph "Joey the Clown" Lombardo.

See also: AIUPPA, JOSEPH; ANDRIACCHI, JOSEPH; CARLISI, SAMUEL; LAPIETRA, ANGELO; LOMBARDO, JOSEPH; MARCELLO, JAMES.

DI IORIO, Nicola (a.k.a. Cola)

Nicola "Cola" Di Iorio was born in Montreal in 1922 and came up through the ranks of the Montreal Mafia under the tutelage of Jimmy Soccio, Diodato Mastracchio, and Giuseppe Cocolicchio.

He rose through the ranks swiftly and was soon Mob boss Vic Cotroni's most brilliant lieutenant.

With his right-hand man Angelo Lanzo, Di Iorio supervised the organization's interests in nightclubs, bar, prostitution, gambling dens, and other rackets. He also had very good political contacts, including donating funds to Pierre Laporte's campaign.

Di Iorio, who owned the Victoria Sporting Club and the Café Métropole on St. Catherine Street, was Vic Cotroni's counselor. Cotroni respected his point-of-view and sought his opinion on the more serious family matters. Associates referred to them as "The Egg" and "The Little Egg" because of their similarities.

On May 29, 1972, Quebec Provincial Police detectives observed an important meeting at the Sirloin Barn restaurant attended by Vic Cotroni, Paolo Violi, Nicola Di Iorio, Angelo Lanzo, Willie Obront, and Irving Goldstein.

A surveillance team from *Connections,* a CBC documentary miniseries that exposed organized crime in Canada in the late 1970s, caught up to Di Iorio one day in a downtown Montreal parking lot. Coproducer Martyn Burke asked how business was, to which Di Iorio responded "Very quiet. It hasn't moved up, it hasn't moved down. It's very quiet." When Burke asked the mob chief what exactly his business was, Di Iorio cleverly retorted "Ah, see, if you don't know, then don't ask me."

Reference

Gary Francoeur. "Nicola 'Cola' Di Iorio." Wiseguy-Wally. Available online. URL: http://www.geocities.com/wiseguywally/NicolaDiIorio.html. Downloaded on July 19, 2004.

—G.F.

DI MAULO, Jos

Jos Di Maulo was born in the early 1940s, and rose to the top of Montreal's Mafia with unprecedented speed. He first came to police attention in September 1960 when he was arrested with Frank Cotroni and Michel "the Penguin" DiPaolo in possession of restricted firearms. He was also reportedly involved in the organization's battle with French-Canadian gangster Richard "Le Chat" Blass and his small band of followers. On March 12, 1971, at age 28, Di Maulo was charged in a triple homicide at the popular nightclub he owned, La Casa Loma. André Vaillancourt, the club's director of personnel, Jacques

Verrier, and Jean-Claude Rioux were killed, and police arrested Di Maulo, Julio Ciamarro, Joseph Tozzi, and Jean-Marc Morin in connection with the slayings.

In November 1971, after a 12-week trial, the three accused were found guilty of first-degree murder. The men appealed the jury's decision and, on February 1, 1973, Di Maulo, Ciamarro, and Tozzi were acquitted. In a separate trial, Jean-Marc Morin was also cleared of the murders. Jos Di Maulo was moving up in the organization. On November 11, 1973, he and his brother-in-law Raynald Desjardins accompanied Paolo Violi to New York City to participate in the election of Phil Rastelli as the new boss of the Bonanno crime family. According to informant Réal Simard, with Frank Cotroni behind bars in Lewisburg in the late seventies for drug trafficking, tensions rose between Di Maulo and Cotroni's brother-in-law Claude Faber concerning the control of Local 31 of the Hotel and Restaurant Workers' Union, which was situated in downtown Montreal. Simard said Cotroni eventually settled the quarrel from prison through numerous telephone calls with his principal lieutenants. The Montreal newspaper *La Presse* reported in 1993 that Di Maulo and Vito Rizzuto, the reputed head of the family, were trying to liquidate $3 billion worth of gold belonging to the late Filipino dictator Ferdinand Marcos, who died in 1989. Jos Di Maulo was arrested along with Valentino Morielli, Fernando De Francesco, Richardo Di Massimo, and Micheline Kemp-Di Maulo on August 17, 1995, on charges of offering a Royal Canadian Mounted Police (RCMP) officer $100,000 to destroy evidence against Jos's brother, Vincenzo, who faced a lengthy sentence stemming from a cocaine-smuggling and money-laundering operation.

But the RCMP was forced to release Di Maulo and Morielli for lack of evidence. The reputed mobster mocked law enforcement when he told reporters "Two (days) in jail, in a 10 foot by 40 foot cell, it wasn't pleasant but I love to follow the law." Police pulled over Di Maulo as he drove down Montreal's St. Lawrence Boulevard on September 22, 1998. The agents suspected the automobile was stolen (it was not), and as they questioned him, they said they smelled alcohol on his breath. But Di Maulo refused to take a breathalizer, so he was charged with driving while under the influence. Judge Pierre Gaston acquitted Di Maulo of the charge in April 2001.

Police say Di Maulo continues to be involved in Montreal's underworld and has acquired almost a dozen businesses in downtown Montreal and Saint-Leonard.

Reference

Gary Francoeur. "Jos Di Maulo." WiseguyWally. Available online. URL: http://www.geocities.com/ wiseguy-wally/JosDiMaulo.html. Downloaded on July 19, 2004.

—G.F.

DI MAULO, Vincenzo

Vincenzo "Jimmy" Di Maulo, Jos's older brother, was born in the late 1930s. He became very successful and, by the 1960s, owned a tavern, the Di Maulo '67, and a nightclub, Le Petit Baril.

Di Maulo played an important role in the Montreal Mafia's war against Richard "the Chat" Blass and his violent band. On May 4, 1968, Blass's henchmen Gilles Bienvenue and Albert Ouimet were shot to death by masked gunmen after exiting Jimmy's nightclub.

Three days later, on May 7, Roger Larue, a member of Blass's gang who had vowed revenge for the death of his comrades, had a heated argument with the Di Maulo brothers at the Le Petit Baril night club. Larue was killed hours later.

Next came Robert Allard, recognized as Blass's right-hand man. On May 6, 1969, Vincenzo Di Maulo, Joseph Armini, and Nicola Leo pumped a dozen bullets into Allard in front of a bar. Dozens of people witnessed the killing, and the three were arrested. Di Maulo, who had no criminal record, pleaded guilty to first degree murder in April 1970 and was sentenced to life imprisonment. Armini and Leo fought the charge but were also convicted.

Di Maulo was paroled in May 1981 and began to build a financial empire that the RCMP would evaluate at $15 million. He established 18 companies, including a condominium complex, as well as several properties. Through his businesses, police claimed, he laundered large sums of cash for many mobsters, including members of the Dubois clan and an influential member of the West End Gang. He also socialized with businessmen, lawyers, and politicians and made many generous contributions to charities, including an annual golf tournament where profits went to a Saint-Laurent hospital.

Di Maulo was among the 57 underworld figures arrested on August 30, 1994, the results of a four-year RCMP undercover sting. The Mounties established a phony money-change house at the corner of Peel Street in 1990 that successfully lured some of Montreal's top criminals. Five hundred fifty-eight kilograms of cocaine were also seized in the operation. Di Maulo was charged with 46 counts of money laundering and drug trafficking.

With Jimmy Di Maulo facing a lengthy prison sentence, loyal friends did what they could to help him. On July 4, 1995, Fernando De Francesco approached police officer Jocelyn Chagnon and promised $100,000 for convincing the prosecutor to reduce from 12 to eight years the sentence he was pursuing.

Chagnon feigned interest and met with De Francesco and Ricardo Di Massimo several times. All the meetings were filmed by police. The negotiations concluded with Micheline Kemp, Di Maulo's wife, delivering $15,000 as a down payment.

Police arrested Kemp, De Francesco, Di Massimo, Valentino Morielli, and Jimmy's brother Jos on August 17, 1995, on bribery charges. The proof against Jos Di Maulo and Valentino Morielli was paper thin, and the two were released for lack of evidence. Kemp pled guilty on June 26, 1997, and was liberated on "time served." De Francesco and Di Massimo each received an 18-month prison sentence.

Jimmy Di Maulo admitted on March 12, 1996, to laundering more than $10.5 million from 1990 to 1994 through the RCMP's phony money-change house. He also recognized his role in an operation to import 2,500 kilograms of cocaine from Colombia into the country. He was sentenced to 12 years.

Reference

Gary Francoeur. "Vincenzo 'Jimmy' Di Maulo." Wiseguy-Wally. Available online. URL: http://www.geocities.com/ wiseguywally/VincenzoDiMaulo.html. Downloaded on July 19, 2004.

—G.F.

DIMES, Albert

"Italian" Albert Dimes was the big enforcer and right-hand man of William Billy Hill, a London gangland leader of the 1940s and 1950s.

See also: CORNELL, GEORGE; FRASER, FRANK; KRAY TWINS; RICHARDSON GANG.

DIONICIO Martínez, Ramón

During the 1970s Ramón Dionicio Martínez, also known as José Luis Sánchez and "El Lechero," formed an illegal narcotics distribution ring in the Rio Grande Valley. Dionicio and his fellow conspirators imported huge quantities of marijuana from Mexico and distributed the marijuana to dealers across the United States. From the sale of these illegal drugs, Dionicio derived a large income. He invested much of this income in real estate, frequently using sham or fraudulent transactions to conceal his involvement. In December 1986 Dionicio purchased a residence in Edinburg, Texas, with proceeds derived from the sale of illegal narcotics.

El Lechero means "the Milkman." Dionicio, a major marijuana trafficker, and 17 other codefendants pleaded guilty to narcotic and money-laundering offenses in a case that was concluded in 1996. He was nicknamed *"lechero"* because he delivered milk as well as bundles of marijuana to his customers. The operation expanded to the point that the "milkman" was transporting tons of marijuana; he admitted distributing more than 200,000 pounds of marijuana, which was transported via trailers, using produce and aluminum cans to cover the illicit cargo. The marijuana was obtained from sources in Colombia and Mexico.

Dionicio cooperated with U.S. authorities and provided information leading to the identification of the Mexican supplier, who maintained an extensive network of bank accounts in the United States and Mexico. The supplier also owned a Mexican currency-exchange house, used to launder drug proceeds. The Mexican supplier and eight other defendants were indicted for importing more than 100,000 pounds of marijuana and 2.5 tons of cocaine into the United States. The supplier was also indicted on charges of laundering approximately $12 million in narcotics proceeds; he pleaded guilty to both trafficking and money-laundering charges and was sentenced to 240 months in prison.

Information provided by the supplier led to the investigation of a Hidalgo County, Texas, sheriff who was alleged to have provided high-level narcotics traffickers with special treatment while they were incarcerated. After bribing jail employees to provide favors, the Mexican supplier paid the sheriff a fee of $5,000 per month and $1,000 for every visit by his family or girlfriend. The sheriff, who also received sports cars, watches, and a flat-bed trailer,

was given about a total of $200,000, part of which was used to construct a pavilion on the sheriff's cattle ranch. The sheriff and three other personnel were indicted on charges of racketeering, bribery, and money laundering, among others. The sheriff was found guilty, was sentenced to 84 months in prison, and was fined $20,000, in addition to paying a judgment of $151,000 on the racketeering conviction.

Reference

United States of America vs. Cindy Gabbard Adams, a.k.a Cindy Sánchez, United States Court of Appeals for the Fifth Circuit, No. 91-2408 and the International Narcotics Control Strategy Report, U.S. Department of State, 1996.

DONMEZ, Osman

Osman Donmez is the key advisor to Onur Ozbizerdik, the well-known scion of Turkish criminal royalty, as he is both the son of Turkish Mafia don Alaatin Cakici and grandson of the most famous Turkish Mafia don ever, Dundar Kilic. Donmez has served Onur since Onur's mother, Ungar, was murdered in 1995 by his father's former bodyguard, supposedly for carrying on an affair during the course of their marriage. Some have suspected that she was somehow plotting against him with her father or some of his advisors. Donmez and Alaatin Cakici had been close in the past, but a political dispute ended their relationship. With his defection from Cakici, the aging and famed mafia don Dundar Kilic quickly swept Donmez into his group. Kilic entrusted Donmez with advising his grandson on criminal business matters. The two are extremely loyal to one another.

"The August 1999 death of Dundar Kilic left Donmez in a position of great power with his influence over the youthful don of the group," reported http://geocities.com/OrganizedCrimeSyndicates. "His new stature in the gang also made him a target of Alaatin Cakici. Donmez was shot and seriously wounded in September 1999 in an attack carried out by the nephew of Alaatin Cakici. Donmez lay close to death for days before finally recovering. He swore to exact his revenge. Revenge came in the form of two high profile attacks: one claiming the life of the man who almost killed him, the other the brother of the man responsible for the attack on him and the murder of his young protégé's mother."

Donmez's control of the former Dundar Kilic's empire makes him currently the most feared and most powerful man in underworld Turkey and a formidable opponent for both illegal competitors and for government authorities.

See also: BASAK, HUSEYIN; KILIC, DUNDAR; OZBIZ-ERDIK, ONUR; UGURLU, ABUZER.

DRUG Enforcement Administration (DEA)

The history of federal drug law enforcement traces back to before the turn of the century when the federal government began to institute gradual restrictions and controls on newly discovered "wonder drugs" such as heroin and cocaine. During the next half-century, the United States would continue to grapple with the negative effects of drugs on society. Multiple government agencies would be charged with monitoring and enforcing the drug laws of the United States. During the past several decades, the federal government's role in fighting the war against drugs has increased. As the organizations that deal in drugs have grown larger and more sophisticated, so too has America's commitment and ability to combat these groups throughout the country and around the world.

The long, proud, and honorable tradition of federal drug law enforcement began in 1915 with the Bureau of Internal Revenue. In the following decades, several federal agencies had drug law-enforcement responsibilities. By the 1960s the two agencies charged with drug law enforcement were the Bureau of Drug Abuse Control (BDAC) and the Federal Bureau of Narcotics (FBN). It was during this period that America underwent a significant change. The introduction of drugs into American culture and the efforts to "normalize" drug use started to take a terrible toll on the nation. Nevertheless, American children could still walk to school in relative safety, worrying only about report cards or the neighborhood bully. Today, however, as children approach their schools they see barbed wire, metal detectors, and signs warning drug dealers that school property is a "drug-free zone." In too many communities drug dealers and gunfire force decent, law-abiding citizens to seek refuge behind locked doors.

In 1960, only 4 million Americans had ever tried drugs. Currently, that number has risen to more than 74 million. Behind these statistics are the stories of countless families, communities, and individuals who were adversely affected by drug abuse and drug trafficking.

Prior to the 1960s, Americans did not see drug use as acceptable behavior, nor did they believe that drug use was an inevitable fact of life. Indeed, tolerance of drug use resulted in terrible increases in crime between the 1960s and the early 1990s, and the landscape of America was altered forever.

By the early 1970s, drug use had not yet reached its all-time peak, but the problem was sufficiently serious to warrant a serious response. Consequently, the Drug Enforcement Administration (DEA) was created in 1973 to deal with America's growing drug problem.

At that time, the well-organized international drug-trafficking syndicates headquartered in Colombia and Mexico had not yet assumed their place on the world stage as the preeminent drug suppliers. All of the heroin and cocaine and most of the marijuana that entered the United States was being trafficked by lesser international drug dealers who had targeted cities and towns within the nation. Major law-enforcement investigations, such as the French Connection, made by agents in the DEA's predecessor agency, the Bureau of Narcotics and Dangerous Drugs (BNDD), graphically illustrated the complexity and scope of America's heroin problem.

In the years prior to 1973 several important developments took place that would ultimately have a significant impact on the DEA and federal drug-control efforts for years to come. By the time that the DEA was created by Executive Order in July 1973 to establish a single unified command, the United States was beginning to see signs of the drug and crime epidemic that lay ahead. To appreciate how the DEA has evolved into the important law-enforcement institution it is today, it must be understood that many of its programs have roots in predecessor agencies.

On July 1, 1973, President Richard Nixon created the Drug Enforcement Administration by merging its predecessor agency, the Bureau of Narcotics and Dangerous Drugs (BNDD) with various law enforcement and intelligence-gathering agencies. The DEA was charged with the responsibility of enforcing the nation's federal drug laws, and it works closely with local, state, federal, and international law enforcement organizations to identify, target and bring to justice the most significant drug traffickers in the world.

Today, the DEA has grown to an agency of more than 9,000 dedicated employees with more than 4,500 special agents located in communities across the United States and in countries around the world. To meet the challenges posed by sophisticated international drug-trafficking organizations, the DEA has developed state-of-the-art investigative tools and techniques that are used in 22 field divisions, offices in more than 50 foreign countries, and high-tech laboratories around the nation.

The DEA's continuing commitment is to serve the United States by providing the very best federal drug law-enforcement assistance to communities besieged by drugs and to partner with members of the international community in targeting the highest levels of drug Mafias.

Since its establishment the DEA has succeeded in large part in its fight against crime. It has had many successes and has been the United States's police arm around the world through cooperation with other branches of the U.S. government, foreign governments, and foreign police agencies to cull the swelling ranks of those who would import drugs or other illegal paraphernalia into the country.

See also: BLACK TUNA GANG; CAMARENA, ENRIQUE; DUARTE, JOSÉ IVAN; FRENCH CONNECTION, THE; HERRERA NEVARES, JAIME, SR.; LEHDER-RIVA, CARLOS; NORIEGA, MANUEL; OPERATION DINERO; OPERATION FOXHUNT; OPERATION GREEN ICE II; OPERATION LEYENDAL; OPERATION OPBAT; OPERATION PISCES; OPERATION PIPELINE; OPERATION SNOWCAP; OPERATION SWORDFISH; OPERATION TIGER TRAP; OPERATION ZORRO II; SYLMAR SEIZURE.

Reference

U.S. Drug Enforcement Adminisrtation, U.S. Department of Justice. "A Tradition of Excellence, DEA History 1985–1900." Available online. URL: http://www.dea.gov/pubs/history/index.html. Downloaded on July 28, 2004.

DUARTE, José Ivan

In 1982, José Ivan Duarte and his conspirator René Benitez were hired by Colombian drug traffickers to plan and execute the kidnaping of Drug Enforcement Administration (DEA) Special Agents Charles Martinez and Kelly McCullough. The agents were taken from their hotel in Cartagena, Colombia, and were transported by car to a secluded area 15 miles away.

Agent Martinez was shot for the first time while still within city limits. Then Duarte and Benitez stopped the car and shot Martinez again. At that point McCullough fled. He was shot as he ran into the jungle. Martinez escaped when his captors' gun jammed as they attempted to shoot him for a third time. Both Martinez and McCullough managed to escape despite their wounds. They reached Cartagena the next day and phoned the U.S. Embassy for assistance. They were airlifted out of the country by a U.S. air force plane from Panama.

Both Duarte and Benitez eluded capture. Warrants for their arrests were issued in June 1982. Benitez was eventually captured in Colombia, extradited, and imprisoned in Miami in 1995. Duarte continued to evade authorities until August 1997 when he was detained in Ecuador. The Ecuadoran government expelled the fugitive, and he was then transported to the United States to stand trial. His capture marked the end of a 15-year investigation and search. According to Administrator Constantine, Duarte's expulsion by the Ecuadoran government showed great courage and commitment to battling drugs.

Reference

U.S. Drug Enforcement Administration, U.S. Department of Justice. "A Tradition of Excellence, DEA History 1985–1990." Available online. URL: http://www.dea.gov/pubs/ history/index.html. Downloaded on July 28, 2004.

DUBOIS, Adrien

The youngest of the infamous Dubois brothers, Adrien was born on January 18, 1946. He grew up on the mean streets of Saint-Henri, a poor neighborhood in Montreal. He followed his brothers into crime and would become one of the city's most important drug traffickers and loan sharks.

In the 1960s Adrien and Boxer Di Francesco took control of the Harlem Paradise, a nightclub on Saint-Antoine Street. The business soon became a center for prostitution and generated a lot of cash for Adrien. Several black pimps, who had long controlled the area's sex trade, opposed Dubois, but they were dealt with swiftly.

Adrien grew in power in the 1970s. With the exception of Claude, he was the most prosperous Dubois brother. From his base of operations in Verdun, police said he ran an extremely successful loan-sharking operation and a large-scale drug network, which stretched as far as Hull, where he supplied much of the area's marijuana, hashish, amphetamines, and cocaine.

Adrien Dubois was the main suspect behind the disappearance of Yvon Bertin, a well-connected criminal and friend of Richard Désormiers. He was dragged out of his home in underwear on November 26, 1971, and forced into an automobile. Bertin had begun to deal drugs on Dubois's turf without permission. His body was never found.

Dubois also led the gang in its 1974–75 war with the McSween Gang. Dubbed the War of the West in newspapers, the two groups battled for drug turf in the city's west end. Nine people were killed, and more than a dozen were wounded in the struggle before the Dubois gang was victorious.

During his brother Claude's trial on first-degree murder charges in 1982, Adrien Dubois, in an attempt to keep former gang hit man Donald Lavoie from testifying, allegedly arranged to have the informant's brother-in-law killed. He supposedly contacted Frank Peter "Dunie" Ryan, leader of the West End Gang, to help him carry out the plot. Ryan hired members of the Hells Angels Montreal Chapter for the hit, but police learned of the contract and took the necessary precautions to protect the intended victim.

Using information from Claude Jodoin, an informer within the gang, police raided a south-shore home on March 3, 1982, and discovered a ton of hashish hidden inside the building's walls. A Dubois henchman was arrested in the bust and sentenced to four years in prison on drug-trafficking charges. According to Jodoin, the drug had belonged to Adrien Dubois, and he lost his $350,000 investment with the seizure.

Police arrested Adrien Dubois on June 29, 1982, and charged him with the murder of Jacques McSween, shot to death in Longueuil on October 5, 1974. Adrien's brother Jean-Guy, who was already behind bars on a murder conviction, and Claude Dubeau, who was also jailed awaiting trial for the murder of Richard Désormiers, were also charged with the murder.

The trail began on February 1, 1983, and featured testimony from several underworld informants. Donald Lavoie claimed to have been present during McSween's murder and described the event in vivid detail. Paul Pomerleau, a small-time extortionist, and Claude Jodoin, a former Dubois Gang member, also provided damaging testimony. But not all of the jury believed what the informants spewed, and the trial, which lasted two and a half months, ended in a deadlock. A new trial was agreed upon.

Adrien Dubois's lawyer Léo-René Maranda managed to have his client freed on bail until the second trial started. On June 1, 1983, while liberated, Dubois was arrested in a hotel on Sherbrooke Street and charged with importing 480 kilograms of hashish.

The second McSween murder trial began soon after and consisted of the same three government witnesses. The jury gave little credibility to the informants and took little time reaching their decision. Adrien, his brother Jean-Guy, and Claude Dubeau were acquitted of murder on June 14, 1985. Friends and family of the defendants applauded loudly as the superior-court jury brought down its verdict.

See also: DUBOIS, CLAUDE; DUBOIS, JEAN-GUY; DUBOIS GANG; LAVOIE, DONALD.

Reference

Gary Francoeur. "Adrien Dubois." WiseguyWally. Available online. URL: http://www.geocities.com/wiseguywally/ AdrienDubois.html. Downloaded on July 19, 2004.

—G.F.

DUBOIS, Claude

Claude Dubois, who would become the most famous of the Dubois brothers, was born on November 15, 1936. The family grew up in the neighborhood of Saint-Henri. The family was extremely poor and just scraped by on their father's $25 a week job at the Black Horse Tavern in downtown Montreal.

The Dubois children basically grew up on the streets, doing what they could to survive. During World War II the neighborhood kids would gather outside the nearby train station and scramble for the loose change that the passing Canadian soldiers would throw. The boys were soon stealing fruit from merchants and selling them around the neighborhood at half the price.

Dubois dropped out of school after finishing the eighth grade and found work as a construction worker, where he developed into a muscular and intimidating young man. One day a police cruiser happened to pull up as Claude and a friend were stealing bags of chips out of a delivery truck on Delinelle Street. He was arrested and, for the fourth time in two years, made an appearance before a court. The judge decided to teach the young man a lesson, and Claude, at the age of 16, received a two-year prison sentence.

On his release Claude began to work as a maitre d' at the Jazz Hot club where he met Harry Smith, a well-known Montreal loan shark. Smith had heard of Dubois's fierce reputation and offered him a job as a collector. The two soon became partners, with $75,000 on the street split between 250 customers. On Smith's death Dubois took over the entire operation.

The Dubois brothers, with Claude at the head, expanded their influence and by the late 1960s had become one of the city's top criminal organizations. Police said the brothers had a large gang of enforcers and had become highly involved in drug trafficking, extortion, and prostitution. They often worked with the city's Mafia and Frank Peter "Dunie" Ryan, the West End Gang's drug kingpin.

In 1972, Richard Désormiers, Frank Cotroni's brother-in-law, began to make trouble in Dubois-controlled bars. This went on for more than a year, and Claude held several meetings with Cotroni to rectify the situation, but nothing was ever done. Finally, to save face, the Dubois brothers decided to act.

On July 20, 1973, Claude Dubois, wearing a huge hat and dressed in an odd Mexican-style costume, broke the window of a Chinese restaurant on Saint-Catherine Street and assaulted a man with a crowbar. He was arrested and jailed. The incident and the costume had been cleverly orchestrated by Dubois and his accomplices to provide him with a solid alibi for when Désormiers would be killed.

But the hit did not occur that night, and Dubois was furious. He refused to delay it any longer and, two nights later, Donald Lavoie and Claude Dubeau walked into the Mon Pays bar and pumped several shots into Désormiers. When Jacques-André Bourassa, the manager, tried to intercede, he was also killed. As all this happened inside, Yvon Belzil's responsibility was to steal Désormiers' white Cadillac.

By the mid-1970s Dubois headed an organization that many considered more powerful than the city's Mafia. On April 21, 1976, in an interview he granted to the producers of the Canadian Broadcasting Corporation's *Connections*, team, Claude Dubois demonstrated how fearless he was: "The only difference between us and the Cotronis is the Cotronis, when they saw it hot with the police, they run away.

Claude Dubois, head of a powerful Montreal criminal organization in the 1970s (*Montreal Gazette*)

When it's hot we stay there, we're gonna face the fuckin' thing."

In that same interview Claude openly told the world his true feelings for Mafia boss Paolo Violi: "They put Violi as a big king; to me Violi's a punk. He tried to go and collect a guy for $100 a week with a punch on the nose. You don't call that a king. For me, he's a punk, no?"

Claude Dubois's world was shattered in 1980 when Donald Lavoie, a trusted associate who had participated in the Désormiers slaying, turned informant after overhearing that there was a contract on his life.

With the information Lavoie provided, Dubois, Yvon Belzil, and Claude Dubeau were charged with the murders of Richard Désormiers and Jacques-André Bourassa. On April 8, 1982, the antigang police squad arrested Dubois at his home in Écho Lake, in the Laurentians, and Belzil at his Saint-Léonard home. Claude Dubeau, 40, who was already behind bars, was informed of the new charges. The next morning, the three accused appeared before the judge and pleaded not guilty to charges of first-degree murder.

Lavoie's testimony was staggering. He admitted to shooting Bourassa and claimed that Dubeau killed Désormiers, all on Dubois's orders. Claude Jodoin, a former *Journal de Montreal* reporter who had

Claude Dubois *(Montreal Gazette)*

become close to the gang, also testified against his former friends. Dubois took the stand in his own defense. He denied having known Désormiers and alleged to have heard about his death in the newspapers. He also denied being in conflict with Frank Cotroni and described him as a "friend."

On November 12, 1982, after a 10-week trial, the three gangsters were found guilty. A month later, on December 8, Dubois, Dubeau, and Belzil were sentenced to life imprisonment. The three, wearing leg irons and handcuffs, showed no emotion when their sentences were handed down.

The Quebec Court of Appeals reduced their sentences to 10 years in March 1989 because, they ruled, that Jacques-André Bourassa's murder had not been premeditated. Dubois was released in the early 1990s and has since kept a low profile.

See also: DUBOIS, ANDRE; DUBOIS, JEAN-GUY; DUBOIS GANG; LAVOIE, DONALD.

Reference

Gary Francoeur. "Claude Dubois." WiseguyWally. Available online. URL: http://www.geocities.com/ wiseguywally/ClaudeDubois.html. Downloaded on July 19, 2004.

—G.F.

DUBOIS, Jean-Guy

Jean-Guy Dubois was born on July 1, 1933 and is the second-oldest of the Dubois brothers. Like many Canadian children, he loved to play hockey, but his father could not afford the necessary gear, so Jean-Guy put together a couple of petty scams to rack up money to buy the equipment. He would later move on to more profitable rackets.

The Dubois brothers' reputation around the neighborhood increased as the years progressed. They were tough, violent, and extremely loyal to one another.

Jean-Guy's brother Normand had a fling with the girlfriend of Rosaire Forgues, a hood with a reputation as the toughest street fighter in the neighborhood. When Forgues found out about the affair, he talked about how he would get even with Normand. The threat got back to the Dubois brothers and Jean-Guy, Claude, and Normand confronted Forgues, who was accompanied by Robert Miron, Ti-Mand Auger, and Roger Provençal. Words quickly turned into fists, and Jean-Guy delivered Forgues a vicious beating. The fight enhanced his reputation on the streets.

The next day, the brothers learned that Robert Miron had told people around the neighborhood that he was going to shoot down Normand. Jean-Guy, Claude, Normand, and René tracked Miron down at the Chez Maurice tavern, where Jean-Guy dropped him quickly.

After the incident, the Dubois brothers learned that Gilles Petit, a young bystander, had been shot down by Miron. Jean-Guy, Claude, Normand, and René were arrested, and Miron was picked up at the scene. Miron admitted to the shooting but claimed that it was only out of fear for the Dubois brothers. Jean-Guy was eventually acquitted of the shooting, but received a two-year prison sentence for assault and possession of an illegal weapon.

After his release, Jean-Guy Dubois found a job as a maitre d' at the Sahara Club. The position gave him the chance to rub shoulders with some of Montreal's most important underworld figures. He also established a successful loan-sharking operation in downtown Montreal and developed a crew of loyal underlings. He contacted members of the Montreal Mafia, who brought in hashish by the ton, and he allegedly set up a lucrative hashish network.

Dubois also bought the Robert Bar Salon on Notre-Dame Street with his brother Adrien and Yvon Belzil. The three made a lot of money from the place and eventually sold it in the late 1970s for $40,000.

In the early 1970s Richard Désormiers, Frank "The Big Guy" Cotroni's brother-in-law, began to stir up trouble in Dubois-protected bars and clubs.

One night Désormiers had the misfortune of starting problems in a club where Jean-Guy was. Dubois decided to teach him a lesson. He got a firearm from André Durocher, a gang henchman, and pointed it at Désormiers. Jean-Guy forced him to get on his knees and placed the gun against his temple. The act cooled Désormiers off for awhile, but he continued to cause problems for the Dubois Gang. He was later gunned down by Claude Dubeau and Donald Lavoie on Claude Dubois's orders.

Late October 22, 1975, police spotted Jean-Guy Dubois and Jacques Ouimet along the Lachine Canal. When they could not explain their presence at the river, the police brought them down to the station. Bloodstains were discovered on Dubois's pant leg, and when police returned to the scene, more crimson drops were detected. Divers searched the water where Dubois and Ouimet had been spotted and discovered the body of Jean-Guy Fournier, an employee at the Hotel Iroquois in Old Montreal. Dubois and Ouimet were charged with the first-degree murder. The first trial was aborted after it was uncovered that a juror had been threatened. A new trial was held, and it resulted with the convictions of both defendants. Both men were handed life sentences.

On June 29, 1982, from his jail cell, Dubois received more bad news. He, his brother Adrien, and Claude Dubeau were being charged with the 1974 first-degree murder of Jacques McSween. The trial began on February 1, 1983, and received great notoriety in the press. Informants Claude Jodoin, Donald Lavoie, and Paul Pomerleau testified for the government, but the jury did not believe their stories. Since the evidence relied solely on the witnesses, the trial ended in a deadlock.

A second trial was held, and Jean-Guy, Adrien, and Claude Dubeau were acquitted on June 14, 1985. Jean-Guy smothered the three defense lawyers with hugs after the judge handed down the verdict. Dubois spent 14 years in jail for the murder of Fournier before being paroled in October 1989.

Jean-Guy Dubois and eight associates—William Bykerdike, Gérard Bourque, Gilles Saint-Amand, Gary Wooley, Israel Meyer Randolph, Stephen Maron, Michel Boisvert, and Lauren Hickman—were arrested on June 28, 1991, and charged with drug trafficking and conspiracy to traffic in narcotics. Police seized 100 kilograms of hashish, 400 marijuana plants, and $500,000 in cash. Dubois was denied bail on July 5 by Judge François Doyon.

Dubois surprised everyone on March 31, 1992, by pleading guilty to charges of trafficking and possession of 44 kilograms of hashish. The evidence accumulated by investigators revealed how Dubois received $6,000 for every kilogram sold to Bykerdike, who then sold the merchandise for $6,500 to Bourque. Bourque then distributed the hashish to the other members of the ring for $7,000 a kilogram.

Dubois was sentenced to seven years on April 14, 1992. He has since been paroled and is back on the streets. His son Alain followed in his father's footsteps and became a full-fledged member of the Rockers motorcycle gang.

See also: DUBOIS, ADRIEN; DUBOIS, CLAUDE; DUBOIS, JEAN-PAUL; DUBOIS GANG.

Reference

Gary Francoeur. "Jean-Guy Dubois." WiseguyWally. Available online. URL: http://www.geocities.com/wiseguywally/JeanGuyDubois.html. Downloaded on July 19, 2004.

—G.F.

DUBOIS, Jean-Paul

Jean-Paul Dubois, the seventh born of the famous Dubois brothers, would become a major loan shark in his home neighborhood of Saint-Henri and was allegedly involved in drug trafficking and extortion. He also purchased Les Deux Mouches bar with "Coco" Laramée.

One night, as Jean-Paul exited the Bar des Copains, a Dubois gang hangout, he was ambushed by two disgruntled loan-sharking customers. They opened fire on him, but fortunately for Dubois, most of the bullets missed their mark. He was slightly injured.

Retaliation was swift. Police found the bodies of Roger Bonenfant and Michel Marleau, the men suspected of the attempted murder of Jean-Paul Dubois, early one morning in February 1968. The corpses were left in the open as an example.

On September 29, 1974, during the organization's vicious war with the McSween Gang, rival gang members barged into Les Deux Mouches bar and fired several shots at Dubois. Luckily for him, the bullets missed.

Jean-Paul was allegedly among the Dubois Gang members, who participated in the brutal August 1975 killing of Mario Saint-Pierre and his girlfriend

Marie Talbot. Saint-Pierre, an associate of Devils Disciples biker gang leader Claude "Johnny Holliday" Ellefsen, and his girlfriend were lured to a meeting at a Saint-Michel-de-Wentworth chalet owned by Dubois. Once there, he was interrogated and beaten for hours with the purpose of extracting Ellefsen's whereabouts. He was then stabbed to death, and Talbot was killed with a hatchet. Their bodies have never been found.

When Donald Lavoie, who had been one of those present during the slayings of Saint-Pierre and Talbot, decided to flip on December 23, 1980, life for Dubois became stressful. When he heard in 1983 that he was going to be charged of the double murder, Jean-Paul went into hiding. Police were stumped: Jean-Paul seemed to have disappeared into thin air.

In May 1988, after five years on the run, Jean-Paul Dubois surrendered to police at the Saint-Jerome Court House. He pled guilty the next day to a reduced charge of manslaughter and was sentenced to three years in prison. He has since been released.

See also: DUBOIS, ADRIEN; DUBOIS, CLAUDE; DUBOIS, JEAN-GUY; DUBOIS GANG.

Reference

Gary Francoeur. "Jean-Paul Dubois." WiseguyWally. Available online. URL: http://www.geocities.com/wiseguywally/JeanPaulDubois.html. Downloaded on July 19, 2004.

—*G.F.*

DUBOIS Gang

The nine Dubois brothers—Raymond, Jean-Guy, Normand, Claude, René, Roland, Jean-Paul, Maurice, and Adrien—grew up in the tough working-class Montreal neighborhood of Saint-Henri and earned a reputation as one of the most vicious, ruthless outfits anywhere in Canada.

The organization rose to the top of Montreal's underworld in the 1960s, vigorously participating in loan sharking, drug trafficking, extortion, and prostitution. Those who refused to fall in line were threatened, battered and, when necessary, eliminated. The Devils Disciples motorcycle gang and the McSween Gang were left helpless as the organization took over their territories.

According to police, between 1968 and 1982, the Dubois Gang was responsible for 63 murders, including 12 who were going to testify against the group and two stool pigeons. Their bloodiest carnage occurred on February 14, 1975, when gang hit men burst into the Hotel Lapinière, a popular McSween hangout, and opened fire. Four men were killed and several others were wounded.

Numerous informers in the early 1980s practically decimated the clan. Several of the brothers and their top subordinates received lengthy prison sentences, and their influence diminished greatly in Montreal.

See also: DUBOIS, ADRIEN; DUBOIS, CLAUDE; DUBOIS, JEAN-GUY; DUBOIS, JEAN-PAUL.

Reference

Gary Francoeur. "The Dubois Gang." WiseguyWally. Available online. URL: http://www.geocities.com/wiseguywally/DuboisGang.html. Downloaded on July 19, 2004.

—*G.F.*

DUNKIRK Boys Posse (a.k.a. Kirkys)

The Dunkirk Boys Posse, also known as Kirkys, has been under the leadership of Dennis (Stickman) Smith since 1977. Traditionally, this posse has been mixed politically but has many members who support the People's National Party (PNP) in Jamaica. From 1987 through 1988 the Dunkirk Boys in New York City were at war with the Spangler Posse, but eventually a truce was declared. The Kirkys were one of the largest drug networks in the mid-Atlantic states, used by international traffickers for distribution.

Some members and associates of the Dunkirk Boys who did not wish to participate in the New York war moved into Englewood, New Jersey, in 1987, selling marijuana, cocaine, crack, and weapons. However, the group has been virtually eliminated from that area because of arrests of their street dealers and midlevel suppliers by the Englewood Police Department and the Bergen County Narcotics Task Force. Ledlo (Blacker) Gillings, who operated in conjunction with this cell of Dunkirk Boys, was sentenced to federal prison on March 3, 1989, on charges of conspiracy to distribute cocaine. The other members of this cell split, some moving their operations to Boston, others to Richmond, Virginia. Intelligence information indicated that in 1988 several members of the Dunkirk Boys who left New York City went to the New Brunswick area. These persons, who were only known by their street names, were not reported to be involved in drug distribution. Instead, they were using New Brunswick only as a safe area.

There were 29 members and associates of the Dunkirk Boys Posse identified as operating or controlling drug distribution networks in New Jersey in 1988. At the present time, however, there is no known network of this posse actively operating in New Jersey.

See also: E'PORT POSSE; FIVE PERCENTERS; TEL AVIV POSSE; WATERHOUSE POSSE.

Reference

New Jersey State Commission of Investigation, Robert J. Clark, Francis A. Betzler, Bruce C. Best, and Debra. A. Sowney. "Afro-Lineal Organized Crime." November 29, 1990. Available online. URL: http://www.state.nj.us/sci/pdf/afro.pdf. Accessed on November 24, 2004.

18TH Street Gang

The 18th Street Gang was created in the late 1960s in the Rampart area of Los Angeles. Many gang experts consider them to be the most violent and aggressive street gang. The 18th Street Gang is currently the largest and fastest-growing gang in the country.

As with most gangs, 18th Street Gang members can be easily identified by their tattoos. Common tattoos include the number 666 (three times six equals 18). Also seen is the number 18 represented in Roman numerals (XVIII). Members also engage in graffiti vandalism to mark their territory using similar symbols.

Although 18th Street maintains a stronghold in several southern California cities, they have continued to spread to numerous cities across the country. Although they claim 18th Street by name, they are actually a collection of several smaller gangs who use 18th Street as their gang's moniker.

18th Street is heavily populated with illegal immigrants but also has numerous Asian, Black, Indian, and Caucasian members. The 18th Street Gang is well established and is involved in all areas of criminal activity. Some members have even become involved in producing fraudulent immigration and naturalization identification cards and even food stamps. Several members also have evolved into a higher level of sophistication and organization than other gangs. This progression is credited to the gang's close relationship with Mexican and Colombian drug cartels.

Reference

Know Gangs. "18th Street Gang." Available online. URL: http://www.knowgangs.com/gang_resources/18th/18th_001.htm. Downloaded on July 19, 2004.

—G.F.

EL Rukins   *See* FORT, JEFF.

ELSON, Monya

Monya Elson was the reputed leader of a Russian crime group involved in counterfeiting, drug trafficking, and other criminal activities. He was allegedly involved in the murders of Elbrous Evdoev and the Lyubarskys.

Elson survived many murder attempts. The first attempt was in Brighton Beach (Brooklyn), New York, on May 14, 1991, when he was shot. This attempt was suspected to have been in retaliation for the attempt on Vyacheslav Lyubarsky, another Brighton Beach-based criminal. Elson, however, was successful in killing Lyubarsky.

Vyacheslav Lyubarsky ("Slava") and his son, Vadim, were shot to death on January 12, 1992, in the hallway outside their Brighton Beach apartment. After returning from dinner with Slava's wife, Nellie, they

Members of the 18th Street Gang in El Salvador celebrate the signing of a peace agreement with a rival gang. (AP)

were ambushed by an assassin who emerged from the hallway shadows and shot both men, but not Nellie.

Another victim of Elson's was Alexander Slepinin. Slepinin was shot to death in his car on June 23, 1992. Allegedly responsible for the death of Efrim Ostrovsky, an associate of Elson's, Slepinin was shot numerous times in the head and back. In 1995 Monya Elson and others were charged in a federal indictment for this and other murders.

Elson ordered a hit on Russian émigré Elbrous Evdoev, also a known criminal. Evdoev was shot in the shoulder and hand on July 4, 1992, in New York City. Evdoev survived. Evdoev told police the shooting had been ordered by Monya Elson.

Later that same year, Elson was shot in the forearm by an unknown assailant in Los Angeles on November 6, 1992. Elson was driven by Leonyard Kanterkantetes to a hospital, where he was treated and released. Two days later an Armenian attempt-

ing to assassinate Elson, was critically injured when the bomb he was planting under Kanterkantetes's car detonated prematurely.

Allegedly, Elson gained some measure of revenge against his enemies in 1993. The body of Elbrous Evdoev was found, fully dressed, frozen solid in a snow bank at an auto salvage yard in Pine Brook, New Jersey, on March 6, 1993. He had been shot three times in the head. Evdoev had been the target of two previous shootings.

In the next year Elson was besieged again. Russian criminal forces attempted to murder Elson again. Elson, his wife, and bodyguard Oleg Zapinakmine were shot in front of Elson's Brooklyn home by Boris Grigoriev on July 26, 1993. All three were treated and released after a brief stay at a local hospital. The attempts on Elson's life resulted from a dispute between Elson and other criminal factions in Brighton Beach.

On September 24, 1993, two months after the failed attempt on Monya, his bodyguard Oleg Zapinakmine was shot once in the back and killed by an unknown assailant. At the time he was shot, Zapinakmine was checking a flat tire on his car in front of his Brooklyn home.

Elson also allegedly ordered the murder of Alexander Levichitz, also known as Sasha Pinya. Levichitz was shot three times in the head near the Arbat Restaurant in Brighton Beach on the evening of January 17, 1994, but miraculously, he survived. He was allegedly a close friend of Monya Elson. Elson was arrested in Fano, Italy, in 1995 and extradicted to the United States to stand trial for three murders. He was convicted and is now serving time in the United States.

See also: EVDOEV, ELBROUS; RUSSIAN MAFYIA; SLEPININ, ALEXANDER.

Reference

New Jersey State Commission of Investigation, New York Organized Crime Task Force, New York State Commission of Investigation, Pennsylvania Crime Commission, with Rutgers University. "The Tri-State Joint Soviet-Émigré Organized Crime Project." 1992. Available online. URL: http://www.state.nj.us/sci/pdf/russian.pdf. Accessed on November 24, 2004.

ENG, Johnny

The government charged Johnny Eng with running a heroin-trafficking operation that imported heroin from Hong Kong for distribution in the United States from 1987 to 1988. The evidence showed that Eng employed three different methods to import the drugs—possession by couriers who flew into John F. Kennedy International Airport, packaging in parcels mailed from Hong Kong, and concealment inside a bean-sprout washing machine imported from Hong Kong.

In early 1987, Eng paid Wah Tom Lee $50,000 for each of six shipments of heroin that she picked up from couriers traveling through Kennedy Airport. The total amount of heroin delivered through this method was 66 kilograms. The bean-sprout washing machine was used to conceal 78 kilograms of heroin sent from Hong Kong. Though Eng was acquitted of the charges related to the washing-machine importation scheme, the 78 kilograms of heroin were considered by the judge at sentencing.

The details of the mail-package smuggling scheme are pertinent to the evidentiary issue in this case.

Sometime in mid-1987 Eng asked Wah Tom Lee and Michael Yu to recruit individuals to receive drugs sent in parcels from Hong Kong. Yu and Lee procured the names of three individuals, Tina Wong, Cathy Leung, and a woman known as Helen (or "Ah Ling"), who were willing to receive the packages in return for $20,000 apiece. After Wong received the first parcel, Eng instructed Yu and Lee to go to Wong's apartment to inspect it. They found that the parcel contained stuffed animals, peppers, and numerous tea boxes. The tea boxes contained seven kilograms of heroin. Several days later, Eng instructed Lee to deliver the heroin to him near a bakery in New York City's Chinatown. At Lee's instruction, Wong brought the heroin to a meeting place near the bakery, met Wong and Eng there, and then transferred the package to Eng. Eng paid Lee and Yu $50,000, of which $20,000 was given to Wong.

A week later, Eng called Lee to inform her that a second parcel would arrive soon. Lee, in turn, called Tina Wong, who notified Cathy Leung. After receiving the package, Leung took it to Wong's apartment. Wong examined its contents and informed Lee how much heroin it contained. Lee called Eng to confirm the delivery. Eng instructed her to leave the heroin in Wong's apartment. Later, at a party at his house, Eng asked Lee to deliver the parcel to someone named *Lap*. Lee arranged for Wong to deliver the heroin to Lap the following day. Eng again gave Lee and Yu $50,000 for the delivery, and Lee in turn gave $20,000 to Leung and $10,000 to Wong.

Following the second delivery, Lee and Yu accompanied Eng to Hong Kong at Eng's expense. Eng introduced Lee and Yu to "Ming," the person who was sending the heroin parcels, and told Ming to contact Yu and Lee if he was not available. Lee provided Eng with a list of four more people willing to receive packages.

Shortly after the group returned from Hong Kong, four more packages were delivered, each containing seven kilograms of heroin. The third parcel was delivered to Cathy Leung's residence. With Eng's permission, Lee sold a portion of the heroin to Ching-Yi Chen. Sometime around the delivery of the third parcel, Lee and Yu, with Eng's permission, began to sell the heroin themselves. Also, at about this time, Lee and Yu again traveled to Hong Kong at Eng's direction, this time accompanied by Tina Wong and two other women. The five of them concealed more than half a million dollars on their persons for delivery to Ming.

The fourth parcel was delivered to "Helen" and then transferred to Wong's residence. Lee again sold part of the heroin in this parcel to Ching-Yi Chen. The fifth parcel arrived at Agnes Chin's residence and was stored in Wong's house. Once again, Lee sold part of the heroin in the parcel to Chen. The sixth parcel was delivered in December 1987 or January 1988 to "Helen," who transferred it to Lee. The seventh parcel arrived at Gwendolyn Chan's residence and was later delivered by Lee to a man named Dai Gow.

The eighth shipment arrived in January or February of 1988 at Agnes Chin's residence. The package was transferred to Lee, who delivered it to Eng by placing it in his jeep.

On February 9–10, 1988, three more boxes from Hong Kong containing heroin and addressed to residences in the New York metropolitan area arrived at customs in California. One of these packages was marked for delivery to a "M. Hsieh" at Gwendolyn Chan's address. The Drug Enforcement Administration then conducted a "controlled delivery," which resulted in Chan's arrest when she accepted delivery of the parcel. Chan agreed to cooperate, and the conspiracy began to unravel. Chan's cooperation led to the arrest of Leung, who also agreed to cooperate. Leung's cooperation led to the arrest of Lee, Yu, and Tina Wong in early March 1988.

The government presented a somewhat different version of events in *United States v. Michael Yu et al.*, No. 88-CR-138(S) (E.D.N.Y. August 31, 1988). In that case, the government prosecuted Eng's coconspirators in the heroin importation scheme. The government charged Wah Tom Lee and Michael Yu, along with four others, with conspiracy to distribute drugs and with the importation and distribution of heroin imported via mail parcels shipped to the United States from Hong Kong. The charges stemmed from the same mail-parcel deliveries that formed the basis for the indictment against Eng.

In Yu, the government argued that Tina Wong had delivered the first two packages to Ching-Yi Chen, while in the instant case the government claimed that Wong delivered the first package to Eng (via Lee) and the second package to Lap (at Eng's direction). In the government's version of events as portrayed at the instant trial, Ching-Yi Chen showed up as a buyer only late in the scheme when Yu and Lee had begun to sell the drugs themselves.

The government explained its changed version of Chen's role as resulting from a reevaluation of Tina Wong's veracity. After the Yu trial, the government interviewed Wong and gave her a polygraph examination. Following its reconsideration of Wong's testimony, the government agreed to the vacation of Ching-Yi Chen's conviction in light of the new information. On this appeal, the government admits that Johnny Eng's name was not mentioned in the earlier trial: "At no time during the Yu trial was Johnny Eng's name mentioned, since Lee and Yu were the persons in the heroin conspiracy with the most direct dealings with Eng, and they were defendants."

Eng was in custody in Hong Kong from August 16, 1989, until he was extradited to the United States on November 1, 1991. He was convicted following a four-week jury trial on all counts related to the drug-courier and mail package importation schemes, but he was acquitted on the charges stemming from the alleged bean-sprout-machine scheme. Eng was convicted of the following crimes: continuing criminal enterprise (CCE), conspiracy to distribute and possess with intent to distribute heroin, importation of heroin, and distribution and possession with intent to distribute heroin. He was sentenced on the "continuing a criminal enterprise" count under the 1987 version of the sentencing guidelines to 151 months imprisonment followed by three years of supervised release. He was sentenced on each of counts three through 14 (the substantive drug offenses) to 292 months imprisonment followed by a life term of supervised release. All the sentences run concurrently.

Reference

United States Court of Appeals for the Second Circuit, No.229—August Term 1993, Argued: October 15, 1993. Decided: Docket No. 93-1197.

E'PORT Posse

At the New Jersey Afro-Lineal Organized Crime Commission's public hearing Elizabeth police detective Thomas G. Swan testified about a particularly vicious group of young African-American males that operated a cocaine-trafficking network in Elizabeth and the Clinton Avenue area of Newark. In March 1988, working with the Union County Narcotics Strike Force and the State Police, the Elizabeth Police Detective Division began to make a series of undercover narcotics buys from street-level dealers near the Pioneer Homes housing project in Elizabeth. The investigation was dubbed Operation Pioneer.

After search warrants and arrests in November 1988, Detective Swan was able to develop a confidential informant, Mutah Sessoms, who revealed that the vast majority of those arrested in Operation Pioneer were part of organizations controlled by two brothers, Robert and Bilal Pretlow. After the arrests, the two groups merged under the leadership of the younger brother, Bilal. Organization members called themselves the E'Port Posse, Phase II, after the Elizabeth Seaport and modeled themselves after Jamaican posses, often dressing in flamboyant style, arming themselves with sophisticated weapons and investing in expensive jewelry. Several expensive cars driven by group members were placed in the names of their acquaintances or relatives.

Starting out as a marijuana dealer in high school, Bilal Pretlow eventually grabbed the drug market for his and his brother Robert's organization and ran rival gangs out of Elizabeth, occasionally with shootouts—some in broad daylight. Detective Swan testified as to the grandiose style in which Bilal Pretlow pursued his goal to expand: Bilal convened a meeting of drug dealers from all over Elizabeth in a central New Jersey restaurant. There he indicated his intention to control drug trafficking in the Elizabeth area and threatened that those who would not go along would face reprisals.

Detective Swan testified that the group's cocaine supply came from a Dominican by the name of Benson, who was located in New York City. The cocaine was generally transported to Elizabeth in taxicabs. In 1989 the group was distributing many kilograms of cocaine, resulting in profits up to $100,000 a week.

Law enforcement strengthened its resolve to deal with the E'Port Posse as the violence surrounding its operations escalated: Mutah Sessoms, the informant, was murdered in June 1989; Robert Pretlow was slain by a rival gang on July 9, 1989; the next day, a third Pretlow brother, Thomas, killed Bobby Ray Davis, a Newark drug trafficker with designs on the Pretlow turf, in retaliation for Robert Pretlow's death. The federal Drug Enforcement Administration, Union County sheriff's office, Newark police, and Essex County sheriff's office joined the Elizabeth police, state police, and Union County prosecutor's office in the investigation. Sessoms's description of an organized criminal enterprise was taken seriously at all levels.

Detective Swan testified how Bilal Pretlow continued to run the operation even while incarcerated: At the time of the November 1988 and subsequent arrests, Bilal Pretlow had paid bail and attorneys fees for his group members. While in the Union County Jail on various drug charges, he continued to run his organization by calling telephones equipped with speed-dialing, call-forwarding, and conference-call capabilities. Telephone toll records to the apartment used by Shawn Hartwell, his first lieutenant who ran the operation in his absence, showed nearly 400 collect calls from the Union County Jail from December 1988 to early February 1989. Many of these calls were for extended periods of time: Some lasted more than an hour, and one or two lasted three and a half hours.

Normally the inmates were allowed to use the public telephone at the jail during a specific eight-hour period, and each was restricted to approximately five to 10 minutes to make a call. Bilal Pretlow, however, ingratiated himself with other inmates by getting his underlings to post bail for them. He bought them gifts and promised them jobs upon his release. Those jobs were in his drug-distribution operation. In one instance he bought $70 Reebok sneakers for the more than 35 inmates on his tier. The inmates returned favors by giving up their allotted telephone time to Pretlow. This alone, though, does not adequately explain the extensive use of the telephone.

On January 18, 1991, Thomas Pretlow was convicted of manslaughter in the fatal shooting of Bobby Ray Davis. Federal charges were brought by the United States Attorney for New Jersey against Bilal Pretlow and eight other members of his group. Rather than face the death penalty, Bilal killed himself in a Federal lockup in 1990.

In December 1990 Husamiddi Williams was sentenced to 13 years in federal prison after pleading guilty to charges of possession of cocaine with intention to distribute and possession of weapons in furtherance of illegal drug activity. Williams ran a "franchise" at Sixth and South Park Streets in Elizabeth for the E'Port Posse for more than a year until he was arrested in August 1989. He employed at least four juveniles to assist in the drug sales. Williams was apprehended by Elizabeth detectives after a shootout between Williams and rival drug dealers. Detective Swan testified that police seized $270,000 in cash, 19 guns, five cars, and about $30,000 in jewelry from Bilal Pretlow and his underlings. With Williams and the Pretlows disposed of by the police, E'Port Posse was effectively shut down.

See also: DUNKIRK BOYS POSSE; FIVE PERCENTERS; TEL AVIV POSSE; WATERHOUSE POSSE.

Reference

New Jersey State Commission of Investigation, Robert J. Clark, Francis A. Betzler, Bruce C. Best, and Debra. A. Sowney. "Afro-Lineal Organized Crime." November 29, 1990. Available online. URL: http://www.state.nj. us/sci/pdf/afro.pdf. Accessed on November 24, 2004.

ESCOBAR, Pablo (a.k.a. El Doctor)

Pablo Escobar rose from a small-time gangster, barely making ends meet while stealing cars, to the towering Colossus of Colombian crime and international terror. He was possibly the wealthiest and most violent organized-crime leader in the history of the free world. *Forbes* magazine in 1989 listed him as the seventh richest man in the world. Escobar entered and then came to dominate the Medellín

Pablo Escobar (left), leader of the Medellín drug cartel, with an unidentified bodyguard in 1983 (AP)

cocaine-manufacturing industry. It was then that he began to establish his own brand of popularity among the poor and disadvantaged. By 1983 he became congressman from Antiquia, his home state. In the late 1980s the U.S. government estimated that Escobar controlled 80 percent of the cocaine being exported from Colombia.

However, in 1984 things began to unravel for Escobar. The government of the United States, the main country into which Escobar exported, demanded that the Colombian government extradite its most notorious drug dealer to the United States for trial. The Colombian government reluctantly began to extradite smaller exporters, but Escobar remained elusive.

Along with his brother Roberto Escobar, Pablo ruled a vast and rich empire. He was known to be a habitual smoker of marijuana, and his personal style was casual and relaxed. However, with foes—whether a competing drug manufacturer, business partners that no longer proved useful, or dedicated law enforcement officials—Escobar was ruthless and brutal. Bounties were placed on the heads of local and federal police and judges who were beyond the reach of bribes. He resorted to bribery, kidnapping, murder, and bombings for the next nine years.

It was alleged that Escobar went so far as to assassinate several presidential candidates who took the wrong position on the Pablo Escobar question—whether to extradite or not. He is also said to have instigated a takeover of the Palace of Justice in Bogotá in 1986, which resulted in the death of 11 supreme court justices and 79 other people. Escobar entered the realm of world-feared terrorist when in November 1989 a bomb blew up an Avianca airliner in Colombia, killing 110 passengers.

By the late 1980s, the U.S. government starting to send covert funds to the Colombian government to help that government cover the costs of the manhunt. By 1991 Escobar had become such an issue to his government and to those around the world that he eventually surrendered. But this was all for show. Escobar's jail was more like a guarded nightclub: he had satellite television, gourmet foods, and a string of beautiful women, and all the time, he was still running his cartel and moving millions of dollars worth of cocaine into the United States. He continued to order killings and to run his business in the same ruthless way.

However, the government continued to pursue his business, and Escobar grew tired of the charade. In

DEA Administrator Robert Bonner (center) announces charges in 1992 against Pablo Escobar for the 1989 terrorist bombing, in the skies over Colombia, of an Avianca Airlines jet that killed 110 people. (AP)

July 1992 he literally walked out of "jail." The "escape" gave the U.S. government the opportunity it had been looking for, and authorities insisted on participating in Escobar's capture.

A combination of the U.S. military, the Colombian government intent on ridding themselves of this embarrassment, and a large vigilante group of citizens who had been wronged by Escobar finally began to shrink the empire "el Doctor" had created. Slowly, the Medellín cartel was reduced to ruins. Escobar fought to the death, bringing down with him more and more victims through bloody murders and bombings. Escobar was eventually killed on December 2, 1993; he was 44 years old. Despite his involvement in countless murders and brutal violence against his people, huge crowds mourned him in his home city.

See also: ESCOBAR, ROBERTO; MEDELLÍN CARTEL.

ESCOBAR, Roberto (a.k.a. El Osito)

Roberto Escobar was the brother of Pablo Escobar. Roberto helped Pablo run the Medellín cartel, making it into one of the largest organized-crime syndicates in the history of organized crime. Roberto was his brother's right-hand man but was especially well known for his business acumen. As such, he was entrusted with the cartel's money. He was responsible for cash flow, money laundering, and investment. He was also responsible for the payroll, which included law-enforcement officials and judges in many countries. The payroll ranged from low-level policemen to the heights of the highest office, including Peruvian president Alberto Fujimori, who took a million-dollar contribution from Escobar during his first campaign.

Less violent than his brother, Roberto el Osito ("the little bear") surrendered to the Colombian authorities in 1992. In 1993 he received a letter bomb that left him partially blind. He recently published his memoir, *My Brother Pablo,* in which he compares his brother to Robin Hood.

See also: ESCOBAR, PABLO; MEDELLÍN CARTEL.

ESPARRAGOZA Moreno, Juan José (a.k.a. El Azul)

Esparragoza Moreno became one of the top lieutenants of Amado Carrillo Fuentes and a partner with Amado's younger brother Vicente Carrillo Fuentes, the leader of the Juárez cartel. According to Peter Lupsha, who wrote "Transnational Narco Corruption and Narco-Investment: A Focus on Mexico," in 1995 for PBS's *Frontline,* "Only Juan José Esparragoza Moreno ('El Azul') is now free and a very important 'statesman' in Colombian/Mexican drug trafficking circles." Lupsha has documented the competition and bloodshed between the competing cartels. Further, he has theorized that of all the Mexican and Colombian Mafia dons, only Esparragoza had the power, connections, and clout to create a "Paz del Norte" among the major trafficking organizations, 50 that "a further symbiosos of narco power into the Mexican economic and political system will likely occur." However, by February 27, 1998, Sam Dillon in the *New York Times* reported that two different U.S. officials identified Rafael Muñoz Talavera as the "new leader" of the Juárez cartel and "that rivals Vicente Carrillo and Juan José Esparragoza 'El Azul' Moreno had 'fallen off of the radar.'" However, by September 1998 Talavera was found dead in the back of an armored Jeep in Ciudad Juárez, Mexico. He had been shot four times in the head, and his body was left in the busy downtown area (apparently he had been killed elsewhere) as a sign by Vicente and Juan José, "the blue one," to show that they were the victors in a bloody civil war within the drug world.

See also: GUADALAJARA CARTEL; JUÁREZ CARTEL.

EUGENE Terry Group

Eugene Terry, Sr., is the leader of a black gambling syndicate in Jersey City, New Jersey, which also operates in conjunction with the Genovese–Gigante crime family. Terry, along with his brother, Steven (Buzz) Terry, is also involved in the financing of a cocaine-distribution network. Steven was arrested on July 1, 2003, and bail was set at $100,000. He was named as one of the top-100 fugitive felons in New Jersey.

Reference

New Jersey State Commission of Investigation, Robert J. Clark, Francis A. Betzler, Bruce C. Best, and Debra. A. Sowney. "Afro-Lineal Organized Crime." November 29, 1990. Available online. URL: http://www.state.nj.us/sci/pdf/afro.pdf. Accessed on November 24, 2004.

EUROPOL

Europol was established by the European Union (EU) convention Council Act of July 26, 1995, which established a European Police Office (Europol Convention) to be located in The Hague, the Netherlands. The objective was to improve police cooperation between the member states to combat terrorism, illicit traffic in drugs, and other serious forms of international crime.

Europol's task is to improve their effectiveness in an increasing number of areas, such as preventing and combating terrorism, unlawful drug trafficking, trafficking in human beings, crimes involving clandestine immigration networks, illicit trafficking in radioactive and nuclear substances, illicit vehicle trafficking, the counterfeiting of the euro, and money-laundering associated with international criminal activities.

Europol has the following principal tasks:

- to facilite the exchange of information between member states
- to obtain, collate, and analyze information and intelligence
- to notify the competent authorities of the member states without delay of information concerning them and of any connections identified between criminal offenses
- to aid investigations in the member states
- to maintain a computerized system of collected information.

Each member state establishes or designates a national unit to carry out the tasks listed above. The national unit is the only liaison body between Europol and the competent national authorities. It sends Europol at least one liaison officer, who is instructed by the national unit to represent its interests within Europol.

To perform its tasks, Europol maintains a computerized information system. Data are entered into the system that is directly accessible for consultation by national units, liaison officers, the Director, the Deputy Directors, and duly empowered Europol officials. The information system may be used to store nonpersonal as well as personal data. The creation of a computerized personal data file by Europol is subject to an instruction approved by the Management Board. Personal data retrieved from the information system can only be transmitted or used by the competent services of the member states to prevent and combat both crime coming under the competence of Europol, as well as other serious criminal offenses. Any individual wishing to obtain data relating to him stored within Europol may make a request, free of charge, to the national competent authority in any member state one wishes.

An independent joint supervisory body is responsible for monitoring the activities of Europol to ensure that the rights of the individual are not violated by the storage, processing, and utilization of the data held by Europol.

The organs of Europol are: the Management Board, composed of a representative of each member state, chaired by the representative of the member state holding the presidency of the council; the Director who is appointed by the council for a four-year period which is renewable once; the Director and Deputy Directors who may be dismissed by the council after obtaining the opinion of the Management Board.

The budget is financed by contributions from the member states and other occasional receipts. The accounts in respect of all income and expenditure entered in the budget together, with the balance sheet showing that Europol's assets and liabilities are subject to an annual audit. The audit is carried out by a joint audit committee, made up of three members appointed by the court of auditors of the European communities.

Each member state is liable for any damage caused to an individual as a result of legal or factual errors in data stored or processed within Europol. Only the member state in which the event which gave rise to the damage occurred may be the subject of an action for compensation by the injured party.

Reprinted courtesy EEU, © European Communities, 1995–2003.

EVDOEV, Elbrous

A Russian mobster who was allegedly involved in prostitution, among other illegal activities, Elbrous Evdoev was shot in the jaw and back in New York City on June 5, 1992. He survived this attempt on his life.

A month later, on July 4, 1992, he was shot again, this time in the shoulder and hand in New York City. Again, he survived. It was at this time that Evdoev told police that the shooting had been ordered by reputed Russian criminal Monya Elson.

But Evdoev's luck did not hold out. His body was found fully dressed, frozen solid, in a snowbank at an auto salvage yard in Pine Brook, New Jersey, on March 6, 1993. He had been shot three times in the head. Monya Elson allegedly ordered the murder.

Reprinted courtesy EEU, © European Communities, 1995–2003.

See also: ELSON, MONYA; RUSSIAN MAFYIA.

Reference

New Jersey State Commission of Investigation, New York Organized Crime Task Force, New York State Commission of Investigation, Pennsylvania Crime Commission, with Rutgers University. "The Tri-State Joint Soviet-Émigré Organized Crime Project." 1992. Available online. URL: http://www.state.nj.us/sci/pdf/russian.pdf. Accessed on November 24, 2004.

FAINBERG, Ludwig (a.k.a. Tarzan)

Ludwig "Tarzan" Fainberg was the Russian Mafia leader of South Florida. He started like many other Russian gangsters, with extortion and fraud, and made it to the big time when he began to ship cocaine for the Colombian drug cartels. Fainberg was not a really tough gangster; he was not even really working with the backing of a major family, but he cornered the market just a bit faster than the rest and used his cocaine money well, supplying the Colombians with Russian helicopters and one time even trying to get them a Russian army submarine.

Fainberg was born in Odessa, Russia, in 1958 to a family of Russian Jews. At age three his family moved to Tsjernovich, where he grew up. He sang in a national boys choir and trained as a boxer for the Russian army until in 1972. When he was 13 the family moved again, this time to Israel. In Israel Fainberg was given his nickname when he jumped from a building to get some attention. Eventually he joined the Israeli marines and tried to become the Israeli equivalent of a U.S. Navy Seal, but he did not complete basic training. He then wanted to become an army officer but failed the exam.

In 1980 Fainberg moved to East Berlin, where he met with some of his Russian friends and joined a crew that was involved in credit-card fraud and extortion. The crew was headed by the notorious Efim Laskin, a criminal who sold weapons to the Red Brigade. Laskin assigned Fainberg to shake down a Berlin banker. With two henchmen, Fainberg went to the bank and pushed the victim into the trunk of their car and threatened him with death if he did not pay. The banker claimed that he could get the money at closing time. The three men waited in the car; after a while Fainberg stepped out to take a walk and smoke a cigarette when all of a sudden four Mercedes Benzes pulled up beside the car, which now only held the two other men. A bunch of other Russian gangsters stepped out of the car and gave the two men a beating. Fearing for his life and hoping for wider horizons, Fainberg decided to go to America.

He settled in Brighton Beach, but it was not the paradise he had hoped for. According to him it was like the Wild West, so he carried a gun at all times. Soon Fainberg established himself by marrying a Russian Mafia princess whose grandfather, ex-husband, and brother-in-law all were Russian gangsters, all going by the same nickname: Psycho. Yet he remained uninvolved. His wife would not allow him to take part in criminal activity. She wanted him home, where they lived off the money from her ex-husband, who was doing seven years in a German prison for extortion. Fainberg's wife bought him expensive suits, took him out to dinner, and watched soap operas with him.

Fed up with this lush existence, Fainberg grew restless, and so he joined another Russian gangster named Grecia Roizes. Their families had close ties, and the two men had been born in the same town.

Roizes had done a three-year term in a Siberian prison because he had hit a man hard enough to reopen a scar on his belly, left by a recent operation. Now Roizes was the head of the most feared crew in Brighton Beach. He had furniture stores in New York, Italy, and Russia that were fronts for a heroin ring used by the Russian Mafia, the Gambino crime family, and the Genovese crime family. Fainberg started to work in one of these stores. One day, when an old lady was treated rudely by one of the young thugs who worked there, he stepped in and offered the old woman free furniture. The next day a muscular Italian man walked into the store, introduced himself as Frankie, and said that the old lady from the day before was his mother and that if Fainberg ever needed anything he should call him. Fainberg was impressed by Frankie's power. Later in 1987 he read the newspaper and finally learned the full name of his new friend, who was now dead—Frank Santora, a made member of the Colombo crime family.

In 1990 Fainberg moved to Florida, which attracted many Russians who either had money to spend or money to make. Ex-KGB agents and other ex-government officials settled there and bought entire buildings with money taken when the Sovet Union collapsed. In South Florida Fainberg opened his club, Porky's, which became a meeting place for Russian gangsters. By this time he was in the drug business and had marijuana fields in the Everglades with a landing strip for airplanes. Soon the marijuana was not enough, so he moved on to cocaine, setting up links with Colombian drug cartels. Business was booming, and the money came flowing in. He was top dog in Florida.

Fainberg's favorite thing was extortion; his second favorite was humiliating women. He would beat them and sexually assault them, and on one occasion he chased a stripper down the street, beat her up, and made her eat stones. But he made so much money that he could get away with anything.

His Russian connections also served him well. In 1993 Fainberg and his Colombian friends bought six M18 Russian helicopters for $1 million apiece. The Colombians tore out the seats to make more room in which to smuggle drugs. Later they negotiated to buy a Russian submarine. The whole thing, including crew, would have cost them $5.5 million, but before the deal went through, he was arrested in Florida.

When business went well for Fainberg, the FBI noticed and they started to look into his past and his friends. They really had nothing on him, and he was not easy to follow, traveling to Colombia and Russia a lot of the time. But then the feds got a break: his friend Roizes (who had earned the nickname "The Cannibal" because he bit off the nose of someone who insulted him) decided to flip and help the FBI so he could get some time out of prison. Fainberg trusted Roizes to the fullest and told him much about his business. He liked to boast; it made him feel tough—until the feds arrested him. On October 17, 1999, he was convicted on RICO charges and deported back to Israel. But Fainberg had nothing bad to say about America: "I love America; it's so easy to steal something here. I think I'm going to Cuba now, a few of my Russian friends have hotels there I'm gonna get rich. . . ."

Reference

David Amoruso. "Ludwig Fainberg." Gangsters Incorporated. Available online. URL: http://www.gangstersinc. tripodcom/Tarzan.html. Downloaded on July 19, 2004.

—D.A.

FALCONE, Giovanni

Famed Italian judge Giovanni Falcone of Sicily specialized in Mafia crimes. Born in a poor area of Palermo, he had a career as a well-loved, crusading, anti-Mafia judge. Falcone's much publicized death drew the ire of the entire world. Falcone was killed in his car as he was driving, when an explosive that had been placed inside the asphalt vaporized the car. When passing over the explosive, Falcone was driving his car at an estimated speed of 160 kmh. He was killed along with his wife and bodyguards in Capaci, on the motorway between Palermo and the city's airport, on May 23, 1992.

It is alleged that the assassination was ordered by Totò Riina, head of the Corleone crime family. The assassination further fueled public resentment against the Mafia and encouraged the Italian government to step in and oversee the jailing of numerous Mafia bosses throughout the country.

See also: AGLIERI, PIETRO; BARGARELLA, LEOLUCA; BRUSCA, GIOVANNI; CORLEONE CLAN; PALAZZOLO, GIUSEPPE; PROVENZANO, BERNARDO; RIINA, SALVATORE; SPERA, BENEDETTO.

FAUCHER, Frédéric

Frédéric Faucher was born on December 16, 1969. Not much is known of his early years, but he grew up in and around Quebec City, and by the early 1990s he was an up-and-coming member of the Rock Machine motorcycle gang's Quebec chapter.

On July 14, 1994, Faucher and four Rock Machine associates were arrested in a hotel room as they planned an attack on members of the Evil Ones, a Hells Angels puppet gang. Police confiscated two pistols, three radio-detonated bombs, and 12 pounds of dynamite. Faucher was convicted and received a short jail sentence.

The Rock Machine associates were obsessed with becoming a member of one of the "big five" biker gangs—the Hells Angels, the Outlaws, the Bandidos, the Pagans, and the Sons of Silence. Faucher settled on the Texas-based Bandidos MC, wrote to Swedish members, and explained the violent war taking place between the Rock Machine and Hells Angels.

Faucher, accompanied by fellow Rock Machine members Johnny Plescio and Robert "Toutou" Léger, tried to enter Sweden on June 18, 1997, to attend the Bandidos Helsingborg memory run for fallen comrades. However, their trip was cut short when Swedish police refused them entry because of their criminal records. The bikers were detained for 24 hours and then deported back to Canada.

But Faucher remained determined. On July 14, 1997, with members Johnny Plescio and Paul "Sasquatch" Porter (who has since aligned himself with the Hells Angels) flanking him, Faucher attended a bike show in Luxembourg. There, the Canadian was seen meeting with top members of the Bandidos Motorcycle Club.

Fred Faucher was reportedly a police suspect in the July 24, 1997, attempted murder of Hells Angels Nomad member Louis "Mélou" Roy. Roy survived, despite being shot four times, and no one was brought up on charges.

On September 11, 1997, the club's president, Claude "Ti-Loup" Vézina, was arrested, and Faucher became the leader of the club's Quebec City activities.

Police raided the home of Faucher's brother, Jean-Judes, also a member of Rock Machine, in December 1999. Within the residence, police found photo albums stuffed with pictures of Hells Angels members and associates.

When law enforcement discussed a new antigang law, Faucher and Maurice "Mom" Boucher, leader of the Hells Angels, called a truce. Accompanied by lieutenants, the biker leaders first met in Quebec City's courthouse and then at the trendy Bleu Marin restaurant on Montreal's Crescent Street to come to an agreement. A photographer from the crime tabloid *Allo Police* was invited to capture the moment, and he did so, snapping a now infamous picture of Faucher and Boucher in a friendly handshake. The peace did not last long, and less than two months later, gang members were back to shooting one another in the streets.

Fred Faucher was arrested with Marcel "Le Maire" Demers, a founding Rock Machine member, on December 6, 2000. Police reported that Faucher was at the head of a drug ring that distributed two kilograms of cocaine a month in the Montreal area. The biker boss was, police say, earning $250,000 a year from cocaine trafficking alone. He pleaded guilty to 28 charges and, on May 11, 2001 was sentenced to 12 years in prison.

See also: HELLS ANGELS.

Reference

Gary Francoeur. "Frédéric Faucher." WiseguyWally. Available online. URL: http://www.geocities.com/wiseguywally/ FredericFaucher.html. Downloaded on July 19, 2004.

—G.F.

FEDERAL Bureau of Investigation (FBI)

ORIGINS

Though most often associated with domestic crimes, the Federal Bureau of Investigation has a long history of tackling international threats and rackets. The FBI originated from a force of special agents created in 1908 by Attorney General Charles Bonaparte during the presidency of Theodore Roosevelt. The two men first met when they both spoke at a meeting of the Baltimore Civil Service Reform Association. Roosevelt, then civil-service commissioner, boasted of his reforms in federal law enforcement. It was 1892, a time when law enforcement was often political rather than professional. Roosevelt spoke with pride of his insistence that border-patrol applicants pass marksmanship tests, with the most accurate being hired. Following Roosevelt on the program, Bonaparte countered, tongue in cheek, that target shooting was not the way to get the best men. "Roosevelt should have had the men shoot at each other, and given the jobs to the survivors."

Roosevelt and Bonaparte both were progressives. They shared the conviction that efficiency and expertise, not political connections, should determine who could best serve in government. Theodore Roosevelt became president of the United States in 1901; four years later, he appointed Bonaparte to be attorney general. In 1908, Bonaparte applied that progressive philosophy to the Department of Justice by creating a corps of special agents. It had neither a name nor an officially designated leader other than the attorney general. Yet, these former detectives and secret-service men were the forerunners of the FBI.

Today, most Americans take a federal investigative service for granted, but in 1908, the establishment of this kind of agency at a national level was highly controversial. The U.S. Constitution is based on federalism: a national government with jurisdiction over matters that crossed boundaries, like interstate commerce and foreign affairs, with all other powers reserved to the states. Through the 1800s, Americans usually looked to cities, counties, and states to fulfill most government responsibilities. However, by the 20th century, easier transportation and communications had created a climate of opinion favorable to federal-government establishment of a strong investigative tradition.

The impulse among the American people toward a responsive federal government, coupled with an idealistic, reformist spirit, characterized what is known as the Progressive era, from approximately 1900 to 1918. The progressive generation believed that government intervention was necessary to produce justice in an industrial society. Moreover, it looked to "experts" in all phases of industry and government to produce that just society.

President Roosevelt personified progressivism at the national level. A federal investigative force consisting of well-disciplined experts and designed to fight corruption and crime fit Roosevelt's progressive scheme of government. Attorney General Bonaparte shared his president's progressive philosophy. However, the Department of Justice under Bonaparte had no investigators of its own, except for a few special agents who carried out specific assignments for the attorney general and a force of examiners (trained as accountants) who reviewed the financial transactions of the federal courts. Since its beginning in 1870, the Department of Justice used funds appropriated to investigate federal crimes to hire private detectives first and, later, investigators from other federal agencies. (Federal crimes are those that were considered interstate or occurred on federal government reservations.)

By 1907, the Department of Justice most frequently called upon secret-service "operatives" to conduct investigations. These men were well trained, dedicated, and expensive. Moreover, they reported not to the attorney general, but to the chief of the secret service. This situation frustrated Bonaparte, who wanted complete control of investigations under his jurisdiction. Congress provided the impetus for Bonaparte to acquire his own force. On May 27, 1908, it enacted a law preventing the Department of Justice from engaging secret-service operatives.

The following month, Attorney General Bonaparte appointed a force of special agents within the Department of Justice. Accordingly, ten former secret-service employees and a number of Department of Justice peonage (compulsory servitude) investigators became special agents of the Department of Justice. On July 26, 1908, Bonaparte ordered them to report to Chief Examiner Stanley W. Finch. This action is considered to mark the beginning of the FBI.

Both Attorney General Bonaparte and President Theodore Roosevelt, who completed their terms in March 1909, recommended that the force of 34 agents become a permanent part of the Department of Justice. Attorney General George Wickersham, Bonaparte's successor, named the force the Bureau of Investigation on March 16, 1909. At that time, the title of chief examiner was changed to chief of the Bureau of Investigation.

EARLY DAYS

When the bureau was established, there were few federal crimes. The Bureau of Investigation primarily investigated violations of laws involving national banking, bankruptcy, naturalization, antitrust, peonage, and land fraud. Because the early bureau provided no formal training, previous law-enforcement experience or a background in the law was considered desirable.

The first major expansion in bureau jurisdiction came in June 1910 when the Mann ("White Slave") Act was passed, making it a crime to transport women over state lines for immoral purposes. It also provided a tool by which the federal government could investigate criminals who evaded state laws but had no other federal violations. Finch became commissioner of White Slavery Act violations in 1912, and former Special Examiner A. Bruce Bielaski became the new Bureau of Investigation chief.

During the next few years, the number of special agents grew to more than 300, and these individuals were complemented by another 300 support employees. Field offices existed from the bureau's inception. Each field operation was controlled by a special agent in charge who was responsible to Washington. Most field offices were located in major cities. However, several were located near the Mexican border where they concentrated on smuggling, neutrality violations, and intelligence collection, often in connection with the Mexican revolution.

With the April 1917 entry of the United States into World War I during Woodrow Wilson's administration, the bureau's work was increased again. As a result of the war, the bureau acquired responsibility for the Espionage, Selective Service, and Sabotage Acts and assisted the Department of Labor by investigating enemy aliens. During these years special agents with general investigative experience and facility in certain languages augmented the bureau.

William J. Flynn, former head of the secret service, became director of the Bureau of Investigation in July 1919 and was the first to use that title. In October 1919, passage of the National Motor Vehicle Theft Act gave the Bureau of Investigation another tool by which to prosecute criminals who previously evaded the law by crossing state lines. With the return of the country to "normalcy" under President Warren G. Harding in 1921, the Bureau of Investigation returned to its prewar role of fighting the few federal crimes.

THE "LAWLESS YEARS"

The years from 1921 to 1933 were sometimes called the "lawless years" because of gangsterism and the public disregard for Prohibition, which made it illegal to sell or import intoxicating beverages. Prohibition created a new federal medium for fighting crime, but the Department of the Treasury, not the Department of Justice, had jurisdiction for these violations.

Attacking crimes that were federal in scope but local in jurisdiction called for creative solutions. The Bureau of Investigation had limited success using its narrow jurisdiction to investigate some of the criminals of "the gangster era." For example, it investigated Al Capone as a "fugitive federal witness." Federal investigation of a resurgent white-supremacy movement also required creativity. The Ku Klux Klan (KKK), dormant since the late 1800s, was revived in part to counteract the economic gains made by African Americans during World War I. The Bureau of Investigation used the Mann Act to bring Louisiana's philandering KKK "Imperial Kleagle" to justice.

Through these investigations and through more traditional investigations of neutrality violations and antitrust violations, the Bureau of Investigation gained stature. Although the Harding Administration suffered from unqualified and sometimes corrupt officials, the Progressive era reform tradition continued among the professional Department of Justice special agents. The new Bureau of Investigation director, William J. Burns, who had previously run his own detective agency, appointed 26-year-old J. Edgar Hoover as assistant director. Hoover, a graduate of George Washington University Law School, had worked for the Department of Justice since 1917, where he headed the enemy alien operations during World War I and assisted in the General Intelligence Division under Attorney General A. Mitchell Palmer, investigating suspected anarchists and communists.

After Harding died in 1923, his successor, Calvin Coolidge, appointed replacements for Harding's cronies in the Cabinet. For the new attorney general, Coolidge appointed attorney Harlan Fiske Stone. Stone then, on May 10, 1924, selected Hoover to head the Bureau of Investigation. By inclination and training, Hoover embodied the progressive tradition. His appointment ensured that the Bureau of Investigation would keep that tradition alive.

When Hoover took over, the Bureau of Investigation had approximately 650 employees, including 441 special agents who worked in field offices in nine cities. By the end of the decade, there were approximately 30 field offices, with divisional headquarters in New York, Baltimore, Atlanta, Cincinnati, Chicago, Kansas City, San Antonio, San Francisco, and Portland. He immediately fired those agents whom he considered unqualified and proceeded to professionalize the organization. For example, Hoover abolished the seniority rule of promotion and introduced uniform performance appraisals. At the beginning of the decade, the Bureau of Investigation established field offices in nine cities. He also scheduled regular inspections of the operations in all field offices. Then, in January 1928, Hoover established a formal training course for new agents, including the requirement that new agents had to be in the 25–35 year range to apply. He also returned to the earlier preference for special agents with law or accounting experience.

The new director was also keenly aware that the Bureau of Investigation could not fight crime without public support. In remarks prepared for the attorney general in 1925, he wrote, "The Agents of the Bureau of Investigation have been impressed with the fact that the real problem of law enforcement is in trying to obtain the cooperation and sympathy of the public and that they cannot hope to get such cooperation until they themselves merit the respect of the public." Also in 1925, Agent Edwin C. Shanahan became the first agent to be killed in the line of duty when he was murdered by a car thief.

In the early days of Hoover's directorship, a long held goal of American law enforcement was achieved: the establishment of an identification division. Tracking criminals by means of identification records had been considered a crucial tool of law enforcement since the 19th century, and matching fingerprints was considered the most accurate method. By 1922, many large cities had started their own fingerprint collections.

In keeping with the Progressive era tradition of federal assistance to localities, the Department of Justice created a Bureau of Criminal Identification in 1905 to provide a centralized reference collection of fingerprint cards. In 1907, the collection was moved, as a money-saving measure, to Leavenworth Federal Penitentiary, where it was staffed by convicts. Understandably suspicious of this arrangement, police departments formed their own centralized identification bureau maintained by the International Association of Chiefs of Police. It refused to share its data with the Bureau of Criminal Investigation. In 1924, Congress was persuaded to merge the two collections in Washington, D.C., under Bureau of Investigation administration. As a result, law-enforcement agencies across the country began to contribute fingerprint cards to the Bureau of Investigation by 1926.

By the end of the decade, special-agent training was institutionalized, the field office inspection system was solidly in place, and the National Division of Identification and Information was collecting and compiling uniform crime statistics for the entire United States. In addition, studies were underway that would lead to the creation of the Technical Laboratory and Uniform Crime Reports. The bureau was equipped to end the "lawless years."

THE NEW DEAL

The 1929 stock market crash and the Great Depression brought hard times to America. Hard times, in turn, created more criminals—and also led Americans to escape their troubles through newspapers, radio, and movies.

To combat the crime wave, President Franklin D. Roosevelt influenced Congress in his first administration to expand federal jurisdiction, and his attorney general, Homer Cummings, fought an unrelenting campaign against rampant crime. One case highlighting the rampant crime included the swindling and murder of members of the Osage Indian tribe in Oklahoma for the rights to their oil fields.

Noting the widespread interest of the media in this war against crime, Hoover carried the message of FBI work through them to the American people; for example, in 1932 the first issue of the *FBI Law Enforcement Bulletin*—then called *Fugitives Wanted by Police*—was published. Hoover became as adept at publicizing his agency's work as he was at administering it. Prior to 1933, bureau agents had developed an esprit de corps, but the public considered them interchangeable with other federal investigators. Three years later, mere identification with the FBI was a source of special pride to its employees and commanded instant recognition and respect from the public. By the end of the decade, the bureau had field offices in 42 cities and employed 654 special agents and 1141 support employees.

During the early and mid-1930s several crucial decisions solidified the bureau's position as the nation's premier law-enforcement agency. Responding to the kidnapping of the Lindbergh baby, in 1932, Congress passed a federal kidnapping statute. Then in May and June 1934, with such gangsters as John Dillinger evading capture by crossing over state lines, it passed a number of federal crime laws that significantly enhanced the bureau's jurisdiction. In the wake of the Kansas City Massacre, Congress also gave bureau agents statutory authority to carry guns and make arrests.

The Bureau of Investigation was renamed the United States Bureau of Investigation on July 1,

1932. Then, beginning July 1, 1933, the Department of Justice experimented for almost two years with a Division of Investigation that included the Bureau of Prohibition. Public confusion between Bureau of Investigation special agents and Prohibition agents led to a permanent name change in 1935 for the agency composed of Department of Justice's investigators: the Federal Bureau of Investigation was thus born.

Contributing to its forensic expertise, the bureau established its Technical Laboratory in 1932. Journalist Rex Collier called it "a novel research laboratory where government criminologists will match wits with underworld cunning." Originally the small laboratory operated strictly as a research facility. However, it benefited from expanded federal funding, eventually housing specialized microscopes and extensive reference collections of guns, watermarks, typefaces, and automobile-tire designs.

In 1935, the FBI National Academy was established to train police officers in modern investigative methods since at that time only a few states and localities provided formal training to their peace officers. The National Academy taught investigative techniques to police officials throughout the United States and, starting in the 1940s, from all over the world.

The legal tools given to the FBI by Congress, as well as bureau initiatives to upgrade its own professionalism and that of law enforcement, resulted in the arrest or demise of all the major gangsters by 1936. By that time, however, fascism in Adolf Hitler's Germany and Benito Mussolini's Italy, and communism in Joseph Stalin's Soviet Union threatened American democratic principles. With war on the horizon, a new set of challenges faced the FBI.

WORLD WAR II PERIOD

Germany, Italy, and Japan embarked on an unchecked series of invasions during the late 1930s. Hitler and Mussolini supported the Spanish Falangists in their successful civil war against the "Loyalist" Spanish government (1937–39). Although many Europeans and North Americans considered the Spanish Civil War an opportunity to destroy fascism, the United States, Great Britain, and France remained neutral; only Russia supported the Loyalists. To the shock of those who admired Russia for its active opposition to fascism, Stalin and Hitler signed a nonaggression pact in August 1939. The following month Germany and Soviet Russia seized Poland. A

short time later, Russia overran the Baltic States. Finland, while maintaining its independence, lost western Karelia to Russia. Great Britain and France declared war on Germany, which formed the Axis with Japan and Italy—and World War II began. The United States, however, continued to adhere to the Neutrality Acts, passed in the mid-1930s.

As these events unfolded in Europe, the Great Depression continued. The depression provided as fertile an environment for radicalism in the United States as it did in Europe. European fascists had their counterparts and supporters in the United States in the German-American Bund, the Silver Shirts, and similar groups. At the same time, labor unrest, racial disturbances, and sympathy for the Spanish Loyalists presented an unparalleled opportunity for the American Communist Party to gain adherents. The FBI was alert to these fascist and communist groups as threats to American security.

Authority to investigate these organizations came in 1936 with President Roosevelt's authorization through Secretary of State Cordell Hull. A 1939 presidential directive further strengthened the FBI's authority to investigate subversives in the United States, and Congress reinforced it by passing the Smith Act in 1940, outlawing advocacy of violent overthrow of the government.

With the actual outbreak of war in 1939, the responsibilities of the FBI escalated. Subversion, sabotage, and espionage became major concerns. In addition to agents trained in general intelligence work, at least one agent trained in defense-plant protection was placed in each of the FBI's 42 field offices. The FBI also developed a network of informational sources, often using members of fraternal or veterans' organizations. With leads developed by these intelligence networks and through their own work, special agents investigated potential threats to national security.

Great Britain stood virtually alone against the Axis powers after France fell to the Germans in 1940. An Axis victory in Europe and Asia would threaten democracy in North America. Because of the Nazi–Soviet Pact, the American Communist Party and its sympathizers posed a double-edged threat to American interests. Under the direction of Russia, the American Communist Party vigorously advocated continued neutrality for the United States.

In 1940 and 1941, the United States moved further and further away from neutrality, actively aiding the Allies. In late 1940, Congress reestablished the draft. The FBI was responsible for locating draft evaders and deserters.

Without warning, the Germans attacked Russia on June 22, 1941. Thereafter, the FBI focused its internal security efforts on potentially dangerous German, Italian, and Japanese nationals as well as on native-born Americans whose beliefs and activities aided the Axis powers.

The FBI also participated in intelligence collection. Here the Technical Laboratory played a pioneering role. Its highly skilled and inventive staff cooperated with engineers, scientists, and cryptographers in other agencies to enable the United States to penetrate and sometimes control the flow of information from the belligerents in the Western Hemisphere.

Sabotage investigations were another FBI responsibility. In June 1942, a major, yet unsuccessful, attempt at sabotage was made on American soil. Two German submarines let off four saboteurs each at Amagansett, Long Island (New York), and Ponte Vedra Beach, Florida. These men had been trained by Germany in explosives, chemistry, secret writing, and how to blend into American surroundings. While still in German clothes, the New York group encountered a Coast Guard sentinel patrolling the beach, who ultimately allowed them to pass. However, afraid of capture, saboteur George Dasch turned himself in and assisted the FBI in locating and arresting the rest of the team. The swift capture of these Nazi saboteurs helped to allay fear of Axis subversion and bolstered Americans' faith in the FBI.

Also, before U.S. entry into the war, the FBI uncovered another major espionage ring. This group, the Frederick Duquesne spy ring, was the largest discovered up to that time. The FBI was assisted by a loyal American with German relatives who acted as a double agent. For nearly two years the FBI ran a radio station for him, learning what Germany was sending to its spies in the United States while controlling the information that was being transmitted to Germany. The investigation led to the arrest and conviction of 33 spies.

War for the United States began on December 7, 1941, when Japanese air forces attacked ships and facilities at Pearl Harbor, Hawaii. The United States immediately declared war on Japan, and the next day Germany and Italy declared war on the United States. By 9:30 P.M., Eastern Standard Time, on December 7, the FBI was in a wartime mode. FBI

Headquarters and the 54 field offices were placed on 24-hour schedules. On December 7 and 8, the FBI arrested previously identified aliens who threatened national security and turned them over to military or immigration authorities.

At this time, the FBI augmented its agent force with National Academy graduates, who took an abbreviated training course. As a result, the total number of FBI employees rose from 7,400 to more than 13,000, including approximately 4,000 agents, by the end of 1943.

Traditional war-related investigations did not occupy all the FBI's time. For example, the bureau continued to carry out civil-rights investigations. Segregation, which was legal at the time, was the rule in the armed services and in virtually the entire defense industry in the 1940s. Under pressure from African-American organizations, the president appointed a Fair Employment Practices Commission (FEPC). The FEPC had no enforcement authority; however, the FBI could arrest individuals who impeded the war effort. The bureau assisted the FEPC when a Philadelphia transit workers' union went out on strike against an FEPC desegregation order. The strike ended when it appeared that the FBI was about to arrest its leaders.

The most serious discrimination during World War II was the decision to evacuate Japanese nationals and American citizens of Japanese descent from the West Coast and send them to internment camps. Because the FBI had arrested the individuals whom it considered security threats, FBI Director Hoover took the position that confining others was unnecessary. The president and the attorney general, however, chose to support the military assessment that evacuation and internment were imperative. Ultimately, the FBI became responsible for arresting curfew and evacuation violators.

While most FBI personnel during the war worked traditional war-related or criminal cases, one contingent of agents was unique. Separated from bureau rolls, these agents, with the help of FBI legal attachés, composed the Special Intelligence Service (SIS) in Latin America. Established by President Roosevelt in 1940, the SIS was to provide information on Axis activities in South America and to destroy its intelligence and propaganda networks. Several hundred thousand Germans or German descendants and numerous Japanese lived in South America. They provided pro-Axis pressure and cover for Axis communications facilities. Nevertheless, in every South American country, the SIS was instrumental in bringing about a situation in which, by 1944, continued support for the Nazis became intolerable or impractical.

Nonwar acts were not limited to civil-rights cases. In 1940, the FBI Disaster Squad was created when the FBI Identification Division was called on to identify some bureau employees who were on a flight that had crashed near Lovettsville, Virginia.

In April 1945, President Roosevelt died, and Vice President Harry Truman took office as president. Before the end of the month, Hitler committed suicide and the German commander in Italy surrendered. Although the May 1945 surrender of Germany ended the war in Europe, war continued in the Pacific until August 14, 1945.

The world that the FBI faced in September 1945 was very different from the world of 1939 when the war began. American isolationism had effectively ended, and, economically, the United States had become the world's most powerful nation. At home, organized labor had achieved a strong foothold; African Americans and women, having tasted equality during wartime labor shortages, had developed aspirations and the means of achieving the goals that these groups had lacked before the war. The American Communist Party possessed an unparalleled confidence, while overseas the Soviet Union strengthened its grasp on the countries it had wrested from German occupation—making it plain that its plans to expand communist influence had not abated. Finally, hanging over the euphoria of a world once more at peace was the mushroom cloud of atomic weaponry.

POSTWAR AMERICA

In February 1946 Stalin gave a public address in which he implied that future wars were inevitable until communism replaced capitalism worldwide. Events in Europe and North America convinced Congress that Stalin was well on his way to achieving his goal. The Russian veto prevented the United Nations from curbing Soviet expansion under its auspices.

Americans feared that communist expansion was not limited to Europe. By 1947, ample evidence existed that pro-Soviet individuals had infiltrated the American government. In June 1945, the FBI raided the offices of *Amerasia,* a magazine concerned with the Far East, and discovered a large number of classified State Department documents. Several months later the Canadians arrested 22 people for trying to steal atomic secrets. Previously, Americans felt secure behind their monopoly of the atomic bomb. Fear of a Russian bomb now came to dominate American thinking. The Soviets detonated their own bomb in 1949.

Counteracting the communist threat became a paramount focus of government at all levels, as well as the private sector. While U.S. foreign policy concentrated on defeating communist expansion abroad, many U.S. citizens sought to defeat the communist threat at home. The American Communist Party worked through front organizations or influenced other Americans who agreed with their current propaganda ("fellow travelers").

Since 1917 the FBI and its predecessor agencies had investigated suspected acts of espionage and sabotage. In 1939 and again in 1943, presidential directives had authorized the FBI to carry out investigations of threats to national security. This role was clarified and expanded under Presidents Truman and Dwight D. Eisenhower. Any public or private agency or individual with information about subversive activities was urged to report it to the FBI. A poster to that effect was distributed to police departments throughout the country. At the same time, it warned Americans to "avoid reporting malicious gossip or idle rumors." The FBI's authority to conduct background investigations on present and prospective government employees also expanded dramatically in the postwar years. The 1946 Atomic Energy Act gave the FBI "responsibility for determining the loyalty of individuals . . . having access to restricted Atomic Energy data." Later, executive orders from both Presidents Truman and Eisenhower gave the FBI responsibility for investigating allegations of disloyalty among federal employees. In these cases, the agency requesting the investigation made the final determination; the FBI only conducted the investigation and reported the results. Many suspected and convicted spies, such as Julius and Ethel Rosenberg, had been federal employees. Therefore, background investigations were considered to be just as vital as cracking major espionage cases.

Despite the threats to the United States of subversion and espionage, the FBI's extended jurisdiction, and the time-consuming nature of background investigations, the bureau did not surpass the number of agents it had during World War II—or its yearly wartime budget—until the Korean War in the early 1950s. After the Korean War ended, the number of agents stabilized at about 6,200, while the budget began a steady climb in 1957.

Several factors converged to undermine domestic communism in the 1950s. Situations such as the Soviet defeat of the Hungarian rebellion in 1956 caused many members to abandon the American Communist Party. However, the FBI also played a role in diminishing party influence. The bureau was responsible for the investigation and arrest of alleged spies and Smith Act violators, most of whom were convicted. Through Hoover's speeches, articles, testimony, and books like *Masters of Deceit,* the FBI helped alert the public to the communist threat.

The FBI's role in fighting crime also expanded in the postwar period through its assistance to state and local law enforcement and through increased jurisdictional responsibility. On March 14, 1950, the FBI began its "Ten Most Wanted Fugitives" List to increase law-enforcement's ability to capture dangerous fugitives. Advances in forensic science and technical development enabled the FBI to devote a significant proportion of its resources to assisting state and local law-enforcement agencies.

A dramatic example of aid to a state occurred after the midair explosion of a plane over Colorado in 1955. The FBI Laboratory examined hundreds of airplane parts, pieces of cargo, and the personal effects of passengers. It pieced together evidence of a bomb explosion from passenger luggage and then painstakingly looked into the backgrounds of the 44 victims. Ultimately, agents identified the perpetrator and secured his confession; then they turned the case over to Colorado authorities who successfully prosecuted it in a state court.

At the same time, Congress gave the FBI new federal laws with which to fight civil-rights violations, racketeering, and gambling. These new laws included the Civil Rights Acts of 1960 and 1964; the 1961 Crimes Aboard Aircraft Act, an expanded Federal Fugitive Act, and the Sports Bribery Act of 1964.

Up to this time, the interpretation of federal civil-rights statutes by the Supreme Court was so narrow that few crimes, however heinous, qualified to be investigated by federal agents.

The turning point in federal civil-rights actions occurred in the summer of 1964, with the murder of voting-registration workers Michael Schwerner,

Andrew Goodman, and James Chaney near Philadelphia, Mississippi. At the Department of Justice's request, the FBI conducted the investigation as it had in previous, less-publicized racial incidents. The case against the perpetrators took years to go through the courts. Only after 1966, when the Supreme Court made it clear that federal law could be used to prosecute civil-rights violations, were seven men found guilty. By the late 1960s the confluence of unambiguous federal authority and local support for civil-rights prosecutions allowed the FBI to play an influential role in enabling African Americans to vote, serve on juries, and use public accommodations on an equal basis.

Other civil-rights investigations included the assassination of Martin Luther King, Jr., with the arrest of James Earl Ray, and the murder of Medger Evers, Mississippi field secretary of the NAACP, with the arrest of Byron De La Beckwith who, after two acquittals, was finally found guilty in 1994.

Involvement of the FBI in organized-crime investigations also was hampered by the lack of possible federal laws covering crimes perpetrated by racketeers. After Prohibition, many mob activities were carried out locally, or if interstate they did not constitute major violations within the bureau's jurisdiction.

An impetus for federal legislation occurred in 1957 with the discovery by Sergeant Croswell of the New York State police that many of the best-known mobsters in the United States had met together in upstate New York. The FBI collected information on all the individuals identified at the meeting, confirming the existence of a national organized-crime network. However, it was not until an FBI agent persuaded mob insider Joseph Valachi to testify that the public learned firsthand of the nature of La Cosa Nostra, the American Mafia.

On the heels of Valachi's disclosures, Congress passed two new laws to strengthen federal racketeering and gambling statutes that had been passed in the 1950s and early 1960s to aid the bureau's fight against mob influence. The Omnibus Crime Control and Safe Streets Act of 1968 provided for the use of court-ordered electronic surveillance in the investigation of certain specified violations. The Racketeer Influenced and Corrupt Organizations (RICO) Statute of 1970 allowed organized groups to be prosecuted for all of their diverse criminal activities, without the crimes being linked by a perpetrator or all-encompassing conspiracy. Along with greater use of agents for undercover work by the late 1970s, these provisions helped the FBI develop cases that in the 1980s put almost all the major traditional crime-family heads in prison.

By the end of the 1960s the bureau employed 6,703 special agents and 9,320 support personnel in 58 field offices and 12 legal-attaché offices.

A national tragedy produced another expansion of FBI jurisdiction. When President Kennedy was assassinated, the crime was a local homicide; no federal law addressed the murder of a president. Nevertheless, President Lyndon B. Johnson tasked the bureau with conducting the investigation. Congress then passed a new law to ensure that any such act in the future would be a federal crime.

THE VIETNAM WAR ERA

President Kennedy's assassination introduced the violent aspect of the late 20th century. This period was characterized by idealism but also by increased urban crime and a propensity for some groups to resort to violence in challenging the "establishment."

Most Americans objecting to U.S. involvement in Vietnam or to other policies wrote to Congress or carried peace signs in orderly demonstrations. Nevertheless, in 1970 alone, an estimated 3,000 bombings and 50,000 bomb threats occurred in the United States.

Opposition to the war in Vietnam brought together numerous antiestablishment groups and gave them a common goal. The convergence of crime, violence, civil-rights issues, and potential national-security issues ensured that the FBI played a significant role during this troubled period.

Presidents Johnson and Nixon and Director Hoover shared with many Americans a perception of the potential dangers to this country from some who opposed its policies in Vietnam. As Hoover observed in a 1966 *PTA Magazine* article, the United States was confronted with "a new style in conspiracy—conspiracy that is extremely subtle and devious and hence difficult to understand . . . a conspiracy reflected by questionable moods and attitudes, by unrestrained individualism, by nonconformism in dress and speech, even by obscene language, rather than by formal membership in specific organizations."

The New Left movement's "romance with violence" involved, among others, four young men living in Madison, Wisconsin. Antiwar sentiment was widespread at the University of Wisconsin (UW), where two of them were students. During the very early morning of August 24, 1970, the four used a powerful homemade bomb to blow up Sterling Hall, which housed the Army Math Research Center at UW. A graduate student was killed, and three others were injured.

That crime occurred a few months after National Guardsmen killed four students and wounded several others during an antiwar demonstration at Kent State University. The FBI investigated both incidents. Together, these events helped end the "romance with violence" for all but a handful of hardcore New Left revolutionaries. Draft dodging and property damage had been tolerable to many antiwar sympathizers; deaths were not.

By 1971, with few exceptions, the most extreme members of the antiwar movement concentrated on more peaceable, yet still radical tactics, such as the publication of *The Pentagon Papers*. However, the violent Weathermen and its successor groups continued to challenge the FBI into the 1980s.

No specific guidelines for FBI agents covering national-security investigations had been developed by the administration or by Congress; these, in fact, were not issued until 1976. Therefore, the FBI addressed the threats from the militant New Left as it had those from communists in the 1950s and the KKK in the 1960s. It used both traditional investigative techniques and counterintelligence programs ("Cointelpro") to counteract domestic terrorism and conduct investigations of individuals and organizations who threatened terroristic violence. Wiretapping and other intrusive techniques were discouraged by Hoover in the mid-1960s and eventually were forbidden completely unless they conformed to the Omnibus Crime Control Act. Hoover formally terminated all Cointelpro operations on April 28, 1971.

FBI Director J. Edgar Hoover died on May 2, 1972, just shy of 48 years as the FBI director. He was 77. The next day his body lay in state in the rotunda of the Capitol, an honor accorded only 21 other Americans.

Hoover's successor would have to contend with the complex turmoil of that troubled time. In 1972, unlike 1924 when Attorney General Harlan Fiske Stone selected Hoover, the president appointed the FBI director with confirmation by the Senate. President Nixon appointed L. Patrick Gray as acting director the day after Hoover's death. After retiring from a distinguished naval career, Gray had continued in public service as the Department of Justice's assistant attorney general for the Civil Division. As acting director, Gray appointed the first women as special agents since the 1920s.

Shortly after Gray became acting director, five men were arrested photographing documents at the Democratic National Headquarters in the Watergate Office Building in Washington, D.C. The break-in had been authorized by Republican Party officials. Within hours, the White House began its effort to cover up its role, and the new acting FBI director was inadvertently drawn into it. FBI agents undertook a thorough investigation of the break-in and related events. However, when Gray's questionable personal role was revealed, he withdrew his name from the Senate's consideration to be director. He was replaced hours after he resigned on April 27, 1973, by William Ruckleshaus, a former congressman and the first head of the Environmental Protection Agency, who remained until Clarence Kelley's appointment as director on July 9, 1973. Kelley, who was Kansas City police chief when he received the appointment, had been an FBI agent from 1940 to 1961.

THE AFTERMATH OF WATERGATE

Three days after Director Kelley's appointment, top aides in the Nixon administration resigned amid charges of White House efforts to obstruct justice in the Watergate case. Vice President Spiro T. Agnew resigned in October, following charges of tax evasion. Then, following impeachment hearings that were broadcast over television to the American public throughout 1974, President Nixon resigned on August 9, 1974. Vice President Gerald R. Ford was sworn in as president that same day. In granting an unconditional pardon to ex-President Nixon one month later, he vowed to heal the nation.

Director Kelley similarly sought to restore public trust in the FBI and in law enforcement. He instituted numerous policy changes that targeted the training and selection of FBI and law-enforcement leaders, the procedures of investigative intelligence collection, and the prioritizing of criminal programs. All of this was done while continuing open investigations. One such case was the Patty Hearst kidnapping investigation.

In 1974, Kelley instituted Career Review Boards and programs to identify and train potential managers. For upper management of the entire law-enforcement community, the FBI, in cooperation with the International Association of Chiefs of Police and the Major Cities Chief Administrators, started the National Executive Institute, which provided high-level executive training and encouraged future operational cooperation.

Kelley also responded to scrutiny by Congress and the media on whether FBI methods of collecting intelligence in domestic security and counterintelligence investigations abridged Constitutional rights. The FBI had traditionally used its own criteria for intelligence collection, based on executive orders and blanket authority granted by attorney generals. After congressional hearings, Attorney General Edward Levi established finely detailed guidelines for the first time. The guidelines for FBI foreign counterintelligence investigations went into effect on March 10, 1976, and for domestic security investigations on April 5, 1976 (the latter were superseded March 21, 1983).

Kelley's most significant management innovation, however, was implementing the concept of "quality-over-quantity" investigations. He directed each field office to set priorities based on the types of cases most important in its territory and to concentrate resources on those priority matters. Strengthening the Quality-over-Quantity concept, the FBI as a whole established three national priorities: foreign counterintelligence, organized crime, and white-collar crime. To handle the last priority, the bureau intensified its recruitment of accountants. It also stepped up its use of undercover operations in major cases.

During Kelley's tenure as director, the FBI made a strong effort to develop an agent force with more women and one that was more reflective of the ethnic composition of the United States. By the late 1970s nearly 8,000 special agents and 11,000 support employees worked in 59 field offices and 13 legal-attaché offices.

THE RISE OF INTERNATIONAL CRIME

In 1978, Director Kelley resigned and was replaced by former federal Judge William H. Webster. At the time of his appointment, Webster was serving as judge of the U.S. Court of Appeals for the Eighth Circuit. He had previously been a judge of the U.S. District Court for the Eastern District of Missouri. Also in 1978, the FBI began to use laser technology in the Identification Division to detect latent crime-scene fingerprints.

In 1982, following an explosion of terrorist incidents worldwide, Webster made counterterrorism a fourth national priority. He also expanded FBI efforts in the three others: foreign counterintelligence, organized crime, and white-collar crime. Part of this expansion was the creation of the National Center for the Analysis of Violent Crime.

The FBI solved so many espionage cases during the mid-1980s that the press dubbed 1985 "the year of the spy." The most serious espionage damage uncovered by the FBI was perpetrated by the John Walker spy ring and by former National Security Agency employee William Pelton.

Throughout the 1980s, the illegal drug trade severely challenged the resources of American law enforcement. To ease this challenge, in 1982 the attorney general gave the FBI concurrent jurisdiction with the Drug Enforcement Administration over narcotics violations in the United States. The expanded Department of Justice attention to drug crimes resulted in the confiscation of millions of dollars in controlled substances, the arrests of major narcotics figures, and the dismantling of important drug rings. One of the most publicized, dubbed "the Pizza Connection" case, involved the heroin trade in the United States and Italy. It resulted in 18 convictions, including a former leader of the Sicilian Mafia.

On another front, Webster strengthened the FBI's response to white-collar crimes. Public corruption was attacked nationwide. Convictions resulting from FBI investigations included members of Congress (ABSCAM), the judiciary (GREYLORD), and state legislatures in California and South Carolina. A major investigation culminating in 1988 unveiled corruption in defense procurement (ILLWIND).

As the United States faced a financial crisis in the failures of savings-and-loan associations during the 1980s, the FBI uncovered instances of fraud that lay behind many of those failures. It was perhaps the single largest investigative effort undertaken by the FBI to that date: From investigating 10 bank failures in 1981, it had 282 bank failures under investigation by February 1987. Resources to investigate fraud during the savings-and-loan crisis were provided by the Financial Institution Reform, Recovery and Enhancement Act.

In 1984 the FBI acted as lead agency for security of the Los Angeles Olympics. In the course of its efforts to anticipate and prepare for acts of terrorism and street crime, it built important bridges of interaction and cooperation with local, state, and other fed-

eral agencies, as well as agencies of other countries. It also unveiled the FBI's Hostage Rescue Team as a domestic force capable of responding to complex hostage situations such as tragically occurred in Munich at the 1972 games.

Perhaps as a result of the bureau's emphasis on combating terrorism, such acts within the United States decreased dramatically during the 1980s. In 1986, Congress had expanded FBI jurisdiction to cover terrorist acts against U.S. citizens outside the U.S. boundaries. Later, in 1989, the Department of Justice authorized the FBI to arrest terrorists, drug traffickers, and other fugitives abroad without the consent of the foreign country in which they resided.

Expanded resources were not limited to "established" crime areas such as terrorism and violent crime. In 1984, the FBI established the Computer Analysis and Response Team (CART) to retrieve evidence from computers.

On May 26, 1987, Judge Webster left the FBI to become director of the Central Intelligence Agency. Executive Assistant Director John E. Otto became acting director and served in that position until November 2, 1987. During his tenure, Acting Director Otto designated drug investigations as the FBI's fifth national priority.

On November 2, 1987, former federal Judge William Steele Sessions was sworn in as FBI director. Prior to his appointment as FBI director, Sessions served as the chief judge of the U.S. District Court for the Western District of Texas. He had previously served as a district judge and as U.S. attorney for that district.

Under director Sessions, crime prevention efforts, in place since director Kelley's tenure, were expanded to include a drug demand reduction program. FBI offices nationwide began to work closely with local school and civic groups to educate young people to the dangers of drugs. Subsequent nationwide community-outreach efforts under that program evolved and expanded through such initiatives as the Adopt-A-School/Junior G-Man Program. The expansion in initiatives required a larger workforce, and by 1988 the FBI employed 9,663 special agents and 13,651 support employees in 58 field offices and 15 legal-attaché offices.

THE END OF THE COLD WAR

The dismantling of the Berlin Wall in November 1989 electrified the world and dramatically rang up the iron curtain on the final act in the cold war: the formal dissolution of the Soviet Union, which occurred on December 25, 1991.

While world leaders scrambled to reposition their foreign policies and redefine national-security parameters, the FBI responded as an agency in January 1992 by reassigning 300 special agents from foreign-counterintelligence duties to violent-crime investigations across the country. It was an unprecedented opportunity to intensify efforts in burgeoning domestic-crime problems and at the same time to rethink and retool FBI national security programs in counterintelligence and counterterrorism.

In response to a 40 percent increase in crimes of violence during the previous 10 years, Director Sessions had designated the investigation of violent crime as the FBI's sixth national priority program in 1989. By November 1991 the FBI had created Operation Safe Streets in Washington, D.C.—a concept of federal, state, and local police task forces targeting fugitives and gangs. Therefore, it was now ready to expand this operational assistance to police nationwide.

At the same time, the FBI Laboratory helped change the face of violent-criminal identification. Its breakthrough use of DNA technology enabled genetic crime-scene evidence to positively identify—or rule out—suspects by comparing their particular DNA patterns. This unique identifier enabled the creation of a national DNA Index, similar to the fingerprint index, which had been implemented in 1924.

The FBI also strengthened its response to white-collar crimes. Popularized as "crime in the suites," these nonviolent crimes had steadily increased as automation in and deregulation of industries had created new environments for fraud. Resources were, accordingly, redirected to combat the new wave of large-scale insider bank fraud and financial crimes; to address criminal sanctions in new federal environmental legislation; and to establish long-term investigations of complex health-care frauds.

At the same time, the FBI reassessed its strategies in defending national security, now no longer defined as the containment of communism and the prevention of nuclear war.

By creating the National Security Threat List, which was approved by the attorney general in 1991, it changed its approach from defending against hostile intelligence agencies to protecting U.S. information and technologies. It thus identified all countries—not just hostile intelligence services—that pose a continuing and serious intelligence threat to the United States. It also defined expanded threat issues, including the proliferation of chemical, biological, and nuclear weapons; the loss of critical technologies; and the improper collection of trade secrets and proprietary information. As President Clinton was to note in 1994, with the dramatic expansion of the global economy, "national security now means economic security."

Two events occurred in late 1992 and early 1993 that were to have a major impact on FBI policies and operations. In August 1992 the FBI responded to the shooting death of Deputy U.S. Marshal William Degan, who was killed at Ruby Ridge, Idaho, while participating in a surveillance of federal fugitive Randall Weaver. In the course of the standoff, Weaver's wife was accidentally shot and killed by an FBI sniper.

Eight months later, at a remote compound outside Waco, Texas, FBI agents sought to end a 51-day standoff with members of a heavily armed religious sect who had killed four officers of the Bureau of Alcohol, Tobacco and Firearms. Instead, as agents watched in horror, the compound burned to the ground from fires lit by members of the sect. Eighty persons, including children, died in the blaze.

These two events set the stage for public and congressional inquiries into the FBI's ability to respond to crisis situations.

On July 19, 1993, following allegations of ethics violations committed by director Sessions, President Clinton removed him from office and appointed Deputy Director Floyd I. Clarke as acting FBI director. The president noted that director Sessions's most significant achievement was broadening the FBI to include more women and minorities.

THE RISE OF A WIRED WORLD: 1993–2001

Louis J. Freeh was sworn in as director of the FBI on September 1, 1993. Freeh had served as an FBI agent from 1975 to 1981. He was appointed U.S. District Court judge for the Southern District of New York in 1991 and served on that court until he was nominated to be director of the FBI during the summer of 1993.

Freeh began his tenure with a clearly articulated agenda to respond to deepening and evolving crime problems both at home and abroad. During the summer of 1994, determined to forge strong, international police partnerships, Freeh led a delegation of high-level diplomatic and federal law-enforcement officials to meet with senior officials of 11 European nations on international crime issues. At the outset, Richard Holbrooke, U.S. ambassador to Germany, declared, "This is the evolving American foreign policy. Law Enforcement is at the forefront of our national interest in this part of the world." On July 4, 1994, Freeh officially announced the opening of an FBI Legal Attaché Office in Moscow, the old seat of Russian communism.

Subsequently, the bureau sharpened joint efforts against organized crime, drug trafficking, and terrorism, and it expanded standardized training of international police in investigative processes, ethics, leadership, and professionalism, including in April 1995, the opening of the first International Law Enforcement Academy (ILEA) in Budapest, Hungary. The bureau also expanded its international presence by opening 21 new legal-attaché offices overseas.

The bureau also mounted aggressive programs in specific criminal areas. During the years 1993 through 1996 these efforts paid off in successful investigations as diverse as the World Trade Center bombing in New York City (1993); the bombing of the Alfred P. Murrah Federal Building in Oklahoma City (1995); the Unabomber, Theodore Kaczynski (1996); and the arrests of Mexican drug-trafficker Juan Garcia-Abrego (1996) and Russian crime boss Vyacheslav Ivankov (1995). In response to public outcry over the tragedies at Ruby Ridge, Idaho, and Waco, Texas, the bureau formed the Critical Incident Response Group (CIRG) to deal more efficiently with crisis situations.

As computers and access to the Internet became commonplace in homes across the United States, the FBI began to put in place measures to address crime in cyberspace. It created the Computer Investigations and Infrastructure Threat Assessment Center (CITAC) to respond to physical and cyber attacks against the U.S. infrastructure. The FBI has also played a crucial role in the investigation and prevention of computer crimes. In 1991 the FBI's Computer Analysis and Response Teams (CART) began to provide investigators with the technical expertise necessary to obtain evidence from the computers of suspects. In 1998, the FBI's National Infrastructure Protection Center (NIPC) was created to monitor the dissemination of computer viruses, worms, and other malicious programs and to warn government and business-computer users of these dangers. In addition, having begun in the FBI's Baltimore Division in 1995 but branching

out to most FBI field offices, the Bureau's Innocent Images Program has successfully identified and stopped large numbers of pedophiles who have used the Internet to purvey child pornography and to lure children into situations where they could be harmed.

Between 1993 and 2001 the FBI's mission and resources expanded to address the increasingly international nature of crime in U.S. localities. The FBI's budget grew by more than $1.27 billion as the bureau hired 5,029 new agents and more than 4,000 new support personnel. To prepare the FBI for both domestic and foreign lawlessness in the 21st century, Freeh spearheaded the effort by law enforcement to ensure its ability to carry out court-authorized electronic surveillance in major investigations that affected public safety and national security in the face of telecommunications advances. Important legislation passed during this period included the Communications Assistance for Law Enforcement Act (CALEA) of 1994, the Health Insurance Portability and Accountability Act of 1996, and the Economic Espionage Act of 1996. Freeh left the bureau in June 2001 for a position in the private sector.

CHANGE OF MANDATE: 2001–PRESENT

On September 4, 2001, former U.S. attorney Robert S. Mueller III was sworn in as FBI director with a specific mandate to upgrade the bureau's information technology infrastructure, to address records-management issues, and to enhance FBI foreign counterintelligence analysis and security in the wake of the damage done by former special agent and convicted spy Robert Hanssen.

Within days of his entering on duty, however, the September 11 terrorist attacks were launched against New York and Washington. Mueller led the FBI's massive investigative efforts in partnership with all U.S. law enforcement, the federal government, and allies overseas. On October 26, 2001, President George W. Bush signed into law the USA PATRIOT Act, which granted new provisions to address the threat of terrorism, and Mueller accordingly accepted on behalf of the Bureau responsibility for protecting the American people against future terrorist attacks. On May 29, 2002, the attorney general issued revised investigative guidelines to assist the bureau's counterterrorism efforts.

To support the bureau's change in mission and to meet newly articulated strategic priorities, Mueller called for a reengineering of FBI structure and operations to closely focus the bureau on prevention of terrorist attacks, on countering foreign intelligence operations against the United States, and on addressing cybercrime-based attacks and other high-technology crimes. In addition, the bureau remains dedicated to protecting civil rights, combatting public corruption, organized crime, white-collar crime, and major acts of violent crime. The bureau has also strengthened its support to federal, county, municipal, and international law-enforcement partners and has dedicated itself to upgrading its technological infrastructure to meet each of its priorities successfully.

At the start of the new millennium, the FBI stands dedicated to its core values and "Bright Line" ethical standards. Commitment to these values and standards ensures that the FBI effectively carries out its mission: To protect and defend the United States against terrorist and foreign intelligence threats; to uphold and enforce the criminal laws of the United States; and to provide leadership and criminal justice services to federal, state, municipal, and international agencies and partners.

Reference

Federal Bureau of Investigation. Available online. URL: http://www.fbi.gov. Downloaded on July 19, 2004.

FÉLIX Gallardo, Miguel Angel

Miguel Angel Félix Gallardo was a major drug trafficker operating from his base in the Mexican state of Sinaloa. He is considered the founder of the Tijuana Cartel. According to Robert Caldwell, in "Mexico: History of a Bloody Drug Cartel" (*San Diego Union,* July 9, 2000) "In 1989, Gallardo was imprisoned in Mexico for complicity in the 1985 kidnapping, torture and murder of U.S. DEA agent Enrique "Kiki" Camarena. When Gallardo went to prison, his drug-trafficking empire was divided among his lieutenants." A major war among his lieutenants, vying for power, resulted. Eventually they, too, were brought to justice.

See also: ARELLANO FÉLIX, RAMÓN; CAMARENA, ENRIQUE; TIJUANA CARTEL.

FIRST Street Crew

In Washington, D.C., after three years of intense investigation, the Drug Enforcement Administration and local homicide detectives brought five leaders of one of the city's most notorious crack-cocaine organizations—the First Street Crew—to justice.

After four months of testimony, the jury found four members of the First Street Crew, including gang leader Antone White, guilty on narcotics and racketeering charges. That the number of killings in the area in which the gang operated has diminished since the convictions is stark evidence of the success of the investigation and trial.

Reference

Janet Reno. "1995 Annual Report of the Attorney General of the United States." U.S. Department of Justice. Available online. URL: http://www.usdoj.gov/ag/annualreports/ar95/toc.htm. Posted in April 1995.

FIVE Percenters

At its public hearing the New Jersey State Commission of Investigation heard testimony from an electronically disguised former member of a group that variously calls itself the Five Percenters, the Five Percent Nation, or the Gods. Also, Louis L. Jordan, an investigator with the Monmouth County prosecutor's office with extensive experience in tracking the group's members and activities, testified at length.

Particularly troubling about the Five Percenters is the existence of racist attitudes and criminal activities behind the facade of a culture with religious overtones. The dogma underlying the group originated in New York City in 1964 when the late Malcolm X expelled Clarence 13X from the Nation of Islam (better known as the Black Muslims) for adulterating the beliefs of that movement. While the Black Muslims believe that blacks should respect themselves and their fellow human beings and that blacks should take their rightful place in society, Clarence 13X postulated that black men (and not women) are gods, that black men are the sole creators and controllers of the Earth, and that whites are devils.

Clarence 13X's teachings included the dogma that 85 percent of the world's population are blacks who, like cattle, have strayed away from "true teachings." Ten percent are the white "devils," who are not to be trusted. The remaining 5 percent are the "pure righteous teachers" or "originals" who must lead the cattle back to the "true way." Thus, the group came to be called Five Percenters, or Gods. Some Hispanics and Sicilians are allowed into Five Percenter groups, as they may be considered to be "half-originals," tracing themselves to black ancestry or relations.

In the 1980s the Five Percenters migrated from New York to New Jersey and several other states. They became active in Asbury Park, Long Branch, Red Bank, Freehold Borough, Bradley Beach, Aberdeen, Lakewood, Matawan, Elizabeth, Linden, Irvington, parts of Newark, Jersey City, Camden, Atlantic City, Trenton, Paterson, Plainfield, Mount Holly, and Pemberton Township. They are presently concentrated in Monmouth and Ocean Counties with approximately 14 chapters, numbering about 300 to 400 members in Monmouth County, according to Detective Jordan.

In addition to developing a prejudiced and demeaning cultural dogma, the Five Percenters became a haven for those engaged in criminal activities, primarily narcotics distribution. They became a solid organization that international drug smugglers came to rely on for large distribution. Investigator Jordan testified that investigations have revealed Five Percenters "involved in everything from criminal mischief to murder, arson, burglary, robbery, aggravated assault, possession of a weapon. . . ." He emphasized that religious teachings are only a nominal part of the movement:

"I have met, in my experience since 1980 of tracking, two families that have not been involved in any way, form or fashion with the negative aspects. However, the rest I've found to be all involved in criminal activity. . . ."

UNIVERSAL RALLIES

Investigator Jordan says, "That's normally a place set up by someone in that movement where they go and they have meetings. One of the key places where they go to have these rallies is in New York City. We have also tracked them since 1980 as having their rallies down in Florida, Great Adventure [amusement park] in Jackson [Township, New Jersey] and also several parks [within] the State of New Jersey, such as Shark River Park in Neptune and several other parks in Monmouth, Middlesex and Ocean counties.

"The purpose is supposedly to educate the young men [and] young women in the better understanding of their culture. We have found that a lot of them are involved in narcotics trafficking, . . . that is, that they are going out, instead of attending the meetings; for example, the bus takes them from here to New York City; some will attend the rallies, the others will stray away and be involved in a lot of narcotics trafficking and bringing the drugs back across the line.

"Certain members use the rally for certain things like to make connections for drugs, guns, or whatever they are into at that time." The Five Percenters have run into some barriers to the spread of their organization. In answer to Commissioner Kenneth D. Merin's questions, Investigator Jordan testified that Five Percenters "initially . . . would go in and set up in places where there is a constant denial of their existence, just giving them a lever to operate. . . ." He explained one reason why they are not well established in some places, such as Newark: "[I]n Newark there is the Muslim faith, which is very strong there, as well as in New York; and they denounce what the Five Percenters are doing. And as a result of that it is very difficult for the Five Percenters to get a foothold. You have to understand also that it is taboo in the Muslim faith to call yourself a god, so here you have these gentlemen calling themselves gods and the Muslim community just does not want to hear that, so they denounce what they are doing." Investigator Jordan described the subservient role of women in the organization: Women, for the most part, are basically an auxiliary. "They are used, for the most part, to be impregnated, to have the children . . . to keep the movement going. . . . [W]e've found that [those on welfare or state aid turn it] over to the movement. Part of that is then given back to them. A majority of it is turned over into narcotics trafficking. . . ."

Five Percenters are apparently not consistently responsive to a centralized leadership. Leaders in the movement may be called ministers, Allah, Father Teacher, Father Allah, and the like, according to Investigator Jordan.

"[W]e look for the graffiti around the buildings, public places, and the telephone booths, the curbing. We look for the negative attitude by the members. At one time they were easily identifiable. They used to wear the knitted skull caps and [lens]less glasses. . . . Now we are identifying them with a half crescent moon and star with a number 7 in it, which is their logo, which represents the Five Percenter Nation."

See also: DUNKIRK BOYS POSSE; E'PORT POSSE; TEL AVIV POSSE; WATERHOUSE POSSE.

Reference
New Jersey State Commission of Investigation, Robert J. Clark, Francis A. Betzler, Bruce C. Best, and Debra. A. Sowney. "Afro-Lineal Organized Crime." November 29, 1990. Available online. URL: http://www.state.nj. us/sci/pdf/afro.pdf. Accessed on November 24, 2004.

FLAMING Eagles

One of the largest and most powerful Chinese-based gangs in the United States, this splinter group from the Big Circle Gang was founded by the notorious Johnny Kon. The Flaming Eagles dominate the U.S. heroin trade.

See also: BIG CIRCLE GANG; KON, JOHNNY.

Reference

Parliamentary Joint Committee on the National Crime Authority. *Asian Organised Crime in Australia: A Discussion Paper by the Parliamentary Joint Committee on the National Crime Authority.* Available online. URL: http://www.aph.gov.au/senate/committee/acc_ctte/completed_inquiries/pre1996/ncaaoc/report/report5.htm. Accessed on November 24, 2004.

FONG, Joe

A Chinese gang leader in San Francisco in the 1970s, Fong was the leader of the Joe Boys, so named because they followed him. Joe Fong began as a young member of the Wa Ching in the Chinatown section of San Francisco. According to Brockman Morris, in *Bamboo Tigers* Fong "joined his older brother, Kit Fong, in the Yao Lei, taking with him such people as Gary Pang, the 'bad' Wayne Yee and others."

Morris pointed out that Fong took some ideas from the Black Panthers' playbook, when he became a political activist, demanding on City Hall's steps better living conditions for Chinatown youths. In reality he used it as a way to increase his power and influence and to swell the ranks of his gang. In October 1972 Joe Fong "was alleged to have participated in a shooting against rival Wah Ching. His defense, carried through several appeals. . . . He was sentenced to life in prison for conspiracy to commit murder." His followers, the Joe Fong Boys, which they later shortened to the Joe Boys, were eventually involved in the Golden Dragon Massacre.

See also: JOE BOYS.

FORT, Jeff

Jeff Fort was born and raised in Chicago on the city's South Side. By 1968 Fort had become, at a young age, the leader of what was then known as one of the most violent and feared street gangs in the country, the Black P-Stone Nation. Fort united the leaders of more than 50 local street gangs into a single organization, which he called the Black P-Stone Nation. Controlled by a 21-man commission, the "Main 21" as they were known projected the group of gangs as a socially conscious, self-help organization.

In 1972, Fort was convicted of defrauding the government of $1.4 million. Fort had created a phony organization that devised programs for underprivileged children and former gang members. This organization then received funding from the Office of Economic Opportunity to the tune of $1 million. Fort was sent to jail but was paroled four years later.

On his release he moved to Milwaukee, Wisconsin, and assumed the name of Chief Prince Malik after joining the Moorish Temple of America. In 1978 Fort returned to Chicago and renamed his gang the El Rukins. For years the El Rukins were the dominant organized-crime group in Chicago's black community. The gang went on to become a major force in drug smuggling on the city's South Side. In 1983, Fort was convicted of selling cocaine and, while serving time in a Texas prison, was tried on federal racketeering charges stemming from an alleged agreement with the government of Libya to commit terrorist acts. According to the testimony of former El Rukin general Trammel Davis, Fort was offered $2.5 million by the Libyan government to plant bombs on American airplanes. Fort was convicted and sentenced to an additional eight years in prison.

Reference

Gary W. Potter. "Unit # 9: Domestic Organized Crime, African-American OC, Youth Gangs, and Outlaw Motorcycle Gangs." Available online. URL: http://www.policestudies.eku.edu/POTTER/crj401_9.htm. Accessed on November 24, 2004.

FOUR Seas Gang

The Four Seas Gang is one of the largest organized-crime groups in Taiwan. They are the second-largest in Taiwan behind the Bamboo Union, Taiwan's largest gang, which has a membership of more than 10,000 Taiwanese. The Four Seas group is approximately 2,000 members strong and is involved with construction. In the last decade, the gang was led most notably by Yang Kuang-nan, who was suspected of shooting the previous leader of the Four Seas Gang, Chen Yung-ho, in 1996.

In 1997, sought by the Taiwanese government as he was a "suspect in several crimes in Taiwan ranging from bid-rigging to murder," according to the *Taipei Times,* Kuang-nan fled to Macau.

In 2001 Kuang-nan was repatriated to Taiwan and was convicted under the Organized Crime Prevention Act on July 18, 2001. He was sentenced to 22

A reputed leader of the Four Seas Gang, Tsai Kuan-lun (center), was arrested in 1996 as part of Taiwan's crackdown on organized crime. (AP)

months, a lenient sentence. The court cited his lack of involvement during his time on mainland China.

See also: KUANG-NAN, YANG; YUNG-HO, CHEN.

Reference

"Repatriated Gang Chief Sentenced to 22 Months." *Taipei Times.* July 18, 2001.

14K Triads

The 14k triad is the largest triad worldwide. It was formed after the Second World War by Nationalists fleeing Communist China. With roughly 20,000 members, the 14K originated with the fight by the Guomintang against communism. Chiang Kai-shek ordered that a league of all triad societies be established and used to fight communist forces using guerrilla tactics. The *14* in the name refers to the address of the original headquarters of this effort. There are more than 30 subgroups to the 14K, and it remains one of the most powerful triads internationally. They are traditionally involved in drug trafficking, alien smuggling, credit-card fraud, theft of computer equipment and automobiles, piracy of intellectual property, and money laundering.

See also: TRIADS.

FRASER, Frank (a.k.a. Mad Frankie)

"Mad" Frankie Fraser is one of the most notorious and highly celebrated of Britain's professional criminals. Fraser was involved in various parts of organized crime from the late 1930s to the early 1980s, despite many convictions and jail stints.

Fraser was a drinking buddy with the Kray twins' father, Charlie, when the boys were still in school. According to MadFrankieFraser.co.uk, the enforcer and thief was by turns an associate or cell mate of "racecourse swindlers, train robbers and racketeers. . . . Frank has been a contract strong arm, club owner, club minder, company director, Broadmoor inmate, firebomber, and prison rioter but—first and last—a thief. 26 convictions. 42 years inside."

One highlight was that he joined the Richardson Gang against the Krays. Fraser is now a minor celebrity and raconteur in Britain.

See also: CORNELL, GEORGE; FRASER, FRANK; KRAY TWINS; MCVITE, JACK; RICHARDSON, CHARLIE; RICHARDSON, EDDIE; RICHARDSON GANG.

FRENCH Connection, The

Illegal heroin labs were first discovered near Marseilles, France, in 1937. These labs were run by the legendary Corsican gang leader Paul Carbone. For years, the French underworld had been involved in the manufacturing and trafficking of illegal heroin abroad, primarily in the United States. It was this heroin network that eventually became known as the French Connection.

Historically, the raw material for most of the heroin consumed in the United States came from Turkey. Turkish farmers were licensed to grow opium poppies for sale to legal drug companies, but many sold their excess to the underworld market, where it was manufactured into heroin and transported to the United States. It was refined in Corsican laboratories in Marseilles, one of the busiest ports in the western Mediterranean. Marseilles served as a perfect shipping point for all types of illegal goods, including the excess opium that Turkish farmers cultivated for profit.

The convenience of the port at Marseilles and the frequent arrival of ships from opium-producing countries made it easy to smuggle the morphine base to Marseilles from the Far East or the Near East. The French underground would then ship large quantities of heroin from Marseilles to Manhattan, New York. The first significant post–World War II seizure was made in New York on February 5, 1947, when seven pounds of heroin were seized from a Corsican seaman disembarking from a vessel that had just arrived from France.

It soon became clear that the French underground was increasing not only its participation in the illegal trade of opium but also its expertise and efficiency in heroin trafficking. On March 17, 1947, 28 pounds of heroin were found on the French liner *St.-Tropez*. On January 7, 1949, more than 50 pounds of opium and heroin were seized on the French ship *Batista*.

The first major French Connection case occurred in 1960. In June an informant told a drug agent in Lebanon that Mauricio Rosal, the Guatemalan ambassador to Belgium, the Netherlands, and Luxembourg, was smuggling morphine base from Beirut, Lebanon, to Marseilles. Narcotics agents had been seizing about 200 pounds of heroin in a typical year, but intelligence showed that the Corsican traffickers were smuggling in 200 pounds every other week. Rosal alone, in one year, had used his diplomatic status to bring in about 440 pounds.

The Federal Bureau of Narcotics' 1960 annual report estimated that from 2,600 to 5,000 pounds of heroin were coming into the United States annually from France. The French traffickers continued to exploit the demand for their illegal product, and by 1969 they were supplying the United States with 80 to 90 percent of the heroin consumed by addicts. The heroin they supplied was approximately 85 percent pure.

Because of this increasing volume, heroin became readily available throughout the United States. In an effort to limit the source, U.S. officials went to Turkey to negotiate the phasing out of opium production. Initially, the Turkish government agreed to limit their opium production starting with the 1968 crop.

Following five subsequent years of concessions, combined with international cooperation, the Turkish government finally agreed in 1971 to a complete ban on the growing of Turkish opium, effective June 30, 1972. During these protracted negotiations, law-enforcement personnel went into action. One of the major roundups began on January 4, 1972, when Bureau of Narcotics and Dangerous Drugs (BNDD) agents and French authorities seized 110 pounds of heroin at the Paris airport. Subsequently, traffickers Jean-Baptiste Croce and Joseph Mari were arrested in Marseilles.

In February 1972, French traffickers offered a U.S. Army sergeant $96,000 to smuggle 240 pounds of heroin into the United States. He informed his superior, who in turn notified the BNDD. As a result of this investigation, five men in New York and two in Paris were arrested with 264 pounds of heroin, which had a street value of $50 million. In a 14-month period, starting in February 1972, six major illicit heroin laboratories were seized and dismantled in the suburbs of Marseilles by French national narcotics police in collaboration with U.S. drug agents. On February 29, 1972, French authorities seized the shrimp boat *Caprice de Temps* as it put to sea near Marseilles heading toward Miami. It was carrying 415 kilograms of heroin. Drug arrests in France skyrocketed from 57 in 1970 to 3,016 in 1972. The French Connection investigation demonstrated that international trafficking networks were best disabled by the combined efforts of drug-enforcement agencies from multiple countries. In this case, agents from the United States, Canada, Italy, and France had worked together to achieve success.

Reference

U.S. Drug Enforcement Administration, U.S. Department of Justice. "A Tradition of Excellence, DEA History 1985–1990." Available online. URL: http://www.dea.gov/pubs/history/ index.html. Downloaded on July 28, 2004.

FUKIENESE

The Fukienese are an emerging Asian-based organized-crime group that dominates the New York City Asian crime scene. In the last 10 years, Toronto's Fukienese population has grown to 7,000–8,000, with a corresponding increase in criminal activity. Fukienese criminals are involved in migrant smuggling, charging up to US$35,000 per head to smuggle people from the Fuchow area of China into Canada and the United States. These fees are rarely paid in whole before the client is brought to Canada, and illegal migrants often become the victims of extortion. Female migrants may be gang raped or sold into prostitution.

In recent times Fukienese groups in Toronto have also been responsible for at least two home-invasion murders and a kidnapping for ransom. Police anticipate that there will be an increase in their level of criminal activities as the local Fukienese population grows.

Reference

Criminal Intelligence Service Canada. "Asian-Based Organized Crime." *1998 National Organized Crime Priorities.* Available online. URL: http://www.cisc.gc.ca/AnnualReport1998/Cisc1998en/asian98.htm. Accessed on November 24, 2004.

FUK Yee Hing

The Fuk Yee Hing are one of the main group of triad societies that have been in existence since the 1930s. The Fuk Yee Hings claimed themselves to be a registered benevolent society for workers. They had 12 branch offices and a membership of 10,000.

While they maintain their position as a benevolent society, today they are known for much more, including bribery, extortion, and prostitution. In Hong Kong they are known to have recruited women to work as prostitutes on the streets, work as prostitutes in or from "villas" (brothels); the women are recruited to work in other jobs and are forced into prostitution on their arrival in Hong Kong; they are recruited to work in nightclubs in Hong Kong and to provide "escort services." They have also been known to work with their counterparts in "Thailand and the Philippines, in bringing women into Hong Kong on two-week tourist visas to work from villas as 'running girls'" according to Hong Kong government sources.

GALIFFI, Agata (a.k.a. Flor de la Mafia)

Agata Galiffi was among the most prominent Mafia dons in the Western Hemisphere in the 1930s and 1940s. Agata was born in Italy, the daughter of Juan Galiffi, a prominent Italian Mafioso. For professional as well as health reasons, Galiffi moved to Buenos Aires when Agata was still a young child.

She was raised in Argentinean high society, going to the top finishing schools, and hanging out with the smart set. However, her father was deported in April 1935 and was sentenced to a jail in Milan for falsifying records and for counterfeiting money. When that happened, Agata decided to run her father's business in South America. Known as the Flower of the Mafia, she was particularly fond of horse racing, and her gang fixed many races as well as running their own bookmaking operation.

From the late 1930s to 1944, Agata was one of the biggest celebrities in South America. She was young, beautiful, and flamboyant—and she was a Mafia don. Her ruthless operation was adept at extortion, counterfeiting, theft, and murder.

She was arrested in 1944 and sentenced to prison but remains a popular icon in South American culture.

GAMBINO, Carlo

Carlo Gambino was born on August 24, 1902, in Palermo, Sicily. He arrived in the United States in 1921 to live in Brooklyn with help of relatives and friends who had already settled in. He would later help his two brothers when they arrived in the United States. Gambino became involved in organized crime and in 1930 was arrested for larceny. By the 1930s he was heavily involved in bootlegging. From the money he made through bootlegging, he bought restaurants and other legit fronts. After Prohibition, in 1939, Carlo Gambino continued bootlegging and in May 23, 1939, received a 22-month sentence and a $2,500 fine for conspiracy to defraud the United States of liquor taxes. Eight months later the conviction was thrown out, and Gambino was a free man again. During the Second World War Gambino made millions from ration stamps. The stamps came out of the Office of Price Administration (O.P.A.) offices. First Gambino's thugs would steal them. When the government started to hide them in banks, he made contact, and the O.P.A. men sold him the stamps." All in all, by the war's end Gambino had made millions through the stamps and the bootlegging.

Gambino was also involved in the narcotics trade. He traveled to Palermo several times to set up the routes and make the deals and, using Sicilians, imported the narcotics into the United States. By 1957 Carlo Gambino had moved up in the Mangano crime family, having become underboss of Albert Anastasia. He also had a loving wife Catherine and three children (two sons and one daughter).

Gambino had a great year in 1957. On October 24 his boss Anastasia was killed while being shaved in the barber shop of the Park Sheraton Hotel. With Anastasia gone Gambino assumed leadership of the Mangano family, exactly his plan since it was Gambino who was behind the Anastasia hit. Listed as a labor consultant to the outside world, Gambino was leading his crime family into better times.

Gambino was making loads of money by now. In addition to illegal income, Gambino garnered a profit from his legal businesses: meat markets, bakeries, restaurants, nightclubs, linen-supply companies, and on and on. Life was great for Gambino. His health was not good, but with both his families doing well and money pouring in, he did not mind. The Racketeer Influenced and Corrupt Organization Act (RICO) had not appeared on the Mafia scene yet, and turncoats were not as common as they would be during the '90s. The government knew who Gambino was and what he did for a living, but to get to him was impossible. Gambino, who entered the United States as an illegal alien but still had not become a U.S. citizen, fought charges by the Immigration and Naturalization Service (INS). They failed time after time. In 1971 Gambino's wife Catharine died. His health deteriorated quickly after that, and by 1975 Gambino felt it was time to appoint a successor.

In doing this, Gambino made the only mistake during his reign as boss of the Mangano/Gambino family. He chose Paul Castellano over his underboss Neil Dellacroce. This decision split the Gambino family into two factions and created a power struggle a decade later. But in the end Carlo Gambino was considered one of the great La Cosa Nostra bosses. He died on October 15, 1976, of natural causes in his Massapequa, New York, home.

See also: CASTELLANO, PAUL; D'ARCO, ALPHONSE; GOTTI, JOHN; GRAVANO, SALVATORE.

Reference

David Amoruso. "Carlo 'Don Carlo' Gambino." Gangsters Incorporated. Available online. URL: http://gangstersinc.tripod.com/Carlo.html. Downloaded on July 19, 2004.

—D.A.

GAMBINO Crime Family

The Gambino crime family has been the most powerful Mafia family in the United States for the last few decades. In recent years it has been decimated by the Federal Bureau of Investigation (FBI), and all their bosses are either in jail or under indictment. They are however still very powerful, with an estimated membership of about 180. The family's first don was Vince Mangano.

The Gambinos' primary illegal activities include narcotics trafficking, gambling, and car theft. The number and power of their stolen-car outlets in Kuwait have led several newspapers to brand the country "Gambino, Inc." Under the command of bosses Carlo Gambino and Paul Castellano, the Gambino family became the most powerful crime family in the country.

The current boss became Peter Gotti, brother of famed don John Gotti. But the former Gotti was in jail. The acting boss is Arnold "Zeke" Squitieri. On John Gotti's arrest, John "Junior" Gotti was acting boss with Corozzo, Peter Gotti and Jackie D'Amico as advisers. By late 1996, when John Gotti had lost most of his appeals, the Commission (a board made up of the ruling dons) pressured Gotti to officially step down and be permanently replaced by someone other than Junior or Peter Gotti when his final appeal was resolved. Federal Bureau of Investigation (FBI) reports indicate that Corozzo was picked as the new point man, but before his official election, he was caught up in an FBI sting, hit with racketeering charges, and jailed to await trial.

Junior Gotti, who showed little evidence of possessing the cunning and intelligence that served Carlo Gambino so well, continued to serve as acting boss until, shortly after, he was indicted on racketeering charges in 1998. He began a federal prison sentence for racketeering in October 1999. As the new millennium began, the family was headed by the onetime Dapper Don's older brother Peter, who when John Gotti died on June 10, 2002, was considered boss.

See also: BONANNO CRIME FAMILY; COLOMBO CRIME FAMILY; COMMISSION, THE; GENOVESE CRIME FAMILY; LUCCHESE CRIME FAMILY.

Reference

David Amoruso. "Gambino Crime Family." Gangsters Incorporated. Available online. URL: http://gangstersinc.tripod.com/Gambino.html. Downloaded on July 19, 2004.

—D.A.

GARCÍA, Francisco, Sr., and Francisco, Jr.

An investigation was initiated after customs agents learned that Francisco García, Sr., and Francisco García, Jr., were smuggling marijuana into the United States. At about the same time, Internal Revenue Service (IRS) officials learned the Garcías were using the bank accounts of their business, Radio Pantera AM 1450, to structure cash deposits. The Garcías acquired the property in 1991.

Customs and IRS agents began to work together on the case, resulting in the October 23, 1993, seizure of 325 pounds of marijuana and $250,000 in Columbus, Ohio. The seizure was linked to the García organization.

As a result of that enforcement action, Radio Pantera and its owners were indicted on marijuana-trafficking and money-laundering charges in March 1994. Several weeks later, search and arrest warrants were executed against the Garcías, their residences, and the radio station. Vehicles purchased with drug proceeds were seized one week after the arrests.

The criminal trial of Francisco García, Sr., and Francisco García, Jr., began in the U.S. District Court in Tucson on May 16, 1995. On June 2 a jury found the defendants guilty of one count each of conspiracy to launder monetary instruments, one count each of conspiracy to engage in monetary transactions in property derived from specified unlawful activities, and one count each of conspiracy to possess with intent to distribute marijuana.

As a result, a forfeiture order was entered against Francisco García, Sr. for $3,130,500 and his interest in Radio Pantera to the government. He was sentenced to 300 months in prison, to be followed by 60 months of supervised release. A forfeiture order was also entered against Francisco García, Jr., for $1,450,500 and his interest in Radio Pantera to the government. He was sentenced to 190 months in prison, following completion of an eight-year Arizona sentence on an unrelated charge.

Additionally, in August 1994, a federal grand jury in Columbus, Ohio, indicted eight people on multiple drug-trafficking and money-laundering charges. The Garcías supplied and transported marijuana to this organization. By January 1995 all the defendants in the Columbus case had pleaded guilty.

Estimates are that sales exceeded 12,000 pounds of marijuana valued at more than $5.6 million. Analysis of the radio station's bank account revealed the owners to have deposited $750,000 into the accounts in cash and cashiers checks.

During the course of the trial, employees of the radio station testified that the owners would bring in large sums of cash at least once a month. The employees were directed to purchase cashier's checks in amounts of less than $10,000. The cashier's checks would then be deposited in the radio station's bank accounts. An accountant testified that he had personally prepared and filed income tax returns with the Secretariá de Hacienda (Mexican finance secretariat) on behalf of the radio-station owners. These statements were made in an effort to show that the large sums of cash received by the owners were proceeds of legitimate economic activity in Mexico on which taxes had already been paid. The accountant further testified that the bank records came from his files and were authentic. A representative of Hacienda was called to testify and refute the accountant's testimony. The Mexican official testified that no documents had been prepared and filed by the accountant on behalf of the station owners. The official also found that the Hacienda tax stamps were fraudulent and that the bank records were not authentic. The accountant was arrested following his testimony, was indicted, and later was found guilty on seven counts of false declarations.

Reference

Department of the Treasury. *International Narcotics Control Strategy Report, October 2, 1996.* Washington, D.C.: U.S. Department of State.

GARCÍA Abrego, Humberto

Humberto García Abrego is the brother of Juan García Abrego and is a suspected drug boss as well. He was arrested numerous times but inexplicably was let go. He was thought to be an organizer and key to the money-laundering operations. In October 1994 he was arrested by Mexican police, as he was a well-known member of the Gulf cartel. After hours of questioning, he was released. Then, again, in February 1997 García Abrego was arrested and placed in prison. His downtown Mexico City cell was infamous, as it was reported to be a six-room suite, complete with telephone and cable television. But on February 28, hours after President Clinton approved aid to Mexico after certifying that the Mexican government was a reliable drug war ally, García Abrego walked out of his Mexican jail.

See also: GARCÍA ABREGO, JUAN; GULF CARTEL.

GARCÍA Abrego, Juan

Juan García Abrego was known as the leader of the Gulf cartel, a powerful drug ring based in Mexico. The movie *Traffic* was in part based on his story. García Abrego's Gulf cartel trafficked mostly in cocaine and marijuana, and it was thought that he was paying off many officials high in the Mexican government. "Documents from the Office of the Attorney General (PGR) and the National Anti-Drug Institute (ICND) reveal that Raúl Salinas de Gortari (brother of the former President of Mexico) had ties with druglords in Mexico as early as 1987," claimed PBS's *Frontline* on May 22, 1996.

García Abrego was born in La Paloma, Texas, in 1944 and claimed dual citizenship in the United States and Mexico. At 6 feet tall and 200 pounds, the portly Abrego was an imposing figure, with brown eyes and brown hair. The cartel began to operate from the early 1980s. García was its chief up to and into the time of his eventual capture in the mid-1990s. It was estimated by U.S. officials that he was paying $50 million a month in bribes and was notorious for ordering killings on the 17th

of each month. He was also known by a host of pseudonyms, including the Doll, the Lord, the Engineer, the Director, the Patient One, the Man, and the Boss.

The U.S. investigation of Juan García Abrego began in 1986. The case broke wide open when "Claude de la O," who posed as a corrupt Federal Bureau of Investigation (FBI) agent, took payoffs as high as $100,000 from García Abrego. It was by using Claude de la O's observations and taped conversations that law enforcement was able to build a case against him.

He was eventually indicted in the United States in Dallas, Texas, in 1990 and was again indicted in Houston, Texas, in 1993. In early 1995 he was placed on the Top Ten Wanted List of the FBI, the first international drug trafficker to be placed on the list. He was eventually apprehended in Monterrey, Mexico, on January 14, 1996, by Mexican authorities and was expelled to the United States to face charges. Many Mexican citizens were upset by García's swift extradition, pointing out that the government failed to address the number of Mexican citizens who had been murdered or shaken down by the Mexican drug kingpin, or about the Mexican political corruption that was seemingly so vast, according to U.S. officials.

Juan Antonio Ortiz, a member of the Gulf cartel who worked for Juan García Abrego, testified during the trial in Houston that he organized the transportation of 10 tons of cocaine over the U.S.-Mexico border during a period of several years. Juan Antonio Ortiz confirmed that the Gulf cartel had in fact bribed officials at all levels of the Mexican government, including its highest reaches.

Juan García Abrego was convicted of drug-trafficking charges in October 1996 in a Houston, Texas, court and is currently serving 11 life sentences in a U.S. jail for his drug trafficking.

At the time of the trial, it was estimated that the cartel smuggled more than 15 tons of cocaine and 23 tons of marijuana from Mexico into the United States. It was also estimated that García personally laundered about $10.5 million in drug money in the United States. The U.S. government estimates that he made more than $1.05 billion in his lifetime from the sales of drugs into the United States. However, a U.S. jury awarded the government only $350 million from his personal fortune.

See also: GARCÍA ABREGO, HUMBERTO; GULF CARTEL.

Juan García Abrego, leader of the Gulf cartel, is escorted out of FBI headquarters in Houston in 1996 after being arrested in Mexico and deported to the United States. (AP)

GENDLER, Lev

Lev Gendler's criminal history included arrests in the United States and Israel for counterfeiting, extortion, kidnapping, and bank fraud. He was connected to the Russian Mafiya. Gendler was found dead in his apartment on March 23, 1993. He had been shot numerous times in the head and body.

See also: RUSSIAN MAFIYA.

Reference

New Jersey State Commission of Investigation, New York Organized Crime Task Force, New York State Commission of Investigation, Pennsylvania Crime Commission, with Rutgers University. "The Tri-State Joint Soviet-Émigré Organized Crime Project." 1992. Available online. URL: http://www.state.nj.us/sci/pdf/russian.pdf. Accessed on November 24, 2004.

GENOVESE Crime Family

The Genovese crime family has been called the ivy league of organized crime. They are presently the strongest and richest Mafia family in the United States with an estimated membership of about 200. The family's first don was Charles "Lucky" Luciano.

The most powerful and wealthy crime family in the New York area and perhaps the entire country, the Genovese family maintains major stakes in narcotics, loan-sharking, extortion rackets, pornography, labor-union racketeering, restaurants, seafood distribution, and vending machines. They are known for doing everything quietly and for the reserved manner in which they conduct business. In December 2001 34 Genovese mobsters were indicted when an undercover agent penetrated their organization.

The current boss is Vincent "the Chin" Gigante, who was arraigned in 1996 on federal murder, labor-racketeering, and other charges. Gigante is serving a 12-year sentence in a Fort Worth, Texas, prison hospital. He has reputedly delegated many duties but still maintains control of the organization.

The current acting bosses are Ernie Muscarella and Dominick "Quiet Dom" Cirillo. The family's consigliere is allegedly James "Jimmy" Ida.

See also: BONANNO CRIME FAMILY; COLOMBO CRIME FAMILY; COMMISSION, THE; GAMBINO CRIME FAMILY; LUCCHESE CRIME FAMILY.

Reference

David Amoruso. "Genovese Crime Family." Gangsters Incorporated. Available online. URL: http://gangstersinc. tripod.com/Gen.html. Downloaded on July 19, 2004.

—D.A.

GENYOSHA (a.k.a. Dark Ocean Society; Black Ocean Society)

The Genyosha dates as far back as 1881 when various samurai societies, left out of the administration or regime of boy emperor Mutsuhito (Meiji), banded together. These *ronin,* or masterless samurai, felt that the power around the emperor was too western minded, bent on modernization in what was still feudal Japan.

Genyosha means the "Black Ocean Society," which took its name from the Genaki Nada strait (the strait of the Black Ocean) which separates Kyushu from the Korean Peninsula. They took this name because they intended to invade Korea (and then China) and place it under Japanese colonial rule. Eventually, the Korean invasion was called off by the palace, and the Samurai grew restless. In the immediate years afterward, the samurai pledged allegiance to the emperor, being of the samurai class. However, as the years went on, the society grew ideas of its own and often tried to blackmail or extort influential government officials when the society's political views were not met with approving administration acceptance.

The tide turned when Mitsru Toyama gained control of the Genyosha. His personal habits included intimidation and gambling. He frequented brothels and gambling houses and yet had many influential friends. He was constantly pursued by authorities but eluded or evaded capture.

Eventually, the Genyosha were turned into a gang that used their skill at violence on innocent people. They were used in breaking up miner strikes, and Toyama, who eventually grew rich by employing Genyosha in various schemes to make money, became wealthy. Genyosha members eventually became involved in gambling, prostitution, extortion, opium smuggling, and pornography operations.

In 1895 ninja-trained Genyosha slipped into the Korean palace and eventually killed the queen. This was at the behest of the Japanese minister of war. With Korea in turmoil, Japan invaded and would remain there for 50 years.

The Genyosha eventually were surpassed by the Black Dragon Society, founded by Toyama's right-hand man, Ryohei Uchida, as a quasi-government/Yakuza hybrid the government would use to infiltrate into other nefarious schemes, whether in politics or illegal businesses.

GHOST Shadows

Four New York City street-gang enforcers for the On Leong Tong make up the Ghost Shadows as a whole: the Mott Street Ghost Shadows, the Bayard Street faction, and the Ghost Shadows that run Baxter and upper Mott Street past Canal Street.

See also: CHAN, WING YOUNG; ON LEONG; TONGS.

Reference

Mark C. Gribben. "Moon Festival Shakedown." Reprinted by permission.

—*M.G.*

GIGANTE, Vincent (a.k.a. the Chin)

Vincent "the Chin" Gigante is one of the oddest gangsters: He is famous for wandering through the streets in his bathrobe and for mumbling and talking to himself. Some people said the ex-boxer just took one punch to the head too many and was clearly losing his sanity. But he was also suspected of faking, and, like all acts, this one, too, lost its audience, and from 1997 onward Gigante had a difficult time making people believe that he was not boss of the Genovese crime family.

Vincent Gigante was born in New York on March 29, 1928, and lived most of his life in the Greenwich Village area of lower Manhattan. Gigante started out fine in life. He completed ninth grade, then attended a vocational high school, but quit to work in a variety of odd jobs. He began to box in 1946. His career saw 24 fights and 23 wins; however, only one was by a knockout. After some bad fights Gigante called it quits and took to a life of crime.

He was classified 4F for military service "because of antisocial behavior." In 1950, he married Olympia Grippa, and they had five children. He also managed to find a mistress with the same first name, Olympia Esposito, and fathered three children by her. Gigante's rise to stardom came when he was chosen by his capo Tommy Eboli to go out and whack then Genovese family boss Frank Costello.

Gigante was not the most intelligent and capable mobster. He spent hours every day target shooting in a secure Greenwich Village basement, and when he was assigned a hit, Gigante should have done well, but he botched it. Gigante went up to Costello in a hotel lobby with a shotgun and shot him in the head. Gigante thought that he had done his job well and left Costello in a pool of blood, but the shot only grazed Costello. The hit took place because Vito Genovese wanted sole power over the family. Even though Costello was not killed in the hit, he still got the message and stepped down. After such a failed hit it was assumed that Gigante's time was up or that at least he would never attain any higher level than soldier.

Instead Gigante became a capo himself in the 1970s. In the early 1980s he moved up to consigliere status as the consigliere of Tony Salerno. In 1981 Genovese family boss Tony Salerno had a stroke and was hospitalized; he then retired to his farm for a six-month recuperation. On his return, however, it is suspected that the family appointed Gigante as boss. Salerno would serve as a front until he was put away in the Commission Case. Salerno eventually died of a stroke in July 1992.

With the arrest and conviction of Anthony Salerno, Vincent Gigante had to come out in the open. With no one to hide behind, Gigante continued a routine he had picked up early on in his criminal career—he acted as if he were crazy. In 1970, he first began to feign mental illness to beat a conspiracy rap. That year he was accused of bribing the police force of Old Tappan, New Jersey. Psychiatrists told the court that Gigante was a "paranoid schizophrenic, suffering from hallucinations." The bribery charges were eventually dropped. The success of this crazy act encouraged Gigante to use his mental frailty as a device to confuse, obfuscate, and elude the law. He entered St. Vincent's Psychiatric Hospital in Harrison, New York, 22 times voluntarily between 1969 and 1990. As he grew older, he became a familiar sight, wandering around the streets of Greenwich Village, a shabby, demented old man. Dressed in striped pajamas, slippers, and a royal blue robe, grinning and talking to himself and looking like an injured old bird. "God is my lawyer," he told a psychiatrist. "He will defend me."

His brother, the Rev. Louis Gigante, told reporters on one occasion, "Vincent is a paranoid schizophrenic. He hallucinates. He's been that way since 1968 or 1969. Look at the medication he takes each day." The reverend then showed a list that he said was his brother's daily intake: five milligrams of Valium, 100 milligrams of Thorazine, and 30 milligrams of Dalmane. When told that her son was being indicted for being the boss of the biggest, most powerful Cosa Nostra family in America, his then 88-year-old mother shouted, "Vincenzo? He is the boss of the toilet!" However, Tony Salerno said it best one time when he was caught on a Federal Bureau of Investigation (FBI) tape as saying: "If 'Chin' gets pinched, all those years in that fuckin' asylum would be for nothing."

At first his acting seemed to pay off. The FBI couldn't convict him though, when they arrested him in 1990, he was charged with 41 different racketeering and conspiracy charges. He would not be convicted until 1997 when he was 69 years old. As he was being closely monitored by the FBI, and guards, he sometimes stopped acting. He apparently looked after himself, made his own bed, shadowboxed in his cell, and despite his advancing years commanded respect from the other inmates. During one conversation with a prison guard, he was asked if other inmates were harassing him. "Gigante looked at me," the guard said, "and replied, 'Nobody fucks with me.'" Not a smart thing to do, especially not when his crazy act was working like it was. However, it was not Gigante's shadowboxing or his normal behavior that did him in: Several turncoat mobsters came to the courtroom to testify that Gigante was not crazy and that he in fact was boss of the Genovese crime family. After that, Gigante was found guilty and convicted. He is due to be released in 2007 when he will be 79.

On January 23, 2002, Gigante's son Andrew and six others were indicted. It became known inside that Gigante's son was his messenger and main guy, even though he was not a made guy. Gigante has, since his conviction, dropped the crazy man act and used his son and others to carry out his directives.

See also: PERSICO, CARMINE.

Reference

David Amoruso. "Vincent 'Chin' Gigante." Gangsters Incorporated. Available online. URL: http://gangstersinc. tripod.com/Gigante.html. Downloaded on July 19, 2004.

—D.A.

GOGA, Irfan

Irfan Goga was an internationally known organized criminal with a violent and successful past. He was at first a protégé and then partner to internationally infamous Mumbai master criminal Dawood Ibrahim (who is based in Karachi). Goga was from Azamgarh in Uttar Pradesh, also the native land of Dawood and career criminal Abu Salem. In his youth he moved to Mumbai but kept close ties to his homeland.

Goga was an enforcer and a hit man; he was also a master kidnapper and an extortionist. At Ibrahim's whim, Goga would easily, quickly and efficiently make Ibrahim's rivals disappear. He was known to be ruthless, and his victims never resurfaced. In his early years Goga's associate was Babloo Srivastava, an internationally known contract killer. Babloo killed Dawood's associate Mirza Dilshad Beg in Nepal in 1997. Goga tried to shield Babloo from Dawood's revenge. Dawood informed on Babloo to Interpol agents, who arrested Babloo, who eventually ended up in Naini jail in Allahabad.

Goga had become well connected in international organized-crime circles. He had at one point befriended the Kuala Lumpur–based Chhota Rajan, also a friend of Babloo. Rajan swore revenge on Dawood.

On November 9, 1998, Goga, who had hosted a card party for more than 31 people, left his Dubai home with Anis Abrahim, Dawood's brother, and another man. He told his wife he would be right back. No one ever saw him again.

See also: ANSARI, AFTAB; BAKSH, NOOR; IBRAHIM, DAWOOD; RAJAN, CHHOTA; SHAKEEL, CHHOTA; SINGH, SANJAY.

Reference

Batabyal, Somnath. "The Vanishing Act." *The Week,* December 6, 1998.

GOLDEN Crescent

Southwest Asia and Southeast Asia remained the principal regions of illicit poppy cultivation in the world, despite eradication of crops and crop-substitution programs carried out in these regions. The area in Southwest Asia, which includes the borders of Afghanistan and Pakistan, is known as the Golden Crescent.

In 1999, the total illegal production of opium was estimated to be 6,600 tons against 4,000 tons during 1998. The increase is attributed to the explosion in Southwest Asia of Afghan poppy crops (estimated to be 4,600 tons against 2,100 tons in 1998.)

See also: GOLDEN TRIANGLE; HEROIN.

GOLDEN Triangle

Southwest Asia and Southeast Asia remained the principal regions of illicit poppy cultivation in the world, despite eradication of crops and crop-substitution

Iranian armed villagers stand in formation in June 2001 in a village near the border with Afghanistan. Sandwiched in the "Golden Crescent" of drug trafficking between Afghanistan and Pakistan, Iran has become a major thoroughfare for drugs headed to Europe and the Gulf States. (AP)

programs carried out in these regions. The Southeast Asian region area is called the Golden Triangle. It is located where Myanmar, Thailand and Laos join. Myanmar remains the major opium producing country (the production is estimated to be approximately 1,500 tons) in this region.

In 1999 the total illegal production of opium was estimated to be 6,600 tons against 4,000 tons during 1998. Most of the extra production came from the Golden Crescent.

See also: GOLDEN CRESCENT; HEROIN.

GÓMEZ BUSTAMANTE, Luis Hernando

Luis Hernando Gómez Bustamante (a.k.a. "Rasguno") is a major North Valle trafficker closely aligned with the Henao Montoya brothers. Although they have worked together for decades, Gómez Bustamente runs a separate and distinct criminal organization. He owns cocaine-hydrochloride conversion laboratories in the Valle Del Cauca region, many of which are concealed on his farms. He also is involved in smuggling cocaine via aircraft to the United States where he is wanted on drug-trafficking charges.

See also: HENAO MONTOYA, ARCÁNGEL DE JESÚS AND JOSÉ ORLANDO.

Reference

Thomas A. Constantine. "International Organized Crime Syndicates and Their Impact on the U.S." U.S. Drug Enforcement Administration. Available online. URL: http://www.dea.gov/pubs/cngrtest/ct980226.htm. Downloaded on July 15, 2004.

GÓMEZ PATINO, Denis

Denis Gómez Patino has been involved in the transportation of cocaine base from Bolivia and Peru to Colombia for decades. Since the arrest of the Rodríguez Orejuela brothers, he has aligned himself with the Henao Montoya brothers and emerged as a major trafficker in his own right.

See also: HENAO MONTOYA, ARCÁNGEL DE JESÚS AND JOSÉ ORLANDO; NORTHERN VALLE ORGANIZATION; RODRÍGUEZ GOREJULA, MIGUEL ANGEL.

Reference

Thomas A. Constantine. "International Organized Crime Syndicates and Their Impact on the U.S." U.S. Drug Enforcement Administration. Available online. URL: http://www.dea.gov/pubs/cngrtest/ct980226.htm. Downloaded on July 15, 2004.

GONZÁLEZ QUIRARTE, Eduardo

Eduardo González Quirarte has been identified as a key manager for the Carrillo Fuentes organization along the border. He is responsible for arranging shipments of cocaine across the border and ensuring that money is transferred back into Mexico. He has links to the Mexican military and law enforcement officials which may make him a significant leader in future Carrillo Fuentes operations.

See also: CARRILLO FUENTES, AMADO; JUÁREZ CARTEL.

Reference

Thomas A. Constantine. "International Organized Crime Syndicates and Their Impact on the U.S." U.S. Drug Enforcement Agency. Available online. URL: http://www.dea.gov/pubs/cngrtest/ct980226.htm. Downloaded on July 15, 2004.

GOTTI, John (a.k.a. the Dapper Don; the Teflon Don)

John Gotti was born October 27, 1940, in the Bronx, New York. When Gotti was 12, he and his family moved to a rough neighborhood in Brooklyn where Gotti took to the streets more and dropped out of school in the eighth grade. Gotti became involved with gangs, committed several small crimes, and eventually started to move up in the underworld. By 1966 he had hooked up with the Gambino crime family. Gotti's specialty was hijacking trucks; he made plenty of money for the Gambinos by hijacking freight from Kennedy Airport. As he moved up in stature inside the Gambino family, he became close to Gambino underboss Neil Dellacroce. It became

clear Gotti was going places, but before he continued his ascent he was arrested in 1969 for a hijacking and sentenced to three years in prison.

When he was released, Gotti continued his life of crime and decided that it was time to take some more steps forward. In 1973 he took on the contract of James McBratney, alleged killer of Carlo Gambino's nephew. After the killing the police closed in on Gotti again. Present at the murder had been two eyewitnesses. Gotti was arrested, but he somehow managed to have the charge against him reduced to second-degree manslaughter and served only two years in prison. While serving his time inside, serious changes took place within the Gambino family outside. Carlo Gambino was on his deathbed and appointed Paul Castellano as his successor. Gotti supported his mentor Neil Dellacroce for the top job and was angered to see the job go to Castellano. That anger would never die down and would be one of the ingredients that would fuel Gotti's drive to power.

When Gotti was released from prison, he went back to work. Already unhappy with Castellano, Gotti experienced tragedy in 1980 when his son Frank died in a car accident. Frank was driving his bike when a Gotti neighbor drove his car down the street and hit the boy. Frank died, and the neighbor was considered a dead man. After receiving several threats via mail and phone and one time being attacked by Gotti's wife with a baseball bat, Gotti's neighbor decided to move. But before he could occupy his new home, a van filled with Gotti goons pulled him off the street. He was never seen again. At the time of this murder, Gotti and his wife were in Florida. Gotti was never charged with the killing.

Throughout the '80s Gotti moved up within the Gambino crime family, eventually becoming capo. Gotti still only saw one man as the rightful boss of the Gambino family, Neil Dellacroce. Under the protection of Dellacroce, Gotti ran his narcotics trade with his crew. Castellano knew about it and wanted it to stop. He wanted to demote Gotti or have him murdered, but Dellacroce always kept the peace. On the other side Gotti wanted Dellacroce to step up and demand his position as boss, but Dellacroce again kept the peace and told Gotti to keep quiet.

In 1985 things came to a boiling point. Castellano was indicted in the Commission Case in which wiretap evidence from bugs from within the Castellano mansion were used. Members of Gotti's crew were indicted on narcotics trafficking. Castellano wanted evidence about the narcotics trafficking so he could have Gotti's crew killed or disbanded and demoted, but Dellacroce kept stalling for time. Gotti on the other hand started to say that Castellano might flip under the Federal Bureau of Investigation (FBI) pressure and that he should be murdered. Dellacroce kept the two sides from hitting each other, but when he died in 1985, it became clear that the hit on Gotti or Castellano was near.

Gotti acted first and won support from the other capos in the Gambino crime family. He also received support from three of the four other New York families. Gotti assembled a hit team and on December 16, 1985, Castellano and his new underboss Tommy Bilotti were gunned down in front of Sparks Steak House in Manhattan. After this, Gotti became the new boss of the Gambino family.

Running his empire from the Ravenite Social Club, Gotti made clear that he was not a low-profile gangster. At his trials he did not shun the media: He showed up wearing flashy $2,000 suits and smiled for the cameras. After winning several trials (one thanks to a bribe by his underboss Salvatore Gravano), Gotti became a media icon. He got nicknamed the "Teflon Don" and the "Dapper Don." He was on the cover of *Time* magazine.

While conducting his business out of his social club, Gotti wanted all his employees to come by to pay their respects. When asked if that would bring unwanted attention from the feds, he answered "What's weird, just some Italians getting together; it's our tradition." So it went ahead. People who did not show ended up dead or had some serious explaining to do; the ones who showed had their picture taken by the FBI.

After several years of observing and listening (the FBI eventually bugged the whole Ravenite building and taped Gotti's conversations), the feds moved on Gotti for the final blow. He was indicted and told that they had him on tape. When Gravano heard Gotti badmouth him on one of the tapes, it pushed him to testify against Gotti. With the evidence from the bugs and the photos and the testimony of Gravano, Gotti's fate was sealed and on April 2, 1992, he was convicted on charges that included five murders and was sentenced to life in prison without parole. In prison Gotti did heavy time, he spent more than nine years in 23-hour lockdown; several years into his sentence, he contracted cancer. Gotti however kept fighting—the cancer, the system, and the

feds. On June 10, 2002, Gotti died of cancer. A big funeral was held in New York attended by about 130 members of the Gambino crime family and his personal family and friends.

See also: CASTELLANO, PAUL; D'ARCO, ALPHONSE; GAMBINO, CARLO; GRAVANO, SALVATORE.

Reference
David Amoruso. "John 'The Dapper Don' Gotti." Gangsters Incorporated. Available online. URL: http://gangstersinc. tripod.com/ John.html. Downloaded on July 19, 2004.

—*D.A.*

GRAJALES-LEMOS (a.k.a. Grajales-Posso Organization)

One of the five major gangs that went on to comprise the Cali cartel. Other member organizations are: the Rodríguez Orejuela brothers; José Santa Cruz Londono (deceased); Helmer Herrera Buitrago; and the Urdinola Grajales brothers.

See also: CALI CARTEL.

GRAVANO, Salvatore (a.k.a. Sammy the Bull)

Sammy "the Bull" Gravano has gone down in Mafia history as the underworld's most well-known informant. He is also the most notorious cooperator in the Federal Witness Protection program. Sammy is despised by everyone on both sides of the law for the same reason: He double-crossed them.

Salvatore Gravano was born on March 12, 1945, the last of five children born to his parents, who were both from Sicily. The Gravano family lived on 78th Street in the Bensonhurst section of Brooklyn, New York. Both of his parents were honest, hard-working Americans, but Gravano went in a different direction. At school Gravano had enormous trouble with reading and learning the material. It was later determined that he was dyslexic. As a result of his slow learning Gravano became the kid in the class who everybody made fun of, until he decided to use violence to shut them up. Once when he had a fight with two older kids, there were two neighborhood wiseguys standing near observing the tussle. Gravano was a small kid who took on older and bigger kids, so the wiseguys gave him the nickname "the Bull" because of his looks and the way he fought. Pretty soon Gravano started with gang life and ran into trouble with the New York Police Department.

As a teenager Sammy got involved with the Rampers gang. He also picked up boxing and body building. The Rampers committed burglaries and stole cars. As time passed Gravano became more violent: He was involved in a shootout and not long after that was arrested for assaulting a police officer. Thanks to a good lawyer Gravano walked, but he was soon back in court, arrested on a burglary charge. The judge gave Gravano the choice: Enlist with the army or go to prison. Gravano chose the army, thinking that he would not be drafted, but he was wrong and was inducted into service at Fort Jackson, South Carolina. When Gravano was discharged, he went back to his Rampers gang and trouble again: While stealing a car with a Ramper pal, Gravano was caught by the owner, who pulled his gun and fired shots at the two gang members. Gravano was hit by the side of the head but survived.

Gravano, now 23, had proven skills and moxie and was ready for the next phase of his career. Wanting to be successful in crime, he decided to join the Mafia. After a short talk with Thomas "Shorty" Spero, Gravano decided to work for the Colombo crime family. He opened a club of his own in Bensonhurst and started a loan-sharking business soon after. A percentage of the money was kicked upstairs to the family bosses who protected him. Gravano was doing well and making money for the Colombo crime family when he received the order to murder Joseph Colucci a member of Shorty Spero's crew. In his book Gravano details the hit: "Joe Colucci was going to die. I was going to kill him because he was plotting to kill me. I felt the rage inside me. . . . Even if I wasn't directly behind him, I felt invisible. I pointed the gun at the back of his head. Everything went in slow motion. I could almost feel the bullet leaving the gun and entering his skull. It was strange. I didn't hear the first shot. I didn't see any blood. His head didn't seem to move, like it was a blank instead of a real bullet. I knew I couldn't have missed, the gun was only inches from his head, but I felt like I was a million miles away, like this was all a dream. . . . I shot a second time in the same spot. This time everything was different. I saw the flash. I smelt the gunpowder. The noise was deafening. Now I saw his head jerk back, his body convulse and slip sideways. I saw the blood. Joe Colucci was dead. He looked like he was sleeping. He looked peaceful. You going to blow me away now? I thought." This was

Gravano's first murder; 18 followed on his road to Mafia history.

After some problems with the Colombos, Gravano was transferred to the Gambino crime family and put under the wing of Salvatore "Toddo" Aurello, a capo in that family. After a period with the Gambinos, Gravano took one last shot at life the legit and honest way: He went into the construction business and did pretty well until he was indicted for murder. Gravano had nothing to do with the murder, but a man he knew had tied him to it, and so Gravano was indicted. The costs of the lawyer were too high for Gravano to pay, and so Gravano quit his construction job, and he and a friend (also indicted in the case) went on a robbing rampage for a year and a half. He also reconnected with the Gambino crime family. Gravano survived the case. He was acquitted, but his life was now definitely pointed in one direction: to become a Mafioso.

His capo Aurello proposed him for membership and in about 1975 Gravano became a made guy in the Gambino crime family. Gravano soon found himself in a great position. As his involvement in construction grew, Aurello told Gravano to take all construction dealings directly to the boss. The boss at the time was Paul Castellano, and Castellano always had more interest in construction. This put Sammy in a nice place. As the years went on Gravano moved toward becoming acting capo of Toddo Aurello's crew. He was doing well, but he too saw that all was not well in the Gambino family. Ever since Carlo Gambino appointed Castellano as new boss instead of the more streetwise Dellacroce, the Gambino family had been divided. Castellano knew this, but did not care and chose to ignore it. His underlings had mixed feelings about their boss: He was smart and ran the family well financially, but he was not a gangster, and he did not show any respect for his soldiers who did the work. After a while things reached a boiling point. The only thing keeping Castellano alive was Neil Dellacroce, his underboss.

Neil Dellacroce had a protégé named John Gotti. Gotti already had expressed his feelings about Castellano, but Dellacroce managed to keep him quiet. Until he died. Gotti had already been acting capo for Dellacroce's crew, but now things would change. Castellano did not like Gotti and could have had him demoted or killed for drug dealing. Now that Dellacroce was gone, Gotti had plans of his own, and when Castellano failed to show at Dellacroce's wake and pay his respects, his fate was sealed. Gotti had already been reaching out throughout the family for support to murder Castellano and had enough backup. When Gravano was asked to join, he decided to go along with the hit and helped plan it. So the hit on Castellano went through, and Castellano and his underboss Bilotti were both assassinated on the streets of New York. The hit put John Gotti in the position of boss and Gravano close to the power.

During Gotti's reign Toddo Aurello decided to step down, and Gravano became official capo. Since the hit on the boss was against Mafia rules and one family, the Genovese, was not included in the preparations, Gotti and friends still had to watch their steps. Gigante, boss of the Genoveses, was a friend of Castellano and did not like the new boss. He would take revenge for his dead ally. Gotti's underboss and Gravano's friend Frank DeCicco was killed by a car bomb. Gotti was supposed to be killed as well but did not attend the meeting, so only DeCicco was blown up. DeCicco's death left a position open, and Gotti appointed Gravano and Ruggiero as underbosses. Under Gotti the Gambino family came under enormous pressure from the Federal Bureau of Investigation (FBI) and it would not be long before Gotti would go down.

In September 1986 Gotti was in court, fighting the federal government, and won. It was not because of his lawyer but because Gravano got to the jury pool and managed to bribe one of them. As time passed Gravano became more successful in his legitimate businesses. He could sense some jealousy from John Gotti, despite the fact that Sammy claimed he was kicking up $2 million a year to him from his dealings with the Teamsters alone. At this point, 1986 or 1987, while Gotti was actually out of prison for a few years, Gravano was named official consigliere, and Frank Locascio became acting underboss of the family. Life under Gotti was faster than it ever was for Gravano. Before Gotti, Gravano had murdered eight people in 14 years. Under Gotti he killed 11 people in six years. Between November 30, 1989, and January 24, 1990, Gotti would spill enough of the family's secrets to finally bring the walls crashing down.

In January 1990 Gotti went to trial for ordering an assault on carpenter's union boss John O'Connor; on February 9, 1990, he was acquitted. Overnight the Dapper Don had become the Teflon Don, and his ego would grow even bigger. But the federal government had one more case up its sleeve. The feds had

Gotti's headquarters bugged and had him on tape discussing hits, his people, and his organization. They even had him on tape bad-mouthing Gravano.

When Gravano heard the tapes of Gotti bad-mouthing him, he almost surrendered to the FBI. But he had second thoughts until he learned that Gotti wanted to let him take the fall for the rash of murders by claiming that Gravano had run wild and murdered people on his own accord. Then the Bull decided to testify against Gotti. He turned to the FBI and told them all they wanted to know. He would send Gotti to prison for life. Scores of other mobsters went to prison because of Gravano's testimony, and he was granted a deal for turning over the evidence. He got a second life.

After serving minimal time for 19 murders, Gravano was released, went into the Witness Protection Program, and started his new life in Arizona. Most people on both sides of the law would give a lot to have the second chance that Sammy did, but Gravano thought nothing of it and was not satisfied. He wanted more, and so he started his own Ecstasy organization with the help of his son, his wife, his daughter, and a local Nazi organization known as the Devil Dogs. Together they ruled the Arizona drug trade. Life was great for Gravano—he got away with 19 murders, he escaped Gotti's hit men, and his own drug organization was raking in more than $200,000 a year. But then the bubble burst.

On February 24, 2000, Gravano, his wife, his son, his daughter, and his son-in-law were arrested on drug charges by Arizona authorities. Ten months later, federal prosecutors in Brooklyn charged Gravano and his son Gerard with buying thousands of Ecstasy tablets in Brooklyn for distribution in Arizona. On May 25, 2001, two weeks before his federal drug-trafficking trial was set to begin, Gravano and Gerard pleaded guilty to drug-conspiracy charges that carry about 12 years in prison, according to federal sentencing guidelines. Their prison terms will be concurrent—served at the same time—as whatever sentences they ultimately receive for their crimes in Arizona.

See also: CASTELLANO, PAUL; D'ARCO, ALPHONSE; GAMBINO, CARLO; GOTTI, JOHN.

Reference

David Amoruso. "Salvatore 'Sammy the Bull' Gravano." Gangsters Incorporated. Available online. URL: http://gangstersinc.tripod.com/Gravano.html. Downloaded on July 19, 2004.

—D.A.

GREAT Circle Triad

The Great Circle Triad is one of the great six triads that have existed in China for hundreds of years. However, while most have been based in Hong Kong and Taiwan, the Great Circle Triad has always been in Shanghai. Few other triad societies have bothered with Shanghai through the years, but with the explosive growth of China in the last two decades, Shanghai has become an economic giant. This has led to other triad societies making attempts to set up shop in this ancient Chinese city. Officials speculate that much gangland violence is in store for the burgeoning city.

GRECO, Luigi

Luigi Greco, along with his family, emigrated to Canada at a young age and settled in the port city of Montreal. The Sicilian-native refused the new society's laws and regulations and turned to crime to make a living. He became involved in everything from auto theft to bank robbery and served a 13-year prison sentence for armed robbery.

Harry Davis, the biggest drug trafficker in the city at the time, saw Greco's potential and hired him as a bodyguard. He moved up quickly to become one of the trafficker's top men, and when Davis was murdered in 1946, the Sicilian took over many of his rackets. He then hooked up with the Cotroni organization and soon ran the entire west side of the city for the group.

Greco and his partner, Frank Petrula, traveled to Italy in 1951 to meet Charles "Lucky" Luciano and then to New York City to visit Frank Costello, known as the Prime Minister of La Cosa Nostra. The Montrealers wanted to make the port city the heroin smuggling center of North America.

The Sicilian's position in the Montreal underworld rose again and, by the time Bonanno family underboss Carmine "Lilo" Galante arrived, Greco was the number-two man in the organization. Only Calabrian-born Vic "the Egg" Cotroni held more sway. The second-in-command ran his empire from his pizzeria, where he still performed many of the day-to-day chores. He was highly active in gambling, loan sharking, extortion, and drug trafficking and had an entourage of impressive criminal talent, including future Hamilton mob boss "Johnny Pops" Papalia. He was a major financial backer of Giuseppe "Pep" Cotroni's lucrative drug network and was also a partner in the Alpha Investment Corporation with Vic Cotroni, Carmine Galante, Frank Petrula, Max Shapiro, and Harry Ship.

Luigi Greco and Giuseppe Cotroni attended the Appalachin Mafia meeting on November 14, 1957, representing Montreal's interests. They were among the fortunate to avoid embarrassment when police raided the conference. Sixty mobsters were nabbed however, leading to an unprecedented amount of police pressure on U.S. crime families.

In March 1972 Greco suffered a $200,000 loss when British Customs officials seized 3,395 pounds of hashish at the Manchester port. Police in Montreal and Lebanon followed the seizure with 12 arrests. But Greco, who had reportedly financed the shipment, remained unscathed.

Luigi Greco was killed in a horrific accident on December 7, 1972. As he and workers were busily replacing the floor of his pizzeria, a solvent caught fire and he was fatally burned. The funeral attracted an impressive gathering of underworld figures who rushed to pay their respects to the old-school Mafioso.

Reference

Gary Francoeur. "Luigi Greco." WiseguyWally. Available online. URL: http://www.geocities.com/wiseguywally/LuigiGreco.html. Downloaded on July 19, 2004.

—G.F.

GREEN Pang

A Hong Kong triad.

See also: TRIADS.

GRIPALDI, Peter

Peter Gripaldi was a reputed California "hit man" when he arrived in New York City some time in early June 1993. He had worked for U.S.-based crime organizations as well as having ties to international organized crime. On June 10, 1993, Gripaldi entered the store of Michael Libkin. Gripaldi spoke briefly with Libkin, removed a silencer-equipped, automatic handgun from his briefcase, and shot Libkin in the groin.

After a struggle, Libkin took out his own gun, followed Gripaldi out of the store, and shot him in the chest. Both men were taken to Bellevue Hospital and released a few days later. Gripaldi was later convicted for this shooting on the basis of an indictment filed by the Manhattan District Attorney. He has been in prison since that time.

GUADALAJARA Cartel

The Amezcua-Contreras brothers, operating out of Guadalajara, Mexico, allegedly head a methamphetamine production-and-trafficking organization with global dimensions. Directed by Jesús Amezcua and supported by his brothers, Adán and Luis, the Amezcua organization is probably the largest smuggler of ephedrine and clandestine producer of methamphetamine in the world today. Adán was recently arrested in Mexico, on weapons charges. José Osorio-Cabrera, a fugitive from a Los Angeles investigation until his arrest in Bangkok, was a major ephedrine purchaser for the Amezcua organization. The Amezcua organization is said to obtain large quantities of the precursor ephedrine, utilizing contacts in Thailand and India, which they supply to methamphetamine labs in Mexico and the United States.

Authorities believe that this organization has placed trusted associates in the United States to move ephedrine to Mexican methamphetamine traffickers operating there. Amezcua-connected groups are now operating in California, Texas, Georgia, Oklahoma, Iowa, Arkansas, and North Carolina.

The Amezcuas' involvement in the U.S. methamphetamine trade was exemplified by a recently concluded Drug Enforcement Administration (DEA) multidistrict wiretap investigation that targeted a significant U.S. methamphetamine organization. The investigation, which concluded in December 1997, proved that the domestic organization had links to the Amezcua-Contreras organization in Mexico. The Amezcua organization supplied the U.S. elements of the organization not only with methamphetamine and precursor chemicals but also with some of their cocaine. The Amezcuas' precursor chemicals came from Colima, Mexico. Associates of the Amezcua organization were also involved in producing methamphetamine in Los Angeles, California.

This investigation resulted in the arrest of 101 defendants, seizure of 133 pounds of methamphetamine, dismantlement of three methamphetamine laboratories, seizure of 90 gallons of methamphetamine solution (which converts to 270–540 pounds of methamphetamine), 1,100 kilograms of cocaine, and assets totaling more than $2.25 million. One of the seized laboratories was operating within 200 yards of a day-care center and a private school; the other was located almost in the middle of an equestrian center in Acton, California. These laboratories' estimated production capabilities exceeded 300 pounds of methamphetamine. Showing a blatant disregard for public safety, the individuals responsible for the production and manufacturing of the methamphetamine fled the area but continued the potentially dangerous cooking process.

See also: AMEZCUA-CONTRERAS, JESÚS.

Reference

Thomas A. Constantine. "International Organized Crime Syndicates and Their Impact on the U.S." U.S. Drug Enforcement Administration. Available online. URL: http://www.dea.gov/pubs/cngrtest/ct980226.htm. Downloaded on July 15, 2004.

GUERINI, Antoine

The leader of the Corsican Mafia clan known as the Guerini family, which was influential in running heroin in and out of Marseilles, Antoine Guerini was reported to have offered a contract to Christian David (international assassin and well-known French heroin smuggler, as well as sometime employee of several different intelligence agencies) to assassinate President John F. Kennedy. Allegedly he did this at the behest of Clay Shaw and others, who approached him. While it seems plausible, it is not likely. However, the Guerini family had ties to the Central Intelligence Agency dating back to the Office of Strategic Services in World War II.

Reference

Salvador, Astucia. "Opium Lords: Israel, the Golden Triangle, and the Kennedy Assassination." Available online. URL: http://www.jfkmontreal.com. Posted in April 2002.

GULF Cartel

The Gulf cartel operates on both sides of the U.S.-Mexican border and is centered in Matamoros, Tamaulipas, Mexico and more recently in Monterrey, Nuevo-Leon, Mexico. It is recognized by law enforcement authorities in the United States and in Mexico as one of the most powerful drug trafficking organizations in Mexico and derives its power from the use of violence and bribery. Once the drugs cross the border, the organization has distribution cells throughout the United States, including San Antonio, Houston, and New York, and is

Former Gulf cartel chief Juan García Abrego (standing), with his predecessor, Juan Nepomuceno Guerra (left), García Abrego's uncle (AP/Reforma)

known to have had elements in Dallas, Chicago, New Orleans, Oklahoma City, Milwaukee, and Seattle, as well as cities in California, Nevada, Arizona, Alabama, Georgia, and Florida. It was estimated that the Gulf cartel annually earned more than $20 billion a year in its heyday from smuggling cocaine into the United States.

A Drug Enforcement Administration background information statement issued in February 1997 stated that it "received information that this group had smuggled cocaine into the United States in excess of 30 metric tons with a street value of hundreds of millions of dollars."

Once led by longtime chief Juan García Abrego, the Gulf cartel was eventually taken over by Oscar Malherbe de León, a well-known brutal enforcer and hit man, but he was eventually apprehended as well.

See also: GARCÍA ABREGO, HUMBERTO; GARCÍA ABREGO, JUAN.

References

Maria Celia Toro. "The Internationalization of Police: The DEA in Mexico." Indiana University. Available online. URL: http//www.indiana.edu/~jah/mexico/mtoro.html. Downloaded on July 19, 2004.

Murder and Money in Mexico. Public Broadcasting Service. Color. 57 minutes, 2000.

GYPSY Jokers

Located in Australia and New Zealand, the Gypsy Jokers are an outlaw motorcycle gang that is considered extremely dangerous. The have allegedly been known to pull off car bombings, bombings of businesses, and are thought to be involved in other illegal activities. Violence is their calling card. Their more outrageous actions in the last few years, especially the car bombing that also destroyed a local tavern in Perth in retaliation for the murder of one of their members, have drawn the ire of the public and the unwanted attention of the authorities.

HAMEL, Normand (a.k.a. Biff)

Normand Hamel, called Biff by criminal associates, was born in the mid-1950s. He hooked up with the Montreal based SS motorcycle gang in the 1970s and remained a member, along with Maurice "Mom" Boucher and Salvatore Cazzetta, until the group's dissolution in 1984.

He became a prospect for the Hells Angels' Laval-based North chapter, but the North chapter was targeted for death by the rest of the Quebec Angels, and Hamel was present at the March 24, 1985, execution of five North chapter members in Lennoxville. Members held Hamel and prospect Claude "Coco" Roy at gunpoint as their comrades were slaughtered inside.

"Biff" Hamel received his colors—as did Maurice Boucher—days after Death Riders president Martin Huneault was shot to death in a Laval bar on May 4, 1987. It is strongly believed by law enforcement that Hamel and Boucher were behind the Huneault murder and that their reward for it all was their colors.

Hamel would eventually become godfather of the Death Riders gang, nearly 10 years after his induction into the club. He was given the position after Hells Angel Scott Steinert's brutal murder on November 4, 1997. He now supervised the gang's narcotics and prostitution networks in Laval and the lower Laurentians.

His power and influence in the organization continued to grow, and on June 24, 1995, Hamel became one of the nine founding members of the gang's elite Nomads chapter. He was considered by many to be the right-hand man of Maurice "Mom" Boucher, leader of the Nomads.

On April 17, 2000, "Biff" Hamel drove his wife and son to a pediatrician's office on St.-Martin Boulevard in Laval. As he left the building, two armed men chased him through the parking lot and shot him several times. He was pronounced dead on arrival at the hospital. Hamel had ignored months of police warning that the Rock Machine had targeted members of the Nomads chapter. He was 44 years old.

See also: HELLS ANGELS.

Reference

Gary Francoeur. "Normand 'Biff' Hamel." Wiseguy-Wally. Available online. URL: http://www.geocities.com/wiseguywally/NormandHamel.html. Downloaded on July 19, 2004.

—G.F.

HAWALA Banking Scheme

Two Indian nationals pled guilty to the structuring of 39 separate transactions totaling nearly $5 million, through corporate accounts utilizing the "Hawala," or underground banking system. In addition, one defendant pled guilty to conspiracy to launder at least $100,000 in currency from narcotic sales. The defendants were sentenced to 37 and 21 months in prison, respectively, fined $125,000 each, and ordered to forfeit $135,772 to the government. The foundation of the Hawala system is a worldwide extended family that consists of extensive Indian and Pakistani networks spread throughout Europe and the Middle East, as well as south Asia. Historically used as a foreign-worker remittance system, the system has been used in recent times to evade taxes, circumvent currency-exchange restrictions, and launder monies from illegal business.

The case originated with a tip from a local bank which indicated that a number of suspicious currency deposits were being made into two corporate accounts. The investigation revealed that the two defendants had been utilizing a number of personal bank accounts to move currency. However, they had recently switched to corporate accounts after banking authorities had questioned their banking activity. The defendants would transfer monies between the United States and India without regard to the source of the funds. The unique aspect of the case was the method in which funds were transferred to India. Monies were given to the defendants in increments greater than $10,000. These funds were then "structured" into their bank accounts in amounts less than $10,000. A facsimile would be transmitted to India, bearing the names and addresses of the persons in India who were to receive the monies. Their respective counterparts in India would then arrange the delivery of the requisite amount of rupees to the designated individuals. On occasion the defendants periodically would wire-transfer the deposited monies to one of any number of accounts located in Hong Kong or Singapore. Once these transfers were made, individuals would travel from India to Hong Kong or Singapore, withdraw the funds in currency, and purchase gold. The gold was smuggled back into India, where it would be sold on the black market for a substantial profit.

Reference

International Narcotics Control Strategy Report, 1996. Washington, D.C.: U.S. Department of State, 1997.

HEAVEN and Earth Society

The Heaven and Earth Society began in the Fujian province of China, as an "antidynastic secret society," so named by 19th-century Western experts on the regions, according to the *Columbia Encyclopedia, 6th Edition.* The Heaven and Earth Society (*Taendi hui*) was made up mostly of the samurai class in the 17th

century. Their goal was to remove or bring an end to the Manchu Ch'ing dynasty "and to restore the native Chine Ming dynasty." The triad societies today claim that many of the members of the Heaven and Earth Society and similar types of secret societies went on to form the original triad societies. They claim this as their heritage. However it is important to note that the Heaven and Earth Society was the refuge of numerous misplaced or masterless samurai (*ronin*) who held similar political views, and it was both a patriotic and a political membership, not involved originally in organized crime. However, the organization, since it was dedicated to the overthrow of the then-current emperor, was considered subversive by Chinese bureaucrats of the day.

See also: TRIADS.

Reference

Columbia Encyclopedia. 6th Edition. New York: Columbia University Press, 2002.

HELLS Angels

The Canadian version of this well-known motorcycle gang is known to be just as raucous and violent as its American cousin. Many members have died violent deaths and been convicted of crimes ranging from weapons possession to drug trafficking to murder.

HELLS ANGELS MONTREAL CHAPTER

The Hells Angels Montreal chapter, based in Sorel, is Canada's first Hells Angels chapter. The gang, originally known as the Popeyes, participated in a brutal war with the Satan's Choice and Devil's Disciples over drug territory before officially becoming Hells Angels on December 5, 1977.

The Montreal chapter is largely responsible for the organization's current success in Quebec. The Hells Angels expanded its influence across the province in the early '80s and approached several biker gangs. A few would eventually become Hells Angels chapters, and others would remain under the gang's control.

The Hells Angels, with the help of its puppet clubs, continues to be a dominant force in the Montreal underworld. The gang derives millions of dollars a year from illegal activities, mostly drugs and prostitution.

HELLS ANGELS NOMADS CHAPTER

Nine well-respected and dedicated Hells Angels formed the Nomads chapter on June 24, 1995. The

Fortified bunker of the Hells Angels biker gang, Trois-Rivières, Quebec, Canada (AP/CP)

founding members consisted of former members of the Montreal, Trois-Rivières, and Halifax chapters. The faction was the gang's fifth established Quebec chapter and considered by police to consist of the club's elite members.

Unlike the other Hells Angels chapters, the Nomads were not bound to any clubhouse, making it much more difficult for enemies and police to track their actions. The Canadian government has failed, despite numerous convictions, to stop the Nomads from successfully invading Ontario and establishing numerous Hells Angels chapters there. The chapter was decimated in 2001, when police jailed all of its members.

HELLS ANGELS SHERBROOKE CHAPTER

The gang that is now known as the Hells Angels Sherbrooke chapter started out in the 1960s as the Dirty Reich and became the Gitans in 1970. The gang bought drugs from the Popeyes, which would become the Hells Angels Montreal chapter, and supplied local pushers.

Sharing the territory with the Gitans was the Atomes motorcycle gang, led by Réjean "Farmer" Gilbert. War between the two gangs broke out in 1973, and within 12 months, six men were killed, and frequent fights had taken place. An uneasy peace was reached, and the groups agreed to share the area's drug market.

In 1984, the Hells Angels Montreal chapter told the Gitans that they could become a Hells chapter if they eliminated the Atomes. Within a few months, Atomes members Michel "Ballon" Fortier, Jean-Noël Roy, Ronald "Big" Sigouin, and Réjean "Farmer" Gilbert were killed. The Atomes gang disappeared, and the Gitans became an official Hells Angels chapter on December 5, 1984.

From their clubhouse in Lennoxville, the organization's influence grew and, despite police efforts to shut down the club, continues to have a firm hold on the area's drug and prostitution markets.

HELLS ANGELS QUEBEC CITY

The Hells Angels Quebec City chapter was formed on May 26, 1988. The gang consisted of members of two old biker clubs, the Vikings, based on the south shore of Quebec City, and the Iron Coffins, based in La Pocatière.

From their clubhouse in Saint-Nicolas, the Hells Angels took over much of the drug trafficking and prostitution in and around Quebec City. The club's main competition has been the Bandidos Quebec City chapter, formerly part of the Rock Machine, who engaged them in a violent turf war for almost a decade.

HELLS ANGELS SOUTH CHAPTER

The Hells Angels South chapter was created on March 1, 1997, when eight members and two prospects broke away from the Montreal chapter. The founders had no criminal records nor were they members with recent convictions. The reason behind this was to avoid being classified under federal legislation as a criminal organization. Normand "Billy" Labelle, one of the original founders of the club's Montreal chapter, became the South faction's first president.

Their impressive clubhouse was located at 28 Rue Alvares in Saint-Basile-le-Grand and had an estimated worth of $167,500. Unlike the club's other Quebec chapters, Hells Angels South has managed to keep a low profile and is said to be involved primarily in narcotics trafficking, prostitution, and extortion.

HELLS ANGELS TROIS-RIVIÈRES

The gang that became the Hells Angels Trois-Rivières chapter was formed in the late 1960s or early 1970s, known as the Missiles. The group caused chaos throughout the Saguenay-Lac-Saint-Jean area of Quebec. They competed against three other biker gangs for drug turf: the Lacmas, El Conquatcheros, and the Hondix. The Missiles, considered by authorities to be far more dangerous and violent than their competitors, quickly took over and the other clubs faded away. So violent was the club that the mayor publicly stated that the citizens of his small town where the Missiles' clubhouse was located, lived in

constant fear of the gang. After numerous arrests, the Missiles changed their name to the Satan's Guards and moved to Chicoutimi. They later moved to Trois-Rivières where, on June 14, 1991, they became an official Hells Angels chapter. Most of their income derives from drug trafficking and prostitution and, with the help of its puppet gangs, the club has a firm hold over Trois-Rivières and the surrounding areas.

See also: BEAULIEU, GEORGES; BERGER, CLAUDE; BOUCHER, MAURICE; BUTEAU, YVES; CARROLL, DAVID; COULOMBE, GERRY; HAMEL, NORMAND; HOULE, DENNIS; LABELLE, NORMAND; LAJOIE-SMITH, MICHAEL; LANGOLIS, MICHEL; LESSARD, RÉJEAN; MAYRAND, RICHARD; PORTER, PAUL; RICHARD, ROBERT; ROY, LOUIS; STADNIK, WOLODUMY; STEINERT, SCOTT; TOUSIGN, ANDRÉ; VALLEE, RICHARD.

HENAO Montoya, Arcángel De Jesús and José Orlando

The Henao Montoya brothers, Arcángel de Jesús and José Orlando (who has surrendered), run trafficking operations out of the Northern Valle del Cauca region. The Henao Montoyas run the most powerful of the various independent trafficking groups that comprise the North Valle drug cartel. The major North Valle drug organizations are poised to become among the most powerful drug-trafficking groups in Colombia. The Henao Montoya organization has been closely linked to the paramilitary group run by Carlos Castano, a major cocaine trafficker in his own right.

See also: GÓMEZ BUSTAMANTE, LUIS HERNANDO; MONTOYA SÁNCHEZ, DIEGO; NORTHERN VALLE ORGANIZATION.

Reference
Thomas A. Constantine. "Statement before the Senate Foreign Relations Committee, Subcommittee on the Western Hemisphere, Peace Corps, Narcotics, and Terrorism Regarding International Organized Crime Syndicates and Their Impact on the United States." 1998 Congressional Hearings, U.S. Congress. February 26, 1998.

HEROIN *See* OPIUM POPPY.

HERRERA BUITRAGO, Helmer (a.k.a. Pacho; H7)

A high-ranking member of the Cali cartel, Herrera Buitrago was one of several well-known drug kingpins whose assests were frozen in the United States by the Clinton Administration by Executive Order 12978. Herrera Buitrago was named to a list of "Specially Designated Narcotics Traffickers" (SDNTs).

Reference

Thomas A. Constantine. "International Organized Crime Syndicates and Their Impact on the U.S." U.S. Drug Enforcement Administration. Available online. URL: http://www.dea.gov/pubs/cngrtest/ct980226.html. Downloaded on July 15, 2004.

HERRERA NEVARES, Jaime, Jr. *See* HERRERA NEVARES, JAIME, SR.

HERRERA NEVARES, Jaime, Sr.

Jaime Herrera Nevares was the patriarch of a huge criminal syndicate based in the mountaintop village of Los Herreras, Durango, Mexico. As far back as 1957, the Herrera organization ran a "farm-to-the-arm" heroin operation that cultivated opium poppy plants, processed and packaged heroin in Mexico, and transported it to Chicago. There it was either sold locally or distributed to other U.S. cities. This group was extremely difficult to penetrate because family members controlled the entire heroin process from top to bottom.

U.S. law enforcement agencies were well acquainted with the Herrera organization and its "Heroin Highway," a drug-trafficking network that stretched from Durango to Chicago. The family frequently smuggled heroin in their invention, the "Durango drive shaft," a sleevelike device that surrounded the vehicle's drive shaft and held several kilos of heroin. They also used compartmentalized gas tanks and door panels to conceal the contraband.

While criminal syndicates such as the Jaime Herrera organization were trafficking heroin into the United States, cocaine trafficking was also a major problem facing law enforcement officials. In September 1977 Drug Enforcement Administration (DEA) agents at JFK Airport in New York seized 85 pounds of cocaine that had been concealed in 4,500 pounds of chocolate bars. Special Agent Michael J. Tobin displayed how the cocaine had been hidden in the candy bars.

At one time, Chicago-area law enforcement agencies believed that the Herreras controlled as much as 90 percent of local heroin distribution. The DEA estimated that the Herrera organization imported 746 pounds of pure heroin into the United States each year. When cut, this amounted to more than 8 tons of 5 percent pure heroin. The Herreras were considered the largest heroin-trafficking organization in Mexico. They returned the majority of their profits to their home in Mexico, using neighborhood currency exchanges to send money orders back to Durango. In the mid-1970s, the DEA traced slightly less than $2 million from these exchanges and Western Union records. This figure represented approximately 1 percent of the total cash transferred to Mexico by the Herrera organization annually.

By 1978 the Chicago Herreras were grossing $60 million a year and had established branches in Denver, Los Angeles, Miami, and Pittsburgh. By 1980 the family had established connections in South America and had diversified into cocaine. By the mid-1980s the family's gross income had reached approximately $200 million a year.

In 1979 Central Tactical Units, a branch of the DEA, launched CENTAC 19 (the 19th CENTAC operation), which targeted the Herrera family trafficking organization and eventually resulted in the seizure of 39 kilograms of heroin, as well as the arrest and long-term incarceration of three key Chicago-based members of the Herrera organization.

During the 1980s investigations against the Herreras continued. On July 23, 1985, as a result of a two-year investigation called Operation Durango, between 450 and 500 federal, state, and local law-enforcement officers in Chicago, Illinois, and Gary, Indiana, arrested 120 traffickers (of the 132 indicted) connected to the polydrug-trafficking Herrera and Zambrana families. Officers seized 10 pounds of heroin, 13 pounds of cocaine, 47 properties, and $300,000. In August 1988 the Mexican leaders of the organization, Jaime Herrera Nevares, Sr., and Jaime Herrera Nevares, Jr., were arrested in Mexico on drug charges and remain incarcerated in Mexico City. They continued to be listed as DEA fugitives based on prior indictments in Miami, Florida.

Reference

U.S. Drug Enforcement Administration, U.S. Department of Justice. "A Tradition of Excellence, DEA History 1985–1990." Available online. URL: http://www.dea.gov/pubs/history/index.html. Downloaded on July 28, 2004.

HERRERA VÁSQUEZ, Hugo

Hugo Herrera Vásquez heads a Cali-based trafficking organization that moves large quantities of cocaine from Colombia to the United States via Central America and Mexico. The Herrera organization also launders drug money destined for Colombia. Cash, wire transfers, and monetary instruments are used to move drug proceeds from the U.S. southwest border area to Colombia through Mexico and Panama.

Reference

Thomas A. Constantine. "Statement before the Senate Foreign Relations Committee, Subcommittee on the Western Hemisphere, Peace Corps, Narcotics, and Terrorism Regarding International Organized Crime Syndicates and Their Impact on the United States." 1998 Congressional Hearings, U.S. Congress. February 26, 1998.

HILL, Henry

Henry Hill is probably the most famous mob turncoat of them all, immortalized by Martin Scorsese's movie *Goodfellas* in which Henry Hill was played by Ray Liotta. Thanks to this movie, Henry Hill's life in the witness protection program is not as boring as he had anticipated at the end of the movie *Goodfellas*. He had done talk shows, interviews, and appearances on television shows, all thanks to his shady life and the great movie made about that life.

Henry Hill grew up in the Brooklyn area dominated by Lucchese crime-family capos Paul Vario. Paul Vario was one of the more respected capos in the Lucchese crime family. He controlled a lot of the family's rackets and also had a number of criminal innovations that returned even more profit, including a number of automobile chop-shops throughout Brooklyn where the stolen parts were sold to crooked auto suppliers and service centers. Hill was fascinated by the gangsters and Mafiosos. From the moment he saw them, he wanted to become just like them. Hill could not become a full-fledged Mafia member, though, because he was not Italian. (Henry's mother was Italian, but his father was Irish: That was enough to disqualify him.) However, not being Italian did not stop Hill from becoming a close associate and friend of Paul Vario and his crew. In his teenage years Hill would do errands for Vario and his crew, and eventually after becoming best friends with Jimmy "the Gent" Burke and Tommy DeSimone, he moved up from running errands to more serious crimes such as truck hijacking.

Hill's wife Karen bore him two daughters. Henry and Karen had a love–hate relationship. Hill lived up to his gangster image, having a number of affairs and girlfriends, staying out to all hours drinking and partying, playing cards and the like. After beating up a nonpaying gambler (whose sister happened to work at the Federal Bureau of Investigation (FBI) as a typist) Hill was sentenced to jail for 10 years. Once inside Hill soon realized that prison time for wiseguys was different from ordinary convicts as they were treated with respect by the everyday convicts and the prison guards (who were paid off to make the time a little easier for the Mafiosos). Hill found some contacts in the narcotics trade inside whom he would soon seek out on his release.

His release came after four and a quarter years, thanks to Paul Vario; Vario set up a dummy job for him, which also helped when Hill started his probation. It was not long before Hill began to use his narcotics contacts from prison and began to shift large amounts of cocaine from Brooklyn to Pittsburgh, even though Paul Vario forbade any of his crew from dealing drugs. The money though soon came rolling in and, soon he needed help, as his operation grew, so he cut his two best pals, Jimmy "the Gent" and Tommy DeSimone, in on the action. But Hill began to use his own product and became very sloppy. In carefully coordinated raids by the police, authorities arrested Hill and his crew, as well as Hill's Pittsburgh connection. The entire crime ring was brought down in one quick and efficient raid.

Former mobster Henry Hill, whose autobiography inspired the movie *Goodfellas* (AP)

Now Hill was in a sticky position: Vario had banned the use or distribution of drugs due to the stiff penalties imposed by the federal government on drug issues. Henry was worried he would be killed if he turned to Vario. Running would place him and his family in the crosshairs of both the federal government and the mafia. So Henry Hill became a government witness. He identified Burke and Vario among others. Vario was the government's big prize, and so Hill had a deal.

Most of Hill's old associates are dead—they either died in prison (Burke and Vario) or were gunned down in the streets (DeSimone). Telling his story on talk shows, Hill is all too happy now that he, in the end, made one good decision in his life.

Reference

David Amoruso. "Henry Hill." Gangsters Incorporated. Available online. URL: http://gangstersinc.tripod.com/HenryHill.html. Downloaded on July 19, 2004.

—D.A.

HOCK Sair Woey

Hock Sair Woey means "Chinese Underworld." Hock Sair Woey was a violent street gang in San Francisco's Chinatown in the 1970s and 1980s that dominated drug dealing and extortion.

See also: HOP SING BOYS; LOUIE, KEN.

Reference

Lee, Bill. *Chinese Playground: Memoirs from the Underworld.* San Francisco, Calif.: Rhapsody Press, 1999.

HOP Sing Boys

One-time enforcer branch of the Hop Sing Tong, the Hop Sing Boys gang was based in San Francisco's Chinatown. Their heyday was evidenced in "The Golden Dragon Massacre," according to *AsiaWeek* correspondent and book author Bill Lee. "Gang warfare on Chinatown's streets culminated in the Golden Dragon Massacre, named for the restaurant in which some patrons were targeted. Five people died and 11 were injured in the 1977 shootout," wrote Lee's editor at *AsiaWeek*.

In a turf war over illegal fireworks sales in San Francisco during June and July, the Hop Sing Boys and Wah Ching faced off against the J Boys, according to Lee.

"Weapons were drawn and gunfire erupted, with gangsters running up and down the street, ducking behind cars and into doorways, blasting at one another," wrote Lee in "The Golden Dragon Massacre" for *AsiaWeek* magazine, January 28, 1999.

Ken Louie, who was murdered in 1977, was the leader of the gang for a period and was one of its more high-profile members.

See also: HOP SING TONG; LOUIE, KEN; TONGS.

References

Bill Lee, *Chinese Playground: Memoirs from the Underworld.* San Francisco, Calif.: Rhapsody Press, 1999.

———, "Notes Underworld." *AsiaWeek,* January 28, 1999.

Brockman Morris, *Bamboo Tigers of San Francisco: Chinatown's Golden Dragon Massacre 1977.* Available online. URL: http://www.pisgahweb.net/brox/btigers/index. html. Downloaded on November 23, 2003.

HOP Sing Tong

The Hop Sing Tong are based on the West Coast with distribution to such major cities as Chicago, New York City, and Baltimore. The gang consists primarily of Chinese membership; however, the Hop Sing Tongs have been known to affiliate themselves with Vietnamese gangs for muscle.

They are affiliated with the West Coast triads and tongs as well as mainland China tongs. Business affiliates include the large Wah Ching and On Leong Tong; they have also been known to do business with both the Crips and the Bloods.

The Hop Sing Tong derived from early patriotic Chinese associations in the late 19th century that helped immigrants adapt to the United States. They were also involved in various criminal smuggling enterprises. In the 20th century they have spread across the United States. In the beginning the Wah Ching gang was smaller and somewhat under the control of the Hop Sing but no more. The Wo Hop To triad of Hong Kong origin now dominates the Wah Ching.

The Hop Sing rely on money laundering, drugs, gambling, and extortion as means of making money. Other criminal activities include gambling, prostitution, home invasions, drug smuggling, technology theft, and alien smuggling. When it comes to drug smuggling, they deal mostly in heroin. Most of their violence is exerted through Vietnamese gangs.

According to the 1994 Annual Report of the Attorney General of the United States, a 48-count indictment against 19 members and associates of the Wo Hop To, a Hong Kong–based triad, and the Hop Sing Tong, a criminally influenced tong, was returned in San Francisco. The indictment marked the first time that the Racketeer Influenced and Corrupt Organization (RICO) statute had been used on the West Coast against Asian organized-crime figures.

HORVATH, Joseph (a.k.a. Joe Valentine, Little Joe)

The youngest child in a family of Hungarian immigrants, Joseph Horvath was born in 1930. He grew up in Montreal's dangerous red-light district, surrounded by the city's criminal element, became involved in illegal activities as a teenager, worked for some of the biggest names in Montreal's underworld, and would become known as Little Joe and Joe Valentine. His first major conflict with the law came

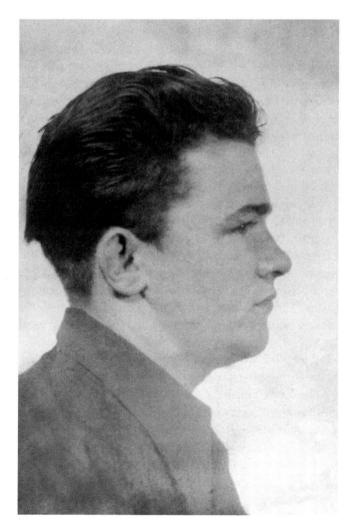

Joseph "Little Joe" Horvath *(Montreal Gazette)*

in 1949 when Horvath was arrested following a violent robbery. He escaped before his trial and, when he was finally captured, received a five-year sentence. On release, Horvath became associated with the Montreal Mafia through lieutenant Nicola "Cola" Di Iorio. He was employed at Di Iorio's Victoria Sporting Club, the mob's most profitable gambling den. He was also said to be a burglary specialist and, later on, moved into drug trafficking, supplying heroin to the Palmer brothers' gang in Vancouver. He moved to the northwest suburb of Pierrefonds and claimed to make a living as a bricklayer.

The Narcotics Squad tracked Horvath as he traveled throughout Europe in July 1969. He was seen meeting with people in London, Barcelona, Rome, and Munich and returned to Montreal on August 5. A week later, he had an important meeting with the Mafia chieftain, Vic "the Egg" Cotroni, most likely to discuss the details of his trip. On March 25, 1970, police listened in on a telephone conversation between "Little Joe" and fellow mobster Frank Dasti. Although they used codes, it was obvious that the two were discussing drug shipments. During the next few months, the Narcotics Squad recorded dozens of such conversations about drugs and meetings. Because of increased police attention, Horvath withdrew from trafficking heroin and cocaine and became highly involved in importing of hundreds of kilograms of hashish. The drug was imported from Afghanistan and distributed to members of the Satan's Choice biker gang.

The Royal Canadian Mounted Police exposed Horvath's hashish network on May 11, 1972. He and six underlings were arrested and charged with conspiring to import hashish. They were arraigned the same day and released on $5,000 bail each. While out, Horvath resumed his heroin trafficking activities with the organization. He was arrested again on March 1, 1974, after a federal grand jury in Milwaukee, Wisconsin, indicted him for conspiring to traffic in narcotics. Joe Horvath died of throat cancer in Saint-Luc Hospital on April 10, 1974. He remained loyal to his associates until the end, planning to take the entire blame for the Milwaukee charges, but he passed away before he could do that. He was 45 years old.

Reference

Gary Francoeur. "Joseph 'Little Joe' Horvath." Wiseguy-Wally. Available online. URL: http://www.geocities.com/wiseguywally/JoeHorvath.html. Downloaded on July 19, 2004.

—G.F.

HOULE, Denis (a.k.a. Pas Fiable)

Denis Houle was born in 1954 and became a member of the Hells Angels Montreal chapter in the early 1980s. Sometimes known as Pas Fiable, he was charged in 1982 with assault and conspiracy to commit assault. The charges were dropped.

Houle played a role in the 1985 slaughter of five North chapter members, according to a biker informant. Gerry "the Cat" Coulombe, said he, overheard Houle, Réjean "Zig-Zag" Lessard, Luc "Sam" Michaud, and Jean-Yves "Boule" Tremblay planning the massacre at the gang's Sorel clubhouse.

Coulombe also told authorities that Houle and fellow Hells Angel Jacques "La Pelle" Pelletier had supplied the firearms that were eventually used to gun down Laurent "L'Anglais" Viau, Jean-Pierre "Matt Le Crosseur" Mathieu, Jean-Guy "Brutus" Geoffrion, Michel "Willie" Mayrand, and Guy-Louis "Chop" Adam. Houle was arrested and, on March 14, 1988, pleaded guilty to five charges, including being an accessory after the fact and culpable homicide.

On May 5, 1995, Houle was convicted of impaired driving and possession of narcotics. One day as he and fellow Hells Angel Richard "Bob" Hudon walked through the prison yard, Rock Machine hit men, stationed near the person's fence, fired at them with semiautomatic rifles. Neither Angel was harmed, and the attackers fled in an automobile.

On June 24, 1995, still behind bars, Houle left the club's Montreal chapter to become one of the founders of the Nomads chapter. This new charter comprised the organization's best, and it would handle the war with the Rock Machine.

Houle's wife was wounded by gunshots outside the couple's Piedmont home on September 20, 1999. A gunman, hidden in a forest near the house, fired several bullets and fled to a nearby highway. Houle, who was away hunting at the time of the vicious attack, assured her safety by reportedly placing armed associates outside her Hôtel Dieu hospital room around the clock until she recovered.

On February 15, 2001, Houle was arrested along with fellow Nomads members Normand Robitaille, Gilles "Trooper" Mathieu, Richard "Dick" Mayrand, Michel Rose, Nomads prospects Luc "Bordel" Bordeleau and Jean-Claude Larivière, and Rockers member Kenny Bédard at the Holiday Inn on Sherbrooke Street West in Montreal. All eight men were carrying firearms, and pictures of eight Rock Machine/probationary Bandidos were found.

The bikers' pocket money, totaling $39,197, was confiscated. Rather than face charges of gangsterism and a lengthy trial, the accused agreed to plead guilty to weapons charges and were sentenced to one year in prison.

Things got worse for Houle as he learned on March 28, 2001, when Opération Printemps 2001 came to a close. The government seized the biker's three homes and charged him with 13 counts of murder, gangsterism, and narcotics trafficking.

In September 2003 Houle and eight others, including three other full-patch members of the Nomads, brought an abrupt end to the 11-month trial by pleading guilty to charges of conspiracy to commit murder, drug trafficking, and gangsterism. The following week, the bikers received sentences ranging from 15 to 20 years in prison. Houle was sentenced to 20 years, with the condition that he serve half before being eligible for parole.

See also: HELLS ANGELS.

Reference

Gary Francoeur. "Denis 'Pas Fiable' Houle." Wiseguy-Wally. Available online. URL: http://www.geocities.com/wiseguywally/DenisHoule.html. Downloaded on July 19, 2004.

—G.F.

HUMAN Trafficking

"People smuggling has become the preferred trade of a growing number of criminal networks worldwide which are showing an increasing sophistication in regard to moving larger numbers of people at higher profits than ever," according to an Interpol report. It is acknowledged that smuggling of people is a continuously growing phenomenon and the issue of a global nature not only as a transnational crime but also as an enormous violation of human rights and a contemporary form of slavery. Currently, economic discomfort appears to be the main reason for illegal migration movement throughout the world.

Nevertheless, many of the willing migrants undertake the hazardous travel to their destination country with criminal syndicates services that specialize in people smuggling. These syndicates will arrange everything for the migrants but at a high price. Very often the traveling conditions are inhumane, the migrants being cramped into trucks or boats, and fatal accidents occur quite frequently.

After their arrival in their destination country, the illegal status of the migrants puts them at the mercy of their smugglers, who often force them for years to work in the illegal labor market to pay off the debts incurred as a result of their transportation. If the migrants are not able to pay, the syndicates may threaten to torture or kill the migrant family members.

People-smuggling syndicates benefit from weak legislation, huge profits, and the relatively low risk of detection, prosecution, and arrest compared to other activities of transnational organized crime. That creates the need for a structure that enables police and other law enforcement agencies to cooperate on a global basis. Interpol fulfills that role, and considerable efforts are being made to develop the services that it can offer.

Potential victims need to be warned about the risks related to trafficking and the truth behind the vague promises of a too-good-to-be-true job in Europe or North America. The general public and criminal justice practitioners need to become more aware of this growing crime. Additionally, the demand side of trafficking should be addressed and potential users informed of the possibility of using services that victims of trafficking are forced to provide.

The Coalition to Abolish Slavery and Trafficking, based in Los Angeles, California, reports that 1.5 million Asian women are working abroad as legal or illegal workers. Countries of origin report an outflow of 800,000 female migrant workers a year, and the number is increasing steadily. Researchers have found that women increasingly migrate to support their families and that they usually migrate alone.

Parallel to legitimate immigration there are well-organized underground syndicates engaged in trafficking immigrants. Women who enter countries illegally or overstay their visas are particularly vulnerable to exploitation. These naïve and desperate young women sold into sexual bondage are often too frightened to seek help regarding rapes, beatings, and druggings received at the hands of their captors. These violations of human rights more often than not are the norm. The United Nations reports that 4 million people a year are traded against their will to work in one or another form of servitude.

Surveys show that the majority of Asian women who now offer themselves as sex workers first entered the sex trade unwillingly. One survey of sex workers found that

- 3 percent were sold by a boyfriend.
- 4 percent were raped and sold.
- 5 percent were raped by a stepfather and sold.
- 32 percent were tricked and sold by a nonfamily member.
- 8 percent were sold by parents to pay debts.
- 4 percent went to the city to find a job and were then sold.

Recent cases of trafficked women found in a sweatshop in El Monte and a brothel in Westminster are considered the "tip of the iceberg" by law enforcement. There are between 4,000 and 5,000 women from the People's Republic of China engaged in prostitution in Los Angeles; many if not most of those women have been trafficked. There are large numbers of women from Korea, Thailand, and other Southeast Asian countries working in brothels or sweatshops in Los Angeles. It is not known how many have been trafficked and held in peonage or slave-like conditions.

UN GLOBAL PROGRAM AGAINST TRAFFICKING IN HUMAN BEINGS

The Global Program against Trafficking in Human Beings was designed by the Center for International Crime Prevention (CICP) in collaboration with the United Nations Interregional Crime and Justice Research Institute (UNICRI) and launched in March 1999. The program assists member states in their efforts to combat trafficking in human beings. It highlights the involvement of organized criminal groups in human trafficking and promotes the development of effective ways of cracking down on perpetrators.

The global program's overarching objective is to bring to the foreground the involvement of organized criminal groups in human trafficking and to promote the development of effective criminal-justice-related responses. As the only entity focusing on the criminal justice element, the program, working through CICP, brings special advantages to the fight against trafficking.

OUTLINE OF THE PROGRAM

The program's key components are data collection, assessment, and technical cooperation.

The assessment component of the Program, performed in cooperation with UNICRI, includes data collection on various smuggling routes and the methods used by organized criminal groups in trafficking.

The UN is also collecting "best practices" used to combat trafficking and the involvement of organized crime. A database containing trafficking trends and routes as well as information about victims and traffickers has been established so that policymakers, practitioners, researchers, and the NGO community can use the collected data.

Countries involved in the program are selected from Asia, Europe, Africa, and Latin America and will be assessed according to:

- smuggling routes and forms of exploitation of trafficked people

- cooperation among law enforcement, prosecution, and judiciary

- government efforts to respond, including recent legislative reforms.

On the basis of the assessments, seven countries are now involved in technical cooperation projects. Specific intervention measures are being introduced that are designed to strengthen the capacity to combat forms of trafficking at the national and international levels. These measures will assist countries of origin, transit, and destination to develop joint strategies and practical actions.

At the national level the program aims to:

- raise awareness (such as through public campaigns) of trafficking in human beings and especially strengthen institutional capacity

- train law enforcement officers, prosecutors, and judges

- advise on drafting and revising relevant legislation

- provide advice and assistance on establishing and strengthening antitrafficking elements; and

- strengthen victim and witness support.

At the international level the program aims to:

- provide assistance to agencies, institutions, and governments as part of an interdisciplinary effort to design effective measures against trafficking in human beings.

The program cooperates closely with other intergovernmental and nongovernmental organizations in the implementation of its activities, including on awareness raising.

SMUGGLING ROUTES

Changing methods of the people-smuggling networks as a response to legislative and law-enforcement activities are necessary for the survival of this network. Flexibility is thus one of the main characteristics of transportation and the choice of routes. This means that the routes used by people smugglers may sometimes be simple and direct but at other times circuitous. The time between departure and arrival may thus vary from some days to several months or even years. Smuggling is carried out either by land, air, or sea.

Migrants from the Asian region are mainly using the route via the Commonwealth of Independent States (CIS, a federation of 12 former USSR republics). Migrants travel from Kazakhstan, Kyrgyzstan, Uzbekistan, Tajikistan, and Turkmenistan to Russia and from there via the Ukraine and Slovakia and the Czech Republic to western European countries or even farther, to the United States and Canada.

At the same time the classic Balkan route from Asian countries via Iran and Turkey and from there

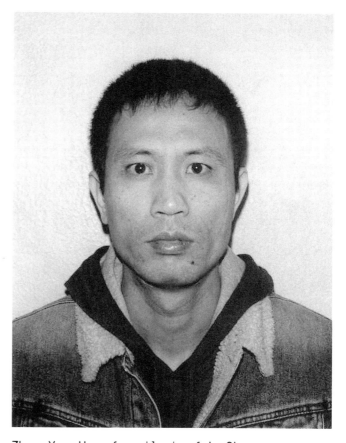

Zhang Yong Hui, a feared leader of the Chinese Snakeheads (a gang notorious for smuggling asylum seekers into Britain), made millions of pounds before being caught. (European Pressphoto Agency, PA)

via the Balkan states to western Europe is used for the smuggling of migrants as well as for the smuggling of all other kinds of illegal goods such as drugs and firearms.

Especially during summer months, Spain faces the arrival of thousands of illegal immigrants originating from the sub-Saharan region on the African continent. These willing immigrants undertake the hazardous trip to travel from Morocco to southern Spain by using the narrow Strait of Gibraltar, where only 21 kilometers separate Europe and Africa. Many people traveling in small, overcrowded boats have drowned in their desperate try to reach Europe.

During recent years, Australia has faced a growing number of illegal immigrants, mostly from the Middle East and South Asia, landing at its western coasts, especially on Christmas Island, which is located relatively close to the Indonesian Archipelago. Most of the refugees originating mainly from the Near East first enter Malaysia, where they are taken to the south before making a short ferry crossing to the Indonesian island of Batam. From there it is not difficult to reach Jakarta and go on to the southern Indonesian islands of Bali, Flores, or Lombok, where they embark for Australia.

Smuggling migrants to the United States is mostly achieved by putting them on planes. Ships with migrants on board are mainly bound for the West Coast, but the use of this route has dropped considerably. Smuggling networks seem to focus more and more on Central and South America, where they entertain the necessary links to Mexican people smugglers to move the illegal migrants via Mexico to the United States.

INCREASING NUMBERS OF SMUGGLED MIGRANTS

It was recently established that people smugglers are making higher profits by smuggling increasing numbers of migrants at the same time.

What had been an exception just one year ago had a rise in media attention. Cases such as the arrival of the vessel *East Sea* that ran aground on the coast of southern France carrying 894 illegal immigrants in February 2001 have now become a sad reality. Daily news reports now frequently mention such vessels with hundreds of migrants crammed on board.

Hygiene is often impossible on board these vessels, as no toilet facilities exist. The vessels are mostly insufficiently equipped with drinking water and food. The treatment of the migrants by the crew and guards can be extremely violent, and sick people might be thrown overboard.

NEW ROUTE VIA SOUTH AFRICA

South Africa is becoming more and more a transit country, but it is also a destination country for mostly Asian migrants, particularly for Chinese nationals. Much of this migration seems to be connected to Southeast Asian smuggling networks. A large number of Chinese nationals are traveling to the country with fraudulent documents or making questionable journeys to contact countries like Swaziland, Lesotho, or Mozambique.

From South Africa the willing immigrants often continue their journey to the United States and also to European countries by plane.

Air smuggling from South Africa has existed for several years, and it appears that the route is being tested again.

Reprinted by permission of the United Nations, 2004.

See also: OPERATION SUNFLOWER.

References

Coalition to Abolish Slavery and Trafficking. Available online. URL: http://www.castla.org. Downloaded on August 9, 2004.

Interpol. "Children and Human Trafficking." Available online. URL: http://www.interpol.int/public/THB/default.asp. Downloaded on July 19, 2004.

HUNG League

One of the many antidynastic secret societies that were formed during the 17th century whose main purpose was to overthrow the Chi'ing Dynasty and return the Ming back to power, the Hung League is the first-known triad society, according to several sources. Originally the society took to bribing and coercing Chi'ing administrators and bureaucrats. However, after 1911, most of these secret societies eventually became more involved with their nefarious businesses than with the politics of the era in which they lived. The Hung League was especially active in Britain at the turn of the 20th century.

See also: HEAVEN AND EARTH SOCIETY; TRIADS.

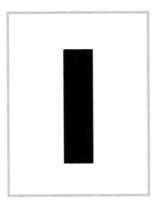

IBRAHIM, Dawood

Based in Karachi, Pakistan, Dawood Ibrahim is one of the most notorious and powerful dons on the Asian subcontinent and is best known for being the mastermind and muscle behind the Mumbai serial bombings that racked India.

Soon after the bombings, Ibrahim and his gang set up shop in Karachi, where the new residents immediately created a stir with local citizens. Ibrahim took up residence in a posh 5,000-square-foot plot in the Clifton area of Karachi, complete with swimming pool, gymnasium, and tennis court. Ibrahim's most violent enforcer, Abdul Razzak Memon, better known as Tiger Memon, received an equally palatial spread. Second-in-command Shakeel Ahmad Babu, better known as Chhota Shakeel, received a similar premises in the Defense Housing Authority enclave. All three are heavily guarded, and unsettled citizens were told to mind their own business.

All of these men are believed to be benefiting from both the generosity and the protection of the Pakistani government since India has demanded their extradition, but Pakistan claims the men cannot be found. Ibrahim and his associates, however, are known to be hiding under the protection of Mullah Rahman, a *jehadi* leader in the countryside. All three have been known to have traveled with passports furnished by the Pakistani government, using false names.

Ibrahim and his associates for many years had operated out of Dubai and Mumbai, where they practiced murder and extortion as well a smuggling of all kinds. Ibrahim has always been able to rely on a wide-ranging network of associates throughout Asia to carry out his highly organized and violent plans. He has the region's film industry, real estate, and many other businesses that he either owns, controls, or extorts. He has also been influential in cricket betting in India, a huge business, since 1999. Of course, Ibrahim's biggest business was smuggling drugs through the entire Asian subcontinent, with Karachi as a main hub of most of this trade for some time.

Dawood usually likes to start off the day with a game of tennis or snooker and then end the day with a night filled with Black Label, gambling, and performances by female dancers. He likes to party until dawn, make the first of his prayers, and then end the revelry of that evening.

On September 15, 2000, Ibrahim had attempted to assassinate his closest rival, Chhota Rajan. Rajan had been an employee of Ibrahim who eventually went off separately and created his own gang. Ibrahim and Chhota Shakeel had accused Rajan of stealing money from them before his departure. No one can be sure whether this is true or not. Regardless, neither man could stand the other, and several associates between them had been killed by either side. Ibrahim had assailants set up in four countries, just waiting to find out where Chhota Rajan was. He was finally identified in Bangkok, where six men stormed the house and a gun battle ensued. Rajan jumped out a second-story window but broke his back when he landed badly. Ibrahim's men shot him from a balcony. He was rushed to the hospital and was assumed dead by many, but he survived. Later, while still in a hospital in Bangkok with a broken back, Chhota bribed nine Thai guards and escaped to freedom. Ibrahim had firmly established himself as the biggest king of the hill and had sent a message to the rest of the world that he could kill anyone at any time. Still, there are numerous underworld adversaries who would just as soon see Ibrahim eliminated from the field of competition, and Rajan is bent on revenge.

It is believed that the Pakistani officials are on the payroll of Ibrahim, as he funds several terrorist

Twelve bombs exploded across Bombay on March 12, 1993, including this explosion in the Bombay Stock Exchange, killing hundreds. The attacks were attributed to Dawood Ibrahim. (AP)

groups, and that he will not be extradited any time soon. It has also been speculated in the Indian press that Ibrahim used a combination of his considerable wealth, along with that of the Pakistani governments, to purchase or to help the Pakistani government acquire nuclear missile technology. Regardless, there is no question that Pakistan has made him what underworld experts call an "economic citizen," or one who pays for refuge.

The Indian Central Bureau of Investigation has opined that if any will get Ibrahim, it will be a combination of the current Pakistani government and/or a competitor. In many circles it is known that Ibrahim and the Pakistani government have become so close that the Pakistani government cannot afford to let Ibrahim out of its control. He simply knows too many of the wrong kinds of details.

See also: ANSARI, AFTAB; BAKSH, NOOR; GOGA, IRFAN; RAJAN, CHHOTA; SHAKEEL, CHHOTA; SINGH, SANJAY.

Reference

Praveen Swami. "Disappearing Act." Frontline 19, no. 3 (February 2, 2002). Available online. URL: http://www. flonnet.com/fl1903/19030300.htm. Accessed on November 24, 2004.

ICHIWA-KAI

A Japanese crime clan founded by former Yamaguchi-gumi leader Hiroshi Yamamoto in 1983. Yamamoto bolted the Yamaguchi when his rival, Masahisa Takenaka, was named Oyabun of the famed crime family when famed Japanese mobster Kazuo Taoka died.

In 1985–86 a huge war between the two rival gangs led to the Ichiwa-kai seeking restraining orders against their rivals from Japanese police. This resulted from Yamamoto's successful assassination of Takenaka, with which he hoped to assume the leadership role of the Yamaguchi. However, with the successful hit, Yamamoto became a marked man. Several of his hit men were killed in theatrical and famous shootings in Japan, including Susumu Akasaka, who was killed by two cross-dressing Yamaguchi hit men who had gained his confidence, one a pistol-packing faux torch singer who fired from the stage during the hit in which Akasaka was killed by five bullets in his head and body.

According to Japanese crime expert Ed Jacob, in *Yakuza Blood Baths,* "Neither assassin was ever

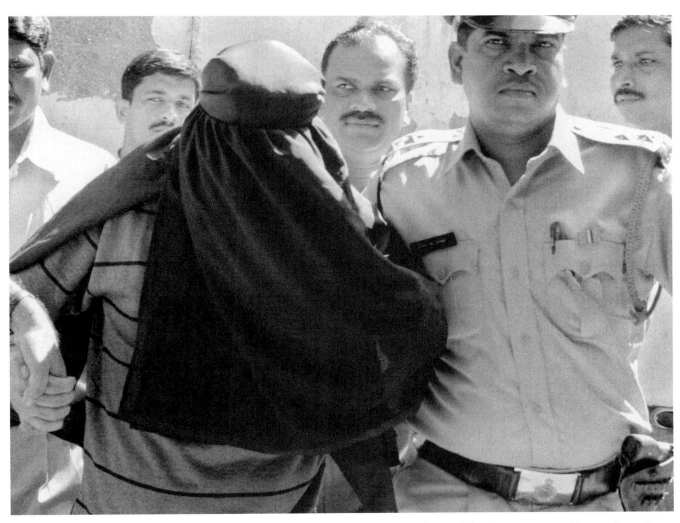

Iqbal Kaskar (face covered), younger brother of India's most wanted gangster Dawood Ibrahim, is escorted by a police officer after being questioned by federal investigators and police officials. (AP)

caught and the killing has gone down as one of the most unusual in yakuza history."

Reference

Ed Jacob. "Crime and Conspiracies: Yakuza Blood Baths." The Quirky Japan Home Page. Available online. URL: http://www.quirkyjapan.or.tv. Downloaded on October 28, 2002.

IMPERIAL Blood Brothers and Blood Brother Unified Nation

Imperial Blood Brothers and Blood Brother Unified Nation are primarily located throughout all of Connecticut and some parts of New York. Plans to establish chapters nationwide are under way, and both male and female members are accepted.

Female members are referred to as Blood Sisters but are nicknamed Diamonds. Gang makeup is primarily African American, with Asians, Hispanics, and some Whites. There is an established hierarchy with strict rules of adherence to the organization and laws.

Members wear red and black. Red represents blood; black represents African Americans (or other minorities). The meaning of the colors is the endless cycle of bloodshed (red) between people of color (black). Another meaning is knowledge (red) and ignorance (black).

Newcomers wear all black beads, all red for agents of death, or six black followed by six red for members. The president's executive staff wears two sets of beads: Each set is six red followed by six black. The president may wear any/or all sequences of beads and as many as 20+ sets.

Gang tattoos or signs may include three pointed crowns, fighting monks, a sword and scroll with the words *warrior* above it and *scholar* below it; the letters *IBB*, *BBUN*, or *BB*; A drip of blood with the words *one love* above the drip and *one blood* below the drip.

The groups keep alliances with Folk Nation and CK (Cop Killas) and are rivals with People Nation. Their criminal activities include narcotics, weapons, extortion, assaults, and intimidation.

The C.O.D. (Children of the Damned) was a family gang started in Windsor, Connecticut, in the mid-1980s. Originally a group consisting of five friends that watched one anothers' back, they occasionally, would do battle with others to protect themselves. During these battles C.O.D. earned a well-respected reputation for attracting wanna-be members. By the late '80s, C.O.D. consisted of more than 100 members, with the five founders leading the group.

In the early '90s, C.O.D. gave birth to a new family that was mostly known for fighting and killing, so it was named the Blood Brothers. Members were also involved in robberies, assassinations for other families, and selling drugs. Members quickly gained respect, although the family's name was not well known. By 1992 the C.O.D. lost power, and the most of the members went on to join other groups. None of the original members took any interest in continuing the Blood Brothers except two.

One led the Blood Brothers, and the other wanted to do something more positive resulting in a division. The structure of the Blood Brothers was changed, several aspects of the family in more positive ways. On January 1, 1993 the Blood Brothers Underground Nation was created in Hartford, Connecticut. This version was created to be more positive, however; this did not mean the end of the original Blood Brothers. Today there are two families that, although different in beliefs, act as one large powerful family.

Members of the Blood Brothers are known to beat and kill members who have been judged disloyal to the family. Nonmembers who disrespect the family are also beaten and killed.

Members of the Imperial Blood Brothers and Blood Brother Unified Nation have exhibited violence both inside correctional facilities and on the streets of Connecticut, New York, New Jersey, Georgia, and other states. Violence includes assaults on staff, inmates, and gang members who do not conduct themselves in a manner in accordance to the gang's rules. Brotherhood members have also assaulted inmates who refuse to join their gang.

The main source of income for the Imperial Blood Brothers and Blood Brother Unified Nation is the sale of drugs.

The Imperial Blood Brothers and Blood Brother Unified Nation have a highly organized and formalized rank structure which includes one elder, an executive staff, security, a secretary of communications, region commanders, chapter leaders, and a defense team.

The Imperial Blood Brothers and Blood Brother Unified Nation have established local leadership in areas where they set up camp. Each chapter leader must report to the region's commander.

Automatic weapons are standard for most members. Knives, poison, and explosives are used by assassins.

All those interested in becoming members must fill out applications that are then reviewed by the executive staff; they must receive final approval by the elder.

In 1998 the Blood Brothers Underground Nation and the Blood Brothers came together to form what is now called the Imperial Blood Brothers and Blood Brother Unified Nation. Showing of the beads has become less visible, but some member have been seen with them.

Reference

Southeastern Connecticut Gang Activities Group (SEGAG). "Imperial Blood Brothers & Blood Brother Unified Nation." Available online. URL: http://www.segag.org. Downloaded on July 19, 2004.

INAGAWA, Kakuji

A lifelong criminal, Kakuji Inagawa came to power in the 1940s and remained a key Japanese underworld figure until the mid-1980s. He founded the Ingawa-kai in 1945 to rival his old master's gang. His main source of income came from gambling casinos, but his gang also ventured into prostitution, loan sharking, and extortion, as well as drug distribution. Their main base of operations was Kanagawa.

Inagawa was well placed in the world of conservative politics, and in 1960 the party in power in Japan, the Liberal Democratic Party, paid Inagawa to recruit a mob of Yakuza and fanatical nationalists to oppose the U.S.-Japan security treaty. In Japan, having lived to a ripe old age despite numerous jail sentences, Inagawa is considered one of the most well-known Japanese gangsters of all time.

INAGAWA-KAI

The Inagawa-kai is reputed to be the largest gang in Tokyo, with more than 8,000 gang members, and is the second-largest gang in Japan. The Inagawa-kai is known for having created most of its wealth from sophisticated business scams. However, it is also known for prostitution, extortion, and drug distribution. Muscle work is often subcontracted out to smaller gangs.

The Inagawa-kai is classified under the Boryoku-dan, the modern version of the traditional Japanese Yakuza organization. Inagawa-kai has now become incorporated, acting as an operating company known as Inagawa Industries.

See also: BORYOKUDAN; INAGAWA, KAKUJI; SUMIYOSHI-KAI; YAMAGUCHI-GUMI.

Reference

Asian Parliamentary Joint Committee on the National Crime Authority. *Organised Crime in Australia, A Discussion Paper by the Parliamentary Joint Committee on the National Crime Authority.*

INTERPOL

Interpol, founded in Vienna in 1923, was disbanded in 1938 and then reconstituted in Paris in 1946. The name *Interpol* was once the telegraphic name for the International Criminal Police Organization. It was officially adopted as the organization's name in 1956 and has since become synonymous with international police cooperation and investigation.

Interpol states that it was "set up for globally enhancing and facilitating cross-border criminal police co-operation. Today, it is the second biggest international organization after the United Nations, with 181 member countries spread over five continents. . . . With the escalation of serious transnational crime, the need for a global police co-operation response has never been more acute."

Interpol's main "mission" is to enhance international police cooperation. Interpol helps introduce, coordinate, and cooperate in helping law-enforcement officials from different police forces, nations,

languages and cultures to cooperate with one another and work together to solve crime. Interpol has only one caveat—since it is an international organization, it must remain above politics. Its charter does not permit the organization or its employees to engage in any investigation or coordination of a political, military, religious, or racial character. The organization says: "Interpol deals only with international crime and not with national crime, i.e., crimes that overlap one or several member countries. . . . Interpol's work covers many specialized areas but its current work is largely related to public safety and terrorism, organized crime, illicit drug production and trafficking, weapons smuggling, trafficking in human beings, money laundering, financial and high-tech crime and corruption."

Located now in Lyon, France, the organization works simultaneously in English, French, Spanish, and Arabic. Interpol receives, stores, analyzes, and circulates criminal intelligence with its more than 181 member nations. Interpol does this 24/7, making it the single largest international criminal database in the world, which can be accessed at any time of the day or night by police forces of member countries anywhere in the world.

Interpol provides the following services, among others, to its member nations:

- maintains a 24-hour remote access to its international database
- posts wanted notices for dangerous or wanted criminals
- posts missing persons notices
- posts unidentified body notices
- publishes world crime statistics
- publishes notices on drug trafficking, currency counterfeiting, sex offenders, murderers, and so on
- hosts international police symposiums
- hosts information exchanges for improving investigative techniques

The General Assembly, Interpol's supreme governing body, meets once a year and makes all the major decisions affecting general policy. It is composed of delegates appointed by the governments of member countries. Each represented member country has one vote.

The executive committee supervises the execution of the decisions of the General Assembly and the work of the secretary general. The secretary general is the organization's chief executive and senior full-time official. He is nominated by the executive committee and elected by a two-thirds majority of the General Assembly to serve a five-year term of office. Interpol is financed by its 181 member countries, whose governments pay annual contributions. These are calculated on a sliding scale according to their gross national product (GNP).

In 2001 Interpol helped or participated in 1,400 arrests or identification of wanted persons whereabouts. Every country that participates in Interpol has an office called the National Central Bureau, that is staffed by that country's own law-enforcement officials. This bureau provides a contact point for international cooperation with offices from other countries.

At any one time, Interpol posts between 6,000 and 7,000 wanted notices from around the world, and the database experiences more than 6,000 searches every month. In 2000, Interpol trafficked 2.5 million messages between nations concerning crime and crime prevention.

"Contrary to popular belief, Interpol officers do not travel around the world investigating cases in different countries. Each member country employs its own officers to operate on its own territory and in accordance with its own national laws," claims the organization.

Reprinted with permission of Interpol, 2004.

Reference

Interpol. "Fact Sheets/Overview." Available online. URL: http://www.interpol.int/Public/icpo/introduction. asp. Downloaded on July 19, 2004.

The former head of Europol, Jurgen Storbeck (left), and Sally M. Light (right), the deputy chief of the U.S. Mission in Denmark, sign an agreement in December 2002 authorizing exchange of personal data of terrorism suspects between the United States and Europe. Europol has also signed a cooperation agreement with Interpol. (AP)

ISHII, Susumu

Susumu Ishii was the reputed boss of the Inagawa-kai, the second largest Yakuza organization in Asia and the largest in Japan. In 1989 Ishii was involved in a scam wherein he sold exclusive memberships to what later turned out to be a pubic golf course. He netted $27.4 million in the scam, selling these shares to major corporations, and he got away with it. In fact as the head of Inagawa-kai he had long done business with many major corporations in Japan. His stock-holdings in major Japanese companies amounted to more than 33 billion yen ($250 billion) and included such prestigious names as Tokyo Corp., Honshu Paper, Nippon Telegraph & Telephone, Nippon Steel, Mitsui Mining, Janome Sewing Machine, Kokusai Kogyo, and Miyaji Iron Works.

Major companies made loans to him (from several million dollars to almost $100 million) to make legitimate business investments, and he repaid them by perpetrating stock scams, driving up company share prices on the Japanese stock market. In 1989 alone, he helped drive up one company stock from $7 to $22. He cashed a portion of his stocks, clearing almost $6 million from the scam, before the stock's price plummeted back down.

He died in 1990 due to brain cancer, and his monies went to his heirs.

See also: INAGAWA-KAI; YAKUZA.

Reference

"Know Your Fellow Investor: A Portrait of Susumu Ishii." 1998 Asset International, Inc. Global Custodian, March 1992.

IVANKOV, Vyacheslav (a.k.a. Little Japanese)

Vyacheslav Ivankov, nicknamed Yaponchik ("Little Japanese"), was, from shortly after his arrival in the United States in 1992 until his arrest by the Federal Bureau of Investigation (FBI) in 1995, a mysterious and even mythical figure. The speculations tossed around about him created an image of a man who was called the father of extortion and the Soviet Union's most influential *vor* (the Russian equivalent of a "made man" in the Italian-American Mafia). He was the "leading crime boss of the Russian Far East" and was reported in the largest Russian-language newspaper in New York City to be the "Red godfather" sent to New York by his fellow *vory* (his fellow made men) to organize and control Russian criminal activities there. U.S. authorities, especially the Federal Bureau of Investigation, certainly acted as if Ivankov were a major crime boss.

Who was this man Ivankov, also known as Yaponchik? What was he doing here? And was he really the Russian crime boss? The Ivankov/Yaponchik case may be the quintessential illustration of how and why a Mafia is created.

Yaponchik was allegedly born in the Soviet Republic of Georgia and grew up in Moscow. He was a champion amateur wrestler in his youth who first went to jail after a bar fight in which (according to his Moscow lawyer) he was defending the honor of a woman. After his release, he began to climb up the Soviet crime ladder—like so many others—by dealing stolen goods on the black market. According to Russian law enforcement authorities. Ivankov formed a criminal organization (called Solsnetskaya) in approximately 1980. Among its activities, this group used false police documents to search the homes of wealthy individuals and steal money and other valuables. In 1982 Yaponchik was caught and convicted for robbery, possession of firearms, forgery, and drug trafficking. He was sentenced to 14 years in prison and served 10. During his imprisonment he was supposedly initiated as a *vor v zakone,* or a "made man" in the Russian Mafiya.

According to Ivankov himself, his prison activities during this period antagonized the Russian Ministry of Internal Affairs, which subsequently conspired with the FBI against him. In a 1995 interview with a Moscow correspondent, Ivankov said that the ministry could not forgive his efforts to reform the Soviet prison system while he was locked up in Siberia—efforts that were in support of his lifelong resistance to communism. The FBI, he says, was taken in by the criminal authorities who run the criminal state that was Soviet Russia. That Vyacheslav Ivankov might not be just any ordinary Russian criminal could be surmised from his supposed acquaintance with Yuri Churbanov, the Brezhnev son-in-law who was involved in the Uzbek cotton scandal. Ivankov's early release from prison in 1991 reportedly resulted from the intervention of a powerful politician and the bribery of a judge on the Russian Supreme Court.

Ivankov came to the United States in March 1992 with a regular business visa indicating that he would be working in the movie industry. How was a man with a felony conviction, 10 years in prison, and a reputation as one of the most powerful criminals in Russia able to receive a visa readily to come to the United States? U.S. Immigration and Naturalization officials claimed that immigration officials in Moscow were overwhelmed and had neither the time nor resources to investigate the criminal backgrounds of all visa applicants. U.S. officials had to depend on both inept and corrupt Russian authorities for this background information. The real reason for Ivankov's being here is open to some dispute. The Russian Ministry of Internal Affairs advised the FBI in January 1993 that Ivankov had come to the United States to "manage and control ROC [Russian organized-crime] activities in this country." Handelman says, however, that his American police sources initially denied that they had received any such warning. Nonetheless, this advice was ultimately taken to heart by the FBI. Alexander Grant, news editor for *Noovoye Russkoye Slovo,* told us in 1994 that Ivankov was indeed the highest-ranking Russian criminal in the United States but that he was "not criminally active here." Grant said that Ivankov had to get out of Russia because "it became too dangerous for him there—dangerous because of the new criminal entrepreneurs who don't respect the likes of Yaponchik." Whatever his original reason for coming, Yaponchik was indeed criminally active after he arrived in the United States, but, as with so much else about him, the scope of his criminal activity is open to controversy. One view is that "Ivankov's New York branch of the Solntsevskaya gang had about 100 members and was recognized on the street as the premier Russian crime group in Brooklyn" and, further, that Ivankov's was the strongest of the Russian organized-crime groups in this country. Similarly relying on FBI sources, Sterling concluded that "[m]uch as Lucky Luciano did with the American mafia sixty-odd years ago, Ivankov is turning an assortment of unruly and loosely articulated Russian gangs on American soil into a modern, nationwide crime corporation." If there is any evidence to support any such assessment, however, it is not apparent.

When he was arrested by the FBI in June 1995, Ivankov was charged with supervising the extortion of several million dollars from an investment advisory firm run by two Russian businessmen. He and three codefendants were convicted of this extortion in July 1996. On the face of it, there was nothing particularly sophisticated about the crime; in fact, one is led to wonder why—if Ivankov was indeed the boss of a large criminal organization and the most powerful Russian mobster in the United States—he was directly involved in arranging and negotiating with the extortion victims. Organized-crime bosses are usually insulated from this sort of direct involvement. Further, it was alleged in the FBI's arrest complaint that the murder in Moscow of the father of one of the victims was part of the threat used to further the extortion. Yet in a telephone conversation dealing with this murder—a conversation that was a part of the arrest complaint—Ivankov, who was supposedly masterminding the scheme, seems ignorant of the murder. Finally, if Ivankov were the new Lucky Luciano, where were the other charges that one might expect could have been derived from his more than two years of high-level criminal activity before the particular extortion began in November 1994?

Ivankov is clearly a serious criminal. Information from Russian authorities, his prison experience, and even his tattoos all suggest that he is a *vor*. He probably is the toughest Russian criminal in the United States, but it is doubtful that he is or was the head of a major criminal organization or a Mafia boss. There is no evidence that he attempted to gain monopoly control over any criminal activities or that he systematically used violence or corruption. On the basis of this single crime, it is difficult to assess the economic, physical, psychological, and societal harm caused by his offenses. The description of the crime itself, however, suggests that it was a rather blundering effort. Finally, returning to one of our Mafia criteria of organizational capacity for harm, Ivankov was said to have had only a loosely affiliated group of some 10 people and not an extensive and sophisticated criminal organization.

In the meantime, Ivankov has been sentenced to U.S. federal prison for nine years and seven months. In a recent interview from prison, Ivankov accuses the FBI of feeding the myth of a Russian Mafia to prove the usefulness of their Russian section. They are, he says, "only tilting with windmills." According to Ivankov, there is no myth about organized crime in Russia because everyone knows that "Russia is one uninterrupted criminal swamp." The criminals are in the Kremlin and the Duma (the legislature), and anyone who thinks that someone like him is the head of all these "bandits" is delirious.

Reference

David Amoruso. "Vyacheslav Ivankov." Gangsters Inc. Available online. URL: http://gangstersinc.tripod.com/ Ivankov.html Downloaded on July 16, 2004.

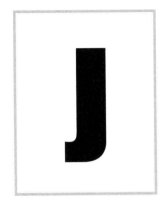

JAMAICAN Posse

The Jamaican Posse is known to operate in New York City and surrounding areas such as southern Connecticut and New Jersey. Membership consists mostly of Jamaican males, but there is little evidence to indicate a formal posse hierarchy within the different branches of the posse. There appears to be a self-identification with other Jamaicans who share similar values (inclination toward criminal and anti-social behavior) that leads to the appearance of a formal body. However, within the various posses, there does exist strong individual leadership, especially among those engaged in terrorist activities or sophisticated criminal activity.

There are more than 40 different posses. Colors that may be associated with posse members are yellow, green, and red. Posses may have working relationships with West Coast street gangs, Colombians, La Cosa Nostra, and have been known to associate with 20 Luv, YBY, and the Brotherhood. Rival ethnic groups include blacks, Caribbean Hispanic, Puerto Rican, whites, and Rastafarians. Illicit activities include illegal drug and weapons, possession and smuggling illegal aliens into the United States.

The Jamaican Posse entered the drug and weapons scene in the early 1980s. Prior to 1986 they were involved in guns and marijuana. They now have also entered the crack market. The centers of trafficking are New York and Miami, with Connecticut's major cities as secondary distribution points (Hartford, New Haven, Bridgeport).

Posse members do not associate with Rastafarians, and some basic ideological differences exist between the two. In the early 1970s, Rastafarians controlled a good portion of the New York drug market. The same market in the 1980s and 1990s appeared to be in control of posse members. Recent information indicates the the major rift between the two groups occurred over cocaine production in Jamaica. The posse is for cocaine production and The Rastafarians are against cocaine but for the production and sale of marijuana in Jamaica.

There are two basic posses, the Spangler Posse and the Shower Posse. All posses are politically aligned with either the People's National Party (PNP), a group said to have socialist tendencies and is rumored to be aligned with Fidel Castro or the Jamaican Labor Party (JLP), reportedly involved with the United States Central Intelligence Agency. The Spangler Posse is aligned with PNP, and the Shower Posse is aligned with JLP.

Posse members are known for drive-by shootings in disputes with rival gangs over drug turf and for ritualized killings of members who "rip off" profits on drugs. The killing ritual usually involves shooting the individual five times; four to the chest and one to the head. Posse members have little regard for public safety or human life. Posse violence can be directed at anyone who they feel has crossed them or who is in their way. Posse members are known to show a lack of respect for law enforcement and corrections personnel. They are usually well informed of the laws and rights of individuals, and they have proven that they will take whatever steps necessary to avoid arrest, commit violent acts while in custody, murder witnesses, and effect an escape by any means possible. Posse members are known to falsify documents and will attempt to gain false credentials of police officers, federal agents, military officers, and intelligence officers.

JHERI-CURL Gang

The Jheri-Curl Gang was a Dominican underworld crime organization in the late 1980s and early 1990s established by career criminal Rafael Martinez. Martinez and his brothers Augusto, Loren, Daniel, and Pepin operated in New York City on West 157th Street from Broadway to the Hudson River. The gang was so named because of the way Martinez and other gang leaders coiffed their hair.

Although extortion and intimidation were their calling cards, the source of their income was from dealing drugs. Allegedly, their supplier was the infamous Pedro Corporan. Estimates by the New York Drug Enforcement Task Force state that Corporan was delivering up to 10 kilos of cocaine weekly to the Jheri Curls.

The group was flashy, riding in gold luxury cars and waving guns. They were known for their special brand of random violence, often shooting or intimidating local civilians for no reason other than for the sheer joy of it. Twenty-three members were arrested in 1991, effectively crippling and then shutting down the gang.

JOE Boys (a.k.a. Joe Fong Boys, JBs, Jelly Beans)

This violent Asian street gang in San Francisco's Chinatown was a rival of the Wah Ching, who remain the dominant force in Asian-based crime in Chinatown. Originally called the Joe Fong Boys, as the leader of the gang was Joe Fong, they became the Joe Boys after Joe Fong was convicted and sent to jail. Before Joe Fong, the gang had been known as the Chung Ching Yee.

"On July 4, 1977, a long standing feud between Chinatown gangs Joe Boys and Wah Ching led to a botched assassination attempt at the Golden Dragon Restaurant, 841 Washington Street. Members of Joe Boys were enraged after Wah Ching vandalized the graves of Joy Boys members. Five innocent bystanders, including two tourists, were killed and 11 injured when Joe Boys descended on the Golden Dragon to avenge their dead," wrote journalist Hank Donat. This infamous event in San Francisco history became known as the Golden Dragon Massacre. The massacre eventually led to the formation of the San Francisco Police Department's Gang Task Force.

See also: WAH CHING.

Reference

Mister SF. "Notorious SF: Golden Dragon Massacre." Available online. URL: http://www.mistersf.com. Downloaded on July 16, 2004.

JOMPHE, Renaud (a.k.a. King of Verdun)

Renaud Jomphe was born in 1959 and grew up in Verdun, Quebec. He hooked up with the Cazzetta brothers and was a founder of the Rock Machine motorcycle club. By the early 1990s, Jomphe ran a thriving drug-trafficking network and had earned the label "the king of Verdun."

The biker was highly respected by other members. He was described as a natural leader and a mentor. Unlike most criminals, Jomphe was seen as a negotiator and considered violence as a last resort. That's why when the gang's leader, Salvatore Cazzetta, was jailed for drug trafficking, Jomphe was considered the ideal choice to take over as leader.

When 11-year-old Daniel Desrochers became a victim of the Rock Machine/Hells Angels turf war, Jomphe told the *Journal de Montreal*'s Michel Auger that "we don't attack, and we certainly don't kill, children." He also labeled the Hells Angels as a "bunch of goons on a power trip."

The day after the interview, a motorcycle shop co-owned by Jomphe was shot up by rivals. The store's manager was injured and a customer was killed. Neither victim was connected to the Rock Machine.

Renaud Jomphe became a victim of the biker war on October 18, 1996. The Rock Machine leader was seated with member Christian Deschenes and associate Raymond Laureau in a booth at the rear of Restaurant Kim Hoa on Wellington Street when a man approached the table, fired several shots, and fled out the back door. Jomphe and Deschenes were killed; Laureau was wounded in the shoulder.

Rock Machine member turned informant Peter Paradis, who was also at the restaurant at the time of Jomphe's murder, later said in court that Jomphe's cousin was responsible for the ambush. According to Paradis, the cousin sold them out to their Hells Angels enemies.

Renaud Jomphe's funeral was held on October 24, 1996. The night before, police arrested a member of the Rowdy Crew biker gang, a Hells Angels puppet club, loitering near the funeral home, so the family canceled the church services. Instead, Jomphe's body, followed by five limousines and 11 Cadillacs carrying yellow-and-black floral arrangements, was taken to an east-end crematorium.

See also: BANDIDOS.

Reference

Gary Francoeur. "Renaud Jomphe." Wiseguy Wally. Available online. URL: http://www.geocities.com/wiseguywally/RenaudJomphe.html. Downloaded on July 16, 2004.

—G.F.

JUÁREZ Cartel (a.k.a. Carrillo Fuentes Organization)

Amado Carrillo Fuentes, based in Ciudad Juárez, Mexico, was known as the Lord of the Skies because of his renown in transporting plane loads of cocaine for Colombian traffickers. Amado Carrillo Fuentes had extensive ties to a number of officials in law enforcement and the military, up to and including the former commissioner of the now-disbanded National Institute to Combat Drugs (NICD) General Jesús Gutiérrez Rebollo. Before his death in July 1997 and after the arrest of General Gutiérrez Rebollo in March, Amado Carrillo Fuentes was under pressure from law enforcement in the United States and Mexico. As a consequence, he made efforts to disguise his appearance through cosmetic surgery and to relocate some of his operations to Chile. Amado's brother, Vicente, has been indicted in the western district of Texas for cocaine violations and a warrant was issued for his arrest in late 1993. He has not yet been apprehended.

The Carrillo Fuentes organization is based in Juárez and is associated with the Cali Rodríguez Orejuela organization and the Ochoa brothers of Medellín. This organization, which is also involved in heroin and marijuana trafficking, handles large cocaine shipments from Colombia. Their regional bases in Guadalajara, Hermosillo, and Torreon serve as storage locations where later, the drugs are moved closer to the border for eventual shipment into the United States. The scope of the Carrillo Fuentes network is staggering; it reportedly forwards $20–$30 million to Colombia for each major operation and generates tens of millions of dollars in profits per week.

Two major Drug Enforcement Administration investigations in 1997 demonstrated the impact that the Carrillo Fuentes cocaine-distribution organization has on U.S. citizens. The first investigation showed that just one Juárez-based organized crime cell shipped more than 30 tons of cocaine into U.S. communities and returned more than $100 million in profits to Mexico in less than two years. Distribution of multiton quantities of cocaine, once dominated by the Cali-based drug traffickers, is now controlled from Mexico in cities such as Chicago, Dallas, Denver, Houston, Los Angeles, Phoenix, San Diego, San Francisco, and Seattle. The Carrillo Fuentes organization is also beginning to make inroads into the distribution of cocaine in the East Coast, particularly New York City, the traditional stronghold of the Cali drug cartel.

In April 1997 two agents assigned to Mexico's new Organized Crime Unit were kidnapped and killed. The agents, who had investigated Carrillo Fuentes, were kidnapped on April 4 and found on April 25 in the trunk of a car in Mexico City. Both had been bound, gagged, beaten, and shot in the face. Reportedly, the two agents were killed because of the unit's raid on the home of Carrillo Fuentes's son. The OCU's primary function is to execute the modern investigative techniques provided for by the 1997 Organized Crime Laws enacted in the United States and Mexico.

A second investigation targeted a Chicago-based transportation and distribution cell of the Carrillo Fuentes organization. This cell was responsible for the monthly smuggling of at least one and a half tons of cocaine from Mexico to the United States. The investigation resulted in the arrest of a Mexican distribution cell operating in New York which delivered hundreds of kilograms of cocaine to Dominican and Colombian traffickers in the New York area. The investigation culminated with the seizure of more than 1,600 kilograms of cocaine and $1.3 million from the Mexican organization in New York.

These investigations revealed the manner in which new drug-trafficking routes are established by the

Carrillo Fuentes cells in the United States. This trend is constantly growing and changing. Despite increased intelligence efforts targeting the command and control and identifying the leaders of the Carrillo Fuentes organization, key lieutenants have not been apprehended in Mexico. For example, Eduardo González Quirarte has been identified as a key manager for the Carrillo Fuentes organization along the border. He is responsible for arranging shipments of cocaine across the border and ensuring that money is transferred back into Mexico. He has links to the Mexican military and law enforcement officials, which make him a significant leader in future Carrillo Fuentes operations.

Like their Colombian counterparts, the Carillo Fuentes traffickers use sophisticated technology and countersurveillance methods. The syndicate employs state-of-the-art communications devices to conduct business. Attempts by the Carrillo Fuentes organization to expand his operations into the lucrative East Coast market that has traditionally been dominated by traffickers from Colombia have been documented.

Since Amado Carrillo Fuentes's death in July 1997, a violent power struggle has ensued as rivals and associates sorted out business arrangements and turf in an effort to control the lucrative Juárez smuggling corridor. Another major Mexican trafficking organization—the Muñoz Talavera organization—is apparently attempting to capitalize on the perceived weakened state of the Amado Carrillo Fuentes organization. The ensuing power struggle has resulted in nearly 50 drug-related murders in the Juárez area since Amado Carrillo Fuentes's death. The victims of these murders have included four doctors, two attorneys, and one federal comandante. The violence associated with these murders was never more apparent than during the gangland-style machine-gun shooting at the Max Fin Restaurant in August 1997. This shooting resulted in the murders of six known drug traffickers and two innocent bystanders. It is now understood that Vicente Carrillo Fuentes runs the organization and has largely been successful in marginalizing the Muñoz-Talavera organization.

Reference

Thomas A. Constantine. "International Organized Crime Syndicates and Their Impact on the U.S." U.S. Drug Enforcement Administration. Available online. URL: http:// www.dea.gov/pubs/cngrtest/ct980226.htm. Downloaded on July 15, 2004.

JUNGLE Boys

The Jungle Boys originally came from New Britain, Connecticut starting about 1976 or 1977. They have recently surfaced in New Haven, Connecticut, facilities as a result of several major drug and homicide arrests in the New Haven area in the last couple of years. On June 22, 1992, 18 members were arrested in a major drug raid in New Haven involving federal, state, and local law-enforcement agencies.

In Connecticut's adult correctional facilities, the Jungle Boys and other New Haven gangs usually band together to form the Elm Street Incorporated. At Manson Youth Institution (MYI), the combining of the Jungle Boys and Kensington Street Incorporated (KSI) is known as the Elm Street Gang.

Membership is made up mostly of black males. Established hierarchy and chain of command include a boss, an underboss, lieutenants, and soldiers. There are no known documented bylaws or charter for the Jungle Boys. As customary with corporate drug gangs, the Jungle Boys do not display any gang colors. Hand sign is all fingers extended except for the ring finger which is bent; however, Jungle Boys members like to display their jewelry as a sign of status.

They have no particular alliances on the streets. The Jungle Boys and other New Haven-based gangs will align with 20 Lov inside correctional facilities. Rivals are the Island Brothers and Bridgeport-based gangs (Nation and Brotherhood).

The Jungle Boys are primarily involved in the trafficking and distribution of cocaine and marijuana in the New Haven area and were a longtime, effective means for sales and distribution of drugs. They worked with many different drug cartels over the years.

In addition to the drugs, the Jungle Boys have been linked to six homicides that are considered drug related. Jungle Boy members are also known to carry firearms and have been linked to several drive-by shootings.

RECENT HISTORY

The Jungle Boys have dominated the Church Street South Housing Project in New Haven since the mid-1980s, and this area is considered the gang's turf. The Jungle Boys are considered one of the five major drug gangs functioning in New Haven, having been linked to being a major part of the city's drug-trafficking activity and gang membership. The main source of income for the Jungle Boys are funds derived from the sale of cocaine and marijuana.

The Jungle Boys have been responsible for six homicides in New Haven and have been linked to numerous drive-by shootings. In correctional facilities, they have been involved in several incidents involving rival gangs from Bridgeport (Brotherhood and Nation).

The primary leaders of the Jungle Boys are presently incarcerated. When incarcerated, members of the Jungle Boys will tend to align themselves with other New Haven-based gangs to obtain a numerical power base.

Reference

Southeastern Connecticut Gang Activities Group (SEGAG). "Jungle Boys." Available online. URL: http://www.segag.org. Updated on October 14, 2003.

JUNIOR Black Mafia

Based in Philadelphia, the Junior Black Mafia (JBM) is involved primarily in the distribution of drugs, mainly cocaine; it also offers murder contract services. The JBM cooperates with associates of the Bruno-Scarfo Mafia crime family in the distribution of cocaine and appears to have modeled its criminal methods after that organization, relying heavily on violence and extortion to further its drug enterprises.

The JBM came into existence in 1985 to counter a sudden migration of New York-based Jamaican posses into the Philadelphia drug scene. Original members of the 1960s Black Mafia (and later Black, Inc.) organized African-American youths into the JBM to thwart the Jamaican influence and to regain from the Jamaicans control of drug distribution in the affected areas of Philadelphia.

The JBM is estimated to have approximately 100 members and about 300 street-level associates. Its members drive expensive cars and often wear gold jewelry and rings with the JBM initials encrusted in diamonds. Originally, admission into the group required a $1,000 initiation fee, lack of a criminal record, and the operation of an established illegal activity.

In Philadelphia the JBM has sought to expand its drug-trafficking profits by offering independent narcotics dealers membership in the JBM. The Pennsylvania Crime Commission documented two 1989 incidents in which the JBM targeted for death dealers who turned down such offers. Like most local gangs, the JBM supplied sales and distribution services in the U.S.'s sixth largest city to major international drug-smuggling cartels, enabling these cartels to grow.

Information regarding the JBM's influence or activity in New Jersey has been limited due to the lack of a coordinated intelligence-collection effort. The commission has been able to document at least two members and eight associates living in Camden and Burlington counties. On February 20, 1991, five associates of the JBM from Philadelphia were arrested in Camden County by the Philadelphia office of the Drug Enforcement Administration (DEA) while transporting a kilogram of cocaine intended for sale in Philadelphia. Just as the old Black Mafia from Philadelphia eventually spread into Camden, Burlington, Gloucester, Cumberland, and Atlantic Counties, it is likely that this new group of African-American organized criminals will follow suit.

Reference

New Jersey State Commission of Investigation, Robert J. Clark, Francis A. Betzler, Bruce C. Best, and Debra A. Sowney. "Afro-Lineal Organized Crime." November 29, 1990. Available online. URL: http://www.state.nj.us/sci/pdf/afro.pdf. Accessed on November 24, 2004.

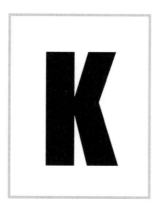

KAYA Clan

In September 1992 in Duisburg, Germany, 20.3 kilos of heroin were discovered aboard a semitrailer. The two drivers were Nezir Kaya, born in 1966 in Nusaybin, Turkey, and Hasib Kaya, born in 1969 in the same town. The vehicle belonged to the trucking company of Osman Kaya, Nezir's brother and Hasib's cousin, which was located in Icel. Tipped off by their German colleagues, the Turkish police raided the company's premises in May 1993. They found 18 Kalashnikovs and 4,000 cartridges in a secret compartment in a tanker truck, bound for a PKK (Partiya Karkaren Kurdistan, or Kurdistan Workers' Party) guerrilla unit.

See also: BAYBASIN CLAN; DEMIR CLAN; KITAY CLAN; SAKIK CLAN; KONUKLU-AY CLAN; KURDISH CRIMINAL CLANS AND THE PKK; SENAR CLAN.

Reference

Based on articles about Kaya Clan from former website of the Center for the Study of the Contemporary Criminal Menace, part of Institut de Criminologie, Université Pantheon-Assas, Le centre Panthéon, 12, place du Panthéon 7531 Paris, France.

KENNY Gang, James

On November 14, 2001, Royal Canadian Mounted Police raided 24 locations in Ottawa, Hull, Gatineau, Laval, Eastern Ontario, and Halifax, arresting 19 suspects allegedly involved in a major drug ring with links in Eastern Canada and overseas. The ring supplied hashish to the Ottawa and Outaouais areas as well as to contacts in the Montreal area. During the investigation, police seized 45 kilograms of hash and $36,000 in cash. During the raids, police seized $173,000 in cash, 48 kilograms of hash, 1 kilograms marijuana, 45 grams of cocaine, five vehicles, and firearms including a handgun, an assault rifle, and various hunting rifles. They also restrained seven properties and two boats. The total amount of items seized and restrained exceeds $1,200,000.

The investigation was the culmination of Project Angle, a one-year joint task-force operation led by the Ottawa RCMP's Integrated Proceeds of Crime Section and the Ottawa Police Service.

The main targets of this investigation were ringleader James Kenny, 47 years old, of Ottawa, and his brother, Brian Kenny, 52, of Ottawa. They and the other suspects were charged with numerous counts of drug-related charges, including trafficking and importing drugs, possession of proceeds of crime, and money laundering.

The hashish was allegedly imported by the Kenny organization from Spain, where one of the suspects lived. Boats were chartered to sail the drugs from Spain to Halifax, where other suspects purportedly provided assistance. The drugs were then allegedly shipped overland to the Ottawa and Outaouais regions and sometimes sold to connections in Montreal.

Reference

Royal Canadian Mounted Police. "RCMP-GRC, 2003-01-16 Important Notices." Available online. URL:

177

KHERI, Chilla

Chilla Kheri is from Jaffna, India. He is alleged to be the kingpin of an international drug-smuggling racket operating in different parts of India. He was connected with the Liberation Tigers of Tamil Eelam, a violent separatist force in Sri Lanka headed by Velupillai Pirapaharan.

He was living in Bhopal under the name Ravi Kumar and engaged in illicit traffic of drugs derived from the opium poppy, cultivated in the western belt of Madhya Pradesh. Chilla Kheri had confessed during interrogation that he had committed two murders in Delhi and Chennai. He was also wanted by Delhi and Chennai police for illicit trafficking in drugs.

Preliminary investigations by Bhopal police revealed that Chilla Kheri was the main conduit for smuggling "brown sugar" (heroin) to Chennai and other points in the southern parts of India. He had named some small-time actors from the south saying that they used to visit Bhopal to buy brown sugar and cannabis procured from the western belt of Madhya Pradesh and Rajastan border. Chilla Kheri has admitted that he was part of an international drug-smugglers' racket operating from south India.

See also: LIBERATION TIGERS OF TAMIL EELAM.

KILIC, Dundar

Dundar Kilic was easily the most powerful and most feared Turkish don in the history of that country's underworld. In some circles he was referred to as the godfather of godfathers. His career as an organized-crime legend spanned four decades, which spoke for his power as well as his cunning in creating and surviving for so long in a business that specializes in early retirement plans. Turkish authorities first noticed him when he was arrested for the first time at age 14; after that he rose quickly through the ranks of Turkey's varied and violent underworld. Kilic was alleged to have killed three people personally, while shooting and injuring dozens more throughout his career. This violent streak helped him establish himself as a man to be reckoned with among the Mafia dons of his youth and garnered for him the respect he needed to operate his vast underworld empire.

Dundar Kilic was a complicated man. He assisted many high-ranking Turkish Mafiosos to succeed

before his death at age 64. There were several of note, the most notable being Alaatin Cakici. Cakici was Dundar's son-in-law. Alaatin had married his daughter Ugur. However, there were rumors of an affair while she was married to Alaatin, and he had his former chauffeur assassinate his wife right in front of Cakici's son Onur. The real reason was that Ugur was talking too much; whether to competing dons or to authorities was never really clear. But one thing was clear: Dundar sought no revenge for the murder. It is unknown whether he refused to make his grandson a complete orphan or could not argue his daughter's assassination due to her own malfeasance. Many people expected Dundar and Alaatin to go to war, but no such bloodshed ever materialized.

In old age, Dundar became seriously depressed, and his sole purpose in life became to educate and establish his grandson as the new Turkish Mafia chieftain. According to http://www.geocities.com/OrganizedCrimeSyndicates, "Dundar was instrumental in the rise of Onur as a mafia power as well as the ascension of another young mafia leader in thirty something Huseyin Basak." Basak was assigned to watch over Onur and teach him the ways of the Mafia. The two have been very loyal to one another, and Basak has taken Onur under his wing in a most genuine way. The young Onur was arrested and is serving jail time. Basak is now quietly running Turkey's largest criminal empire.

"Aged and ailing, Dundar suffering from eye cancer, lung and heart troubles, the don died in August of 1999 at the age of 64," OrganizedCrimeSyndicates continued. "Following his death, it became apparent that Kilic was a man with a big heart as news of several charitable donations he had made over the years circulated through the press. He provided an opportunity for an estimated 10,000 students to obtain extended education degrees through the years."

See also: BASAK, HUSEYIN; DONMEZ, OSMAN; OZBIZERDIK, ONUR; UGURLU, ABUZER.

KILIC Gang   *See* KILIC, DUNDAR.

KIMURA, Tokutaro

Tokutaro Kimura held high-ranking offices in the Japanese government and in the justice system in the years just after World War II. He was the minister of justice and later the head of the Self-Defense Force. He used these positions to help the Yakuza. His friend, the man who recommended him to the position, was Yoshio Kodama, one of the biggest Yakuza bosses in history. Kimura used his position to get early releases for Yakuza prisoners that had been taken into custody.

KITAY Clan

Hakki Kitay was arrested on September 1, 1993, at a Turkish border checkpoint in Kapikule, en route from Bulgaria, based on a tip from the Dutch, German, and British police, following the seizure of 14.8 kilograms of heroin in the Turkish city of Icel on October 29, 1992. Sentenced in Turkey on October 19, 1993, to 10 years in prison for drug trafficking, Hakki was tied to 22 cases involving the importation of a total of 1.2 tons of heroin into Germany between 1990 and 1993. His clan was also connected. While under surveillance during a business trip to Germany, on October 23, 1992, Hakki contacted Emin Uysal and Selim Curukkaya, also known as Tilki Selim (Selim the fox), top managers of the Partiya Karkaren Kurdistan, or Kurdistan Workers' Party (PKK) financial operations in Germany. Hakki is the brother of Vahdettin Kitay, also known as Veli, head of a regional PKK guerrilla operation, who was killed in October 1989 in a clash with the Turkish Police during which one police officer was killed. Hakki is the father of Nizamettin Kitay, also known as Vedat, who trained at the PKK's "military academy" in Lebanon, and is a cadre in the PKK's guerrilla unit in Bingol Province, led by Mahmut Curukkaya, also known as Doctor Suleiman, who is the brother of Tilki Selim. Between May and November 1993, German police dismantled a network between Hamburg and Bremen of 22 "political refugees" or "asylum seekers" in possession of 16 kilograms of heroin. Among them were Ihsan and Senol Kitay; the latter, Hakki's son, was murdered in Germany shortly thereafter. Also arrested in the case were Sehabettin, a former head of the PKK for the city of Elazig, and two other known party militants. In this instance too, the other Kitays had drug-trafficking records in several European countries.

See also: BAYBASIN CLAN; DEMIR CLAN; KAYA CLAN; KONUKLU-AY CLAN; KURDISH CRIMINAL CLANS AND THE PKK; SAKIK CLAN; SENAR CLAN.

Reference

Department for the Study of the Contemporary Criminal Menace. "Two Typical 'Degenerate Guerilla Groups': The Liberation Tigers of Emil Eelam and the Kurdistan Worker's Party." *Notes and Etudes* ("Terrorism and Political Violence" special) 32 (June 1996). Available online. URL: http://www.drmcc.org/docs/ne32.pdf. Accessed on December 16, 2004.

KODAMA, Yoshio

Yoshio Kodama was born in 1911 and grew up in a poor family. He spent most of his childhood living with relatives in Korea. At an early age Kodama showed much interest in politics and at age 21 started his own right-wing ultranationalist political group. The main objective of this group was to assassinate the prime minister and top cabinet ministers. Before his group could do this, however, Kodama's plans were discovered, and he was arrested and imprisoned for three-and-a-half years.

When Kodama was released from prison, he started to work for that same government he had wanted to destroy, serving as an espionage agent, and he maintained an extensive network of spies throughout Asia. He saw to it that countless shipments filled with nickel, cobalt, copper, and radium arrived in Japan to strengthen the war effort. Kodama did not totally play by the rules, however: Together with the normal shipments he included heroin. For his work on behalf of the Japanese government, Kodama was awarded the title of rear admiral. When the war was over, Kodama was worth an estimated $175 million.

Despite all the money, Kodama was in big trouble. After the war he was classified a class-A war criminal by the allied powers and was sentenced to two years in prison. Later, he was released on a general amnesty. Out of prison, Kodama started to work for the allied powers as a go-between for the G-2 section of the allied forces and the Yakuza. Kodama supplied Yakuza muscle to take out orders by the political party and allied forces. Kodama and his connections were branched out throughout Japan and Asia; he had enormous power. In the early 1960s Kodama used his power to organize a truce between several warring Yakuza clans. He made an alliance between Kazuo Taoka, boss of the Yamaguchi Gumi, and Hisayuki Machii, a Korean boss in charge of the Tosei Kai. After the truce Kodama was looked upon as the underworld's visionary godfather and made peace between several other warring Yakuza clans.

In the mid-1970s Kodama used his power to give Lockheed Corporation an opening in the Japanese market. In return for a $2.1 million dollar bribe, Kodamo discredited an All Nippon Airways president who resigned and thereby made way for Lockheed. It became a big scandal when the truth came out and

Kodama's good name was dragged through the mud. While awaiting trial Kodama suffered a stroke and in January 1984 died peacefully. He is still looked at as the big peacemaker of the Japanese underworld.

See also: YAKUZA.

Reference

David Amoruso. "Yoshio Kodama." Gangsters Inc. Available online. URL: http://gangstersinc.tripod.com/Kodama.html Downloaded on July 16, 2004.

—*D.A.*

KON, Johnny

Johnny Kon is a former Big Circle associate and a convicted heroin smuggler. He testified that he helped organize a group of Big Circle Gang members into a tightly organized and disciplined group known as the Flaming Eagles, which expanded from jewelry-store robberies in Hong Kong to a worldwide heroin distribution network. All of Kon's Big Circle associates were also members of other triads. The Flaming Eagles, one of the largest Chinese gangs, have seized control of the U.S. heroin trade in a difficult war with the U.S. Mafia.

See also: BIG CIRCLE GANG; FLAMING EAGLES.

Reference

Parliamentary Joint Committee on the National Crime Authority. "Asian Organised Crime in Australia: A Discussion Paper by the Parliamentary Joint Committee on the National Crime Authority." Available online. URL: http://www.aph.gov.au/senate/committee/acc_ctte/completed_inquiries/pre1996/ncaaoc/report/report5.htm. Accessed on November 24, 2004.

KONUKLU-AY Clan

On March 8, 1995, following several months of surveillance, the police uncovered two heroin-refining labs near the village of Saray, in the Turkish province of Tekirdag, and arrested 14 members, or allies, of the Konuklu and Ay clans. The labs were found to contain 92 kilograms of heroin, 336 kilograms of Afghan morphine base, and 32 kilograms of acetic anhydride, in addition to two Kalashnikovs, various handguns, and internal Partiya Karkaren Kurdistan, or Kurdistan Workers' Party (PKK) documents. One of the farms belonged to the Konuklu, specifically Mrs. Gulistan Konuklu, herself a daughter of Nasrullah Ay, a PKK cadre. In the Konuklu clan, headed by Mehmet Ali Konuklu, Nihat, Ramazan, and Sahin Konuklu are believed to

manage the heroin production operations, and Yusuf Konuklu handles overseas sales and marketing. The second lab was owned by Nusrettin Ay. His sons, Hikmet and Kurbettin, are said to produce the drug, while two other sons, Heybet and Ali, sell it overseas. Documents found on the scene showed that part of the profits go to the PKK. Some members of these clans are also active in the PKK logistical unit: care for the wounded; supplying radios, runners, propaganda distribution; and so on.

See also: BAYBASIN CLAN; DEMIR CLAN; KAYA CLAN; KITAY CLAN; KONUKLU-AY CLAN; KURDISH CRIMINAL CLANS AND THE PKK; SAKIK CLAN; SENAR CLAN.

Reference

Department for the Study of the Contemporary Criminal Menace. "Two Typical 'Degenerate Guerilla Groups': The Liberation Tigers of Emil Eelam and the Kurdistan Worker's Party." *Notes and Etudes* ("Terrorism and Political Violence" special) 32 (June 1996). Available online. URL: http://www.drmcc.org/docs/ne32.pdf. Accessed on December 16, 2004.

KORATAEV, Oleg

Oleg Korataev was a former Soviet boxer known to be a brutal mob enforcer. He was shot to death on January 12, 1994, near the Arbat Restaurant in Brighton Beach, Brooklyn, New York. He was attending a party at the restaurant and was shot in the back of the head as he stepped outside to get some air.

See also: RUSSIAN MAFIYA.

Reference

New Jersey State Commission of Investigation, New York Organized Crime Task Force, New York State Commission of Investigation, Pennsylvania Crime Commission, with Rutgers University. "The Tri-State Joint Soviet-Émigré Organized Crime Project." 1992. Available online. URL: http://www.state.nj.us/sci/pdf/russian.pdf. Accessed on November 24, 2004.

KRAY Twins

Ronnie and Reggie Kray were popular and violent mobsters in the 1960s in Britain. The two impeccably dressed twins were known for a personal brand of violence. They were known for theft, professional enforcement, extortion, and murder. Well-known club owners, the Krays owned outright or had interest in more than 30 clubs and bars. Many that they owned outright were bought for little since they had

Funeral procession for Reggie Kray in London on October 11, 2000 (AP)

suffered some kind of fire damage due to arson prior to the Krays buying those establishments.

They were born on October 24, 1933. Reggie was always the brighter and more sociable of the two. Ronnie was more of a loner, who liked animals. Ronnie had a short temper and was extremely violent. Ronnie was very feared because of his strength and sadism.

Ronnie was well known in homosexual circles, sharing quarters with royalty and other highly placed persons. Reggie, on the other hand, was a ladies' man and a highly sought bachelor.

The two were well known in London and were often celebrated and glamorized by Fleet Street newspapers. However, the murders of George Cornell and Jack "the Hat" McVite helped to put the Krays away. The Krays received lengthy sentences. Ronnie died in jail, and Reggie died not long after his release after 25 years in prison.

See also: CORNELL, GEORGE; FRASER, FRANK; MCVITE, JACK; RICHARDSON, CHARLIE; RICHARDSON, EDDIE; RICHARDSON GANG.

KUANG-NAN, Yang

Aggressive leader of the Four Seas Gang, one of the most powerful gangs in Taiwan. Kuang-nan was a trusted lieutenant of Chen Yung-ho. According to the *Taipei Times*, "Yang is suspected of involvement in two unsolved murders—the 1996 slaying of the former head of the Four Seas Gang, Chen Yung-ho, who was shot dead in a Taipei restaurant, and the 1998 killing of Huang Nai-hsuan, deputy general manager of Yuanta Securities."

Kuang-nan fled Taiwan in 1997 to Macau to escape prosecution by the Taiwanese government. The Four Seas gang is known as an extremely violent gang: They have been suspected of extortion, murder, and other nefarious activities. In December 2000, Yang was repatriated to Taiwan. According to the *Taipei Times*, "The Taoyuan District Court had convicted him and sentenced Yang to two years for joining a criminal gang—a Criminal Code offense punishable by a maximum of three years in prison." But the Taiwan High Court convicted him under the Organized Crime Prevention

PKK leader Abdullah Ocalan
(AP/Hurriyet)

Osman Ocalan (left), a top commander of the PKK and brother of PKK leader Abdullah Ocalan, in a camp in northern Iraq in 1998 (AP/Hurriyet)

Act instead on July 18, 2001, and handed down a 22-month sentence. The high court reasoned that Yang had not been able to run his organization from Macau, and so it it did not hand down a sentence that could easily have been much stiffer.

See also: FOUR SEAS GANG; YUNG-HO, CHEN.

Reference

"Repatriated Gang Chief Sentenced to 22 Months." *Taipei Times,* July 18, 2001.

KURDISH Criminal Clans and the PKK

A symbiotic relationship links the Partiya Karkaren Kurdistan, or Kurdistan Workers' Party (PKK) to the crime clans of southeastern Anatolia, who in turn resemble the Mafia "families" of Sicily: a tradition of rebellion against the state, secrecy, and impermeability obtained by an intermingling of biological and criminal ties. There are about a dozen of these clans: the Aksoy, Aydinli, Baybasin, Canturk, Guven, Kitay, Kocakaya, Koylan, Ozdemir, Polat, Toprak, Ugur, and Yildrim, among others. In Europe, some of them sell, for approximately FF800,000 a kilogram wholesale, the heroin that they buy in the "Golden Crescent" for

FF15,000 a kilogram. Others control the entire process, from producing the powder from Asian morphine base all the way to running the "street dealing" in Western Europe, always in sizable quantities.

See also: BAYBASIN CLAN; DEMIR CLAN; KAYA CLAN; KITAY CLAN; KONUKLU-AY CLAN; KURDISH CRIMINAL CLANS AND THE PKK; SAKIK CLAN; SENAR CLAN.

Reference

Department for the Study of the Contemporary Criminal Menace. "Two Typical 'Degenerate Guerilla Groups': The Liberation Tigers of Emil Eelam and the Kurdistan Worker's Party." *Notes and Etudes* ("Terrorism and Political Violence" special) 32 (June 1996). Available online. URL: http://www.drmcc.org/docs/ne32.pdf. Accessed on December 16, 2004.

KYOKUTO-KAI

A prominent Tokyo-based crime gang that has been known to work with Russian counterparts for car smuggling. Just after the turn of 21st century, a war broke out between the Matsuba-kai and the Kyokuto-kai over gangland territory in which several high-ranking lieutenants were killed.

LABELLE, Normand (a.k.a. Billy; Dog)

Normand Labelle, called Billy or Dog by associates, was born in the mid-1950s and joined the Popeyes motorcycle gang at a young age. On September 14, 1974, at the age of 19, he and fellow Popeye Gilles "Le Nez" Lachance walked into the Chaufferie discotheque and reportedly brutally beat Brian Levitt and shot his brother Gary. The brothers had made the mistake of getting into a traffic dispute with the two bikers. Labelle was not charged, but Lachance was convicted of manslaughter and sentenced to seven years in prison.

Three years later, on December 5, 1977, Labelle became a founding member of Canada's first Hells Angels chapter when the Montreal club was absorbed by the Big Red Machine, as the Hells Angels are sometimes known. He was among the 15 members who purchased the club's impressive clubhouse in Sorel.

Labelle, who would become close to Hells Angels Michel "Sky" Langlois and Michael "L'Animal" Lajoie-Smith, took on a characteristic that is uncommon among the club: the ability to keep a low profile. His name has rarely made the papers.

Police arrested Dark Circle members Salvatore Brunetti, Normand Paré, Jean-Jacques Roy, André Désormeaux, Michel Duclos, Louis-Jacques Deschenes, Franco Fondacaro, Serge Bruneau, Michel Possa, Jean-René Roy, André Bureau, Marcel Gauthier, Claude Joannette, Roger Lavigne, Jean Rosa, and Pierre Bastien in November 1995 and charged them with, between August 15 and September 30, 1995, conspiring to murder Billy Labelle. Dark Circle was the hit squad of the Rock Machine motorcycle club, which was competing in Montreal for narcotics distribution with Hells Angels. All were eventually convicted.

On March 1, 1997, eight members and two prospects broke away from the Montreal chapter and formed the South Chapter. The South Chapter is alleged to traffic narcotics throughout the region. They ordered new patches from Vorarlberg, Austria, where all the club's patches are made, and set up shop in Saint-Basile-le-Grand. Labelle, who is active primarily in Laval and the Laurentians, became the chapter's first president.

See also: HELLS ANGELS.

Reference

Gary Francoeur. "Normand 'Billy' Labelle." Wiseguy-Wally. Available online. URL: http://www.geocities.com/wiseguywally/NormandLabelle.html. Downloaded on July 15, 2004.

—G.F.

LAGACÉ, Richard (a.k.a. Bam Bam)

Richard Lagacé, called Bam Bam, was born in 1959 and was among the founding members of the Cazzetta brothers' Rock Machine gang. Described by the media as a "Rock Machine leader," Lagacé commanded respect from the other members of the group.

Police arrested a major figure in the Hells Angels Trois-Rivieres chapter, a member of the Rowdy Crew's Lanaudiere branch, and a Hells Angels sympathizer on December 7, 1995, and charged them with conspiring to murder Lagacé, Rock Machine Paul "Sasquatch" Porter, and Dark Circle member Louis-Jacques Deschenes.

On October 28, 1998, police arrested 25 suspected Rock Machine members and associates as they dined in the restaurant of a downtown hotel. The men were forced to lie on the ground while they were searched and then were taken away in handcuffs. Lagacé and fellow Rock Machine Denis Belleau, who were among those arrested, were freed the next day after swearing to stay away from the others who were picked up by police.

Lagacé was shot to death on July 30, 1999, as he left the Ben Weider Health Club in Saint-Lin, north of Montreal. The two killers then forced their way into a house, held a woman at gunpoint while they stole her car keys, and sped away in her red Nissan. The car was later found abandoned in a Saint-Sophie cemetery. The firearm used in the murder was also retrieved by police.

Police watched and took notes as almost 60 Rock Machine members and associates attended Lagacé's funeral four days later. The men crowded in a Saint-Lin church and paid homage to one of the original members of the biker gang.

See also: BANDIDOS.

Reference

Gary Francoeur. "Richard 'Bam Bam' Lagacé." Wiseguy-Wally. Available online. URL: http://www.geocities.com/wiseguywally/RichardLagace.htm. Downloaded on July 15, 2004.

LAJOIE-SMITH, Michael (a.k.a. L'Animal)

Michael Lajoie-Smith, nicknamed "L'Animal," was born in the early 1960s. He joined the Hells Angels Montreal chapter in the early 1980s and in 1987 allegedly became the gang's godfather to their Laval-based puppet club, the Death Riders. Lajoie-Smith was now the head of a crew of drug dealers and thugs who intimidated bar owners into allowing the gang's drug pushers into their establishments.

When the war with the Rock Machine erupted in 1994, Lajoie-Smith was said to be responsible for battles fought on the north shore of the Mille-Îles River, in such towns as Terrebonne, Lachenaie, and Mascouche.

On July 22, 1995, Lajoie-Smith viciously beat Alain Cadieux, an innocent bystander, in the Le Marsolais bar in Cartierville. The 32-year-old man was beaten so badly that he was left in a permanent vegetative state.

A few months later, on October 13, 1995, Lajoie-Smith was arrested outside a bar in Montreal's north end with a loaded 9-mm firearm. He was convicted of possession of a restricted weapon and sentenced to five months in prison.

Things only got worse for "L'Animal." The Hells Angel's righthand man Martin "Satan" Lacroix became an informant after his October 26, 1995, arrest and told police the names of Lajoie-Smith's crew. He also said that Lajoie-Smith had paid him $400 to plant a bomb in the Le Gascon strip club in Terrebonne.

On August 30, 1996, Lajoie-Smith pleaded guilty to plotting to blow up Le Gascon bar and about three months later, on December 5, 1996, admitted to maliciously battering Alain Cadieux. He was sentenced to six years in prison.

With Lajoie-Smith behind bars, police, using the possession of goods obtained with the proceeds of crime, seized the biker's two houses, jewelry, a Cadillac, and two Harley-Davidson motorcycles. His bank accounts were also frozen. On November 27, 1998, Lajoie-Smith's luxurious Laval home was burned down. The house had 13 rooms, an outdoor swimming pool, a two-car garage, and security cameras. It was torched shortly before the government had listed it for sale.

Lajoie-Smith became eligible for parole in August 2001, but his request was denied.

See also: HELLS ANGELS.

Reference

Gary Francoeur. "Michael Lajoie-Smith." Wiseguy-Wally. Available online. URL: http://www.geocities.com/wiseguywally/Lajoie-Smith.htm. Downloaded on July 15, 2004.

LANGLOIS, Michel (a.k.a. Sky)

Michel "Sky" Langlois was born in 1946 and joined the Montreal-based Popeyes biker gang when he was in his early twenties. He became a Hells Angel on December 7, 1977, when the Popeyes became Canada's first Hells Angels chapter. He earned the name Sky because he possessed a pilot's license and owned an aircraft.

When the club's president, Yves "Le Boss" Buteau, was shot to death on September 8, 1983, Langlois replaced him as the Hells Angels' Canadian national president.

Langlois played a passive role in the March 24, 1985, slaughter of five members of the club's north chapter in Lennoxville. When police put out a warrant for his arrest, Langlois disappeared. He vanished into Morocco, where he lived the life of a fugitive for two years.

On April 13, 1988, Langlois and fellow Angels René "Canisse" Hébert and Guy "Junior" Auclair showed up at the Sûreté du Québec headquarters in Sherbrooke and surrendered. Langlois received a two-year prison sentence. Sky Langlois, along with seven members and two prospects, left the Montreal chapter on March 1, 1997, and created the south chapter. None of the members had been convicted within the last five years; this avoided their being classified under federal legislation as a criminal organization.

On January 18, 1998, Robert Savard, 44, was arrested at the Lacolle border crossing in southern Quebec. Police found 178 kilograms of cocaine, worth an estimated $71 million, hidden in the walls of the trailer he pulled behind his van. The drug was brought from Mexico and was intended to be distributed in Montreal. Savard was eventually sentenced to seven and a half years in prison.

Langlois was arrested at his Longueuil home on October 14, 1998, and charged with importing and conspiring to import the 178 kilograms of cocaine seized in January. Through the efforts of a double agent, police discovered that Langlois had allegedly bankrolled 15 percent of the drug operation. A man Langlois called Le Grand Manitou provided the rest of the funds.

In the hope of convincing the judge to grant Langlois bail, his lawyer presented the court with four witnesses, including the biker's girlfriend. Micheline Blanchard, who was the girlfriend of Hells Angels president Yves "Le Boss" Buteau before he was gunned down in 1983, described him as a good father and a man of his word. She also offered to put up their family home in Longueuil as security.

The bullet-riddled body of one of Langlois's alleged accomplices, 29-year-old Genevieve Dubois, was found in a forest in Saint-Hubert on February 12, 1999. A drug courier for the Hells Angels, police said they suspected that she was killed because the bikers feared she would "flip," or testify against the gang.

Evidence against Langlois, who is only one of three of the founding members of the Hells Angels in Canada still alive, included videotaped meetings. He was convicted and sentenced to five years in prison and a $20,000 fine on July 9, 1999.

See also: HELLS ANGELS.

Reference
Gary Francoeur. "Michel 'Sky' Langlois." Wiseguy-Wally. Available online. URL: http://www.geocities.com/wiseguywally/MichelLanglois.htm. Downloaded on July 15, 2004.

LANZO, Angelo

Angelo Lanzo, a colossus of a man, started out as a doorman at a club run by Canadian mobster Jimmy Orlando and collecting loan-shark payments for Giuseppe Cocolicchio in Montreal. He impressed his superiors and was placed in charge of several of the mob's gambling joints. He was convicted in 1952 of running the Ramsay Club on Bullion Street, one of the city's biggest gambling dens, and was sentenced to two months in prison. When mob lieutenant Nicola "Cola" Di Iorio noticed Lanzo's talent, his importance in the organization increased considerably. He became Di Iorio's closest confidant, privileged to the inner secrets of the Mafia's top members. He was seen meeting with Vic Cotroni, the groups' leader, with whom only high-ranking members could meet, and was placed in charge of several clubs, including the Café Métropole, the Little Club, and the Casa Del Sol.

Police arrested 20 individuals during a raid at Lanzo's apartment on Broadway Street in Nôtre-Dame-de-Grace in November 1966. According to authorities, the purpose of the meeting was to set up a network of bookmaking joints throughout the city for Expo '67. In January 1970 police observed as Lanzo, Di Iorio, and Frank Dasti made a trip to Miami, Florida, where they had several meetings with Gambino wiseguy Guido Penosi to discuss and arrange the shipments of the drugs from Montreal to New York City. On May 29, 1972, police observed an important meeting at the Sirloin Barn between leaders of the organization. Present were Lanzo, Vic Cotroni, Paolo Violi, Nicola Di Iorio, William Obront, and Irving Goldstein. Sûreté du Québec officers testified at the

Quebec Inquiry into Organized Crime (CECO) that Lanzo, along with Vic and Frank Cotroni, Paolo Violi, Nicola Di Iorio, Luigi Greco, and Michel Pozza, made up the hierarchy of the Montreal Mafia. When the commission subpoenaed Lanzo to appear before them, the mobster went into hiding. He died of a coronary thrombosis on May 19, 1974, in an apartment where he was hiding out from testifying before the committee.

Reference

Gary Francoeur. "Angelo Lanzo." WiseguyWally. Available online. URL: http://www.geocities.com/wiseguywally/Lanzo.htm. Downloaded on July 15, 2004.

LAPIETRA, Angelo (a.k.a. the Hook)

Angelo "the Hook" LaPietra was a top crime-syndicate counselor. He was sentenced to prison in 1986 and was released in just before he died in 1999.

See also: AIUPPA, JOSEPH; ANDRIACCHI, JOSEPH; CARLISI, SAMUEL; DIFRONZO, JOHN; LOMBARDO, JOSEPH; MARCELLO, JAMES.

LATIN Kings *See* ALMIGHTY LATIN KING NATION.

LEBLANC, Gilles

Gilles Leblanc was one of the Dubois Gang's lesser-known members, even though he was extremely active in Montreal during the 1970s. As a loyal soldier for the gang's leader, Claude Dubois, Leblanc was primarily involved in strong-arming, extortion, and armed robbery.

When Richard Désormiers began to cause trouble in a club run by the Dubois Gang, Leblanc and Claude Lesage were sent to teach him a lesson. The two were supposed to give Désormiers a beating but, once on the scene, changed their minds. They knew that assaulting the brother-in-law of mob boss Frank Cotroni was like playing with fire. Leblanc and Lesage were later reprimanded by the Dubois brothers for not following his orders.

Leblanc, along with Dubois soldiers Yvon Belzil, Réal Lévesque, and Claude Dubeau, provided security when Claude Dubois met with Frank Cotroni numerous times to discuss the Désormiers problem.

When no resolution could be reached, Dubois decided to take care of business. He gave the mission

of killing the troublesome Désormiers to Leblanc and Claude Lesage. The two enforcers were supposed to kill him and make his body disappear. When Leblanc and Lesage could not fulfill the task, a frustrated Dubois allegedly gave the contract to trusted aides Yvon Belzil and Claude Dubeau. Désormiers was gunned down in the Mon Pays bar on July 22, 1973.

In autumn 1975 Jacques Lemieux and Gérald Mayer opened the Honest John Theatrical Agency near the Agence Calcé, a booking agency for exotic dancers that was under the protection of Claude Dubois. Dubois, who collected $250 a week from the Agence Calcé, did not like the extra competition. One evening, when Lemieux and Mayer and their secretary Denise Adam were dining at the Giusitini steak house in Saint-Léonard, Leblanc and several Dubois Gang members charged into the restaurant and attacked the group. Lemieux and Mayer were severely beaten, and before exiting, Leblanc fired two shots at Denise Adam, a former employee of Agence Calcé.

Leblanc, along with Dubois soldier Michel Bernard, was shot to death in the l'Index night club on March 12, 1976. The gang was furious and sought blood. Normand Perras, who they suspected was one of killers, was later killed in a tavern on Ontario Street.

See also: DUBOIS GANG.

Reference

Gary Francoeur. "Gilles Leblanc." WiseguyWally. Available online. URL: http://www.geocities.com/wiseguywally/Leblanc.htm. Downloaded on July 28, 2004.

—*G.F.*

LEHDER-RIVA, Carlos

Carlos Lehder-Riva was drawn to drug trafficking for two reasons: profits and politics. Lehder-Riva was an admirer of such political figures as Ernesto "Che" Guevara and Adolf Hitler. A Colombian, he was also intensely anti-American. While in a U.S. prison in the mid-1970s, he conceived of the idea of smuggling cocaine into the United States the same way marijuana was smuggled.

Rather than hiding small amounts of cocaine in luggage or on airline passengers, Lehder-Riva planned to transport it in large quantities on small private aircraft. The huge profits he expected to realize from this plan would finance his political ambitions in his native Colombia. Out of prison in 1976, Lehder-Riva eventually bought a sizable portion of Norman's Cay, a Bahamian island about 225 miles southeast of Miami.

On this small island he built an airstrip as a refueling stop for the light planes that transported his cocaine to secret airstrips in the United States.

Lehder-Riva conceived the idea of transporting loads of cocaine from Colombia to the United States. In 1981, he was indicted on U.S. federal charges in Jacksonville, Florida, and a request for his extradition from Colombia was formally presented to that government in 1983. Up until that time, no extradition requests had been honored by the Colombian government. Lehder-Riva, a major cocaine trafficker, had formed his own political party and adopted a platform that was vehemently opposed to extradition. He viewed cocaine as a very powerful weapon that could be used against the United States and referred to the substance as an atomic bomb. Lehder-Riva also claimed that he was allied with the Colombian guerrilla movement M-19, in an effort to protect Colombian sovereignty.

His inclination to use violence eventually tripped him up when he was suspected of involvement in the 1984 assassination of Colombia's justice minister, Rodrigo Lara Bonilla. Outraged by the terrorist tactics employed by the Medellín organization, the Colombian government turned Lehder-Riva over to the Drug Enforcement Administration (DEA) and extradited him to the United States in February 1987.

Lehder-Riva was convicted and sentenced to 135 years in federal prison. He subsequently cooperated in the U.S. investigation of Panama dictator Manuel Noriega and received a reduced sentence in return for his testimony.

References

David Amoruso. "Carlos Lehder-Riva." Gangsters Inc. Available online. URL: http://gangstersinc.tripod.com/lehder-riva. Downloaded on July 15, 2004.

U.S. Drug Enforcement Administration, U.S. Department of Justice. "A Tradition of Excellence: DEA History 1975 to 1990." Available online. URL: http://www.usdoj.gov/dea/pubs/history/index.html. Downloaded on July 15, 2004.

LESSARD, Réjean (a.k.a. Zig-Zag)

Réjean Lessard grew up in the Eastern Townships and was among the original members of the Marauders biker gang in Asbestos, Quebec. He was called "Zig-Zag" by his biker buddies. The gang sold drugs, held drag races, assaulted citizens, and partied.

In 1979 the Marauders disbanded, and many members, including Lessard and Michel Mayrand, joined the Hells Angels. As a member of the club's North chapter, Lessard's stock rose quickly. He began to make more money and spent much of that cash on partying and cocaine.

Lessard's drug abuse finally caught up to him in 1983 when he suffered repeated epileptic seizures. He stopped using cocaine and began to focus his attention on business.

Frustrated by the North chapter's constant partying and reckless behavior, Lessard, Luc "Sam" Michaud, and Robert "Tiny" Richard quit and joined the Montreal chapter in summer 1983. When Yves "Le Boss" Buteau was gunned down on September 8, Lessard became the chapter's new president.

Lessard continued to be unhappy with the North chapter, which he felt had grown reckless. A meeting was set up at the Sherbrooke chapter's clubhouse in Lennoxville on March 24, 1985. Five members of the North chapter were shot to death, wrapped in sleeping bags, and dumped in the St. Lawrence River. The others were absorbed into the Montreal chapter.

The next day, Lessard called a meeting of all Hells Angels in Quebec, as well as the members of the Halifax chapter, at the Montreal chapter's bunker in Sorel. He explained the slayings and the reasons behind them and sent members to British Columbia to explain the situation to that province's chapters.

After police fished out the bodies of the five Hells Angels from the St. Lawrence, a warrant was put out for Lessard and fellow Hells Angels Robert "Tiny" Richard, Jacques "La Pelle" Pelletier, and Luc "Sam" Michaud on charges of first-degree murder.

Police officer Jacques Ghilbault pulled over Lessard and Richard "Dick" Mayrand on September 1, 1985, after they made an illegal left turn on a stolen motorcycle. Two stolen firearms and a silencer-equipped submachine gun were found on them.

The four Hells Angels were kept behind a glass cage during the trial, and observers were frisked and prodded with a metal detector before entering the courtroom. The evidence against the accused was overwhelming and, after 16 days of deliberation, the jury convicted Lessard, Pelletier, and Michaud of first-degree murder. The three received life sentences. Richard was acquitted.

See also: HELLS ANGELS.

LIBERATION Tigers of Tamil Eelam (LTTE)

Founded in 1976, the Liberation Tigers of Tamil Eelam (LTTE) is the most powerful Tamil group in Sri Lanka and uses overt and illegal methods to raise funds, acquire weapons, and publicize its cause of establishing an independent Tamil state. The LTTE began its armed conflict with the Sri Lankan government in 1983 and relies on a guerrilla strategy that includes the use of terrorist tactics.

The Tigers have integrated a battlefield insurgent strategy with a terrorist program that targets not only key personnel in the countryside but also senior Sri Lankan political and military leaders in Colombo and other urban centers. The Tigers are most notorious for their cadre of suicide bombers, the Black Tigers. Political assassinations and bombings are commonplace. The LTTE has refrained from targeting foreign diplomatic and commercial establishments.

Exact strength is unknown, but the LTTE is estimated to have 8,000 to 10,000 armed combatants in Sri Lanka, with a core of trained fighters of approximately 3,000 to 6,000. The LTTE also has a significant overseas support structure for fund raising, weapons procurement, and propaganda activities.

The Tigers control most of the northern and eastern coastal areas of Sri Lanka but have conducted operations throughout the island. Headquartered in northern Sri Lanka, LTTE leader Velupillai Prabhakaran has established an extensive network of checkpoints and informants to keep track of any outsiders who enter the group's area of control.

The LTTE's overt organizations support Tamil separatism by lobbying foreign governments and the United Nations. The LTTE also uses its international contacts to procure weapons, communications, and any other equipment and supplies it needs. The LTTE exploits large Tamil communities in North America, Europe, and Asia to obtain funds and supplies for its fighters in Sri Lanka often through false claims or even extortion.

Other known front organizations include: World Tamil Association (WTA); World Tamil Movement (WTM); Federation of Associations of Canadian Tamils (FACT); The Ellalan Force; and The Sangillan Force.

See also: KHERI, CHILLA.

Reference

U.S. Department of State. "Patterns of Global Terrorism, 2001." May 2001. Available online. URL: http://www.state.gov/s/ct/rls/pgtrpt/2001. Accessed on November 24, 2004.

LICCIARDI, Maria (a.k.a. La Piccolina)

When people are asked what they think of Maria Licciardi, they answer several things. They will say she was charismatic, calm, highly intelligent, ruthless, and more important, they will say she was the *capo di tutti capo* of the Camorra, the boss of bosses in the Mafia organization based in Naples.

Maria Licciardi was born March 24, 1951, in Naples, Italy. Naples is the third-largest city in Italy and is home to the Camorra. The Camorra is the Neapolitan answer to the Sicilian Mafia. The Camorra started its hold on the city in the years after World War II, when it took control of the weapon- and cigarette-smuggling operations. During the years it expanded into real estate and the drug trade. Maria Licciardi knew from early on what the Camorra was and who ran it. She grew up in a family of killers and Camorra members. All her brothers were active Camorra members; one of them, her brother Gennaro "the Monkey" Licciardi, had become boss and ruled supreme. Her husband Antonio Teghemié was also a member.

Growing up, Maria Licciardi expected to one day play the role of wife, and in the mob world the role of the wife was to be loyal, tight lipped, cook, clean, and raise the children. But the Italian government's crackdown on organized crime put countless members and bosses behind bars and led to bloody wars that decimated the clans and families. The role of the woman began to change. With most qualified men in prison, dead, or too young, women slowly took over the seats of power of the Camorra.

Maria's life as a *capo di tutti capo* was not easy. In 1993 assassins killed her brother Gennaro Licciardi in prison, and soon after her two brothers, Pietro and Vincenzo, and her husband Antonio Teghemié were murdered as well. The way was clear for Maria to take control. She had lost her brothers and husband and now had to prove her qualities to the other bosses and, more important, to her soldiers. She set up meetings with rival Camorra clans and told them that the fighting over territory and power had to stop. The wars meant that they lost money. Licciardi proposed that the clans carve up the city and work together to expand cigarette smuggling, drug trade, and racketeering. The other bosses agreed to work together and made peace.

Maria Licciardi's first victory was behind her, and she was now fully in control. As her next act Licciardi established her family in the prostitution trade, which until then they had always avoided because of a sense of honor. They brought girls from the Albanian Mafia, put them on the street, and collected the money. Many of the girls were kept addicted to drugs so they would not become informants or run away, and when they became too old, they were killed. Maria also expanded the drug trade. The Camorra ruled the Neapolitan suburbs and used young drug dealers to sell heroin and cocaine. One police officer described it as "one big web, they constantly change people and locations, and the police have a lot of trouble breaking down the Camorra organization." Many people who live in these suburbs support the Camorra. Unemployment is high, and one of the main employers is the Camorra. They provide money for the community, and some people fear them.

Licciardi's reign had been relatively quiet and free of problems until a Camorra clan, unhappy with Licciardi, decided to deny an order. The disagreement came over a shipment of pure, unrefined heroin. Licciardi said that the heroin would kill all the customers and bring heat from the public and law enforcement. She ordered it not to be sold. Behind her back a Camorra clan named Lo Russo decided otherwise and made the shipment ready for sale on the streets. After a few days Licciardi's prophecy came true, and drug addicts began to die from the heroin. Public opinion and law enforcement came down aggressively on the Camorra clans. The alliance that Licciardi realized early on in her career fell apart, and wars among the clans erupted. Businesses were taken over or destroyed, and more than a hundred mobsters were killed. The war forced law-enforcement agents to hunt for the leaders.

Now Licciardi was under pressure from both rivals as well as law enforcement and had earned a place on the "30 most wanted Italians" list. She went into hiding but continued to run the Camorra and fight her wars. When Maria felt that prosecutor Luigi Bobbio and his team were getting a bit too close to her family soldiers and herself, she decided to take action. In January 2001 she bombed Bobbio's office building as a warning, but it didn't help her. Bobbio continued his fight and under massive protection he started to break down the wall surrounding Licciardi.

Seventy of her men were arrested, but all maintained a code of silence and accepted their prison terms. Licciardi seemed untouchable. Italian authorities only had one photograph of her. They distributed it despite concerns that Licciardi might have had plastic surgery or changed her hair color. They kept up pressure, and Licciardi's hide out became known. A team was set in place to arrest her.

Licciardi was hiding in a Neapolitan suburb. She felt safe knowing the people living there would not give her up to the police, but on June 14, 2001 the Mobile Squad of Naples and special operations team from the police raided Licciardi's hideout and arrested her. She did not resist. At her arrest police noticed she looked just like the photo that was released years earlier. At age 50 Maria Licciardi ended her reign as boss.

Although still uncommon in Sicily and unheard of in the United States, female Mafia bosses in Italy are on the rise. Statistics show that in 1990 one woman was indicted for Mafia connections while in 1995 there were 89 such indictments. The emergence of women as bosses is far more noticeable in Naples than Sicily. The police attribute it to cultural differences. "Family ties are very tight here, and women have always had a far more dominant role in the family here than in Sicily," said Giuseppe Donno, a spokesman for the police department of the province of Naples. "They say that behind every great man there is a strong woman, and that is true in crime families as well."

Reference

David Amoruso. "Maria 'La Piccolina' Licciardi." Gangsters Inc. Available online. URL: http://gangstersinc.tripod.com/MariaLicciardi.html. Downloaded on July 16, 2004.

LIMPY Ho (a.k.a. Ng Sikho)

Limpy Ho was born in mainland China. In the 1960s he fled to Hong Kong. He rose to great prominence in the underworld, becoming a minor celebrity in the 1960s and early 1970s. Extremely violent and very cunning, he became a well-known 14K Triad leader, along with flamboyant leader Ma Sik-yu. He was into extortion, prostitution, and drug distribution. Arrested in 1974 he was sentenced to 30 years in jail. While in jail he was asked to pay on monies earned on his illegal activities that were still in operation. He died in prison.

See also: TRIADS.

LOMBARDO, Joseph (a.k.a. Joe Padula, Joey the Clown)

Joseph "Joey the Clown" Lombardo was a longtime Outfit lieutenant. A crew boss on Chicago's West Side, he has been involved in loan sharking, extortion, and arson and has allegedly approved the murder of dozens of men. Sentenced to prison in 1982 for attempting to bribe a U.S. senator, he was released in 1992. It is alleged that at more than 73 years of age, he is currently the head of the Outfit, along with John "No Nose" DiFronzo and Joe "the Builder" Andriacchi.

See also: AIUPPA, JOSEPH; ANDRIACCHI, JOSEPH; CARLISI, SAMUEL; DIFRONZO, JOHN; LAPIETRA, ANGELO; MARCELLO, JAMES.

LOTUS Gang

The Lotus Gang, with more than 100 members and connections to the Hells Angels and Indo-Canadian-based crime groups, has been active in the Vancouver area with cocaine and heroin importation and trafficking, credit-card fraud, extortion, and cellular-telephone cloning. Asian- and aboriginal-based drug traffickers are also cooperating in the Winnipeg drug trade, and there are indications that the Lotus Gang from Vancouver is taking an interest in the Winnipeg market.

Reference

Criminal Intelligence Service Canada. "Asian-Based Organized Crime." Available online. URL: http://www.cisc.gc.ca/AnnualReports/1998/Cisc1998/asian1998.htm. Downloaded on July 16, 2004.

LOUIE, Ken

Flashy leader of the Hop Sing Boys, a one-time enforcer branch of the Hop Sing Tongs, Louie was a well-known enforcer himself and was known for violence and extortion.

Louie was gunned down outside his home on May 31, 1977, when an assassin fired at him while he tried to make a getaway in his car. According to *Asia Week* magazine writer and book author Bill Lee in his article "The Golden Dragon Massacre" (January 28, 1999), "His killer approached from the passenger side and fired into the vehicle. After Ken was wounded, the assassin reached in through the shattered window and continued blasting away. Most of the dozen shots fired from the Walther automatic hit their mark." He was pronounced dead at the scene of the crime.

See also: HOP SING BOYS; HOP SING TONG; TONGS.

Reference

Lee, Bill. *Chinese Playground: Memoirs from the Underworld.* San Francisco, Calif.: Rhapsody Press, 1999.

LUCAS, Charles

Like many other African-American organized crime figures, Charles Lucas began his career in the numbers racket, but it was the Vietnam War that provided Lucas with the opportunity to become a major figure in his own right. He established a heroin importation and distribution network made up of black Vietnam veterans, primarily relatives, which enabled him to move heroin directly from Southeast Asia to the streets of the United States.

In addition to seeking control of wholesale drug markets in Indochina, the Lucas heroin network covered the Bronx, New Jersey, Chicago, North Carolina, and Los Angeles. All the trademarks of astute organization were apparent in the Lucas organization: Personnel were selected because they were trustworthy, not merely because of some sentimental friendship or childhood attachment; a division of labor among personnel was constructed such that one knew only what was necessary to function; state-of-the-art technologies in transport, processing, and packaging were used.

Lucas and his brother Alphonso were arrested in 1991, incarcerated, and sentenced to serve jail time. Their conviction was overturned in 1995.

Reference

Gary W. Potter. "Unit #9: Domestic Organized Crime, African-American OC, Youth Gangs, and Outlaw Motorcycle Gangs." Available online. URL: http://www.policestudies.eku.edu/POTTER/crj401_9.htm. Accessed on November 24, 2004.

LUCCHESE Crime Family

The Lucchese crime family is famous as the family behind the 1978 Lufthansa heist. They have been depicted in the movie *Goodfellas* and the book *Wiseguy,* but now the family is infested with turncoats. Many of its members are either in prison or in the witness-protection center, and some are being treated by prison psychologists.

Current membership is estimated at approximately 100. The family's first Don was Tom Gagliano. Their primary activities include narcotics trafficking, gambling, loan sharking, waste management, construction, and involvement in the garment industry.

The current but incarcerated boss is Louis "Louie Bagels" Daidone. The current acting boss is Steven Crea. He is presently facing state charges of enterprise corruption after being arrested on September 6,

2000. Crea was jailed on Rikers Island pending bail hearing but continued to preside over a family in increasing disarray. The family was thrown into further disarray when Daidone was sentenced to life imprisonment in 2004 after a January 23, 2004 conviction on four courts.

See also: BONANNO CRIME FAMILY; COLOMBO CRIME FAMILY; COMMISSION, THE; GAMBINO CRIME FAMILY; GENOVESE CRIME FAMILY.

Reference

David Amoruso. "Lucchese Crime Family." Gangsters Inc. Available online. URL: http://gangstersinc.tripod.com/Luc.html. Downloaded on July 16, 2004.

LUEN Group

The Luen Group is based out of Hong Kong. They are the fourth largest of the groups based there. They are a triad society that includes more than 8,000 members and has four subgroups.

LYUBARSKY, Vyacheslav (a.k.a. Slava)

Vyacheslav Lyubarsky was shot in the buttocks by an unknown assailant on March 3, 1991, in the hall outside his apartment in Brooklyn. He was allegedly a member of a Soviet narcotics trafficking group that imported heroin into the United States through Bangkok, Poland, and Brussels. He survived his wounds.

In retaliation for the attempt on Lyubarksy's life, Monya Elson was shot in Brighton Beach on May 14, 1991. Elson was a reputed leader of a crime group that dealt in counterfeiting, drug trafficking, and other criminal activities. He was allegedly involved in the murders of Elbrous Evdoev and later the Lubarsky brothers. This was only one of many failed attempts on Elson's life.

Vyacheslav ("Slava") Lyubarsky and his son, Vadim, were shot to death on January 12, 1992, in the hallway outside their Brighton Beach apartment. After returning from dinner with Slava's wife, Nellie, they were ambushed by an assassin who emerged from the hallway shadows and shot both men, but not Nellie. In 1995, Monya Elson and others were charged in a federal indictment for these and other murders and were convicted after Monya was extradicted from Italy where he was hiding.

Reference

New Jersey State Commission of Investigation, New York Organized Crime Task Force, New York State Commission of Investigation, Pennsylvania Crime Commission, with Rutgers University. "The Tri-State Joint Soviet-Émigré Organized Crime Project." 1992. Available online. URL: http://www.state.nj.us/sci/pdf/russian.pdf. Accessed on November 24, 2004.

MACHII, Hisayuki

Hisayuki Machii was born Ching Gwon Yong, in 1923 in Korea and was raised in Japanese-controlled Korea. Machii worked in the U.S. Counterintelligence Corps after the war in Japan. In the years after the war, Machii established himself as a recognized leader in the Japanese underworld, especially while Japanese Yakuza leaders were being detained by U.S. officials. When the Japanese godfathers were freed, Machii joined forces with them rather than fight them as rivals. This was a trailblazing path, as no Koreans had made such headway before in the Japanese Yakuza. Also, he befriended such established leaders as Yoshio Kodama.

Machii established his own gang, the Voice of the East Gang (also known as Tosei-kai), which rivaled the powerful Yamaguchi-gumi, who were forced to consummate a deal with the upstarts rather than fight. Machii proved valuable to the Japanese Yakuza because he could bridge the gaps between the Korean and Japanese underworlds. He retired at the turn of the century to spend time in Japan and Hawaii.

See also: KODAMA, YOSHIO; YAKUZA.

MANCHEKAR, Suresh

Suresh Manchekar is a notorious Mumbai gangster, well known for violence and extortion. Manchekar and another young alleged gangster, Guru Satam, banded together when they were young, becoming a very formidable pair, known for cunning and violence.

Today they are bitter rivals, competing against one another on the same feeding grounds, that is, construction, films, and local businesses. Both resort to extortion and violence. Manchekar was incarcerated in the early 1990s, and in his absence, he appointed Sunil Askolar the de facto boss. Askolar was a worthy associate, and the business thrived. However, he was killed in 1998, and Manchekar was released the same year. Since his release, the reporting of crimes, especially extortion, has grown steadily.

Manchekar was killed in a shootout with Thane (Mumbai) police on August 15, 2003. During an attempted arrest, Manchekar waited until police drew near before firing a .38-caliber pistol. Police returned fire, killing him. According to the *Times of India*, he was "the most wanted gangster from Thane." He was 42 at the time of his death. So involved was his life of crime that the Indian government prosecuted his 72-year-old mother, citing her involvement in a 1998 gangland murder case.

See also: ASKOLAR, SUNIL; BAKSH, NOOR; IBRAHIM, DAWOOD; GOGA, IRFAN; RAJAN, CHHOTA; SATAM, GURU; SHAKEEL, CHHOTA; SINGH, SANJAY.

MARA Salvatrucha (a.k.a. MS-13)

The Mara Salvatrucha gang, commonly referred to as MS-13, enforces an extensive hierarchy. Each local gang is divided into "cliques," which are further divided into small groups. Members range from 12 year olds to adults. MS-13 now includes members from Ecuador, Guatemala, Honduras, and Mexico. Common identifiers include the number 13 and also *sureño,* a Spanish word meaning "southerner." Other marks include "M" or "MS," or "Salvadoran Pride." Members often make the hand sign "M."

The gang is active in Central America, the United States, Mexico, and Canada. Since Mara Salvatrucha's inception in California and Washington, D.C., members have plagued many American cities. Many MS members continue to have close connections with El Salvador.

Mara Salvatrucha gang members are known to be involved in all aspects of criminal activity. Because of their ties to their former homeland, they have access to sophisticated military weapons, thus making firearms trafficking one of their main criminal enterprises. Other law enforcement agencies have reported MS-13 members were exporting stolen cars to South America. As with nearly all street gangs, the MS-13 is also involved in drug sales, murder, and other common gang crimes.

Reference
Know Gangs. "Mara Salvatrucha." Available online. URL: http://www.knowgangs.com/gang_resources/ms/ms_001.htm. Downloaded on July 16, 2004.

MARKOWITZ, Michael

A Romanian émigré, Michael Markowitz was well known in Brighton Beach, Brooklyn, New York, as an accomplished gas-fraud and scam criminal. Throughout the course of his career, he was aligned with many different organized-crime groups, but as his run neared its end, he was also hounded by law-enforcement authorities. This pressure made him a hunted man by both law enforcement officials and organized-criminal elements who feared he might cooperate with police.

His friend and longtime associate Philip Moskowitz, also an expert in gas-fraud schemes, was found dead in North Brunswick, New Jersey, on December 5, 1987. Moskowitz's body exhibited signs that he had been tortured prior to his death.

Michael Markowitz was shot to death in a car on May 2, 1989, after being taken into police custody. Arrested in connection with the bootleg gas scams, he was allegedly killed on orders from La Cosa Nostra to prevent his cooperation with police.

Reference
New Jersey State Commission of Investigation, New York Organized Crime Task Force, New York State Commission of Investigation, Pennsylvania Crime Commission, with Rutgers University. "The Tri-State Joint Soviet-Émigré Organized Crime Project." 1992. Available online. URL: http://www.state.nj.us/sci/pdf/russian.pdf. Accessed on November 24, 2004.

MASSINO, Joseph

Massino is the current boss of the Bonanno crime family, and unlike the bosses of the other four New York crime families, Massino is not serving time in a prison. That is something special for a Mafia boss in recent times. Massino reputedly has the support of the family, and since he took over as boss, the Bonanno crime family has been making a comeback of sorts. They are rumored by some to now be the second-most-powerful Mafia family in New York, behind only the Genovese family.

Joey Massino began his underworld career as a truck hijacker and quietly rose up the ranks. When then Bonanno family boss Carmine Galante was assassinated in July 1979, Massino was a capo. The slaying of Carmine Galante meant that the Bonanno family had to select a new boss. This decision cut the family into two factions: One supported proposed new boss Philip "Rusty" Rastelli, and the other was against him. Massino supported Rusty Rastelli and aligned himself with him, joining such Bonnano family contemporaries as capo Sonny "Sonny Black" Napolitano, Sally Farrugia, and consiglieri Steve Cannone.

The faction that opposed Rusy Rastelli included capos Caesar Bonventre, Philip "Philip Lucky" Giaccone, Dominick "Big Trin" Trinchera, and Alphonse "Sonny Red" Indelicato. Eventually the faction supporting Rastelli won, killing three capos of the other faction in a shotgun ambush. It has been rumored that Massino was among the shooters. Rastelli became boss, and it seemed that finally all would be well within the ranks of the Bonanno family.

Things began to fall apart when the F.B.I. paid Sonny Black a visit. They had a message for the family: For six years they had hidden an undercover F.B.I. agent within their ranks. Donnie Brasco (real name Joseph D. Pistone) had infiltrated the Bonanno crime family and before the Bonanno members realized what happened they were deluged with indictments. Several members were murdered in the aftermath. Sonny Black, blamed for bringing Donnie

Brasco too close to the family, was found shot to death with his hands cut off.

Massino survived to face the charges, and in 1986 he was convicted and sent to prison for crimes connected to the Bonannos' control of Teamsters Local 814, the union that represents furniture movers. During his trial, when Pistone walked past Massino on his way to the witness stand to testify against him, the adversaries eyed each other. "Hey, Donnie," Massino reportedly said. "Who'd you get to play me in the movie?" Unfortunately for Massino, the movie, *Donnie Brasco* with Al Pacino and Johnny Depp, was more about Sonny Black's crew than his.

When Philip "Rusty" Rastelli died in 1991, Massino was the obvious choice for new boss. When Massino went to prison, the Bonanno family was on its way to extinction. Its members, considered mob "outlaws," did not have a seat on the Mafia's fabled Commission, the governing group that oversees the city's five crime families. An internal war left several members dead. Rampant drug dealing in the family had brought intense pressure from the Drug Enforcement Administration and the Federal Bureau of Investigation.

When Massino was released from prison in 1993, he had a lot of work to do. He ran the Bonanno family with his brother-in-law Salvatore A. Vitale as underboss and 73-year-old Anthony Spero as consiglieri. Under Massino's lead the Bonanno crime family turned around completely. Massino became known as an electronics whiz with a penchant for secrecy and discretion. He lives modestly with his wife in Howard Beach, Queens, a few blocks from the former home of his friend, the imprisoned-for-life late Gambino crime boss John Gotti. "He's careful. He's a very smart guy," said one NYPD organized-crime detective about Massino. "He's wise to surveillance, and he lives by the old-school rules. He believes in keeping La Cosa Nostra secret."

Massino's levelheaded leadership stopped the erosion of the family power. He shut down the Bonanno social clubs and avoided other situations that might invite surveillance. Massino has denied any involvement in La Cosa Nostra and has accused the federal government of bias against Italian Americans. His principal source of legitimate income, authorities say, is King Caterers, a Farmingdale, New York, business that provides food to street vendors. He also is part owner of the Casablanca Restaurant in Maspeth, Queens, where he likes to enjoy the Italian cuisine.

Despite some initial tension, Massino's reign was a successful one, run with tight fists and tight lips. The Bonanno family regained its seat on the Commission and its crews have beefed up longtime interests in narcotics trafficking, unions, loan sharking, gambling and illegal vending machines. Massino appeared untouchable and so did the Bonanno family.

However, things around Massino started to crumble. His underboss and consiglieri both were arrested, convicted, and sent to prison. Spero was indicted on a racketeering and murder charge, found guilty in 2001, and sentenced to life in prison. Underboss Vitale was also indicted in 2001 on loan-sharking, bank-fraud, and money-laundering charges. Massino did not panic and replaced his administration. Anthony "T.G." Graziano was promoted to consigliere and was seen in company of Massino on flights to Mexico and Italy. Unfortunately for Massino, Graziano was indicted in 2002 on murder, murder conspiracy, drug trafficking, extortion, and illegal gambling charges allegedly committed in the past 12 years. Massino was not indicted in any of these high profile cases. As his administration, his capos and his soldiers go to prison, Massino remains the boss and continues to run his empire.

Today, Joe Massino is still the alleged boss of the Bonanno crime family, living in freedom and running his operation. The Bonanno crime family is proof that the Mafia will not just die.

Reference

David Amoruso. "Joseph Massino." Gangsters Inc. Available online. URL: http://gangstersinc.tripod.com/JoeMassino.html. Downloaded on July 16, 2004.

MATSUBA-KAI

This prominent Tokyo-based crime gang has been known to work with Russian counterparts for car smuggling. Just after the turn of the 21st century, a war broke out between the Matsuba-kai and the Kyokuto-kai over gangland territory. Several high-ranking lieutenants have been killed.

MATTA Ballesteros, Juan Ramón

Juan Ramón Matta Ballesteros first attracted the U.S. government's attention in 1970 when he was arrested at Dulles Airport for carrying drugs; he was sentenced to five years. He fled the United States before he served a day. In 1978 Matta backed a coup d'état of the government in Honduras. The successful move put a military regime into power that was willing to turn the country into a transit stop for transporting the cocaine northward to Hondoras, then to Mexico, and then into the United States.

The Drug Enforcement Administration (DEA) first identified Honduran drug trafficker Juan Ramón Matta Ballesteros in 1985 as one of the leaders of one of the largest cocaine cartels in South America. It was believed at the time that Matta's group was responsible for trafficking up to one-third of all the cocaine in the United States coming from Colombia.

However, the Central Intelligence Agency was working with Matta, who was trafficking arms to the Contras, and so it has been conjectured that they helped defer any action against him for some time. Their protection was made null and void when DEA agent Enrique Camarena was tortured and murdered in Mexico, and the DEA moved against Matta in 1988.

See also: CAMARENA, ENRIQUE.

MATTHEWS, Frank

Frank Matthews is the leader of a violent international drug organization. Matthews is said to be responsible for the importation and sale of large amounts of heroin and cocaine into the United States, and he also allegedly ordered the murder of several associates. He has been at large for 27 years.

Frank Matthews was born and raised in Durham, North Carolina. As a youth he became a numbers runner. He later moved to Philadelphia, where he ran his own numbers operation before moving to the Bedford-Stuyvesant section of Brooklyn in the 1960s. Matthews created a successful numbers business and eventually branched out into the heroin industry as the street distributor for the famous "French Connection" operatives who were trafficking through Marseilles, France. Between 1967 and 1970, Matthews built what was then the largest domestic distribution of heroin within the United States.

Police received an anonymous tip that led to his arrest in December 1972. The bail was set at $2.5 million by a federal magistrate. Matthews was last seen in a Brooklyn Federal Court in 1973. He posted $325,000 in cash and property and then proceeded to jump bail. It was alleged that he ran off with $5 million in cash and had a strong network of friends. He is still considered at-large, and a reward of $50,000 has been offered for any information that will lead to his capture and arrest.

MAYRAND, Richard

Richard "Dick" Mayrand was born in 1964. He followed his older brother, Michel "Willie" Mayrand, into the Hells Angels North chapter and received his colors in his early or mid-twenties.

He was present at the now infamous March 24, 1985, slaughter at the Sherbrooke chapter's Lennoxville clubhouse. Mayrand and others were held at gunpoint while members of the organization's Montreal and Halifax chapters gunned down five North members. Mayrand's brother Michel was among the casualties.

Following the annihilation of the Hells Angels North chapter, Mayrand became a member of the club's Montreal chapter. When his brother's body was pulled from the St. Lawrence River, Richard did not attend his funeral service in Asbestos, Quebec.

On September 1, 1985, Mayrand and Montreal chapter president Réjean "Zig-Zag" Lessard were stopped by a police officer as they roared down a street on a stolen motorcycle. Two firearms and a silencer, all reported stolen, were found in their possession.

Arrested for possession of 52,500 capsules of LSD, Mayrand was pronounced guilty of drug trafficking on March 6, 1987, but the conviction was overturned in June 1989 after a judge concluded that the crown's evidence relied solely on the testimony of informants Clermont Paquet and Gerry "the Cat" Coulombe.

Mayrand remained a member of the Hells Angels Montreal chapter until 1997 or 1998, when he transferred over to the club's Nomads chapter. The upward move symbolized the influence and power Mayrand held in the organization.

Mayrand, who had avoided newspaper headlines since the 1980s, was arrested on February 16, 2001, along with fellow Nomads Gilles "Trooper" Mathieu, Denis "Pas Fiable" Houle, Normand Robitaille, and Michel Rose, as well as prospects Luc Bordeleau, Richard Lariviere, and Rocker Kenny Bedard. The bikers had gathered at the Holiday Inn on Sherbrooke Street with pictures of several of their Rock Machine rivals. Mayrand was arrested along with Bordeleau as they left the hotel to retrieve their cars. Both had firearms on them. The others, who were also armed, were picked up inside the building. To avoid gangsterism charges, the group pled guilty to illegal firearms possession on February 21, 2000, and each received a one-year prison sentence.

On March 29, 2001, Mayrand, who is the club's national president, was informed from behind bars that he was being charged with murder, narcotics trafficking, and gangsterism as part of Opération Printemps 2001. Mayrand and eight associates were found guilty in March 2004. He was sentenced to 22 years in prison.

See also: HELLS ANGELS.

Reference

Gary Francoeur. "Richard 'Dick' Mayrand." Wiseguy-Wally. Available online. URL: http://www.geocities.com/wiseguywally/RichardMayrand. Downloaded on July 16, 2004.

MAZARA Del Vallo

This Sicilian Mafia clan was recently run by the late Francesco Messina. The operations are now controlled by Matteo Messina Denaro, his son.

See also: DENARO, MATTEO MESSINA.

McVITE, Jack (a.k.a. the Hat)

A sometime enforcer and hit man for the Firm, as the Kray Gang was known in England, Jack McVite was well known for wearing fancy hats to hide his balding scalp. By the 1960s he was a drug dealer and user, as well as a heavy drinker. His loud and obnoxious ways proved to be too much for the Kray twins, whose associates and business connections McVite harassed. After numerous warnings by the Krays, McVite was invited to a "party" that turned out to be an execution. He was stabbed to death by Reggie Kray in 1965.

See also: CORNELL, GEORGE; FRASER, FRANK; RICHARDSON, CHARLIE; RICHARDSON, EDDIE; RICHARDSON GANG.

MEDELLÍN Cartel

Based out of Medellín, Colombia, this cartel was founded by Pablo Escobar. A former car thief, Esco-bar fought a constant pitched battle to control the manufacture of cocaine in Medellín, as well as throughout Colombia. As Escobar rose, many in the city profited from his largesse or by being on his payroll. Medellín became a company town, and the cartel became the richest in history.

The Medellín cartel bought and manufactured cocaine from numerous places throughout South America. It was well known that the cartel purchased semiprocessed cocaine from Peru. Officials on the cartel's payroll then turned a blind eye to planes and fishing boats packed with coca paste that were destined for Colombia for refining.

The organization was also run by brother Roberto Escobar who handled many of the money matters concerning the cartel. Charged with running the cash flow and payroll, the Escobars had thousands of law-enforcement personnel and judges on their payroll throughout the Western Hemisphere.

The cartel was by far the most sophisticated as well as the most deadly of all the cartels. They were known for their brutality and violence, as well as for their massive wealth and flashy expenditures. The cartel suffered greatly when Escobar became too big a liability to the Colombian government and brought them under withering condemnation from many nations, especially the United States. The U.S. market was the cartel's main market, and it held the largest market share.

Pablo Escobar offered himself up for arrest and detention to the Colombian government in 1991, but his life behind bars hardly put a crimp in his style. The "jail" that held Escobar was anything but, equipped with television and a gourmet chef. He was even supplied with a string of beautiful women. Escobar gave the government the ability to say that it had captured its biggest problem and that it had the cocaine trade under control. But many knew it was a farce, as Pablo and his brother Roberto continued to run their empire and quench their bloodlust.

In July 1992, Escobar walked out of jail to the horrors of the international community. Even the surrender of Roberto in 1992 did not mollify the desire of the Colombian and U.S. governments, who were now working jointly, to capture Pablo. Together, the two governments and a home-grown vigilante movement led to the downfall of the cartel and the death of Pablo in 1993.

See also: ESCOBAR, PABLO; ESCOBAR, ROBERTO.

Fábio Ochoa, a leader in the once-powerful Medellín drug cartel, is escorted by police officers after his arrest on October 13, 1999. (AP)

MEJÍA MUNERA, Miguel and Victor

Miguel and Victor Mejía Munera (a.k.a. "the Twins" or "los Mellizos") are identical twins who allegedly run a major cocaine trafficking organization that transports cocaine to the United States and Europe. The Mejía Munera brothers are said to have links to both the North Valle and Cali syndicates. The Drug Enforcement Administration believes that the Mejía brothers are "up and coming" traffickers who will attempt to fill the void created by the arrest of the Rodríguez Orejuela brothers.

Reference

Thomas A. Constantine. "International Organized Crime Syndicates and Their Impact on the U.S." U.S. Drug Enforcement Administration. Available online. URL: http://www.dea.gov/pubs/cngrtest/ct980226.htm. Downloaded on July 15, 2004.

MESSINA Brothers

The Messina brothers were one of the most notorious British underworld syndicates ever to be created and prosper in that country. They ruled London's criminal underworld for more than two decades, and their power was as great as any Sicilian mob on the continent or in America. World War II was surely a factor in their longevity, as the British authorities were busy trying to defend and then, postwar, rebuild the brutally bombed capital. In that era, the

Messina brothers had a hand in almost every black-market transaction.

The Messina brothers' father held the surname DeBono, and their mother was an Arab. Salvatore, Carmelo, Alfredo, Attilio, and Eugene were born in Alexandria, Egypt. The brothers took their name from the Sicilian region known as Messina, one of the most trafficked parts of Sicily, both in the history of industry and war. According to http://www.geocities.com/OrganizedCrimeSyndicates, "As far back as the early 1900s, their father was linked to the white slave trade—forced prostitution. The brothers eventually gravitated towards the racket, deceiving local women who thought they were promised marriage and more opportunities. The women eventually were forced to sell their bodies on London's notorious West End. The brothers would eventually relocate to London, proclaiming themselves kings of the English underworld and raising the eyebrow of Scotland Yard."

John Alexander Falconer joined the Metropolitan Police in 1948. He has written, "On the 9th July, 1957 . . . I was . . . posted to West End Central, the busiest station in the U.K. with 400 PCs. This was affectionately known as the 'Factory.' At that time prostitution was flourishing with soliciting in the street commonplace. Amongst the well-known 'ladies' of the era were two women who were run by the notorious Messina brothers." It was well known that many local constables were paid to look the other way in the areas of Bond, Queen, and Stafford Streets. However, soon Scotland Yard entered the picture, and the brothers began to flee the country before the end of the 1950s.

Eugene and Carmelo surfaced in Belgium, where they were arrested for prostitution and pimping in 1955, and were both sentenced to jail time of varying length. Carmelo was banned from the country. Alfredo was arrested in England and charged with running a prostitution ring and was sentenced to serve hard time. Brother Attilio, obviously the least bright, was caught trying to reenter the country and was sentenced to four years in prison in 1959.

"With the exception of Salvatore Messina, who never emerged after fleeing, all the brothers were hammered by the British justice system. Following their releases the Messina brothers would never recapture their power and all are believed to have since passed away," according to http://www.geocities.com/OrganizedCrimeSyndicate.

See also: COMER, JACK; KRAY TWINS; RICHARDSON, CHARLIE; RICHARDSON, EDDIE.

MEXICAN Mafia (a.k.a. Sureño)

The creation and success of the Mexican Mafia has been credited to Rodolfo Cadena and Joe Morgan. While serving time at the Duel Vocational Institute in Tracy, California, they heard several inmates complain of the abuse and racism of the California prison system. At that time white prison gangs such as the Blue Bird Gang controlled all activities within the prison walls. In response the Mexican-American inmates created a gang to protect themselves from the other inmates. They soon became the most powerful organization in the California prison system, controlling all illegal activities behind bars. The Mexican Mafia remained unmolested until 1968 when their rivals, NUESTRA FAMILIA was formed. As a direct result of the growing control and threat of the Mexican Mafia, the Black Guerrilla Family and the Aryan Brotherhood also emerged. Southern California street gangs banded together in prison to combat the unified Northern California street gangs. Young street-gang members began to call themselves *sureños* (Spanish for "southerner"). Once the Sureño street-gang members are arrested and imprisoned, they too will join the Mexican Mafia.

Sureño street gang members openly identify themselves with the symbols XIII, X3, 13 and 3 dots. This refers to the 13th letter of the alphabet, *M*, which stands for Mexican Mafia. The gang identifies with the color blue and the words *Sureño, Sur,* and *Southerner.* Other symbols include a black hand, *La Eme* (meaning the *M* in Spanish) and MM (Mexican Mafia). Members of the Mexican Mafia have been known to align themselves with the Aryan Brotherhood and the Italian Mafia.

The Mexican Mafia has been identified in every state penal institution in the United States, and the group maintains numerous contacts throughout Mexico. Sureño street gangs have been identified in several states throughout the country. They are involved in drug smuggling, drug dealing, gun running, and other illegal activities.

Reference

KnowGangs. "Mexican Mafia." Available online. URL: http://www.knowgangs.com/gang_resources/sureno/sureno_001.htm. Downloaded on July 16, 2004.

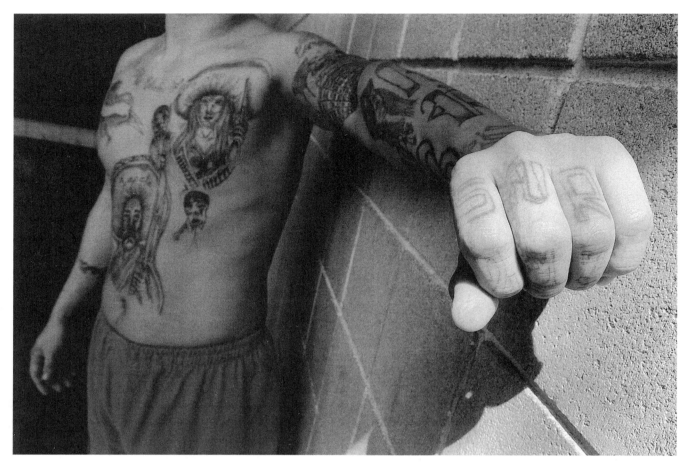

A tattoo on this inmate's hand indicates that he is a member of the Sureño 13 gang, also known as the Mexican Mafia. (AP/The Observer)

MICHAILOV, Yevgeni

Michailov, a Russian émigré, was a reputed criminal, involved in jewelry theft and fraud. He was abducted in Brooklyn on July 8, 1991, and his body was found in a lot near Kennedy Airport in New York City on August 27, 1991. He had been shot four times in the head.

See also: RUSSIAN MAFIYA.

Reference

New Jersey State Commission of Investigation, New York Organized Crime Task Force, New York State Commission of Investigation, Pennsylvania Crime Commission, with Rutgers University. "The Tri-State Joint Soviet-Émigré Organized Crime Project." 1992. Available online. URL: http://www.state.nj.us/sci/pdf/russian.pdf. Accessed on November 24, 2004.

MIKHAILOV, Sergei

Sergei Mikhailov is one of the most powerful Russian mobsters. He is the boss of the Moscow-based Solsnetskaya Organization, the biggest and most powerful Mafia organization in Russia and probably the world, counting 5,000 members. Mikhailov's power reaches from Moscow to Miami to Geneva to the Middle East and beyond.

Sergei Anatoliavic Mikhailov was born on February 7, 1958, in Moscow, Russia. He grew up in an atmosphere where doing crime was doing business. According to Mikhailov the real criminals were the police and the politicians who murdered and tortured anyone who dared sing a different tune than the one approved by the communist government. Mikhailov, or Mikhas as he was called, did not dive into a life of crime right away: He first worked as a waiter in several Moscow restaurants, but the pay was not good, and so soon Mikhailov turned to crime full time. After some time without being caught, his luck ran out. In 1984, at the age of 26, Mikhailov was charged with theft and fraud and sentenced to six months in a Russian prison, or gulag. In the gulag Mikhailov made good contacts with other Russian gangsters, including members of the *vory v zakone*, the Russian Mafia. The contacts made in prison would serve Mikhailov well.

When released from prison, Mikhailov was a hardened criminal with a feared reputation. He was ready to begin his rise to power. He began his own organization and named it after a neighborhood in Moscow: The Solsnetskaya Organization. In the beginning Mikhailov and his organization's main activities were extortion, counterfeiting, drug trafficking, and blackmail. As business grew, they soon clashed with rival organizations over territory. Several wars were fought, and every time Mikhailov and his Solsnetskaya Organization came out on top.

With the rival organizations out of the way, Mikhailov had total control. He soon expanded his rackets to include arms dealing, infiltration of legitimate businesses, and money laundering. Pretty soon the Solsnetskaya Organization was the biggest, most organized, most powerful, and most feared criminal group in Russia. The money rolled in, and Mikhailov's power was enormous. When he was arrested in 1989 on extortion charges, he served 18 months in a Russian detention center awaiting his trial. When the trial finally took place, the main witness refused to testify, and Mikhas walked out a free man that same day, eager to expand his criminal empire.

When the Soviet Union collapsed and the iron curtain fell, Russia was in total chaos. Where there is chaos, there is opportunity, and Mikhailov and the other Russian Mafia bosses took full advantage of the confusion to gain control of politicians and government resources. There was nothing left to stop the Russian Mafia from assuming total control of what the government left behind. Pretty soon Mikhailov's organization owned banks, casinos, car dealerships, and even the Vnoekovo Airport.

Operating from their new headquarters, a stylish building along the Leninsky Prospekt, Mikhailov's organization controlled prostitution, gambling, and weapons dealing. Mikhailov had taken control of Russia and now felt that it was time to expand his operation on to the international scene.

In 1994 while Mikhailov sent his soldiers all over the world to set up bases, he himself decided to go to Israel. Israel is a popular residence among Russian mobsters because of its law that allows Jews from all over the world to return there without being refused, even if they are on the run from the law. Thus many Jewish Russian mobsters live in Israel, and many non-Jewish Russians take advantage to obtain a fake passport. One such man was Sergei Mikhailov. While living in Israel, Mikhailov watched his empire expand. His organization was now active all over the world. He did business with other criminal organizations including the Colombian cartels and Italian Mafias both in the United States and Italy.

Mikhailov's power was enormous. He maintained hit teams, called combat brigades, on standby in Miami and flew them around the world whenever somebody had to be assassinated. The team took care of the hit and then returned to Miami to wait for a new assignment. In the meantime they ran some U.S.-based operations for the organization in New York, Los Angeles, and Houston.

In 1995 Mikhailov decided to move to Switzerland. There he started to build up a web of bank accounts and companies with respectable directors. According to Swiss court documents, Russian mobsters laundered $60 billion through Swiss banks. Mikhailov was doing well and showed it. He sent his children to a good private school, bought a castle near Geneva, drove a beautiful Rolls Royce, and spent about $15,000 dollars a month on clothing. Life was good until Swiss authorities decided to put some pressure on the Russian mobsters who were moving to Switzerland.

In October 1996 Mikhailov was arrested and charged with being boss of a criminal organization,

Russian mobster Sergei Mikhailov (center) arrives at the Court of Justice in Geneva, Switzerland, on December 3, 1998. (AP)

using false documents, and breaking a Swiss law restricting foreigners from buying property. In his mansion police found Israeli military bugging equipment which Mikhailov used to listen in on secret Swiss police radio transmissions. The police also found loads of documents in the names of bogus companies that were used for laundering money from drugs and weapon sales. Detectives also found out that Mikhailov invested millions in the United States, where he had bought nightclubs in New York and Los Angeles and a car dealership in Houston. Mikhailov denied that he was a criminal and said that he was just a "simple businessman." The Swiss authorities did not believe it and locked him in a prison to await his trial.

As the Swiss prosecutors began to gather evidence, Mikhailov's associates tried to make sure that there was little evidence left. Several people who had done business with Mikhailov were found dead. In Holland a father and his son were murdered: The father was stabbed in his eye and bled to death. Another man in Amsterdam was shot. Shortly thereafter the head of the Moscow police department fled to Switzerland and claimed he was threatened by some of Mikhailov's men. Even the media was intimidated: A Belgian journalist who wrote several columns about Mikhailov was warned by the local police that there was a contract on his life; eventually the police stopped the plot when they arrested a corrupt Belgian policeman who was about to take on the contract. Finally after two years the trial started on November 30, 1998. Eighty witnesses wearing bulletproof vests were called in to testify, and Mikhailov faced up to seven years in prison if convicted.

The trial turned out to be a major success for Mikhailov and a major blow to the Swiss authorities. Despite all the evidence found at Mikhailov's home and the testimony of the 80 witnesses, the Swiss prosecutors could not gain a conviction. The big obstacle was the Russian government. When asked to provide certain documents that would show that Mikhailov was the head of a criminal empire, they refused. As a result Mikhailov was acquitted on the most serious charges and found guilty on a minor charge, for which he was not sentenced because he already had served two years awaiting his trial.

Mikhailov immediately thanked the jury, crying: "My heart is full of gratitude. . . . I love you, I love you, I love you." Later, in a statement, he added: "You have shown to the whole world that democ-

racy, law, and justice exists in this country." After being set free in December 1998, Mikhailov returned to Russia and sued Geneva for his lost income in the two years he had spent in prison. He won. In July 1999 a Geneva court awarded Mikhailov the full amount he had claimed, although the authorities appealed against the decision.

Living in freedom Mikhailov allegedly leads his criminal empire that stretches from Asia to Canada back to Moscow and Western Europe. There is no place on this world that is safe from his organization. He continues to make billions of dollars and expands his power constantly.

See also: RUSSIAN MAFIYA.

Reference

David Amoruso. "Sergei 'Mikhas' Mikhailov." Gangsters Inc. Available online. URL: http://gangstersinc.tripod. com/Mikas.html. Downloaded on July 16, 2004.

MOCK Sai Wing (a.k.a. Mock Duck, Clay Pigeon)

Hip Sing Tong leader, and one of New York's most famous gang leaders. Mock Duck ruled the Hip Sing Tong based in Manhattan's Chinatown during the first three decades of the 20th century. Mock Duck's Tong wars with the On Leong Tong (Peaceful Dragon Parlor) are legendary. During the 1930s Mock Duck retired and moved to Brooklyn, where he died of natural causes. Before he came to Chinatown, the On Leong Tong and its owner, Tom Lee, faced only token opposition. Based at 15 Pell Street, the On Leong Tong took over from the Chee Kung, helped Chinese immigrants acclimate to the United States, and controlled the Chinatown opium dens and, most importantly, the gambling proceeds. From 1885 to 1900 they operated unmolested. In 1900, local reformers, led by Dr. Charles Parkhurst, started to publicize the graft and corruption that came out of Chinatown. "Simultaneously there appeared a certain Mock Duck, once an On Leong man, a cherubic, ever-smiling, moon-faced Machiavelli, who looked upon Tom Lee's profits, decided Tom was a wicked man, and said as much to Dr. Parkhurst. By some miracle Mock Duck escaped with his life to become the father of the Hip Sing Tong and a rival of the On Leongs for control of the gambling privileges in Chinatown. He used to lisp in explaining the name of the organization, 'means plospelous, and Sing is Chinese word for union. We plospelous union all lite.'

And he would beam in an irresistible way of which only your Chinese politician has the secret," according to the *Brooklyn Daily Eagle*, October 19, 1924. "Out from the East by way of the West came little Mock Duck. He had the fat smile of a Chinese cherub. But there was a desperately impudent glint in his eye which not even Chinese stolidity could film over. He joined Wong Get [a rival tong]. He knew by tradition of the threat of Tom Lee to use the white man's meddling as a foil to the devices of his Chinese enemies."

Mock Duck went about his business methodically. He went before Tom Lee with dogged purpose set in his childlike, fat features and stated his case. There was only veneration in his posture and his voice for the eminence of the goat-whiskered patriarch to whom he made his astounding proposal. Translated, it was not complicated: Literally it was "50–50 or fight" as reported in *The World*, December 4, 1924. Seventeen years of sporadic violence, murder, arson, and kidnapping followed. Through all the gunfire, Mock Duck was hit only once, in 1904, and spent three weeks in a hospital as a result. There were two major "tong wars" under his watch, from 1904 to 1906 and from 1909 to 1913. The phrase *hatchet man* comes from these battles because their assassins carried small axes in their long sleeves. Tom Lee weathered it all and died a natural death in 1917 at the age of 76. Both the On Leong and Hip Sing tongs have burial spaces in "The Evergreens Cemetery, which borders Brooklyn and Queens."

Mock Duck was described as "a curious mixture of bravery and cowardice. He wore a shirt of chain mail, carried two guns and a hatchet and, although notoriously a poor marksman, earned a reputation for bravery for the utter disregard for his own safety he displayed when squatting on his haunches in the street with both eyes shut and firing at a surrounding circle of On Leongs," reported the *Brooklyn Eagle* on February 29, 1932.

During the height of Mock Duck's prosperity, agents of the New York Society for the Prevention of Cruelty to Children investigated a report that his adopted daughter, Ha Oi, was a white girl. The courts found that she was the daughter of one Lizzie Smith, who had married a Chinaman. She was taken away from Mock Duck. The Hip Sing leader was frantic, for he loved the girl tenderly. He carried the case to the appellate division but lost. Then, to drown his sorrow, he began to gamble recklessly as

he roamed aimlessly to Chicago and San Francisco and throughout the Midwest. His despair was such that he did not care whether he won or lost. He made large winnings and returned to New York with diamond studs blazing from his shirt front and $30,000 in his pockets. The old tong guns began to blaze again, and hatchets gleamed. Mock Duck was arrested many times but was not convicted until 1912 when he was sent to Sing Sing for operating a policy game. When he emerged from prison, he announced he was through with the old life and intended to become a respectable citizen of Brooklyn.

See also: HOP SING TONG; ON LEONG TONG.

Reference

Fodor, J. "Mock Duck." *Brooklyn Daily Eagle,* February 29, 1932.

MOGILEVICH, Semion

Semion Mogilevich was born on June 30, 1946, in Kiev, Ukraine. Not much is known about his early years, and he did not become known to the police until the 1970s. In the early 1970s Mogilevich was part of the Lyubertskaya group in Moscow. He was a small-time crook, trying to stay ahead of the communist government, getting by with petty theft and fraud. During this career of crime, he served three years in prison for selling currencies on the black market and another four years for currency dealing offenses. All this petty crime hardly made Mogilevich any money.

His first big accomplishment came in the 1980s when scores of Russian Jews emigrated to Israel and the United States. He offered to buy their possessions and sell them so that he could send them some nice money from the deals, but in reality he sent nothing and made loads of money off of the Jews who were trying to leave. By the 1990s Mogilevich had made several millions. He had invested the money he had stolen from Jewish refugees and made more through weapons smuggling, prostitution, gambling, drugs, and black-market items. In the 1990s the Soviet Union was collapsing, and the organized crime groups were becoming more powerful than ever before. Wars between these mobsters erupted, and Mogilevich, along with his top employees, decided to leave Moscow for Israel.

In Israel, Mogilevich became an Israeli citizen and remained inconspicuous. He made contacts with other Russian and Israeli organized-crime groups, ran his foreign businesses, and expanded his criminal empire. Mogilevich invested all of his illegal money and bought nightclubs, precious-stones factories, art, liquor factories, and more. He used some of these companies as fronts to expand his illegal empire. Among his purchases was a weapons factory. According to Mogilevich, he "bought that factory in Hungary in 1992 and it still hasn't sold one single armament." The factory produces antiaircraft guns and missiles and mortars.

In 1991 Mogilevich married his Hungarian girlfriend Katalin Papp. This marriage allowed him to move to Hungary and live there. Once he arrived in Budapest, he set up his criminal organization by buying nightclubs and restaurants. According to Federal Bureau of Investigation (FBI) records, he built up an organization of 250 members modeled after the Italian Mafia.

Budapest looked like the paradise that Mogilevich needed, but even though he had most of the politicians and the police in his pocket or too scared to resist him, the Hungarian government decided to show Mogilevich that he and his criminal friends were not welcome. On May 31, 1995, police raided a restaurant called U Holubu that belonged to a company owned by Mogilevich. Hungarian criminal intelligence said that two Russian-speaking criminal organizations—one from Moscow and one from the Ukraine—were meeting there. All men present were arrested and later released. Mogilevich did not attend the meeting. When asked about the meeting, Mogilevich said: "Yes, on May the 31st 1995, my comrade Victor Averin had his 38th birthday. And he got together his friends (who had agreed on this with him) and their wives and children, to celebrate his birthday in the Czech Republic at the U Holubu restaurant."

When asked if he was planning to attend, Mogilevich said yes. When questioned as to why he had not and if he had been tipped off, he answered that his plane was "running more than 45 minutes late. I was meant to be at the restaurant for 9:30 P.M., that's what we'd agreed over the phone. At 10:45 P.M. I had only just landed. By the time I arrived at U Holubu, the raid was already in full swing. I went to the neighboring hotel and sat in the bar there until about five or six in the morning. Then I got in a taxi and went to Budapest." The raid was little trouble for Mogilevich and his organization. It was a desperate police action by a government that needed to do something to maintain its authority and power over increasingly powerful criminals.

Mogilevich's criminal empire currently operates in continental Europe (including Italy, the Czech Republic, and Switzerland), the United States, the Ukraine, Israel, and the United Kingdom. He also has dealings with organizations in South America, Pakistan, and Japan. Mogilevich is considered one of the smartest and most powerful gangsters in the world, and so far no one has been able to stop him.

In 2000 it became known that the F.B.I. had set up a joint task force with the Hungarian police to combat organized crime in the region and Eastern Europe in general. Chances are however that the F.B.I. arrived too late. It looks as if Mogilevich has become too powerful, even as he keeps insisting that he only sells grain and wheat.

Reference

David Amoruso. "Semion 'The Brainy Don' Mogilevich." Gangsters Inc. Available online. URL: http://gangstersinc. tripod.com/Mog.html. Downloaded on July 16, 2004.

MOHAWK Warrior Society

"The Mohawk Warrior Society is the archetype for militant Canadian aboriginals. In less than twenty-five years, the Society emerged, armed itself, grew corrupt, and collapsed—an evolution which provides a near-perfect example of the means by which an insurgent group can subvert itself," reported the Mackenzie Institute in June 1996.

Originally, this was an organization created to advance Native American peoples and extol their traditions. Many individuals came from the Mohawk, Oneida, Tuscarora, and Seneca nations. However, like the Black Panthers of the United States, they took on a more militant attitude and decided to arm themselves in order to protect themselves from what they considered harassment and brutality at the hands of the Canadian government and Canadian authorities.

By the 1980s they began to grow their cache of firearms to include .50-caliber sniping rifles and machine guns, grenade launchers, plastic explosives, and, allegedly, antitank rockets. The Canadian authorities identified in 1985 several suspects that they knew were dealing illegal drugs from the Mohawk reserve under the protection offered by the Warrior Society for a fee.

Other Mohawks were uncomfortable with the new Warrior Society businesses. Tensions between the Mohawk nation and the Warrior Society eventually grew, as the Warrior Society exhibited such techniques as extortion and violence against their own people to protect their illicit businesses. It is alleged that the Warrior Society had alliances and dealings with a variety of other organized-crime groups, including the Montreal underworld, Vietnamese gangsters and the Chinese triads, the Russian Mafiya, Jamaican Posses, and East Indian gangs.

"The Warriors have come a long way from the inspired militants of 1973. In the process, they have terrorized their own communities, facilitated a multibillion dollar smuggling industry," stated the Mackenzie Institute report.

Reference

The Mackenzie Institute. "The Long Fall of the Mohawk Warriors." Available online. URL: http://www. mackenzieinstitute.com/1996_06_military_mohawks. html. Downloaded on July 16, 2004.

MONTOYA Sánchez, Diego

Diego Montoya Sánchez allegedly heads a North Valle trafficking organization that transports cocaine base from Peru to Colombia and produces multiton quantities of cocaine hydrochloride for export to the United States and Europe. The Drug Enforcement Administration considers Montoya Sánchez to be one of the most significant cocaine traffickers in Colombia today.

Reference

Peter Huston. "A New Threat to England—The Indians Want to Send Us Back Now." *Bizarre Magazine.* Available online. URL: http://www.capital.net/~phuston/ mobi.html. Downloaded on July 16, 2004.

MONTREAL

Montreal's most powerful criminal organization is, arguably, the Mafia. Active in Quebec since the early 1900s, the group has been able to develop a nearly impregnable hierarchy and establish international drug networks.

The organization was, for many years, a branch office of New York City's powerful Bonanno crime family. The group, led by the influential Vic "The Egg" Cotroni, ran huge gambling rings, corrupted politicians, and smuggled millions worth of narcotics into the U.S. market. The profits of these illicit activities were laundered through legitimate businesses, further expanding the organization's influence.

A power struggle erupted between the Calabrian and Sicilian factions of the family in the late 1970s. Several mobsters would lose their lives before the war was ended with the assassination of boss Paolo Violi. Vito Rizzuto, of the Sicilian wing, assumed control. He broke the family with the Bonannos and established close ties with the powerful Caruana/ Cuntrera family.

The Mafia, along with the predominantly Irish West End Gang and the Hells Angels, make up Montreal's consortium. The group determines the price of drugs, the amounts that are imported, and to whom it is sold. Vito Rizzuto remains in control and leads an extremely powerful, secretive, and disciplined group.

Reference

Gary Francoeur. "Montreal Mafia." Wiseguy Wally. Available online. URL: http://www.geocities.com/wiseguywally. Downloaded on July 19, 2004.

—G.F.

MORPHINE   *See* OPIUM POPPY.

MOTORCYCLE Gangs

With World War II over in 1945, thousands of veterans returned home to take up their lives again. However, many missed the excitement of the war. One of the ways they sought to recreate this excitement was by riding a Harley Davidson or Indian motorcycle. Biker gangs started in the 1950s as loosely knit, rowdy groups. They gained popularity and status in the 1960s and are now recognized as dangerous criminal groups. According to the American Motorcycle Association (A.M.A.), these outlaw bikers represent about one percent of the nation's motorcycle riders. The outlaw bikers are involved in murder, rape, assault, burglary, narcotics, theft, prostitution, weapons offenses, and intimidation of the public and witnesses. They pose a threat to society in general and to law enforcement because they possess expertise in sophisticated weapons and an intricate intelligence network.

Not all outlaw gangs are complex criminal organizations. Only four appear to have the large national impact that warrants investigation under the federal

"Racketeer Influenced and Corrupt Organizations" (RICO) statute. They are the Hells Angels, the Outlaws, the Pagans, and the Bandidos, often referred to as the "Big Four." All four motorcycle clubs have chapters in several states. The Hells Angels also have chapters in Canada, throughout Europe, Australia, and New Zealand. The Pagans have a chapter in Australia.

Legend holds that the genesis of the outlaw biker gangs took place in Hollister, California, on July 4th weekend in 1946. The American Motorcycle Association (A.M.A.) was sponsoring the Annual Motorcycle Dirt Hill Climb Races in Hollister, a small town with a police force of seven.

The town filled with bikers. Two of the larger motorcycle groups to attend were the "Pissed Off Bastards of Bloomington" (P.O.B.O.B.) and the "Market Street Commandoes." During the evenings, drag races and bar and street fights were common. One member of the P.O.B.O.B. was arrested and jailed. A large mob gathered and demanded his release. When local authorities refused, the estimated mob of 750 reportedly tore the small community apart, although well-publicized photos of the mayhem were later found to have been staged.

The Hollister incident contributed three biker traditions that survive to this day: the 4th of July run, the one-percenter image, and calling anyone not part of the biker subculture, "citizen."

After Hollister, the P.O.B.O.B.'s membership started to increase, and the new blood came with new ideas. After much consideration one idea was a name change. The new identity they chose was "Hells Angels."

Though there are many different motorcycle gangs, many of them share similar organizational structures. Numerous gangs have chapters in various cities and states around the nation, and some have chapters in several countries. Typical organization includes:

National President—Usually the founder of the club. He will usually be located at or near the national headquarters. He will be surrounded by bodyguards and organizational enforcers.

Territorial or Regional Representatives—In some cases called the national vice president in charge of a specific region or state.

National Secretary/Treasurer—He is responsible for the club's money and collecting dues from local chapters. He also records any by-law changes and any minutes.

National Enforcer—This person answers directly to the national president. He acts as a bodyguard and administers punishment for club violations. He has also been known to locate former members to retrieve colors or remove the club's tattoo from them.

Chapter President—This person has either claimed the position or has been voted in. He has final authority over all chapter business and members.

Vice President—This person is second in command. He presides over club affairs in the absence of the president. Normally, he is hand picked by the chapter president.

Secretary/Treasurer—This is usually the member with the best writing skills and probably the most education. He will maintain the chapter roster and accounting system. He is also responsible for collecting dues, keeping minutes, and paying any bills that the chapter accumulates.

Sergeant at Arms—This person maintains order at club meetings. Because of the violent nature of outlaw gangs, this person is normally the strongest member physically and is loyal to the chapter president. He may administer beatings to fellow members for violations of club rules. He is the club enforcer.

Road Captain—This person fulfills the role of a logistician and security chief for club-sponsored runs or outings. The Road Captain maps out routes to be taken during runs and arranges refueling, food, and maintenance stops. He carries the club's money and uses it for bail, if necessary.

Members—The rank and file, fully accepted, dues-paying members of the gang. They are the individuals who carry out the president's orders and have sworn to live by the club's bylaws.

Probate or Prospective Member—These are the club's hopefuls, who spend from one month to one year in a probationary status. They must prove during that time that they are worthy of becoming members. Some clubs have the probate commit a felony with fellow members observing in an effort to weed out the weak and stop infiltration by law enforcement. Probates must be nominated by a regular member and receive a unanimous vote for acceptance. They are known to carry weapons for other club members and stand guard at club functions. The probate wears no colors and has no voting rights.

Associates or Honorary Members—An individual who has proved his value or usefulness to the gang. These individuals may be professional people who have in some manner helped the club. Some of the more noted are attorneys, bail bondsmen, motorcycle-shop owners, and auto wrecking-yard owners. These people are allowed to party with the gang, either in town or on their runs; however, they do not have a voting status or wear colors.

All outlaw motorcycle clubs have bylaws or a constitution that sets an acceptable standard of conduct and administrative procedures for the club. The bylaws cover matters such as membership requirements, penalties for misconduct, and acceptable behavior during runs or meetings. While bylaws differ from club to club, the following are examples of common bylaws:

All members must be male and at least 18 years of age.

All prospective new members must be sponsored by a current member.

All prospective new members must complete a probation period.

All members pay monthly dues, and all new members will pay initiation fees to the national headquarters.

No member shall transfer from one chapter to another without the permission of both presidents and will pay a transfer fee to the national treasury.

When a member is in another jurisdiction, he will abide by their bylaws and president.

Any member caught using intravenous drugs will lose his colors and everything that goes with them.

Members may only ride Harley-Davidson or Indian motorcycles.

Outlaw motorcycle gangs are male dominated and highly chauvinistic. Women are treated as playthings and property. Women are generally forced into prostitution or street-level drug trafficking and are quite often physically and sexually abused. In the outlaw biker's society, women are bought, sold, traded, or given away within the club.

Selling drugs in the mid-1960s taught the outlaw biker the basics of supply and demand. When they learned that men would pay, they put their women to work as prostitutes. In the violent, profit-oriented society inhabited by the outlaw biker, a woman is a piece of property to rent or trade.

Women take up with outlaw bikers for different reasons: Some are hungry, some need a warm place to stay, and others feel safe in the gang. While outlaw bikers have been known to abduct and rape women, most women attach themselves voluntarily to the club and everything it stands for—drugs, alcohol, parties, fast bikes and cars, cheap thrills, and sex. Rebellious teenagers, bored businesswomen, and uneducated and homeless women have all been attracted to the biker-gang lifestyle, whether for excitement or for a sense of security.

A woman's main value to an outlaw biker, aside from providing sexual gratification, is to make money. She must give all her money to her "old man." Bikers put their women to work in massage parlors, topless bars, cocktail lounges, and strip clubs. Most are covers for prostitution, which is the bikers' most lucrative source of income after drugs.

Another area where the women are used effectively is intelligence gathering. They may enter a community and take jobs at city, county, and state offices where they have access to blank birth certificates, driver's licenses, and other useful documentations. Women will also seek work as police records clerks, telephone operators, employees in welfare offices, and in prison institutions. They will even sleep with police to compromise them or gather intelligence.

Women of motorcycle gangs mainly fall into three categories:

Mama or Sheep—These are women who belong to the club at large. They belong to every member and are expected to consent to the sexual desires of anyone at any time. They perform menial tasks around the clubhouse but do not attend club meetings. Some clubs permit these women to wear "colors" with the inscription "Property of (club name)" embroidered on the back.

Old Lady—These are the wives or steady girlfriends of club members. An old lady is the property of one biker and cannot be used or abused by other club members. An old lady is not a club member and is not permitted to attend club meetings. She also will in some clubs wear "Property of" colors, however, with the name of the biker she belongs to rather than the club name.

Broad—A female who is used for onetime sexual gratification, a one-night stand, or a rape victim, who is later discarded.

Women are expected to help the outlaw biker get ahead. For example, several Hells Angels have their old ladies turn tricks in topless bars in North and South Carolina. The bars are near military bases, and the old ladies use their connections to get all the weapons the club needs. The Cleveland chapter got three light antitank weapon (LAW) rockets through their old ladies. Other chapters have gotten .45 caliber pistols and hand grenades from their women.

The Big Four outlaw gangs claim to be the 1 percent of motorcyclists who will not conform to society's laws and morals ethics. They are the Hells Angels, the Outlaws, the Pagans, and the Bandidos. All of them are U.S.-based and have international chapters, with the exception of the Pagans.

The Big Four are guided by their own code of terror. They strive to maintain their reputation as outlaws by instilling in people a fear they interpret as respect. The gangs keep members in line and eliminate the opposition with squads of killers: the Hells Angels Filthy Few, the Outlaws SS, the Pagans Black T-Shirt Squad, and the Bandidos nomad chapter.

The Big Four earn most of their money making and selling drugs. They control 75 percent of the North American methamphetamine market. Prostitution, extortion, theft, arson, robbery, bombings, and contract murders are among the crimes that bring in millions more. The Big Four are paramilitary operations fueled by greed and run on fear. Members are armed with the latest in military technology and protected by the best lawyers.

Two of the Big Four motorcycle gangs have been locked in a death battle since 1974. The Hells Angels and Outlaws kill each other's members at every opportunity. They also encourage smaller clubs to expand their territory and bolster their strength. Gangs that resist takeovers do not last long; their drug supplies dry up or they are destroyed.

See also: BANDIDOS; HELLS ANGELS; OUTLAWS; PAGANS.

Reference
Southeastern Connecticut Gang Activities Group (SEGAG). "Motorcycle Gangs." Available online. URL: http://www.segag.org. Downloaded on July 15, 2004.

MOUSSOTOV, Said Amin

Said Amin Moussotov was a former Soviet kickboxer. Moussotov was reputed to be a vicious enforcer and a member of a violent Chechen crime group. He was a high-ranking and much-feared Russian mobster whose muscle and special brand of violence did not come cheap. It is suspected that he was involved in the murder of Fima Laskin.

Efim Laskin was stabbed to death in Munich on September 27, 1991. Laskin's associate Fima Miller was murdered two months before him inside a Brooklyn jewelry store on July 27, 1991. He was alleged to be an associate of Namik Karafov.

Moussotov himself was shot to death by two unknown gunmen on May 8, 1992, in the hallway of his home in Palisades Park, New Jersey.

See also: RUSSIAN MAFIYA.

Reference
New Jersey State Commission of Investigation, New York Organized Crime Task Force, New York State Commission of Investigation, Pennsylvania Crime Commission, with Rutgers University. "The Tri-State Joint Soviet-Émigré Organized Crime Project." 1992. Available online. URL: http://www.state.nj.us/sci/pdf/russian.pdf. Accessed on November 24, 2004.

MOY, Wilson

In the heart of the 22nd Street Chinatown community in Chicago, the magnificent terra-cotta designed On Leong Merchants Building towers over the street. Years ago, Chinese immigrants found temporary lodging here and were assisted by the On Leong organization, a tong gang that slowly evolved into a fraternalistic body deeply rooted in the customs of imperial China.

More recently, the upper floors of this historic building were transformed into a gambling casino, sponsoring fan tan, bung-loo, and other games that appealed to the Chinese residents of the community. The operation pulled in more than $11.5 million in revenue, which sent up a red flag to the syndicate. Frank "the German" Schweihs, enforcer and an outfit heavyweight, "consulted" with Yu Lip Moy, national president of the Merchants Association in 1984. The deal the Chinese gamblers arrived at with Schweihs and John LaRocca, the leader of the Pittsburgh mob, was a 75-25 split of the protection money the association was to pay to organized crime. Pittsburgh was to receive $1,500. Schweihs collected $4,000 a month for the outfit's First Ward operation, headed by James "Jimmy L." LaPietra.

Wilson Moy, described at various times as the "Mayor of Chinatown," was one of 11 men indicted for overseeing this interstate gambling operation, which allegedly was protected by several high-ranking Chicago police officers. During the 1991 trial Yu Lip Moy testified in federal court that Chicago police officer Joseph Carone, considered to be an authority on Asian street crime, stood guard outside the Merchant's Building at 2216 Wentworth while the games were in progress. Carone was later transferred to the Chicago Lawn District and was never charged in connection with the On Leong cases.

The outfit is seemingly unfazed by the padlocking of the On Leong building. Under the direction of John "No Nose" DiFronzo, boss of the Elmwood Park crew, plans were undertaken in the fall of 1989 to set up poker, blackjack games, and a sports book for Asian gamblers in a private club setting in the suburbs. Help-wanted ads did not appear in the Sunday classifieds, but the word soon went out on the streets: "Asian front men wanted. Must be prepared to relocate at a moment's notice."

See also: MOCK SAI WING; ON LEONG TONG.

Reference

Illinois Police & Sheriff's News. "Asian Street Gangs and Organized Crime in Focus: Arising Threat from the Far East." Available online. URL: http://www.ipsn.org/asg08107. html. Downloaded on July 16, 2004.

NAKAJIMA-KAI

This Kyoto-based crime organization has been known to work with other gangs. The Nakajima-kai is one of the prominent gangs in Kyoto.

NAKANISHI, Kazuo

Kazuo Nakanishi became the *oyabun,* or head, for Yamaguchi-gumi in 1985 in the middle of a bloody gang war with the Ichiwa-kai. Hundreds of mobsters were killed and thousands arrested in the course of the war. He ruled the Yamaguchi-gumi for five years and eventually stepped down, ceding control to Yoshinori Watanabe. Kazuo Nakanishi became a *saiko komon,* or a senior advisor, to Watanabe. Nakanishi now lives in Osaka. He rules more than 439 members, who are divided into 15 subgangs.

See also: WATANABE, YOSHINORI; YAKUZA; YAM-AGUCHI-GUMI.

NAM Cam (a.k.a. Nam Cam Gang, Truong Van Cam)

Truong Van Cam is infamously known as Nam Cam. He is the crime boss of an underworld gang that operates out of Ho Chi Minh City, Vietnam. Nam Cam and his gang have been accused of everything from murder and assault to gambling, fraud, and bribery in Ho Chi Minh City as well as throughout Vietnam. He is also considered a formidable force within the Golden Triangle.

Nam Cam was dishonorably discharged from the Army of the Republic of Vietnam (ARVN) in Qui Nhon before 1975. He has a long personal history of law breaking. After his discharge, he settled in Saigon, where he improved his contacts in the Vietnamese underworld and developed a large base of people with excellent connections to the government. By the 1980s Cam Nam was wealthy and a major donor to communist officials. He was considered a citizen in good standing.

Through the 1980s and 1990s, Cam built a vast organized-crime empire that stretched from Saigon to Hanoi. He had already earned several million dollars by the time he was arrested in 1995 and continued his money-making operations after he was released in 1997.

Nam Cam was first arrested in May 1995. After his conviction, he was sent to a Vietnamese reeducation camp. By 1998 he was back out on the streets. He was arrested not long after on charges of murder, gambling syndication, drug trafficking, prostitution, and extortion.

Bay Sy, one of Nam Cam's most trusted lieutenants, is also his brother-in-law. Cam trusted Bay Sy to run a large and popular gambling house in Ho Chi Minh City. The illegal casino was well known and operated successfully despite the complaints of local residents. Deputy chief of the Ho Chi Minh City police, Mang, was unable to stop the gang's activities, which included protection rackets, organizing gambling houses, and other criminal enterprises.

In August 2002 scandal rocked Vietnam. Widespread corruption led to arrests and dismissals within the Vietnamese police force from street police to police-force officials, as well as to two Vietnamese government cabinet members.

Vietnamese president Tran Duc Luong signed a declaration dismissing Pham Si Chien from his posts as deputy chief of the Supreme People's Procuracy (SPP) and prosecutor of the SPP. He was a top state prosecutor. A senior Ho Chi Minh City police official, Colonel Vo Van Mang, Ho Chi Minh City's deputy chief of police bureau was also fired from his job. Both were expelled from the Communist Party of Vietnam (CPV) due to dereliction of duty and their relationship with several members of the organized-crime gang of Nam Cam.

Two Vietnamese communist chiefs were also ousted. Two Central Committee members were Tran Mai Hanh, director general of the official Voice of Vietnam radio, and deputy police minister Bui Quoc Huy. They were also linked to Nam Cam, and as a result the crime lord was once again arrested.

"Some officials had overcome numerous sufferings and risked their lives during the past wars of resistance, but they have succumbed to the temptation of illegal money and other things in life . . . and even lent a helping hand to criminals," the official Vietnam News Agency (VNA) quoted Vietnam's Communist Party chief Nong Duc Manh, in the wake of the scandals.

The internationally watched trial of Nam Cam and his gang began in Ho Chi Minh City in December 2002. Prosecutions were made against 156 suspects, facing 24 charges including murder, organized gambling, bribery, organizing illegal emigrations, abuse of power, drug trafficking, usury, extortion, aiding and abetting, and irresponsibility causing serious consequences. The list of defendants included 20 former state and government officials: 108 were in custody at the time of trial, and 48 others out on bail. Truong Van Cam himself faced seven charges of murder, as well as charges of organized gambling, assault, organizing illegal emigrations, aiding and abetting criminals, bribery, and usury.

See also: VIETNAM; VIETNAMESE GANGS.

Reference

Ulhas Joglekar. "Vietnam Ousts Top Communist Party Cadres for Mafia Links." The Times of India. Available online. URL: http://csf.colorado.edu/mail/pen-1/2002111/msg00802.html. Downloaded on July 16, 2004.

NASSER David, Julio Cesar

Nasser David headed a major drug-trafficking and money-laundering organization based out of Colombia's North Coast. His organization smuggled tons of cocaine and marijuana via regular shipping channels and cargo containers. In August 1997 Julio Cesar Nasser David was arrested by the Colombian National Police.

Reference

Thomas A. Constantine. "Drug Interdiction and Other Matters Related to the National Drug Control Policy." Hearing before the Subcommittee on Coast Guard and Maritime Transportation of the Committee on Transportation and Infrastructure, House of Representatives, 104th Congress, 2nd Session, September 12, 1996. Joint Hearing with Senate Caucus on International Narcotics Control. Washington, D.C.: U.S. Government Printing Office, 1997, 104–169.

NATALE, Ralph

Ralph Natale was proof that the Philadelphia crime family was at its end and in deep trouble. Natale would become the first Mafia boss to flip (turn government witness) and testify against his former employees. But was he really the top guy or just a high-profile patsy at whom the feds could aim their guns?

Ralph Natale started out as an absolute nobody. He was not a killer or a tough guy, and he was not street smart either. Natale was the guy who hung around mobsters but never truly became part of the crew. One member of the crew was Philadelphia crime boss Angelo "the Gentle Don" Bruno, who started Natale as a bartender at the Rickshaw Inn in Cherry Hill. Tending bar, Natale came into contact with many lower-level guys but never really joined the action. A few years later Natale's first big break came when Local 170, the bartenders union to which he belonged, was in chaos. Three of the union leaders who were controlled by Angelo Bruno were arrested and convicted of extortion. Bruno decided that Natale would become the guy who would take his orders at the union. In his new position Natale diverted hundreds of thousands of dollars from the union's health benefit plans to Bruno. Things were going great for Natale. Finally he was a somebody with some power, and he was not going to let anybody take that away from him. So when former Local 170 official Joey McGreal was released from prison and wanted Natale's spot, Natale ordered his first murder and stayed on top as head of the union. The murder further inflated his ego, and he became involved in other rackets.

One day a lawyer working for Mr. Living Room, a furniture store in Marlton, New Jersey, approached Natale to help him out with an insurance scam. Natale was asked to firebomb the place, and in turn he would receive 25 percent from the million-dollar insurance settlement. Natale firebombed the place but was already thinking out a plot that would give him the full 100 percent. Natale contacted a hit man named Charlie Allen and asked him to help him murder a business partner that owed him money. Natale told Allen, "I'm gonna take him down by the waterfront. . . . I'm gonna dump him. That guy's stealing my . . . money. . . ." However, Charlie Allen was a police informer who wore a wire at every meeting he had with Natale. Natale had no clue and told Allen all about his rackets, the help he needed, and more. Natale talked about how he was a no-show employee for the largest beer distributorship in Philadelphia. In 1978 Natale was arrested for the Mr. Living Room arson and convicted a year later. While he was out on bail, Natale used Allen (who again was wearing a wire) to sell 4,000 quaaludes and arrange a meeting between his cocaine suppliers and Allen's buyers (who were federal agents working undercover). So Natale was arrested again in January 1979 and convicted of smuggling cocaine in July 1980.

How Natale dealt with prison is difficult to say. The story he told his associates was that he was "the man" in there and that every group feared him. But all of that seems to be an attempt to impress his associates rather than the truth. He said about his life behind bars: "It was like like being inside an x-ray machine. Prison shows you who is a real man, how they handle themselves. You see how they act at Christmas with no family or friends around, locked up like that. You see how they do their time. You see who breaks, who bends, and who is a stand-up guy."

Inside Natale eventually shared a cell in Erie County, Pennsylvania, with Joseph Merlino, a young Philadelphia mobster. Natale discovered the two had a lot in common as they both hated the former boss Nicky Scarfo and the way he had run the Philadelphia crime family. Merlino hated Scarfo for demoting his father Salvatore "Chuckie" Merlino from underboss to soldier, and Natale was angry when Scarfo grabbed his illegal proceeds and never took care of his family while he was in prison. Natale found he had authority and seniority and that with the help of Merlino and his crew of youngsters he could become boss. After a few years Merlino got out and found that Scarfo had been replaced with the Sicilian born John Stanfa. After all his talks about leadership with Natale, Merlino was not about to let his plans be stopped by this old Sicilian out-of-towner. Merlino readied for war.

As Merlino and his group of youngsters fought Stanfa, Natale was safe in prison, sometimes calling Merlino to give him a pep talk and promise him that things would be great when they were in power. After several mobsters on both sides were killed the Federal Bureau of Investigation (FBI) decided to put a stop to the war and take Stanfa and his crew off the streets. Now Natale and Merlino could take the top positions. In 1995 Natale was released from prison and took the top spot after Merlino made him. Now Natale who never had done any real Mafia work in his gangster life was the head of the Philadelphia crime family just after becoming a made guy, and he had the backing of the New York families.

Natale was a happy man, but right away things began to go wrong. Merlino continued to act as he had done under Stanfa and carried out a lot of activity without talking to Natale first. People were being whacked without Natale's permission, and there was more and more proof that Merlino was running his own organization. One former Natale associate said: "They tried to leave Ralph out, but he knew. People would drop money or other things off for Joey but Joey would not be there, and Ralph was. So Ralph would say, 'I'll hold onto it.' Then he'd check it out and find money or something from a scheme nobody had told him about. This was about 1995, less than a year in his position, that Natale began to suspect Merlino and his friends were very disloyal. They were cutting him out of deals and going behind his back to make money. Natale was letting them get comfortable and bury themselves." His former associates also say that Stanfa was planning on taking the whole Merlino crew out with the help of a North Jersey crew run by Pete Caprio.

Because he was left out of business deals, Natale, who probably needed more money for his girlfriend (besides his wife), decided to sell some drugs by himself to make up for what Merlino was holding back. Acting all by himself and out of touch with current events, it did not take the feds long to arrest Natale. Looking at 20 to life and with nothing but hate toward Merlino and his crew, Natale decided to save his own skin and burn theirs by becoming a government witness and testify against his former family, thereby becoming the first Mafia boss to ever turn on his own family.

After word got out that Natale had flipped, people began to leak stories to the press that Natale knew nothing, that he was nothing but a puppet on a string, and that he was kept out of all the major business. They also said that he was never formally inducted but that he bought his way into La Cosa Nostra. This may all have been to discredit Natale, but he had them tricked first when he made them fight his war. When he flipped he seemed to have tricked them all again because he escaped both prison and mob retribution.

See also: STANFA, JOHN.

NAVARRO-LARA, Alfredo

General Alfredo Navarro-Lara of the Mexican national army was arrested by Mexican authorities on March 17, 1997, for making bribes on behalf of the Arellano Félix organization. Navarro-Lara approached the Delegado for Tijuana with an offer from the Arellano Félix organization for bribe money in the amount of $1.5 million per month—or $18 million per year. He was sentenced to 15 years in a Mexican prison.

See also: TIJUANA ORGANIZATION.

Reference

Thomas A. Constantine. "Drug Interdiction and Other Matters Related to the National Drug Control Policy." Hearing before the Subcommittee on Coast Guard and Maritime Transportation of the Committee on Transportation and Infrastructure, House of Representatives, 104th Congress, 2nd Session, September 12, 1996. Joint Hearing with Senate Caucus on International Narcotics Control. Washington, D.C.: U.S. Government Printing Office, 1997, 104–169.

NAZI Low Riders

Although the Nazi Low Riders (NLR) originated in the California prison system and still derive much of their power from inside corrections facilities, the group has also become a vicious street gang in several areas in California.

The Nazi Low Riders first gained recognition as a street gang in Costa Mesa in the early 1990s. Since then, NLR street units have sprung up in other cities and areas throughout Southern California. More recently, NLR members, who are mostly in their teens and early 20s, have begun to move into Central and Northern California and are slowly traveling east when they are released on parole. Today, NLR is probably the fastest-growing white gang in California, and the group is already spilling beyond state lines.

While the group is still considered to be in its formative stages, it is continually expanding. In 1996, there were only 28 confirmed NLR members. In 1998, that number had risen to 331, with an estimated additional 1,000 members.

The gang's explosive growth is a concern for several reasons. First, some members have been known to be heavily involved in the production and trade of methamphetamine, a highly addictive stimulant that promotes violent tendencies in users. Second, gang members have also developed a reputation for being ruthlessly violent. Finally, the Nazi Low Riders are vicious white supremacists.

NLR members exhibit extremely violent criminal behavior both in prison and on the streets. They have developed a strong network within their own ranks and with other white-power gangs. Unlike earlier, loosely affiliated racist skinheads, NLR is organized and motivated by profit. During the past seven years, NLR's tight criminal operations have helped to position it as the "gang of gangs" among white supremacists and a major force in the West Coast criminal world.

The Nazi Low Riders trace their roots to the Aryan Brotherhood (AB), a notoriously violent white supremacist prison gang. John Stinson, an AB member, was instrumental in the formation of NLR. In the late 1970s or early 1980s, looking for people to act as middlemen for the AB's criminal operations, Stinson turned to young skinheads incarcerated by the California Youth Authority at the Preston facility and in Chino at the Youth Training School. At that point, NLR was just beginning to establish itself as a white gang for inmates, and AB was still the leading white gang in prisons. The term *Nazi Low Riders* is a perverse twist on the use of *low riders,* a common slang phrase for Hispanic gang members.

With a limited membership, NLR led a quiet existence for several years and eluded the watchful eye of law enforcement until the early 1990s. By then, the California Department of Corrections had successfully disrupted and virtually suppressed AB activities.

NLR's role as middlemen for AB's criminal operations allowed it to begin filling AB's shoes within the prison system and gave NLR the opportunity to become the principal white gang within the prisons.

Several NLR members come from families with a gang history. It is not uncommon for an NLR member's father to have been a member of a motorcycle gang. Furthermore, many NLR members have grown up in families that preached intolerance and white supremacy.

Although some observers argue that NLR's actions are based more on criminal motivation than racist ideology, both play an important role in the gang's profile. The two fundamental requirements for NLR membership are that an individual is a proven criminal and that he or she is willing to show loyalty to the "white race." The gang's white power message has also become an integral factor in the violent acts members commit. As one NLR member said, "Hate is survival."

NLR members generally tend to focus their hatred on blacks and "race traitors," defined as people who are involved in interracial relationships. They have also expressed hatred for Jews, Asians, and other minorities. There appears to be an unusual paradox within the NLR—a few NLR members have Hispanic surnames, and members who have Hispanic girlfriends or wives are accepted into the ranks. However, this is true only for Hispanics. Blacks and other nonwhites are not tolerated. Some authorities have attributed this "alliance" between whites and Hispanics to a shared hatred of blacks. Others have concluded that NLR opposes only Northern Californian Hispanics because of criminal gang rivalries. The alliance might also be explained by the fact that NLR members often live in primarily Latino neighborhoods where they are outnumbered. One former NLR member explained, "You must have at least half white blood but no black blood."

Like most of those in gangs, NLR members have created a self-contained culture that includes graffiti, hand signals, tattoos, a dress code, and language. Much of it is based on Nazi symbolism and icons, but the exact symbols of the gang vary from place to place. For example, an NLR member in Huntington Beach might dress differently from one in Lancaster. The "NLR" tattoo may be found on almost any part of a gang member's body, including the back of the head. Nazi Low Riders do not adhere to specific rules on tattoos or dress, making immediate identification of gang members more difficult for law enforcement.

Although there is no single tattoo required of NLR members, symbols like the swastika, the "SS" lightning bolts, and other Nazi-related images, including pictures of Hitler, are widespread in the gang. Some NLR members prefer eagles, skulls, and demons. Tattoos or patches with the numeral "88" (the eighth letter of the alphabet is *H,* hence 88 signifies *HH* or "Heil Hitler") and *WP* (White Power) are also popular. Abbreviations representing white-power phrases such as *WSU* (White Student Union) and *AYM* (Aryan Youth Movement) are common as well.

In addition to Nazi and white-power-related tattoos that have been popular among other white supremacist gang members, NLR has its own versions. A tattoo consisting of the letters *NLR* is quite common and often appears on the stomach, back, and neck or in small letters above the eyebrows and on the knuckles. Some prefer the full words *Nazi Low Riders,* often written in Old English script. For some, the runic alphabet (characters of any of several alphabets used by the Germanic peoples from about the third to the 13th centuries) is becoming a popular way of encoding a message about their white-power gang affiliation. Recently, NLR members have been more reticent about admitting their NLR association, realizing that it can be a liability. Some have claimed that NLR signifies "never lose respect" or "no longer racist." Although most members tend to wear their tattoos proudly in visible places, some now opt for smaller, less conspicuous images in less visible spots.

With regard to dress, NLR members frequently wear white supremacist or Nazi paraphernalia such as T-shirts printed with a white-power band logo, but they are becoming savvy enough to hide such clothes from law-enforcement officials and the public.

Reprinted by Permission of Anti-Defamation League

ÑETA

Carlos Torres-Irriarte, also known as "La Sombra," created Ñeta while serving time in the Río Piedras prison in Puerto Rico in 1970. He started the gang to stop the feuding gangs in prison. In Puerto Rico when a baby is born, traditional Puerto Ricans would exult "Ñeta! Ñeta!" La Sombra used the name for his newly formed organization. Some believe that *Ñeta* stands for "Never Tolerate Abuse." Ñeta stresses national Puerto Rican pride.

Members identify with the colors red, white, and blue. Black is sometimes substituted for blue. These colors can be seen on their head, necklaces, and clothing. Probationary members wear all white beads until they are considered loyal; then, they can wear black beads among the white, plus one red one. Members usually display the Puerto Rican flag and are known to carry Ñeta identification cards. The Ñeta emblem is a heart pierced by two crossing Puerto Rican flags with a shackled right hand with the middle and index fingers crossed. Members salute each other by holding the crossed fingers of their right hands over their heart. This hand signal has the meaning N in sign language; it also means togetherness and unity.

Ñeta has a stronghold in large cities across the United States. Its presence can be found in most correctional institutions across the country and in Puerto Rico. Although members commonly engage in criminal activity for the benefit of the gang, they use the façade that the group is merely a cultural organization. They have strong ties to several other street gangs, and many members also claim allegiance to Los Macheteros, a revolutionary group fighting for independence of Puerto Rico. Members see themselves as oppressed people who are unwilling to be governed by the United States. Any disrespect shown to an individual Ñeta member is looked upon as disrespect to the group and is usually dealt with violently. Members are required to procure 20 prospective recruits, and all come together in observance of their fallen members on the 30th of each month.

Reference

KnowGangs. "Netas." Available online. URL: http://www.knowgangs.com. Downloaded on July 16, 2004.

NIBIKI-KAI

The Nibiki-kai was based in Hachioji, Japan. They gained international fame in 1990 when they were involved in a very ugly, violent, and public war with the very large Yamaguchi-gumi in western Tokyo.

"This conflict was significant in that the Yamaguchi-gumi had a long-standing agreement with the Inagawa-kai not to set up gang offices in Tokyo, and the Tokyo police were particularly keen to maintain this situation," wrote Peter Hill, an Oxford University sociologist, in *Heisei Yakuza: Burst Bubble and Botaiho*.

See also: INAGAWA-KAI; YAMAGUCHI-GUMI.

NIGERIAN Letter Scams

On July 10, 2001, the Royal Canadian Mounted Police (RCMP), Toronto West Detachment, Commercial Crime Section announced the results of a three-year investigation that successfully dismantled a highly sophisticated international criminal organization, controlled by three individuals operating in the greater Toronto area and victimizing people around the world.

This alleged criminal group had been perpetrating a large-scale international fraud known as the West African–based Organized Advance Fee Fraud, or more commonly known as the "Nigerian letter scam." The RCMP alleges that the criminal group was part of a larger criminal organization based in Nigeria. At that time, the RCMP had identified more than 300 victims, most of whom were citizens of the United States. The victims included successful business people from all walks of life, including "a cattle rancher, an insurance agent, a hotel-chain owner, a brewery consultant, an importer-exporter, and a recreational vehicle salesperson."

In 1998, while investigating a complaint, "common elements surfaced concerning several ongoing investigations in both Canada by the RCMP and in the United States by the FBI and the U.S. Secret Service." The three agencies coordinated investigations, exchanged information, and zeroed in on groups they thought were conducting fraudulent cross-border telemarketing activity.

West African-based Nigerian letter scams normally occur in two phases. "Typically, in the first phase of this type of fraud, intended victims receive a letter either by mail or fax allegedly from officials of a large Nigerian institution, such as the Nigerian National Petroleum Corporation or the Central Bank of Nigeria." Most of the victims receive a mailing culled by the perpetrators from directories of highly touted corporations, professional groups (unions, guilds, etc.), or from business publications.

The first stage of this fraud was to convince the potential victim to let some unknown but trustworthy Nigerian civil servant to hide or store large sums of cash (usually in the millions of dollars) in an offshore account in the name of the victim, where the sum could remain hidden for an unspecified period of time. In return for letting the sender hide money in the victim's account, the recipient was eventually offered a percentage of the amount transferred into his or her account. The letter required the recipient to return an e-mail or a phone call to transfer important account information, with a fee sometimes attached somewhere in the neighborhood of $10,000 "supposedly for legal fees and administration costs in order to secure the business arrangement."

During the second stage of the scam, the victim received a phone call from the members of the organized-crime group posing as Nigerian bankers. "The victim is falsely advised that the total contract funds have cleared Nigeria and are now in an alleged clearing house or mercantile bank in North America." False banks or clearing houses in Toronto, Detroit, New York City, Chicago, and Nassau, Bahamas were identified by the callers. Although the numbers given for return calls or forwarding institutions were peculiar to their cities, all "were call-forwarded to a 'boiler room' in the Greater Toronto Area."

When the victims called these numbers, they were informed of further fees and legal expenses (sometimes as high as $50,000), which were in huge sums, and they were bled of funds until they were broke, with the fraudulent transaction never taking place.

This confidence scam made use of fictitious companies and false documentation. The telephone contacts were "knowledgeable in international banking" and were "well-spoken and professional in their dialogue and behavior with the victims."

Reference

Royal Canadian Mounted Police, Communication Canada. "RCMP, FBI and U.S. Secret Service Crumple 'Nigerian Letter Scam.'" *Canadian Government Publishing Directorate*. July 10, 2001.

NIGERIANS

Bernard J. Murphy, assistant special agent-in-charge of the Newark office of the Federal Bureau of Investigation (FBI), testified at the commission's public hearing about highly mobile Nigerian criminals engaged in organized schemes to defraud banks and other financial institutions. Special Agent Murphy detailed several examples in which Nigerians, using high-quality fabricated identification, engaged in sophisticated frauds in New Jersey: In early 1987 a group of New Jersey bankers requested FBI assistance in investigating a series of frauds that were being committed by Nigerians against New Jersey financial institutions. On initial investigation these crimes appeared to be widespread and isolated; how-

ever, a detailed examination of the individual frauds revealed a complex scheme that employed similar styles, all of which were interconnected.

A detailed examination of one of these frauds revealed that an individual using an alias opened accounts in four banks in Marlboro, Old Bridge, and Freehold, New Jersey. All of the accounts were opened with a minimal cash deposit, normally $50–$100, and each bank was provided with a home address, a place of employment, and a New Jersey photo driver's license for identification. The customer also requested and received an automatic teller machine (ATM) card for each bank account. The banks, following their normal procedure for new account verification, did not discover any invalid information, and, therefore, opened the accounts.

Shortly after the accounts were opened, a series of checks drawn on banks in Florida, Georgia, Maryland, and New York were deposited into these accounts via the ATMs. The accounts were monitored remotely via ATM, and when the money was released into the account the Nigerian visited several branches of each bank during a two- to three-day period and withdrew most of the funds. Finally, all of the deposited checks were later returned unpaid, causing the banks to suffer losses.

The investigation revealed that the address given by the Nigerian customer was, in reality, a self-storage facility. The self-storage facility also offered private mail-receiving services. The employment reference that he had provided was contacted by the bank, and it was determined to be a telephone answering service. The alias name and the Social Security number used by the defrauder were traced to a real person who was an executive with a New York financial institution.

In yet another case, in May 1988, an individual attempted to open a bank account in Middletown, New Jersey. An alert customer-service representative questioned the individual, who then fled the bank. The service representative obtained the license plate of his vehicle and contacted local police, who then arrested the suspect within a few blocks of the bank. Although this individual was alone when he left the bank, he had a passenger in his car at the time of his arrest. The passenger was later identified through fingerprints as a Nigerian national who was a federal fugitive. The original charges against the passenger were also for fraudulent activity. The driver of the vehicle posted a $10,000 bond and was released the same day.

The name given by the driver was, in fact, an alias of yet another Nigerian national. The alias given to the Middletown Police Department in Monmouth County was the same name used to defraud another bank in Millstone, New Jersey. Further investigation determined that all the aliases were stolen identities of bank employees from New York City.

An in-depth investigation by the FBI revealed that he had used nine different aliases in Jersey City, Passaic, Belleville, North Arlington, Perth Amboy, Bellmawr, Edison, Iselin, Haddon Township, and Blackwood, New Jersey, and had defrauded banks in those areas of $225,000. It was also determined that the driver had applied for and obtained credit cards from a local department store under a false name and credit history. He had obtained another $60,000 in cash and merchandise with these credit cards.

In little more than a year, the driver obtained almost $300,000 in cash and merchandise from New Jersey businessmen. There is no way to calculate the driver's total financial gain from his fraudulent activities, but his extensive travel up and down the East Coast and as far away as California is documented. Also known is that the checks deposited by the driver were used by other Nigerians to commit similar frauds.

Another individual, while on bail for a $40,000 fraud committed against the New Jersey Department of Labor, engaged in an eight-month fraudulent spree that netted him well in excess of $100,000, using the Social Security accounts and true names of New Jersey residents. Again, one of the individuals victimized was a senior executive at a New Jersey financial institution.

These and similar investigations reveal a pattern of widespread fraudulent activity, including bank fraud, credit-card fraud, student-loan fraud, unemployment fraud, insurance fraud, rental-car fraud, and the like.

These frauds all have a common denominator, the false identification card. The card is a prerequisite to all of the fraudulent activity. Nigerian criminal elements will seek to infiltrate major companies to obtain biographical data on the company's legitimate employees. They will normally apply for positions as security guards or cleaning personnel or for positions with temporary employment agencies, even in white-collar capacities, such as accountants. The security guards and cleaning personnel, for example, during periods of minimal presence by company employees, will attempt to obtain information on payroll and human-resource records, which will, of course, contain biographical data on legitimate company employees. If they are not successful in penetrating these areas of the company, they will look for information on individual employees, normally supervisory or management position employees, which will also enable them to obtain the biographical data and credit lines based on the true employee's biographical data.

In March 1990, accounts were opened at two banks in Princeton, New Jersey, under the name of Moneyline Investment. A series of checks drawn on an attorney trust account in Georgia were deposited into the accounts with money withdrawn prior to checks being returned unpaid, causing a $25,000 loss.

The month before, an individual had attempted to obtain a $3,000 cash advance on a credit card in West Windsor, New Jersey. At that time an alert teller called the credit-card company for authorization, and the customer spoke with the security department of the credit-card company. The customer was asked a series of questions, one of which was fictitious and designed to be so, and when he responded, the security department told the bank to seize the card. The bank also seized the driver's license used for identification. The individual fled the bank and the police obtained a John Doe warrant for this individual.

A few months later, in September 1990, the Plainsboro, New Jersey, police department arrested a woman who had attempted to open a bank account under an alias name. The woman was later identified to be a Nigerian from Maryland. In her possession was a check drawn on the same Georgia attorney's trust account, the one that was used in Princeton under the Moneyline Investment account name. This woman is believed to have been working in concert with the West Windsor, New Jersey, John Doe.

Once the link between the West Windsor and the Plainsboro incidents was developed, further investigation determined that this John Doe customer had obtained a safe deposit box at yet another branch of the same bank in East Orange, New Jersey. Again in September this John Doe customer went to the East Orange bank to close his safe deposit box. The only warrant for him was the local John Doe warrant for the attempted cash advances. Two local officers were in the bank parking lot taking a report on another incident, and they took the individual into custody. The same vehicle that had been used at the bank in Plainsboro was located in the parking lot.

In May 1990, a set of Interceptor tires was put on this vehicle and charged to a fraudulently obtained American Express credit card. When the tires were put on, the car, the mileage was 56,000 miles. When the arrest was made in mid-September, the mileage was in excess of 90,000 miles. He had put 35,000 miles on the car in a little more than four months. How would this individual put so many miles on the car in four months? What developed as a result of this arrest was the identification of mail drops in Alexandria, Virginia, the District of Columbia, Maryland, and five more in New Jersey. Additionally, it was determined that this individual had been employed through a temporary accounting service at a company in New Jersey. While working for the company, he stole 10 blank checks of a subsidiary company from the back of a checkbook and a legitimate accounts payable check in the amount of $28,000. This check was negotiated at a bank in Virginia where a fraudulent account had been established. One of the blank checks was also negotiated in Massachusetts. Additional deposits in the Massachusetts accounts were drawn on a federal credit union in Bladensburg, Maryland. In Bladensburg, Maryland, it was determined that that credit union had been victimized, and a series of 700 checks were stolen from that institution. The credit union in Maryland suffered more than $100,000 worth of losses. Special Agent Murphy described what he called "controlling cells," operating in various regions of the country, that suggest the presence of centralized leadership for Nigerian organized crime: The information that is obtained by cell workers in similar scenarios is furnished to a cell leader, who controls access and distribution. The cell leader interacts and exchanges information with leaders in other states. The exchange of information, checks, and identification provides these groups with a constant supply of new information, which allows them to perpetrate new frauds without readily being detected.

Special Agent Murphy said, "Nigerians present a unique problem for law enforcement, in that their fraudulent activities are committed against government agencies where benefits can be obtained, against financial institutions, department stores, credit card companies and insurance companies. They also impact heavily on the general public with

increased costs from frauds being passed on to them in higher interest rates and taxes. The individual victim whose personal credit history has been victimized faces a long battle to get his personal credit history back to normal with the fraudulent charges deleted.

"The Commission has learned that Nigerians are also involved in organized smuggling of heroin into the United States. In this country a person called a 'God Father' controls four to six 'mules' who transport drugs and money. The typical smuggling process starts in Nigeria when the mule—usually a woman or juvenile—goes to a 'Black Magic House' to receive instructions and swallow the contraband drugs, which are sealed in condoms for transport to the United States. Nigerians obtain most of their heroin from Southeast Asia where 70 percent of the heroin available in the United States is produced. Three out of five couriers arrested in Thailand in possession of heroin are from Nigeria. Historically, the source of heroin in the black community has been La Cosa Nostra—trafficking in Southwest Asian heroin. Today, the major source is ethnic Chinese organized criminals dealing in Southeast Asian heroin. Of course, the evidence of Nigerian smuggling clearly indicates that Chinese criminals are not the lone suppliers of Southeast Asian heroin in the United States."

Reference

New Jersey State Commission of Investigation, Robert J. Clark, Francis A. Betzler, Bruce C. Best, and Debra. A. Sowney. "Afro-Lineal Organized Crime." November 29, 1990. Available online. URL: http://www.state.nj.us/sci/pdf/afro.pdf. Accessed on November 24, 2004.

NORIEGA, Manuel

On February 4, 1989, Manuel A. Noriega and 15 defendants were indicted by the grand jury in Miami, Florida. The structure of the Racketeer Influenced and Corrupt Organizations statute indictment alleged that Noriega was a drug facilitator for the Medellín cartel. Noriega had utilized his position as the commander of the Panamanian Defense Forces and as the ruler of Panama to assist the Medellín cartel in shipping cocaine; procuring precursor chemicals for the manufacture of cocaine; providing a safe haven for cartel members following the assassination of Colombian minister of justice Rodrigo Lara-Bonilla on April 30, 1984; and sponsoring the laundering of narcotics proceeds in Panamanian banks.

When the United States invaded the country of Panama on December 20, 1989, Noriega eluded

Panamanian general Manuel Noriega (AP)

capture by the U.S. military for the next several weeks. General Manuel Antonio Noriega surrendered to U.S. authorities on January 3, 1990, in Panama and was immediately taken to Miami to answer the indictment. During the next 21 months, enforcement Group 9 in Miami interviewed hundreds of individuals and reviewed reams of seized papers in the United States and Panama. In September 1991, the "drug trial of the century" began.

During the next eight months, more than 100 prosecution witnesses, including Carlos Lehder-Riva, former Drug Enforcement Administration administrators Bensinger, Mullen, and Lawn, an ex-Panamanian attorney general, cartel leader Pepe Cabrera, and others testified at the trial. In supporting the prosecution, the DEA had special agents deployed in 15 countries around the world, including Panama, Colombia, Spain, Luxembourg, Germany, France, and Cuba.

Finally, on April 9, 1992, the jury returned a verdict of guilty on eight of the 10 counts in the indictment. Noriega, who had become Panama's political leader in 1988 after President Eric Arturo Delvalle was ousted, was convicted on racketeering and cocaine-trafficking charges for protecting Colombian smugglers who had routed drugs through Panama. On July 9, 1992, Manuel Noriega was sentenced to 40 years in federal prison.

On April 6, 1998, he failed to overturn his drug-trafficking conviction and the 40-year prison sentence it drew. Noriega's appeal contended that the drug cartel had paid $1.25 million to a witness to testify falsely against him and that the government must be held responsible for the alleged bribe. The U.S. Supreme Court, acting without comment, let stand a ruling that said Noriega received a fair trial. The Noriega case was the most notorious drug trial in U.S. history and demonstrated to the American public the global scope of corruption that accompanied international drug smuggling.

Reference

U.S. Drug Enforcement Administration, U.S. Department of Justice. "A Tradition of Excellence, DEA History 1985–1990." Available online. URL: http://www.dea.gov/pubs/history/index.html. Downloaded on July 28, 2004.

NORTHERN Valle Organization   *See* MONTOYA SÁNCHEZ, DIEGO.

NUESTRA Familia/Norteños

The Nuestra Familia (NF, or Our Family) was organized by Robert "Babo" Sosa in California's Folsom State Prison in 1968. Sosa and his associates were tired of the abuse and victimization at the hands of the Mexican Mafia (MF). Most of the original members of NF were from northern California. As the NF and the MF engaged in a bitter prison war, new prisoners were recruited into the NF while Southern California inmates joined the Mexican Mafia. By the late 1970s, after numerous prison riots and murders, an official dividing point emerged between the gangs in Delano, California, near Bakersfield. Those living north of this location were known as Norteños. The Nuestro Familia were the first prison gang to ever be federally indicted for violation of the Racketeer Influenced and Corrupt Organizations (RICO) act in the early 1980s. The gang has a written constitution, rules (known as the 14 bonds) and an organized leadership structure. Nearly all California Hispanic gangs identify themselves as being Norteños (Northerners) or Sureños (Southerners), an indication of who they will join when they go to prison.

Norteño street gang members often identify with the symbols XIV, X4, 14, and 4 dots. Fourteen refers to the 14th letter of the alphabet, *N,* which stands for Norteño or Nuestra Familia. The gang associates with the color red and the words *Norteño, Norte,* or

220

Northerner. Other symbols include a five-pointed star, symbolizing the North Star or the Huelga bird, the symbol used by the United Farm Workers Union. These two tattoos, the star and bird, must be earned by committing an assault or murder on their enemies, the Sureños.

The Nuestra Familia has a large chain of command that oversees every Norteño gang in Northern California. Norteños have been identified in nearly every state in the United States as well as several European countries. At the direction of the Nuestra Familia, a pro-Norteño gangster rap group compiled two music CDs entitled *GUN (Generation of United Norteño)* and *Quete* ("gun" in Spanish). The CDs were distributed to Norteño street gang members. According to federal authorities, the purpose of the CDs was to raise money for the gang and to promote unity among individual Norteño street gangs. Norteños continue to be heavily involved in drug sales and murders. They remain bitter enemies of the Mexican Mafia prison gang and Sureño street gangs.

Reference

KnowGangs. "Netas." Available online. URL: http://www.knowgangs.com/gang_resources/nuetra_familia/nf_001.htm. Downloaded on July 16, 2004.

O

OBRONT, William (Willie Obie)

William "Willie Obie" Obront, who was named in organized-crime inquiries as the Canadian equivalent of Meyer Lansky, was born in Montreal on March 27, 1924. He first came to police attention when he was in his twenties and would assume a position that was nearly impossible: a Jew at the top of Montreal's Mafia.

Obront became Vic Cotroni's chief money launderer. His job was allegedly to hide funds derived through gambling, narcotics smuggling, loan sharking, and other illicit activities. He also invested the money, creating even more revenues. The Quebec Crime Probe of 1977 revealed how Obront had washed more than $89 million in two years for the organization through various schemes.

He also ran a thriving loan-sharking business that supposedly generated millions of dollars in profit. In late 1973, Obront successfully took over all gambling in the Ottawa-Hull area for the Montreal mob. Police estimated that the group took 25 percent of a bookmaking operation that generated $50,000 a day. Obront sat at the head of 38 companies. He was president of Certes Holding Ltd. and owned shares in the Béret Bleu club with Roméo Bucci, Peter Adamo, and Frank Dasti. He, along with two associates, also managed to have the only meat-storage facilities on the Expo '67 site, as well as 500 vending machines on the property. Willie Obie became so wealthy that he was known to wager $50,000 on U.S. football games.

The organization's primary money launderer successfully avoided the spotlight and moved to Hallendale, Florida, in the 1970s; things fell apart for Willie Obie on July 21, 1983. He was named with Vic Cotroni's son Nick in an indictment following a joint investigation from the Royal Canadian Mounted Police, the Drug Enforcement Administration, and the Federal Bureau of Investigation. Obront headed a $50-million-a-year drug ring that brought millions of phoney quaaludes into the United States. The network was enormous. Obront and Cotroni were arrested with 20 Canadians, 27 Americans, and two Colombians. The gang was responsible for trafficking 70 percent of the Quaalude market in the United States and shipped an estimated 35 to 40 kilograms of cocaine into Canada between 1981 and 1986. A kilogram of cocaine was seized outside Obront's home on the day he was arrested.

Obront was sentenced to 20 years in prison. On March 7, 2002, the 78-year-old Obront was released.

Reference

Gary Francoeur. "William 'Willie Obie' Obront." Wiseguy-Wally. Available online. URL: http://www.geocities.com/wiseguywally/WilliamObront.htm. Downloaded on July 19, 2004.

—G.F.

OCHOA Restrepo, Fábio

"Fabio Ochoa Restrepo was the patriarch of one of Colombia's most important drug trafficking families," according to the *Miami Herald,* on February 19, 2002. His three sons were all top lieutenants in the Medellín cartel, one of the richest and most successful drug operations in the history of such businesses.

However, the well-connected and highly respected Ochoa Restrepo was never accused or indicted on drug-trafficking charges, either by the Colombian or the U.S. government, and up to the time of his death, he defended the reputation of his sons and his family.

Fábio Ochoa Restrepo was a famed horse breeder and the patriarch of one of Colombia's most important drug-trafficking families. (AP)

Ochoa Restrepo was a renowned South American horse breeder and was considered to be a very wealthy man. He and his family lived on a large ranch called La Loma. He was in ill health for most of his adult life and died at 78 years of age of kidney failure on February 18, 2002.

References

"Fabio Ochoa Restrepo, Drug Family Patriarch." *The Miami Herald,* February 19, 2002, AP

Phil Gunson. "Fabio Ochoa Restrepo." *The Guardian,* April 29, 2002.

OCHOA Vásquez, Fábio

Fábio Ochoa Vásquez is the youngest son of Fábio Ochoa Restrepo.

Fábio Ochoa Vásquez was allegedly involved with the Medellín cartel, a Colombian drug cartel once headed by Pablo Escobar. Jorge Luis and Fábio Ochoa Vásquez were both top-ranking lieutenants in the organization.

On February 19, 2002, Fábio Ochoa Vásquez turned himself in to authorities and urged his brothers to do the same, hoping he could cut a deal with the Colombian government.

All three brothers ended up serving time in Colombian prisons, spending five years a piece for their involvement with the Medellín cartel. All three brothers were released in 1996 and vowed that they would never involve themselves in the cocaine business again. But the temptations of the family's business were too great for Fábio, who became involved with a Mexican group smuggling and distributing in Florida. Fábio was indicted by a federal court and extradited to the United States. He was convicted on May 27, 2003, and sentenced to time in a Florida prison.

OCHOA Vásquez, Jorge Luis

A son of Fábio Ochoa Restrepo, an alleged major drug-trafficking operative in and supplier to the Medellín cartel. Ochoa Vásquez was known for a variety of aliases, including, El Gordo, Los Pablos, Moises Moreno Miranda, Jorge Luis Azquez, El Niño, El Ocho, and Jorge Luis Ochoa Arismendez.

Jorge Luis Ochoa Vásquez was allegedly involved with the Medellín cartel, a Colombian drug cartel once headed by Pablo Escobar. Jorge Luis and Fábio Ochoa Vásquez were both top-

Pablo Escobar (left) and Jorge Luis Ochoa (right, with hat), the two leaders of the Medellín cocaine cartel, attending a bullfight in Medellín, Colombia, in 1984 (AP)

ranking lieutenants in the organization. Jorge Luis was wanted for drug trafficking and murder as far back as 1984.

According to the *Miami Herald* on February 19, 2002, "[Fábio] Ochoa Vasquez was the first major trafficker to turn himself in to authorities in exchange for a promise he would not be extradited for past crimes. His surrender opened the way for his two older brothers to also turn themselves in."

The deal was subsequently canceled by the Colombian government and replaced with a new one after Pablo Escobar was killed in a shootout with police in 1993. "A December 1997 constitutional change reinstated extradition but only for crimes committed after that date," the paper also stated.

All three brothers ended up serving time in Colombian prisons, spending five years a piece for their involvement with the Medellín cartel. All three brothers were released in 1996 and vowed that they would never involve themselves in the cocaine business again.

Since then, Jorge Luis has remained in Colombia and has not been sought for any other drug-trafficking businesses. He helped his father run their horse-breeding operations until his death in February 2002.

OCHOA Vásquez, Juan

Juan Ochoa Vásquez was released from prison in July after serving five months of a six-year sentence. He is the son of Fábio Ochoa Restrepo and the brother of Fábio Ochoa Vásquez and Jorge Luis Ochoa Vásquez. Juan Ochoa is wanted in the United States for the 1986 slaying of a Drug Enforcement Administration informant. He has not left Colombia and has not been identified recently by the U.S. government as being involved in any current drug businesses.

OGAWA, Kaoru

Kaoru Ogawa is one of the most notorious of the Japanese *sokaiya* in Japan's history. Sokaiya are corporate extortionists. They work closely with Yakuza groups, accumulating negative information on company transgressions and personal transgressions of the company's executives. They trade on the currency of possible exposure, blackmailing the company's executives. They often take part in stock-pricing scams and other ways of using legitimate companies to create and reap ill-gotten gains. Mostly, large corporations would pay large sums of money just to keep the sokaiya away. Executives who spurned these interruptions had their dirty laundry aired in public when the sokaiya would rise to speak at public shareholder meetings.

In 1997 the Japanese government cracked down on these corporate blackmailers and many sokaiya were put out of business. Many were placed in jail. All of them have been banned from shareholder meetings, and the government has done everything it could to discredit these men and their sources of information.

Stephanie Strom wrote in the *New York Times* on August 11, 1999, "Mr. Ogawa is the most prominent of the survivors of the Japanese Government's war on the sokaiya, as Japan's oddly high-profile corporate extortionists are known. At a shareholders meeting in June, he proudly introduced himself as the famous sokaiya who had been recently released from jail. . . . Kaoru Ogawa, old-time sokaiya, now suggests he serves as 'Japanese Ralph Nader' by encouraging shareholders to force corporations to get their businesses in order."

References

Stephanie Strom. "International Business: Dead End on Shakedown Street; Crackdown Spurs a Makeover of Japan's Corporate Racketeers." *New York Times,* August 11, 1999; "'Famous' Racketeer Busted for Fraud." *Mainichi Daily News,* May 13, 2002.

ONG, Benny (a.k.a. Uncle 7)

Benny Ong was known as the "godfather" of the Chinese organized-crime world in New York City. He was the head of the Hop Sing Tong gang in Chinatown from 1974 until his death. He was tried and convicted by Edward J. Kuriansky of racketeering. He died aged 87 in August 1994.

ON Leong Tong

On Leong Tong is "an extension of the merchant associations that were first organized [by Chinese immigrants] in 1847 in San Francisco as a means of preserving cultural identity and providing a social outlet." Not all members of On Leong are connected with organized crime; in fact, the On Leong Tong have very credible businessmen and trade unions that are supposed to be some of the most successful in their sphere of influence.

However, some members are very much involved in organized crime. The On Leong have strong posts in San Francisco, Boston, New York, and Chicago, as well as in other cities. The Chicago faction allegedly runs one of the best underground casinos, which was broken up several times, most notably in 1986. The early 1990s saw a federal racketeering trial that illustrated the tight ties between the On Leong and the Chicago mob, or "the Outfit." Together, they had been running a gambling ring worth millions.

The New York On Leong, among the most notorious of the factions, was run by Wing Young Chan, who was both the head of the On Leong Merchants Organizations as well as a leading underworld figure. The On Leong have been involved in murder and drug trafficking and distribution. The On Leong Tong also trafficked in human beings, bringing illegal aliens to America, as well as supplying On Leong Tong–run brothels with sex slaves smuggled in from mainland China.

See also: CHA, WING YOUNG; GHOST SHADOWS; TONGS.

References

Richard C. Lindberg. "Spotlight on Asian Organized Crime." *Search International.* Available online. URL: http://www.search-international.com/WhatsNew/WNasiangangs.htm. Accessed on November 24, 2004.

Mark C. Gribben. "Moon Festival Shakedown." Reprinted by permission.

—*M.G.*

OPERATION Artus

The U.S. Customs Service announced on March 20, 2002, the execution of seven search warrants on eight individuals in the United States and as many as 30 simultaneous warrants in 10 foreign countries on members of a private Internet group exchanging and downloading child pornography over the Internet. The foreign countries serving search warrants included the United Kingdom, Canada, France, Germany, Switzerland, Spain, Japan, Finland, Austria, and Sweden. One arrest was made in the United States, but additional charges were leveled.

The U.S. Customs Service, assisted by various local, state, and federal agencies, began to execute search warrants in the early morning hours on the East Coast. Warrants were eventually executed in New York, Pennsylvania, Ohio, Tennessee, Nevada, Oregon, and Alaska.

The U.S. targets of the investigation included a U.S. military pilot, a network administrator for a publishing company, a registered nurse, an artist, and several other individuals. U.S. Customs agents seized 12 computers, more than 600 CDs, floppy disks and external drives, more than 200 videos, one digital camcorder, and a book on how to seduce children. Three of the individuals were identified as previously unknown members of the notorious Wonderland Club child pornography ring that was dismantled in 1998.

The investigation, dubbed "Operation Artus," began in November 2001 when agents of the German national police, assisted by local police in Muenster, Germany, executed a search warrant on a German citizen suspected of distributing child pornography. German authorities subsequently discovered that the man had been exchanging child pornography over the Internet through a private Internet Relay Chat (IRC) channel. With the man's consent and cooperation, German National Police were provided the nicknames of some of the members of the group.

German national police and U.S. Customs determined that a common aim of the members was to find and exchange child pornography in DVD-quality movie-file format. As a requirement, members had to offer new child pornography material from time to time to remain part of the group. This raised concerns among law enforcement that members were involved in the actual production of child pornography.

As a result of the German investigation, law enforcement from 10 countries identified 46 targets including eight in the United States. The U.S. Customs Cyber Smuggling Center in Fairfax, Virginia, identified the names and addresses of the U.S. targets and coordinated the U.S. enforcement actions with the Department of Justice Child Exploitation Section.

See also: OPERATION BLUE ORCHID; OPERATION CANDYLAND; OPERATION ORE; OPERATION TWINS; WONDERLAND CLUB.

Reference

Interpol. "12 Arrests in Interpol-Coordinated Action against Pedophile Ring." Available online. URL: http://www.interpol.com. Posted on March 20, 2002.

OPERATION Banco   *See* BLACK TUNA GANG.

OPERATION Blast Furnace

In July 1986, the Drug Enforcement Administration (DEA) launched Operation Blast Furnace, a joint operation, in which DEA personnel and Bolivian Narcotics Strike Force troops launched a series of raids against cocaine laboratories in Bolivia. This enforcement effort was supported with intelligence provided by the DEA that specifically targeted coca paste and cocaine production in Bolivia, one of the major cocaine-producing nations of the world. Prior to the operation, DEA intelligence analysts had been sent to La Paz where they developed daily situation reports and drafted a strategic intelligence report. In addition, their analysis of ledgers found at three laboratory sites helped identify several major Bolivian violators. On the day of the law enforcement action, six U.S. military Black Hawk helicopters, operated by U.S. Army pilots and support personnel, transported the strike teams to the suspected laboratory sites. Eight cocaine laboratories and one shipment location were located and destroyed. Some of the labs destroyed had been capable of producing 1,000 kilograms of cocaine per week. At least one lab had been in operation since 1982. Operation Blast Furnace brought cocaine production to a virtual standstill in Bolivia. Traffickers fled the country, and coca-paste buyers from Colombia stayed away. The coca-leaf market collapsed, and quantities that had previously sold for $1.50 dropped to 10 cents. Following the success of Operation Blast Furnace, many coca farmers approached the U.S. Agency for International Development asking for assistance in planting legal substitute crops.

Reference

U.S. Drug Enforcement Administration, U.S. Department of Justice. "A Tradition of Excellence, DEA History 1985–1990." Available online. URL: http://www.dea.gov/pubs/history/html. Downloaded on July 28, 2004.

OPERATION Blue Orchid

For one year U.S. and Russian law enforcement began to cooperate to crack a major transnational child pornography ring known as "Blue Orchid," which offered an Internet site depicting the physical and sexual abuse of children. The U.S. Customs Service and the Moscow City Police succeeded in dismantling this operation. As a result of their work, five people were arrested in Russia and four were arrested in the United States. In addition, U.S. authorities executed 15 search warrants in the United States. Others were arrested across Europe. Investigations remain ongoing.

Because of the success of cooperation in taking down the Blue Orchid network and two previous distribution networks, the U.S. Department of State dedicated $100,000 to assist the Moscow City Police in enforcement actions against child pornography on the Internet. This cooperation strengthened the mutual assistance in fighting the production, distribution, and acquisition of child pornography.

"The project will provide training and consultations at the U.S. Customs Cybersmuggling Center in Fairfax, Virginia, as well as some equipment and other technology necessary to investigate Internet purveyors of this material. The Department of State also funded training on Internet child pornography investigative techniques for the Moscow City Police in July 2000 at the Cybersmuggling Center in Virginia," according to the U.S. State Department.

Several Blue Orchid collaborators were discovered in 1996, which led to authorities discovery of the Wonderland Club and its later dismantling in 1996.

See also: OPERATION ARTUS; OPERATION CANDYLAND; OPERATION ORE; OPERATION TWINS; WONDERLAND CLUB.

Reference

Richard Boucher. "U.S.-Russian Law Enforcement Cooperation Cracks Child Pornography Ring." U.S. Department of State Press Release, March 26, 2001. Available online. URL: http://www.state.gov/r/pa/prs/ps/2001/1684.htm. Accessed on November 24, 2004.

OPERATION Candyman

On March 18, 2002 the Federal Bureau of Investigation (FBI) announced that it had dismantled a computer-based pornography ring and arrested scores of its members. U.S. Attorney General John Ashcroft announced in Washington that Operation Candyman, began in January 2001 and that it would continue.

Twenty-seven individuals were arrested and admitted to abusing 36 children, Ashcroft reported. He said at the briefing that the investigation had uncovered an estimated 7,000 members of the group, including some 2,400 outside the United States.

In a 14-month period, all 56 national FBI field offices investigated hundreds of individuals who were subscribers of "The Candyman" e-group. These individuals were spread across the country, according to Ashcroft, and some held positions of trust by parents such as bus drivers, teachers, or other educational roles.

"Forty individuals in 20 states are now in custody, with another 50 expected by week's end," FBI Executive Assistant Director Bruce Gebhardt said. "They include members of the clergy, law enforcement officers, a nurse, a teachers aide, a school bus driver, and others entrusted with protecting, nurturing and educating the American youth."

"Unfortunately, some in this country have used the internet to exploit America's young people by creating e-mail groups to promote and trade pictures of children being sexually exploited, and abused. It is clear that a new marketplace for child pornography has emerged in the dark corners of cyberspace. There, in e-groups hidden in the vastness of the internet, innocent boys and girls have been targeted by offenders who view them as sexual objects. These offenders have tried to use the technology and anonymity of the internet to trade child pornography, and they must be stopped," said Ashcroft.

See also: OPERATION ARTUS; OPERATION BLUE ORCHID; OPERATION ORE; OPERATION TWINS; WONDERLAND CLUB.

Reference

U.S. Department of State. "FBI Dismantles International Internet Child Pornography Ring." Available online. URL: http://www.usembassy.it/file2002_03/alia/a2031805.htm. Posted March 18, 2002.

OPERATION Cathedral   *See* WONDERLAND CLUB.

OPERATION Cheshire Cat   *See* WONDERLAND CLUB.

OPERATION Dinero

Operation Dinero, a joint Drug Enforcement Administration (DEA)/Internal Revenue Service (IRS) operation, was launched by the DEA's Atlanta Division in 1992. In this investigation, the U.S. government successfully operated a financial institution in Anguilla for the purpose of targeting the financial networks of international drug organizations. In addition, a number of undercover corporations were established in different jurisdictions as multiservice "front" businesses designed to supply "money-laundering" services, such as loans, cashier's checks, wire transfers, and peso exchanges, or to establish holding companies or shell corporations for the trafficking groups. Believing these services were legitimate, the Cali Mafia engaged the bank to sell three paintings, a Picasso, a Rubens, and a Reynolds. These paintings, estimated to have a combined value of $15 million, were seized by the DEA and the IRS in 1994. The operation resulted in 116 arrests in the United States, Spain, Italy, and Canada, and seizure of nine tons of cocaine, and the seizure of more than $90 million in cash and other property. The two-year joint enforcement operation was coordinated by the DEA, the IRS, Immigration and Naturalization Services (INS), and the Federal Bureau of Investigation (FBI), and international law enforcement counterparts in the United Kingdom, Canada, Italy, and Spain.

See also: CALI CARTEL.

Reference

U.S. Drug Enforcement Administration, U.S. Department of Justice. "A Tradition of Excellence, DEA History 1985–1990." Available online. URL: http://www.dea.gov/pubs/history/index/html. Downloaded on July 28, 2004.

OPERATION Durango

In 1985, the Drug Enforcement Administration, Chicago Division, investigated for more than six months the relationship between Chicago, Illinois, and Durango, Mexico. The investigation was called Operation Durango. The six-month investigation of the Durango, Mexico–based drug trafficking group led to the arrest of 120 defendants and the seizure of heroin, cocaine, marijuana, and $25 million in assets.

Reference

U.S. Drug Enforcement Administration, U.S. Department of Justice. "A Tradition of Excellence, DEA History 1985–1990." Available online. URL: http://www.dea.gov/pubs/history/index/html. Downloaded on July 28, 2004.

OPERATION Foxhunt (a.k.a. Operation Zorro)

Under Operation Foxhunt, while investigating the domestic operations of the Helmer Herrera Buitrago organization, the Drug Enforcement Administration (DEA) developed a "cluster" of investigations nationwide from cooperating-individual information, intelligence leads, and wire intercepts. The organizations being targeted were part of a national and international, multifaceted cocaine transportation/distribution organization. This investigation touched on several concurrent investigative efforts in numerous U.S. cities and resulted in a 31-case cluster investigation that produced the arrest of 198 defendants, the seizure of more than 6.5 tons of cocaine, and in excess of $13.5 million of assets.

In September 1994 the DEA concluded Operation Foxhunt, a two-year investigation of a major Cali Mafia transportation operation based in Los Angeles. The investigation targeted two Colombian cell transportation directors who were responsible for the movement of multiton quantities of cocaine from main distribution points in Los Angeles to wholesale distribution centers in New York City, San Francisco, and Chicago. The drugs were then moved to consumer distribution points in such cities as St. Louis, Missouri; Newark, New Jersey; San Antonio, Texas; Washington, D.C.; and New Orleans, Louisiana. The operation took its name from one of the investigation's primary targets, Diego Fernando Salazar-Izquierdo, a Cali transportation cell director in Los Angeles, known as Zorro, which is Spanish for "fox." The second cell director, Over Arturo Acuna, referred to as Arturo, directed parallel drug operations in Los Angeles. Both Zorro and Arturo reported directly to drug lords in Cali, Colombia. It took 31 concurrent investigations and two years to identify and arrest Zorro because the Cali operatives used sophisticated systems of fax lines and cellular communications to foil wiretaps. They also used computer software to "clone," or steal, the telephone numbers of unsus-

pecting individuals and segmented organizations to avoid detection. By the time the investigation concluded, 6.5 tons of cocaine and more than $13.5 million had been seized, and 191 suspects had been arrested. Fifty-five federal, state, and local agencies had participated in this investigation.

See also: CALI CARTEL.

References

U.S. Department of Justice. "1995 Annual Report of the Attorney General of the United States." Available online. URL: http://www.usdoj.gov/ag/annualreports/ar95/toc.htm. Downloaded on July 28, 2004.

U.S. Drug Enforcement Administration, U.S. Department of Justice. "A Tradition of Excellence, DEA History 1985–1990." Available online. URL: http://www.dea.gov/pubs/history/index.html. Downloaded on July 28, 2004.

OPERATION Green Ice

By the late 1980s, the Drug Enforcement Administration financial investigative skills had evolved to such a high degree that the agency set up its own bank to lure drug traffickers looking to launder their profits. In 1989, the investigative team created Trans America Ventures Associates and established its credentials in the financial community. The result was so convincing that *Hispanic Business Weekly* listed it as one of the top 500 Hispanic corporations in America. Undercover agents then posed as money launderers and offered to pick up funds anywhere in the world. They used informants to identify drug money brokers from Colombia who acted as middlemen between Cali Mafia kingpins and money laundering operations in the United States.

Beginning in San Diego and Los Angeles, the investigations took undercover agents to Houston, Ft. Lauderdale, Miami, Chicago, and New York to pick up money and to establish "fronts," such as leather-goods shops, in these cities. During the course of the investigation, DEA agents laundered more than $20 million for the Colombia-based cartels. As the investigation developed, cartel operatives asked the undercover agents to provide money-laundering services in Europe, Canada, and the Caribbean. Consequently, Operation Green Ice was expanded into a coordinated international law-enforcement effort involving Canada, the Cayman Islands, Colombia, Costa Rica, Italy, Spain, the United Kingdom, and the United States.

In September 1992 undercover agents finally arranged a meeting with top-ranking Cali financial managers at locations in the United States, Italy, Spain, and Costa Rica. The drug lords arrived, expecting to discuss plans for their criminal business but instead were arrested. Operation Green Ice was an unprecedented collaboration of talent and financial expertise that successfully formed the first international task force to attack the monetary networks of the Cali Mafia. Operation Green Ice led to the arrest of seven of the Cali Mafia's top financial managers, the seizure of more than $50 million in assets worldwide, and the arrest of 177 persons, including 44 in the United States.

See also: CALI CARTEL.

References

U.S. Department of Justice. "1995 Annual Report of the Attorney General of the United States." Available online. URL: http://www.usdoj.gov/ag/annualreports/ar95/toc.htm. Downloaded on July 28, 2004.

U.S. Drug Enforcement Administration, U.S. Department of Justice. "A Tradition of Excellence, DEA History 1985–1990." Available online. URL: http://www.dea.gov/pubs/history/index.html. Downloaded on July 28, 2004.

OPERATION Green Ice II

Green Ice II, a spin-off of the successful 1992 Green Ice investigation, culminated in April 1995 with the arrest of 109 individuals and the seizure of 13,882 pounds of cocaine, 16 pounds of heroin, and $15.6 million in cash. This second phase operation concentrated on the Cali Mafia's money brokers and cocaine distribution networks from Mexico to the United States. Once again, the Drug Enforcement Administration (DEA) established storefront operations and bank accounts throughout the world and then convinced drug traffickers that undercover DEA agents had connections to launder their drug proceeds. Most of the individuals arrested were high-ranking Cali cell leaders or money brokers in the United States. Green Ice II had three distinct phases. The first targeted certain Casas de Cambio and check-cashing institutions along the Southwest border. Casas de Cambio are legal, unregulated money-exchange houses that operated much like banks. These organizations wire-transferred large sums of money and did not keep records of the source or owner of the funds. Second, the DEA

agents working on this case created their own money-exchange houses and also infiltrated existing Casas de Cambio to identify major narcotic traffickers, money launderers, and the financial institutions used by the traffickers. The third portion of the investigation followed the money into Colombia and linked specific cartel members with the narcotics proceeds. Ultimately, more than 200 federal agents from 27 federal, state, and foreign law-enforcement agencies contributed to the indictment of over 80 individuals. In addition, Operation Green Ice II enabled the DEA to gain a wealth of knowledge on wire-transfer information, bank accounts, and identification of money couriers/brokers. It also proved that corrupt businessmen, bankers, and attorneys had created an alliance with drug dealers to funnel their drug profits back to them.

Reference

U.S. Drug Enforcement Administration, U.S. Department of Justice. "A Tradition of Excellence, DEA History 1985–1990." Available online. URL: http://www.dea.gov/pubs/history/index.html. Downloaded on July 28, 2004.

OPERATION Leyenda

On March 14, 1985, the Drug Enforcement Administration (DEA) was notified by Mexican Federal Judicial Police (MFJP) officials that they had taken into custody five Jalisco state police officers who were believed to have participated in the abduction of Special Agent Enrique Camarena. However, the DEA was neither advised in advance of this operation nor invited to participate in the subsequent interviews of the suspected Jalisco state police officers.

Under Mexican police questioning, the Jalisco officers gave statements implicating themselves and others in the abduction of Special Agent Camarena. One suspect died during the interrogation. The statements of the Jalisco officers implicated Caro-Quintero and Fonseca-Carrillo, among others, in planning and ordering the abduction of Special Agent Camarena.

On March 17, 1985, Mexican newspapers reported that 11 individuals had been arrested by the MFJP for the kidnapping of Special Agent Camarena. Arrest orders were also issued for seven international drug traffickers, including Rafael Caro-Quintero, on kidnapping and murder charges.

The DEA subsequently discovered that Caro-Quintero was in Costa Rica. On April 4, 1985, the DEA office in San Jose, in conjunction with the local authorities in Costa Rica, located and apprehended Caro-Quintero and seven of his associates. The Mexican government then sent MFJP officials to Costa Rica after persuading the Costa Rican government to expel Caro-Quintero to Mexico on immigration violations. On April 5, 1985, Caro-Quintero and the others arrested with him left Costa Rica for Mexico aboard two jets belonging to the Mexican government. In Mexico City, Caro-Quintero was interrogated for several days by police officials. Ultimately he gave a statement implicating himself and others in the abduction of Special Agent Camarena.

But Caro-Quintero denied any knowledge of who actually killed Special Agent Camarena or how he died. He also denied any knowledge of the abduction and death of Captain Alfredo Zavala, a Mexican pilot, who was also part of the antidrug investigation.

On April 7, 1985, drug trafficker Ernesto Fonseca-Carrillo and several of his bodyguards were arrested by Mexican police officials and military forces in Puerto Vallarta and taken to Mexico City for questioning. Fonseca and his right-hand man, Samuel Ramirez-Razo, gave statements to the MFJP implicating themselves in the abduction of Special Agent Camarena. However, neither individual admitted having any knowledge of Camarena's death or Captain Zavala's abduction.

Rafael Caro-Quintero was implicated in Special Agent Camarena's death. In 1985 he was arrested in Costa Rica and deported to Mexico. Caro-Quintero was tried and convicted in February 1989 for narcotics trafficking and weapons violations. He was sentenced to 34 years.

Although there were some discrepancies in the testimony of Caro-Quintero, Fonseca-Carrillo, and Ramirez-Razo, all claimed that they had nothing to do with the death of the DEA agent and further stated that these crimes were probably the work of another narcotics trafficker, Miguel Angel Félix Gallardo.

Meanwhile, in April 1985, the DEA learned that certain members of the Mexican government had in their possession a series of audio tapes of Camarena's torture and interrogation. These tapes allegedly had been seized by Mexican military authorities from Fonseca during his arrest in Puerto Vallarta. When the DEA confirmed that the voice on the tape was Camarena, the Mexican government, after great pressure from the U.S. government, turned over copies of all five tapes.

On April 12, 1985, a team of one DEA and four Federal Bureau of Investigation (FBI) agents arrived in Guadalajara, Jalisco, Mexico, via DEA aircraft. These agents were advised that the house where Special Agent Camarena was alleged to have been taken after his abduction had been located by the MFJP in Guadalajara.

On May 3, 1985, a new DEA investigative team was established to coordinate and investigate the abduction of Camarena and Captain Zavala. This investigation was given the name Operation Leyenda. Through evidence gained from cooperating individuals and relentless investigative pursuit, this team was able to ascertain that five individuals abducted Special Agent Camarena and took him to a house at 881 Lope de Vega in Guadalajara on February 7, 1985. Ultimately, the agents were successful in securing the indictments of several individuals connected to the abduction and murder. The hard work, long hours, and total agency commitment had yielded positive results.

In retrospect, Operation Leyenda was a long and complex investigation, made more difficult by the fact that the crime was committed on foreign soil and involved major drug traffickers and government officials from Mexico. It took several years to develop the facts, to apprehend the perpetrators, and finally to bring them to justice.

See also: CAMARENA, ENRIQUE; CARO-QUINTERO, RAFAEL.

Reference

U.S. Drug Enforcement Administration, U.S. Department of Justice. "A Tradition of Excellence, DEA History 1985–1990." Available online. URL: http://www.dea.gov/pubs/history/index.html. Downloaded on July 28, 2004.

OPERATION Mercure

From March 20 to March 26, 2002, Europol conducted a big international operation on ecstasy trafficking. Customs services from France, Germany, and The Netherlands organized the operation, which was coordinated from Europol's Headquarters in The Hague. Liaison officers of the participating countries worked together and were equipped with the necessary communication tools. The drugs unit of Europol supported the operation.

Involved in the operation were Canada, Australia, the United States, Switzerland, Iceland, and most of the European Union member states. The operation focused on air passengers traveling from Europe to the United States, Canada, and Australia. The aim of the operation was the identification and arrest of those couriers who smuggle synthetic drugs (especially ecstasy). The operation was successful and about 335,000 pills were seized, plus 13 persons were arrested.

The seizures took place at many different airports: Amsterdam-Schiphol (89,000), Frankfurt/Main (83,000), Zürich (40,000), Madrid (27,000), Brussels (10,000), Paris–Charles de Gaulle (26,500), and Miami (59,000). The street value of one ecstasy pill is about 23 EUR. The street value of all the pills seized in the United States and Canada was approximately 7.75 million EUR.

Europol facilitated Operation Mercure by providing the Operational Coordination Unit (OCU), headed by Dutch customs officers and including all necessary equipment and communications. Furthermore additional support was given by the Drugs Unit of Europol in the form of expertise, available 24 hours a day, plus the use of a specialized system enabling the linking of seizures.

Reference

"Joint Strike against Trafficking, Seizure of 335,000 XTC Pills." *The Hague*, March 28, 2002.

OPERATION Oceano

Operation Oceano represented the first time the Drug Enforcement Administration (DEA) had worked with the Nicaraguan National Police on a joint interdiction operation in Nicaraguan territory. The seizure of 990 pounds of cocaine from an airdrop off the Pacific coast of Nicaragua provided the evidence the DEA needed to confirm that Colombian cartels had been using this smuggling route.

Reference

Reno, Janet. *1995 Annual Report to the Attorney General of the United States,* Washington, D.C.: U.S. Department of Justice, 1996.

OPERATION Opbat

Operation Bahamas and Turks and Caicos Islands (OPBAT), launched by the U.S. State Department in 1982, continued in the 1990s to combat the flow of illegal drugs through the Caribbean into the southeastern United States. The United States had an excellent working relationship with both the Commonwealth of the Bahamas and the government of the Turks and Caicos Islands (as a dependent territory of the United Kingdom). The Drug Enforcement Administration (DEA) along with U.S. Coast Guard and Departments of State, Army, Customs Service, Southern and Atlantic Military Commands, actively supported the Royal Bahamas police force and Royal Turk and Caicos police forces in combating drug trafficking through 100,000 square miles of open water surrounding 700 islands with a landmass of 5,382 square miles. With increasingly effective law-enforcement efforts along the Mexican border, there had been a resurgence of smuggling through the Caribbean. The traffickers used turboprop twin-engine aircraft, large, fast high-powered vessels, global positioning systems, cellular telephones, and Cuban territorial air and seas as cover for their trade. All of these factors made OPBAT's law-enforcement operations exceedingly difficult. They have been very successful in combating crime. In 2001 OPBAT officials made 133 arrests and seized 2.4 metric tons of cocaine and 13 metric tons of marijuana.

Reference

U.S. Drug Enforcement Administration, U.S. Department of Justice. "A Tradition of Excellence, DEA History 1985–1990." Available online. URL: http://www.dea.gov/pubs/history/index.html. Downloaded on July 28, 2004.

OPERATION Ore

On December 17, 2002, more than 250 police officers from the Metropolitan Police's (Scotland Yard) Serious Crime Group (SCG) executed 45 warrants on suspects' homes as part of Operation Ore—an investigation into people in the United Kingdom suspected of accessing child pornography Web sites. Following many weeks of intelligence gathering and analysis on each case, officers from the SCG entered addresses across the city and arrested 35 people. A large amount of computer equipment and other evidence was seized.

Operation Ore was a nationwide investigation in response to information supplied by U.S. law enforcement about a large number of suspected users of paid-for child pornography sites. Lists of suspects had been collated by National Criminal Intelligence Service (UK) NCIS and developed further by National Criminal Service, and was then passed on to police forces across the United Kingdom for further investigation.

It was the single largest operation mounted in a child protection capacity so far by Scotland Yard and displayed a continuing commitment to child protection issues. To support this and other operations, the Child Protection Command increased its own computer forensic capabilities and was assisted by a number of other agencies with the required specialist skills and equipment. This forensic capability was further enhanced in January 2003 with a preliminary phase in the creation of the Child Protection High Tech Crime Unit at Scotland Yard as part of Specialist Operating Group 5 (SO5). This unit concentrates on online investigations and includes officers previously attached to the Met's Clubs and Vice Unit.

See also: OPERATION ARTUS; OPERATION BLUE ORCHID; OPERATION CANDYLAND; OPERATION TWINS; WONDERLAND CLUB.

Reference

Scotland Yard. "35 Arrested in Internet Child Pornography Raids." *Bulletin 2002/0246*. December 17, 2002.

OPERATION Pipeline

As drug traffickers established their networks within U.S. borders, they began to rely heavily on the highway system to move their wares from entry points to distribution hubs around the country. Beginning in the early 1980s, New Mexico state troopers grew suspicious when they noticed a sharp increase in the number of motor vehicle violations that resulted in drug seizures and arrests. At the same time, and unknown to the troopers in New Mexico, troopers in New Jersey began making similar seizures during highway stops along the Interstate 95 "drug corridor" from Florida to the northeast. Independently, troopers in New Mexico and New Jersey established their own highway drug-interdiction programs. Over time, as their seizures mounted, law-enforcement officers found that highway drug couriers shared many characteristics, tendencies, and methods. Highway law-enforcement officers began to ask key questions to help determine whether or not motorists they had stopped for traffic violations were also carrying drugs. These interview techniques proved extremely effective. The road patrol officers

also found it beneficial to share their observations and experiences in highway interdiction.

The success of the highway interdiction programs in New Jersey and New Mexico led to the creation of Operation Pipeline in 1984. This Drug Enforcement Administration (DEA)–funded training program featured state police and highway-patrol officers with expertise in highway interdiction who provided training to other officers throughout the country. Pipeline, a nationwide highway interdiction program, was one of DEA's most effective operations and continued to provide essential cooperation between the DEA and state and local law-enforcement agencies. The operation was composed of three elements: training, real-time communication, and analytic support. Each year, state and local highway officers delivered dozens of training schools across the country to other highway officers. These were intended to inform officers of interdiction laws and policies, to build their knowledge of drug trafficking, and to sharpen their perceptiveness of highway couriers. Training classes focused on: (1) the law, policy, and ethics governing highway stops and drug prosecution; and (2) drug trafficking trends and key characteristics, or indicators, that were shared by drug traffickers. Also, through the Electronic Privacy Information Center (EPIC), state and local agencies shared real-time information with other agencies, obtained immediate results to their record checks, and received detailed analysis of drug seizures to support their investigations.

Operation Pipeline has been tremendously successful in the United States. Between 1986, when EPIC began to keep close records of Operations Pipeline's accomplishments, and August 1998, Operation Pipeline was responsible for more than 34,000 seizures. It led to the confiscation of 350 kilograms of heroin, 105,000 kilograms of cocaine, 460,000 kilograms of methamphetamine, 815,000 kilograms of marijuana, and $471 million in drug profits.

Reference

U.S. Drug Enforcement Administration, U.S. Department of Justice. "A Tradition of Excellence, DEA History 1985–1990." Available online. URL: http://www.dea.gov/pubs/history/index.html. Downloaded on July 28, 2004.

OPERATION Pisces

In 1984, the Drug Enforcement Administration (DEA) set up an undercover money-laundering operation called Operation Pisces with the Internal Revenue Service (IRS) and several state and local agencies.

This two-year, undercover intelligence investigation successfully revealed a direct connection between the Colombian cartels, including drug kingpin Pablo Escobar, and street gangs in the United States, as well as deals negotiated in Denmark and Italy.

During the operation, DEA agents, posing as money launderers, also discovered that the drug lords were moving a ton of cocaine per week and reaping profits of almost $4 million a month. The organizations used check-cashing businesses to launder the enormous proceeds from the sale of cocaine. When the operation ended in 1987, law enforcement had arrested 220 drug dealers and seized $28 million in cash and assets and more than 11,000 lbs. of cocaine in southern California. The investigation was further proof of the continuous flow of drugs and money between Colombia and the United States.

See also: ESCOBAR, PABLO; MEDELLÍN CARTEL.

Reference

A Tradition of Excellence, DEA History 1985–1990, U.S. Department of Justice, Washington, D.C. March 1991.

OPERATION Sentac 19 *See* HERRERA NEVARES, JAIME, SR.

OPERATION Snowcap

Operation Snowcap had six general objectives:

1. To encourage, through diplomatic efforts, coca source countries to participate in crop eradication;
2. To suppress cocaine production through the destruction of clandestine cocaine laboratories and seizure of precursor chemicals, coca paste, cocaine base, and cocaine hydrochloride;
3. To investigate and prosecute major cocaine trafficking organizations and to seize their assets;
4. To support enforcement efforts against cocaine trafficking by providing timely intelligence;
5. To increase personnel and financial and technical assistance dedicated to foreign cocaine enforcement programs;
6. To improve domestic and foreign drug law-enforcement officers' skills through training.

The success of Operation Blast Furnace set the stage for one of the Drug Enforcement Administration's (DEA's) most extensive and unprecedented enforcement efforts—Operation Snowcap. This initiative was developed by the DEA and the Department of State's Bureau of International Narcotics Matters (INM) in 1987 and was designed to disrupt the growing, processing, and transportation systems supporting the cocaine industry.

The DEA and INM coordinated Operation Snowcap operations in 12 countries: Guatemala, Panama, Costa Rica, Argentina, Brazil, Chile, Venezuela, Colombia, Ecuador, Bolivia, Peru, and Mexico. The U.S. Department of Defense and the border patrol also participated in the operation. The majority of Snowcap activity was concentrated in Bolivia, Peru, and Ecuador because of the prevalence of coca processing in these nations.

Planning for Operation Snowcap began in September 1986, two months before Operation Blast Furnace was concluded. When the 1987 operation was launched, there was a smooth transition of responsibility for air operations from the U.S. Army to the government of Bolivia. Six Bell UH-1 Huey helicopters, loaned by the U.S. Army to the INM, and a U.S. Army training team arrived on the same C5-A transport that withdrew the Blast Furnace equipment from Bolivia.

Besides coca-suppression operations, the Snowcap strategy included chemical control, vehicular interdiction, and marine law-enforcement interdiction operations. The marine law-enforcement and vehicular interdiction concepts mirrored successful programs in the United States. The marine law-enforcement operations grew from the DEA's close coordination with the U.S. Coast Guard, while vehicular interdiction originated from the DEA's Operation Pipeline, the Electronic Privacy Information Centre's (EPIC's) national highway interdiction program.

Operation Snowcap depended on agents who volunteered for temporary assignments in foreign countries. These special agents left domestic field divisions for temporary tour of duty assignments to work closely with host country law-enforcement counterparts. As envisioned, Operation Snowcap was designed to be a temporary program to assist law-enforcement entities in Latin America with training and investigative work.

Reference

U.S. Drug Enforcement Administration, U.S. Department of Justice. "A Tradition of Excellence, DEA History 1985–1990." Available online. URL: http://www.dea.gov/pubs/history/index.html. Downloaded on July 28, 2004.

OPERATION Sunflower

An international organized criminal network involved in trafficking women for sexual exploitation was smashed on February 10, 2002. In an international operation, coordinated by Europol and by the Italian Carabinieri, about 80 arrests were carried out simultaneously in several European countries.

The operation under the code name *Girasole,* or "Sunflower" was led by the Italian authorities and progressively involved other countries in cooperation with Europol. The operation focused on dismantling an organized criminal network engaged in smuggling young women mainly from eastern European countries. Intensive investigations revealed that individuals and travel companies based in Ukraine were the major operators in promoting and facilitating the smuggling of women by obtaining visas fraudulently.

Based on information sent by the participating countries, Europol conducted an operational analysis using sophisticated methodology. These techniques supported the Italian judicial investigations and identified a highly active criminal network composed of a large number of Ukrainian travel companies in cooperation with partner travel agencies and hotels, mainly based in Austria, Italy, Germany, France, and Spain. The analysis also determined the major links between the travel companies, hotels, executives, and their modus operandi.

Director of Europol, Jürgen Storbeck, expressed his thanks to all participating countries and especially to the Italian authorities for their effective and efficient cooperation. He stated, "Operation Girasole, was a strong blow against those making illegal profits by exploiting the human desire for a better life. Europol will continue to strengthen its efforts, in cooperation with the Member States and other international organizations, in fighting this devastating criminal phenomenon."

The participating countries were Austria, Belgium, France, Germany, Italy, Portugal, Spain, Netherlands, Albania, the Czech Republic, Poland, Romania, Switzerland, Russia, and Ukraine.

See also: HUMAN TRAFFICKING.

Reference

U.S. Drug Enforcement Administration, U.S. Department of Justice. "A Tradition of Excellence, DEA History 1985–1990." Available online. URL: http://www.dea.gov/pubs/history/ index.html. Downloaded on July 28, 2004.

OPERATION Swordfish

In December 1980, the Drug Enforcement Administration (DEA) launched a major investigation in Miami aimed against international drug organizations. The operation was dubbed Operation Swordfish because it was intended to snare the "big fish" in the drug trade. The DEA set up a bogus money-laundering corporation in suburban Miami Lakes that was called Dean International Investments, Inc. The DEA agents teamed up with a Cuban exile who had fallen on hard times and was willing to lure Colombian traffickers to the bogus bank. In addition to spending time in Cuban prisons after the Bay of Pigs invasion, the exile had also served jail time in the United States for tax fraud and was heavily in debt to the U.S. Internal Revenue Service. During the 18-month investigation, agents were able to gather enough evidence for a federal grand jury to indict 67 U.S. and Colombian citizens. At the conclusion of the operation, drug agents seized 100 kilograms of cocaine, 250,000 methaqualone pills, tons of marijuana, and $800,000 in cash, cars, land, and Miami bank accounts. Operation Swordfish was a significant attack on South Florida's flourishing drug trade.

Reference

U.S. Drug Enforcement Administration, U.S. Department of Justice. "A Tradition of Excellence, DEA History 1985–1990." Available online. URL: http://www.dea.gov/pubs/history/index.html. Downloaded on July 28, 2004.

OPERATION Tiger Trap

Operation Tiger Trap was conceived at Drug Enforcement Administration's (DEA's) Bangkok office during June 1994 with the goal of identifying and targeting the major heroin traffickers in the region. Operation Tiger Trap was the first of its kind, a multiagency international operation designed to dismantle or disrupt the trafficking activities of the world's largest heroin-trafficking organization, the Shan United Army (SUA). Also known as the Mong Tai Army, it was located primarily in the areas of Burma adjacent to the northern border provinces of Thailand. The SUA warlord Khun Sa claimed that his army, which was financed primarily through heroin trafficking, was fighting the Burmese for independence for the Shan people.

The SUA controlled the cultivation, production, and transportation of heroin from the Shan state. Although other insurgent groups in Burma also trafficked heroin, the SUA had been the dominant force in worldwide distribution. Prior to Operation Tiger Trap, the percentage of Southeast Asian heroin from the DEA's Heroin Signature Program rose from 9 percent in 1977 to 58 percent in 1991. On December 3, 1993, law-enforcement authorities seized 315 kilograms of heroin in Pae, Thailand.

Tiger Trap was divided into phases that would all target key functionaries. On November 27, 1994, the operation culminated when teams of Royal Thai Police, Office of Narcotics Control Board Officers, and Royal Thai Army Special Forces Soldiers, working with DEA agents, lured targets in Burma into Thailand where they were then arrested. This action significantly damaged the ability of the SUA to distribute heroin. The Royal Thai Army then worked with the Thai Border Patrol Police to close the Burma border to "commercial quantities" of goods entering the Shan state.

When law-enforcement authorities had completed their operations, 13 senior SUA traffickers were arrested, and all were pursued for extradition/expulsion to the United States. These 13 principal defendants in Operation Tiger Trap included some of the most persistent and high-level heroin traffickers operating out of Thailand. Khun Sa's men included Chang Tetsa, Liu Fangte, Meedian Pathummee, Kuo Fa Mou, Ma Tsai Kuei, and Chao Fusheng, all subjects of U.S. indictments in the Eastern District of New York EDNY. The defendants were a mixture of three distinct categories: those who were eligible for expulsion (illegal aliens in Thailand); those who possessed fraudulent identification; and authentic Thai citizens.

Reference

U.S. Drug Enforcement Administration, U.S. Department of Justice. "A Tradition of Excellence, DEA History 1985–1990." Available online. URL: http://www.dea.gov/pubs/history/index.html. Downloaded on July 28, 2004.

OPERATION Twins

A major Internet-based pedophile network was smashed on July 2, 2002, by an international police operation. The operation, led by the United Kingdom's National Hi-Tech Crime Unit (NHTCU), started by an initiative from the Swedish National Criminal Intelligence Service and was fully supported and coordinated by Europol. The countries involved in Operation Twins are Belgium, Canada, Denmark, Germany, Italy, Netherlands, Romania, Spain, Sweden, Switzerland, the United States, and the United Kingdom.

The operation was the result of a 12-month intelligence-led effort and focused on a criminal organization, whose activities included the production and distribution of child pornography and live time abuse of children. Worldwide dawn raids carried out simultaneously across seven countries, targeted members of a prolific pedophile gang. Around 50 premises have been searched and in all cases the occupants were implicated in crimes relating to child abuse and pornography. A substantial quantity of equipment was seized, including computers and laptops containing images of child abuse, videos, and CDs. The main emphasis of operational measures carried out was in Germany where 31 of the 50 suspects lived. The German Federal Criminal Police Office (BKA) set up a special information and coordination point, and the Council of the Prosecutor in Frankfurt/Main led the investigation.

Europol played a central supporting and coordinating role in the operation. A dedicated team of intelligence analysts, working in a secure operations room equipped with the latest technology, processed information received on a daily basis from investigations being carried out in the different participating states. The data reviewed during the investigation numbered hundreds and thousands of images, and thousands of videos depicting hundreds of child victims, most of whom remain unidentified.

Europol's Deputy Director Gilles Leclair, Head of Serious Crime Department, stated: "Child pornography constitutes a disgrace of the human dignity. Criminal groups take advantage of the high-tech technology to attack the principles and the values of our democratic systems but, once more, the international law-enforcement cooperation proved very effective and gave a strong and decisive answer against organized crime. Europol will continue to consider child pornography, along with the trafficking in human beings, within its immediate priorities, as decided by the JHA Council, and support the investigations of the competent national law-enforcement authorities with a rapid exchange of information as well as with a high and sophisticated level of intelligence analysis."

Detective Chief Superintendent Len Hynds, head of the NHTCU, said: "Operation Twins has exposed the complex, sophisticated and organized hierarchical structure that online paedophile groups are now using to protect themselves, including their identities and the atrocious activities they are involved in, from those in the wider community, and in particular law enforcement." He added, "Today's results illustrates an excellent example of how international law enforcement works in partnership, across multigeographical jurisdictions to identify and bring to justice those responsible for and engaged in sexual abuse of children."

Reprinted by permission of Interpol, 2004.

See also: OPERATION ARTUS; OPERATION BLUE ORCHID; OPERATION CANDYMAN; WONDERLAND CLUB.

Reference

"Internet Based Pedophile Gang Smashed in Worldwide Police Swoop." *The Hague,* July 2, 2002.

OPERATION Zorro II

As part of the Southwest Border Initiative that was launched in 1994, the Zorro II investigation targeted Mexico-based cocaine smuggling and distribution organizations, as well as the partnership groups based in Colombia. Working together, these organizations were responsible for importing and distributing almost six metric tons of cocaine throughout the United States. Zorro II was a bit of a misnomer since the operation was officially known as Operation Foxhunt. Zorro referred to Carlo Ledher, who was known as Zorro by his confederates. Since much of the operations seemed a continuation of Zorro, the agents popularly called it Zorro II.

Zorro II illustrated the close and efficient partnership that existed between the drug organizations from Mexico and Colombia. More important, this case showed that the international drug trade was a seamless continuum, a criminal enterprise that stretched, without interruption, from the jungles of South America across transit zones, such as Mexico, to the cities and communities of the United States.

Zorro II was particularly important because, for the first time, law enforcement dismantled not only a Colombian organization that produced the cocaine,

but also the organization in Mexico that provided the transportation. During the course of the eight-month investigation, law-enforcement officers coordinated and shared information gleaned from more than 90 court-authorized wiretaps. The operation involved 10 federal agencies, 42 state and local agencies, and 14 Drug Enforcement Administration field divisions across the country. As a result of the investigation, more than $17 million and almost 5,600 kilograms of cocaine were seized, and 156 people were arrested. Zorro II confirmed that Mexico-based traffickers were not just transporters but had their own distribution networks throughout the United States.

See also: OPERATION FOXHUNT.

Reference

U.S. Drug Enforcement Administration, U.S. Department of Justice. "A Tradition of Excellence, DEA History 1985–1990." Available online. URL: http://www.dea.gov/pubs/history/index.html. Downloaded on July 28, 2004.

OPIUM

ORIGIN AND HISTORY OF THE OPIUM POPPY

The source of opium is the opium poppy, *Papaver somniferum,* one of the few species of *Papaver* that produces opium. Through centuries of cultivation and breeding, a species of the plant was developed that is now known as *Papaver somniferum.* The genus, *Papaver,* is the Greek word for "poppy." The species, *somniferum,* is Latin for "sleep-inducing."

The psychological effects of opium may have been known to the ancient Sumerians (circa 4000 B.C.) whose symbols for the poppy were *hul* (joy) and *gil* (plant). The plant was known in Europe at least 4,000 years ago, as evidenced by fossil remains of poppy-seed cake and poppy pods found in the Swiss lake dwellings of the Neolithic Age. Opium was probably consumed by the ancient Egyptians and was known to the Greeks as well. References to the poppy are found in Homer's works *The Iliad* and *The Odyssey.* Hippocrates (460–357 B.C.), the father of medicine, recommended drinking the juice of the white poppy mixed with the seed of nettle.

The opium poppy probably reached China in about the seventh century A.D. through the efforts of Arab traders who advocated its use for medicinal purposes. In Chinese literature, however, there are earlier references to its use. The noted Chinese surgeon Hua To of the Three Kingdoms (A.D 220–264) had patients swallow opium preparations and *Cannabis indica* before undergoing major surgery.

The beginning of widespread opium use in China has been associated by some historians with the introduction of tobacco into that country by the Dutch from Java in the 17th century. The Chinese were reported to mix opium with tobacco. The practice was adopted throughout the area and eventually resulted in increased opium smoking, both with and without tobacco.

In 1803, the German pharmacist F. W. Serturner isolated and described the principal alkaloid in opium, which he named morphium after Morpheus, the Greek god of dreams. The invention of the syringe and the discovery of other alkaloids of opium soon followed: codeine in 1832 and papaverine in 1848. By the 1850s, the medicinal use of pure alkaloids, rather than crude opium preparations, was common in Europe.

In the United States, opium preparations became widely available in the 19th century, and morphine was used extensively as a painkiller for wounded soldiers during the Civil War. The inevitable result was opium addiction, contemporarily called "the army disease" or "soldier's disease." These opium and morphine abuse problems prompted a scientific

search for potent, but nonaddictive, painkillers. In the 1870s, chemists developed an opium-based and supposedly nonaddictive substitute for morphine. The Bayer Pharmaceutical Company of Germany was the first to produce the new drug in large quantities under the brand name Heroin. This product was obtained by the acetylation of morphine. Soon thereafter, studies showed heroin to have narcotic and addictive properties far exceeding those of morphine. Although heroin has been used in the United Kingdom in the treatment of the terminally ill, its "medical value" is a subject of intense controversy.

THE OPIUM POPPY PLANT

The opium poppy, *Papaver somniferum,* is an annual plant; that is, the plant matures one time and does not regenerate itself. New seed must be planted each season. From a small seed, it grows, flowers, and bears fruit (a pod) only once. The entire growth cycle for most varieties of this plant takes about 120 days. The tiny seeds (like the seeds on a poppy seed roll) germinate quickly in warm air and sufficient soil moisture. In less than six weeks, the young plant emerges from the soil, grows a set of four leaves, and resembles a small cabbage in appearance. The lobed, dentate (jagged-edged) leaves are glaucous green with a dull gray or blue tint.

Within two months, the plant will grow from one to two feet in height with one primary long, smooth stem. The upper portion of this stem is without leaves and is called the peduncle. One or more secondary stems, called tillers, may grow from the main stem of the plant. Single poppy plants in Southeast Asia often have more than one tiller.

The main stem of a fully matured *Papaver somniferum* ranges between two and five feet in height. The green leaves are oblong, toothed, and lobed and vary between four to 15 inches in length at maturity. The mature leaves have no commercial value except for use as animal fodder.

As the plant grows tall, the main stem and each tiller terminate in a flower bud. During the development of the bud, the peduncle portion of the stem elongates and forms a distinctive "hook" that causes the bud to be turned upside down. As the flower develops, the peduncle straightens and the buds point upward. A day or two after the buds first point upward, the two outer segments of the bud, called sepals, fall away, exposing the flower petals. At first, the exposed flower blossom is crushed and crinkled,

The bulb of a poppy contains the syrup used to make heroin. (AP)

Pakistan's Anti-Narcotic Force soldiers guard a shipment of 1,430 pounds of heroin and 550 pounds of morphine, seized in early January 2002 in Turbat, Pakistan. (AP)

but the petals soon expand and become smooth in the sun. Poppy flowers have four petals. The petals may be single or double and are either white, pink, reddish purple, crimson red, or variegated.

Opium poppies generally flower after about 90 days of growth and continue to flower for two to three weeks. The petals eventually drop to reveal a small round green pod which continues to develop. These pods (also called seed pods, capsules, bulbs, or poppy heads) are either oblate, elongated, or globular and mature to about the size of a chicken egg. The oblate-shaped pods are more common in Southeast Asia.

Only the pod portion of the plant can produce opium alkaloids. The skin of the poppy pod encloses the wall of the pod ovary. The ovary wall consists of three layers: the outer, middle, and inner layers. The plant's latex (raw opium gum) is produced within the ovary wall and drains into the middle layer through a system of vessels and tubes within the pod. The cells of the middle layer secrete more than 95 percent of the plant's opium when the pod is scored and harvested.

Farmers harvest the opium from each pod while it remains on the plant by making vertical incisions with a specially designed homemade knife. After the opium is collected, the pods are allowed to dry on the stem. Once dry, the largest and most productive pods are cut from the stem, and the seeds are removed and dried in the sun before storing for the following year's planting. An alternative method of collecting seeds for planting is to collect them from intentionally unscored pods because scoring may diminish the quality of the seeds. Aside from being used as planting seed, poppy seed may also be pressed to produce cooking oil. Poppy-seed oil may also be used in the manufacture of paints and perfumes. Poppyseed oil is straw yellow in color, odorless, and has a pleasant, almondlike taste.

OPIUM POPPY GROWING AREAS

The opium poppy thrives in temperate, warm climates with low humidity, and requires only a moderate amount of water before and during the early stages of growth.

The opium poppy plant can be grown in a variety of soils—clay, sandy loam, sandy, and sandy clay—but it grows best in a sandy loam soil. This type of soil has good moisture-retentive and nutrient-retentive properties, is easily cultivated, and has a favorable structure for root development. Clay soil types are hard and difficult to pulverize into a good soil texture. The roots of a young poppy plant cannot readily penetrate clay soils, and growth is inhibited. Sand soil, by contrast, does not retain sufficient water or nutrients for proper growth of the plant.

Excessive moisture or extremely arid conditions will affect the poppy plant's growth adversely, thus reducing the alkaloid content. Poppy plants can become waterlogged and die after a heavy rainfall in poorly drained soil. Heavy rainfall in the second and third months of growth can leach alkaloids from the plant and spoil the harvest. Dull, rainy, or cloudy weather during this growth stage may reduce both the quantity and the quality of the alkaloid content.

The major legal opium production areas in the world today are in government-regulated opium farms in India, Turkey, and Tasmania (Australia). The major illegal growing areas are in Southwest Asia (Afghanistan, Pakistan, and Iran) and in the highlands of mainland Southeast Asia (Burma, Laos, Vietnam, and Thailand)—popularly known as the Golden Triangle. Opium poppy is also grown in Colombia, Mexico, and Lebanon.

Opium poppies containing small amounts of opium alkaloids were, at one time, widely grown as an ornamental plant and for seeds in the United States. The possession of this plant was declared illegal by the Opium Poppy Control Act of 1942.

The highlands of Mainland Southeast Asia, at elevations of 800 meters or more above sea level, are prime poppy-growing areas. Generally speaking, these poppy-farming areas do not require irrigation, fertilizer, or insecticides for successful opium yields. Most of the opium poppies of Southeast Asia are found in Burma, specifically in the Wa and Kokang areas, which are in the northeastern quadrant of the Shan State of Burma. Laos is the second-largest illicit-opium-producing country in Southeast Asia and third-

largest in the world behind Afghanistan and Burma. In Laos poppy is cultivated extensively in Houaphan and Xiangkhoang Provinces, in addition to the six northern provinces of Bokeo, Louangnamtha, Louangphabang, Oudomxai, Phongsali, and Xaignabouli. Poppy is also grown in many of the remote, mountainous areas of northern Thailand, particularly in Chiang Mai, Chiang Rai, Mae Hong Son, Nan, and Tak Provinces. Successful eradication programs together with highland programs of agricultural development and crop substitution in northern Thailand have reduced poppy cultivation to minimal levels.

Lai Chau Province, situated between China and Laos, is a major opium-poppy cultivation area in Vietnam, as is Nghe An Province, in the areas bordering Laos. In China, small crops of opium poppies are cultivated by ethnic minority groups in the mountainous frontier regions of Yunnan Province, particularly along the border area with Burma's Kokang area in Shan State.

It is noteworthy that the dominant ethnic groups of mainland Southeast Asia are not poppy cultivators. The Burmans and Shan of Burma, the Lao of Laos, the Thai of Thailand, the Han Chinese of Yunnan, China, and the Vietnamese of Vietnam are lowlanders and do not traditionally cultivate opium poppies. Rather, it is the ethnic minority highlander groups, such as the Wa, Pa-O, Palaung, Lahu, Lisu, Hmong, and Akha who grow poppies in the highlands of mainland Southeast Asia.

A typical household of mainland Southeast Asian highlanders averages between five and 10 persons, including two to five adults. Such a household of poppy farmers can cultivate and harvest about 1 acre of opium poppy per year. Most of the more fertile fields can support opium-poppy cultivation for 10 years or more without fertilization or insecticides before the soil is depleted and new fields must be cleared.

CONCLUSION

Opium may be used in many forms. It can be eaten, smoked, or dissolved in alcohol or water for drinking. Opium can also be used to make heroin, morphine, and other potent drugs, which may be injected or ingested orally. In many regions of the world where illegal opium farms operate, laboratories are also set up to process opium into forms of the drug suitable for sale on the global illicit drug market. Much of the difficulty in eliminating the illegal opium trade can be attributed to the substantial profit opium growers can achieve on even relatively small harvests.

Reference

U.S. Drug Enforcement Administration. "Opium Poppy Cultivation and Heroin Processing in Southeast Asia." *Drug Enforcement Agency document, DEA-20026.* Available online. URL: http://www.usdoj.gov/dea/pubs/intel/20026/20026.html. Downloaded on July 16, 2004.

ORLANDEZ Gamboa, Alberto (a.k.a. Caracol)

Alberto Orlandez Gamboa (a.k.a. Caracol) is said to run the most powerful drug trafficking organization on the north coast of Colombia. Orlandez Gamboa reputedly exploits maritime and air routes to the Dominican Republic, Haiti, Puerto Rico, and other Caribbean islands to smuggle tons of cocaine and marijuana into the United States. Orlandez Gamboa also uses front companies and banks to launder millions of dollars in drug proceeds.

Reference

Thomas A. Constantine. "International Organized Crime Syndicates and Their Impact on the U.S." U.S. Department of Justice. Available online. URL: http://www.dea.gov/pubs/cngrtest/ct980226.htm. Downloaded on July 28, 2004.

ORTIZ, Juan Antonio

Juan Antonio Ortiz was a member of the Gulf cartel, which operated out of Mexico and distributed cocaine and marijuana into the United States for more than 10 years. He worked for Juan García Abrego. Ortiz was highly placed in García Abrego's organization. He had knowledge of payments to high officials in office and personally supervised the shipment of drugs across the borders. He claimed that in a several year span, he transported more than 10 tons of cocaine into the United States.

In 1996 he testified against his former boss during Abrego's Houston trial.

See also: GARCÍA ABREGO, JUAN.

OSANO, Kenji

Kenji Osano was a Japanese underworld kingpin and chairman of Kokusai Kogyo Company. A long time Yakuza higher-up, he was a lifelong friend of Kakuei Tanaka, a legendary Japanese political leader with ties to the underworld. He was linked to a kickback scandal in the 1970s concerning other Japanese government officials and the Lockheed corporation. One of the largest holders of hotel beachfront properties in Hawaii, Osano died in 1986.

OUTLAWS

The Outlaws Motorcycle Club, also called the American Outlaw Association, was founded by John Davis in 1959 in Chicago, Illinois. The club has about 34 chapters in the United States and Canada with about 900 members, it is not a nationwide association. It is regional. Mostly located from just a little west of the Mississippi to the east coast. The club also has chapters in Australia. Their westernmost chapter is in Oklahoma City, the headquarters for the south region. Chicago is the headquarters for the central region, and Detroit is the headquarters for the northern region. Detroit has been the mother chapter since 1984, having moved from Chicago when a new national club president was elected.

The Outlaws' colors are affectionately known as "Charlie," a white skull with crossed pistons on a black background—a modern Jolly Roger. The skull has beady red eyes, which are supposed to look out for trouble behind the wearer's back. The pistons are outlined in red. Charlie is borrowed from the back of Marlon Brando's black leather jacket in the *The Wild One.* The emblem is briefly visible in a fight scene as Brando falls backwards. The club motto is simple: "God forgives, Outlaws don't."

While Outlaws chapters operate independently, regional and national officers control drug trafficking, relations with other motorcycle gangs, and the distribution of the club's profits. The Outlaws are involved in extortion, contract murders, motor vehicle thefts, gun- and explosives running, armed robbery, rape, and mail fraud, in addition to drug trafficking and prostitution.

Outlaws members must sell drugs and own at least one handgun. Members work in pairs to avoid screw-ups and to avoid situations where the club may be humiliated or disgraced. A lone biker is a tempting target for punks trying to impress someone.

Drug trafficking is the Outlaws' main source of income. "Canadian Blue," diazepam (Valium), is manufactured in clandestine Ontario laboratories and smuggled across the border, usually to Chicago. It is then distributed to different chapters. Some pay cash for the drugs, others trade weapons, women, or methamphetamine. The Florida chapters buy the club's cocaine from Colombian and Cuban suppliers. The Outlaws also manufacture and distribute cocaine and methamphetamine in the Fort Lauderdale area. They own property in south Florida where smugglers dock and unload their boats. The Milwaukee chapter controls the methamphetamine market in Wisconsin. The Outlaws also control methamphetamine laboratories in Georgia.

Like the Hells Angels, the Outlaws today claim they are a motorcycle club interested in motorcycle gatherings where enthusiasts meet and exchange information and enjoy the camaraderie of other motorcycle riders. However, Outlaws members have also been linked in the United States and elsewhere with violence, including extortion, drug distribution, and even murder.

One incident occurred on September 27, 2002, according to the *St. Petersburg Times,* as reported by Graham Brink: "Federal agents . . . arrested the club's international president James 'Frank' Wheeler, who faces a six-count indictment that accuses him of racketeering, murder, extortion, drug dealing and obstruction of justice. National vice president Dennis Pellegrini, 44, was arrested in Michigan and faces drug conspiracy charges."

Harry Joseph Bowman, another top ranking Outlaws president, made the Federal Bureau of Investigation's (FBI's) Top Ten Most Wanted list on March 14, 1998, with charges including, "Racketeering Influenced Corrupt Organizations (RICO); RICO Conspiracy; Conspiracy to Distribute Controlled Substances; Use of Violent Crimes in Aid of Racketeering; Distribution and Possession with Intent to Distribute Controlled Substances; Malicious Damage or Destruction by Explosive of Property Affecting Interstate Commerce; Possession of a Firearm by a Convicted Felon," according to his "wanted" poster. Bowman was apprehended and arrested on June 8, 1999 by FBI officers in suburban Sterling Heights, Michigan, at a residence.

In another example, on October 25, 2002, in London, Ontario, the Royal Canadian Mounted Police hit the Outlaws chapter in a predawn raid. According to the Canadian Press reporting on that same day, "By day's end, 56 suspected members of Ontario's second-largest bike gang and their associates faced 173 charges." Included in that cadre of detainees was Canadian national president Mario Parente.

See also: MOTORCYCLE GANGS.

Reference

Southeastern Connecticut Gang Activities Group (SEGAG). "Outlaws." Available online. URL: http://www.segag.org. Downloaded on July 16, 2004.

OZBIZERDIK, Onur

Onur Ozbizerdik is the stepson of Alaatin Cakici, one of Turkey's most notorious and feared godfathers. Alaatin was married to Ugur Kilic, daughter of Dundar Kilic; however, the couple became estranged. She was on a ski vacation in Uludag, at a posh resort. "When Ugur Kilic saw Keskin, who had previously been Cakici's chauffeur, she asked him what he was doing there at the hotel reception desk. The reply came in the form of bullets from Keskin's gun. Onur, who was still 12 years old, watched in terror as his mother was cut down. He swore that one day he would take vengeance for his mother," reported the *Turkish Daily News* (December 12, 1999). "Cakici justified the murder of his former wife by saying, 'She was talking too much.'"

Onur was committed to joining the same career as his father and grandfather. The elder Kilic even hired an underworld tutor for young Onur, Osman Donmez. He was initiated into the family business at 14, the same age as his grandfather, when he stabbed an unsuspecting passerby. He later shot a barman, wounding him in the genitals. It soon became apparent that Onur was a sociopath and an up-and-comer.

According to http://wwwgeocities.com/OrganizedCrimeSyndicates, "Three months following the death of his grandfather Onur marked his ascent by shooting Gencay Cakici and his wife in an attack aimed at Alaatin. This attack was meant to settle the score between not only Onur and Alaatin but Cakici and Onur's new mentor Osman Donmez. Donmez had been shot by Cakici's nephew Kenan Ali Gursel in an attack ordered by the powerful mafia don Alaatin Cakici."

Onur was arrested, charged, and convicted in the attack of Cakici and his wife, both of whom survived. Onur is now a Mafia don to be reckoned with, and the Turkish underworld is collectively holding its breath as it watches some of its older dons die off, and its younger dons ascend.

See also: BASAK, HUSEYIN; DONMEZ, OSMAN; KILIC, DUNDAR; UGURLU, ABUZER.

OZU, Kinosuke

This Japanese crime lord experienced his golden age during the American Occupation following World War II. He became famous for creating a series of speakeasies in the area known then as Harmonica Alley (Harmonica Yokocho), near the Shinjuku area of Tokyo, not far from the red light district. None of them survive today. At one point, immediately following World War II, Ozu, leader of the Ozu-guni, controlled 45,000 black-market open-air stands in and around Tokyo, employing almost 500,000 people.

PAGANS

The Pagans gang ranks among the fiercest outlaw bikers in the United States, with about 900 members in 44 chapters between New York and Florida. They are the only major gang without international chapters, although they have ties to gangs in Canada. Most chapters are in New Jersey, Pennsylvania, Delaware, and Maryland.

The Pagans are more nomadic than other clubs. Chapters have been known to move overnight. The club also does not have a geographically fixed mother chapter as do the Hells Angels in Oakland, the Outlaws in Detroit, and the Bandidos in Corpus Christi. Instead Pagan operations are guided by a mother club made up of 13 to 20 former chapter presidents, who wear a black number 13 on the back of their colors to indicate their special status. The mother club alternates meetings between Suffolk and Nassau Counties in Long Island, New York. Members meet at each other's homes or elsewhere rather than at clubhouses. The Pagan president and vice president are figureheads who really do not run the club, although the president sets the price of the drugs that the gangs sells. As a show of class, the Pagans give their president, Paul "Ooch" Ferry, the same salary paid to the president of the United States, about $200,000 a year.

Prostitution is an extremely profitable operation. Many of the Pagan girlfriends or female associates generate money for the club by selling themselves. Many of the women the Pagans put to work as prostitutes are runaways. The biker gangs rape them and call it training. Sometimes the Pagans photograph them for blackmail. Some girls are abused and then let go; some stay with the club; others are never found.

The Pagans' propensity for violence and their proximity to mob turf has earned the club the best connections to traditional organized crime among the Big Four motorcycle gangs. Pagans act as drug couriers, enforcers, bodyguards, and hit men for the mob, mostly in Pennsylvania and New Jersey. They associate with the Genovese and Gambino families. Cooperation between the groups proceeds slowly. Two prospects may be asked to prove that they are worthy by clubbing a trade unionist with baseball bats when he fails to vote the way the mob wants him to. Pagans and mobsters gradually cooperate in extortions, counterfeiting, car theft, and drug trafficking.

The Pagans make and distribute most of the methamphetamine and PCP in the northeastern United States—amounts worth about $15 million a year. They have their own chemists and laboratories that supply dealers in Connecticut, New York, New Jersey, Pennsylvania, Virginia, Maryland, and Ohio. They also deal in cocaine, marijuana, and killerweed (parsley sprinkled with PCP).

They have also been known to bring in drugs from the West Coast. In 1997 sources indicated that the majority of the nation's PCP supply was manufactured and distributed by Los Angeles–based street gangs. While buses, trains, and airlines are used to transport PCP from California manufacturers, private automobiles are believed to be the primary means for transporting PCP across the country. Female couriers are also used, along with the U.S. mail system. Places to conceal PCP and other drugs include tires, behind radios, in antennas, and wrapped in plastic inside the gas tanks.

The Pagan enforcement team is a gang of 13 members, the Black T-shirt Gang. When problems arise, members load into two vans and are said to be "TCB" (taking care of business). Reprisal from a Pagan usually consists of two shots in the back of the head from a .38-caliber double automatic Colt and being stamped on. That is the telltale sign of a Pagan hit.

In June 1998 a group of Pagans was arrested in Pennsylvania for selling and distributing drugs to members of an Amish community. In 2002 a highly violent confrontation between Hells Angels and Pagans members resulted in national headlines and confirmed that both gangs were still very strongly tied to their outlaw traditions.

See also: RICHTER, KEITH EDWARD.

Reference

Southeastern Connecticut Gang Activities Group (SEGAG). "Pagans." Available online. URL: http://www.segag.org. Downloaded on July 16, 2004.

PALAZZOLO, Giuseppe

"Police believe the arrest of Giuseppe Palazzolo brings them closer to their ultimate target—the 'boss of bosses' Bernardo Provenzano, who is believed to head the Sicilian Mafia," the BBC reported when Palazzolo was arrested on March 13, 2001. The BBC also reported that letters from Provenzano's wife were found, giving clues about his hideout. The BBC continued, "Mr. Palazzolo is accused of being a Mafia middleman whose alleged role included buying property on behalf of Mr. Provenzano."

Provenzano is Italy's most powerful and most elusive Mafia don. He has been on the run for more than 40 years, and at one point underworld associates had the Italian authorities believing that Provenzano might even be dead, but the arrest of Palazzolo put that

rumor to rest. Palazzolo was his financial link to the outside world. Palazzolo enabled Provenzano to secure lines of credit and consumate some of his biggest deals. According to http://www.geocities.com/OrganizedCrimeSyndicates, "Palazzolo often met with Provenzano and discussed his financial dealings many of which involved the heads of other clans throughout the country. In one such encounter, Palazzolo sat and discussed with Provenzano investing in an agricultural business with Salvatore Biondo and Toto Riina."

Palazzolo was aged 51 at the time of his arrest in Caltanissetta. His capture was easily the biggest blow in bringing down the most elusive Mafia don on the European continent today.

See also: AGLIERI, PIETRO; BARGARELLA, LEOLUCA; BRUSCA, GIOVANNI; CORLEONE CLAN; FALCONE, GIOVANNI; PROVENZANO, BERNARDO; RIINA, SALVATORE; SPERA, BENEDETTO.

PARADIS, Peter (a.k.a. Buddy)

Peter Paradis, nicknamed Buddy, was born in the mid-1960s and began to dance in Montreal strip clubs at the age of 16. By age 18 Paradis had entered a far more profitable career: drug trafficking.

In 1994 Paradis was approached by Renaud Jomphe, who was often called the King of Verdun. Jomphe, one of the Rock Machine motorcycle gang's founding members, wanted Paradis to work for him. Sensing the potential for big profits, the former stripper turned drug trafficker agreed.

On October 18, 1996, as the war between the Rock Machine and the Hells Angels raged, Renaud Jomphe was assassinated. Jomphe, accompanied by fellow Rock Machine Christian Deschenes and associate Raymond Laureau, were dining at the Kim Hoa Restaurant in Verdun when a Hells Angels hit man approached their table and blasted away. Deschenes was also killed, while Laureau was struck in the shoulder.

Upon Jomphe's death, Paradis took over his drug distribution network. This enabled him to quickly move up through the ranks of the organization, and in early 1997 Paradis became a member of the Rock Machine. As a member, Paradis had to pay $1,000 a month for the gang's lawyer's fees, but he could easily afford it. As the head of the organization's Verdun operations, his salary had skyrocketed from $2,000 a week to $7,000 a week.

On April 11, 1997, while Paradis drove along Montreal with associates Mario "Marteau" Filion and Simon "Chiki" Lambert, the trio noticed Hells Angels sympathizer and drug dealer Raymond Vincent walking along the street. Paradis later said that Lambert, wearing a ski mask, got out of the automobile and fired three shots at Vincent, who later died from the wounds.

One of Paradis's pushers approached him with the complaint that Hells Angels sympathizer Éric Perfechino was stealing his business. The Rock Machine advised him to "do what you have to do" and furnished him with a gun. Perfechino was killed on January 3, 1998.

On August 10, 1998, after being dropped off in front of his Lasalle home by bodyguard Daniel "Poutine" Leclerc, Paradis was shot four times by Hells Angels associates. He barely escaped death but spent eight days in the hospital.

Things got worse in March 1999 for Paradis, as he, along with eight associates, were arrested on drug-trafficking charges.

In July 2000 Paradis became the first Rock Machine member to turn government witness when he testified against his eight codefendants. All were found guilty, four on Canada's first antigang prosecution. Paradis was a confident witness and was sentenced to 12 years for his crimes. He has since written a book about his experience in a biker gang.

See also: BANDIDOS.

Reference

Gary Francoeur. "Peter 'Buddy' Paradis." Wiseguy-Wally. Available online. URL: http://www.geocities.com/wiseguywally/PeterParadis.html. Downloaded on July 16, 2004.

—G.F.

PATINO-FOMEQUE, Victor

Victor Patino-Fomeque, who surrendered to Colombian authorities in June 1995, had managed the Cali drug Mafia's maritime drug-smuggling operations in Buenaventura, Colombia. In May 1996 Patino-Fomeque received a 12-year prison sentence. Due to Colombia's lenient penal codes, however, Patino-Fomeque probably will not be required to serve out his full sentence. Furthermore, Patino-Fomeque allegedly continues to direct his drug-trafficking organization from prison.

Reference

David Amoruso. "Victor Patino-Foque." Gangsters Inc. Available online. URL://gangstersinc.tripod.com/Patino-Foque. Downloaded on July 16, 2004.

—D.A.

PECKERWOODS

A term first used in the South to deride white racists, today *Peckerwoods* also refers to organized racist activity in and out of the nation's prisons. In the late 1980s, recruitment of young men and women in many of the nation's prisons helped lead to the emergence of white-power street gangs similar to the neo-Nazi skinheads, but with one major difference: Many Neo-Nazi skinheads disavow any form of drug use. Peckerwoods, like most gangs, earn their money from drug dealing, clandestine drug labs, and gun running. Women in this movement are called Featherwoods.

The typical Peckerwood gang has approximately five to 20 members, who range in age from the early teens to mid-20s. Most of these gangs lack leadership and structure. Common tattoos include Peckerwood, White Pride, White Power, WP, Wood, SWP (Supreme White Power), and other Nazi-related insignias. The Peckerwood style is derived from Latino gangs (Pendelton shirts and baggy pants) and skinheads (Doc Marten boots, flight jackets, and, in some instances, shaved heads).

Criminal activities perpetrated by Peckerwoods include theft, burglaries, vehicle thefts, weapon charges, and possession and sale of narcotics. They have also been known to participate in numerous racially motivated assaults and murders.

Reference

KnowGangs. "Peckerwoods." Available online. URL: http://www.knowgangs.com. Downloaded on July 16, 2004.

PEDRIOLI, Richard (a.k.a. Alvin Penning)

Fugitive Richard Pedrioli, an international firearms smuggler with links to the Japanese Mafia, surrendered to deputy marshals in Manila, Philippines, in July 1999 after nearly five years on the lam.

Pedrioli, an Oakland, California, native, was previously convicted of unlawfully exporting munitions.

When he violated his supervised release by leaving the United States, the Marshals Service was called in to find him.

Deputies from eastern California tracked Pedrioli, 56, to the island nation of the Philippines. With the assistance of the Philippine National Police and the State Department Diplomatic Security Service, the deputies coordinated the search efforts.

"We had known that he was in Southeast Asia, predominantly the Philippines, since November 1997," lead deputy Dave Hiebert said.

Pedrioli peddled weapons in the Philippines, Vietnam, and Cambodia. He was able to maneuver at will while overseas by using false forms of identification and bogus passports.

The fugitive's penchant for arms smuggling can be traced back to his arrest by agents of the U.S. Bureau of Alcohol, Tobacco and Firearms (ATF) in 1988. Documentation indicates that he had smuggled more than 3,500 guns into the Philippines. He pleaded guilty to that charge but was rearrested prior to his sentencing after he fraudulently obtained another individual's passport and attempted to smuggle 70 additional firearms into the islands in 1989.

He was subsequently sent to prison in Lompoc, California, to serve his federal sentence. However, he allegedly continued to operate a weapons-smuggling operation while in prison.

He was later released from the Lompoc prison and placed on probation, but he purchased yet another large quantity of firearms in 1994 using a fictitious name. Hiebert said that when he learned that the ATF was going to press new charges against him, he fled the country.

This is when the Marshals Service took over. Pedrioli was quickly elevated to the agency's "15 Most Wanted" list because of his extensive international ties to arms dealers and organized criminal enterprises such as the Yakuza, or Japanese Mafia.

"He was juiced into everything," Hiebert said, referring to Pedrioli's links to gun running, drug trafficking, jewel theft, and extortion.

Philippine authorities linked Pedrioli to the assassination of an executive of the Sumitomo Bank of Japan. The fugitive allegedly sold the firearms to Yakuza members, who in turn carried out the murder.

In September 1994 Pedrioli, under the name Alvin Penning, tried to raise money by demanding a massive payment from the management of the New World Hotel in Makati City, Philippines. The extor-

tionist was foiled, however, when the hotel establishment worked with the Makati City Police. Local officers arrested Pedrioli along with two others during an entrapment operation, but Pedrioli never did any time because the hotel managers failed to follow up and attend the trial hearings.

Hiebert and fellow eastern California deputy Gary Yandell, along with Filipino law-enforcement authorities, worked diligently to shut off Pedrioli's support base in both the United States and the Philippines. The deputies were aided by the second-in-command of the Philippines immigration department. This individual, 10 years earlier; had attended a training course at the Marshals Service's Special Operations Group headquarters in Louisiana. Hiebert had been one of the instructors. Because of this unique connection, Hiebert was able to call upon this official for invaluable assistance.

"He put 12 agents at our disposal," Hiebert said. "We had carte blanche."

The unrelenting pressure of the combined law-enforcement efforts to cut off the fugitive from his associates proved the deciding factor. Described by investigators as "the ultimate con man," Pedrioli soon burned all his bridges by double-crossing and angering close associates.

With nobody else to turn to, he began to beg his family for money. But it was Pedrioli's family that was feeding investigators information on a daily basis.

"We had run down all his aliases, his family and friends," Hiebert said. "He kept pissing people off and they got tired of his scams and being used."

The crafty fugitive, unable to escape this stranglehold, eventually surrendered to deputies in Manila and was arrested without incident.

"Basically, we ran him out of resources," Hiebert said. "That's how we caught him."

Pedrioli was then debriefed by a number of domestic and foreign law-enforcement agencies. His sentencing is pending.

Reference

Marshal's Monitor. "Deputies Corner Firearms Smuggler in Manila." U.S. Department of Justice. July 1999. Available online. URL: http://www.usmarshals.gov/monitor/july-1999/jul99-2.html. Downloaded on December 16, 2004.

PERAFAN, Justo Pastor (a.k.a. the Big Boss)

According to the Drug Enforcement Administration, Perafan was the boss of the now-defunct Bogotá cartel, and his personal wealth is said to be about $10 billion. Perafan's trafficking organization smuggled multiton quantities of cocaine to the United States and Europe via containerized maritime cargo. Perafan was a fugitive dating back to 1994 when a U.S. grand jury indicted him. He was also fleeing a similar indictment from his native Colombia. Interpol agents and Colombian National Police apprehended Perafan in a shopping mall in Venezuela in May 1996, but it was not until November 1997, after a long and politically sensitive extradition, that he arrived in the United States to face trial on charges of having smuggled more than 30 tons of cocaine between 1988 and 1997. He was tried in New York City.

Perafan, who liked to be known as the big boss, was convicted on June 21, 1998. He was considered the last of the major drug lords—his lifestyle and brutal violence epitomized the zenith of power of the Colombian drug lords. A short, stocky, dark-haired man, Perafan was visited by his 10 children during his trial. At the age of 51, in 1998, Perafan was sentenced to no more than 30 years in prison, the fullest extent of the sentence under the extradition agreement with Venezuela.

See also: BERNAL-MADRIGAL, ALEJANDRO; BOGOTÁ CARTEL.

PERSICO, Carmine (a.k.a. Junior, the Snake)

Carmine Persico, Jr. was born in 1937 in Brooklyn. His father, Carmine, Sr., was a soldier in the Genovese crime family. To his friends Carmine Persico was known on the streets as Junior, and to his enemies he was known as the Snake. As a teenager he became the leader of a group of young thugs and terrorists called The Garfield Boys. At age 17 he reputedly killed his first victim, but before he could be convicted on the testimony of a state witness known only as the Blue Angel, his older brother Alphonse confessed to the murder and went to prison for 18 years.

Carmine Persico was one of the main enforcers for the Colombo family. When he was a capo he had a crew that consisted of many heavy hit men such as: Alphonse "Ally Boy" Persico (Carmine's brother), Gennaro Langella, Anthony Abbatemarco, Joey Brancato, and associate Hugh "Apples" McIntosh. Even though Apples could not become a made man, he still was a very successful enforcer for the family and ultimately became Carmine Persico's bodyguard.

Carmine Persico was a genuine tough guy. Small in stature, scrawny, and ugly in appearance, with one hand twisted from a bullet wound, he had also been shot in the face during the first Gallo war. The incident, famous in mob lore, placed him and a partner in crime, Alphonse D'Ambrosia, sitting in a car as a group of Gallo hoods drove by. The Gallos opened fire with an M-1 carbine. Ambrosia was shot in the chest and the Snake got one in the face but spat the bullet out and then drove them both to the hospital.

Persico became boss for the first time at the end of the second Gallo war. Although it has not been proven, most people believe that he pulled the strings from prison, while Thomas DiBella was appointed acting boss. When Persico was released from prison, DiBella stepped down and handed the seat to Persico. His tenure as boss of the Colombo crime family was marked by his troubles with the law. Of his first 13 years in the seat, he spent 10 of them in prison. When he was out of prison, he operated the family from the Diplomat Social Club on the corner of third Avenue and Carroll Street in the Carroll Gardens neighborhood of Brooklyn. Here were the main players of the Persico faction of the Colombo family: Carmine, when he was out of prison, his brother Ally Boy, Jerry Langella, Hugh MacIntosh, Carmine Franzese (the brother of Sonny), Greg Scarpa, and Anthony, Vincent, and Joe, Jr., the sons of Joseph Colombo.

Throughout the 80s, the Colombo family was under massive pressure as the Federal Bureau of Investigation (FBI) and city and state organized-crime strike forces attacked them and the other four families on all fronts. In 1986 Anthony, Joseph, and Vincent Colombo were convicted for racketeering, conspiracy, and narcotic offenses and went to prison for varying terms. Carmine and Alphonse Persico and Jerry Langella were arrested and convicted for labor and construction racketeering and extortion and were sentenced to terms of 39, 12, and 65 years, respectively. In addition, Carmine and Langella were sentenced to 100 years for crimes under the RICO Act in what became known as the Commission Trial, effectively removing them from the streets of New York forever. But in removing the Snake from his stronghold, the government was helping to set the stage for the third war in the family.

Incarcerated in Lompoc Penitentiary in California, Carmine Persico still exerted control and strong influence over his family. He made Vic Orena acting boss, and in doing so he created the third family war.

After this third war, which totally decimated the Colombo family, Carmine's son Alphonse—"Allie"—was reputedly in charge as acting boss. However, he was quickly arrested by the FBI. If Carmine Persico is a real family man, then he probably is glad to be in prison because the Colombo family is not doing well.

See also: GIGANTE, VINCENT.

Reference

David Amoruso. "Colombo Crime Family." Gangsters Incorporated. Available online. URL: http://gangstersinc.tripod.com/Col.html. Downloaded on July 15, 2004.

—*D.A.*

PHARAON, Gaith Rashad

Born on September 7, 1940, in Saudi Arabia, Gaith Rashad Pharaon is a white male, 175 centimeters in height, and weighs 113 kilograms. He is of stocky build with thinning black hair, graying at the temples. He normally wears a small pointed beard but has been seen with only a mustache. Pharaon is a citizen of Saudi Arabia and travels on a Saudi passport. He speaks Arabic, French, English, and some Greek. He smokes cigars and wears traditional Arab clothing when in Saudi Arabia. In other countries, he usually wears Western-style business attire.

Pharaon owns a yacht named *Le Pharaon* with a picture of the Egyptian Sphinx painted on the stern. Its home port is believed to be London, although there is no indication that this yacht has been there in many years. Since 1992 Pharaon has traveled through Europe, North Africa, the Caribbean and Latin America, and Asia.

Pharaon is extremely wealthy and has numerous contacts within governments around the world. His son competes in international speedboat races, which Pharaon sometimes watches.

Though still at large, Pharaon has been connected to one of the largest commercial frauds and the largest bank failure in history. The fall of the Bank of Credit and Commerce International, or B.C.C.I., took almost $12 billion in depositors' money and left some 250,000 unpaid creditors around the world. Thousands of families lost their life savings in the bank's collapse. B.C.C.I. officials and their agents are charged with bribing bank regulators and central bankers in Pakistan, Nigeria, Morocco, Senegal, Tunisia, Ivory Coast, Congo, Zambia, Argentina, and Peru. In some cases, B.C.C.I. funds were used to defraud lending agencies, including the International Monetary Fund.

In the United States, B.C.C.I. illegally purchased American banks and defrauded American investors and the U.S. government. A key figure in the B.C.C.I. conspiracy was Gaith Rashad Pharaon. On November 15, 1991, a U.S. court in Washington, D.C., issued an arrest warrant for Pharaon, charging him with fraud, conspiracy, and racketeering. The hunt for Pharaon continues.

Reference

U.S. International Broadcasting Bureau. "International Crime Alert: Gaith Rashad Pharaon." Available online. URL: http://www.ibb.gov/fugitives/pharaon.html. Downloaded on July 15, 2004.

PHILADELPHIA Crime Family

The Philadelphia crime family is not doing well. Nicodemo Scarfo and the family are still recovering from the blow that followed when they were decimated by the Federal Bureau of Investigation (FBI) and a wave of soldiers turned informants.

Estimated membership is approximately 100. The family's first Don was Salvatore Sabella, who ruled from 1911 to 1927. Sabella started the family in 1911; with the surge of Italian immigrants in that area, he had no trouble convincing men to do his bidding. He was deported even after being found not guilty for a shooting in 1927.

The family's primary illegal activities include extortion, drug trafficking, and loan sharking. The current reputed boss is Joseph "Skinny Joey" Merlino, who was sentenced to 14 years in prison on December 3, 2001, on racketeering charges. Merlino's underboss is Joseph Ligambi (who may have become acting boss). The family's consigliere is George Borgesi (also sentenced to 14 years in prison for racketeering).

Reference

David Amoruso. "Philadelphia Crime Families." Gangsters Incorporated. Available online. URL: http://www.gangstersinc.tripod.com/Philadelphia.html. Downloaded on July 15, 2004.

—*D.A.*

PING, Zhang Ai (a.k.a. Ah Gow)

Zhang Ai Ping, a.k.a. Ah Gow, was a typical member of a Chinese street gang. He pleaded guilty to a number of federal criminal charges in 2001, not the least of which included kidnapping, rape, and armed robbery. His presentence report prepared for the U.S. Attorney's Office in New York makes him sound like a one-man crime wave.

Ah Gow was born in Fuzhou in the Fujian Province of China on March 11, 1968, the fourth child of Li Mao Ying and Zhang Ho Hua. His parents are former teachers who still live in China. Along with a brother and sister, Ah Gow entered the United States illegally in 1992. He told the probation officer that he no longer had much contact with his family.

He was once treated for noninfectious tuberculosis and told the probation officer that he has limited ability to read and write Chinese and speaks no English. His health remains poor from his bout with TB.

Ah Gow faced a $20,000 debt to the snakeheads (a Chinese gang that specializes in human trafficking) for bringing him to America, but he had no opportunity to learn any kind of meaningful trade. The most money he ever reported earning in a year was a taxable income of $8,400 in 1996. There was nowhere Ah Gow could turn except to crime, and he took to his new career vigorously.

Ah Gow joined the Fukienese Flying Dragons, which the U.S. government considers an ongoing criminal enterprise. He first came to the attention of the government in 1994 when with three other men he robbed a Forsythe Street apartment where approximately 20 people had gathered. It was payday for the workers at a Chinatown restaurant, and the men knew there would be significant cash at the apartment. When one of the workers tried to hide a small amount of his hard-earned wage, Ah Gow beat the man severely. The Flying Dragons escaped with approximately $1,200.

The same month, Ah Gow, Huang Yong, and two other men robbed a mah jongg parlor near Confucius Plaza in Chinatown, again beating one of their victims. The gangsters fled with more than $12,000, some jewelry, and guns. Later in the summer, Ah Gow and a street brother staged a robbery of a delivery truck. The driver had tipped them to the contents of the truck, and Ah Gow stole $6,000.

They later robbed a gambling den run by the rival Tung On gang on Division Street, where they received $40,000. At the same time, the government charged, they were extorting money from a Chinese dentist in Chinatown. Then in an apartment robbery in New Jersey Ah Gow stole immigration documents and between $5,000 and $6,000.

In fall 1994, Ah Gow's *dailo* (a high-ranking member of a Chinese gang), Lin Bo, kidnapped a group of five illegal aliens, and had Ah Gow hold them at gunpoint for several days. The aliens were being held until their snakehead paid a $20,000 ransom. For his part in the scam, Ah Gow received $1,000.

When he reported to prison to begin to serve his 135-month sentence—which would include English as a Second Language and vocational training—Ah Gow left behind a wife and a six-year-old son in Brooklyn.

When the time came for Ah Gow to enter his plea, he was embittered and angry with America and the government, which he thought was persecuting him. After all, he reasoned, the girl he was accused of raping, one of the illegal aliens he was guarding, had not protested that much, and he felt she had it coming.

See also: TONGS.

Reference

Mark C. Gribben. "Ah Gow: Life and Times of a Chinese Gangster." Reprinted by permission.

—M.G.

PIRACY

The U.S. State Department, as does the International Chamber of Commerce, issues warning to both professional shipping companies as well as pleasure-craft operators about the real and constant threat of piracy on the open seas. Current hot spots in the world are the waters off India, around the east coast of Africa, Latin America, the Caribbean, Indonesia, and China. The State Department warns that Americans may be at particular risk of violence in Guatemala. According to the U.S. State Department, "Maritime piracy is a persistent and growing problem . . . targeting both pleasure and commercial vessels. Pleasure yachters are advised to review the current security situation with their local agent when planning itineraries and to exercise particular care when sailing in the Strait of Malacca between Riau Province and Singapore and in the waters north of Sulawesi and Kalimantan."

"Some countries turn a blind eye to the lucrative business of piracy, while others—notably China—have confiscated the stolen ships and turned the pirates loose to rob again," writer Kathleen McKoon-Hennick wrote in *The Modern Face of Piracy.* "A look at the *Weekly Piracy Report* published by the International Chamber of Commerce, illustrates just how common piracy is. Even the United States Merchant Marine Academy at Kings Point has begun training their cadets to deal with pirates." Piracy is defined as any crimes committed against another on the high seas in international waters. While piracy seems like an anachronistic way to make a living, it is a growing and lucrative business for those who have brought piracy back to the forefront. It is now big business, and many nations are taking the threat seriously, especially the United States and Britain.

"Following the economic slump in Southeast Asia and cuts in spending on naval patrols by many countries, including Indonesia, commercial shipowners in the region are complaining that robbery by pirates at sea is becoming increasingly frequent and violent," wrote Michael Richardson in an article entitled "Sea Piracy." "They warn that unless governments take more effective and coordinated action, pirate attacks could cause a major disaster in a crowded international sea-lane, such as the Straits of Malacca or the Strait of Singapore, which are among the world's busiest shipping channels."

"Piracy is arguably the single greatest menace to modern shipping today," Singapore Shipping Association president Lua Cheng Eng said in a recent report to a meeting of Asian shipowners in Tokyo. "Asia has become featured widely as a piracy hot spot. This is a matter of serious concern to us in the shipping and trading community."

Pirates generally come alongside in fast speedboats under cover of darkness. They clamber aboard using grappling hooks as ships slow down to avoid accidents.

The need to address the rising tide of piracy made itself shockingly apparent in 2001 when famed sporting sailor Sir Peter Blake was murdered at the mouth of the Amazon River. Blake has been the daring and dashing yachtsman who had won the America's Cup for New Zealand. On December 6, Blake's 119 foot schooner *Seamster* was boarded by pirates. After threatening the life of crew members, pirates began to withdraw from Blake's boat with their ill-gotten gains. Blake fired on the pirates with a handgun but was shot and killed himself. The murder drew international attention, and the focus for a more meaningful governmental and world policy soon became the talk in many political bodies around the world.

"Pirates continue to operate in areas of the world marked by poverty, political upheaval and war," McKoon-Hendrick wrote. "Rather than fading from the seas along with cutlasses and caravels, reported incidents of piracy are on the rise, and pirates are better equipped and informed than ever. As with piracy of old, merchant ships are favored targets of organized criminal operations, but small time criminals," known as river rats, can be extremely dangerous as well.

In 1999 it did not go unnoticed that pirates were becoming more violent. The Associated Press reported in 1999 that pirates had killed 67 people in 1998 as "compared to 51 in 1997, according to statistics from the London-based International Maritime Bureau. The actual number of reported pirate attacks worldwide fell to 198 in 1998 from an all-time high of 247 in 1997, the bureau said in earlier reports."

There appears to be a strong commitment to address piracy. . . . Much more must be done at the national, regional and global levels in order to suppress this modern threat to international peace and security," Maureen O. Walker, the acting deputy director of the Office of Oceans Affairs of the U.S. State Department, told the United Nations in New York on May 10, 2001. "In our view there are three ways that this can be undertaken. First, national governments should consider establishing inter-ministerial bodies to draw up action plans for preventing such attacks as well as plans for steps to be taken in the event of an attack. Second, surveillance efforts should be augmented. Third, port security should be enhanced through better training in law enforcement and the ability to identify phantom ships.

On the matter of definitions, not all of these attacks on the high seas or in an EEZ [Exclusive Economic Zone] can be classified as traditional acts of piracy, over which all States may exercise jurisdiction. When they occur in port or at anchorage they are more likely proscribed and should be punishable by local criminal law. When the acts endanger the safety of navigation and occur on board foreign flag ships while underway in the territorial sea, international straits or international waters, these acts are frequently not proscribed nor punishable by the criminal law of the coastal State.

The Convention for the Suppression of Unlawful Acts Against the Safety of Maritime Navigation, with its Protocol for the Suppression of Unlawful Acts Against the Safety of Fixed Platforms Located on the Continental Shelf, done at Rome 10 March 1988, was adopted under the IMO's auspices. These instruments can fill many of the jurisdictional gaps highlighted when the acts endanger the safety of international navigation and occur on board national or foreign flag ships while underway in the territorial sea, international straits, or international waters. The Convention requires States parties to criminalize such acts under national law and to cooperate in the investigation and prosecution of their perpetrators. . . .

While we recognize the impending urgency of the calls for action the U.S. also acknowledges that developing countries cannot deal with this on their own. . . . Bilateral and multilateral assistance must begin to address these needs. We believe that this process, which is designed to facilitate coordination and cooperation among UN agencies to promote peaceful uses of the seas, can play a role in alerting donor agencies to this issue and raise awareness in the developing world that such requests should be given a priority by them. UNDP [United Nations Development Program] and other agencies must begin to appreciate the fact that developing countries need support in addressing two issues: enhancing enforcement capability and implementation of port security measures. Donor institutions should be encouraged to engage in a dialogue with developing countries to assess the needs identified to address piracy and report their findings to the Secretary-General.

Capacity can be increased in the developing world to suppress piracy and armed robbery at sea through increased force protection and enhancement of local maritime law enforcement efforts. An increased presence in these locations by cooperating navies and maritime law enforcement vessels may be needed to supplement these efforts. In that connection serious consideration should be given by states sharing borders in areas threatened by piracy to establish bilateral/regional cooperation arrangement. . . .

As piracy and armed robbery at sea are just one aspect of international crime, including transnational organized crime, coordination with the United States Federal Bureau of Investigation (FBI) could enhance regional training efforts. The FBI has expanded its cooperative programs with the police of up to 44 nations. This includes an important training component. In the past five years more than 3,000 international trainees were trained by the FBI in the U.S., and nearly 15,000 were trained in other countries.

More attention should be paid to vessel tracking in terms of current technology. Home port verification should also be studied. Article 110 of the Law of the Sea Convention provides a basis for boarding vessels flying questionable flags. Consideration should be given to increasing the onus on Flag States to make sure they do not register stolen vessels.

There are a number of ways to improve port security so that officials can prevent acts of armed robbery against ships at anchor or in port, to identify stolen vessels and to assist in the apprehension of the criminals. The experience of Brazil is instructive and we commend the Brazilian authorities on their success.

Port personnel need training from the Captain of the Port to the dock workers. The most comprehensive training for Captains of the Port is at the World Maritime University, Malmo, Sweden. The two-year course offered at this institution is world-renowned. The U.S. Agency for International Development has advised that it can fund requests for attendance at this University by developing countries if the request is identified as a priority.

The Coast Guard is available to teach and instruct law enforcement tactics and port security measures and enhancements to member nations. This can serve to reduce and mitigate the piracy threat. Member nations may send their personnel to the United States for training or the Coast Guard can send international training detachments to member nations.

References

Associated Press. "Joint Sea Patrols As Piracy Surges." *Hong Kong Standard*. Available online. URL: http://www.hkstandard.com/online/news/001/asia/news005.htm. Downloaded on July 15, 2004.

BBC. "Call to Combat Asian Sea Piracy." Available online. URL: http://news.bbc.co.uk/1/hi/world/south_asia/1172160.stm. Posted on February 16, 2001.

Kathleen McKoon-Hennick. "The Modern Face of Piracy." About.com. Available online. URL: http://sailing.about.com/library/weekly/aa121401a.htm. Downloaded on July 15, 2004.

Maureen Walker. "Statement at Oceans and Law of the Sea Open-Ended Informal Consultative Process Pursuant to General Assembly Resolution 54/33." United Nations. Available online. URL: http://www.un.int/usa/00_066.htm. Downloaded on July 15, 2004.

UN Atlas of the Oceans. "Piracy and Armed Robbery at Sea." Oceansatlas.org. Available online. URL: http://www.oceansatlas.org/unatlas_gifs/offsiteframe.jsp?url.htm. Downloaded on July 15, 2004.

PIZZA Connection

In the 1960s both the American and Sicilian Mafias discovered that pizza parlors were ideal locations for setting up heroin distribution centers. Afghan, Pakistan, and Turkish opium was processed in Sicily and then transported to the United States. The pizza parlors provided the cover of walk-in traffic with regular customers, and the cash flow of the pizzerias also provided distributors with an easy way to launder their cash. The connection's effects were vast, as the ring was able to press distribution from Boston, Massachusetts, to Milton, Wisconsin.

The ring was forged between the Bonanno family and Gaetano Badalamanti, the top boss of the Ciucull Mafia of Palermo, Sicily. In the 1980s the ring was busted, and more than 150 Mafia members on both sides of the Atlantic were arrested.

Tommaso Buscetta was the government's star witness whose testimony at the New York trial made the difference in the case. He died at an undisclosed location under the witness-protection program, April 2, 2000, after helping to bring down $1.6 billion drug-smuggling operation. The trial lasted 17 months and saw hundreds of witnesses, hours of bugged conversations, and thousands of documents. It significantly crippled the Sicilian heroin trade for sometime, but did not completely destroy it.

Some history professors have opined that the Central Intelligence Agency (CIA) allowed the trade to

help fund the Afghan rebels against the communist Russian intervention. In 1997, Professor Alfred McCoy published *The Politics of Heroin: CIA Complicity in the Global Drug Trade*. According to McCoy, "Former CIA operatives have admitted that this operation led to an expansion of the Pakistan-Afghanistan heroin trade. In 1995 the former CIA director of this Afghan operation, Charles Cogan, admitted sacrificing the drug war to fight the cold war. "'Our main mission was to do as much damage to the Soviets. We didn't really have the resources or the time to devote to an investigation of the drug trade,' he told Australian television."

Reference

Shana Alexander. *The Pizza Connection: Lawyers, Money, Drugs, Mafia.* New York: Weidenfeld & Nicolson, 1988.

PLESCIO, Johnny

Johnny Plescio was born in the mid-1960s and became a founding member of the Rock Machine motorcycle gang in the 1980s. He became known for his strong-arm tactics and was widely respected within the gang.

Plescio was arrested in summer 1993 on a charge of threatening a Montreal police officer. The trial was delayed until February 18, 1994, because Plescio's lawyer, Gary Martin, was also defending a witness in the case, Eric Toupin, a Rock Machine associate who turned informant after being arrested on drug-trafficking charges.

Agent Michel Chartrand testified that, on July 7, 1993, he overheard Plescio telling two acolytes that he was going to "get" officer Jeffrey Stern. Plescio was sentenced to three months in prison on December 7, 1995. That day, while the men were awaiting sentencing, a fight broke out between Plescio, three Rock Machine members, and two members of the Jokers, a Hells Angels puppet club. Plescio, Luc Gauthier, Paul Magnan, and the Paradis brothers, Paul and Robert, were arrested and charged with disturbing the peace.

On June 18, 1997, Johnny Plescio and fellow Rock Machine member Frederic Faucher and Robert "Tout Tout" Léger flew to Helsingborg, Sweden to attend the Bandidos memorial run for deceased members, but Swedish police learned of the trip and, because of their criminal records, refused the Canadians entry into their country. They were detained 24 hours and shipped back to Canada.

Gaetano Badalamanti, top boss of the Ciucull Mafia of Palermo, Sicily, which formed half of the "pizza connection" drug ring (AP)

Plescio and Fred Faucher traveled to Europe again less than a month later, on July 14, 1997, this time with Rock Machine member Paul "Sasquatch" Porter. The three attended a bike show in Luxembourg and were seen meeting with high-ranking members of the Bandidos motorcycle club.

But Johnny Plescio did not live long enough to see his dream of seeing the Rock Machine become a Bandidos chapter. He was riddled with 16 bullets in his Laval home on September 8, 1998. He was 34 years old. A burned car that contained two machine guns was found in the neighborhood.

Sixty-five people attended his funeral on September 15 to pay their respects to the fallen Rock Machine biker. Police guarded the entrance of the Loreto funeral home in Saint Leonard, and all who entered had to provide identification. Among the visitors, according to police, were Rock Machine members Frederic Faucher, Serge "Merlin" Cyr, and Alain Brunette.

See also: BANDIDOS.

Reference

Gary Francoeur. "Rock Machine/Bandidos." Wiseguy-Wally. Available online. URL: http://www.geocities.com/wiseguywally/RockMachine.html. Downloaded on July 15, 2004.

—G.F.

POISON Clan

The Poison Clan was a drug-smuggling gang based in Jamaica. The organization extensively smuggled mainly crack cocaine into the United States. It trafficked the illegal drug mostly to cities up and down the East Coast and, to a lesser extent, to other cities around the country.

In 1997 authorities successfully prosecuted 30 members the Poison Clan. They were convicted of having committed more than 10 homicides in Virginia and New York.

PORTER, Paul (a.k.a. Sasquatch)

Paul Porter, born in Canada in the early 1960s, is nicknamed Sasquatch because of his size and girth. He allied himself with the Cazzetta brothers in the 1980s and was a founding member of their motorcycle gang, the Rock Machine. An intelligent man, he kept a low profile and moved up to become one of the most powerful members of the gang.

Devon Dale "Chubby" Beckford is led away after arraignment in federal court in July 1997. He and his brother, Dean, were accused of leading the New York City-based Poison Clan. (AP/Democrat and Chronicle)

When a vicious war broke out between the Rock Machine and Hells Angels in 1994, Porter became a target. On May 31, 1997, as he drove down Highway 125 near L'Epiphanie, a car pulled up beside him and someone fired at him. After grazing his left arm, the slug settled in Porter's bulletproof vest. It saved his life.

A few weeks later, on July 17, "Sasquatch" traveled with Rock Machine members Fred Faucher and Johnny Plescio to Luxembourg to meet with the Bandidos international president from Texas, the European president, and chapter presidents from Australia and France during the Bandidos Euro run.

By early 2000, Porter was the third-most-powerful man in the Rock Machine. Only Fred Faucher, head of the Quebec City chapter, and Serge "Merlin" Cyr, leader of the Montreal operations, held more influence. Porter's opinion was respected among members and often sought on serious matters. He left Quebec and helped establish the gang in Ontario. He sponsored the Kingston chapter and became its first president.

Porter also played a major role in forging the truce with the Hells Angels in late 2000 at the Bleu Marin restaurant in Montreal. He was one of the Rock Machine members to accompany Faucher to the meeting. Quebec's six-year biker war, which resulted in the deaths of more than 150 people, came to an end, but the peace would not last.

It seems that Porter was unhappy when his gang became probationary Bandidos on December 1,

2000. While congratulations from Bandidos around the world poured into the Rock Machine's website, Porter's message was quite the opposite: "Hello to all the RMMC. I whish [sic] you all the best with your new colors. Bye my brothers." He then defected to the Hells Angels, taking bikers Johnny "Mini-Me" Spezzano and Steve Burns along with him.

Sasquatch Porter is now a member of the Ontario Nomads chapter, based in Ottawa, and is believed to have been a key player in the patchover, or recruitment, of 168 Ontario bikers to the Hells Angels.

See also: BANDIDOS; HELLS ANGELS.

Reference

Gary Francoeur. "Rock Machine/Bandidos." Wiseguy-Wally. Available online. URL: http://www.geocities.com/wiseguywally/RockMachine.html. Downloaded on July 15, 2004.

—G.F.

POSADAS-OCAMPO, Cardinal Juan Jesus

"The Tijuana Cartel was among the most violent of the Mexican organizations and has been connected by Mexican officials to the violent death of Cardinal Juan Jesus Posadas-Ocampo who was killed in the cross fire of rival drug gangs at the Guadalajara Airport in 1993. During 1994, this group was engaged in a turf battle over methamphetamine territory in San Diego," said Thomas A. Constantine, Drug Enforcement Administration administrator before the Senate Foreign Relations Committee on February 26, 1998. "Twenty-six homicides were committed during one summer as rival groups battled over trafficking regions."

During a Mass celebrated on January 25, 1999, in the chapel of the new apostolic nunciature in Mexico City, Pope John Paul II asked those present—some 200 people, including economic and political personalities—not to forget the sacrifice of Cardinal Juan Jesus Posadas-Ocampo.

Five years after the shocking assassination of the cardinal, who was archbishop of Guadalajara, the murder mystery has not been solved. Civil authorities and church leaders sharply disagree in their theories of the motive for the assassination.

Several different motives for the slaying have been advanced. Cardinal Posadas-Ocampo took the lead role in negotiating new accords by which the Mexican government granted juridical recognition for the Catholic Church—a cause which was highly unpopular among radical groups in Mexico. His Guadalajara diocese was and is one of the main Mexican centers of the international drug traffic which was denounced on various occasions by the cardinal and the Mexican bishops' conference. Newspapers reported that the cardinal himself was in possession of "dangerous information" which could expose government officials who were involved in the drug trade. But in fact government investigators have declined to pursue the possibility that the cardinal's killers may have been motivated by any of those facts.

On May 23, 1993, Cardinal Posadas-Ocampo, accompanied by his driver, was at Guadalajara airport to welcome the nuncio, Archbishop Girolamo Prigione, who was arriving from Mexico City. As the cardinal stepped out of the car, two men ran up and shot both the cardinal and his driver; both died instantly. The shooting continued in the airport parking lot, and five other people were killed.

According to the chief government investigator on the case, the cardinal was the victim of a "crossfire" in an airport confrontation between two rival drug-trading gangs. A few days after the assassination, however, a postmortem confirmed that the bullets that killed the cardinal and his driver had been fired at point-blank range. Obviously the killers were aiming at their target and had an opportunity to see his face.

Faced with these results, the government changed its story and announced that the cardinal had been mistaken for the head of a drug-trafficking gang, Joaquin Loera Guzman, nicknamed El Chapo. The killers were said to be the Arellano Felix brothers, gunmen for a rival gang based in San Diego, California.

Church leaders in Mexico continued to express doubts: How could the gunmen mistake Cardinal Posadas-Ocampo—a well-known public figure—for a drug dealer? Moreover, they pointed out that in physical appearance the cardinal—middle-aged, tall, robust, and wearing a prominent pectoral cross—could not realistically be mistaken for Joaquin Loera Guzman, who was young, short, and slim. So Cardinal Juan Sandoval Iniguez, successor to Cardinal Posadas-Ocampo in Guadalajara, firmly insists that the killers were conscious of their victim's identity.

Investigators have challenged church leaders to provide some evidence for their suspicions that the killing was an intentional attack on the cardinal. The Mexican episcopal conference replied that eyewitnesses had observed "strange movements" at the airport on the day of the assassination: weapons were brought in, and troops and police were mobilized, as if something special were afoot. Yet the gunmen escaped, boarded another plane, flew across country, and still were not intercepted when they landed on Mexican soil. However, the church refused to identify the eyewitnesses, citing concerns for their safety, and the officials heading the government investigation refused to accept "secret" testimony.

The Arellano Félix brothers, still the government's prime suspects, have denied taking part in the killing in separate interviews with the press and with the apostolic nuncio in Mexico.

Both the case and the investigation itself are now confused. On May 24, 1998, an Inter-Institutional Commission—made up of representatives of both the state government of Jalisco and the Guadalajara archdiocese—was set up. By November 30, 1998, that commission had collected 46 personal testimonies, 14 psychiatric reports, and 11 judicial reports. An on-site inquiry had used laser beams to determine the bullets' trajectory. There was an examination into the position of the bullets in the victims' bodies, to ascertain the exact position of the criminals at the time of the shooting. Investigators did their utmost to re-create the scene of the killings precisely.

The investigation has spawned a series of related actions. There have been 18 local and federal trials and 81 investigative reports. Criminal charges have been filed against 73 people, for a variety of alleged offenses; 36 people have been arrested, and 35 are now wanted (two suspects have died). The entire proceedings of the investigation now fills 47 volumes.

The Inter-Institutional Commission had been expected to examine all possible evidence and reach a final conclusion before November 30, 1998. But when that date arrived the commission decided to extend its work "only for a few weeks" in hope of finding a final resolution. For the Mexican government, it was a top priority to bring this case to a definitive close before the arrival of the pope on January 22, 1999. Finally, on November 15, 2002, a Mexican federal judged dismissed the charges, claiming there was not enough to convict

Arellano Félix, who remained in jail on other charges. To the eyes of Sandoval, this confirmed, he said publicly, that the federal government was somehow involved in the assassination. No other charges have been brought up in the case. It remained unsolved.

References

Catholic World News. "Murder of Mexican Cardinal Still Unsolved." Available online. URL: http://www.cwnews.com/news/viewstory.ctm?recnum=9477. Downloaded on July 15, 2004.

Thomas A. Constantine. "International Organized Crime Syndicates and Their Impact on the U.S." U.S. Drug Enforcement Administration. Available online. URL: http://www.dea.gov/pubs/cngrtest/ct980226.htm. Downloaded on July 15, 2004.

POTATO Bag Gang

In 1975 Russian immigrants from the Odessa region of Russia were committing a series of frauds that created a media stir. Preying on other recent Russian immigrants across the country, the "Potato Bag Gang" told the victims that they were selling them a sack of gold coins at a deep discount because the money was illegally gotten. When the victims purchased the bags with real cash, they discovered that the money bags were filled with potatoes.

POZZA, Michel

Michel Corrado Celestino Pozza was born in the northern Italian city of Trento and immigrated to Canada at a young age. University educated and gifted with a superior intelligence, Pozza was not an average mobster. Luigi Greco, the second-in-command of the Montreal Mafia, saw Pozza's potential and took him under his wing. By the 1960s he was considered to be Greco's right-hand man. One of the organization's chief money launderers, he moved about freely between the family's Calabrian and Sicilian wings.

When Paolo Violi married Grazia Luppino in Hamilton on July 10, 1965, Pozza accompanied Luigi Greco to the ceremony. Also making the journey from Montreal was Vic Cotroni, who acted as Violi's best man, and Jos Di Maulo.

In 1973, police officials affirmed to the Commission d'enquete sur le crime organisé (CECO) that Pozza was in fact an important and influential member of the Calabrian faction of the Montreal Mafia.

Through Salvatore Catalano of the Bonanno family, Pozza first met with Vito Ciancimino, the former mayor of Palermo, in 1979. The meeting took place in Mondello, near Palermo. The two allegedly met to discuss drug trafficking.

In the late 1970s as the Sicilian and Calabrian factions of the Montreal Mafia battled for control, Pozza was seen more and more around the Rizzutos and less around the Cotronis.

In November 1980 Pozza, Vito and Nick Rizzuto, and Joe Lopresti were among the guests at the wedding of Sicilian mob boss Giuseppe Bono at the Hotel Pierre in New York. Bono, at the time, was the leader of the Bolognetta family in Milan.

Pozza was called to a meeting with Vic Cotroni in the early 1980s to explain his relationship with the Sicilian faction. The gathering proved unproductive and, as they left, Frank Cotroni turned to Réal, who later turned informant, and allegedly explained that "something has to be done about him."

In 1982, as Pozza worked as the treasurer for the C&C Credit Company on Papineau Avenue, the CECO began to investigate organized crime ties in the garment industry. Because of his relationship with the International Ladies Garment Workers Union, Pozza was among those set to be called to testify.

But Pozza never had to go before the commission. On the night of September 17, 1982, he met Réal Simard for a drink. The next morning, as the two talked in front of Pozza's Mont-Rolland home, Simard produced a .22-calibre pistol and shot the money launderer several times, including twice in the head. He was 57 years old.

Pozza had been kept under police surveillance, but the watch had been called off that night because of a shortage of manpower. Inside his home, police found phone numbers and addresses in Palermo and a check worth $5 million with the signature of Vito Ciancimino, one of Sicily's most famous politicians. The money, according to police, was the proceeds of narcotics trafficking.

Reference
Gary Francoeur. "Michel Pozza." WiseguyWally. Available online. URL: http://www.geocities.com/wiseguywally/MichelPozza.html. Downloaded on July 15, 2004.

—G.F.

PROJECT Angle   See JAMES KENNY GANG.

PROVENZANO, Bernardo (a.k.a. the Tractor)

Bernardo Provenzano was born on January 31, 1933, in Corleone. After the Second World War Provenzano joined the Mafia family of boss Michele Navarra and became an enforcer for Luciano Liggio in that family. In a short time Provenzano and another young man named Salvatore "Totò" Riina, who would later become known as one of the most vicious Mafia bosses ever, became Liggio's most trusted enforcers. They were feared and had a reputation. Liggio said of Provenzano: "He has the brains of a chicken but shoots like an angel." He also gained the nickname the Tractor because "he mows people down." With people like Riina and Provenzano and his own fearsome reputation, Liggio grew more powerful and eventually became a threat to Navarra. Navarra acknowledged the threat and decided it was time to eliminate Liggio so he could continue his rule. Navarra sent a group of his men to ambush Liggio and whack him; they failed and only wounded him. With the help of Riina, he escaped.

Now it was Liggio's turn to strike. He put together a group of hit men including Provenzano and Riina to take out Navarra, and Liggio's group of hit men succeeded where Navarra's men failed, Liggio's group ambushed Navarra while he was driving back from a meeting. The group of young assassins riddled the car in which Navarra sat with bullets; in the end the car was pumped with 112 bullets, and Navarra and another person who happened to be along for the ride were dead. With Navarra out of the way Luciano Liggio became the new godfather.

Navarra's death made a lot of Mafiosi unhappy, not only because they lost an ally but also because it was a breach of the Mafia code that you did not whack your boss. These Mafiosi as well as Navarra supporters who wanted to avenge their boss made it very dangerous for Liggio and his two enforcers, Provenzano and Riina. In the early 1960s the heat became too much for Provenzano. Sensing that he would soon be arrested or whacked he took off and disappeared in the countryside of Sicily. While he was on the run, he fathered two sons but spent his days looking over his shoulder. The Italian authorities had declared him a missing person and eventually thought he was whacked and that his body would soon be found, but they could not be further from the truth.

While on the run, Provenzano continued his criminal career, a career that came to new heights when his old pal Totò Riina became the new boss. While Riina took care of the violent aspect of mob business and stepped into the front, Provenzano was hidden, taking care of the money. Provenzano made sure everybody paid and all the Mafiosi got their share.

As the drug money came flowing in, a power struggle started over who was to control it. Riina went on a rampage in a war that would leave 800 Mafiosi dead. When the government decided to crack down on the Mafia, Riina hit back. Two top prosecutors were killed by bombs, and anyone else who opposed the Mafia was found dead. The campaign of terror that was supposed to scare off the people and government had the opposite effect: The government went on even harder, and the public was now in their favor. The people had seen the brutal image of the Mafia and were sickened by it. As the hunt for Riina became more intense, Provenzano was still hidden from everybody and presumed dead. In 1992 his wife and children returned from the countryside. Talk about Provenzano's death flared up, but without a body, no one could be sure.

On January 15, 1993, in Palermo, Sicily, Totò Riina was arrested by Italian police. The arrest of Riina placed Provenzano at the top of a criminal empire under fire by competition and law enforcement. Changes needed to be made. Under Provenzano the Sicilian Mafia steered away from its terror tactics toward the government and went back into the underworld. Out of sight the Mafia restructured, returning to its roots. Under Provenzano the Sicilian Mafia has once again became the invisible power and expanded its interests while keeping clear from law enforcement. Provenzano commands his troops via cryptic, handwritten notes transported by key members. There are occasional visits and very occasional summits with Mafia leaders, but otherwise Provenzano is a ghost, presumed dead but feared to be running the most powerful Sicilian Mafia in decades.

Police believe he spends most of his time in western and central Sicily, going from one safe house to

Paolo Palazzolo, brother-in-law of fugitive Mafia boss Bernardo Provenzano, was arrested for alleged ties to the Mafia in January 2002. (AP/Police Handout)

another. In January 2001 police intercepted several letters by Provenzano to his family, proof that he was still very alive. The letters were as close as police would get. Provenzano seems unfindable to this day. While other bosses and Mafiosi have been caught one by one, Provenzano has been on the run for almost 40 years. Untouched by Italian police and for a long time presumed dead, one can only assume that that will be the way Italian law enforcement will find Provenzano, presumably dead, somewhere in a safe house in Sicily.

See also: AGLIERI, PIETRO; BARGARELLA, LEOLUCA; BRUSCA, GIOVANNI; CORLEONE CLAN; FALCONE, GIOVANNI; PALAZZOLO, GIUSEPPE; RIINA, SALVATORE; SPERA, BENEDETTO.

Reference

David Amoruso. "Bernardo 'The Tractor' Provenzano." Gangsters Incorporated. Available online. URL: http://gangstersinc.tripod.com/BernardoProvenzano.html. Downloaded on July 15, 2004.

—D.A.

PUZYRETSKY, Emil

Emil Puzyretsky was a Russian mob enforcer in Brooklyn who was known for his use of knives. He was also involved in bootleg gas scams, among other things. Puzyretsky was shot to death on May 11, 1991, inside the National Restaurant in Brighton Beach. With a silencer-equipped handgun, a gunman shot him twice at close range and several additional times after he fell to the floor.

See also: RUSSIAN MAFIYA.

Reference

New Jersey State Commission of Investigation, New York Organized Crime Task Force, New York State Commission of Investigation, Pennsylvania Crime Commission, with Rutgers University. "The Tri-State Joint Soviet-Émigré Organized Crime Project." 1992. Available online. URL: http://www.state.nj.us/sci/pdf/russian.pdf. Accessed on November 24, 2004.

QUINTERO-PAYAN, Emilio

Emilio was the brother of Juan José Quintero-Payan and a fellow leader of the Mexican Juárez cartel. Both Quintero-Payans were uncles of Rafael Caro-Quintero. Caro-Quintero was convicted in 1988 of the murder of Enrique Camarena Salazar, a Drug Enforcement Administration agent.

See also: CAMARENA, ENRIQUE; CARO-QUINTERO, RAFAEL; ESPARRAGOZA MORENO, JUAN JOSÉ; JUÁREZ CARTEL; QUINTERO-PAYAN, JUAN JOSÉ.

QUINTERO-PAYAN, Juan José

Juan José Quintero-Payan was a leader of the Juárez cartel, one of Mexico's biggest and most profitable drug-smuggling organizations. Quintero-Payan had risen to be one of the top three leaders of the Juárez cartel after the death of Cartel chief Amado Carrillo Fuentes in July 1997.

He and his brother Emilio, who was also a Juárez cartel leader, were the uncles of Caro-Quintero, who was convicted in the murder of Enrique Camarena Salazar, a Drug Enforcement Administration agent, in 1988.

Quintero-Payan, was among Mexico's oldest drug traffickers. According to the *Los Angeles Times* on October 31, 1999, he had "served as tutor to such other notorious traffickers as Juan José Esparragoza. Quintero-Payan, nicknamed Don Juanjo, was born in Guadalajara, in western Mexico, and kept his power base there, running the Pacific Coast cell of the Juárez cartel."

Quintero-Payan had a violent history in drug smuggling. According to the *Times,* "News reports said he was indicted in the United States in 1985 for marijuana smuggling along with his brother Emilio, though neither was caught at the time. The indictment stated that the brothers held U.S. bank accounts worth nearly $20 million and that they were responsible for shooting an informant who was gathering information on them." Quintero-Payan was arrested on October 29, 1999, in the state of Jalisco in Mexico by Mexican police.

See also: CAMARENA, ENRIQUE; CARO-QUINTERO, RAFAEL; ESPARRAGOZA MORENO, JUAN JOSÉ; JUÁREZ CARTEL; QUINTERO-PAYAN, EMILIO.

Reference

James F. Smith. "Mexico Arrests Alleged Drug Cartel Kingpin; Smuggling: Veteran Boss Brought Cocaine from Colombia, Prosecutor Says." StreetGangs.Com. Available online. URL: http://www.streetgangs.com/topics/1999/103199mexdg.html. Posted on October 31, 1999.

RACKETEER Influenced and Corrupt Organizations Act (RICO)

The Organized Crime Control Act of 1970 amended the then current federal racketeering statutes. In doing so, the Racketeer Influenced and Corrupt Organizations Act (RICO) was turned into law.

According to "Prosecuting Criminal Enterprises: Federal Offense And Offenders November 1993" by K. Carlson and P. Finn (ABT Associates Inc.) "RICO specifically prohibits four activities: (a) investing the proceeds of a pattern of racketeering activity (as defined below) in an enterprise that engages in interstate or foreign commerce; (b) acquiring or maintaining an interest in such an enterprise by means of a pattern of racketeering activity; (c) using a pattern of racketeering activity in conducting the affairs of such an enterprise; or (d) conspiracy to do (a), (b), or (c)."

Any one of 27 types of activities may be considered a violation of the laws laid down in the statute, including eight of which are considered state felonies. Carlson and Finn write, "The 27 Federal offenses include specific types of gambling, prostitution, drug offenses, obscenity, theft, fraud, extortion, counterfeiting, bribery, obstruction of justice, cigarette boot-legging, and labor law violations. State predicate crimes include murder, kidnapping, gambling, arson, robbery, bribery, extortion, and drug offenses."

The law broadly includes any conspiracy or group, legal and legitimate as well, or any other kind of association that it feels can be cited in such proceedings.

The RICO laws made it possible for prosecutors to obtain sentences against organized-crime members of up to 20 years in prison and the forfeiture of ill-gotten gains. The law also provides prosecutors the ability to gain injunctions against indicted persons who attempt to move any kind of assets to prevent government seizure.

The RICO statutes also provide a means for U.S. citizens to sue those convicted of the RICO statutes for damages incurred during their reign of power, according to Finn, "If it can be shown that the plaintiff was injured in his or her business or property and that those injuries resulted from a pattern of racketeering activity." Finn also goes on to point out that many objections have been made amongst those in the legal profession that many plaintiffs have used these means in "divorce proceedings, religious disputes, and contractual disputes between business people."

While many underworld organized-crime members have been charged and sentenced under the RICO statutes, many citizens have used the statutes to go after corrupt corporation executives, against corporations that have acted unseemingly, and even against the U.S. Supreme Court.

According to Jeff E. Grell, a lawyer and promoter of RICOAct.com, who has both prosecuted and defended RICO cases, "Since the mid-1980's, The

Act has been applied to circumstances originally believed by many to be beyond the scope of The Act. The Act has not only been successfully used against members of organized crime groups such as the Mafia, but also against legitimate business persons, against spouses in contested divorce cases, and against attorneys, bankers, accountants, and protest organizations, to name just a few of the individuals or groups who have been surprised to find themselves a named defendant in a RICO case."

While attempts to have the RICO statute declared unlawful, on the whole, have been unsuccessful, over the years, numerous amendments have been added to the statutes to make it more just and inclusive.

References

K. Carlson and P. Finn. "Prosecuting Criminal Enterprises: Federal Offense And Offenders." Electric Law Library. Available online. URL: http://www.lectlaw.com/files/cri18.htm. Downloaded on July 15, 2004.

U.S. Department of Justice, Criminal Division. "Organized Crime and Racketeering Section." Available online. URL: http://www.usdoj.org/criminal/ocrs.html. Downloaded on July 15, 2004.

RAJAN, Chhota (a.k.a. Rajendra Nikhalje)

Chhota Rajan is one of the most famous and violent of the Asian subcontinent's colorful world of gangsters. Rajan has suffered a series of defeats and defections and has suffered and survived them all. Rajan has been known to smuggle cars, arms, and drugs; to order murders and kidnappings; and has resorted to extortion and other violence to obtain any goal he desires.

Chhota operated out of Mumbai, India, and eventually moved out after extreme pressure from Dawood Ibrahim for whom he had previously worked. Ibrahim, lieutenant and former Rajan friend, told Rediff's Sheel Bhatt, "His father was a sweeper in a company. He had no money to even eat. At that time he came to us begging for some work. So we hired him. . . . When his mentor Bada Rajan [Rajan Nair] died [in 1983], we gave him shelter and money. He was nobody before joining us."

But he quickly became somebody. By the late 1999s Rajan was Ibrahim's largest and strongest competitor. But Rajan could not compete with Ibrahim after a bloody turf war in the streets of Mumbai. He relocated to Malaysia and Australia and then went to Thailand under the name Vijay Daman. He was seeking a business visa so that he could stay and operate a dried-fish export business he had established, presumably to use as a front for his other nefarious activities. It is assumed that he was looking to establish himself in Bangkok.

However, despite his tightly held address and highly secure building, Ibrahim's men found Rajan. He was living in Sukumit area, 26th Street. His house had a big iron gate. "The bastard did not come out of his house for three full months. My guys were waiting outside for him."

Six men charged his house armed with 10 automatic weapons. A wild gun battle ensued. With nowhere else to go, Rajan leapt from his palatial apartment suite and broke his back in the fall. News of his death shot through Asia.

Chhota Shakeel, who masterminded the assassination attempt, talked freely with newspapers from an undisclosed location from an untraceable cell phone. "We had not planned to kill him so easily," crowed Chhota Shakeel. Shakeel had admitted that the plan was to kidnap Rajan, take him to a boat waiting on the water in Bangkok and bring him to Karachi, where he would be tortured and murdered.

This proved to be just slightly premature. It turned out Rajan had survived the fall and was still alive. He remained in a highly guarded hospital room in Bangkok, under the eye of nine Thai guards. He escaped. Initial reports in November claimed that the injured gangster had climbed down a set of bed sheets more than three stories. The truth was even more fantastic. In return for more than $1 million, Rajan walked out. He eventually fled Thailand, and his whereabouts are unknown.

It has been speculated that Guru Satam, a close associate of Rajan's was the traitor who gave away Rajan's address. This speculation occurred when Satam and his gang decided to form a separate rogue gang.

Rajan also suffered the loss of his closest strong men, Dilip Maratha and Asif Amdavadi, in an encounter near Lajpor in Surat.

Rajan is largely believed to be behind the attempted assassination of Chhota Shakeel, whose apartment was bombed by a live grenade tossed through an opened window. The blast killed two persons and gravely injured Shakeel, but he too survived.

While Rajan has remained hidden away, he has continued to press his causes where necessary, arranging an attempted shooting of a Bollywood (India's filmmaking capital) producer, as well as pressing smuggling operations and other businesses.

See also: BAKSH, NOOR; GOGA, IRFAN; IBRAHIM, DAWOOD; SATAM, GURU; SHAKEEL, CHHOTA; SINGH, SANJAY.

References

Sheela Bhatt. "Chhota Rajan Shot Dead in Bangkok." Rediff. Available online. URL: http://www.rediff.com/news/2000/sep/15chhota.htm. Downloaded on July 15, 2004.

Sheela Bhatt. "We Had Planned Not to Kill Him So Easily." Rediff. Available online. URL: http://www.rediff.com/news/2000/sep/15rajan.htm. Downloaded on July 15, 2004.

RAMIREZ-ABADIA, Juan Carlos (a.k.a. Chupeta)

In March 1996 Juan Carlos Ramirez-Abadia (a.k.a. Chupeta) surrendered to Colombian authorities. Chupeta is believed to have surrendered, in part, for fear of his personal safety and to be eligible for a more lenient prison sentence. In December 1996 Chupeta was sentenced to 24 years in prison but may actually serve as few as seven and a half years. In March 1998 a reliable Drug Enforcement Administration (DEA) source reported that Jorge Orlando Rodriguez, a.k.a. El Mono, had assumed control of the day-to-day operations of the Chupeta organization. However, Ramirez-Abadia continues to be involved in the major decisions involving the organization's activities. The DEA also reported that Chupeta's net worth was approximately $2.6 billion.

Reference

David Amoruso. "Juan Carlos Ramirez-Abadia." Gangsters Incorporated. Available online. URL: http://gangstersinc.tripod.com. Downloaded on July 15, 2004.

—D.A.

REZNIKOV, Vladimir

Vladimir Reznikov was a Russian émigré to New York who was involved in various illegal activities, including many types of gas scams. He was a vicious criminal. One of his well-known exploits was the murder of Rachmel Dementev. On January 1, 1981, he shot Dementev to death after Dementev referred to Reznikov as an informant.

Reznikov also killed Ilya Zeltzer in the Platinum Energy gas-distribution offices in Brooklyn, New York. Allegedly, the murder happened while the two argued over bootleg gas.

In front of the Odessa Restaurant in Brighton Beach, Brooklyn, New York, he himself was shot to death on June 13, 1986, while getting into his car. Allegedly, he was murdered by La Cosa Nostra at the request of several other Russian criminals. These Russians were also involved in the bootleg-gas scams.

RICHARD, Robert (a.k.a. Tiny)

Robert "Tiny" Richard was a member of the Montreal-based Popeyes motorcycle gang when the group was absorbed and became the first Canadian Hells Angels chapter in 1977. Richard was extremely dedicated and loyal to the club. He sported 11 tattoos, including "Filthy Few," which, according to reports, is worn by members who have killed for the club.

The Montreal chapter became so large that it was divided in two on September 14, 1979. The north chapter, based in Laval, was created, and Richard, as well as most of the club's original members, joined the new chapter.

But the north faction was reckless. The majority of members were crazed drug addicts who were not reliable and could not be trusted. They kept poor records and skimmed profits. Richard, Réjean "Zig-Zag" Lessard, and Luc "Sam" Michaud left the group and returned to the Montreal chapter.

The Montreal chapter became outraged by north's constant cocaine use and decided to "take care of business." North chapter members were invited to a club meeting at the Sherbrooke chapter's Lennoxville clubhouse on March 24, 1985. The north faction was liquidated and the victims were wrapped in sleeping bags and tossed into the St. Lawrence River.

Richard, along with Hells Angels Jacques Pelletier, Luc "Sam" Michaud, and Réjean "Zig-Zag" Lessard, were brought up on charges of the first-degree murder of their fellow gang members. The four Hells Angels were imprisoned behind a $40,000 glass cage, and observers were frisked and prodded with a metal detector before being allowed into the courtroom. Pelletier, Michaud, and Lessard were convicted of first-degree murder, but Richard was eventually acquitted of all charges.

Richard, who became the national leader of the organization, was in trouble with the law again in September 1995 when he tossed around a television reporter at the funeral of Hells Angel Louis "Ti-Oui" Lapierre. Lapierre, who had been convicted of the north chapter massacre, had taken his own life.

"Tiny" Richard died of a heart attack at his home on February 23, 1996. The 46-year-old biker stood more than six feet tall and, at one time, weighed more than 300 pounds. By the time of his death, the Hells Angel had worked his weight down to 230 pounds. Approximately 350 bikers and friends attended Richard's funeral on February 28, 1996, a clear sign that the man was well respected within the gang.

See also: HELLS ANGELS.

Reference

Gary Francoeur. "Robert 'Tiny' Richard." Wiseguy-Wally. Available online. URL: http://www.geocities.com/wiseguywally/RobertRichard.html. Downloaded on July 15, 2004.

—*G.F.*

RICHARDSON, Charlie

Charlie Richardson, along with Brother Eddie, was a scrap-metal dealer and a notorious gang leader. The Richardson gang were the Kray twins' biggest rivals in England in the 1960s. The rival gangs had many skirmishes over the south London neighborhoods. The Richardsons were pursued eagerly by the London police and the Krays and were effectively finished by the end of 1965.

Businessmen and criminals, the Richardsons had a series of legitimate businesses including five scrap-metal yards and a metal works, and they owned part of a South African diamond mine.

See also: CORNELL, GEORGE; FRASER, FRANK; KRAY TWINS; MCVITE, JACK; RICHARDSON, EDDIE.

RICHARDSON, Eddie

Coleader of the Richardson Gang in 1960s London, he was also the brother of Charlie Richardson.

See also: CORNELL, GEORGE; FRASER, FRANK; KRAY TWINS; MCVITE, JACK; RICHARDSON, CHARLIE.

RICHARDSON Gang

The Richardson gang ran south London and the West End in the 1960s.

See also: CORNELL, GEORGE; FRASER, FRANK; KRAY TWINS; MCVITE, JACK; RICHARDSON, CHARLIE; RICHARDSON, EDDIE.

RICHTER, Keith Edward (a.k.a. Conan)

Born on January 1, 1959, in Bayshore, New York, Richter grew to become an allegedly high-ranking official in the Pagans Motorcycle Club. He was arrested Saturday, December 6, 1997, at 4:30 P.M. at the Hollywood Motel in Farmingdale, Long Island.

Federal criminal charges alleged Richter to be the "Mother Club Adviser" of the four Long Island chapters of the Pagans. The complaint alleged that a cooperating witness, thoroughly familiar with the Pagans, advised investigators that the Pagans had been engaged in extorting the proprietors and performers of Long Island topless dancing establishments. The witness alledged that the Pagans had been unsuccessful in extorting the Carousel, a topless club in Huntington, because Sean McCarthy, the club's manager and bouncer, had not only withstood attempts to intimidate him, but he had beaten or otherwise injured several Pagans.

In October 1996 Richter, also known as "Conan," supposedly instructed another Pagan, Franklin Alexander Frank, to kill McCarthy, but Frank was arrested on separate charges before the plot could be carried out.

According to charges filed, a second cooperating witness indicated that as mother club adviser, Richter oversaw the illegal activities of the four Long Island chapters, including extortion of topless clubs. This complaint also alleged that in March or April 1997, many members of the Pagans were given maps of McCarthy's residence and neighborhood. In July 1997 a Pagan offered to talk to McCarthy to settle the dispute, but Richter reportedly told the member that no Pagan was to see McCarthy unless he had "a nine millimeter in his hand."

Also implicated in Richter's arrest was Joseph Spring, a.k.a. "Joey Dogs," a Pagan and a close associate of Richter, who was arrested on July 29, 1997. The complaint alleged that at the time of his arrest, Spring had in his possession records of payments extorted from exotic dancers; a vehicle search revealed two copies of a document containing personal information about McCarthy, a description of his cars and home, and a map and directions to that home.

Richter is currently incarcerated in the federal penitentiary in Lewisburg, Pennsylvania, serving a 16-year sentence. He will be released in 2011. Spring testified against Conan at his trial.

See also: PAGANS.

Reference

FBI National Press Office. "Arrest of Keith Edward Richter." Department of Justice, December 8, 1997.

RICO *See* RACKETEER INFLUENCED AND CORRUPT ORGANIZATIONS ACT.

RIINA, Salvatore (a.k.a. Totò Riina)

Salvatore Riina (also called Totò Riina) is the most famous Mafia villain in the recent history of Sicily. He supposedly organized the death of Giovanni Falcone, the "Giudice"—judge—who fought against the Mafia until his death on May 23, 1992. Riina is now

Italian Mafia boss Salvatore Riina (AP)

in prison for life. Corleone was his home city and is often mentioned with his name.

See also: AGLIERI, PIETRO; BARGARELLA, LEOLUCA; BRUSCA, GIOVANNI; CORLEONE CLAN; FALCONE, GIOVANNI; PALAZZOLO, GIUSEPPE; PROVENZANO, BERNARDO; SPERA, BENEDETTO.

Reference

Wikipedia. "Toto Riina." Available online. URL: http://en. wikipedia.org/wiki/Toto_Riina. Accessed on November 24, 2004.

RIVARD, Lucien

Lucien Rivard became a leader of the Canadian drug trade in the 1940s. He was considered to be a superior organizer and earned great respect in the Montreal crime world. He possessed international connections and often worked with the Cotroni brothers. His main lieutenants were Jean-Louis "Blackie" Bisson, who handled Rivard's Montreal activities, and Bob Tremblay, who distributed Rivard's heroin in Vancouver.

By the 1950s Rivard was the number-one man in the heroin trafficking throughout the country. He expanded his business in 1954 when he became partners with Giuseppe "Pep" Cotroni. While Rivard had better heroin contacts at the time, the Mafia had much better connections in the U.S. narcotics market.

In the late 1950s Rivard moved to Cuba, where he continued to run his empire. He was seen meeting with Corsican traffickers Jean-Baptiste Croce and Paul Mondolini, and when they were forced to return to France on criminal charges, Rivard took over their interests.

In Cuba Rivard also ran a large-scale gambling ring and smuggled thousands of firearms into Canada. He was often followed as he met with influential underworld leaders, including Salvatore "Little Sal" Giglio of the New York based Bonanno crime family. Rivard even served as Giglio's best man at his March 22, 1957, wedding to Florence Anderson.

On January 8, 1958, during a visit to Montreal, Rivard and his lieutenant Jean-Louis "Blackie" Bisson were arrested for illegal possession of firearms. He was released the next morning after he provided a registration certificate for his gun. Bisson pleaded guilty and paid a $50 fine.

Canadian drug trafficker Lucien Rivard *(Montreal Gazette)*

Rivard's stay in Cuba came to an end when Fidel Castro overthrew the military dictatorship of Fulgencio Batista. A clean up against mobsters ensued, and Rivard and many others, including Meyer Lansky, were imprisoned. Learning that Rivard had paid Batista $20,000 a week to operate freely, Castro wanted him executed, but Montreal lawyer Raymond Daoust contacted the minister of External Affairs in Ottawa and intervened. Rivard was released and shipped to Montreal on June 24, 1959.

After Rivard's partner, Giuseppe Cotroni, was sentenced to 10 years in prison in November 1959, Rivard completely took over the importation of heroin in Canada. He began to rake in enormous profits.

In 1960 Rivard and Gerry Turenne purchased a large summer resort center in Auteuil, Quebec. The property, valued at more than $200,000, included a marina, cottages, dance hall, swimming pool, restaurant, bar, and a beach. Rivard ran the business and even did much of the repairs himself.

Quebec Provincial Police arrested Rivard and associates Gilles Brochu and Roger Beauchamp on March 7, 1962, for robbing and beating Gaétan Raymond, who had criticized the heroin trafficker. As Rivard was being led out in shackles, five thugs, led by gangster Réjean Lavoie, allegedly ambushed him and beat him severely before police could intervene. Lavoie was murdered just four days after he was paroled.

Rivard avoided a jail sentence when the man he, Brochu, and Beauchamp had beaten, Gaétan Raymond, failed to identify them as his attackers. They were freed for lack of evidence.

On January 17, 1964, a U.S. federal grand jury, based mainly on the information of former Rivard henchmen Michel Caron, indicted the French-Canadian mobster on international heroin-trafficking charges. He was arrested and placed in Montreal's Bordeaux Jail while awaiting extradition. Three of his followers were also indicted on similar charges.

On March 2, 1965, while Rivard was still incarcerated in Bordeaux awaiting extradition, he and fellow prisoner André Durocher asked a guard for permission to get hoses from the furnace room to water the outdoor rink. When they entered the utility room, Durocher pulled out a gun (which was actually nothing more than a carved piece of wood blackened with shoe polish) and the two gangsters tied everyone up. They managed to sneak up behind the guard posted on the west wall and restrained him. The two French-Canadians then used a ladder to climb the small interior wall and hoses to get over the large exterior wall. They hijacked a man's automobile but not before giving him cab fare. He was called a half hour later by Rivard and told where he could find his car.

"The Rivard Affair," as the prison escape became known, gathered national attention. The Canadian government put out a large reward for the drug trafficker's capture and the Royal Canadian Mounted Police cooperated with the Federal Bureau of Investigation, Interpol, U.S. Bureau of Narcotics, and U.S. Customs from the first hours after the escape.

Reports placed Rivard and Durocher in Florida, in Peru, in Mexico, in Spain, in New Brunswick, in Trois-Rivières, and even in Montreal. Rivard enjoyed the attention and sent several letters to authorities, including an amusing postcard to the prime minister of Canada, Lester B. Pearson.

André Durocher, Rivard's companion, was apprehended by police on May 28, 1965, after an anonymous call placed the fugitive in a Montreal apartment. Rivard was finally caught on July 16, 1965, in a Woodlands cottage near Chateauguay. He and associates Fred Cadieux and Sébastien Boucher were lounging around in bathing suits when police burst into the cottage.

After 136 days on the run, Rivard was brought back to Montreal where the crown agreed to withdraw charges of escaping and armed robbery so that the trafficker could be extradited to the United States as soon as possible.

He was escorted to Houston, Texas, where his three coaccused were already jailed. The trial lasted only seven days, and after only three hours of deliberation, the jury declared Rivard guilty. He was sentenced to 20 years in prison and fined $20,000. Lucien Rivard was paroled on January 17, 1975. He returned to Montreal where, police claim, he continued to run his empire. He kept a low profile until his death on February 3, 2002. He was 86 years old.

Reference
Gary Francoeur. "Lucas Rivard." WiseguyWally. Available online. URL: http://www.geocities.com/wiseguywally/Rivard.html. Downloaded on July 15, 2004.

—G.F.

RIZZUTO, Vito

Vito Rizzuto, son of Nicolo Rizzuto and Libertina Manno, was born on February 21, 1946, in the Sicilian province of Agrigento. The family immigrated to Canada in 1954 and settled in Montreal, Quebec. Rather than enter the legitimate working world, Vito followed in his father's footsteps as a "man of respect."

Rizzuto married Giovanna Cammalleni and had three children. His eldest son, Nicolo, was followed by Leonardo and daughter Libertina.

In 1965, at the age of 19, Rizzuto was convicted of disturbing the peace and fined $25. He was again convicted in 1972, this time with his brother-in-law Paolo Renda, for conspiracy to commit arson. He was sentenced to two years in prison. Renda received four years.

In the 1970s, war broke out between the Montreal Mafia's Calabrian and Sicilian factions, and Nicolo Rizzuto relocated to Venezuela. Vito remained behind. The conflict endured until 1981, resulting with more than 20 casualties in Montreal and Italy. Nick and Vito Rizzuto, father and son, allegedly came out of the conflict as leaders of the Montreal Mafia.

Rizzuto was seen meeting with Michel Pozza, close associate of Vic "the Egg" Cotroni and financial advisor of the organization. A few days later Pozza was shot to death outside his Laurentian home on September 28, 1982.

On November 30, 1987, the Royal Canadian Mounted Police seized 16 tons of hashish. The drug, with an estimated street value of $350 million, was apprehended on an island off Newfoundland's northeast coast. Rizzuto was arrested and charged with conspiring to traffic in narcotics, but he was absolved of all charges in November 1990 when Newfoundland Supreme Court Judge Leo Barry ruled that the evidence against the Mafia godfather had been obtained illegally. Five other men were charged after the bust; four were convicted and received sentences ranging from five to nine years in jail.

In 1988, while out on bail from his 1987 arrest, Rizzuto was nabbed once again. He was charged with conspiring to smuggle 32 tons of Lebanese hashish into the country. He was acquitted on December 18, 1989, when informant Normand Dupuis refused to testify. Dupuis, who claimed he was offered $1 million not to take the stand, changed his mind after his family began to receive death threats. Rizzuto walked out free once again while Dupuis received a 32-month jail sentence on an obstruction-of-justice charge.

On May 23, 1993, Vito Rizzuto and two dozen friends and family members greeted his father at a Montreal airport. Nick Rizzuto, who served five years in a Venezuelan jail on cocaine trafficking, was released on parole after Montreal mobster Domenic Tozzi delivered a $800,000 bribe to Venezuelan officials. Nick Rizzuto has become his son's advisor on the family business.

Rizzuto, considered by many to be the most powerful mobster in Canada, was among 30 Mafia suspects arrested on January 20, 2004. He was accused of being the lead gunman in the May 1981 murders of high-ranking New York mobsters Philip Giaccone, Alphonse Indelicato, and Dominick Trinchera. He is currently in prison awaiting extradition to the United States.

See also: COTRONI, VIC; POZZA, MICHEL.

Reference
Gary Francoeur. "Vito Rizzuto." WiseguyWally. Available online. URL: http://www.geocities.com/wiseguywally/VitoRizzuto.html. Downloaded on July 15, 2004.

—G.F.

ROCK Machine   *See* BANDIDOS/ROCK MACHINE.

RODRÍGUEZ GACHA, José Gonzalo

In the early 1980s the Ochoa family, Pablo Escobar, Carlos Lehder-Riva, and José Gonzalo Rodríguez Gacha formed an alliance that later became known as the Medellín cartel. These Colombian underworld figures coordinated the manufacturing, distribution, and marketing of cocaine.

Rodríguez Gacha went so far as to hire an Israeli counterterrorism officer, Yair Klein, who trained the Medellín cartel's paramilitary personnel and assassins. It was alleged that Klein even taught the cartel's people how to make bombs. The *Palm Beach Sunday Post,* on May 27, 1990, reported that "According to the Colombian intelligence reports, Rodríguez Gacha, in 'early January 1989' made arrangements for a ship to 'pick up an arms shipment destined to Colombia via Panama. The shipment would have no difficulty because everything had been arranged with certain Israeli authorities.'" But problems developed quickly. The first vessel selected was apparently too full to pick up the additional load, according to the documents. A second vessel then developed engine trouble, and it, too, had to be scrapped.

In 1984 Carlos Lehder-Riva, Pablo Escobar, Jorge Luis Ochoa Vásquez, and José Gonzalo Rodríguez Gacha were indicted by a Miami federal grand jury based on evidence obtained by Drug Enforcement Administration informant Barry Seal. Seal was assassinated in February 1986. On December 15, 1989, Colombian police raided Rodríguez Gacha's ranch in Tolu. He was killed during the raid.

See also: CALI CARTEL; MEDELLÍN CARTEL.

RODRÍGUEZ Orejuela, Gilberto (a.k.a. the Chess Player)

Gilberto Rodríguez Orejuela was known as a smooth operator. He posed as a legitimate businessman, but Gilberto and his younger brother Miguel founded the Colombian Cali cartel in the 1970s with José Santa Cruz Londono. Gilberto was the man with impeccable manners and exceptional business acumen. Miguel was responsible for the day-to-day business and operations.

The rival Medellín cartel was the more successful and the more violent of the two groups. Meanwhile the Cali cartel relied on bribery and smooth business dealings and gained respect in the region. A bright and excellent businessman, Gilberto used brains rather than brawn to gain advantages in business dealings as well as to outwit his opponents. However, from time to time the two major cartels clashed in bloody battles. While the Medellín was actively pursued by the Colombian government due to bribes and relationships with high-ranking government officials, the Cali cartel remained lower on the radar. Their bribery was said to have reached the highest office in Colombia.

The death of Pablo Escobar placed the Cali cartel in a unique position, giving them a monopoly on South American drug trade. In the mid-1990s Drug Enforcement Administration (DEA) estimated that the Rodríguez Orejuela brothers' combined wealth was $205 billion, earned from drug profits over a 10-year period. At this time the DEA estimated that only 20 percent of the cocaine in the United States was not imported by the Cali cartel and that they were clearing nearly $8 billion a year.

But with the Medellín cartel out of the way, the U.S. government and Colombian government both focused on the Cali and the two brothers. Gilberto was arrested first when Colombian police surrounded his apartment in Cali and stormed it on June 9, 1995. He was found hiding in an armoire.

"The United States and Colombia have worked closely together to target and capture these Cali mafia leaders. Rodriguez-Orejuela is a major kingpin in the world cocaine trade," said DEA Administrator Thomas A. Constantine. "Rodriguez-Orejuela who is known as the 'Chess Player' has been backed into a corner. Thanks to the Colombian Government he has no moves left." Miguel, and six other leaders, were arrested in 1996, and the cartel was smashed.

Gilberto was released early from prison on good behavior on November 8, 2002, despite protestations from Colombian president Alvaro Uribe.

See also: CALI CARTEL; MEDELLÍN CARTEL; MEJÍA-MUNERA, MIGUEL AND VICTOR; RODRÍGUEZ OREJUELA, MIGUEL ANGEL; SANTA CRUZ LONDONO, JOSÉ.

Reference

U.S. Drug Enforcement Administration, U.S. Department of Justice. "Arrest of Cali Mafia Leader Gilberto Rodriguez-Orejuela." Available online. URL: http://www.usdoj.gov/dea/pubs/pressrel/pr950609.html. Posted on June 9, 2004.

RODRÍGUEZ Orejuela, Miguel Angel (a.k.a. the Master)

One of the cofounders of the Cali cartel, he is brother to Gilberto Rodríguez Orejuela, who was the brains behind the Cali cartel. While Gilberto (known as the Chess Player) was the visionary laying out the major groundwork for the organization, Miguel was known for handling day-to-day operations. Miguel was referred to as "the Master." It was he who made sure payrolls were met, men recruited, bribes efficiently taken care of, shipments moved, and security arranged.

Miguel, also known as the "Transportation Specialist," micromanaged all aspects of their multifaceted trafficking ventures, which included production, transportation, wholesale distribution, and money laundering.

Born in 1943 in Cali, Miguel had been involved in drug trafficking since approximately 1980. He was responsible for smuggling multiton quantities of cocaine from Colombia into the United States, Canada, and Europe using a wide variety of sophisticated transportation and smuggling techniques. Seventy percent of the cocaine destined for the U.S. market is smuggled through Mexico.

Said Drug Enforcement Administrator Thomas A. Constantine, "Combined with brother Gilberto's capture on July 9 and that of Jose Santacruz-Londono's on July 5, these three arrests strike a mortal blow against the unholy trinity who lead the Cali mafia. This is the capstone in a series of arrests of major leaders of the Cali drug mafia, perhaps the most significant criminal entity the world has ever seen."

See also: CALI CARTEL; MEDELLÍN CARTEL; MEJÍA-MUNERA, MIGUEL AND VICTOR; RODRÍGUEZ ORE-JUELA, GILBERTO; SANTA CRUZ LONDONO, JOSÉ.

ROMERO de Velasco, Flavio

The former state governor of Jalisco, Mexico, Flavio Romero de Velasco was jailed on January 24, 1998, in connection with his ties to drug lords Rigoberto Gaxiola Medina and Jorge Abrego Reyna Castro. Romero is accused of laundering drug money, accepting bribes, and providing a safe haven for drug lords in his western state between 1977 and 1983. In February 1998, the Drug Enforcement Administration arrested Jorge Alejandro Abrego Reyna Castro in Phoenix. The Mexican government had ordered Abrego Reyna's arrest on criminal-association and money-laundering charges in connection with the case of former Jalisco governor Flavio Romero de Velasco and requested his extradition.

On July 15, 2001, Romero de Velasco was cleared of all charges and was set free, ending a three-year battle with Mexico City prosecutors.

Reference
Thomas A. Constantine. "International Organized Crime Syndicates and Their Impact on the U.S." U.S. Department of Justice. Available online. URL: http://www.dea.gov/pubs/cngrtest/ct980226.htm. Downloaded on July 28, 2004.

ROY, Louis (a.k.a. Mélou)

Louis "Mélou" Roy was believed by police to be Quebec's second-most-powerful and influential Hells Angel, only behind Maurice "Mom" Boucher. He received his colors in 1991 and served as president of the Trois-Rivières chapter before founding the elite Nomads chapter in 1995.

Roy was the organization's principal contact with the Montreal Mafia and believed to be the richest Hells Angel in the province. Law enforcement estimated that he was responsible for importing at least 5,200 kilograms of hashish from Jamaica, India, South Africa, Belgium, Holland, and Switzerland. He was also active in other rackets, including large-scale importation of other drugs.

Along with fellow Nomad Richard "Rick" Vallee, Roy was charged with trafficking in cocaine in 1995. The charges were later dropped.

Roy and Hells Angel Sylvain "Baptiste" Thiffault were brought up on charges of ordering the 1995 deaths of drug dealers Richard Delcourt and Jacques Ferland. Hit man Serge Quesnel, who admitted to the shootings, turned informant and agreed to testify against his former employer.

April 4, 1997, proved to be a great day for Roy. He and Thiffault were on their way to court to learn their verdict when police shoved Rock Machine associate Roger Hardy in the paddy wagon with them. The Hells Angels beat the man severely and then, later in the day, were acquitted of all charges. The jury felt Quesnel was not a credible witness.

But Mélou Roy was back in court again, charged with ordering the 1995 slaying of Claude "Le Pic" Rivard. He was granted bail, and on August 23, 1997, while exiting his Mercedes in the parking lot of his father's motel in Jonquiere, Roy was shot four times by a masked assailant. He refused to cooperate with police and underwent major surgery, eventually recovering fully.

Four members of the Hells Angels Trois-Rivières chapter and a member of the Blatnois puppet gang agreed to plead guilty on murder conspiracy charges if prosecutors withdrew the charges against Roy.

On September 18, 1998, Roy pled guilty to one count of federal tax evasion and was ordered to pay $20,000 for not declaring any revenue between 1990 and 1993. Authorities calculated that Roy had not reported $190,000 in revenue in that time period.

Roy disappeared on June 24, 2000, the fifth anniversary of the Hells Angels Nomads chapter. His Mercedes-Benz was found on a busy street in downtown Montreal weeks later. Just days before his disappearance, he had been present in Trois-Rivières as provincial police arrested almost the entire Blatnois biker gang, a Hells Angels puppet club. Police believe that the Hells Angels were behind Roy's disappearance, murdering him because he wanted to reduce drug prices. He was 41 years old.

See also: HELLS ANGELS.

Reference

Gary Francoeur. "Louis 'Mélou' Roy." WiseguyWally. Available online. URL: http://www.geocities.com/wiseguywally/LouisRoy.html. Downloaded on July 15, 2004.

—G.F.

ROYAL Canadian Mounted Police (RCMP)

According to the Royal Canadian Mounted Police, it was Sir John A. Macdonald, Canada's first prime minister and minister of justice, who first conceived of the famed police force. Macdonald's main objective was "to bring law, order and Canadian authority to the North-West Territories (present-day Alberta and Saskatchewan)." The Canadian Mounted Police force was modeled on several different police forces of the day, including the Royal Irish Constabulary, and the horse cavalry of the U.S.

Canada's most famed lawmen were made legal by an Act of Parliament on May 23, 1873. Officers and recruits were in the field by July 1874. "General law enforcement detachments were established throughout the prairies and a patrol system instituted in

order to police effectively the entire region . . . established friendly relations with the First Nations, contained the whisky trade and enforced prohibition, supervised treaties between First Nations and the federal government assisted the settlement process by ensuring the welfare of immigrants, fighting prairie fires, disease and destitution," according to the RCMP's own history.

By the close of the century, the renamed and reorganized Northwest Mounted Police jurisdiction stretched from Alberta and Saskatchewan all the way through the farthest reaches of the Yukon and then to the Arctic coast. The prefix *Royal* was "conferred on the NWMP by King Edward VII in June 1904." In 1920 they were renamed the Royal Canadian Mounted Police, and despite a rash of changes from smaller to larger to larger in terms of their jurisdiction, the RCMP would be forever known to millions around the world. A naval branch was even developed to patrol coastal waters.

The RCMP, known for their unique uniforms, which include their red military tunics (with black and gold adornment) and broad-brimmed forestry-style hat, became known as Mounties. By the 1930s, the RCMP were developing the techniques that other national law-enforcement agencies were perfecting elsewhere, such as fingerprinting, crime indexing, photo indexing, forensic sciences, information exchanges, and transportation modifications, making them an elite police unit. By 1950, having survived numerous reconfigurations, the RCMP severed metropolitan and wilderness alike throughout Canada. During the 1970s, the RCMP also became responsible for "airport policing, VIP security, drug enforcement, economic crime" and more. In the 1990s, the RCMP went through an "expansion of international police duties," including such countries as Bosnia/Herzegovina, Croatia, East Timor, Guatemala, Haiti, Kosovo, Namibia, Western Sahara, and Yugoslavia. The RCMP are considered one of the best elite national police forces in the world.

Reprinted by permission of the Royal Canadian Mounted Police, 2004.

Reference

Royal Canadian Mounted Police. "Communication Canada, Canadian Government Publishing Directorate." Available online. URL: http://www.rcmp-grc.gc.ca/index_e.htm. Downloaded on July 15, 2004.

RUSSIAN Mafiya (a.k.a. the Russian mob)

Gangsters from the former Soviet Union have established a strong and abiding presence in the New York/New Jersey/Pennsylvania region, engaging in a wide array of crimes that range from sophisticated financial frauds to narcotics trafficking to murder. Evidence also shows that members of disparate Russian-émigré crime groups here have the potential to develop into one of the most formidable organized-crime challenges to law enforcement since the advent of La Cosa Nostra.

The Russian-émigré crime networks have grown from their core base in the Brighton Beach section of Brooklyn to their current reach well beyond the New York metropolitan area into the counties of central New Jersey and the suburbs of Philadelphia. One of the most troubling aspects is evidence of links between individuals here and criminal elements in the former Soviet Union, a phenomenon that lends a disturbing and complex international dimension to this emerging domestic law-enforcement problem. The range of criminal and illicit activities linked to these groups is impressive.

During the first two decades of the 20th century, more than 2.5 million Russians entered this country along with millions of other European immigrants. This first large wave of Russian immigration slowed dramatically, however, after the 1917 Bolshevik revolution. Since then, the rate of Russian immigration into the United States has depended largely upon the political relationship between the two countries. When the United States and the Soviet Union were allied against Germany during World War II, many Russians were able to leave the Soviet Union. During the cold-war period immediately following the conclusion of the war, however, Russian emigration was again stifled as Soviet leaders closed the "iron curtain" and permitted few people to leave that country. Russian emigration remained at a low level until the early 1970s when the Soviet government liberalized its emigration policy and permitted certain citizens to leave the country. The first wave of émigrés consisted mainly of Soviet Jews fleeing religious persecution, most of whom emigrated to Israel or the United States. After that, the number of Russians permitted to migrate rose steadily as the Soviet Union, nearing its collapse, began to ease travel and emigration restrictions.

The tristate region of New York, New Jersey, and Pennsylvania has long been one of the top areas in the United States for the relocation of Russian émigrés. In New York City, Russian émigrés settled predominantly in Brighton Beach, the oldest and most prominent Russian community in the United States. A longtime, working-class Jewish community located near Coney Island in the southern part of Brooklyn, Brighton Beach is currently home to about 30,000 Russian émigrés. Philadelphia's Russian community is located in the northeast section of the city near Bustleton Avenue. By the mid-1980s, as the Russian communities in New York and Philadelphia were starting to become crowded, Russian émigrés began to move out of the cities and into the surrounding areas.

From New York, they moved eastward into Nassau and Suffolk Counties on Long Island and westward into Essex, Bergen, Middlesex, and Monmouth Counties in New Jersey. At the same time, Russian émigrés began to populate several counties outside Philadelphia, including Bucks and Montgomery Counties in Pennsylvania, and Camden and Burlington Counties in New Jersey. Simultaneously, law-enforcement agents began to see increasing evidence of Russian-émigré crime within these communities. The specific nature and seriousness of this criminal activity and the degree to which it might be organized were, at the time, largely unknown. Prior to the mid-1980s few law-enforcement agencies in the tri state region had taken notice of the growing problem of Russian éemigré crime. The scant information then available in records maintained by these agencies reflected the lack of any serious dedication to the problem. Agencies that sought to attack the problem could barely afford to assign more than one detective to the task of tracking Russian-émigré criminals. Those assigned often were provided with little assistance while facing formidable investigative roadblocks. Much of the information available at that time concerned the number and size of local Russian organized-crime groups. Various federal agencies reported that 12 Russian émigré crime groups, with an estimated membership of 400–500 persons, were operating in New York City, while the New York Police Department listed about 500 Russian émigrés as being suspected of criminal activities.

At the same time, the Philadelphia Police Department had identified about fifty Russian émigré criminals, many of whom traveled regularly between New York City and Philadelphia. Similarly, Russian émigré crime in the United States attracted little academic attention. Prior to 1992, there had been only one serious study of Russian émigré crime in the United States. In 1986, Lydia Rosier, a professor at the John Jay College of Criminal Justice in New York City, published a book about Russian émigré crime based upon a four-year study of crime in Brighton Beach. In her book, Rosier stated that a "vast amount of at least informally organized crime" existed in Brighton Beach. She attributed this crime to networks of interconnected criminals acting in conjunction with each other. Rosier did not, however, attempt to determine whether the crime she had uncovered was part of a structured network of national or international criminal activities or whether it was being controlled by persons in the United States or the Soviet Union. As Russian émigré crime increased, law-enforcement agencies in the tristate region and across the nation realized they needed to evaluate this growing problem. Although the criminal activities attributed to Russian émigrés included such common predatory street crimes as burglary, robbery, theft, arson, prostitution, and low-level narcotics trafficking, they also included murder and a number of more complex and sophisticated crimes. Russian émigré criminals were linked to forgery, counterfeiting, tax and insurance fraud, confidence schemes, and sophisticated extortions. Some forged ties with members of La Cosa Nostra.

Russian émigré criminals were associated in various ways with the Colombo, Gambino, Genovese, and Lucchese families in New York and New Jersey. The relatively few United States law-enforcement agencies that had concerned themselves with this issue offered varying explanations for the emergence of Russian émigré criminal activity. One was that Soviet officials had intentionally released criminals from its prisons and commingled them with Jewish émigrés who were permitted to leave the Soviet Union in the mid-1970s. Another was that members of organized-crime groups in Odessa, Ukraine, had smuggled themselves out of the country by assuming the identities of Soviet Jews who were either dead or in jail. Still another explanation offered was that the Soviet intelligence agency, the KGB, allowed the criminals to emigrate so as to undermine legitimate Russian communities in other countries and make them unattractive to Soviet citizens.

For several reasons, all of these explanations proved inadequate. First, each assumes that Russian émigré crime in the United States is largely a product of a professional criminal class that has imported its criminal ways onto our shores. Several of the criminals known to have operated in Brighton Beach during the 1980s and 1990s, such as Evsei Agron, Marat Balagula, Emil Puzyretsky, and Boris Nayfeld, provide support for this assertion as they were, in fact, products of the Soviet prison system. Nevertheless, the actual number of known Russian émigré criminals who entered the United States in the 1970s and 1980s, either with or without the consent of Soviet officials, was relatively small and, in general, their crimes have been very localized.

No matter how aggressive or vicious they may be individually, they have neither the critical mass nor the criminal sophistication to create a major local or regional threat, much less a national or international one. Second, none of the explanations takes into account the effect that the collapse of the Soviet Union has had in the United States. History has shown that the growth of organized crime in any community is invariably linked to the recent migration into that community by ethnic groups having weak ties to the dominant political culture. During the years immediately prior to and even more so after the collapse of the Soviet Union, the number of persons permitted to emigrate to the United States from former Soviet republics increased dramatically. For example, in 1992, 129,500 nonimmigrant visas were issued to persons from Russia, Belarus, and Ukraine. In 1988, just four years earlier, only 3,000 such visas were issued. Currently, about 350,000 Russian émigrés reside in the United States, as compared to about 75,000 just 10 years ago. Much of this growing population is concentrated in a few cities like New York and Philadelphia. In addition, it has been estimated that a large number of Russian émigrés have overstayed their visitors' visas and are living illegally in the United States.

Thus, the rise in crime in Russian émigré communities is more likely attributable to the increased numbers of Russians living in this country than to a small number of violent criminals. Finally, the proponents of these explanations fail to recognize and understand the peculiarities of the societal environment of the Soviet Union. As is true in all societies, people are conditioned by the moral, social, and economic environment in which they live. Soviet citizens were reared by a government which, although unable to provide basic necessities adequately for its people, lavishly rewarded high-ranking and loyal members of its dominant political party. Thus, to survive, many Soviet citizens were forced to find ways to "beat the system" without being caught. Actions such as bribing an official to do a favor, paying a premium to obtain desired goods, or buying necessities from black-market sellers became common practices accepted by the general population as necessary for survival. Consequently, many Russian émigrés are well schooled in this type of behavior. Lydia Rosier observed that "immigration from the Soviet Union brought to America's shores many people for whom crime [is] but ordinary behavior."

According to Rosier, some Russian émigrés are criminals who, out of necessity, manipulate the system to survive. They do not consider themselves to be criminals, even though they regularly break the law. Others are professional criminals, those already pointed to as the core of Russian crime in the United States. Both types know very well how to skirt the bureaucracy and adapt governmental services for private gain. This is not to suggest that all Russian émigrés either came to the United States for the purpose of committing crimes or became criminals after arriving. It does suggest, however, that the potential crime problem should not be considered as being limited to the professional criminals. Crime in general—and organized crime in particular—have traditionally provided routes of upward mobility for immigrants in the United States.

Immigrants who turned to crime often did so out of frustration at being blocked from other avenues for advancement. Russian émigrés differ considerably, however, from prior immigrant groups in their ability to take advantage of both legitimate and illegitimate routes to success. Unlike the farmers and unskilled laborers who comprised the majority of earlier immigrations to this country, Russian émigrés are generally urban in origin, well educated, and industrially and technologically skilled. Despite a language barrier, they have marketable skills and have not been closed off from the legitimate ladders of upward mobility. In sum, Russian-émigré crime in the United States did not grow out of the same cultural alienation and economic disparity experienced by other immigrant groups.

Russian émigré criminals did not begin their criminal careers as members of adolescent street gangs in ethnic ghettos, as did many Irish, Italian, Jewish, African-American, Latino, and, more recently, Chinese and Vietnamese criminals. Instead, they engage in a variety of frauds, scams, and swindles because those are the kinds of crimes that most closely build upon their previous experience in the former Soviet Union. Unlike their ethnic predecessors in crime, Russian émigrés do not have to go through any developmental or learning process to break into the criminal world in this country. They are able to operate almost immediately upon their arrival.

One of the central challenges in combatting the Russian Mafiya is gaining an understanding of the underlying nature of the types of crimes committed by Russian émigrés. Analysis of the information by authorities has revealed that Russian émigrés are involved in a broad variety of crimes ranging from simple theft to sophisticated fraud to murder. Some of these crimes are being committed by individual criminals; others bear some indicia of organized criminal activity. As illustrated by the examples set forth below, Russian-émigré crimes often involve extensive planning within varying networks of individuals. The most common types of crime being committed by Russian émigrés are those that involve some form of deception.

Many of these crimes, such as jewelry switching, are simple scams perpetrated by low-level street criminals. Others, such as insurance fraud, are much more complex and sophisticated. To succeed, complex crimes require great deal of coordination among criminals, as well as infiltration of legitimate areas of the economy.

MOTOR-FUEL TAX FRAUD

The largest and most publicized frauds involving Russian émigrés have been motor fuel tax scams—frauds in which the perpetrators sell and resell gasoline and diesel fuel without paying required excise taxes. These frauds have cost the government an estimated $1 billion annually in lost tax revenues during the last decade. Much of this money has been diverted to La Cosa Nostra and its Russian émigré partners. Prior to 1982, New York State required individual gas stations to be responsible for the collection of fuel taxes. Many of the stations, however, sold their fuel, failed to pay the required taxes, and then either went out of business or changed corporate ownership before revenue officials were able to collect the taxes due. To end this practice, New York shifted tax collection responsibility from retailer to wholesaler. Lost tax revenues continued, though, as unscrupulous criminals quickly identified a way to take advantage of the new law.

The estimated national average of federal, state, and sales tax for gasoline is .35 cents a gallon. Licensed fuel companies began to purchase bulk fuel and move it through bogus "sales" to a series of dummy wholesale companies. This created what came to be known as a daisy chain. The fuels never actually moved. The dummy companies simply filed invoices with the government, along with fraudulent tax-exemption forms stating that the company had bought and sold fuel. One of the dummy companies along the daisy chain was a "burn company" that was ostensibly responsible for paying the taxes but that, instead, went out of business without doing so. Revenue collectors were left with a complex trail of paper that led to a dead end.

In New Jersey, the most significant motor fuel tax scams involve the purchase and sale of diesel fuel, which is used to power diesel engines in trucks and other vehicles. Diesel fuel is virtually identical in chemical composition to home heating oil. At the refinery, both diesel fuel and heating oil are designated as number-two fuel. When purchased for resale as home heating oil, the fuel is not taxable. When purchased as diesel fuel, however, it is subject to state and federal motor fuel excise taxes. Russian émigré criminals and other scam artists have found various ways to take advantage of this distinction. Typically, tax evaders buy number-two fuel and sell it as diesel fuel to retailers, at a price that includes state and federal taxes, without remitting the taxes to the government. Sometimes, daisy chain is used to commit the scam, and the fuel is sold to several dummy companies, all or some of which file falsified invoices indicating the required taxes have been paid. Other times, scam operators simply purchase nontaxable heating oil and sell it as diesel fuel. Either way, the opportunity for illicit gain is great. In New Jersey, the total tax due on the sale of diesel fuel is 41.9 cents per gallon.

Recently, the state of New Jersey recognized its motor fuel tax law needed revision. Prior to July 1, 1992, state law required that wholesalers collect motor fuel excise taxes. New Jersey's legislature changed this, however, in response to recommendations that resulted from a New Jersey State Commission of Investigation public hearing in the fall of 1991. State law now mandates that retail sellers of diesel fuel collect the required taxes. The daisy chain scam not only costs the government a great deal of money but has the added effect of forcing many legitimate fuel wholesalers and retailers out of business. This is because the unpaid federal and state taxes are not entirely pocketed by the perpetrators of this fraud. Rather, a percentage of these illicit profits, in the form of lower wholesale prices, is passed on to retailers who take part in the scam. Legitimate fuel retailers are unable to compete with the lower prices offered by the bootleggers.

The self-admitted originator of the daisy-chain fraud was Lawrence Iorizzo, a Long Island businessman. In the early 1980s Iorizzo began to sell untaxed motor fuel through wholesale and retail companies he owned. In 1981 Iorizzo's businesses were threatened by a local gang of thugs, and he contacted Colombo crime-family member Michael Franzese for help. In return for protection from La Cosa Nostra, Iorizzo offered Franzese a partnership in the profitable business of selling untaxed gasoline.

Contemporaneous with the development of the Iorizzo/Franzese partnership, Michael Markowitz, a Rumanian, was running his own daisy-chain operation in Brooklyn. In addition, several Russian émigrés were also running fuel scams. When the Markowitz operation became the subject of scrutiny by authorities, Markowitz found it necessary to align his network with the Iorizzo/Franzese operation. Eventually, all the daisy-chain operations in the New York area, many of which involved Russian émigrés, came under control of La Cosa Nostra, which regulated the operations as a cartel, mediated disputes between members, and appropriated a percentage of the profits. The fuel-tax scam gradually expanded beyond the New York–New Jersey market to Pennsylvania, Ohio, Texas, California, Georgia, and Florida.

During the past few years, a number of joint investigations by the Internal Revenue Service, the Federal Bureau of Investigation, and various state agencies have focused on motor fuel tax evasion. These investigations have led to the indictment and conviction of numerous Russian émigrés from the tristate region. In April 1993 a federal grand jury indicted fifteen individuals and two businesses involved in a $15 million Pennsylvania tax-fraud scam. That same year, similar indictments were brought in New Jersey, where the federal government charged six Russian émigrés and several members of La Cosa Nostra in connection with a $60 million motor fuel tax scam, and in New York, where 18 individuals, including five Russian émigrés, were charged in connection with a $34 million gas-tax scam.

In 1995, 25 defendants, including 15 Russian émigrés, were charged in a federal indictment filed in New Jersey with defrauding the government of more than $140 million in fuel tax.

INSURANCE AND ENTITLEMENT FRAUD

Insurance fraud is another complex crime frequently committed by Russian émigré criminals. One of the largest medical insurance frauds ever perpetrated in the United States was masterminded by a group of Russian émigrés in California during the middle to late 1980s. Led by Michael Smushkevich, the group set up phony medical clinics and mobile laboratories and solicited patients with promises of free physical examinations and diagnostic tests. The group then submitted fraudulent bills, supported by falsified medical reports and treatment forms, to insurance companies indicating that the clinics had provided medical services prescribed by doctors. Before being caught in 1991 by federal agents, the group had defrauded California insurance companies of more than $50 million.

The most impressive aspect of this insurance scam was the magnitude of the operation. The group set up more than 250 medical clinics and labs; employed dozens of doctors, technicians, clerical workers, and administrative personnel; submitted thousands of claims totaling more than $1 billion; and laundered illicit proceeds through 500 different shell companies and foreign banks. The group was so brazen that when claims were rejected, they were often rebilled under a different clinic name. In 1991, Smushkevich, his wife, his brother, and 10 others were indicted for racketeering, mail fraud, and money laundering. Russian émigré insurance fraud schemes have not been limited to medical coverage.

In the early 1990s, a group of Russian émigrés in Pennsylvania perpetrated an insurance scam in which they staged auto accidents and submitted more than $1 million in phony claims to various insurance companies. The scam was orchestrated by Alexander Zaverukha who, along with his business partner Victor Tsan, owned a medical clinic in Bucks County, Pennsylvania. Zaverukha recruited other Russian émigrés to take part in the scam, then set up eight different traffic accidents, and brought the "injured" parties to his clinic where they were treated for nonexistent injuries. Zaverukha, Tsan, and seven other persons, including a doctor who worked at the clinic, were indicted in 1995 by a federal grand jury. Government entitlement programs such as Medicare and Medicaid have also been the target of Russian émigré criminals. These programs have reported numerous incidents of fraud involving the submission of bills for services or merchandise that were never provided. The submissions range from medical examinations to transportation in ambulettes to the purchase of medical equipment. In 1986, 13 Russian émigrés fraudulently netted thousands of dollars by selling cheap shoes to Medicare recipients and then billing Medicare for the purchase of expensive orthopedic shoes.

Similarly, a Russian émigré in Pennsylvania tried to defraud the United States Food Stamp Program. Peter Cherepinsky, a resident of Philadelphia who owned a food store in Pennsauken, New Jersey, purchased $45,000 worth of fraudulently obtained food-stamp coupons at a discount price and then deposited the coupons into his business checking account. Cherepinsky was indicted in connection with this scam in 1993.

CONFIDENCE SCHEMES

There also have been many incidents in cities throughout the United States involving Russian émigré criminals engaging in various types of confidence schemes. In many cases, the victims of the schemes have also been Russian. Most of the schemes are common scams such as jewelry switching, in which the perpetrator offers to inspect or appraise the victim's jewelry and then substitutes an inexpensive piece for the real one during the inspection. Philadelphia Police Department intelligence files indicate that, in 1981, the city's jewelry district suffered a rash of gem scams purportedly committed by a group of Russian émigrés. The most egregious scam involved the theft of $80,000 worth of diamonds in which the perpetrator allegedly substituted diamond "look-alikes" for real gems. This case was never prosecuted as the victim subsequently withdrew the complaint.

A recently uncovered scam underscores the ability of Russian émigré criminals to identify and take advantage of weaknesses in workplace security systems. In September 1995 Bella Jakubovicz and Asya Drubich were indicted by a federal grand jury in Brooklyn for allegedly participating in the theft of more than $35 million worth of jewelry from their employer, NGI Precious Metals, a Manhattan jewelry manufacturer. The indictment alleges that the women, who emigrated to the United States from the Soviet Union in the early 1980s, would arrive at work before the company's metal detectors were activated, steal bracelets and other jewelry, hide them in the company locker room, and then return to work. The stolen goods were eventually sold to a fence for cash, which was deposited in several Swiss bank accounts. Although NGI Precious Metals went out of business in 1990, authorities were unable to charge the two women until recently because of the difficulties involved in obtaining Swiss bank records.

Many Russian émigré confidence schemes have international aspects. A favored scheme is to arrange contractual agreements between parties in the United States and representatives of governments or private companies in various parts of the former Soviet Union. The contracts involve multimillion-dollar purchases of U.S. goods or technology. The purchases are either made from U.S. companies, or by U.S. companies on behalf of the buyers. In either case, the U.S. companies, which are managed or influenced by Russian émigrés, require a sizable portion of the contract price prior to producing or delivering the product. Once paid, the companies subsequently default or disappear prior to fulfilling the contract, leaving the foreign entity without its purchase and with little recourse. One of these investigations has recently resulted in the indictment of a group of Russian émigrés who allegedly stole more than $5.7 million from 24 Russian businesses and a charity set up to aid victims of the 1986 Chernobyl nuclear accident.

In March 1996 Lev Breskin and Alexander Korogodsky of New Jersey and Yakov Portnov and George Yosifian of New York City were charged in a federal indictment with conspiracy, wire fraud, and money laundering. The indictment charges that in January 1992 the men set up a phony wholesale company in Manhattan and then attended a trade expo in Russia where they met customers seeking to purchase various U.S. products, such as computers, medicine, and coffee, which are not readily available in that country. The men requested full payment in advance of the purchases but promised to deliver the products at very low prices. It is alleged that, after receiving the money, no goods were ever delivered to the victims.

COUNTERFEITING

Counterfeiting is another crime of deception in which Russian émigrés have been active. Several investigations of Russian émigrés involved in the production of counterfeit credit cards. In addition, Russian émigrés have been found to be expert counterfeiters of checks, passports, visas, and other types of identification documents. Research has revealed there are well-established markets for these products within the local Russian communities and that Russian émigrés are now supplying other criminals with their products.

Counterfeiting of credit cards usually involves altering the magnetic strip on the back of a card. The counterfeiters first obtain account information from legitimate credit cards by stealing legitimate cards, obtaining credit card receipts from dishonest vendors, or copying account numbers while peeking over the shoulder of unsuspecting credit card users. The legitimate account information is then encoded onto the magnetic strip of another card. This may be a stolen card, a card that has exceeded its credit limit, or a bogus card produced by the counterfeiters. The card is then used to buy goods from an unsuspecting vendor or a vendor operating in collusion with the perpetrators. When the vendor slides the card through a magnetic reader, information from the legitimate account encoded on the magnetic strip is transmitted to the credit card issuer. Unaware that a bogus card is being used in the transaction, the issuer authorizes the purchase and the goods are charged to the account of the legitimate credit card holder. Although the issuer also transmits the number of the account that has been charged for the purchase, there is little chance that the counterfeiter will be caught even if the vendor is not part of the scam. Cashiers rarely match the account number transmitted by the issuer to the account number on the credit card. As long as the issuer authorizes the purchase, most vendors will only verify that the card and receipt signatures match.

In August 1989 four Russian émigrés were indicted for and later convicted of manufacturing, possessing, and selling $17 million worth of counterfeit U.S. currency and $4 million worth of bogus traveler's checks. A fifth conspirator, Roman Kolompar, is presently a fugitive. The money and checks had been circulated in New York, Chicago, Los Angeles, and Poland.

Another case involved a group of Russian émigrés who sold counterfeit credit cards. The cards, which were printed in Israel and embossed in the United States, were sold to Russian émigrés in Brighton

Beach. The operation, while successful for a time, did not produce high-quality cards. For example, Visa cards manufactured by the group displayed a hologram of a hawk rather than the "Visa dove," and the cards contained obvious misspellings of the words printed on the reverse side. Members of this group were arrested by the United States Secret Service in 1992. A law-enforcement database was instrumental in identifying the group's printer in Israel, who was arrested by Israeli police in November 1992.

In the early 1990s Alexander Semenov and several other Russian émigrés used reencoded credit cards to purchase more than $120,000 worth of goods in New York, Pennsylvania, Massachusetts, Illinois, and California. Upon arrest in 1993 by the United States Secret Service, Semenov tried to conceal his true identity by changing the spelling of his name and his biographical information. However, law-enforcement officials were able to connect him to other incidents of credit card fraud.

VIOLENT CRIMES

Like others who operate in the underworld, Russian émigré criminals have employed violence in furtherance of their criminal pursuits or as a means of settling disputes. Russian émigré criminals have been implicated in numerous murders, attempted murders, assaults, and extortions. In most instances, police investigating the incidents have been unable to find any witnesses to the crimes. Witnesses who were located and interviewed, including victims, often refused to cooperate.

Investigators have gathered information regarding more than 70 murders and attempted murders involving Russian émigrés committed since 1981. All suggest that the victim, perpetrator or both were involved in ongoing criminal activity. Many of the victims were known criminals who had a prior criminal relationship with either the person who attacked them or the person who ordered the attack. In several cases, intelligence information obtained from confidential sources indicated that the victim was attacked as a result of a dispute between two individual criminals or gangs, or in retaliation for a prior violent act. Many of the homicides appear to have been well planned, and in some instances assassins or "hit men" were used to commit the crime. Those who carried out the attacks often used distractions, decoys, or other tricks to gain an advantage over victims.

Fifty-three homicides involved the use of guns, including automatic, semiautomatic, and silencer-equipped handguns. Victims were often shot either at close range, usually in the head or chest, or from a moving vehicle. One victim, who had been stabbed to death, was found floating in Sheepshead Bay, New York. Another was found frozen stiff in a snow bank at a Morris County, New Jersey auto salvage yard, fully clothed in a suit and tie. He had been shot twice in the temple. During the autopsy, bullet-wound scars were discovered on various parts of the deceased's body, indicating he had been the victim of prior shootings.

EXTORTION AND KIDNAPPING

Extorting Russian émigrés who are successful in legitimate or illegitimate business endeavors is another practice among Russian criminals. A reputed major figure in Russian émigré crime in the United States, Vyacheslav Ivankov, was indicted by a federal grand jury in 1995 and charged with attempting to extort $3.5 million from two Russian émigré businessmen in the United States The indictment alleges that the father of one of the extortion targets was beaten to death and left on a train platform in Moscow after the demands by Ivankov and his associates were not met. Ivankov was arrested after the two businessmen agreed to cooperate with U.S. law enforcement.

In Brighton Beach, a Russian émigré shoplifter was the extortion victim of Alexander Levichitz, also known as "Sasha Pinya," a particularly violent Russian émigré criminal. The basis for this extortion is notable. Pinya and his girlfriend became involved in an argument over Pinya's infidelity based upon information provided to Pinya's girlfriend by the shoplifter. Pinya demanded a monetary settlement from the shoplifter to atone for the problem he had caused. Eventually, a resolution was reached whereby the shoplifter provided Pinya with the names of other low-level criminals in Brighton Beach from whom Pinya could successfully extort money.

In September 1993 Pinya was arrested by the Suffolk County District Attorney's Office. In March 1995 four Russian émigrés from Brooklyn used threats and physical violence in an attempt to extort $25,000 from a Russian émigré auto repair shop owner in Roselle, New Jersey. The four pleaded guilty in May 1995.

In 1992 a group of Russian émigrés in Philadelphia sponsored the arrival of women from the former

USSR, the Commonwealth of Independent States to be employed as live-in domestics. The women were subsequently threatened with deportation if they did not turnover a portion of their weekly earnings to their sponsors.

In other cases, the extortion of Russian émigrés residing in the United States has been accomplished by kidnapping the victim and either demanding a ransom from the victim's family or forcing the victim to withdraw money from bank accounts or to purchase money orders for their captors.

DRUG TRAFFICKING

Since the demise of the Soviet Union, the Federal Bureau of Investigation (FBI) and Drug Enforcement Administration report that many of the new republics are being used as transshipment points for deliveries of Colombian cocaine into western Europe. In 1993, Russian authorities in St. Petersburg intercepted a one-ton shipment of cocaine, packaged in cans of corned beef, believed to be the product of a cooperative arrangement between crime groups in Russia and Colombian cartels.

Russian émigrés are also involved with the Colombian cartels in U.S. drug activity. In the late 1980s and early 1990s Russian émigré Vladimir Beigelman of Brooklyn was known to be involved in cocaine trafficking with the Cali cartel. On December 2, 1993, Beigelman was fatally shot in the face while exiting a van in Queens. Witnesses described the assailants as two Hispanics. Evidence indicates Beigelman was murdered in a dispute over a large quantity of missing cocaine.

In 1992 the United States attorney for the Southern District of New York prosecuted 16 individuals, including Russian émigrés David Podlog and Alexander Moysif, on charges of distributing heroin and cocaine. The next year, 24 individuals led by four Russian émigrés were indicted for the manufacture of crack cocaine vials at factories in New Jersey and Pennsylvania. During the arrests, authorities seized more than $1 million in cash, along with several vehicles, stock portfolios, and other property.

In 1994, another federal indictment was filed against Russian-émigré narcotics traffickers. In this indictment, Boris Nayfeld, Shalva Ukleba, Alexander Mikhailov, Simon Elishakov, and Valery Krutiy were charged with participating in the smuggling, distribution, and sale of heroin that originated in Southeast Asia and was smuggled into the United States via Poland.

MONEY LAUNDERING

The demise of the Soviet Union and its transformation to market economy ignited a great deal of currency exchange activity with the United States and Western Europe by Russia and other former Soviet republics. During the last few years, a massive influx of money originating as rubles has been exchanged for U.S. dollars via financial institutions and front companies in this country and Europe and then transported back to the CIS. Fearful that the funds are being used to support criminal organizations, terrorist groups, and drug cartels, law-enforcement officials are trying to determine how much of this activity is legitimate. There is some evidence that suggests the activity is linked to organized crime. The FBI reports that a substantial percentage of these funds is derived from fraud, theft and other criminal activities in the CIS. In addition, many privately owned banks that have surfaced throughout the former Soviet Union and through which many of the transactions are being made are alleged to be owned by Russian organized-crime operatives. Also, during the past year, more than 30 people involved in the Russian banking system have been murdered. Russian authorities believe these events are the result of organized-crime efforts to control the banking industry.

Conversely, there is evidence that much of the increased activity is legitimate. Many of the transactions involve Russian investment firms, financial institutions, and other businesses engaged in international commerce that need convertible currencies, such as U.S. dollars and German marks, to transact business. In addition, Russian companies seeking to upgrade or expand facilities are forced to deal with the United States and other western nations due to the lack of modern technology in Russia. These businesses also exchange rubles for dollars and marks to purchase equipment.

Several factors make it difficult to determine which currency exchanges are legitimate business ventures and which constitute illegal money laundering schemes. First, based upon U.S. law, the transfer of money from one account to another is legal unless it is done for an illegitimate purpose. Second, most of the currency exchanges are made through banks in other countries both before the funds enter and after they leave the United States. This makes tracing the entire route of the funds nearly impossible. Finally, any crimes connected to the exchanges are usually committed in the country that initiated the transfer. Thus, even if U.S. law enforcement can show the funds are illicit and trace their path through the financial institutions involved in the exchanges, it may be impossible to establish jurisdiction over the crime.

One case illustrated the high-tech sophistication of Russian criminals. In 1994 Vladimir Levin, operating in St. Petersburg, Russia, stole $10 million from Citibank via the bank's electronic money transfer system. Using only his computer hacking abilities and the assistance of several other persons, he was able to circumvent the bank's security system and wire transfer the misappropriated funds to accounts in Finland, Russia, Germany, the Netherlands, Israel, Switzerland, and the United States.

Other money-laundering schemes are less sophisticated. Russian émigrés involved in fuel tax scams have used illicit proceeds to purchase vehicles in the United States, which were then shipped to the CIS and resold at three to four times their U.S. retail prices. On other occasions, Russians have simply smuggled money through international borders by secreting it in clothing or body cavities.

In 1994 Yuri Anatoliyevich Desyatov pleaded guilty to smuggling $1.2 million into the United States. Desyatov was involved with extortion and weapons purchasing in addition to money smuggling. Russian émigrés have also been conducting various types of money-laundering schemes in hotels and casinos in Atlantic City. Casino operators indicate that a significant number of Russian émigrés frequent casinos. Many of them are "high rollers," recognized as favored customers and, as such, have received such perks as limousine service, plush hotel suites, meal and alcohol allowances, and seating for prime events.

One of the schemes observed by various law-enforcement agencies, including the United States Secret Service and the New Jersey State Police, involves the use or attempted use of counterfeit currency and traveler's checks. Russian émigré criminals use the bogus currency in amounts below the federal Currency Transaction Report threshold to obtain cash and/or playing chips. In New York City and other financial centers around the country, the potential for Russian money laundering should not be underestimated. During a recent U.S. House of Representatives Banking Committee hearing, U.S.

Federal Reserve Governor Edward W. Kelley, Jr., estimated that nearly $500 billion is laundered through U.S. banks annually. As the use of electronic international banking grows, the vulnerability of these financial institutions to fraudulent transactions becomes a paramount concern to law enforcement everywhere. Manipulation of these institutions could seriously impact the economic stability of this country. Vice Crimes Project staff members have developed little data concerning Russian émigré vice crimes. Although gambling and prostitution rings exist, they are predominantly small-scale operations in Brighton Beach and other Russian communities. The project found no evidence that Russian émigré criminal organizations are exercising widespread control over these types of criminal activities.

One recent case in New Jersey, however, reveals both the willingness and ability of Russian émigré criminals to maximize profits by transporting criminal activities. Earlier this year, police in North Brunswick, investigating what they believed to be a prostitution ring, arrested several female dancers inside a local go-go bar. One of the females was a Russian juvenile who, police later learned, was an exotic dancer brought from Brooklyn, along with several other young Russian females, to dance in go-go bars and work in massage parlors in central and northern New Jersey. The dancers were being driven to and from New Jersey by a hired driver.

THE NATURE OF RUSSIAN-ÉMIGRÉ CRIME

There is a tendency on the part of some in law enforcement and the media to readily adopt simplistic, stereotypical perceptions of organized crime. This has certainly been true in regard to Russian crime, where terms such as *Russian Mafia* have been loosely applied. Superimposing descriptions that fit other known criminal groups on Russian émigré criminals impedes the ability of law enforcement to identify and address the real problem.

In Russia, criminals typically fall into three major types: (1) the *vory v zakone*; (2) the young entrepreneurs; and (3) the "thieves in authority."

Vory v Zakone

Reputed members of the *vory v zakone*, or "thieves in law," have been said to be the closest thing the ex-Soviets have to being a "made guy" in La Cosa Nostra, and the top *vory* are portrayed as godfatherlike figures. The *vory* are the most sophisticated of the professional criminals. Their roots are generally traced to the Soviet prison system—more specifically, to the far-flung gulag prison network established by Stalin in the 1930s. Most vory have spent the bulk of their lives in prison and profess a complete submission to the criminal life. They maintain their own laws and rules and reject any involvement with or obligation to the legitimate world. According to one Russian expert, the association of vory is a rather loose structure with little differentiation among its members, and with the elite being just the first among equals.

There are an estimated 600 vory in the former Soviet Union, with approximately 200 of them in Russia. The elite make up a Moscow-based politburo of 10–15 vory who govern the criminal world through their representatives. Vyacheslav Ivankov is alleged to be one of the 200 vory in Russia and perhaps even among the top leadership group.

The vory share a number of characteristics with members of La Cosa Nostra: a set of rules, a code of behavior, nicknames, and their own vernacular. They also have a system for mediating and resolving disputes. Whether there is any enforcement mechanism to back-up the resolutions from these meditations is not clear. It should be reiterated, however, that the vory's rules and code of conduct are practiced principally in the closed environment of the Soviet prison system where they have lived most of their lives. Of the three major types of Russian criminals, the vory most resemble the members of La Cosa Nostra. Thus, an argument can be made that they constitute the greatest criminal threat currently presented by Russians in the United States. The credibility of such a threat is conditioned, however, on a number of factors, such as the number of vory presently in the United States, how closely they are linked to the Moscow-based crime leaders, and how successfully they can organize and control the multitude of criminal ventures in which Russians are involved in the United States.

The FBI estimates that there have been as many as five vory in the United States at one time or another. The real potential for harm from the vory will depend on how well internal discipline can be maintained outside the prisons walls where their roots lie. This control will be complicated by the fact that criminal activity is now taking place thousands of miles from Moscow.

Some experts challenge the primacy of the vory, both as present and future threat. It is alleged that the traditional initiation into the vory has been corrupted by the selling of this title. If so, this would affect whether and how well internal discipline can be maintained. The criminal expertise of the vory is also more likely to involve common crimes such as theft, robbery, and extortion. More complex crimes such as international banking and commodities scams, money laundering, and dealing in strategic metals may be beyond the scope of their criminal expertise. The vory are the most astute criminals at present but may constitute less of a problem over the long term. Some experts believe that although the vory still dominate the traditional criminal world in Russia, especially in prison, the gangster bureaucrats, with their intertwined links to the government, will soon dominate the social, economic, and political structures of the former Soviet Union. Russia is currently a very attractive venue for criminal pursuits. As those pursuits grow in size and sophistication, it is expected that these criminals will look to expand their interests internationally.

Young Entrepreneurs

The young entrepreneurs see crime as the easy route to riches. These are people in their late teens to mid-30s who were not criminals before the collapse of the Soviet Union but who, out of necessity, had experience in the Soviet black market and shadow economy. Some are students or graduates of higher education; others were in the military. Few, if any, have attractive job prospects in the legitimate sector. They constitute a pool for recruitment by criminal organizations in Russia or operate within their own small group. Unlike that of the professionals, their criminal behavior is not very well entrenched. They are first generation criminals, and their crimes are most often crimes of opportunity.

Thieves in Authority

The "thieves in authority" or avtoritety, arose during the last few decades of the Soviet Union, beginning during the Brezhnev era. Some were part of the Communist Party and/or were Soviet bureaucrats. They were part of what has been called the Soviet Mafia. Some were deputy directors or former administrators of factories and other business enterprises. Others ran cooperatives during the Gorbachev era or were members of the national security and military establishments. Whatever their background, nearly all are well-educated persons who possess international connections. These "gangster–bureaucrats" operate at the intersection of crime, capitalism, and government in the former Soviet Union. They have the knowledge, experience, sophistication, and contacts needed to run international banking schemes and major commodities deals. They are also the ones best suited to deal in black-market nuclear materials. For these reasons, they have the greatest potential for future harm both within and outside the CIS.

LA COSA NOSTRA AND RUSSIAN-ÉMIGRÉ CRIMINALS

In the view of some, Russian émigré criminals are organized in a continuing structure to conduct a variety of criminal ventures. There have been reports that between three and five Russian émigré organized-crime "families" presently exist in the New York area. Vyacheslav Ivankov's arrival in the United States was seen by many as proof that a centralized Russian criminal organization exists. When he was arrested in 1995, Ivankov was labeled, in La Cosa Nostra terms, the *capo di tutticapi,* or "boss of bosses," of Russian crime in the United States.

An opposing view is that Russian émigré criminals have no defined organizational structure or hierarchy. This view holds that Russian criminals are individuals who do not follow a rigid authoritarian structure. Instead, "like liquid mercury on a countertop," according to an article that appeared in the *New York Daily News* (June 9, 1995), they operate mainly as individual specialists or in fluid groups that occasionally unite to commit a crime.

Based upon its review and assessment of Russian émigré crime, law-enforcement officials believe that the reality lies somewhere between these two positions. With the exception of the *vory v zakone,* it is believed that Russian émigré criminal organizations are not, by and large, like the families of La Cosa Nostra. There is no evidence of either a central "commission" which oversees the various Russian émigré criminal activities or even a few hierarchical groups that engage in specialized criminal activities. Although Russian criminals have shown a propensity for extreme violence and possess the capacity to corrupt, they have yet to assert monopoly power in any of their U.S. criminal activities other than in the fuel frauds where they functioned as partners of La Cosa Nostra.

The professional criminals and opportunists who currently characterize Russian émigré crime in the United States typically mistrust each other. There is generally little or no personal loyalty based upon common ethnic or cultural backgrounds, even though some of the criminals knew each other in the former USSR. The most prevalent network structure is usually an ad hoc team of specialists who are mustered for specific criminal ventures usually pertaining to crimes of deception. These specialists form opportunistic partnerships which are sometimes based on referrals by other Russian criminals. After the criminal objective is attained, the specialists may split up or may move together to other criminal ventures.

Networks of specialists, however, are not the only manner in which Russian émigré criminals organize. Professional criminals who profess a propensity for violence have formed small criminal groups to commit extortions or engage in narcotics trafficking. These groups often center around one or more dominant individuals and the composition of the group is subject to frequent change.

One way to contrast La Cosa Nostra and Russian émigré criminal organizations is to view the former as having a structure—a distinct, definable crime family—that is supported by criminal activities. The structure is continuous, and crime is used to carry out its objectives and maintain its strength and vitality. Russians, however, create floating structures on an as-needed basis to enable them to carry out particular crimes. The criminal opportunities come first, and the necessary structure to take advantage of those opportunities follows. Generally, La Cosa Nostra is structure oriented; members use criminal activities to support the structure. Russian émigré criminals are venture oriented; they use structure to support their criminal activity.

HARM CAPACITY

The critical distinction between organized crime and all other crime lies in its capacity to cause harm. Assessing the harm potential of Russian émigré criminals is, therefore, vital to understanding the Russian criminal threat.

Harm occurs in a variety of ways—economic, physical, psychological, and societal. Economic harm includes monetary losses by victims, illicit gains by criminals, and detrimental effects to the marketplace. Physical harm is the violence used to attain and retain monopoly control over criminal ventures. Psychological harm involves the creation of a climate of fear and intimidation and a perception that criminal networks can avoid apprehension by law enforcement. Societal harm is the undermining of the system, the compromising of the political process, and the corruption of law enforcement and other institutions.

The motor fuel tax scams exhibit most of the harms caused by organized crime. First, economic harm is caused when conspirators keep the tax due and discount the fuel sold to motor fuel retailers. This allows those retailers who purchased their product from the conspirators to undersell their competitors, increase their profits and gain a greater market share. The price advantage enjoyed by these retailers destroys competition in the retail market over time. In this way, predatory pricing can upset the entire distribution system. Second, physical harm is caused. A cartel of motor fuel bootleggers enforces the rules of the cartel through the use of threats and violence. Third, psychological harm is caused when retailers are intimidated into purchasing nontaxed motor fuels from the cartel. Finally, societal harm may be caused if the cartels continue to grow in power and accumulate wealth. This could, eventually, permit them to entrench their position through corruption of the established political structure.

The capacity to cause harm is determined by the size, scope, sophistication, and, especially, continuity of the criminal networks involved. The harm occurs when criminal organizations attempt to monopolize specific areas of the marketplace and employ violence and corruption to attain criminal objectives.

MONOPOLY POWER

Just as a desire for market monopoly exists in the licit marketplace, so it exists in the illicit marketplace as well, and for the same reason—to optimize wealth and power. Monopoly power is attained by forcing out and discouraging competition. This is achieved through the threat and use of force and violence and by obtaining advantages over competitors, such as the ability to underprice, through other criminal activity. Market monopolies permit the accumulation of wealth and power, which can then be used to corrupt the legal and political systems. This, in turn, further solidifies the criminal organization's positioning the marketplace. This is the essence of organized crime. It is the most severe and insidious form of harm caused by organized crime.

La Cosa Nostra has monopolized many different areas of the marketplace. For the past several decades, law enforcement in this country has fought to eradicate La Cosa Nostra's influence over these areas. Conversely, Russian émigré criminals have not yet established monopoly control over any of their U.S. criminal activities. Although Russian émigrés were among the first to take part in the motor fuel tax scams, monopoly control of this activity was not attained until members of La Cosa Nostra became involved.

USE OF VIOLENCE

The demonstrated willingness to use force and violence to attain a monopoly, discourage competition, and intimidate witnesses is also one of the hallmarks of organized crime. It is systematic and functional in that it furthers the interests of the criminal organization. La Cosa Nostra uses violence as a calculated tool for business gain, to enforce mediated agreements, and to organize markets. On the other hand, Russian émigré criminal violence appears to be a mix of the calculated and the ad hoc.

Russian émigrés have shown a willingness to use violent acts to achieve their criminal goals. There have been numerous murders and attempted murders involving Russian émigrés in the tristate region, many of which remain unsolved. Generally, however, these crimes appear to be neither systematic nor designed to protect any particular criminal enterprise; instead, they seem to have been motivated by greed or personal vendetta. For example, in 1995, Monya Elson and a group called Monya's Brigada were indicted by a federal grand jury for, among other crimes, three murders and one attempted murder. This violence reportedly resulted from Elson's desire for recognition and stature. Two of the victims were targeted by Elson because he was jealous of their status in the criminal community.

There have also been numerous extortions of Russian émigrés in the region. Many of these were committed by enforcers, criminals who specialize in extorting Russian-owned businesses in Brighton Beach and elsewhere. The enforcers work for whomever pays them. Although, occasionally, there may be disputes between individuals or groups regarding certain extortion victims, most of the extortions appear to be opportunistic rather than a systematic approach to obtain power or control.

Russian violence is not random in the same sense as the drive-by shootings of street gangs. Russian émigré criminals appear to exercise some care in choosing their victims and avoiding harm to innocent bystanders. Furthermore, several Russian émigré murders and attempted murders resulted from attempts to assert hegemony over various market areas, such as the bootleg motor fuel business, or to settle scores between criminal groups. Nevertheless, there is a view among some in law enforcement that the Russians' reputation for violence exceeds the reality of its use, at least in the United States. As has been true in United States drug markets, a great deal of Russian émigré violence is attributable to the unregulated competition that exists in their criminal ventures.

USE OF CORRUPTION

The threat of Russian émigré criminals using corruption as a means to further their criminal pursuits is more of a potential than an actual harm. La Cosa Nostra uses corruption to facilitate its criminal activities, eliminate competition, and entrench itself in the marketplace. At the present time, Russian émigré criminals in the United States have not cultivated the appropriate political contacts to emulate La Cosa Nostra. Perhaps they presently see no need to maintain corrupt relationships to further criminal objectives. Should the situation change, however, Russian émigrés do possess the capacity to corrupt. They are products of a system that is accustomed to bribing politicians and government officials and in which corruption is a way of life.

In the meantime, the pervasive corruption that exists throughout the governments of the former Soviet republics creates problems for U.S. law-enforcement agencies collaborating with their counterparts in those countries. For example, ascertaining whether a Russian émigré suspect in the United States has a criminal history or is currently under investigation in one of the former Soviet republics is risky because the target may be informed about the inquiry. The U.S. Immigration and Naturalization Service indicates that it is often impossible to find out whether a U.S. visa applicant from one of the former Soviet republics has a criminal background. In these and other ways, corruption in the former Soviet Union may facilitate Russian émigré crime in the United States.

Russian éemigré criminals constitute a serious and evolving crime threat in the United States. At present, Russian émigré criminals do not possess either the organizational or the harm capacity that would warrant considering this threat as critical as the threat posed by South America drug cartels or La Costa Nostra. Nevertheless, given the sophisticated nature of their criminal activities, as well as the extensive planning and coordination those activities require, it may be only a matter of time before the Russian émigré crime threat reaches that level.

Russian émigré criminal groups in the United States do not resemble traditional organized crime, such as La Cosa Nostra. Russian émigré groups lack the structure and permanence found in other crime groups. Instead, Russian émigré criminals operate within an amorphous confederation in which roles are not as clearly defined and relationships among members not as continuous as those within other criminal organizations. Furthermore, other than in connection with the motor-fuel tax scams, that Russian émigré criminals are not employing or attempting to employ violence and corruption to attain monopoly power or organize the marketplaces in which they are functioning. Russian émigré crimes have been and are being committed mainly by individual opportunists or ad hoc criminal groups.

Despite these differences, Russian émigré criminals could very well prove to be more prolific and successful in this country than other more-structured crime groups. Although maintaining a permanent, continuous organization has, in the past, proven to be significantly advantageous in the criminal world, it has also led, in part, to the decline of many criminal groups. The very structure which enables criminal organizations, such as La Cosa Nostra, to survive continuously despite the loss of one or more of its members, also provides law enforcement with a window through which the organization can be attacked. Thus, although there is evidence that some Russian émigré criminals are beginning to develop more structured, hierarchal organizations, the present lack of structure within Russian émigré crime groups may prove to be even more troubling to law enforcement.

In any case, Russian émigré criminals in the United States present a formidable problem for law enforcement. They are generally more intelligent and sophisticated than most criminals and are imbued with a business acumen rarely seen in traditional organized crime groups. Having been "trained" under the black-market and shadow economy of the former Soviet Union, Russian émigré criminals are adept at identifying weaknesses in legal, business, and financial systems and capitalizing on those weaknesses for their financial benefit. They survived under the strict, punitive control of the communists and are clearly willing to continue their criminal ways in this country.

History has shown that criminal networks often evolve into more harmful types of organized crime. The evolution of Russian émigré crime will be governed by the social context in which the criminal groups are operating. Consumer demand for its particular goods and services, its ability to expand, the amount of attention devoted to it by law enforcement, and competition from other crime groups will each influence the domestic growth of Russian émigré crime. The task of American law enforcement is to shape the social context and create obstacles so as to keep Russian criminals from developing the capacity for greater harm.

It is also recognized that the prospective Russian organized-crime problem may have no connection to Russian émigré crime other than a common heritage; yet, it is one that, potentially, may cause severe harm within the United States. Currently, within the CIS, there are numerous criminal organizations that are demonstrating an enormous capacity for harm. They have acquired monopoly control of a broad array of illegal and legal enterprises, including some Russian banks, and have amassed considerable wealth and power within the CIS in a relatively short span of time. These organizations have used violence—against businessmen, journalists, and government and law-enforcement personnel—to acquire and maintain their monopoly control and are also engaging in massive corruption to facilitate their criminal pursuits.

The geographic and political barriers that had impeded the Soviet Union from full participation in the global economy are gone. Ease of travel and enhanced global communications will continue the expansion of international business, both legal and illegal, in the CIS. As criminal organizations and gangster bureaucrats position themselves to further their political power and wealth, their business/criminal activities will continually extend internationally. The proliferation of money laundering between the CIS and the United States is evidence that this expansion is already underway. The task for U.S. law enforcement is to counter both of these Russian crime threats simultaneously. State and local agencies, with assistance and cooperation from federal agencies, must ensure that more permanent and sophisticated criminal networks do not evolve within their jurisdictions. At the same time federal law-enforcement agencies must assume primary responsibility for countering the international organized-crime threat. Together, these efforts can prevent the "Russian Mafia" from becoming the 21st century's La Cosa Nostra.

See also: ELSON, MONYA; IVANKOV, VYACHESLAV; KORATAEV, OLEG; LYUBARSKY, VYACHESLAV; MARKOWITZ, MICHAEL; MIKHAILOV, SERGEI; MICHAILOV, YEVGENI; ZAPINAKMINE, OLEG; ZILBERSTEYN, VLADIMIR.

Reference

New Jersey State Commission of Investigation, New York Organized Crime Task Force, New York State Commission of Investigation, Pennsylvania Crime Commission, with Rutgers University. "The Tri-State Joint Soviet-Émigré Organized Crime Project." 1992. Available online. URL: http://www.state.nj.us/sci/pdf/russian.pdf. Accessed on November 24, 2004.

SA, Khun *See* OPERATION TIGER TRAP.

SABINI, Charles (a.k.a. Darby)
In the period between the First and Second World Wars, Charles "Darby" Sabini lead the Sabini gang. Sabini was known to have 300 armed men at his disposal, as well as a herd of judges, politicians, and senior policemen in his pay at the height of his power. According to some authorities, he built the largest organized-crime enterprise ever seen in the United Kingdom.

Sabini ran the Italian mob in Clerkenwell and was known for importing Sicilian muscle to handle turf disputes when they could not recruit more men locally. He and his gang operated for more than 20 years in the United Kingdom, running extortion rackets, theft rings, and night clubs. They were the first real English organized-crime group to have international connections. They were famous for being involved in horse racing, especially in South England. By the end of World War II, Sabini's influence and muscle gave way to a new breed of organized-crime gangs.

SAKIK Clan
On June 16, 1994, "Servet Ipek." born in 1964, was arrested for murder in Germany. The investigation showed that "Ipek's" real name was Seyyar Sakik, born in Mush in 1962, wanted in Turkey, and on the lam in Germany. It also uncovered that the murder was the end result of the trafficking of 190 kilograms of heroin between Turkey and Germany. Seyyar Sakik's brothers are Sirri Sakik, a DEP (outlawed Turkish Democracy Party) deputy, and Semdin Sakik, until recently head of PKK (Partiya Karkaren Kurdistan, or Kurdistan Workers' Party) guerrilla operations in Tunceli Province, and now regarded as the PKK's number-two "political" leader. In Germany, Idriss Sakik, a cousin of the first two, is in charge of wholesale heroin sales. In Turkey, the Sakik Clan is known for its pro-PKK militantism.

On November 3, 1993, Abdulsamet Sakik was killed by elite Turkish forces. Semdin Sakik was arrested in April of 1998, but suffered serious kidney problems. He was found guilty of armed treason and was sentenced to death in 1999. His sentence was commuted in 2002 to life imprisonment.

See also: BAYBASIN CLAN; DEMIR CLAN; KAYA CLAN; KITAY CLAN; KONUKLU-AY CLAN; KURDISH CRIMINAL CLANS AND THE PKK; SENAR CLAN.

References
Metehan Demir. "Sakik in Intensive Care." *Turkish Daily News.* Available online. URL: http://www.turkishdaily news.com/old_editions/04_21_98/dom.htm#d1. Downloaded on July 15, 2004.
———. "What the European Union Reforms Will Bring." *Turkish Daily News.* Available online. URL: http://www.

turkishdailynews.com/old_editions/08_06_02/dom.htm#d10. Downloaded on July 15, 2004.

SALAZAR-IZQUIERDO, Diego Fernando (a.k.a. Zorro)   *See* OPERATION FOXHUNT.

SALCIDO Uzeta, Manuel (a.k.a. El Cochiloco, The Crazy Pig)

Well-known Sinaloan drug lord Manuel Salcido Uzeta lives in Culiacán, the state capital of the Mexican state of Sinaloa. He has been known to use the port of Manzanillo as his main port for drug trafficking.

"In the post-war years, traffickers from Sinaloa became definitely the most important in the country. They began with opium smuggling, and continued with marihuana, cocaine and methamphetamines, depending on the demand," wrote noted Mexican scholar and journalist Luis Astroga in *Drug Trafficking in Mexico: A First General Assessment*. "In the seventies, Pedro Avilés, Manuel Salcido Uzeta (the "Crazy Pig"), and specially Miguel Angel Félix Gallardo, were the most common names." Astrog noted that the authorities had seized more than 875 tons of cocaine and marijuana as well as intercepting more than 671 kilograms of raw opium.

"In all of these cases, information about the drug and the name of the organizations has not been made public."

SALINAS GUERRA, Hector

On July 17, 1997, Hector Salinas Guerra, a primary witness in a McAllen, Texas, trial of a major Mexican marijuana drug-trafficking organization, was kidnapped by members of this organization at gunpoint from his place of business in McAllen, Texas. His tortured, badly decomposed body was found on July 22, 1997, in an open field in Reynosa, Tamaulipas, Mexico. Salinas was to testify in a trial that was scheduled to begin on July 21, 1997. Subsequently, on July 25, 1997, a jury in McAllen, Texas, reached a verdict of acquittal for the seven defendants in this case. This abduction and murder highlights the violent nature of drug trafficking along the U.S.-Mexico border and the threats posed not only to U.S. and Mexican law officials, but also to cooperating sources and witnesses.

Reference
Thomas A. Constantine. "DEA Congressional Testimony." U.S. Drug Enforcement Administration. Available online. URL: http://www.usdoj.gov/dea/pubs/cngrtest/ct980226.htm. Downloaded on July 28, 2004.

SANTA Cruz Londono, José

José Santa Cruz Londono, the third part of the triumverate that ruled the Cali cartel, ran the organization along with Gilberto and Miguel Angel Rodríguez Orejuela. Records indicate two known arrests for Santa Cruz Londono, the first in 1976 when he traveled from New York to Costa Rica on a U.S. passport, and the second in 1977 when he was arrested in Queens, New York, by the New York City police on weapons charges. He served no jail time. Santa Cruz Londono had been a Drug Enforcement Administration (DEA) fugitive since April 1980 and had been indicted four times in the United States, including as part of Operation Cornerstone in Miami.

Santa Cruz Londono's cocaine-distribution and money-laundering operation centered around the New York metropolitan area. In 1992, the DEA seized two cocaine conversion laboratories in Brooklyn, New York, that were directly linked to Santa Cruz Londono. He was considered one of the most violent members of the Cali Mafia and is an expert manager of worldwide cocaine distribution, production, and money laundering.

The Cali Mafia was responsible for 80 percent of the world's cocaine supply and had an estimated annual income of $7 billion. Financial records indicate Santa Cruz Londono's net worth at several billion dollars at the cartel's height.

Santa Cruz Londono was one of the premier drug traffickers in the world; he had been involved in large-scale cocaine trafficking since 1970. The Santa Cruz organization operated in the United States primarily in New York City, Miami, Los Angeles, San Francisco, Houston, Las Vegas, and Chicago. DEA investigations also have tied Santa Cruz Londono to drug-money-laundering operations in various cities in Europe and the Americas.

In addition to drug trafficking, Santa Cruz was wanted for the 1989 assassination of former Antioquia (Colombia) governor Antonio Roldan Betancur and was linked to the 1992 murder of journalist Manuel de Dios Unanue in New York.

Santa Cruz Londono was taken into custody on July 4 by Colombian National Police at 8:00 P.M. while he dined at the Carbon de Polo Restaurant in Bogotá, Colombia. Thomas A. Constantine, administrator of the Drug Enforcement Administration, said, "In its war against the Cali drug Mafia, the Colombian Government is to be commended for this arrest, and for the recent arrest of Gilberto Rodriguez-Orejuela. However, major mafia leaders like Santa Cruz Londono and Rodriguez-Orejuela must be prosecuted and punished to the extent commensurate with their nefarious criminal acitivities, and cannot be permitted to manage their operations from prison. The arrest of Santa Cruz Londono in Bogotá, Colombia, last night is another crippling blow to the Cali Mafia. Coupled with the arrest last month of Gilberto Rodriguez-Orejuela, this action by the Colombian National Police demonstrates that the Cali Mafia is not invincible. Santa Cruz Londono has long been a vicious player in the international cocaine trade, and his arrest is welcome news to the DEA."

See also: CALI CARTEL; MEDELLÍN CARTEL; MEJÍA-MUNERA, MIGUEL AND VICTOR; OPERATION CORNERSTONE; RODRÍGUEZ OREJUELA, GILBERTO; RODRÍGUEZ OREJUELA, MIGUEL ANGEL.

Reference

U.S. Drug Enforcement Administration, U.S. Department of Justice. "Arrest of Cali Mafia leader Jose Santa Cruz-Londono." Available online. URL: http://www. usdoj.gov/dea/pubs/pressrel/pr950705.htm. Downloaded on July 15, 2004.

SANTAPAOLA, Benedetto "Nitto"

Benedetto Santapaola was a visionary Sicilian mafioso. The head of the Catania clan, he had risen through the ranks as an enforcer and deadly assassin of the much feared and revered Salvatore "Toto" Riina, one of the most powerful of all Italian mobsters of the last 40 years, and served Riina faithfully for three decades from the 1970s through Riina's death. A loyal soldier and respected counselor as well, he was in line to succeed Riina upon the older don's death. However, Nitto was don for only five months.

According to http://www.geocities.com/Organized CrimeSyndicates, "Santapaola, head of the Catania Clan, is credited with building a working relationship with the Columbian cartels leading to the rise of the super Mafia families of the 90s." The Criminal Justice Policy Foundation (June 1999 News Briefs) also weighed in on Santapaola, describing him as "the mastermind of Mafia involvement in the international drug trade, including recent efforts to build a global alliance with Colombian cocaine cartels. The alliance allegedly involved providing the Colombians with access to the Mafia's drug distribution and money laundering channels in return for a major share of European and American cocaine profits."

A member of the regional commission would have participated and then deliberated the massacre of Able when Giovanni Falcone was murdered. Santapaola was arrested on June 18, 1993, at 54 years of age. As recently as October 7, 2000, Tommaso Sum, 41 years old, a high-ranking soldier in the Santapaola clan, was arrested by police officers of Caltagirone. He was a key link to the control and the management of economic activities, concessions, and public contracts. This was thought to be a mortal blow to Nitto's continued operations while he was behind bars.

See also: AGLIERI, PIETRO; BARGARELLA, LEOLUCA; BRUSCA, GIOVANNI; CORLEONE CLAN; FALCONE, GIOVANNI; PALAZZOLO, GIUSEPPE; PROVENZANO, BERNARDO; RIINA, SALVATORE; SPERA, BENEDETTO.

SARTI, Lucien

Lucien Sarti was a Corsican drug trafficker and professional assassin. Christian David, an international drug smuggler and killer, claims that it was Sarti and two other gunmen who killed President John F. Kennedy in 1963. Sarti was part of the Corsican Mafia. He was killed by Mexican police in 1972.

See also: DAVID, CHRISTIAN; FRENCH CONNECTION, THE.

SASAKAWA, Ryoichi

Ryoichi Sasakawa was a political fixer who was expert in the ways of coersion and blackmail. Influential in Japanese politics, Ryoichi was well connected to the Yakuza of his day. A well-known contemporary of Ryoichi was Yoshio Kodama.

As head of the Japan Motorboat Racing Association, Sasakawa became rich while spending most of his time with high-rolling Yakuza mobsters. He was a fervent Japanese nationalist and devoted anticommunist. As a political fixer, Sasakawa exchanged Yakuza money for political power and prestige and made himself wealthier in the meantime.

Reporter Michael McDonagh wrote in "Saluting the Ghosts of the War Dead" for the *Tokyo Journal*, "Sasakawa Ryoichi headed up the post war government-sanctioned motorboat gambling racket and became, in his own words, 'the world's richest fascist' administering the modestly named Sasakawa Peace Foundation."

See also: KODAMA, YOSHIO.

References

Michael McDonagh. "Saluting the Ghosts of the War Dead." *Today on Tokyo Journal.* Available online. URL: http://www.tokyo.to/yasukuni/yasukuni.html. Downloaded on July 15, 2004.

Robert Parry. "The Dark Side of Rev. Moon: Drug Allies." *The Consortium.* Available online. URL: http://www.consortiumnews.com/archive/moon6.html. Downloaded on July 15, 2004.

SATAM, Guru

Guru Satam is a notorious gangster in Mumbai, India. Originally aligned with Chhota Rajan, he split with Rajan in January of 2001. He operates in central Mumbai (Bombay) and is known for making most of his money from drug distribution and extortion.

Satam is believed to have been in an alliance with Ashok Shetty (alias Kathau) who is believed to have informed Chhota Shakeel's henchmen about Rajan's location in Bangkok. The first signs authorities had about the split was how Satam's associates in prison began to distance themselves from those close to Rajan himself.

Satam's defection from Rajan has thrown crime in Mumbai into an unstable business. Alliances are being considered, formed, and dissolved, as the various underworld kingpins vie for more power and control. Satam has several rivals, including Suresh Manchekar, who would love to see him fail.

Satam has been a notorious gangster with no fear of the authorities. He made a name for himself by threatening Indian movie stars and attempting to extort the Indian film industry. It was also one of his henchmen who killed Indian politician Vittal Chavan.

See also: BAKSH, NOOR; GOGA, IRFAN; IBRAHIM, DAWOOD; MANCHEKAR, SURESH; RAJAN, CHHOTA; SHAKEEL, CHHOTA; SINGH, SANJAY.

Reference

J. Dey. "Underworld Tremors As Satam Breaks Away from Chhota Rajan Gang." *Indian Express Newspapers (Bombay) Ltd.* Available online. URL: http://indianexpress.com/ie/daily/20010129/ina29027.html. Downloaded on July 15, 2004.

SENAR Clan

In December 1986 Turgut Senar, who ran a film company in Istanbul, was arrested with 1.6 kilograms of heroin in Van Province and indicted. In September 1989 Istanbul police found nearly 40 kilograms of heroin in a car that belonged to him. He was arrested in September 1991 in Van for participation in PKK (Partiya Karkaren Kurdistan, or Kurdistan Workers' Party) armed operations. PKK "revolutionary tax" receipts totaling 30 million Turkish lira were found on him. Fahit Senar, Turgut's brother, was arrested on October 1992 in Izmir while hiding 81 kilograms of heroin aboard the cargo ship *Florida,* bound for Italy. He is still in custody.

See also: BAYBASIN CLAN; DEMIR CLAN; KAYA CLAN; KITAY CLAN; KONUKLU-AY CLAN; KURDISH CRIMINAL CLANS AND THE PKK; SAKIK CLAN.

Reference

"Terror Organizations in Turkey, Separist Terror Organizations KADEK and Drug Trafficking Drug Trafficking Actions of KADEK." *Terrorism.* Available online. URL: http://www.terror.gen.tr/english/turkey/separatist/drug/trafficking.html. Posted on June 30, 2002.

SERPICO, John

According to the indictment against them, John Serpico and Maria Busillo exercised substantial influence over the operations and financial affairs of the Central States Joint Board (CSJB), located at 1950 West Erie in Chicago; its member locals, whose membership varied but at times was approximately 20,000 union workers; three employee benefit plans affiliated with the CSJB; and the International Union of Allied Novelty and Production Workers (IUANPW), which at times had approximately 30,000 members and in 1995 consolidated its offices with the CSJB. The indictment alleges that the CSJB entities did not regularly hold contested elections and that Serpico and Busillo selected or controlled the selection of candidates who ran unopposed. Separate attachments list the labor-union locals that at times were members of the CSJB, as well as the positions that Serpico and Busillo have held with the CSJB, its member locals, and benefit and pension plans. In addition, Serpico is the chairman of the Illinois International Port District, an appointed post which is unrelated to the charges in the indictment, and Cataldo is a former executive director of the port district.

Gilbert Cataldo, was charged with scheming with Serpico to obtain $333,850 in kickbacks in exchange for a $6.5 million loan commitment made by a pension plan that Serpico controlled to finance a hotel in Champaign, Illinois.

Serpico and Busillo were charged with one count each of racketeering, racketeering conspiracy, bank fraud, and making false statements on a bank-loan application. In addition, Serpico was charged with seven counts of mail fraud, Busillo was charged with two counts of mail fraud, and Cataldo was charged with three counts of mail fraud.

From May 1979 to 1991 Serpico and Busillo defrauded the CSJB entities by soliciting and receiving from banks, including Gladstone-Norwood Bank of Chicago and the former Capitol Bank and Trust, at least nine personal and business loans totaling more than $5 million on terms more favorable than those that the banks offered to other borrowers with similar financial qualifications, in return for causing the CSJB entities to deposit and maintain substantial funds at those banks.

From July 1989 to April 1991 Serpico defrauded the Midwest Pension Plan, the CSJB Staff Pension Plan, and the IUANPW by soliciting and receiving a substantial kickback in exchange for influencing those entities to provide a speculative mortgage loan, initially $6.5 million, for the construction of a hotel in the Trade Center South complex in Champaign, Illinois. In 1990, Serpico caused approximately $100,000 in cash from this kickback to be delivered to Busillo to assist her in the purchase of her $900,000 house in Glenview.

From August through December 1990 Busillo and Serpico defrauded Capitol Bank by making false statements in obtaining an $800,000 loan to Busillo to purchase the Glenview residence. They falsely represented that the purchase price was $800,000, when, in fact, it was $900,000, and they concealed from the bank that Busillo had paid an additional $100,000 cash from an undisclosed source toward the purchase price.

In May 1988 Serpico and Busillo engaged in a series of unlawful financial transactions, including the laundering of more than $10,000 in funds derived from criminal activity and other transactions that were structured in amounts less than $10,000.

Regarding the favorable loans, the indictment alleged that the special terms and conditions that Serpico and Busillo sought and received from the banks included the following, among others: Loans were made on an unsecured basis; they were not fully secured according to lending policies; they were made even though the borrowers could not demonstrate adequate cash flow to service the debt; they were made to finance 100 percent of the purchase price of real estate or of the start-up costs of a business; interim construction loans were made without permanent financing in place; principal payments were amortized over periods longer than usual, thus reducing monthly payments; they were made to cover interest payments on existing loans; business and real-estate development loans were made to principals with little or no expertise in such ventures; and customary charges and fees were reduced and waived.

The indictment listed several allegedly corrupt loans: a loan of approximately $210,000 from Gladstone-Norwood Bank to Serpico in May 1979, in connection with the purchase of a 59-unit apartment building at 3708 North Sheffield, Chicago; a loan of approximately $240,000 from Capitol Bank to Busillo and a relative in August 1986, representing 100 percent of the purchase price of a six-unit apartment building at 3158 North Mobile, Chicago; a loan of approximately $125,000 from Capitol Bank of Westmont to Busillo in January 1987 to refinance a mortgage on a condominium located on Marco Island, Florida; loans of approximately $150,000 and $1.8 million from Capitol Bank for Studio Network, Inc., a business then owned by Serpico and Individual A, in May 1987 and September 1987, to provide financing relating to a film studio located at 1058 West Washington, Chicago; a loan of approximately $195,000 from Capitol Bank to Serpico and Individual B in

November 1988, to provide financing for the start-up of Protective Service Systems, Inc., including 100 percent of the purchase price of a building to be used to house illegal aliens detained by the United States Immigration and Naturalization Service; loans totaling approximately $1.4 million from Capitol Bank to Serpico and two partners, namely Gilbert Cataldo and Individual C, from May 1989 through December 1990, to provide 100 percent financing for the construction of a building at 1101 West Taylor Street, Chicago; a loan of approximately $100,000 from Capitol Bank to Busillo and Individual D in or about June 1989, for the purchase of property at 4913-21 South Racine, Chicago, that formerly had been used as a bus fueling depot; loans totaling approximately $540,000 from Capitol Bank to Serpico and Individual E from December 1989 through June 1990 for the construction of a nine-unit apartment building at 702 South Lytle Street, Chicago.

In November 1996 Capitol Bank was sentenced to pay a fine of $800,000 after the bank pleaded guilty to conspiracy to commit mail fraud and bribery in connection with an employee benefit plan. In addition, Capitol Bank's controlling shareholders at the time were required to sell their interests in the bank's holding company.

Regarding the hotel-venture kickbacks, the indictment alleged that Serpico influenced the Midwest Pension Plan, which then had assets of approximately $39 million, to be the lead lender for the $6.5 million mortgage loan, and the CSJB Staff Pension Plan and the IUANPW to each purchase $1 million interests in the loan, when they had assets totaling $4 million and $3 million, respectively. The indictment alleges the following additional details relating to the $333,850 in kickbacks:

On April 27, 1990, 51 Associates Limited Partnership, a partnership involving Company A in the hotel development, issued a check for $133,850 to Taylor West and Company, a one-person consulting firm under whose name Cataldo did business. The payment purportedly was for construction oversight services that allegedly were never provided by Cataldo or Taylor West.

On June 11, 1990, 51 Associates issued a $100,000 check to Taylor West for architectural and engineering services that Cataldo and Taylor West allegedly never provided. Cataldo deposited the checks into Taylor West bank accounts and used part of the money to pay expenses for a real-estate development in Cicero in which Cataldo and Serpico were partners. Between May 9 and July 24, 1990, Cataldo obtained $126,000 in cash withdrawals, all in amounts less than $10,000. Serpico caused $100,000 of this money to be delivered to Busillo, who used it in August 1990 to make a payment toward the purchase of the Glenview residence. Serpico advised Busillo in connection with the purchase of this house, assisted her in obtaining financing for its purchase from Capitol Bank, and instructed her not to discuss the cash payment. On April 15, 1991, 51 Associates issued another $100,000 check to Taylor West, purportedly for architectural and consulting services, which allegedly were never provided.

"In testimony before the President's Commission on Organized Crime in 1985," wrote Matt O'Connor in the July 17, 2001, *Chicago Tribune,* "Serpico acknowledged friendships with a virtual who's who list of Chicago mobsters, including former Outfit bosses Joseph Aiuppa, Joseph Ferriola and Ernest 'Rocco' Infelice. But Serpico maintained they were all simply childhood friends."

Serpico was convicted on six of 11 counts, and his confederates were also convicted on various charges in July 2001.

References

Matt O'Connor. "Ex-Labor Boss Guilty in Fraud Case." *Chicago Tribune,* July 17, 2001.

———. "Ex-Union Boss Serpico Guilty in Deposits-For-Loans Scheme." *Chicago Tribune,* July 16, 2001.

SHAKEEL, Chhota (a.k.a. Shakeel Ahmad Babu)

Well-known second-in-command to internationally infamous Indian subcontinent Mafia don Dawood Ibrahim, Chhota Shakeel is one of the world's most feared organized-crime leaders.

Shakeel met Ibrahim when they were both in their early twenties on the streets of Mumbai (Bombay). The two have since gone on to become the most powerful organized-crime figures in the region. They rely on an international and diverse group of associates to bring violent and immediate pressure to bear on victims of their choosing.

Whether it be gambling, film, real estate, or whatever, Ibrahim and Shakeel have taken what they wanted and have done so with ruthless efficiency.

Shakeel organized the assassination of Chhota Rajan, the second-most-powerful Mafia don in the region, who was also a sworn enemy of Dawood Ibrahim. "We had our men in four or five countries—Malaysia, Australia, Thailand, India, Dubai, everywhere. . . . He was giving lots of interviews to the Indian press. The Indian media made a hero out of him," Shakeel told Sheel Bhatt of Rediff. "He was nobody before joining us." On September 15, 2000, Shakeel had six men storm a penthouse holding Rajan, a former Ibrahim associate. A gun battle ensued, and Rajan tried to jump to safety from a second floor window. In the fall, he badly injured his back. Shakeel's men shot him from the window. He was taken to the hospital and was believed dead. But Rajan survived. In November while in Bangkok under the protection of the government of Thailand, who had agreed to hand him over to Indian agents, Rajan bribed nine guards who then led him to a remarkable escape. Rajan, with broken back, was still in the hospital. His health today is in serious question, but his desire for revenge is keen.

On September 16, 2001, an attempt was made on Shakeel's life. He was very seriously injured but survived. Ibrahim swore revenge. Many thought it might be revenge for Rajan's assassination, which had been 11 months earlier. Shakeel had been in his house when a motorcycle drove by, tossing a live grenade into an opened window. Despite the deaths of several others, Shakeel survived his rather serious wounds.

See also: ANSARI, AFTAB; BAKSH, NOOR; GOGA, IRFAN; IBRAHIM, DAWOOD; RAJAN, CHHOTA; SINGH, SANJAY.

Reference

Praveen Swami. "Disappearing Act." *Frontline* 19, no. 3 (February 2, 2002). Available online. URL: http://www.flonnet.com/fl1903/19030300.htm. Accessed on November 24, 2004.

SHAN United Army

Drug Enforcement Administration (DEA) agents and Thai police scored a major success in 1995 against the Shan United Army (SUA) and its notorious leader, fugitive drug kingpin Chang Chi Fu (a.k.a. Khun Sa). In December 1994 and continuing into 1995, in an unprecedented operation called "Tiger Trap," DEA Agents and Thai military and police elements arrested 11 key associates of Khun Sa from the Thai/Burma border area and jailed them in Bangkok. All 11 remain incarcerated while extradition proceedings are pending. Those arrested represented the leadership infrastructure of the SUA, and the SUA was dealt a crippling blow.

Reference

U.S. Department of Justice. "1995 Annual Report of the Attorney General of the United States." Available online. URL: http://www.usdoj.gov/ag/annualreports/ar95/toc.htm. Downloaded on July 15, 2004.

SHVARTSMAN, Arkady

Arkady Shvartsman, a well-known Philadelphia based Russian Mafiya member was shot and killed by two gunmen on January 18, 1995, as he sat in his vehicle during the evening rush hour, just a few blocks away from the Philadelphia Police Department headquarters. Shvartsman's briefcase, which contained more than ten thousand dollars, was left untouched by the gunmen on the seat next to Shvartsman.

See also: RUSSIAN MAFIYA.

Reference

New Jersey State Commission of Investigation, New York Organized Crime Task Force, New York State Commission of Investigation, Pennsylvania Crime Commission, with Rutgers University. "The Tri-State Joint Soviet-Émigré Organized Crime Project." 1992. Available online. URL: http://www.state.nj.us/sci/pdf/russian.pdf. Accessed on November 24, 2004.

SICILIA-FALCON, Alberto

Alberto Sicilia-Falcon was a major marijuana-heroin-cocaine dealer whose cartel was earning approximately $3.6 million a week in its heyday. He was suspected as a sometimes employee of the Central Intelligence Agency (CIA). Sicilia-Falcon was also friends with another well-known sometime CIA freelancer, famed Mexican bullfighter Gaston Santos. Jose Egozi, a CIA trained freelancer, was also a friend and adviser to Sicilia-Falcon. Sicilia-Falcon was later captured and tortured, according to James Mills in *The Underground Empire—Where Crime and Governments Embrace* (New York: Doubleday, 1986). In 1975 Sicilia-Falcon, who was arrested by Mexican police (assisted by U.S. drug agents) "is said to confess to CIA drugs and weapons operations intended to destabilize Latin nations. Rearrested after his escape, facing assassination or further torture, Sicilia-Falcon is rescued by a high

Mexican official the CIA later identifies as its 'most important source in Mexico and Central America.'"

SIDROPULO, Georgiy

Georgiy Sidropulo was reputed to be part of a Russian and Hispanic narcotics group known as T.F., which means "Together Forever." Sidropulo was shot three times in the jaw, the chest, and the shoulder while sitting in front of a Brighton Beach, Brooklyn, café on October 20,1993. The shots were fired from a van. He survived the attack.

See also: RUSSIAN MAFIYA.

Reference

New Jersey State Commission of Investigation, New York Organized Crime Task Force, New York State Commission of Investigation, Pennsylvania Crime Commission, with Rutgers University. "The Tri-State Joint Soviet-Émigré Organized Crime Project." 1992. Available online. URL: http://www.state.nj.us/sci/pdf/russian.pdf. Accessed on November 24, 2004.

SINGH, Sanjay (a.k.a. Bunty Gujjar)

Singh's career in organized crime began in 1989, and he became involved in diverting bank funds, kidnappings, extortion, and multiple murders, including murder of Bharatpur jailer Jai Prakash. He also smuggled cars and arms. He was wanted in more than 40 cases in India. In 1997 he escaped from Rajasthan Police—he was wanted by authorities.

He again escaped police custody on January 18, 2000. But on March 26 in Dehli, two spotters, Chander Shoba (alias Pappu) and Hari Om, saw the police arrive and warned Singh of the attempted arrest. Trapped in a house, Singh and two accomplices, Dinesh Gujjar and Subhash, walked out onto the house's terrace and opened fire on police with an AK-56 rifle, a .455 revolver, and a .45 pistol. Police returned the fire, and a violent gun battle ensued. Fifty-eight shots were fired in all, and Singh and his two armed accomplices were killed.

See also: ANSARI, AFTAB; BAKSH, NOOR; GOGA, IRFAN; IBRAHIM, DAWOOD; RAJAN, CHHOTA; SHAKEEL, CHHOTA.

SKINHEADS

Neo-Nazi skinheads have been responsible for at least 43 murders across the nation, most of which have occurred since 1990. A majority of their murder victims have been members of minority groups: Hispanics, blacks, and Asians. Some deaths have resulted from in-group violence with skinheads killing fellow gang members. Skinheads have also committed thousands of other crimes: beatings, stabbings, shootings, thefts, synagogue desecrations, and other forms of mayhem and intimidation.

In recent years the number of skinheads in this country has remained static, ranging from 2,500 to 3,500 members in 40 states. There is no single national skinhead organization in the United States. Instead, loosely linked networks of skinhead gangs operate in scattered communities. During the years, however, the skinheads have tried to align with more organized racists and anti-Semites, including the Ku Klux Klan and other old-line hate groups such as Aryan Nations, the Church of the Creator, and Tom Metzger's White Aryan Resistance (WAR). They have also begun to use the Internet to recruit youngsters and to spread their neo-Nazi propaganda. Those attracted to the movement are almost uniformly white youths between the ages of 13 and 25.

A sample of violent incidents involving neo-Nazi skinheads during the last two years:

- Two neo-Nazi skinheads, soldiers from Fort Bragg, were convicted for the December 1995 murder of a black couple in Fayetteville, North Carolina.
- Two skinhead brothers brutally murdered their mother and father in Allentown, Pennsylvania, in 1995.
- A skinhead in Dallas shot and permanently paralyzed a black motorist in 1995.
- A gang of skinheads from Florida kidnapped a man on Long Island, New York, and robbed and murdered him in 1995. When the skinheads were captured, they were armed with assault rifles, a shotgun, and a pellet gun.
- A black musician was stabbed by a skinhead in Ventura, California, as he and a white woman sat on a pier in 1995.

Despite their static numbers, the skinhead propensity toward violence must be a priority concern of law enforcement and communities across the nation. The arrest and imprisonment of many of the original skinheads involved in violent incidents during the past decade point up law enforcement's effectiveness in bearing down on violent skinhead activity, inhibiting its growth and causing it to disappear in some communities.

Reprinted by permission of Anti-Defamation League.

SLAVE trade *See* HUMAN TRAFFICKING.

SLEPININ, Alexander
An alleged Russian Mafiya member, known for extortion and other racketeering activities, Slepinin was known to be the force behind the murder of Efrim Ostrovsky.

Slepinin was extorting money from Ostrovsky, a businessman with dubious relationships. Ostrovsky was shot to death on January 21, 1992, while exiting his stretch limousine in Queens, New York. The motivations to move against Ostrovsky remain unknown.

Six months later, Slepinin himself was the target. He was murdered in his car on June 23, 1992, shot numerous times in the head and back, killing him. In 1995 Monya Elson and others were charged in a federal indictment for this and other murders.

See also: ELSON, MONYA; RUSSIAN MAFIYA.

Reference
New Jersey State Commission of Investigation, New York Organized Crime Task Force, New York State Commission of Investigation, Pennsylvania Crime Commission, with Rutgers University. "The Tri-State Joint Soviet-Émigré Organized Crime Project." 1992. Available online. URL: http://www.state.nj.us/sci/pdf/russian.pdf. Accessed on November 24, 2004.

SLOBOTKIN, Jerome
This Philadelphia-based criminal testified in court against Nicodemo Scarfo and Scarfo associates in 1988. He claimed to be a victim of a Scarfo protection racket. Slobotkin was shot to death near his Philadelphia home by Antuan Bronshtein on February 19, 1991.

See also: RUSSIAN MAFIYA.

Reference
New Jersey State Commission of Investigation, New York Organized Crime Task Force, New York State Commission of Investigation, Pennsylvania Crime Commission, with Rutgers University. "The Tri-State Joint Soviet-Émigré Organized Crime Project." 1992. Available

online. URL: http://www.state.nj.us/sci/pdf/russian.pdf. Accessed on November 24, 2004.

SOI Fong
The Soi Fong are one of two main organized-crime organizations, or triads, operating in Macau. The other is the 14K. *Soi Fong* means "water room." According to the *South China Morning Post*, in an article entitled "Gangsters Who Have Forgotten the Rules," Harald Brunning wrote, "While some criminologists believe that it is a local offshoot of the regional Wo On Lok conglomerate of secret societies, others regard it as Macau's only 'indigenous' triad, apparently set up by local gangsters on Macau's outlying islands in the 30s. The etymology of its name is unclear." Brunning also pointed out that the name, referring to water, might refer to the plethora of water carriers that used to be employed in Macau many years ago, who the gang might have used to transport goods and money, or who posed as water carriers but were really gang members.

According to a 1997 article appearing in *Asian Today*, "The power of the two main triad groups—the 14K and Soi Fong (Water Room)—is so great that police chiefs admit their ranks have been infiltrated. Commanders now confiscate the mobile phones of police officers prior to crime-busting raids for fear of tipping off the gangsters."

See also: 14K TRIADS; TRIADS.

SONORA Cartel (a.k.a. the Caro-Quintero Organization)
Miguel Caro-Quintero's organization is based in Sonora, Mexico, and focuses its attention on trafficking cocaine and marijuana. Miguel, along with two of his brothers—Jorge and Genaro—run the organization. Miguel himself was arrested in 1992, and the U.S. and Mexican governments cooperated in a bilateral prosecution. Unfortunately, that effort was thwarted when Miguel was able to use a combination of threats and bribes to have his charges dismissed by a federal judge in Hermosillo under questionable circumstances. He has operated freely since that time.

The Caro-Quintero organization specializes primarily in the cultivation, production, and distribution of marijuana, a major cash-crop for drug groups from Mexico. Despite its specialization in marijuana cultivation and distribution, like the other major drug organizations in Mexico, this group is polydrug in nature. It also transports and distributes cocaine and methamphetamine.

Caro-Quintero's drug smuggling is based on his capability to coordinate air operations utilizing small single-engine aircraft to transport marijuana and cocaine from the interior of Mexico to the northern state of Sonora, which borders southern Arizona. There is repeated information that indicates that a variety of municipal, state, and federal officials in Mexico are bribed to allow Caro-Quintero's organization access to airfields throughout the vast desert of Sonora.

Once the narcotics are stored in the northern zone of Sonora, the organization utilizes horses and human backpackers to smuggle multiton quantities per month over desolate sections of the international border, spanning from San Luis Rio Colorado, Sonora, and Yuma, Arizona, in the west to Agua Prieta, Sonora, and Douglas, Arizona, in the east.

On November 23, 1997, a shooting incident occurred at the Nogales, Sonora, Mexico port of entry that left one Mexican Customs official dead and two defendants and one other Mexican official wounded. The incident began when a secondary inspection of a blue-and-gray van revealed a box that contained $123,000. An accomplice appeared, joined the passenger, and together they grabbed the box and ran. Both subjects were subdued and then taken to the Mexican Customs office for processing. About 20 minutes later, eight gunmen, armed with AK47 rifles, and 9mm and .45 caliber handguns, arrived at the customs office and a gun battle erupted. The Nogales, Arizona, port of entry was also hit with gunfire from the Mexican side, but no injuries were inflicted on the U.S. side of the border.

The July 31, 1997, arrest of one of Miguel's immediate relatives, identified as Alberto Caro-Quintero, further illustrated this organization's capability to smuggle ton quantities of cocaine. The investigation leading to Alberto's arrest in Cancun revealed that he was planning to transport 1,500 kilograms of cocaine from the Gulf coast of Mexico to Sonora for ultimate destination in the United States.

See also: CARO-QUINTERO, MIGUEL ANGEL; CARO-QUINTERO, RAFAEL.

Reference

Thomas A. Constantine. "International Organized Crime Syndicates and Their Impact on the U.S." U.S. Drug Enforcement Administration. Available online. URL: http:/www.usdoj.gov/dea/pubs/cngrtest/ct980226.htm. Downloaded on July 28, 2004.

SPEER, Klaus

Known as the Godfather of Berlin, Klaus Speer began, his career in organized crime as a leader of a gang of pimps. He gained a fair amount of notoriety among European police when he and his hoodlum gang "had a Chicago-style shoot out on Berlin's *Bleibtreustrasse* allegedly over shares of the city's prostitution market," according to German organized-crime expert Klaus von Lampe.

Like many other well-placed overseers of organized crime, Speer was able to work his way into a number of legitimate businesses. He became an owner of a gym and also promoted boxers and boxing matches.

Speer was charged with fraud, extortion, assault, loan sharking, gambling, possession of an illegal weapon, and corruption in 1993. "Despite a vigorous defense put up by his lawyer and former prison buddy (convicted on terrorism charges) Horst Mahler, Speer was sentenced to stiff five and a half years in prison for illegal possession of a firearm and bribery," according to von Lampe.

Reference

Klaus von Lampe. "Organized Crime in Germany." Available online. URL: http://people.freenet.de/kvlampe. Downloaded on July 15, 2004.

SPERA, Benedetto

On January 30, 2001, Benedetto Spera was arrested in Palermo. It was the greatest blow yet in the long campaign to bring in Bernardo Provenzano, the Mafia Don in hiding for the last 40 years. Spera was a brutal and deadly assassin in his godfather's stead, as well as a trusted counselor and confidante.

According to Organized Crime Syndicates.com, "Through the talents of men like Spera, Provenzano revamped the Corleonese clans' method of operating. After gaining and maintaining control of the Sicilian underworld through a campaign of terror, Provenzano shifted the group from using brute force to corrupting businesses, politics and in some cases the church."

Spera was also one of those who voted to kill judges Giovanni Falcone and Paolo Borsellino.

SPILOTRO, Anthony (a.k.a. the Ant)

Anthony Spilotro was born on May 19, 1938 in Chicago and grew up in a loving family and seemed to be on track for a good life, but he soon decided that he wanted something else. In his sophomore year at Steinmetz High School, he dropped out and turned to a life of crime, joining forces with other Steinmetz dropouts and engaging in such petty crimes as shoplifting and purse snatching. On January 11, 1955, Spilotro was arrested for the first time, for stealing a shirt. He was fined $10 and put on probation. But after several more arrests Spilotro received special attention from the police. By 1960 Spilotro had been arrested 13 times; at that point he felt he was ready for the next step in his criminal career.

To go anywhere as a criminal in Chicago, you had to be connected to the Outfit, the Chicago family of La Cosa Nostra, and that is exactly what Spilotro did. He hooked up with Outfit enforcer "Mad" Sam DeStefano. Spilotro started out as a debt collector for DeStefano but quickly became involved in bigger crimes. He was involved with the Mafia long enough to eventually be requested to commit a murder. In 1962 Spilotro made his reputation in the M&M killings: Together with mob heavies DeStefano, Felix Alderisio and Chuckie Nicoletti, Spilotro tortured criminals Bill McCartney and Jimmy Miraglia. McCartney's head was put in a vise until his eye popped out. After this gruesome murder Spilotro was considered golden material for the Chicago Outfit. After the M&M murders, in 1963, Spilotro became a made man in the Chicago Outfit, and he left the protective wing of DeStefano and joined Felix Alderisio's crew.

Now a member of the Chicago Outfit, Spilotro was assigned to a bookmaking territory on the northwest side of Chicago. In this territory he controlled a few dozen bookmakers. In 1964 Spilotro was sent to Miami to work with Frank "Lefty" Rosenthal, who was big in sports betting. Rosenthal was sent to Miami to control Chicago Outfit interests there. Spilotro was sent there to see to it that

things ran smoothly and nobody muscled in. By 1967 Spilotro was back in Chicago full time.

In 1971 Spilotro was assigned to Las Vegas, where he replaced Marshall Caifano. Spilotro set himself up in the Circus Casino and operated his business from the gift shop there. Spilotro operated under the name Anthony Stuart, his wife's maiden name. The moment Spilotro arrived in Las Vegas, he started to take care of loose ends. There were five murders where the victims were tortured before they were killed. Several casino employees were found buried in the desert.

However, in September 1972 Spilotro had to come back to Chicago, when he was indicted in the Foreman case. Spilotro was indicted along with DeStefano and his brother Mario DeStefano. Another criminal named Crimaldi, who was present at the Foreman killing, had become an informant for the government and was the star witness. Things looked bad for Spilotro, especially considering "Mad Sam's" crazy court antics. Spilotro and Mario DeStefano figured that they had a chance of beating the case if they could somehow separate their case from Mad Sam's, and so it was decided to eliminate Mad Sam. In May of 1973, Mario DeStefano and Spilotro set up Mad Sam at his home and murdered him with a shotgun. On May 22, 1973, Mario DeStefano was found guilty and Spilotro was acquitted. He went back to Las Vegas.

But his problems were not over yet; new indictments were coming. This time Spilotro was indicted together with Joseph Lombardo. Again there was an eyewitness, but that was not a problem for Spilotro and Lombardo. In September 1974, they found the witness and shot him in the head. Without the witness there was no case, and Spilotro and Lombardo were acquitted of all charges. Spilotro went back to Vegas for the final time.

In Vegas Spilotro ran things smoothly. He saw to it that the skim from the casinos went as planned and that no other mobsters moved in on their operations. Spilotro worked closely with his old partner Frank Rosenthal, who was the boss of the Stardust Casino. But after a few years, things started going bad for Spilotro. In 1979 Spilotro was added to the Las Vegas black book, an exclusion list of people who could not set foot in any of the Las Vegas casinos. Spilotro was outraged but it did not stop him from running his Las Vegas business.

Besides the Casinos, Spilotro also started his own gang named "the Hole in the Wall" gang. This gang

SPIRITO, François

was made up of Spilotro and his brother and their associates. They chose their name because they stole mostly jewelry by making a hole in the wall from a neighboring building. This gang was against the Outfit's orders. The Outfit in Chicago had ordered Spilotro to keep a low profile. His gang was considered a rogue operation by his Outfit associates. It was also rumored that Spilotro was selling drugs and sleeping with the wife of Frank Rosenthal. When word got back to the Outfit bosses, Spilotro's time was up. After several months on June 14, 1986, Spilotro and his brother Michael were summoned to an Outfit meeting. They were driven to an Indiana cornfield and beaten with baseball bats. Eventually they were buried alive.

See also: DESTEFANO, SAM.

Reference

David Amoruso. "Anthony 'The Ant' Spilotro." Gangsters Incorporated. Available online. URL: http://gangstersinc. tripod.com/Spilotro.html. Downloaded on July 15, 2004.

—D.A.

SPIRITO, François

François Spirito was among one of the first modern gangsters in France. Located in Marseilles, Spirito and fellow organized crime associate Paul Bonaventure Carbone set the standard for the French Mafia dons of later years. Originally, Spirito and Carbone worked closely with Marseilles city officials to help organize fascist shock troops to help the French fascist movement of the 1930s. Rounding up hordes of local ne'er-do-wells, Spirito and Carbone sold their violence and mayhem for a price to the fascist and local leaders when communist demonstrations were taking place. However, as the fascist movement in France died, Spirito and Bona venture, who relied on extortion and prostitution for their main source of income, worked their way into new businesses.

With the Spanish civil war in full stride, the two Marseilles smugglers turned into arms dealers, smuggling guns to either side for the highest price. During World War II, with their fascist connections still in place, they were collaborators with the occupying German forces, from whom they made great sums of money and the undying gratitude of local and German government supervisors.

However, Carbone was killed in 1943, and after the war Spirito hid out in Spain. But by the late 1940s, Spirito was the first French mobster to bring heroin into the United States, making him the father of the French Connection routes that would dominate the American drug scene for the next 30 years and a power broker in the Corsican Mafia. It was Meyer Lansky who bought the Turkish opium and had it smuggled to labs in Marseilles, where it would be made into heroin and then transported by Spirito to the United States. However, Spirito was arrested in New York, convicted, and served time. He was then extradited to France where he was prosecuted as a war criminal. After severing time in a French jail, he was released and retired to the French Riviera, where he died in retirement in 1967, an elder statesman of the French underworld.

See also: CARBONE, PAUL BONAVENTURE; CORSICAN MAFIA; FRENCH CONNECTION, THE.

Reference

A. McCoy. *The Politics of Heroin.* Chicago: Lawrence Hill Books, 1991.

STADNICK, Wolodumyer (a.k.a. Nurget, Walter)

Canadian criminal Wolodumyer Stadnick, called "Walter" or "Nurget" by friends, was born on August 3, 1952, to parents Andrew and Valentina. His father worked as a tree cutter, and the family lived in Hamilton's working class North End.

Stadnick, along with his two older brothers, Eric and Gordon, attended Hill Park Secondary School. Classmates remember him as a quiet boy who spent a lot of time in the automotive shop.

After school, Stadnick belonged to a youth gang for a short period before joining the now-defunct Wild Ones motorcycle club. The gang, based in a clubhouse on Hamilton Mountain on West Avenue, sold drugs and was often used as enforcers by the Italian Mafia.

In 1978, Stadnick and another Wild Ones member traveled to Montreal to present themselves to the newly established Montreal Hells Angels Chapter, but the Outlaws biker club, the Hells Angels' archenemy, learned of the meeting and sent a hit squad to Quebec. As Stadnick and his friend sat drinking in an east-end bar, hit men walked into the establishment and blasted at the two Wild Ones. Stadnick was left untouched but his friend was killed.

After three Wild Ones were murdered and another seriously injured in a four-month period, the gang dissolved. Stadnick became an associate of the Hells Angels Montreal Chapter and, on May 26, 1982, he was formally inducted into the organization.

Stadnick was almost killed on September 8, 1984 as he and a group of Angels rode their bikes. A priest, rushing to see the pope's visit to Montreal, ran a stop sign and crashed into the pack. Angels prospect Daniel Matthieu was killed, and Stadnick received severe burns and lost several fingers. The priest escaped unharmed.

As Stadnick lay recovering in Hamilton's St. Joseph's Hospital, members of the 13th Tribe biker gang of Halifax flew over and stood guard during visiting hours. The display earned the club their Hells Angels colors.

Stadnick was arrested on August 23, 1988, at the home of Douglas Freeborn, former president of the Hamilton chapter of the Satan's Choice biker gang. Both individuals were charged with possessing about 11 ounces of hashish for the purpose of trafficking. He was acquitted of all charges in November 1989 when Freeborn admitted that the hash seized belonged to him.

Stadnick was stopped in January 1992 at the Winnipeg airport with more than $80,000 cash. He was charged with possessing the proceeds of crime but was acquitted during the trial.

In 1993 as Stadnick and some associates drank in Winnipeg's Rolling Stone bar, two off-duty police officers entered. The duo allegedly began to taunt the group verbally until the manager kicked them out of the establishment. Later on, when the bikers left, the police were outside waiting. A brawl erupted and Stadnick was again arrested. He was again acquitted, however, when it was discovered that police had started it.

Stadnick, who served eight years as the club's national president and was extremely influential, left the Montreal chapter and was one of the nine founding Nomads chapter members. The group, led by Maurice "Mom" Boucher, comprised the club's elite members, and their mission was to establish Hells Angels chapters in Ontario.

The influential Hells Angel called Hamilton home. Stadnick lived in a modest red-brick bungalow in a quiet neighborhood and also had a residence in Sorel, Quebec. He attended church on Sundays and works out regularly. He owned several Harley-Davidson motorcycles and tailored clothing and custom-made jewelry.

Stadnick, who has successfully avoided serious jail time, was among the more than 100 bikers rounded up in Opération Printemps 2001. He was arrested in Jamaica while lounging by the pool at the Ritz Carlton Hotel in Montego Bay. He faced 13 counts of murder. Stadnick was found guilty on the murder conspiracy charge in June 2004. He was found not guilty on 13 counts of first degree murder and three counts of attempted murder.

See also: HELLS ANGELS.

Reference

Gary Francoeur. "Wolodumyer Stadnick." WiseguyWally. Available online. URL: http://www.geocities.com/wiseguywally/stadnick.html. Downloaded on July 15, 2004.

—*G.F.*

STANFA, John

After the Scarfo years, which crippled the Philadelphia crime family, law enforcement and mobsters alike agreed that if any one could reconstitute the Philadelphia Mafia organization, John Stanfa was the one. Stanfa was Sicilian, low key, and knew the game. Things, of course, would turn out very different.

John Stanfa was born on December 7, 1940, in the tiny mountain village of Caccamo, about 30 miles southeast of Palermo. It was a region of western Sicily long dominated by the Mafia. Stanfa was the youngest of four children. He had two older brothers and one brother-in-law who were members of the Sicilian Mafia. He came to the United States with his wife Nicolena Congialdi, and they moved to Philadelphia. In 1967 their first child Sara would be born, followed by Joseph four years later and Maria in 1976.

Stanfa went by unnoticed in his early years. The Federal Bureau of Investigation had seen him hanging around the wiseguy haunts but did not consider him a significant associate. He was registered as a stonemason and bricklayer by trade. He was set up in business by his friend Carlo Gambino, the New York Mafia boss. Gambino was a friend of Philadelphia Mafia boss Angelo Bruno. Gambino helped Stanfa as a favor for his Sicilian friends. When Bruno was assassinated, Stanfa was in the seat next to him. It has been rumored that Stanfa was in on the plot; however, he has never admitted to this. Not surprisingly, when questioned, he said nothing.

On May 14, 1980, he was indicted on perjury charges. Stanfa took off and went underground. With the help of his Gambino contacts, he set himself up with a girlfriend, leaving his wife and three kids alone to survive on food stamps. After eight months on the lam, Stanfa came out of hiding. On April 21, 1981, he was sentenced to eight years in prison for lying to a grand jury. In the meantime another boss, Testa, was murdered, and a new boss took over: Nicodemo Scarfo. At the end of Scarfo's reign, in about 1987, the family was in big trouble. Scarfo brought enormous heat from law enforcement, and eventually his underlings began to flip to the other side, resulting in lengthy prison sentences for Scarfo and associates.

In 1987 Stanfa got out of prison, and for the next several years kept a low profile. He spent some time in Sicily and New York before returning to Philadelphia in late 1989 or early 1990. At that point, Anthony Piccolo was acting boss and did not like his job. He wanted to step down. With the backing of the Gambino family and the Genovese family, Stanfa became the new boss. Piccolo became his consigliere. Eventually 33-year-old Joseph "Joey Chang" Ciancaglini, Jr. (son of a jailed Scarfo capo) allegedly became underboss. As a boss, Stanfa always talked about the flaws of Scarfo; yet in a lot of ways he did the same things. Stanfa put in place the street tax again. This meant that every criminal had to pay a tax on his activities. This created tension and threats of violence on the streets of Philadelphia. This put in place an atmosphere that would not be good for business.

Stanfa sent out Felix Bocchino to collect the street tax. Things went well at first for Stanfa; the street tax was easy money. Then Felix Bocchino was murdered. The media went crazy. They called it the first mob hit in seven years. At first both Stanfa and the Federal Bureau of Investigation (FBI) had no clue as to who was behind the murder, but pretty soon things became clear. In South Philadelphia there was a group of young thugs—sons, brothers, nephews of Philadelphia mobsters who did not feel connected to the new administration. The youngsters were led by Joseph "Skinny Joey" Merlino, a young, flashy good-looking thug who gave great Christmas parties. Merlino was the son of former Scarfo underboss Salvatore Merlino. Other youngsters in Merlino's group were: Steven Mazzone, Marty Angelina, George Borgesi (whose father was an imprisoned Scarfo hit man), Gaetano "Tommy Horsehead"

Scafidi, and Vince Iannece (whose father was a jailed Scarfo soldier).

Merlino and his friends were already running things and were doing pretty well. They already had the street tax in place, and so when Bocchino came around collecting what they felt was their money, he had to go. The Bocchino hit would be the first casualty in the war between the young mobsters and the old school Cosa Nostra gangsters. Pretty soon Stanfa found out about the "young turks," as they would later be called by the media, and took action. There was a botched hit on Merlino's second in command Michael Ciancaglini. Michael was 29 and the son of a jailed Scarfo capo. His brother was serving seven years for extortion. When asked about the murder attempt, Michael said he knew nothing and did not see anything. At the time of this botched hit, Merlino was in jail.

In the meantime Stanfa decided he could use some new blood and got himself some Sicilian soldiers, two young men named Biagio Adornetto and Rosario Bellocchi. By the fall of 1992 Stanfa began to plot the demise of the Merlino faction. Stanfa operated by the saying: "Keep your friends close but your enemies even closer," and so he and Merlino were seen together on social occasions and mob meetings. In September Stanfa held a secret ceremony in which Merlino, Michael Ciancaglini, and Adornetto were inducted into the Philadelphia family as made members. People around Stanfa warned him that these youngsters were no good and that they would bring the whole operation down, but Stanfa said he knew and would take care of it.

The two Sicilian mobsters that Stanfa had inducted into his family started to make overtures toward his daughter Sara. When Sara rejected Adornetto, the stage was set for another botched hit. Adornetto, after the rejection, began bad-mouthing the administration and Bellocchi. Something had to be done, so Bellocchi went to see his friend with a shotgun. The shotgun would not fire and Adornetto escaped.

Pretty soon Stanfa decided it was time to get rid of the young turk Merlino who had irritated him once again. Merlino liked to bet, but when he lost he would not pay the bookmaker. Stanfa went to war with Merlino, but Merlino was way ahead of Stanfa. On March 2, 1992, in his social club Stanfa's underboss Joey Chang was shot in the head, the neck, and the chest. He survived, but he was too wounded to ever again become an active Mafia member. At the age of 35 Joey Chang retired. Stanfa went crazy. It turned out that Merlino was advised by Joe Ciancaglini, Sr., (Joey Chang's father) and his father Salvatore Merlino.

Merlino also made some contacts in prison. His cellmate was Ralph Natale, a 64-year-old Bruno family member (doing prison time for arson and drug trafficking). Natale would be out on parole in two years and would be a serious rival to Stanfa. Even more troubling was the fact that Natale had ties to New York to parties who would like to see Stanfa go: Merlino was backed by the Genovese family.

Stanfa moved fast and ordered the hit on Merlino and his two top associates, but by summer 1993 Merlino and friends were still alive. They came close to death—one assassination attempt failed when several bombs did not explode as planned. Stanfa had to wait until August 5, 1993. In a drive-by shooting, Merlino and second-in-command Michael Ciancaglini were fired at, killing Ciancaglini but leaving Merlino alive—he was shot in the buttocks and survived.

Even though Merlino survived, Stanfa was a happy man, feeling at ease and on top. He was sure that Merlino would soon fall, and so he became careless. On August 31, 1993, while he was driving to work with his son Joe and a driver, he was ambushed. Stanfa's car was stuck in traffic, a van pulled up beside it, the side doors opened, and bullets came blazing out. Stanfa's son was hit in the face. Stanfa's driver got the car away from the van and managed to escape with Stanfa and his wounded son.

Joe Stanfa survived, but for Stanfa this meant war. The FBI agreed. Mob assassinations in shady back alleys was one thing, but murders on a busy highway was another, so the FBI and other government agencies turned up the heat on the Philadelphia mobsters. Stanfa wanted the entire Merlino faction wiped out. For several weeks hit teams from both factions were on the lookout for targets. Two Merlino associates were murdered, Merlino and his top associates went underground, and one associate even changed sides—Tommy "Horsehead" Scafidi stepped over with info to Stanfa.

On November 15, 1993, Merlino was arrested by the FBI and charged with violating his parole. On November 23, 1993, he went back to jail. Stanfa had even more problems of his own at this time: He discovered that he had an informer among his family. Stanfa ordered the snitch hit, but the informant

escaped—with two bullets in his head! Stanfa knew he was in trouble.

On March 17, 1994, Stanfa and 23 top associates were indicted on racketeering charges that included murder, murder conspiracy, extortion, arson, kidnapping, and obstruction of justice. The FBI had bugged Stanfa from the early weeks of his reign as boss, and the entire war and mob business were caught on tape. The Joey Chang hit was even videotaped. Things worsened for Stanfa and his confederates when several associates turned informant, especially Bellocchi; several others would as well after sentencing. This brought the entire family down. Stanfa knew his time was up. In November 1995 John Stanfa was sentenced to five consecutive life sentences.

See also: NATALE, RALPH.

Reference

David Amoruso. "John Stanfa." Gangsters Incorporated. Available online. URL: http://gangstersinc.tripod.com/JohnStanfa.htm. Downloaded on July 15, 2004.

—D.A.

STEINERT, Scott

Scott Steinert was born in Wisconsin in the early 1960s and relocated to Quebec, Canada, with his family at the age of eight. Not much is known about his early years, but by the early 90s Steinert had become a feared member of the Hells Angels Montreal chapter. He was now extremely influential and owned three stripper agencies and an escort service.

The Hells Angel became godfather to the Laval-based Death Riders motorcycle gang after Michael "L'Animal" Lajoie-Smith's August 30, 1996, conviction for planting a bomb at the Le Gascon strip club in Lachenaie. He now supervised the gang's activities in Laval and the lower Laurentians.

Later that year, Steinert moved into the extravagant Lavigueur mansion on Île-Jésus. He put up an eight-foot-high fence around the property and installed security cameras on the estate. Steinert even had his bodyguard, Donald Magnusen, move into one of the homes on the property.

The Lavigueur estate became his base of operations and Steinert often conducted business with other Hells Angels and members of his puppet club, the Death Riders, there. He also directed and starred in several porno movies on the property, the most famous of which is *Babe's Angel*.

In late August 1997 as the war between the Hells Angels and Rock Machine raged, Steinert's escort service was torched by rivals, but it was only a temporary setback and business continued as usual.

On the evening of November 4, 1997, just weeks after Steinert's marriage, he called his bodyguard, Donald Magnusen, and explained that they had a meeting to attend. Magnusen left his house in tears, and the two never returned.

The Sûreté du Québec, who believed Steinert had went into hiding to escape deportation, issued a warrant for his arrest on January 22, 1998. He was also charged with possessing goods obtained with the proceeds of crime and seized the Lavigueur estate, two houses in Sorel, and a garage.

The truth behind Steinert's disappearance unfolded on May 23, 1998, when police discovered the Magnusen's corpse in the St. Lawrence Seaway. Steinert's body floated to the surface almost a year later, on April 15, 1999. Both men had been beaten to death, wrapped in plastic, and dumped in the river. The motive behind the murders has yet to be revealed.

See also: HELLS ANGELS.

Reference

—G.F.

SUÁREZ GÓMEZ, Roberto

Roberto Suárez Gómez was the undisputed drug kingpin of Bolivia. He was growing, buying, and manufacturing cocaine in the 1970s and 1980s. His fortune was thought to exceed the gross national product of the country in any given year. His paramilitary corps were trained by Klaus Barbie, the "Butcher of Lyon," and his personal fleet of airplanes was said to be more modern than the Bolivian Air Force's own squadrons. His planes could outrun the national defenses.

So rich and so powerful was Suárez Gómez that he backed a coup in Bolivia in 1980. Sometimes called the Cocaine Coup, Suárez Gómez backed his cousin, Bolivian Colonel Luis Arce Gómez, in a military coup d'etat. These generals have been referred to as the Cocaine Generals.

That same year saw a reversal of fortune for Suárez Gómez on the American front—he had lost two operatives and more than 850 pounds of cocaine when in May the Drug Enforcement Administration confiscated it in a bust in Miami. However, his personal wealth was massive: Suárez Gómez owned an estate in the distant jungle of Beni, Bolivia, that was roughly considered to be the same size as the country of Wales. He died in 1988.

SUMIYOSHI-KAI

The Sumiyoshi-kai is the second-largest gang or organized-crime syndicate: it is classified under the Boryokudan, the modern version of the traditional Japanese Yakuza organization. The Sumiyoshi-kai has now become incorporated, acting as an operating company known as Hori Enterprises.

It has more than 7,000 gang members; some estimates range as high as 15,000 members. Its archrival is the yamaguchi-gumi. The Sumiyoshi-kai is involved in a wide range of illegal activities including illegal gambling, prostitution, drug distribution and smuggling, extortion, and murder.

See also: BORYOKUDAN; INAGAWA-KAI; YAMAGUCHI-GUMI.

Reference

SUMIYOSHI-RENGO

Tokyo-based crime organization, the Sumiyoshi-rengo is a subgroup of the Sumiyoshi-kai, Japan's second-largest crime group.

SUNG Lian

Sung Lian is one of the four major triads in Taiwan. They are relatively small, having only 200–300 members. According to an article entitled "Taiwan's Triads" that appeared in the April 1997 of *Asia, Inc.* magazine, they are made up of "mostly second-and third-generation mainland immigrants. Activities: debt collection, massage parlors, brothels, small businesses."

See also: TRIADS.

References
"The Taiwan's Triads." *ASIA, Inc.* Available online. URL: http://members.tripod.com~orgcrime/taiwanstriads.htm. Downloaded on July 15, 2004.
Illuminated Lantern Publishing. "Young and Dangerous 1." Available online. URL: http://www.illuminatedlantern. com/cinema/review/archives/young_and_dangerous_2. php. Downloaded on July 15, 2004.

SUN Ye On

Without question the Sun Ye On is the largest and most powerful of the Hong Kong triads. It has been speculated that the origins of the Sun Ye On date back to the Chiu Chao and Hakka. Headquartered in Hong Kong, it has many subgroups in Asia and around the world, is considered to have 50,000–60,000 members around the world, and has very strong branches in Los Angeles, Miami, New York, and San Francisco.

The main rival is the 14K triad. In an article entitled "Empire of Crime" in the May/June 1995 issue of *Mother Jones,* in a discussion of the triads, Frank Viviano wrote, "Their version of Capone is the Hong Kong-based To Luen-shun, emperor of the Sun Yee On triad and commander of a private army of more than 50,000 thugs. According to the Hong Kong Royal Police, the Sun Ye On controls a huge network of nightclubs, prostitution rings, counterfeiting presses, and drug processing facilities, and moves contraband of every conceivable variety through the People's Republic of China."

The U.S. federal government seemed to echo that same sentiment five years later when in November 2000 the White House released a report that stated, "Sun Yee On members are involved in trafficking heroin and methamphetamine, as well as alien smuggling, to the United States, where the triad has ties to New York's Tung On Gang." The report went on to explain that the Hong Kong-based triad made substantial investments in Canada in the 1990s, and Sun Ye On members have settled in Toronto, Edmonton, and Vancouver.

The Sun Ye On have made friends with the Chinese government. As Fredric Dannen pointed out in *The New Republic* (July 14 and 21, 1997), "Among the most popular ventures shared by Chinese officials and Hong Kong triads are the businesses that triads know best—nightclubs, karaoke bars, and brothels. In Shanghai, where the People's Liberation Army owns a string of nightclubs with the Sun Ye On triad society, and where the Public Security Bureau operates several high-class houses of prostitution (including one called the Protected Secret Club), the parallels to the roaring '20s are unmistakable."

The founder of the Sun Ye On is Heung Wah-yim. An old man now, he is relatively retired, leaving the bulk of running the massive organization to Charles Heung. He is the 10th of 13 Heung children. Charles is now the Grand Dragon and the person with the most power in the organization, but his many brothers are keeping busy.

According to Intellnet.org, "Jimmy Heung is a well-known senior member of Sun Yee On, Hong Kong's largest triad. Heung Wah-yim, Jimmy's older brother, has been identified by the Senate Standing Committee on Asian Organized Crime to be the Dragon Head of Sun Ye On." Wah Sing and Wah Keung entered the Hong Kong film business in an effort to infiltrate the legitimate film industry and to try to legitimize their own operations. Few people are sure if the move was made to further their business interests or for reasons of ego. Many say it was for both reasons. One thing is sure: With the backing of the Sun Ye On, they have plenty of capital behind them to move forward successfully.

See also: 14K TRIADS; TRIADS.

References
Fredric Dannen. "Partners in Crime—Part II: A Means of Maintaining Social Order." *The New Republic,* July 14 & 21, 1997.
Frank Viviano. "The Empire of Crime." *Mother Jones,* May/June 1995.

SYLMAR Seizure

On September 29, 1989, the American public was presented with irrefutable evidence of the enormous volume of cocaine coming into the country when the Drug Enforcement Administration (DEA) raided a warehouse in Sylmar, California, and seized 21.5 tons of cocaine. Such a huge amount of cocaine was amassed at the Sylmar warehouse because of a conflict between Colombia-based distributors and the Mexico-based group they had hired to transport the drug. The group from Mexico had continued to transport cocaine to the warehouse but refused to release it to the Colombian distributors until they were paid for their transportation services. This was the largest cocaine seizure in U.S. history. Colombian drug traffickers responded to the staggering Sylmar seizure by changing the way they compensated transportation groups from Mexico; they began to pay Mexico-based smuggling organizations up to 50 percent of each cocaine shipment in product rather than in cash. This shift to using cocaine as compensation for transportation services radically changed the role and sphere of influence of Mexico-based trafficking organizations in the U.S. cocaine trade. Criminal groups from Mexico became not only transporters but also distributors of cocaine.

Reference

U.S. Drug Enforcement Administration, U.S. Department of Justice. "A Tradition of Excellence, DEA History 1985–1990." Available online. URL: http://www.dea.gov/pubs/history/ index.html. Downloaded on July 28, 2004.

TAKAGI, Takeshi

Takeshi Takagi, a Japanese citizen, and Toyo Tanso, USA Inc., of Troutdale, Oregon, an American subsidiary of a Japanese company, conspired to corner the isostatic graphite business.

According to *Multinational Monitor* (April 2001), "Isostatic graphite is a fine grain carbon product with great strength and resistance to heat and chemical reaction. It is commonly used to produce, among other products, electrodes for electrical discharge machinery, dies for the continuous casting of metals and various products used in the semi-conductor industry." Thus, the company was looking to corner a section of the semiconductor market between July 1993 and February 1998.

The Department of Justice brought suit against Takagi and the company and won. The company was fined $4.5 million and Takagi $10,000. "The case represents the first time a Japanese business executive agreed to face a possible jail sentence for a violation of U.S. antitrust law," claimed *Multinational Monitor*.

TAKENAKA, Masahisa

Masahisa Takenaka was a short-lived *oyabun* ("father" or godfather) of the Yakuza in the early 1980s. A smart political infighter, known for his aggressive approach to underworld activities, the ruling class of Yakuza leaders voted him into power, but his main rival, the cerebral and clever Hiroshi Yamamoto, was infuriated by the decision. With that, Yamamoto took approximately 12,000–13,000 members and started a new organization named the Ichiwa-kai. With this, a bitter turf war ensued that spilled into the streets and onto the nation's front pages. This kind of bloody and violent street war was highly unusual for the Yakuza.

Takenaka was brutally assassinated when four hit men broke into the home of his mistress in Osaka and began to fire. His bodyguard was killed instantly, and Takenaka was taken to a hospital, where he died. Shortly afterward, Kazuo Nakanishi was appointed the new *oyabun*.

See also: YAKUZA.

TAOKA, Kazuo

Kazuo Taoka was boss of the most powerful Yakuza family in Japan, the Yamaguchi-gumi. The toughest and most feared Yakuza boss Japan ever had, under his reign the Yamaguchi-gumi grew more powerful than ever before. Kazuo is considered the most successful Yakuza boss ever, but like most crime bosses Kazuo Taoka also would fall.

Taoka was born in 1913 in Kobe, Japan. His parents could not take care of him, and so, at an early age, to make money Taoka began to work on the docks of Kobe and pretty soon turned to a life of crime to survive. He joined a gang under the leadership of Noboru Yamaguchi. Taoka proved he was fit for a life of crime when he fought in street fights: One of his special moves was to claw his opponent's eyes with his fingers, a move that gave him his nickname *Kuma* or in English "Bear." In 1936 at the age of 23 Taoka was sentenced to eight years in prison for killing a rival Yakuza member. He was released from prison in 1943 and rejoined his pals in the Yamaguchi-gumi clan. In 1946 his boss Noboru Yamaguchi died. At the age of 33 Taoka took over as the new *oyabun* of the Yamaguchi-gumi who, at that time, were decimated by arrests and military draft and were down to an estimated 25 *kobun* (made guys or soldiers). But under Taoka things would improve greatly.

Taoka turned out to be an amazing *oyabun*. Thanks to his organizational skills, the Yamaguchi-gumi's membership soon increased and became strong enough to challenge other groups in the area. First to succumb to the Yamaguchi-gumi's powers were the Honda Kai group. They were a major gambling group in Kobe. Next were the Meiyu Kai from Osaka. With the defeat of the Meiyu Kai the Yamaguchi-gumi took a major share in the Osaka rackets. Taoka was not satisfied yet and ordered his soldiers to take on the Miyamoto-gumi; Under threat the latter decided that it was better to join the Yamaguchi-gumi clan. So the Yamaguchi-gumi had new members and grew even more powerful. Taoka then wanted to move in on Yokohama, but this move did not go through after talks with major Yakuza *oyabun* Kodama. Kodama was one of the most respected Yakuza *oyabuns* of Japan and brokered a pact between the Yamaguchi-gumi and Tokyo's powerful Inagawa Kai clan. This alliance created a Yakuza monopoly with only four of Japan's prefectures free of their control.

By 1978, at the age of 65, Taoka was living the life. He had the power and the money and could sit back and enjoy. However, this was short lived. In July 1978 Taoka was relaxing in a Kyoto nightclub, as always surrounded by his bodyguards, but that did not stop a young man from walking up to Taoka and shooting him with a .38 caliber gun, managing to escape, and leaving Taoka wounded with a gunshot in the neck. Taoka was rushed to a hospital and survived. He found out that the young man who shot him was part of the Matsuda clan. The *oyabun* of the Matsuda clan had been assassinated by the Yamaguchi-gumi. Several of the Matsuda clan's members had vowed to take revenge. This young man tried, failed, and was found dead several weeks later in the woods near Kobe.

Taoka recovered from his wounds and went on to control his criminal empire. These were the glory days for the Yakuza. Within two decades things would change for the worse, just as it would for their Italian counterparts in the United States. But this was not on Taoka's mind; he was still living like an emperor and enjoying his power and wealth. In 1981 Kazuo Taoka died of a heart attack. His funeral was a big affair attended by high-ranking Yamaguchi-gumi members from all over Japan as well as a number of well-known celebrity entertainers. After his death the Yamaguchi-gumi clan had some trouble getting back to normal. During the customary three-month mourning period police took advantage and arrested 900 Yamaguchi-gumi members in the hope of turning some of them informer (and maybe breaking the clan). Taoka had chosen his successor before he died, but at the time he was in prison and could not lead the clan. That being the case, Taoka's widow decided to become *oyabun* for the time being to prevent an internal war. She did not make any major decisions but maintained peace until a permanent new *oyabun* was selected.

See also: YAKUZA.

Reference

David Amoruso. "Kazuo 'The Bear' Taoka." Gangsters Incorporated. Available online. URL: http://gangstersinc. tripod.com/KazuoTaoka.html. Downloaded on July 15, 2004.

—D.A.

TEL Aviv Posse

In late fall 1989 information was developed regarding known members of the Tel Aviv Posse operating in Paterson, New Jersey. This posse originated in the Tellerville section of Kingston, where it was initially known on the streets as the Skulls. Its members support the major Jamaican political party, the Peoples National Party (PNP), and they have been known to associate closely with members of the Jungle Posse. The Spangler Posse has long operated several drug distribution networks in Paterson, and it appears that they are operating independently of and not in conflict with this new posse. Since the Spangler, Jungle, and Tel Aviv posses are all supporters of the PNP, it is possible that they are working together.

See also: DUNKIRK BOYS POSSE; E'PORT POSSE; FIVE PERCENTERS; WATERHOUSE POSSE.

Reference
New Jersey State Commission of Investigation, Robert J. Clark, Francis A. Betzler, Bruce C. Best, and Debra A. Sowney. "Afro-Lineal Organized Crime." November 29, 1990. Available online. URL: http://www.state.nj.us/sci/pdf/afro.pdf. Accessed on November 24, 2004.

TEOLI, Antonio

Antonio "Tony" Teoli was born in the late 1940s and began allegedly a career in the Montreal Mafia as a *picciotto,* or soldier, under mob boss Paolo Violi. According to police, Teoli often sold his swag straight out of Violi's headquarters, the Reggio Bar. In summer 1973 restaurant owner Giovanni Proetti came to Violi for help. Pierre Lafleur, a deliverer whom he had fired, was showing up and making problems in his establishment. Proetti offered Violi $500 to "solve his problem." Teoli and another soldier were sent to "talk" to Lafleur. The harassment soon stopped. A police wiretap picked up Violi scolding Teoli and fellow soldier Pietro Bianco in August 1973. He complained that the two were not productive, having not brought in any money in the last three days. Viola then suggested that they should rob his neighbor, who was away for the weekend.

Teoli, Andrew Scoppa, and Vincenzo Ciancio were picked up on November 14, 1998, and were charged with running an important drug network that distributed cocaine and heroin in restaurants and bars in the city's Villeray and Parc-Extension districts. Teoli and Scoppa were arrested at their homes in Laval, while Ciancio, their drug courier, was picked up at his home in Montreal. Eight kilograms of cocaine, worth an estimated $32 million, was seized in the bust. Police also seized a 9-mm revolver equipped with a silencer, $115,000 in Canadian and American currency, two Jeep Cherokees, and a Chrysler automobile. Police had been investigating the trio for more than a year. Teoli was arrested in the east end of Montreal in December 2003 with $100,000 in cash stuffed into a large bag. Police said he and four others, including Andrew Scioppa, were planning to use the money as a deposit for a purchase of 91 kilograms of cocaine.

Reference
Gary Francoeur. "Antonio 'Tony' Teoli." WiseguyWally. Available online. URL: http://www.geocities.com/wiseguywally/AntonioTeoli.html. Downloaded on July 15, 2004.

—G.F.

TIAN Dao Man

A Taiwan-based triad, Tian Dao Man is approximately 200 to 300 members strong. Their main activities revolve around prostitution, debt collection, and some small legitimate and illegitimate businesses.

See also: TRIADS.

TIJUANA Organization (a.k.a. Arellano Félix Organization)

Based in Tijuana, this organization is one of the most powerful, violent, and aggressive trafficking groups in the world. More than any other major trafficking organization from Mexico, it extends its tentacles directly from high-echelon figures in the law-enforcement and judicial systems in Mexico to street-level individuals in the United States. The Arellano Félix Organization is responsible for the transportation, importation, and distribution of multiton quantities of cocaine and marijuana, as well as large quantities of heroin and methamphetamine in the United States.

The Arellano Félix Organization has been responsible for the murder of several Mexican law-enforcement officials, journalists, and informants, and for threats directed toward Drug Enforcement Administration (DEA) and Federal Bureau of Investigation (FBI) agents and a U.S. prosecutor. They are an extremely powerful and aggressive organization that utilizes San Diego and Tijuana street gangs as assassins and enforcers. They have been known to utilize sophisticated communications equipment, conduct countersurveillance, and maintain a well-equipped and well-trained security force.

The Arellano Félix Organization has been traditionally thought to control drug distribution in the western United States. Interviews of defendant witnesses also reveal that the Arellano Félix Organization is responsible for the importation and distribution of multiton quantities of cocaine annually to these areas. However, recent DEA investigations have shown that the Arellano Félix Organization has expanded its sphere of control and that they are now transporting and distributing drugs to trafficking organizations in Chicago, Kentucky, Ohio, and New York.

The Arellano Félix Organization pays enormous bribes to Mexican law-enforcement officials. Witness statements indicate that the Arellano Félix Organization is paying as much as $1 million every week to federal, state, and local officials in Mexico to ensure that they will not interfere with the group's drug-trafficking activities.

On November 14, 1997, two Mexican military officers assigned to the Federal Judicial Police in Tecate, Baja California Norte, were shot and killed while traveling in an official Mexican government vehicle from Tecate to Tijuana. On arriving at the federal court building in Tijuana, the officers' vehicle was ambushed and sprayed with gunshots from AK-47 and 9-mm weapons. The two officers worked in the same office that was responsible for the November 8, 1997, arrest of Everardo Arturo Paez Martínez, a high-ranking member of the Arellano Félix drug-trafficking organization.

Ramón Eduardo Arellano Félix, considered the most violent of the brothers, organizes and coordinates protection details over which he exerts absolute control. On September 11, 1997, he was added to the FBI's 10 Most Wanted List. Ramón was indicted in San Diego, California, on charges relating to importation and conspiracy to import cocaine and marijuana. A joint task force, composed of the DEA, the FBI in San Diego, California, and state and local officers, is continuing its investigation into the Arellano Félix Organization, including Benjamín Arellano Félix, chairman of the board, for cocaine trafficking. Their goal is to investigate and prosecute the entire Arellano Félix Organization as a continuing criminal enterprise that has sent multiple tons of cocaine from Mexico into the United States in this decade.

The Mexican government secured extradition to Mexico of Alfredo Hodoyan Palacios and Emilio Valdez Mainero to stand trial as paid killers for the Tijuana cartel. Valdez was a top operative of the Arellano Félix Organization. Hodoyan is wanted in connection with the broad-daylight assassination of top federal drug prosecutor Ernesto Ibarra Santes in September 1996. The case was developed in cooperation between the Mexican attorney general and U.S. prosecutors in San Diego. The two had fled to the United States, seeking to frustrate Mexican justice. Hodoyan pled guilty on weapons charges and was sentenced on April 30, 1998. On February 19 Valdez

pled guilty in San Diego on conspiracy charges and possession of 50 kilograms of cocaine.

Reference

Thomas A. Constantine. "International Organized Crime Syndicates and Their Impact on the U.S." U.S. Drug Enforcement Agency. Available online. URL: http://www.usdoj.gov/dea/pubs/cngrtest/ct980226.htm. Downloaded on July 28, 2004.

TINY Rascal Gangsters (a.k.a. TRGs, Tiny Rascal Gang, Tiny Rascals)

The Tiny Rascal Gangsters are the largest Asian street gang in the United States. They originally started out as a Cambodian street gang in the mid-1980s in California, but the organization now includes members from a diverse number of Asian backgrounds. TRGs are especially strong in Long Beach, where they are involved in a turf war with the Eastside Longos (a local Hispanic gang). Since 1991 Long Beach has been a battleground that has seen drive-by shootings and assaults by these two gangs, resulting in nine deaths.

The Tiny Rascal Gangsters have a solid presence on the East Coast in many of the urban centers of Connecticut, Maine, Vermont, and Massachusetts. They are also strong within the prison system in New Hampshire. Two East Coast Tiny Rascal Gangster sets are known as the Grey Rag and the Blue Rag.

TOKHTAKHOUNOV, Alimzhan

Alimzhan Tokhtakhounov was born in 1949 in Tashkent, Uzbekistan. Tokhtakhounov's first setback came when at a young age he lost his father. Not long after his father's death Tokhtakhounov's mother died as well, leaving him alone at age 13 to take care of his younger brother. Growing up as a youngster, one of the few places Tokhtakhounov felt happy was on the soccer field. He loved the sport and played it with a passion. Eventually he played in the first team of the Uzbek team, Pakhtakor. As a football player Tokhtakhounov earned the nickname *Taiwanchik*, which means "little Taiwanese." But as much fun as playing football was, it was not paying the bills, and Tokhtakhounov needed money to take care of his younger brother. Tokhtakhounov began to play cards for money and won big. When he injured his knee during football practice, his career ended, and he decided to test his luck at cards and other operations in the big city: Moscow.

In Moscow Tokhtakhounov started to manage a football team during the day and play cards at night. He also joined the Izmaylovo organized-crime group. He made good money playing cards; during the vacation he went to the resort town of Sochi where he scammed tourists out of their card money. Tokhtakhounov was earning a nice living with his criminal activities, had given up his manager job at the football club, and was now a criminal full time. In 1972 this proved to be a mistake: Tokhtakhounov was arrested for nothing more than being without a job. In Communist Russia those arrests were frequent, and in 1980 Tokhtakhounov was arrested again on similar charges. During his years with the Izmaylovo organization, Tokhtakhounov mingled with Russian celebrities and athletes while working for the Association XXI Century company, a company owned by the powerful mobster Otari Kvantrishvily. Tokhtakhounov's job in this company was to take care of the debtors who refused to pay.

In 1989 he decided to leave Russia and planned on setting up business in East Germany. After having spent three years in East Germany, Tokhtakhounov found that the attention from German authorities became too much. People around Tokhtakhounov were being killed and police questioned him. Tokhtakhounov knew nothing, but fearing for his life, he left Germany in 1993.

While in France Tokhtakhounov continued his criminal ways and in 1994 was involved, according to French authorities, in a money-laundering case involving $70 million dollars. French police also questioned him in connection with the murder of a Russian man because they believed he had ties to the man behind the murder. After all the questioning, Tokhtakhounov had had enough and decided to move again, this time to Israel. He did not stay long though, and after a while he moved back to France, where once again he mingled with celebrities and athletes and others of high social class. It paid off. In 1999 Tokhtakhounov was made a knight in the Order of St. Constantine. The ceremony was attended by several reputed Russian organized-crime figures.

But in 2000 Tokhtakhounov moved to Italy. This time it seemed like a permanent move. He bought houses in Forte dei Marmi, Rome, and Milan. In Italy Tokhtakhounov kept a low profile, or so it

seemed. His friends say he was very busy trying to get a Russian passport but nothing more. On July 31, 2002, the truth of what Tokhtakhounov was doing in Italy became clear: He had fixed the Olympic ice-skating games. On that day, June 31, 2002, Tokhtakhounov was arrested on charges that he fixed the pairs and ice-dancing figure-skating competitions at the Salt Lake City Olympics. According to the FBI, Tokhtakhounov fixed the competition for French couple Marina Anissina and Gwendal Peizerat and made them win by pressuring a Russian juror to vote for them; meanwhile, he pressured a French juror to vote for the Russian pair Elena Berezhnaya and Anton Sikharulidze. Tokhtakhounov did this according to the FBI to obtain a French visa. True or not, Tokhtakhounov was arrested in Italy and kept there. The United States has requested that the Italian authorities hand him over, but so far it seems that Tokhtakhounov will stay put in an Italian prison. If the ice-skating fix turns out to be true, it is yet another example of how far the power of the Russian Mafiya reaches.

See also: RUSSIAN MAFIYA.

TONGS

BOO HOW DOY: THE EARLY HISTORY OF CHINESE TONGS IN NEW YORK

Descended from rebel organizations in China, tongs originated in the United States as "benevolent" merchants' associations designed to shield Chinese Americans by extorting a street tax in exchange for protection. Originally meaning "parlor." the word *tong* came to signify secret societies that engage in illegal activities.

At the turn of the century, tong members were largely composed of merchants, laundry workers, and manual laborers who paid dues to the tong in exchange for financial support and physical protection from business competitors and law enforcement figures. Gradually, tongs developed into a form of organized crime in which the leaders both extorted protection money from its members and raked in profits from opium distribution, prostitution, and illegal gambling rackets.

The first tong in U.S. history is believed to have originated in San Francisco in 1874. This tong was an extension of a merchant association, founded by the Chinese as a means of self-preservation against the vile treatment they received in the United States. The violent persecution of the Chinese, as well as a failed strike against the transcontinental railroad (of which many Chinese were employees) in 1867 and the completion of the railroad in 1869 resulted in an exodus eastward across the country.

In 1870 there were fewer than 100 Chinese in New York. Census figures put the number at 25, while unofficial estimates of the time put the number closer to 75. Despite media persecution and rampant newspaper stories suggesting that the horrors of Chinatown included white women being forcefully addicted to opium and then turned out as sex slaves, there were only three known opium dens at this time.

By 1880, the Chinese population in New York had grown to 800 and continued to increase through the 1890s, when estimates put the number of Chinese immigrants in New York at 13,000. With such a staggering increase and with a population so completely isolated by language, culture, and prejudice, it was inevitable that some type of exploitative force would step in to control the immigrant community. By 1880 the first New York tong had been established.

TOM LEE AND THE ON LEONG TONG

Tom Lee, who appeared in New York around 1870, had his hand in nearly all of Chinatown's opium dens and gambling operations—largely fan-tan, *pigow,* and lotteries. Known as the unofficial mayor of Chinatown, Lee headed the On Leong (Peaceful Dragon) Tong. The On Leong Tong quickly evolved into an organization whose business diversification was strikingly similar to later Mafia operations.

Lee and the On Leong Tong not only extorted protection money from the community, but also controlled the growing number of opium dens in Chinatown and had a monopoly on illegal gambling and prostitution. The On Leongs also learned early on the art of graft, greasing the palms of politicians and patrolmen in exchange for the privilege of continuing their criminal operations.

Rumors concerning vice dens, sexual slavery, and prostitution plagued Chinatown, but it is impossible to know the extent to which the On Leongs were actually involved in prostitution. Although Chinatown history is full of horror stories about Chinese women sold into sexual slavery, it is nearly impossible that the sexual enslavement of Chinese women could have been an ongoing enterprise as there could not have been a fresh supply of Chinese women for such an endeavor; the Chinese Exclusion Act of 1896, which was not lifted until 1942, prohibited the Chinese from entering the United States unless they were proven scholars, highly qualified professionals, or extremely rich. In any case, an 1890 poll shows that 800 New York Chinese worked as laundrymen, while precisely three Chinese women were registered as prostitutes or sexual slaves.

Much more lucrative were the On Leongs' extortion and gambling rackets. The tong gambling syndicate, transliterated as the Bing Ching Union, extorted a 7 percent tax on all winnings at tong-controlled fan-tan and *pi-gow* operations. The tax increased to 14 percent for all winnings above $25. Late payments were assessed a then-exorbitant $10 penalty fee.

Lee also controlled all six of the votes assigned to the Chinese community in elections. A master of political finesse, he would vote these in a bloc as often as his political patrons wanted. Lee's mastery of graft was such that he was even made a deputy sheriff of New York County.

By the 1890s a second tong had been established—the relatively quiet and powerless Hip Sing (Prosperous Union) tong. The Hip Sings were not considered a threat, and Lee's only opposition came in the form of a brief coup by a man named Wong Get, who failed to earn the respect of the community or any of its resultant power. Tom Lee controlled Chinatown unchallenged until the turn of the 20th century.

MOCK DUCK AND THE HIP SING TONG

Around 1900, however, there appeared in Chinatown a man named Mock Duck, later known as the Clay Pigeon of Chinatown because of his uncanny ability to survive myriad assassination attempts.

Like Tom Lee, Mock Duck took to wearing chainmail shirts and walking everywhere with a bodyguard. Mock Duck also carried two .45 revolvers and a hatchet, and he was soon known for his favorite fighting method, in which he would squat in the middle of the street, shut his eyes, and fire both of his guns in a full circle around him.

Mock Duck wanted in on Tom Lee's action and quickly allied himself with both Wong Get and the quiet Hip Sing tong, led by Lem Tong "Charley" Sing, also known as Scarface Charley. Mock Duck demanded half of the revenues from Lee's extensive opium, gambling, and prostitution operations. Lee refused, and two days later Mock Duck and the Hip Sings set fire to an On Leong boarding house, killing two tong members.

The New York "tong wars" began in earnest when Tom Lee retaliated by putting out a $1,000 bounty on Mock Duck and the Hip Sings. Mock Duck, in turn, allied himself with Frank Ross, the attorney for reform crusader Reverend Charles Parkhurst. Claiming that he was an honest businessman who wanted to help Parkhurst save the Chinese from their corrupt ways, he gave Moss a list of addresses of all of the On Leong gambling operations on Pell and Doyer Streets. He withheld the addresses of On Leong operations on Mott Street where the real money was to retain some leverage over Lee.

The On Leongs, meanwhile, had been paying tributes of $16 per week to local police, and the two tongs used their respective patrons to harass each other.

Mock Duck soon succeeded in taking over nearly all of Pell Street, and open warfare ensued. Both the Hop Sings and the On Leongs took to wearing chain-mail shirts and carrying hatchets and revolvers. The white press woke up to the violence in Chinatown and ran stories about the warring "hatchet men," also called *boo how doy* by the Chinese.

The press was so prejudiced and ignorant of the Chinese-American enclave that their sensationalistic accounts about the gang wars of the "highbinders" or "hi-binders," as the tongs were sometimes called, were colored to the point of being nearly worthless.

Certain facts remain about the tong wars, which lasted until the early 1930s with only a few short-lived declarations of peace to break up the action.

In 1904, Mock Duck found himself a new ally. He promised the Four Brothers, one of the oldest and most revered Chinese family guilds at the time, that he would help restore their waning power in exchange for their support. The alliance allowed Mock Dock to step up the violence in his campaign against the On Leongs, and on Chinese New Year in 1905, several Hip Sing enforcers slipped into a crowded theater and shot to death five On Leongs.

Judge Warren W. Foster of the New York Court of General Sessions interceded in 1906 and convinced both sides to sign what was to be the first of several short-lived peace treaties. The treaty lasted one week, until one "hatchet man" decapitated another.

Six months later, another treaty was signed. This one lasted until 1909, which was to be the bloodiest year in the history of the tong wars. By this time, the Hip Sings' consolidated power was far greater than the On Leongs', and the struggle for control of the Chinatown rackets continued to escalate.

BOW KUM AND THE ESCALATION OF THE TONG WARS

On April 15, 1909, the On Leongs abducted and killed Bow Kum ("Sweet Little Flower"), a slave girl who belonged to Low Hee Tong of the Hip Sings. Retaliations for the murder of Bow Kum continued until 1925, and the tong wars escalated to include the widespread use of bombs, a tactic that left at least 50 Chinatown residents dead.

Both Tom Lee and Mock Duck survived the tong wars relatively unscathed. In 1912, Mock Duck was sentenced to two years in Sing Sing on charges of running a policy game. When he was released in 1914, he moved to a remote area of Brooklyn and took up a life of peace and quiet.

An enduring peace eventually ended the tong wars around 1932, though there are two differing accounts as to how it was reached. One theory holds that U.S. and Chinese officials stepped in and politely asked Mock Duck to intervene and make peace between the warring tongs. Another theory holds that the tong wars ceased when U.S. health and immigration officials threatened to deport more than 200 Chinese if the killings continued.

Tom Lee died of natural causes in 1917, at the age of 76. Mock Duck died in Brooklyn in 1942.

While the tong wars that swept across the nation and left more than 350 individuals dead in Chinese enclaves across the country eventually did end, tongs continued to grow in power and influence.

Today, the On Leong and the Hip Sing tongs both operate nationwide with major interests in gambling, money laundering, extortion, prostitution, technology theft, and heroin distribution. While the two do sometimes work together, the On Leongs are primarily allied with the infamous Ghost Shadow gang, while the Hip Sings are affiliated with Chinese triads and the Wah Ching gang.

CHINATOWN (SAN FRANCISCO) TONG WARS OF THE 1920S

The violence of the 1920s was not restricted to bootleggers. Shortly after the World War I armistice,

San Francisco's Chinatown erupted in another kind of gangland warfare. While Chief White's cleanup campaign had succeeded in wiping out the last vestiges of the Barbary Coast, the tongs had continued to operate brothels, gambling parlors, and opium dens and even trafficked in Chinese "slave girls."

Police Chief Daniel O'Brien, who replaced Chief White in 1920, appointed Inspector Jack Manion to take over the Chinatown squad. Manion whose tough persona inspired much of the pulp detective fiction of the 1920s and 30s, was credited with the pacification of the district. He developed a network of informants and used them to conclude a truce among the tongs.

Dan McKlem joined the force in 1925 and drew one of his first assignments in Chinatown. As McKlem remembered, "Manion was a boyhood associate of O'Brien's, and O'Brien picked him to take over Chinatown after he (Manion) had some success with the Black Hand in North Beach, which was the same as the Mafia in those days. Two of us would work north of Washington [Street], and two would work south, and there were two 'straw bosses,' named Johnny Conley and Jack O'Donnell. Your effectiveness depended on your contacts with the Chinese. They had to take a liking to you or they wouldn't give you the time of day. And even then, there were some things they just wouldn't tell you."

McKlem continued: "I remember in the last of the Tong Wars there was a guy named Wong Quong, who was killed on January 6, 1926, in Ross Alley. And on April 20, Ju Shuck was killed in the back of the Chinese Theatre [at 420] Jackson. They were all from different Tongs, and we knew they'd been killed because of a war, but we could never figure out just who did it. The Chinese were a secretive lot anyway, by and large, but none of them could talk about a murder like that. They would have been violating the code."

In spite of the difficulties posed by both the nature of tong code and the veil of secrecy that hung over Chinatown during this period (to say nothing of the language barrier), Manion was able to bring the leaders of the tongs together for a meeting that eventually resulted in a peace treaty. Slowly but surely, Manion's informants provided him with enough material to shut down the slave traffic and to curtail illegal gambling and drug activity.

After 10 years in Chinatown, Manion had become such an institution that the Chinese community adamantly refused to let him return to the Bureau of Inspectors. Bowing to popular demand Manion asked to, and the department let him, remain in Chinatown until his retirement in May 1946.

THE TONGS IN CHICAGO

In the early 1990s, the On Leong Merchant's Association was the focus of a federal racketeering trial that exposed the links between the Chicago outfit and a multimillion-dollar gambling ring headquartered along 22nd Street. On Leong traces its Chicago roots to the 19th century where it existed as a social and benevolent organization to indoctrinate Chinese immigrants to the American way of life.

During the 1991 federal racketeering trial of 11 Chinese businessmen accused of running a gambling game from inside the On Leong "casino"—a continuing enterprise that netted $2 million between 1974 and a police raid in April 1986—prosecutors secured conviction on tax conspiracy charges against Wilson Moy, often described as the unofficial "mayor" of the Chinatown community.

Former mob attorney and federal informant Robert Cooley testified during the trial that Moy and another man gave him $100,000 to pass on to former First Ward Alderman Fred Roti and Pat Marcy, the mobbed-up secretary of the First Ward Democratic Organization to "influence" the outcome of the 1981 William Chin murder case in the Cook County Circuit Court.

The jury failed to reach a verdict on this specific charge in the five-month-long racketeering trial.

Hip Sing has an uptown storefront office. On Leong is still a viable force in the South Side Chinatown neighborhood. There are those who are of the opinion that the organizations are still not divorced from their criminal past and that little has changed.

The rigged gambling games continue, it is said, in a secure location not far from the former On Leong building on Wentworth Avenue where the arrests were originally made. Since the doors were padlocked by the police and the records seized, the On Leong headquarters has been converted into the Pui Tak Center, a religious and cultural meeting place.

Meanwhile, restaurant owners, local merchants, and small-time bookies running popular Chinese gambling games like fan-tan, allegedly continue to pay street taxes to the 26th Street Chinatown "crew," which oversees the outfit's interests in this part of town.

The presence of the Hip Sing and On Leong in Chicago is traced to the early years of this century when the original Chinatown located between Polk Street and Congress relocated to 22nd Street and Wentworth Avenue—following the migration of the Levee vice merchants, gambling bosses, tricksters, and dope fiends from downtown into the South Side badlands.

The affiliated gangs of the Tong are well organized and entrenched in their respective communities, according to Jim Brongiel, an Asian organized-crime specialist for the Office of International Criminal Justice, a University of Illinois think tank that trains Chicago police sergeants and lieutenants through an executive development program, as well as publishing "Criminal Justice International."

"We have seen large amounts of money being laundered through various Chicago banks from businesses that use the word *international* in their dealings," Brongiel explains. "Asian gangs, with close links to sophisticated criminal organizations like the 14K Triad, the largest triad on the Chinese mainland, are involved in money laundering, illegal gambling, counterfeiting, the theft of computer software, and the smuggling of illegal aliens into this country."

TONGS AND THE FUTURE

Tong gangs have fanned out across the United States and are particularly active in Maryland, Los Angeles, and New York City. Houston's Asian community was hit particularly hard in 1996 with numerous drive-by shootings and continuous gang warfare. During the 1970s and 1980s the Wah Ching, a Chinese street gang organized in 1966, came to control most of the criminal vices in the Chinatowns of Los Angeles, New York, and San Francisco. Their extortion and protection rackets are reminiscent of decades-old Mafia activity. The power of the Wah Ching on the West Coast was never seriously threatened until 1989 when a new criminal organization, the Wo Hop To triad of Hong Kong, began to move into the San Francisco Bay Area. In recent years, there has been a consolidation of power between these two groups and the evolution of an Asian "supergang."

Having realized the benefits of applying structure and organization to their criminal endeavors, some West Coast Vietnamese and Chinese "gangsters" are being recruited into the Crips and Bloods gangs. Their presence has been detected in the greater Midwest, notably in Minneapolis-St. Paul and central Wisconsin where Hmong youth have formed a dozen Crip gangs and at least five Blood gangs.

See also: MOCK SAI WING; ON LEONG TONG.

References

Illinois Police and Sheriff's News. "Asian Street Gangs and Organized Crime in Focus: A Rising Threat from the Far East." Available online. URL: http://www.ispn.org/asg08107.html. Downloaded on July 15, 2004.
Andrew Sekeres III. "Institutionalization of the Chinese Tongs in Chicago's Chinatown." Gang Research Net. Available online. URL: http://gangresearch.net/Chicago Gangs/tongs/sek1.html. Downloaded on July 15, 2004.
Virtual Museum of the City of San Francisco. "Chinatown Tong Wars of the 1920s." Available online. URL: http://www.sfmuseum.org/sfpd/sfpd4.html. Downloaded on July 15, 2004.

TOUSIGNANT, André (a.k.a. Toots)

Born in 1964, André "Toots" Tousignant eventually became a major player in the Hells Angels organization in Canada. He joined the Rockers biker club in the early 1990s where, along with fellow Rocker Paul "Fon Fon" Fontaine, he controlled drug trafficking in a Montreal gay neighborhood.

When feared Nomads chapter president Maurice "Mom" Boucher looked for a driver/bodyguard, Tousignant, who stood at an intimidating 5 feet 11 inches and 220 pounds, was the ideal choice. He became responsible for the safety of the most powerful Hells Angel in Canada.

On March 24, 1995, police pulled over Tousignant and Boucher as the two drove to Sherbrooke for a motorcycle show. A loaded 9-mm firearm was found under Boucher's belt, and he was arrested. Tousignant was not charged.

Tousignant and Fontaine were later allegedly assigned the grave task of killing prison guards because Boucher wanted to destabilize the justice system. "Toots" kept watch on Bordeaux prison and photographed the prison guards and noted their work schedules. On June 26, 1997, he and Stéphane "Godasse" Gagné, a Rockers associate, followed prison guard Diane Lavigne, 42, as she drove home from work. On a Japanese motorcycle, they pulled alongside her vehicle and pumped her with bullets.

The bike was abandoned in a parking lot, and the killers fled in a Ford Escort. Another prison guard, Pierre Rondeau, would be gunned down by the group on September 8, 1997.

The murders went down without any problems, and law enforcement was left without leads. The Hells Angels were pleased with Tousignant's work, and he was awarded the status of prospect with the club's elite Nomads chapter.

But Tousignant's world began to crumble on December 4, 1997, when a small-time drug dealer told police that Stéphane Gagné had murdered the two prison guards. Gagné was arrested two days later and, facing a lengthy prison term, confessed to the crimes and chose to cooperate.

With the information provided by Gagné, police struck on December 18, 1997. Maurice Boucher was arrested and charged with two counts of first-degree murder. Warrants were issued for André Tousignant and Paul Fontaine, but they had gone into hiding after hearing of Boucher's arrest.

Police spent the next two months looking for the fugitives but were unsuccessful. "Toots" and "Fon Fon" were reportedly seen in Alberta, where the two were allegedly being hidden by members of the Hells Angels Edmonton Chapter.

The suspense ended on February 27, 1998, when the scorched corpse of André Tousignant was discovered near Bromont, northeast of Montreal. He had been shot several times before his body had been set on fire.

See also: HELLS ANGELS.

Reference

Gary Francoeur. "André 'Toots' Tousignant." Wiseguy-Wally. Available online. URL: http://www.geocities.com/wiseguywally/AndreTousignant.html. Downloaded on July 15, 2004.

—G.F.

TRIADS

The term *triad* was given by the Hong Kong government to Chinese secret societies based on the triangular symbol that once represented such societies. The symbol is the Chinese character *hung,* encased in a triangle, representing the union of heaven, earth, and man. So triads even today are sometimes referred to as the "Hung Society" or the "Heaven and Earth Society." The purpose of these societies, it is said, was the overthrow of the Qing (Ch'ing) empire and the restoration of the Ming. The character *hung,* in addition to meaning the most auspicious and lucky color red, also alludes to the founder of the Ming Dynasty, Hung Wu. Because of the treasonous nature of their enterprise, they developed secret forms of communication and elaborate initiation ceremonies to impress upon new members the need for absolute loyalty and secrecy.

Triads have a rather elaborate history which is partly based on reality, partly on myth. It involves not only a struggle against the Qing dynasty but also a retreat to the Shaolin monastery and the eventual famous burning of the monastery as an integral part. Only five people survived the fire, and these are said to be the "Five Ancestors" of modern triads. They go on to have a number of adventures that are still remembered by triad officials and are sometimes represented in initiation rituals.

Triad-origin mythology holds that when they recruited thousands of people to their cause, including Sun Yat-sen, the Qing dynasty was finally defeated. Whatever the cause of the collapse of the Qing, and whatever the triad's involvement, when it at last fell, triad societies no longer had a dedicated cause and so realigned their purposes. Some became (and in fact had been already) devoted strictly to criminal activities. Others were martial associations. Still others were like labor unions and trading associations. Many were some combination of all of these. Joining a triad did not make a person a criminal. There were many advantages to membership, the greatest advantage being that by joining the triad, an international fraternity of like-minded individuals could then offer assistance and protection when necessary.

It is important to note that the Triads are not synonymous with Chinese criminal syndicates; that is to say, not all syndicate members or criminals are triad members. On the other hand, all triad members are criminals, if only because membership alone is considered a criminal offense under Hong Kong's 1994 Organized and Serious Crimes Ordinance. But even though everyone who is part of a triad is breaking the law through membership alone, most triad members are not otherwise criminally active. So membership in a given triad may be estimated at 20,000, but only 2,000 of those would be designated as active—engaged in criminal activity. On the other hand, a small street-level gang may have no triad affiliation at all. Children who enter a street gang have usually made some triad contacts, already and it is likely they would join for the protection and status that membership provides.

The triads, then, are not at all like the Mafia. The Mafia is known for strong familial ties and a rigid pyramidal hierarchy. Triads, on the other hand, are loose affiliations in the extreme. Although there is a hierarchy to triad leadership: Those lower on the ladder have much more freedom of lateral movement. In fact, the movements and activities of smaller gangs are only rarely directed by the leaders of a triad. Triad members do not typically have to secure permission from the head of a triad to engage in a criminal activity, even if the activity involves partnering with people who are not members of the triad or are even in fact members of a different triad.

Joining a triad can be a great advantage to a person who wishes to engage in criminal activity. Immediately on entering a triad, a person will have greater access to resources and be able to more easily partner with other members of the triad to pull off money-making schemes. Victims of extortion are much less likely to protest when they feel that the powerful and mysterious triads, who have influence all over the world, are leaning on them, as opposed to just feeling picked on by one criminal. Street punks find greater self-respect in the fanciful idea that they belong to a fraternity of noble warriors whose history extends back hundreds of years. Although there is not necessarily a direct benefit to senior members of triad fraternities from the actions of junior members, benefits do move upward, especially through monetary and other gifts given by junior triad members to their seniors on special occasions, such as the Chinese New Year and other holidays.

Although triads originated in mainland China, Hong Kong is the undisputed capital. Triad activity is most concentrated there. Triads do have international scope, however, with members in nearly every country in the world but are especially strong in China, Southeast Asia, and the United States. Triad criminal activity includes but is not limited to street-level crime, such as gambling, extortion, and prostitution, and international activities such as narcotics trafficking, counterfeiting, and smuggling goods and people. In Hong Kong, it is estimated that there are 50 triad societies with a total membership of at least 80,000. Of these societies, about 15 are criminally active. What follows is a list of the largest triads operating in Hong Kong:

Sun Yee On: The largest triad in Hong Kong, with an estimated 25,000 members. In addition to activities in Hong Kong, intelligence reports since 1994 seem to indicate that they dominate the government of Guangdong Province on the mainland.

Wo Group: There are around nine subgroups in this triad grouping with a total membership of around 20,000. Different subgroups have been known to specialize in different activities—the Wo Shing Yee controls dockworkers, the Wo On Lok specializes in loan sharking, the Wo Hop To runs protection rackets, and so on. The original Wo group triad was the Wo Shing Wo, and it is the longest established triad in Hong Kong.

14K Triad: Also with roughly 20,000 members, the 14K originated with the fight by the Guomintang against communism. Chiang Kai-shek ordered that a league of all triad societies be established and used to fight communist forces using guerrilla tactics. The "14" in the name refers to the address of the original headquarters of this effort. There are more than 30 subgroups to the 14K, and it remains one of the most powerful triads internationally.

Big Circle Gang: Former Red Army guards and People's Liberation Army soldiers form a sort of loose affiliation of gangs, though they are not technically a triad society. They enter Hong Kong illegally and are known for violent armed robberies of jewelry stores, banks, and gold dealers. Often they are equipped with military weaponry such as assault rifles and grenade launchers. The name may derive from reeducation detention camps in China to which Red Guards have been sent, from which they have escaped, and which are marked on maps by a large circle.

TRIAD ORGANIZATION

At its most basic level, the hierarchy of triad members matters little except in each individual relationship between two members, each based on ties between the *dai-lo,* or "big brother," and *sai-lo,* or "little brother." The big brothers give work, protection, and advice to the younger brothers, who give loyalty, support, and money in exchange. In many cases, this is the only relationship that matters.

There is a triad hierarchy, but it is not really known to what extent it is still used. Most analysts agree the lower ranks are still commonly in place, but how many triad groups use the more complicated higher rankings and to what extent cannot be accurately measured. Along with the names of each rank, triad ranks also have numbers, all beginning with 4, which represents the four oceans that were said to surround China in ancient times and so signifies the universe as a whole.

489: At the top of the triad hierarchy is the man known as Mountain Lord, First Route Marshal, or Dragon Head. The Dragon Head is an elected position, and the person in this position has final responsibility for the triad organization as a whole, including arbitrating conflict within various branches and guiding the general direction the organization should be taking. His word is law. He is sometimes referred to as a 21 (4+8+9), the character for which reflects the symbol for *hung*, as used to represent the Hung Society as a whole.

438: Below the Dragon Head are a number of positions of equal rank: The Assistant Mountain Lord, the Incense Master, and the Vanguard. The assistant acts as the Dragon Head's proxy in his absence and is often conferred with by the Dragon Head for important decisions. The Incense Master and Vanguard officiate over triad rituals; in this respect they are extremely important in preserving the rituals and ensuring that they remain potent symbols of the triads history and power. In this regard, the number 438 becomes 15 (4+3+8), which further breaks down into 3 × 5, 3 symbolizing creation, and 5 symbolizing longevity. Of course, all this numerological massaging is suspect at best. Although these are common explanations for the rank numbers, it is more likely that the numbers had some significance as part of the ancient mystery rites from which triads developed, long ago, which has long been forgotten and supplanted by explanations based on more recent triad history and numerology.

426: The Red Poles were originally military unit leaders; they are now gang leaders. A Red Pole may have about 50 men under his command. He is the one who takes care of the messy aspects of triad life: If pressure needs to be put on, if someone needs to be rubbed out, the Red Pole is called and he carries out the assignment with his men.

415: At the same level as the Red Pole is the White Paper Fan, or administrative officer. The White Paper Fan is responsible for keeping the books, investing the money, determining legal strategy, and so on. Typically highly educated and not a fighter, he may consult with a Red Pole on strategy.

432: The Straw Sandal, also at the same rank in a triad organization as Red Poles and White Paper Fans, is the triad messenger. Someone need a ransom notice? The Straw Sandal delivers. He also organizes branch meetings and gang fights.

49: At the bottom of the triad hierarchy are the 49s. Almost all triad members belong to this category. They are the footsoldiers of organized crime. 49 becomes 36 (4 × 9), the number of oaths a new recruit must swear before joining the triad.

According to recent police reports, many triads organize themselves out of Red Poles and 49s. The Red Poles might each be branch leaders. A council of Red Poles presides over the triad as a whole, with one of the Red Poles being elected as chairperson, another as treasurer. Most of the other ranks have fallen into disuse.

TRIAD INITIATION CEREMONIES

Elements of triad initiation are derived from all aspects of the history of triad societies. The ritualized aspect derives in part from when triads were more like cults. The swearing of absolute secrecy comes from their tradition of antigovernment activities. Initiation fees are paid, dating from practices in place when triads were more similar to trade guilds or cooperatives. Each element of the initiation ceremony represents some aspect of the myth and occasionally the reality of triad origins.

The initiation ceremony as it was practiced as recently as 20 years ago could take six hours to complete. These days, however, triad officials have little time to conduct such elaborate ceremonies, and fewer and fewer people even know the proper way to conduct one. Instead, new recruits are given a quick,

15-minute ceremony in which they must swear the 36 oaths. The longer ceremonies may still occasionally be conducted for promotions.

It begins with entrance into the triad lodge. The lodge is not a fixed space; rather, it is wherever the ceremony is set up. It could be in someone's basement or even an alleyway. As a result, the layout of the ceremonial chamber is adapted to meet the needs of the situation. The recruit is summoned to the lodge by a notice written on red paper or a strip of bamboo. The recruit must remove his shoes and socks and bare his chest before entering. The Incense Master and the Vanguard preside over the ceremony.

Upon entering the lodge, the initiate must pass through three archways or gates. In front of the first, which bears the warning "On entering the door, do not proceed further if you are not loyal," the initiate does a ritual dance and then passes through. The archway is made of crossed swords, and entering the archway is called Passing the Mountain of Knives. On the other side the Vanguard symbolically records information about his membership, but of course no written records are kept. The second gate is named the Loyalty and Righteousness Hall. A sign on the arch declares "Before the gate of loyalty and righteousness, all men are equal." After passing through this second arch, the initiate pays his initiation fee, handing it over in a little red envelope. Past the third gate is the "Heaven and Earth Circle," and a sign on the arch states, "Through the Heaven and Earth Circle are Born the Hung Heroes." The recruit must pass through the third arch, then the "Heaven and Earth Circle" itself, a bamboo hoop. Passing through the hoop represents a sort of rebirth into triad society. On the other side of the circle the initiate enters the main hall and must then navigate through a series of episodes, symbolizing the history of the triads, with names like The Stepping Stones, The Two Plank Bridge, and The Fiery Pit. Senior triad officials stand on either side, observing the progress of the initiate through the ritual.

At last the initiate stands before the triad altar at the end of the hall, where senior triad leaders recite some triad poetry to him. Books full of triad poetry are carefully guarded and secreted away by some triad members. Then the initiate washes his face and removes his clothes. He is given white robes and straw sandals to wear. His old life washed away, he is now prepared for his rebirth as a triad member. In front of the altar, he swears the 36 oaths and binds the oaths with blood—usually a cock is killed and its blood dripped into a bowl of wine. Then yellow paper is burned and its ash added to the blood wine, and it is tasted by the initiate. The bowl is broken to illustrate what becomes of traitors. The recruit is now a 49. The ceremony ends with a trip to a restaurant for a celebratory feast.

The elaborate ceremony instills respect and fear of the institution into triad recruits. As long as a sense of awe and respect fills his heart, he will be loyal. But ever since the crackdown on triads in Hong Kong, elaborate initiation ceremonies are a dying breed. Nowadays, the new recruit may forgo the entire ceremony, instead swearing to an altar to Guan Yu, the God of War. Although Guan Yu is worshipped by all triads (and police) in Hong Kong, he actually does not figure in the original initiation ceremony, which adheres strictly to symbolism derived from the triad origin myths, in which Guan Yu does not play a part.

THE 36 OATHS

Accounts of the 36 oaths differ widely. The most legitimate list comes from W. P. Morgan's *Triad Societies in Hong Kong* (1960), quoted below. These days the oath taking is much abbreviated, but this list can be considered a list of traditional triad oaths, which the so-called honorable triad men would follow.

1. After having entered the Hung gates I must treat the parents and relatives of my sworn brothers as my own kin. I shall suffer death by five thunderbolts if I do not keep this oath.

2. I shall assist my sworn brothers to bury their parents and brothers by offering financial or physical assistance. I shall be killed by five thunderbolts if I pretend to have no knowledge of their troubles.

3. When Hung brothers visit my house, I shall provide them with board and lodging. I shall be killed by myriads of knives if I treat them as strangers.

4. I will always acknowledge my Hung brothers when they identify themselves. If I ignore them, I will be killed by myriads of swords.

5. I shall not disclose the secrets of the Hung family, not even to my parents, brothers, or wife. I shall never disclose the secrets for money. I will be killed by myriads of swords if I do so.

6. I shall never betray my sworn brothers. If, through a misunderstanding, I have caused the arrest of one of my brothers I must release him immediately. If I break this oath, I will be killed by five thunderbolts.

7. I will offer financial assistance to sworn brothers who are in trouble in order that they may pay their passage fee, etc. If I break this oath, I will be killed by five thunderbolts.

8. I must never cause harm or bring trouble to my sworn brothers or Incense Master. If I do so, I will be killed by myriads of swords.

9. I must never commit any indecent assaults on the wives, sisters, or daughters, of my sworn brothers. I shall be killed by five thunderbolts if I break this oath.

10. I shall never embezzle cash or property from my sworn brothers. If I break this oath I will be killed by myriads of swords.

11. I will take good care of the wives or children of sworn brothers entrusted to my keeping. If I do not, I will be killed by five thunderbolts.

12. If I have supplied false particulars about myself for the purpose of joining the Hung family, I shall be killed by five thunderbolts.

13. If I should change my mind and deny my membership of the Hung family, I will be killed by myriads of swords.

14. If I rob a sworn brother or assist an outsider to do so, I will be killed by five thunderbolts.

15. If I should take advantage of a sworn brother or force unfair business deals upon him, I will be killed by myriads of swords.

16. If I knowingly convert my sworn brother's cash or property to my own use, I shall be killed by five thunderbolts.

17. If I have wrongly taken a sworn brother's cash or property during a robbery, I must return them to him. If I do not, I will be killed by five thunderbolts.

18. If I am arrested after committing an offense, I must accept my punishment and not try to place blame on my sworn brothers. If I do so, I will be killed by five thunderbolts.

19. If any of my sworn brothers are killed or arrested or have departed to some other place, I will assist their wives and children who may be in need. If I pretend to have no knowledge of their difficulties, I will be killed by five thunderbolts.

20. When any of my sworn brothers have been assaulted or blamed by others, I must come forward and help him if he is in the right or advise him to desist if he is wrong. If he has been repeatedly insulted by others, I shall inform our other brothers and arrange to help him physically or financially. If I do not keep this oath, I will be killed by five thunderbolts.

21. If it comes to my knowledge that the government is seeking any of my sworn brothers who has come from other provinces or from overseas, I shall immediately inform him in order that he may make his escape. If I break this oath, I will be killed by five thunderbolts.

22. I must not conspire with outsiders to cheat my sworn brothers at gambling. If I do so, I will be killed by myriads of swords.

23. I shall not cause discord amongst my sworn brothers by spreading false reports about any of them. If I do so, I will be killed by myriads of swords.

24. I shall not appoint myself as Incense Master without authority. After entering the Hung gates for three years, the loyal and faithful ones may be promoted by the Incense Master with the support of his sworn brothers. I shall be killed by five thunderbolts if I make any unauthorized promotions myself.

25. If my natural brothers are involved in a dispute or law suit with my sworn brothers, I must not help either party against the other but must attempt to have the matter settled amicably. If I break this oath, I will be killed by five thunderbolts.

26. After entering the Hung gates, I must forget any previous grudges I may have borne against my sworn brothers. If I do not do so, I will be killed by five thunderbolts.

27. I must not trespass upon the territory occupied by my sworn brothers. I shall be killed by five thunderbolts if I pretend to have no knowledge of my brothers' rights in such matters.

28. I must not covet or seek to share any property or cash obtained by my sworn brothers. If I have such ideas, I will be killed.

29. I must not disclose any address where my sworn brothers keep their wealth, nor must I conspire to make wrong use of such knowledge. If I do so, I will be killed by myriads of swords.

30. I must not give support to outsiders if so doing is against the interests of any of my sworn brothers. If I do not keep this oath, I will be killed by myriads of swords.

31. I must not take advantage of the Hung brotherhood in order to oppress or take violent or unreasonable advantage of others. I must be content and honest. If I break this oath, I will be killed by five thunderbolts.

32. I shall be killed by five thunderbolts if I behave indecently towards small children of my sworn brothers' families.

33. If any of my sworn brothers has committed a big offense, I must not inform upon them to the government for the purposes of obtaining a reward. I shall be killed by five thunderbolts if I break this oath.

34. I must not take to myself the wives and concubines of my sworn brothers nor commit adultery with them. If I do so, I will be killed by myriads of swords.

35. I must never reveal Hung secrets or signs when speaking to outsiders. If I do so, I will be killed by myriads of swords.

36. After entering the Hung gates, I shall be loyal and faithful and shall endeavor to overthrow Ch'ing and restore Ming by coordinating my efforts with those of my sworn brethren, even though my brethren and I may not be in the same professions. Our common aim is to avenge our Five Ancestors.

Reference

W. P. Morgan. *Triad Societies in Hong Kong*. Hong Kong: Government Press, 1960.

—Peter Nempstead

UGURLU, Abuzer

Abuzer Ugurlu became renowned for smuggling weapons, alcohol, and cigarettes in Turkey in the 1980s. In addition, it was claimed that Ugurlu bribed the former prime minister and helped Mehmet Ali Agca, who organized a conspiracy against the pope. Ugurlu was judged in absentia by the Martial Law Court on September 12, 1980.

On October 21, 1999, the Turkish Ministry of Foreign Affairs announced that "Ugurlu was captured at his home by the Drugs Squad yesterday after being on the run for four years. A forged identity card was found on Ugurlu in the name of 'Mehmet Yavuz Altinsir' but no evidence of any other crime could be found."

Abuzer has been a career criminal since the 1960s. He has been linked either by hard fact or by innuendo to every major smuggling crime in Turkey and has been known to be linked to some government officials. He is also known to be associated with the terrorist network that includes an organization known as Ulkuculer, or the Gray Wolves (an outlawed group that smuggles weapons as well as drugs).

Ugurlu enjoyed close ties to well-known Mafioso Abdullah Catli. Catli's henchmen allegedly were couriers for Abuzer Ugurlu, the Turkish mob boss. The thugs traversed the infamous route across Bulgaria that was favored by smugglers believed to have carried NATO military equipment to the Middle East and returned heroin.

Ugurlu was well known for using surrogates to carry out his business and was able to keep an incredibly low profile for a mobster so extremely well known in the Turkish underworld. "This practice paid off in 1981 when a contract was issued by one of Ugurlu's chief lieutenants on the life of Pope John Paul II. Ugurlu reportedly authorized the payment of US \$1.7 million for the murder of the pontiff," reported http://www.geocities.com/Organized CrimeSyndicates. "When the plan failed, Ugurlu's name was rarely uttered and he was even listed as an aide to Bekir Celenk, the man who was ultimately deemed the point man for the entire operation." While Celenk took the heat, with his face appearing in numerous publications, Ugurlu remained in the background. Ugurlu was so clever that he was able to remain almost unnoticed, despite that he was staying in the same floor of the Hotel Vitoshi as Celenk. Ugurlu was briefly interviewed and released.

Ugurlu enjoyed a robust business trading drugs, cigarettes, and weapons until the Susurluk scandal rocked Turkey. This scandal, including top national ministers, precipitated a huge public outcry against the out-of-control Turkish underworld and led to a massive purging of the country's high-ranking criminal element. This eventually led, too, to Ugurlu's arrest despite his desire to keep as low a profile as possible. In spite of this low profile and his penchant for making a fortune several times over from his illegal activities, Organized Crime Syndicates.com claimed that he had "served as the benefactor for such underworld leaders and terrorists as Abdullah Catli, Oral Celik, Mehmut Ali-Agca and Mehmut Sener."

See also: BASAK, HUSEYIN; CATLI, ABDULLAH; DON-MEZ, OSMAN; KILIC, DUNDAR; OZBIZERDIK, ONUR.

ULKUCLER   *See* UGURLU, ABUZER.

UNICORN (a.k.a. Unified Caribbean On-Line Regional Network)

The Unified Caribbean On-Line Regional Network (UNICORN) is an international-crime clearing house for the sharing of information electronically. This special initiative was sponsored by the U.S. Drug Enforcement Administration (DEA). The particular targeted crimes includes money-laundering schemes and drug cartels suspected of smuggling illegal drugs, especially cocaine and heroin. More than 36 Latin American and Caribbean countries were participating in this joint venture. The DEA's participation includes loaning surveillance equipment to help monitor suspected traffickers who are trying to smuggle illegal substances between the different countries as well as into the United States.

According to Jeff Starr, who wrote in "Drug Trade in the Caribbean" for the Council on Hemispheric Affairs, "Two specific operations, Genesis and Columbus, are proof of UNICORN's growing success. Genesis was a tremendous triumph with 126 arrests in Haiti and the Dominican Republic. Previously, both countries had never been able to collaborate with each other's law offices until the advent of UNICORN. . . . The increase in communication among the nations involved displays a level of cooperation that can be much attributed to UNICORN."

UNITED Bamboo

Taiwan is the home base of United Bamboo triad. The triad, the largest among Taiwan's four main triad groups, is said to have more than 10,000 members worldwide. They also have a strong presence in Central and South America as well as in the United States. The U.S. branch of United Bamboo is located in Monterey Park, California. They are one of the most feared of all the triads and are known to be especially violent.

But United Bamboo has continued to expand. A report entitled "Triad Societies and Chinese Organized Crime in South Africa" by Peter Gastrow of the Organized Crime and Corruption Program, Institute for Security Studies, reported, "The National Police Administration in Taiwan recognizes two major Taiwan-based triads. The best known and largest of the two is the United Bamboo Gang, also known as the Chu Lien Pang, with an estimated membership of over 20,000."

The group was founded as the Bamboo Woods League by 17 founding members, the foremost of whom was Chen "Dry Duck" Chi-li. Chi-li was instrumental in building the organization, despite a series of arrests that spanned almost the entirety of his lifetime. Even after he was deported from Taiwan, Chi-li remained the *Dai-lo* (Big Brother), recognized leader, of United Bamboo. He oversees their operation from Cambodia. Chi-li entered the construction business. He has used his legions to strike or otherwise extort or interfere with competitive construction companies, even while working hard on the building projects the company has on its vast slate under construction.

However, United Bamboo has long been involved with extortion and prostitution. It is considered to be one of the largest smugglers of aliens in the world and has enslaved thousands of women into being prostitutes in foreign countries. "Vancouver has become a major point of entry for the smuggling of aliens of Asian descent, not only for Canada, but for the United States as well. A member of the United Bamboo from Los Angeles was involved in smuggling aliens into North America via the People's Republic of China, Hong Kong and Taiwan from staging areas in Vancouver," according to a report from the Canada First Immigration Reform Committee (October, 1993, Immigration: The Sleeper Issue of Election '93).

UNITED BAMBOO MEMBERS' CODE OF ETHICS
(Courtesy Los Angeles County Sheriff's Department)

1. Harmony with the people is the first priority. We have to establish good social and personal connections so as not to create enemies.
2. We have to seek special favors and help from uncommitted gang members by emphasizing our relationships with outside people. Let them publicize us.

3. Gambling is our main financial source. We have to be careful how we handle it.
4. Do not take it upon yourself to start things and make decisions you are not authorized to make. You are to discuss and plan all matters with the group and "Elder Brother."
5. Everyone has their assigned responsibility. Do not create confusion.
6. We do not divulge our plans and affairs to outsiders, for example to our wives, girlfriends, etc. This is for our own safety.
7. We have to be united with all our brothers and obey our Elder Brother's orders.
8. All money earned outside the group must be turned over to the group. You must not keep any of it for yourself. Let the Elder Brother decide.
9. When targeting wealthy prospects, do not act hastily. Furthermore, do not harass or threaten them. Act to prevent suspicion and fear upon their part.
10. If anything unexpected happens, do not abandon your brothers. If arrested, shoulder all responsibility and blame. Do not involve your brothers.

See also: TRIADS.

Reference

Asia, Inc. "Taiwan's Triads." Available online. URL: http://members.tripod.com/~orgcrime/taiwanstriads/htm.

Chen Chi-li, alleged leader of United Bamboo, the most feared of Taiwan's four triads (AP)

URDINOLA Grajales, Jairo Ivan

Jairo Ivan Urdinola Grajales and his brother Julio Fabio Urdinola Grajales head a major drug-trafficking organization associated with the so-called Northern Valle del Cauca drug cartels. The Urdinolas are related by marriage to the Henao Montoya family. The Colombian National Police arrested Ivan in April 1992, while Fabio later surrendered to Colombian authorities in March 1994. The incarceration of the Urdinola Grajales brothers notwithstanding, their organization reportedly remains active in the drug trade.

Reference

Thomas A. Constantine. "International Organized Crime Syndicate and Their Impact on the U.S." U.S. Drug Enforcement Administration. Available online. URL: http://www.usdoj.gov/dea/pubs/cngrtest/ct980226.htm. Downloaded on July 28, 2004.

U.S. Customs Service

The job of protecting 96,000 miles of U.S. land, air, and sea borders and more than 300 ports of entry is entrusted each day to the 20,000 employees of the U.S. Customs Service. U.S. Customs is the principal agency tasked with protecting U.S. borders and is the only border agency with an extensive air, land, and marine interdiction force to carry out their primary mission: Control all carriers, persons, and articles entering and leaving the United States.

The U.S. Customs Service was founded in 1789 to save the struggling new nation from financial collapse. Customs has come to the aid and protection of the United States for more than two centuries. Customs gave America its first source of revenue, became its first federal law-enforcement agency, and has affected and been affected by the nation's history from the earliest days to the present.

After declaring independence in 1776, the United States was soon on the brink of bankruptcy. During the brief period under the Articles of Confederation, in which each state assessed customs duties against its neighbors, Congress learned that the national treasury could not rely on the states for funds.

When, in 1789, Congress first assembled in New York City to launch the United States on its proper course, it had one overriding concern: money—where to find it, how to collect it, how to keep it rolling in. Fighting a revolution had left the national cupboard bare.

James Madison of Virginia proposed the plan that would eventually make the United States solvent: Impose a duty on imports and create a well-managed agency to ensure its due collection. Responding to an urgent need for revenue, the first Congress passed, and President Washington signed, the Tariff Act of July 4, 1789. It established a tariff and a system for collecting duties.

The act was considered so important that the press of the day hailed it as a "second Declaration of Independence." Customs districts, ports of entry, and the machinery for appointing Customs officers and prescribing their duties were established on July 31, 1789—one day before the Tariff Act took effect. President Washington then nominated 59 collectors of customs and more than 40 other officers to staff the new Customs Service.

The entire service was placed under the Treasury Department, headed by 32-year-old Alexander Hamilton. Hamilton's tireless, dedicated commitment to the new service set an early standard for Customs officials.

REGULATORS AND PROTECTORS OF U.S. BORDERS

The prevention of smuggling has been a primary Customs Service assignment, and one of its most hazardous, since its inception. In 1808, when Customs officials were trying to stop the smuggling of dress goods along the Vermont-Canada border, merchants threatened to kill any Customs collector who attempted to enforce the laws. It was in 1808 as well that the infamous *Black Snake,* a ferryboat smeared with tar and turned into a smuggling ship, and manned by a crew of desperados, scorned Customs officers and carried load after load of potash across

Lake Champlain from Canada. Determined to put an end to this traffic, U.S. officials dispatched the *Fly,* a 12-oared cutter manned by Lieutenant Farrington, Sergeant Johnson, and 12 infantry privates who had been detailed to pursue the *Black Snake.*

On August 2, 1808, Lieutenant Farrington and his men boarded the pirate ship. During the ensuing melee, three infantrymen were killed, and Lieutenant Farrington was severely wounded. In a last determined effort, Sergeant Johnson and a detachment of soldiers captured the *Black Snakes'* crew. All were jailed at Burlington, Vermont, and indicted for the killing of three government officials. Three of the crew members were found guilty; one, Cyrus B. Dean, was hanged two weeks later.

When American pioneers moved west, Customs inspectors accompanied the early settlers, enforcing U.S. laws and territorial statutes relating to revenues, immigration, and smuggling. In mountain states along the northern border, primitive enforcement conditions prevailed well into the 1920s, easing only with the coming of the automobile and, later, aerial surveillance. Mounted Customs officers along the Southwest border faced difficult terrain and desperate smugglers. Officer Robert Rumsey was one of many killed in the line of duty.

In 1853, the Secretary of the Treasury authorized the appointment of mounted Customs inspectors for the newly created Paso del Norte district. The mounted patrol was responsible for 1,900 miles of border along the Gulf of Mexico, the U.S.-Mexican border, and the Pacific Ocean. Among these early mounted Customs officers were members of the First U.S. Calvary, better known as Teddy Roosevelt's "Rough Riders."

In the Far West, where Customs has had a continuing presence since the territory's acquisition, Custom's officers managed to preserve their Customhouse flag during the devastating earthquake of 1906.

With the passage in 1920 of the Eighteenth Amendment—prohibiting the importation, possession, and sale of liquor—smuggling in the U.S. reached a new high. Bootleggers worked the borders with boats, trucks, and planes.

Customs countered with seizure after seizure of contraband alcohol. When the rum runners were caught, Customs officers often confiscated their transport vehicles, along with the liquor they carried. During Prohibition, in fact, the U.S. Customs air interdiction fleet consisted wholly of aircraft seized for liquor smuggling.

TODAY'S CUSTOMS SERVICE

The keyword for the U.S. Customs Service at the dawn of the 21st century is *more*. It must deal with more international travelers, more conveyances, more cargo and, unfortunately, more opportunities for those who choose to break U.S. laws. Today's Customs Service continues as a vital and integral part of U.S. security, with a wide array of responsibilities, which includes the enforcement of more than 400 laws and treaties, often on behalf of other federal agencies. In the forefront has been Customs' ability to adapt its responses to the trials of an ever-changing world, modifying its enforcement techniques, technologies, and resources to confront current and future threats to the United States.

NARCOTICS INTERDICTION

With the repeal of Prohibition in 1933, the market for bootleg liquor was gone, but, as the economics of smuggling dictate, a different, deadlier form of contraband began its infiltration onto U.S. shores. Since the 1960s Customs officials have fought the influx of illegal narcotics, such as opium, heroin, hashish, marijuana, and amphetamines into the United States.

The staggering and ever-increasing number of conveyances, cargo, and passengers arriving into the United States each year presents Customs with complex targeting and interdiction challenges, requiring a variety of intelligent, investigative, and operational approaches.

Trying to curb the flood of illegal drugs has proven an arduous task; yet, through diligence, close inspection, sophisticated technology and the sacrifice of lives, Customs has given an excellent account of itself in fighting the flow of illegal drugs into the United States. The U.S. Customs Service is the leading U.S. drug-enforcement agency in terms of the number of illegal narcotics seized and suspects apprehended. In one recent year alone, Customs seized 1.4 million pounds of narcotics bound for domestic distribution.

Customs interdiction efforts, and its unique position at America's frontline, often provide the agency with clear indications of epidemic use of specific drugs. In recent years, sizable seizures of cocaine and new synthetic drugs, such as ecstasy, have tipped law-enforcement authorities to the latest "drugs of choice" and the techniques criminals use to smuggle them.

A distinctive high-profile tool in Customs' arsenal is its force of drug detector dogs, their trainers, and the Customs officers who work with them.

First used on a wide scale in 1970, Customs narcotic detector dogs save countless hours by locating narcotics in vehicles, mail, and unaccompanied baggage on cargo ships and throughout Customs facilities. A dog and its handler can check 500 packages in 30 minutes. It would take a Customs mail examiner several days to inspect as many. At border points, a dog can inspect a vehicle in about two minutes, while the same search by a Customs inspector would take at least 20 minutes.

Technological advances, such as mobile and fixed truck X-ray systems, also assist in Customs' search for illegal substances, while providing expedited movement of cargo. These devices provide an accurate, detailed look at cargo in a fraction of the time needed for a manual search, allowing for a greater number of conveyances to be searched and moved on.

Customs narcotics-interdiction efforts often extend beyond U.S. shores. Customs aircraft fleets, equipped with sophisticated surveillance and tracking devices, coordinate with their high-speed boats to thwart smuggler aircraft as they drop payloads of narcotics off the U.S. coast. Customs also coordinates and participates in counternarcotics missions over high-activity areas, such as the Caribbean and certain South American countries.

MONEY LAUNDERING

Customs agents are experts in the investigation of international money-laundering schemes devised by sophisticated cartels to hide their criminal proceeds. With the passage of the Bank Secrecy Act, which mandates that individuals and corporations disclose certain assets and transactions, those engaged in illegal activities found it increasingly difficult to turn their riches into legitimate commerce. Customs investigators expertly—and often successfully—negotiate the intricate, calculatedly tangled money trail associated with making illegal proceeds escape scrutiny.

Money laundering globally disrupts the legitimate flow of commerce, introducing billions of unregulated dollars into the world's economies, while depriving governments of revenue collected in the form of taxes and duties. The Customs Money Laundering Coordination Center, one of the government's primary weapons tasked with curbing money-laundering activities, is engaged in continuous undercover financial investigations, as evidenced during a recent three-year period when Customs conducted 12,000 investigations leading to 3,150 arrests and the seizure of nearly $1.1 billion.

TRADE FRAUD

Customs special agents are recognized as being among the finest criminal investigators in the world. Their expertise in border investigative methods and techniques has effectively enabled them to consistently solve many complex types of crimes. Customs has investigated every type of smuggling activity imaginable—from narcotics to exotic and endangered animals; Rembrandt paintings; illegal export of munitions of war; international money-laundering schemes; undervaluation schemes; cargo theft and international conspiracies; neutrality violations and child pornography. Another initiative established by Customs is the Forced Child Labor Command Center, which monitors the importation of prohibited goods manufactured by forced or indentured child labor.

STRATEGIC INVESTIGATIONS

Few crimes are more terrifying or potentially more devastating than those involving the importation of arms or explosives intended to do harm to the United States and its citizens. It is the duty of Customs to halt the trafficking of sensitive and controlled commodities, including weapons of mass destruction (WMD) and related technologies, munitions, and firearms. The threat does not end at stopping these items as they enter the United States. Customs also is tasked with preventing the export of technical and military-use commodities to proliferate countries, terrorist groups, and criminal organizations. In the recent past, items seized by Customs include military aircraft, missile parts, night-vision systems, bomb-making devices, Phalanx missiles, and stealth and antimissile technology. Customs additionally enforces violations of economic sanctions and embargoes and the import or export of stolen property.

CYBERSMUGGLING

Customs was assigned the lead in enforcing crimes committed over the Internet and via other electronic media. Among the most heinous crimes investigated by Customs Computer Investigation Specialists is child pornography. In addition to developing and implementing the strategies used to track cyber pornographers, Customs investigators routinely provide training and expertise to prosecutors and law-enforcement officials both in the United States and abroad. Despite the relative newness of this type of crime, Customs has already effected hundreds of arrests in child pornography cases. Among the variety of other media-related crimes Customs investigates is telemarketing fraud (i.e., bogus investments, charities, prize offers, travel packages).

INTELLECTUAL PROPERTY RIGHTS

To secure the rights of creative individuals and those who have a vested interest in their works, Customs protects intellectual property rights (IPR). IPR can be a copyright that protects original creations of authorship, such as books, paintings, music, and movies; a trademark, which is a design, slogan, brand name, or configuration used to identify products as originating from a particular source; a patent, which is issued to protect a novel or useful invention; or a trade name, used to identify a specific business or occupation. Each year, trade in counterfeit or pirated merchandise in violation of IPR costs industry billions of dollars and nearly 750,000 jobs.

Science and analytical research assist Customs officers in their efforts to stop these illegal and fraudulent activities. The Customs Service maintains eight laboratories in the United States and San Juan, Puerto Rico, where sophisticated equipment analyzes certain imports to determine their appropriate classification. These scientific findings provide key, accurate evidence in the effort to prosecute IPR violators.

COMMERCE

With much larger numbers looming, Customs currently processes more than $1 trillion (total imports) in trade each year. Along with human resources and policy initiatives designed to assist the effort, technology is also being put in service protecting the public revenue. Technology is as crucial to Customs' commercial role as it is to law enforcement.

A new automated commercial environment (ACE) in the works will rely on account management to streamline the commercial import process, thus lowering the cost of trade compliance and increasing customer service for the trade community. Inspectors will use this system to make paperless cargo clearances as well as targeting noncompliant cargo for examinations.

Customs current automated system (ACS) helps brokers, Customs agents, the law enforcement community, and, ultimately, users perform a variety of functions, ranging from the assessment and collection of user fees to obtaining instant information on new or changing import quotas, monitoring high-risk shipments, and exchanging enforcement information nationwide. Additionally, computer technology has increased and accelerated Customs' role as registrar of statistics vital to U.S. trade, commerce, and security.

CUSTOMS STATISTICS AND ACCOMPLISHMENTS

In Fiscal Year 2000, the U.S. Customs Service processed 489 million pedestrians and passengers. Processed conveyances, such as passenger vehicles, trucks, private and commercial aircraft, and small boats and vessels amounted to 139.9 million. Of these arriving persons, vehicles, and carriers, Customs staff arrested 23,670 people. They also confiscated the following significant seizures of illegal goods:

- 6.4 million rounds of ammunition
- 150,036 pounds of cocaine
- $60,000,000 in counterfeit goods
- 9.3 million ecstasy tablets
- 39,643 firearms
- 2,555 pounds of heroin
- $204,100,000 in illicit proceeds
- 1,291,487 pounds of marijuana
- $132,243,384 in illegal merchandise
- and 2,872 pounds of methamphetamine

In December 1999 U.S. Customs Service officers disrupted a terrorist plot timed to coincide with the millennium celebrations in the United States. Alert Customs officers on the U.S.-Canadian border arrested an Algerian, Ahmed Ressam, with timing devices and large quantities of explosive materials. Ressam was later convicted for his role in the terror plot, which was intended to bomb Los Angeles International Airport.

The Customs Service arrested 302 individuals in connection with the smuggling of WMD components as well as other sensitive military technology, munitions, and controlled goods. Customs also seized 736

shipments of munitions, technology, and sanctioned items worth $50.7 million.

In August 2000 the U.S. Customs Service announced the results of Operation Journey, a massive, two-year investigation involving authorities from 12 nations. The investigation, which targeted a global maritime drug-transportation organization, resulted in the seizure of 25 tons of cocaine and the arrest of 43 individuals, including the accused ringleader. The probe has since led to the indictment of major cartel figures in Colombia and the August 2001 seizure of $35 million in U.S. currency by Colombian authorities.

The U.S. Customs Service has become one of the leading federal law-enforcement agencies in the fight against the illegal drug ecstasy (MDMA). U.S. Customs formed a special task force and trained several hundred canines to be alert to this drug. U.S. Customs seizures of ecstasy tablets have dramatically increased in recent years—from 3.5 million tablets in Fiscal Year 1999 to 9.3 million tablets in Fiscal Year 2000.

During 2001 Customs strategic cases have resulted in numerous arrests, including individuals attempting to smuggle HAWK missile parts and military aircraft components to Iran, military encryption technology to China, and spy cameras to Pakistan.

In March 2001 the U.S. Customs Service and Russian police took down a global child-pornography Web site, resulting in four arrests and the execution of 15 search warrants in the United States, and five arrests in Russia. The enforcement action, dubbed Operation Blue Orchid after the Russian Web site, went after individuals associated with a Russian Web site selling child-pornography videotapes over the Internet and through the mail. Working together, Moscow city police and U.S. Customs identified a group of Russian child pornographers engaged in the production and distribution of child pornography to customers in the United States and Europe. As a result of the Blue Orchid case, three U.S. Customs special agents were selected by the National Association of Police Organizations as winner's of this year's "Top Police" award in the international category.

Customs joined forces with the Federal Aviation Administration to conduct an operation targeting dangerous goods transported on commercial aircraft. This joint initiative, Operation Clear Sky, was conducted at 19 major airports. During the Operation, there were a total of 1,811 international commercial flights inspected and a total of 268 hazardous materials interdictions. There were also three undeclared currency seizures totaling $218,555.

Reference

"Protectors of Independence." *U.S. Customs Service and Customs Statistics and Accomplishments, U.S. Customs Service, Department of Treasury.* Available online. URL: http://www.customs.ustreas.gov/linkhandler/cgov/toolbox/publications/mission/protectorsofindependence.htm. Downloaded on July 15, 2004.

VALLÉE, Richard (a.k.a. Rick)

Richard "Rick" Vallée was born on November 10, 1957, and became a Hells Angels member when the Satan's Guard biker gang became the Big Red Machine's Trois-Rivières chapter on June 14, 1991. He was soon seen as the right-hand man of Louis "Mélou" Roy, the group's leader.

By then, Vallée was no stranger to law enforcement. He had pleaded guilty to operating a prostitution den on November 30, 1988, and during the next few years twice pleaded guilty to possession of hashish. On May 22, 1992, he was acquitted of the charge of illegally using a firearm, and the next year a charge of possession of an illicit drug was dropped.

In the mid-1990s, Vallée left the Trois-Rivières chapter for the newly formed Nomads chapter. This move was a clear indication of his sway and influence within the gang.

A group of Quebec volunteer firefighters walked into a Champlain, New York, bowling alley in early 1993 and ordered some drinks. One of the men began to talk with the establishment's bartender, Lee Carter, and, after some friendly banter, asked Carter if he wanted to make some fast cash. All he had to do was "mule" loads of cocaine from New York to Montreal. The bartender feigned interest but approached police immediately after and agreed to become an informant.

As a result of Carter's cooperation, two men were arrested and 57 kilograms of cocaine was seized. Police suspected that the drug was destined to be delivered to Vallée and Roy. The two Hells Angels were arrested in Quebec and charged with drug trafficking.

Carter was to be the main witness at the trail, but he never had the opportunity. He was killed on July 23, 1993, when a bomb planted under his Porsche exploded. The explosion tore Carter's right leg from his body; it was found three vehicles away, under another car. Without their star witness, prosecutors did not have enough evidence and dropped the charges in 1997.

Serge Quesnel, a Hells Angels underling, was arrested on April 1, 1995, just before he was going to murder Robert Duduc, a leader of the Jokers biker gang. Quesnel decided to become a government witness and spilled the beans on the Duduc murder contract. Quesnel said the task had been assigned to him by Richard Vallée, who said that he wanted Duduc killed because he was not loyal enough to the Hells Angels.

Vallée was charged with conspiracy to murder. Quesnel testified against his former boss but was less than convincing and the jury did not believe anything he said. Vallée was acquitted on December 17, 1996. Members of the Jokers gang applauded loudly when the verdict against their Hells Angels godfather was revealed. Robert Duduc would be murdered on April 30, 1998.

The Hells Angel was not out of the woods yet. The U.S. marshal issued a warrant for his arrest in connection with the 1993 bombing murder of Lee Carter. Vallée was picked up by police and put back in prison without the possibility of bail.

On January 21, 1997, while in the Rivière-des-Prairies penitentiary, Vallée was attacked by another inmate. He was punched in the face, a blow that broke his jaw. The injury needed treatment, and the Hells Angel was regularly escorted from prison to a hospital for appointments.

On June 5, 1997, Vallée was escorted by two unarmed prison guards to the St.-Luc Hospital for treatment on his jaw. While there, he informed his escorts that he wanted to take a shower. As one guard watched the door, the other accompanied Vallée inside the bathroom. Inside the shower, an armed henchman waited with two guns. When the two entered the room, the henchman jumped the escort and confined him with his own handcuffs. Vallée and his accomplice escaped through another door and ran outside, where two other henchmen waited on motorcycles. The two jumped on the back of the bikes and sped away.

The spectacular escape led to a Canada-wide manhunt. The U.S. marshal was furious and put tremendous pressure on Canadian authorities for Vallée's capture. Vallée was finally arrested on April 17, 2003 as he left a store on St.-Mathieu Street in Montreal. A firearm and cash were found in his car. He had been arrested by Montreal police a week earlier for turning right on a red light. Police did not recognize him, as he had altered his appearance and was carrying a driver's license in the name of Guy Turner. The Hells Angel failed a breathalyzer test and was taken into custody. He was fingerprinted and released, after promising to return for a court appearance. Police then matched his fingerprints, revealing his true identity.

See also: HELLS ANGELS.

Reference

Gary Francoeur. "Richard 'Rick' Vallée." Wiseguy-Wally. Available online. URL: http://www.geocities.com/wiseguywally/RichardVallee.html. Downloaded on July 16, 2004.

—G.F.

VANVERBERGHE, Francis (a.k.a. the Belgian)

Francis Vanverberghe was nicknamed the Belgian and was also known as the gangster with a big heart. Vanverbeghe was born in Marseilles. He became a highly regarded figure in the French and European underworld as the gang leader who dominated the struggle for control of the importation of illegal drugs onto the continent. These battles were part of the famed French Connection and led to the gangster's reputation as a ruthless and cunning operator.

In 1977 he was convicted and sentenced to 12 years of prison for his part in that famed underworld operation. He was released in 1984. He was arrested in Belgium four years later and extradited to France on drug charges. While he spent four years in custody, he was never prosecuted. Eventually he was released, and the government of France was forced to pay $20,000 in reparations for a violation of his civil rights.

On September 28, 2000, two assassins on a motorcycle drove by a Paris betting shop in the tony section of the eighth arrondissement and opened fire. At the age of 54, Vanverberghe was killed.

Reference

John William Tuohy. "Round Up the Usual Suspects." AmericanMafia.com. Available online. URL: http://www.americanmafia.com/Feature_Articles_63.html. Downloaded on July 16, 2004.

VERBITSKY, Garik (a.k.a. Jerry the Razor)

Garik Verbitsky was a reputed Russian Mafiya member. He was a brutal operative, also known as Jerry the Razor.

Verbitsky shot Shaya Kalikman to death on March 3, 1986, in a Brighton Beach, Brooklyn, social club. Almost a year later, Verbitsky would find himself on the wrong side of a gun. Verbitsky was shot to death in a Brighton Beach social club on April 21, 1987.

See also: RUSSIAN MAFIYA.

Reference

New Jersey State Commission of Investigation, New York Organized Crime Task Force, New York State Commission of Investigation, Pennsylvania Crime Commission, with Rutgers University. "The Tri-State Joint Soviet-Émigré Organized Crime Project." 1992. Available online. URL: http://www.state.nj.us/sci/pdf/russian.pdf. Accessed on November 24, 2004.

VICE Lords

The Vice Lords is the oldest and second-largest black street gang in the Chicago area. It was originally formed in the late 1950s as a club in the Illinois State Training School for Boys in St. Charles, Illinois. As members were released, several relocated to the Lawndale area of Chicago, where they gained recognition as a gang. Their main area of power remains the West Side of Chicago in the Altgeld Gardens, the Eden Green development and the Golden Gate development. Since the original formation numerous breakaway factions have been formed. These factions now operate throughout the city of Chicago and outlying areas. Each faction has its own distinctive name and leader. According to the National Drug Intelligence Center, the Vice Lords is one of three main groups that control sales and distribution of cocaine, heroin, and marijuana in Illinois and surrounding states. Since they supply only distribution and retail sales, authorities know that they are consistently dealing with various international drug traffickers who are seeking distribution in major markets.

The Vice Lords utilized gold, black, and red as their colors and the five-pointed star, top hat, martini glass, Playboy bunny, dollar sign, and the cane as their symbols. The different factions use specific graffiti to identify themselves individually. Their common hand sign is a single upraised hand with the thumb, index, and middle fingers to form "VL." Also utilized is the upraised hand with all fingers extended and a separation between the middle and ring fingers. The Vice Lords call other members *People* and use the term *All is well*. Members of the Vice Lords can be seen wearing University of Iowa, Pittsburgh Steelers, Pittsburgh Pirates, Pittsburgh Penguins, University of Texas Longhorns, and Chicago Bulls athletic jackets, T-shirts, and baseball caps. Members also wear Louis Vuitton, (VL reversed) and University of Nevada Las Vegas jackets and caps (UNLV–VLNU reversed, Vice Lord Nation United).

The Vice Lords can be found in the Midwest and in some eastern cities. They continue to have a stronghold over many Chicago neighborhoods. The Vice Lords possess a rank structure within the individual factions which includes General, Minister, Lieutenant, and Foot Soldiers. This structure is similar in all factions of the Vice Lords; however, each faction's leadership is unique and has no power over members of other factions.

VIETNAM

According to the statistics from Standing Office of Drug Control in Vietnam, as reported by the United Nations, the extent and pattern of drug abuse in Vietnam is shifting from the rural older-age groups to the younger-age groups in urban areas. The emergence of amphetamine-type stimulants in Vietnam is also likely to have an impact on the young generation. Amphetamine-type stimulants have become available in large quantities in the major cities and in some of the larger provincial centers. Increasing intravenous drug use and continued practice of needle sharing is helping to fuel the HIV/AIDS epidemic.

At the same time with the increasing drug consumption, crime rates are on the rise in Vietnam. These two phenomena are interlinked since, according to available statistics, as many as 90 percent of the people involved in murder, robbery, and theft have been identified as drug addicts. The majority are young people. Drug-related crimes show an upward trend throughout the country. Unemployment is one of the reasons leading to drug use. In rural areas, underemployment remains higher than in urban centers, with active employment accounting for only 74 percent of the total work time in a year.

Vietnam is still considered a minor drug-producing country, although remarkable success has been achieved in the eradication of poppy plants. The area of opium cultivation in 2000 was estimated to be as small as 428.6 hectares, of which 426.4 hectares have been destroyed, accounting for 99.5 percent of the total planted area. The potential opium output for the year 2000 was four metric tons. There was also minor production of cannabis in the southern provinces of Vietnam. No confirmation but anecdotal evidence points at the possibility that certain precursors have been produced in Vietnam.

In Vietnam, both the seizures made and the number of people involved in drug trafficking has increased and shows an escalation of the drug problem in the country. Drug smuggling is unfolding in an ever more complicated manner. This development may be a consequence of Vietnam's proximity to the Golden Triangle, the recently introduced open-door policy, as well as high profits involved in the drug business. Moreover, Vietnamese law-enforcement authorities are facing difficulties in tackling the escalating situation partly because the long borders and coastal lines have proven to be extremely tricky to patrol.

See also: NAM CAM; VIETNAMESE GANGS.

Reference

United Nations Office on Drugs and Crime. "Vietnam Country Office." Available online. URL: http://www. unodc.org/vietnam/index.html. Downloaded on July 16, 2004.

VIETNAMESE Gangs

After the fall of South Vietnam in the mid-1970s, a large influx of Vietnamese refugees were targeted for resettlement within the United States. A small tract of land in Orange County, California, was identified, and a small community took root. A second group of Vietnamese immigrants, well known in the media as the boat people, also arrived on American shores about five years later. They, too, settled in Orange County. These Vietnamese immigrants formed solid and close-knit communities that are referred to in southern California as Little Saigon. There are approximately 1,000 Vietnamese gang members in Southern California.

Producers Ahrin Mishan and Nick Rothenberg's stunning 1994 documentary, *Bui Doi: Life Like Dust,* is a major exposé of Vietnamese gang life and contributed greatly to understanding of Vietnamese gangs.

As with any influx of immigrant populations, among the hard-working populations were individuals who were more interested in organized crime. The most well-known Vietnamese gangs include the Natoma Boyz, the Santa Ana Boyz, the Chosen Brothers, and Nip Family. These male gangs have their female counterparts such as Natoma Girlz, Chosen Sisters, Innocent Bitch Killers, South Side Scissors, and Midnight Flowers.

Vietnamese gangs, however, are not tied to boundaries of their neighborhoods, a good example being the Santa Ana Boyz, who also have members in San Diego, Los Angeles, Westminster, Garden Grove, Anaheim, Riverside, and Pomona.

Reference

Bui Doi: Life Like Dust. Producers: Ahrin Mishan and Nick Rothenberg. Documentary. 28 mins. 1994.

VIOLI, Francesco

Francesco Violi, the youngest of the infamous Violi brothers, was born in Sinopoli, near Reggio Calabria. He immigrated to Canada in the late 1950s, a few years after his brother Paolo. Continuing in the family tradition, Francesco became involved with criminal

Francesco Violi *(Montreal Gazette)*

activities. When Paolo Violi relocated to Montreal and became involved with the Cotroni mob, he brought Francesco along as his primary enforcer and right-hand man. According to police, Francesco Violi was supposedly intensely feared in the underworld. He was said to have a vicious temper that could be sparked with the slightest perceived threat. That is why when the Sicilian faction targeted Paolo Violi, they knew the intelligent thing to do was to take out his brother first.

On February 9, 1977, as Francesco sat behind his desk at Violi Importing and Distributing Ltd., two masked assailants entered, brandishing firearms. He was backed against the wall and shot in the face with a shotgun. The other attacker pumped several bullets into Violi to make sure he was indeed dead. He was 38 years old. Most of the city's elite underworld figures attended Francesco Violi's funeral, which consisted of 26 flower-bearing automobiles. Less than a year later, his brother Paolo would suffer the same fate. Finally, on October 17, 1980, it was brother Rocco who was murdered by a sniper as he sat at home with his family. Francesco is buried alongside his brothers in Notre Dame des Neiges Cemetery.

Reference

Gary Francoeur. "Francesco Violi." WiseguyWally. Available online. URL: http://www.geocities.com/wiseguywally/FrancescoVioli.html. Downloaded on July 15, 2004.

—G.F.

VIOLI, Paolo

Paolo Violi immigrated from Sinopoli, Italy, to Canada in the 1950s. The family settled in Ontario, and Paolo—along with his brothers Rocco, Francesco, and Giuseppe—became a low-level criminal in the Hamilton area.

On May 24, 1955, Violi and immigrant Natale Brigante chatted in a parking lot in Toronto. Violi produced a .32-caliber firearm and pumped four bullets into Brigante. Police picked Violi up in Welland and charged him with manslaughter. The charges were dropped when Violi claimed self-defense and showed the court a knife wound as proof.

In the early 1960s Violi relocated to Montreal and hooked up with Frank "Le Gros" Cotroni, Vic's younger brother. He ran a successful extortion racket in Montreal's Italian community of St. Leonard, operated a counterfeiting ring, and shipped bootleg whiskey from Montreal to southern Ontario. He began to meet regularly with Vic Cotroni and encountered Bill Bonanno in November 1966.

Violi married into Mafia royalty on July 10, 1965, when he wed Grazia Luppino, daughter of Ontario Mafia godfather Giacomo Luppino, and expanded his influence greatly. Grazia, a loyal wife, would remain by his side until his death. Vic Cotroni and Ontario crime bosses Johnny Papalia and Paul Volpe would become godfather to the couple's children.

Violi continued his successful criminal career and, by the early 1970s, was seen as Cotroni's heir apparent. But the godfather of St. Leonard, as Violi was called, was not as calm as his predecessor. When a war erupted in 1973 between the Cotroni family and the Dubois gang, Violi's proposed solution, overheard on a wiretap, was to "have gone into the club, clients or no clients, lined everybody up against the wall and rat-a-tat-tat." But Cotroni, who now played the role of advisor, was not as brash and decided to make peace with the French-Canadian gang.

In the mid-1970s Paolo Violi's world was invaded once again. Montreal police officer Bob Menard, under the name Bob Wilson, rented the apartment above Violi's headquarters, an ice-cream bar on Jean-Talon East. Menard would bug Violi's base of operations, and the information picked up from the bug was priceless.

Despite being born in Italy, agent Menard learned, Violi was a Canadian nationalist. He hated the separatists. When English teachers in St. Leonard began to receive threatening calls, Violi provided them with bodyguards for protection. The threats soon ceased.

In the late 70s the Sicilian faction of the family, led by Nicolo Rizzuto, decided to make a grab for power. Pietro Sciara, Violi's adviser, was killed on Valentine's Day, 1976, while leaving a theatre with his wife. Ironically, the movie they had seen was *The Godfather*.

Francesco Violi, Paolo's brother, was next. He was murdered on February 8, 1977. Francesco was on the phone in his office at Violi's Importing and Distributing Company when he received a shotgun blast to the face. Several bullets were also fired from a handgun to affirm the man's death. Paolo was behind bars at the time, serving a contempt term.

Paolo Violi was a marked man when he was released from prison that fall. Nick Rizzuto, who had left for Venezuela to avoid Violi's wrath, had placed a contract on his head. Violi refused to run or hide and continued to attend his regular hangouts.

On January 22, 1978, while playing cards at a bar owned by Vincenzo and Giuseppe Randisi, two masked men strolled in with .12 gauge shotguns. One of the assassins placed a gun to the back of Violi's head and fired. Violi was 46 years old.

Violi's funeral featured 31 black Cadillacs loaded with flowers and tributes from mobsters in Italy and North America. Sicilian mobsters Giovanni DiMora, Agostino Cuntrera, and Dominico Manno would plead guilty to plotting Violi's death. DiMora and Manno each received seven years in prison, while Cuntrera got five years.

Upon Violi's death, Nicolo Rizzuto took over the family and became independent.

Reference

Gary Francoeur. "Paolo Violi." WiseguyWally. Available online. URL: http://www.geocities.com/wiseguywally/PaoloVioli.html. Downloaded on July 15, 2004.

—G.F.

WAH Ching Gang

The Wah Ching exemplifies the ability of a gang to evolve into a formidable organized-crime group. From its origin in 1966 as a street gang, the Wah Ching has developed into a sophisticated criminal organization, with multi-international-crime connections. During the 1970s and 1980s, the Wah Ching became an organization that controlled most of the criminal vices in San Francisco's Chinatown and Los Angeles's Chinese communities. During that time, there may have been as many as 200 Wah Ching members and 500 criminal associates in California. Although primarily headquartered in San Francisco, they have developed strong associations with Asian organized-crime groups and gang members in Los Angeles, Seattle, Vancouver, Toronto, Boston, and New York—along with close ties to the Sun Yee On and the 14K Triads in Hong Kong.

Typical criminal activities of the Wah Ching include extortion, burglary, gambling, prostitution, loan sharking, narcotics trafficking, robbery, and murder. Their operations now include legitimate businesses including real-estate investments, jewelry stores, restaurants, nightclubs, travel agencies, and the entertainment industry.

The dominant position of the Wah Ching has not been seriously challenged until recently. Members of a rival criminal organization known as the Wo Hop To Triad from Hong Kong have been moving into the San Francisco Bay Area since 1989.

In 2002 the Wah Ching suffered several defeats. Two prominent members, Vicent Tu and Darius Wong, were indicted and put behind bars. In addition 11 alleged Chinatown gangsters (from the Joe Boyz and the Wah Ching) were arrested for book making and protection rackets and other activities by the U.S. District Attorney's office.

See also: TRIADS; WO HOP TO.

WAN Kuok-Koi (a.k.a. Broken Tooth Koi)

Wan Kuok-koi was one of the most important Yakuza bosses. He was the head of the 14K triad, and his influence stretched from Macau to Hong Kong to Taiwan, where it was involved with prostitution, gambling, extortion, and other illegal businesses. However, Kuok-koi led the 14K into a destructive war with the Shui Fong triads over gambling rackets. A bloody war ensued. The 14K gang allegedly took part in drive-by shootings, car bombings, and attempted assassinations. Kuok-koi became dangerously obsessed with the war, and police thought the war would escalate even further, having killed more than 34 gangsters already. Also, police linked Wan to the attempted assassination of top gambling inspector and former police intelligence officer Lieutenant-Colonel Manuel Antonio Apolinario. Apolinario survived the well-organized but failed hit. Wan was arrested on May 1, 1998, along with brother Wan Kuok-hung, his high-ranking lieutenant. He was sentenced to 15 years in prison after he was arrested and tried on a series of antiracketeering laws in 1999. Seven associates received lesser sentences.

See also: 14K TRIADS; TRIADS.

WARREN, Curtis (a.k.a. Cocky)

Curtis "Cocky" Warren is Britain's biggest and richest drug trafficker, worth an estimated £185 million. Unlike most other drug traffickers or criminals Warren is highly intelligent, does not drink, smoke, or use drugs, and has a photographic memory for telephone numbers and numbers of bank accounts. His organization had contacts with the Colombian Cali cartel and Moroccan and Turkish criminal organizations. Curtis Warren was the main drugs supplier in all of Britain, moving tons of cocaine, heroin, and ecstasy.

Curtis Warren was born on May 31, 1963, in Liverpool, England, and grew up in the Granby district of Toxteth, a tough neighborhood with a bad reputation. At age 11 Warren decided school was not for him and left. He started doing petty crimes and was arrested several times—at age 12 for stealing a car, for example. When he reached his teens, Warren became a bouncer at a Liverpool night club; in this position he had a close look at how the drug trade worked—a bouncer had the power to let the dealers and their drugs in or keep them out. Warren realized that this could be very good business.

After some time, Warren was promoted to the main bouncer and had the task of bossing around the other bouncers. In this position, he could fully exploit the dealers and have a good hold on the drug trade. He started by selling and controlling the drugs. As years passed by Warren became richer and was involved with bigger and bigger deals.

By the late 1980s he teamed up with another English drug trafficker named Brian Charrington from Middlesbrough, England. In September 1991 they flew to Venezuela to set up a big cocaine shipment. They planned to ship the cocaine in steel boxes sealed inside lead ingots, which could not be exposed by X-ray and would make manual inspection difficult. When the shipment hit England, it was held by suspicious customs agents. They cut open one ingot but found nothing and let the shipment through. Moments later they got a tip from the Dutch police that there was cocaine hidden inside the steel boxes

inside the lead ingots, but by now the shipment and Warren were long gone. Lucky for law enforcement a second shipment was on its way, and this time they were waiting.

When the shipment arrived, the cocaine was found, and Warren and Charrington and several others were arrested. It seemed that Warren's criminal career was over and that he was going away to prison for a very long time. Warren and his pal Charrington faced charges of importing shipments of cocaine with a combined worth of £500 million (about $600 million). But Warren was about to catch a lucky break. Two detectives revealed that Charrington was a police informer. The custom agents knew nothing of this informer, and it turned out that Charrington, with help of his informer status, had shipped a lot of drugs to Britain. Warren's case was dropped, and in 1993 Curtis Warren was acquitted of all charges. Legend has it that after he was set free he went back to the customs agents, walked past them, and said: "I'm off to spend my 87 million (English) pounds from the first shipment, and you can't . . . touch me."

Back on the streets of Liverpool, things were becoming dangerous. Several organized-crime figures were found in holes, burned, and with several bullets in their head. Others were found chopped up by machetes. Along with those problems, Warren faced the prospect that the English authorities would come after him with everything they had, especially since their first effort ended in disgrace. With all this in mind Warren thought it was a smart idea to move to a nice safe country, and so in 1995 he moved his headquarters to Holland. Most drug traffickers would choose Amsterdam or Rotterdam as a good place to set up base, but Warren decided the quiet town of Sassenheim would be perfect. He moved into a very nice villa from where he conducted his business and made his deals.

By this time Curtis "Cocky" Warren was a very rich and powerful man. He owned houses, mansions, and office blocks in Britain, casinos in Spain, discos in Turkey, a vineyard in Bulgaria, and his villa in Sassenheim. The rest of his money was stashed away in Swiss bank accounts. Warren could have easily retired to some tropical island, but for some reason he kept on going, setting up more and more drug deals and making more and more money. In the quiet town of Sassenheim, Warren felt safe and relatively hidden from the police. From his home he made phone calls to his friends in England. He didn't know it, but police were listening in—not that that mattered since Warren talked in code. He never named any of his friends by name, only by nicknames such as "macker and tacker," "the egg on legs," "twit and twat," "the werewolf and the vampire," "badger," "boo," and other names. But police continued to watch him closely, hoping that he might slip.

One of Warren's new shipment plans was already set in place. This time the cocaine from Venezuela would be shipped to Bulgaria, where it would be cooked into liquid and held in suspension inside bottles of wine. The cocaine would be put in wine in Bulgaria; from there it would be shipped to Holland and then on to Liverpool to be sold. While Warren waited for his cocaine shipment from Venezuela, he was already thinking of where to stash his new heap of money, but this time people were watching. On October 24, 1996, the shipment from Bulgaria arrived in Holland and that night Dutch S.W.A.T. units raided Warren's home to arrest him. The unit, using stun grenades, totally surprised the sleepy Warren and put him under arrest without problem. Several of the members of his organization were arrested that same night. At the homes they found three guns, ammo, hand grenades, crates with ochlorobenzyliden-malononitrile (teargas) gas canisters, 1,500 kilograms of heroin, 50 kilograms of ecstasy, and $600,000 in cash. The shipment was also caught, which combined with the stashes found before, would be worth £125 million. He was arrested in Holland and put in jail to wait his trial.

At the trial Curtis Warren was charged with importing 800 kilograms of cocaine into Holland, and planning to ship it to the United Kingdom. On July 19, 1997, he was found guilty and sentenced to 12 years in prison. Immediately after his sentencing, authorities started the search for Warren's riches, estimated at £125 million by British authorities. So far they have only traced £20 million, and because of international laws, the British authorities can not touch it. They have not found the more than £100 million that they assume he must be hiding somewhere. The only person who knew where all that money was stashed was Warren, and he never kept any records. He never wrote it down and never kept numbers or accounts in a computer. He had it all in his mind, a photographic memory. As authorities continue their search, the man who knows where

the treasure is buried is serving his 12-year sentence in the maximum security prison Nieuw Vosseveld in Vught, Holland. He was not planning to tell them anything regarding his golden stash.

After serving more than two years of relatively quiet time, Warren made some noise; he kicked in the head of a fellow inmate. It all happened on the afternoon of September 15, 1999, when Warren was walking around the prison yard. While Warren walked around quietly, inmate Cemal Guclu started to yell abuse at Warren. Guclu was serving a 20-year sentence for murder and attempted murder. He walked towards Warren and tried to punch him in the face. Warren evaded the punch and pushed Guclu against the wall, after which Guclu fell to the ground. Guclu tried to punch Warren again, but Warren was one step ahead and kicked him in the head four times. After this, Guclu tried to get up once more before Warren again kicked him in his head, after which Guclu lay motionless in the prison yard, his head a bloody mess. Guclu was dead on the spot.

In February 2001 Warren was back on trial. Warren said he "acted in self defense." The Dutch judge, who did not feel the same way, found Warren guilty of manslaughter adding: "The defendant had used excessive violence." The judge sentenced Warren to four years in prison. Warren now 37 was now getting out in 2014 and would now serve 16 years instead of 12. Dutch authorities then informed Warren he had to pay them 26 million guilders ($14 million) or face an added five-years in prison. After some legal wrangling, an agreement was struck: Warren would pay 15 million guilders ($8 million) and not face an added 5-year term. Dutch authorities agreed and took the money.

Curtis "Cocky" Warren is still in prison serving his time and will be out in 2014. Warren's stash of gold has still not been found, and he remains the wealthiest British criminal, worth an estimated £125 million according to authorities (and £185 million according to insiders). It is all stashed safely, and the combination of the vault is safely locked away in Warren's head.

Reference

David Amoruso. "Curtis 'Cocky' Warren." Gangsters Inc. Available online. URL: http://gangstersinc.tripod.com/CurtisWarren.html. Downloaded on July 15, 2004.

—D.A.

337

WATANABE, Yoshinori

Yoshinori Watanabe was born in 1941 in the Tochigi prefecture north of Tokyo, into a big farming family and had a pretty good life. After finishing middle school he moved to Tokyo and worked in restaurants making noodles. After a couple of years, he grew bored and moved to Kobe where he joined the Yamaken-gumi, a gang that is part of the Yamaguchi-gumi clan. When Watanabe joined the Yamaguchi-gumi sometime around 1960, they were embroiled in a series of deadly turf wars. According to the underworld legends, it was in these wars that Watanabe showed his skills as a leader. He proved to be tough and smart and was, besides a hard worker, lethally efficient in resolving disputes. The bosses recognized his talent, and after the wars Watanabe quickly rose through the ranks.

By the early 1980s the Yamaguchi-gumi clan was in chaos. They had lost their boss in 1981 to a heart attack, his successor to liver failure, and then the next successor to assassins. Then in 1988, it was Watanabe's turn. He became the fifth boss in the history of the Yamaguchi-gumi clan. By now the Yamaguchi-gumi were the biggest Yakuza clan in Japan. However, during the 1980s, they were split into two rival factions. They had lost power during the war that followed, which left 26 members dead. Many people considered the Yamaguchi-gumi finished and expected another Yakuza clan to take over. At first it seemed the expectation would be met when Watanabe did not do much in his first months as top boss.

In the early 1990s, law enforcement began to see dramatic changes in the Yamaguchi-gumi clan. Watanabe started to bring the Yamaguchi-gumi back to the top of Japanese organized crime. He abandoned the centralized power structure and split it into seven semiautonomous regional groups, making it harder for police to monitor them and easier to control internal and external friction. He forged new alliances and cemented existing ones with rival clans nationwide, and he rekindled an earlier leader's dream of making the gang a nationwide power. When Watanabe took charge, the clan had offices in 39 of Japan's 47 prefectures. Today, that number is up to 43. At the same time, Watanabe added 5,000 full-time men to the clan. By 1999, according to police statistics, the Yamaguchi-gumi had 165,000 full-time members, more than five times the size of the entire American Mafia at its peak in the 1950s.

Thanks to Watanabe, the membership was up a third since he took over in 1988.

Under Watanabe the Yamaguchi-gumi also survived the major crackdown on organized crime and the Japanese recession. Where other Yakuza clans were decimated by the police efforts that jailed their leadership or the recession that drove membership down, the Yamaguchi-gumi grabbed what was left and managed to muscle in on the new economy. It was not all good times for Watanabe though. Two of his underbosses were jailed and a third was murdered, but because he is the most powerful Yakuza boss of the moment, police forces are aiming all their resources at him. Putting him behind bars will not be easy: Watanabe is well isolated from actual crimes, and the Yamaguchi-gumi have a strong hold on politics.

During the House Election, the Yamaguchi-gumi helped raise money and delivered votes for scores of politicians. Exactly what such relationships yield is unclear, but they suggest that short of taking on Watanabe's political allies, the police stand little chance of bringing him to his knees. Equally unnerving, in a recent issue of *Shukan Taishu*, a magazine closely read by police and Yakuza alike, an unnamed Yamaguchi-gumi underboss warned that if the police ever threatened the clan in earnest, it would not hesitate to retaliate. Watanabe currently lives in a palatial home in one of Kobe's old-money neighborhoods. He is a simple man, say people who know him, avoids rich food, lifts weights, jogs, hikes in the Kobe hills, has a single-digit golf handicap, skis in winter and jet-skis in summer, is an avid student of Chinese history and Japanese law, and enjoys karaoke. (His repertoire includes a Japanese ballad set to the music from *The Godfather*.)

Those who know him say he sees himself first and foremost as an unorthodox public servant. To his mind, there will always be losers, people incapable of holding down regular jobs. Since the Yakuza provides work for such people and helps keep their aggression and frustrations in check, or at least directed mainly at one another, he thinks of it as a pragmatic solution to an intractable problem. He admits it may not be ideal, but he believes the Yakuza is far better than the alternative—disorganized crime characterized by random attacks such as those that plague other developed nations. He may have a point. Since Japan launched its Yakuza crackdown a decade ago, serious crime has soared by 70 percent. The arrest rate for such crimes has fallen to 70 percent from 90 percent, and the police have been plagued by a snowballing series of cover-ups and scandals.

"If a gang of young thugs turns up and starts causing trouble, the Yakuza go out and sort them out because it's bad for business," says Ichiro Senda, a former mid-ranking Yamaguchi-gumi boss who once worked under Watanabe. "But if the Yakuza are gone who'll there be to make sure punks don't terrorize ordinary people. The police? I wouldn't count on it."

See also: TAOKA, KAZUO; YAKUZA; YAMAGUCHI-GUMI.

Reference

David Amoruso. "Yoshinori Watanabe." Gangsters Incorporated. Available online. URL: http://gangstersinc. tripod.com/Watanabe.html. Downloaded on July 15, 2004.

—*D.A.*

WATERHOUSE Posse

The name of this posse derives from the fact that many of its members are from the Waterhouse area of Kingston, Jamaica. Members and associates of the Waterhouse Posse have been arrested in Jersey City and Mount Laurel, New Jersey. Between 1983 and early 1985 a small cell of the Waterhouse Posse operated a marijuana distribution network in Trenton. The principal operatives of this network were Dennis Derrick Dobson and Daniel Augustus Comrie, both of Willingboro, who were arrested in 1985 for attempting to bribe a Trenton police officer to protect their operation on South Clinton Avenue. On June 4, 1990, Dennis Dobson was arrested by police in Bristol Township, Pennsylvania, for operating a cocaine and crack distribution network out of the Venice-Ashby housing project in the township. Dobson's operation sold cocaine and crack through street operatives in lower Bucks County, Pennsylvania, and Trenton, New Jersey.

Since about 1989 the term *posse* has become popular with non-Jamaican gangs, due to the publicity surrounding the Jamaican groups. In many urban areas, for instance, African-American youth gangs have adopted the term *posse*. Meanwhile, many of the real Jamaican posses have started to call their groups *massives*. Many of the second-tier members have started using the term *crews* to describe their cells or drug distribution networks. For example, at a public hearing a disguised Jamaican witness identi-

fied a New York City group, calling itself the Tower Hill Crew, led by a Jamaican named Bonnie Wizzie. By the end of 1989, entrepreneurial considerations had become more important than political allegiances in running the posses. As members of the old guard of the posse leadership are either killed or jailed, younger members, some of them second-generation immigrants who are less attuned to the gang warfare and politics of Kingston, are taking over. The emphasis now is on practical concerns, such as who is able to supply the drugs and at what price.

See also: DUNKIRK BOYS POSSE; E'PORT POSSE; FIVE PERCENTERS; TEL AVIV POSSE.

Reference

New Jersey State Commission of Investigation, Robert J. Clark, Francis A. Betzler, Bruce C. Best, and Debra A. Sowney. "Afro-Lineal Organized Crime." November 29, 1990. Available online. URL: http://www.state.nj. us/sci/pdf/afro.pdf. Accessed on November 24, 2004.

WAYNE Pack Group

In Trenton an African American known as Wayne Pack conducts an illegal lottery that pays off to Gambino-Gotti La Cosa Nostra (LCN) associate Anthony (Pushy) Pulcinello. Under changing leadership, this operation has been in existence since 1954. In its early years, its leaders dealt with the Bruno-Scarfo LCN family. John Gotti, Jr., currently runs the Gambino family from behind bars.

Reference

New Jersey State Commission of Investigation, Robert J. Clark, Francis A. Betzler, Bruce C. Best, and Debra A. Sowney. "Afro-Lineal Organized Crime." November 29, 1990. Available online. URL: http://www.state.nj. us/sci/pdf/afro.pdf. Accessed on November 24, 2004.

WHITE Lotus Society

A Chinese secret society that was politically motivated but was also involved in illegal activities due to their hiring of street gangs, the White Lotus Society rose up against the Manchu Dynasty, hoping to place the Ming Dynasty back into power. They also were one of the moving forces behind the Boxer Rebellion in Peking in 1896–1900. It is believed today that the White Lotus Society has gone back to its Buddhist roots and is no longer a player in serious gangland enterprises.

WILD Cowboys

In New York City, the Wild Cowboys were a Dominican youth gang known for wild violence. Formed in the mid-1980s out of a Bronx neighborhood crack operation, the gang eventually ran roughshod over the South Bronx and Washington Heights, a neighborhood in upper Manhattan.

The Wild Cowboys, through a reputation of violence and intimidation, were also able to import and distribute large amounts of illegal drugs, throughout their own territory and also become a weigh station for other parts of the East Coast through other Dominican communities.

Rick Chandler wrote, in a review of the book *Gangbusters* by Michael Stone, for *Ironminds* (September 25, 2000), "At its height, the group of Dominicans known as Wild Cowboys were running a $30,000-a-day crack franchise in locations in the South Bronx, Manhattan, and Brooklyn. Prone to savage, unexplainable violence, the Wild Cowboys operated their drug sales much like fast-food franchises—carving out territory, making drugs readily available and cheap. In the areas in which they operated, the Wild Cowboys literally ruled the streets, to the point where even the police were reluctant to go in and nose around."

They were known for extortion and drug dealing, for murdering members of rival gangs and intimidating witnesses in crime investigations, and for their wild shootouts. By 1993 the Wild Cowboys were dismantled by a series of forces including opposing gangs, police arrests (more than 40 gang members eventually were jailed), and the vicious murder of those within the organization.

References

Rick Chandler. "Busting the Gangs." Ironminds. Available online. URL: http://www.ironminds.com/ironminds/issues/000925/bookshelf.shtml. Downloaded on July 16, 2004.

Michael Stone. *Gangbusters*. New York: Doubleday, 2000.

WO Group

The Wo Group is the oldest triad in Hong Kong. The original Wo Group was the triad known as Wo Shing Wo. There are approximately 20,000 members of the Wo Group around the world. Many are of Cantonese descent. Today there are nine different subgroups of the Wo Group.

According to TheIlluminatedLantern.com, "Different subgroups have been known to 'specialize' in different activities; The Wo Shing Yee controls dockworkers, the Wo On Lok specializes in loan-sharking, the Wo Hop To runs protection rackets, and so on."

Many Wo Group members have either visited or are settling in the United States and Canada as well as South Africa in the last decade.

One of the other businesses that the Wo Group is involved in is the smuggling of women for the means of prostitution and sexual enslavement.

See also: TRIADS.

WO Hop To

The Wo Hop To are a triad that immigrated from Hong Kong to San Francisco in hopes of dominating the local Asian-based organized-crime world. The rival gang to the Wah Ching, the Wo Hop To began building its organization as far back as 1989 in the Bay Area and began to recruit members and entire gangs from the area, building a very strong organization. Vietnamese, Crips, and Bloods have been known to join. Wo Hop To then began to recruit members of the rival Wah Ching. Some made the jump, and some did not. These recruiting failures led to a series of killings. In one instance, an entire gang (a small but violent one) joined the Wo Hop To, except for its leader, who was found murdered. The Wah Ching remain the number-one organized-crime syndicate in Asian-based crime in San Francisco, with the Wo Hop To right on their heels.

See also: TRIADS; WAH CHING GANG.

WONDERLAND Club (a.k.a. Operation Cathedral, Operation Chesire Cat)

Operation Cheshire Cat, a U.S. Customs investigation into a child pornography and molestation ring known as the Orchid Club, led Customs agents to the discovery in the United Kingdom of a much larger, more sophisticated child-pornography trading ring known as the Wonderland Club. Wonderland was a members-only club. Each new member had to be sponsored by a current member and was required to have at least 10,000 images of child pornography on his computer. The club had its own rules and membership committee. So far, law enforcement has arrested approximately 100 suspects in 12 countries. Leads in the Wonderland case continue to be generated.

"The Wonderland Club took its name from Lewis Carroll and its alleged clientele from Main Street, U.S.A.—including an engineer from Portland, Maine, a scientist in New Britain, Conn. Other suspected members lived in sleepy towns like Broken Arrow, Okla.; Lawrence, Kans.; and Kennebunk, Maine," wrote Elaine Shannon in *Time* magazine on September 14, 1998. Shannon pointed out that these perpetrators, like "the author of *Alice's Adventures in Wonderland,* had a scandalous predilection for photographing half-clad little girls."

Cheshire Cat was initiated in 1996 and targeted a vile group of child pornographers known as the Wonderland Club, which traded pictures and films on the Internet. "The investigation arose out of leads generated from a prior case that was directed at a similar group known as the Orchid Club. Clues from the orchid case pointed Customs toward London, where we commenced work with British law enforcement. London police executed search warrants and uncovered evidence of Wonderland's vast international connections composed of about 200 pedophiles," Commissioner Raymond W. Kelly of the U.S. Customs Service said in a speech at Georgetown University, Washington, D.C., on May 6, 1999.

The Metropolitan Police (Scotland Yard) named the investigation Operation Cathedral. On September 2, 1998, more than 107 people were simultaneously arrested by 1,500 police officers in Britain, Australia, Austria, Belgium, Finland, France, Italy, Norway, Portugal, Sweden, and the United States. The Wonderland collection contained more than "750,000 pornographic images and 1,800 computerized videos of children suffering sexual abuse," according to Alex Richardson of ABC News. According to authorities, as many as 1,263 children were exposed in the photographs, and at the time, only 17 had been identified, those being six in the United Kingdom, seven in the United States, one in Portugal, one in Chile, and one in Argentina.

Customs targeted the American members of the club. Thirty-nine raids in 32 U.S. cities were initiated, from Glen Carbon, Illinois, to Brooklyn, New York. The diversity of the places and the people involved was truly astonishing. In the end, 35 search warrants were issued, resulting in 13 arrests.

According to Kelly, "Two aspects of this case are particularly noteworthy. First, it was a coordinated, multinational enforcement effort. Simultaneous raids were conducted on the same day at a precise hour in 12 countries, including the U.S., ten western European nations, and Australia. This had to be done so as to prevent members in one country from getting tipped off in advance by members in another country, and giving the perpetrators the time to erase their hard drives before the police could arrive."

The second notable feature of Operation Cheshire Cat was the extreme technological hurdles faced by cyber-crime agents. "Wonderland members were as clever as they were twisted," noted Kelly. "Like the disappearing cat in the Lewis Carroll fantasy *Alice in Wonderland,* they often vanished from one computer server, only to reappear on another server based somewhere else in the world. Hence the origin of the name for our investigation."

The complicated and extremely well thought-out encryption technology that the ring's members used to hide their transmissions posed a substantial block to cyber agents. It turned out to be a system designed by the KGB during the cold war.

The Wonderland Club held pictures, films, and DVD movies of as many as 1,250 children, mostly under the age of 10, and featuring children as young as three months. Wonderland Club was an Internet Relay Channel (IRC) based in England. A search warrant was executed in October 1997 in the United Kingdom on Ian Baldock's home. The search warrant resulted in the seizure of 42,000 images of child pornography. A February 1998 search warrant executed on another British subject, Gary Salt, confirmed the existence of Wonderland and revealed another IRC called "Our Place."

Most of those who participated in the Wonderland Club were from the United Kingdom. Seven were convicted and sentenced to serve time. Ian Baldock, 31, from St. Leonards, East Sussex, was sentenced to two and a half years of jail time. Antoni Skinner, 36, from Cheltenham, Gloucestershire, was sentenced to 18 months. Gavin Seagers, 29, from Dartford, Kent, was sentenced to two years of prison. Ahmet Ali, 30, from Tulse Hill, South London, was jailed for two years. Frederick Stephens, 46, from Hayes, West London, was sentenced to one year's jail time. Andrew Barlow, 25, from Bletchley, Milton Keynes, Buckinghamshire, was sentenced to a two-year prison sentence. David Hines, 30, of Bognor Regis, West Sussex, was sentenced to two and a half years behind bars. Based on their greater participation in the ring, both Baldock and Hines were placed on the sex offenders register for life. The others that were convicted and sentenced also were placed on the sex offender's register but for only seven years.

According to Stephan Cape, BBC crime reporter, several in the United Kingdom were shocked by what many called soft sentences. "You would get a longer sentence for accumulating masses of parking tickets or for burglary. I am absolutely stupefied by this leniency," said Michelle Elliott, director of the child-protection charity Kidscape. "It sends a clear message that these crimes are not being taken seriously."

According to Richardson, Judge Kenneth MacRae said as he sentenced the men at Kingston Crown Court, southwest of London, "The use and abuse of children for your own perverted gratification has horrified all right-minded people." He added, "You have, directly or indirectly, exploited the most vulnerable."

According to *Time*'s Shannon, "A suspect living in a trailer park in St. Charles, Mo., was arrested after agents found, along with child porn, firearms and a stash of the black powder used to make bombs. . . . A law student in New York City threw his hard drive into a neighbor's yard (it was later discovered by a police dog). . . . An alleged club member in Allen, Texas, committed suicide last week after being served with a search warrant."

In September 1998 a search warrant was executed on Shawn C. Moseman's Coast Guard barracks room, his vehicle, and a storage area. Customs agents discovered approximately 40,000 images of child pornography and 475 movies depicting minors engaged in sexual activity. Moseman entered a guilty plea on February 6, 2001. On May 16, 2001 the U.S. attorney for the Eastern District of Virginia announced that Moseman, 30 years old, was sentenced to 135 months imprisonment and three years' supervised release for transporting child pornography.

See also: OPERATION ARTUS; OPERATION BLUE ORCHID; OPERATION CANDYMAN; OPERATION ORE.

References

Stephen Cape. "Paedophiles Jailed for Porn Ring." *BBC.* Available online. URL: http://news.bbc.co.uk/i/hi/uk/1168112.stm. Posted on February 13, 2001.

CNN. "How Police Smashed Child Porn Club." Available online. URL: http://www.cnn.com/2001/WORLD/europe/UK/02/13/paedophile.police/. Posted on February 13, 2001.

Raymond W. Kelly. "Child Pornography." (Remarks given at Georgetown University, Washington, D.C., May 6, 1999).

Elaine Shannon. "Main Street Monsters: A Worldwide Crackdown Reveals That Child Pornographers Might Just Be the People Next Door." *Time.* Available online. URL: http://www.time.com/time/archive/preview/0,19987,1101980914/139940,oo.html. Posted on September 14, 1998.

YAKUZA

HISTORY OF THE YAKUZA—FEUDAL JAPAN

The Yakuza can trace its origins back to as early as 1612, when people known as *kabuki-mono* ("crazy ones") began to attract the attention of local officials. Their odd clothing and haircuts and behavior, along with carrying longswords at their sides, made them quite noticeable. *Kabuki-mono* made a habit of antagonizing and terrorizing anyone at their leisure, even to the point of cutting one down just for sheer pleasure.

The *kabuki-mono* were eccentric samurai, taking outrageous names for their bands and speaking heavily in slang. Their loyalty to one another was remarkable. They would protect each other from any threat, including against their own families.

In fact, the *kabuki-mono* were servants of the shogun, also taking the name of *hatamoto-yakko* ("servants of the shogun"). The groups were comprised of nearly 500,000 samurai that were forced into unemployment during the time of peace during the Tokugawa era, forcing them to become *ronin* ("wave man," a masterless samurai). Many had turned into bandits, looting towns and villages as they wandered throughout Japan.

The *hatamoto-yakko* cannot truly be seen as the forebears of that Yakuza. Instead, the Yakuza see the *machi-yokko* ("servants of the town") as their ancestors. These people were the ones who took up arms and defended the villages and towns from the *hatamoto-yakko*. These people consisted of such occupations as clerks, shopkeepers, innkeepers, laborers, homeless warriors, and other *ronin*. Everyone who was part of the *machi-yokko* was an adept gambler, which helped them develop a closely-knit relationship with each other and their leaders, much like today's Yakuza.

The *machi-yokko* soon became folk heroes, praised by the townspeople for their actions against the *hatamoto-yakko*, though they were, for the most part, untrained and weaker than the *hatamoto-yakko*. They were very similar to England's Robin Hood. Some of the *machi-yokko* were even subjects of stories and plays.

The early Yakuza did not surface until the middle to late 1700s. These members include the *bakuto* (traditional gamblers) and the *tekiya* (street peddlers). These terms are still used today to describe Yakuza members, although a third group, *gurentai* (hoodlums) has been added in the post–World War II era. Everyone in those groups came from the same background: poor, landless, delinquents, and misfits. The groups stuck closely in the same small areas without problems, as the *bakuto* remained mostly along the highways and towns, and the *tekiya* operated in the markets and fairs of Japan.

The Yakuza began to organize into families, adopting a relationship known as *oyabun–kobun* (father-role/child-role). The *oyabun* was the father, providing advice, protection and help; the *kobun* acted as the child, swearing unswerving loyalty and service whenever the *oyabun* needed it.

INITIATION

The initiation ceremony for the Yakuza also developed in this period of time. Instead of the actual bloodletting that was practiced by the Mafia and the triads, the Yakuza exchanged sake cups to symbolize the entrance into the Yakuza and the *oyabun–kobun* relationship. The amounts of sake poured into each cup depended upon one's status, whether the participants were father-son, brother-brother, elder-younger, and so on. The ceremony was usually performed in front of a Shinto altar, giving it religious significance.

TEKIYA

The *tekiya's* history is still widely debated. The most widely accepted theory was that the *tekiya* came from *yashi,* an earlier word meaning "peddler." The *yashi* were traveling merchants of medicine, similar to the American West's snake-oil merchants. In time, *yashi* became a catch-all for all merchants and peddlers.

The *tekiya* united with each other for protection and mutual interest from the Tokugawa regime. They began to control the booths at fairs and markets. Their reputation for shoddy merchandise was well known and well deserved. Their salesmanship was deceptive. They lied about origins and quality of products. They would act drunk and make a show of selling their wares cheaply so that it would appear that they were unaware of what they were doing. They would delude the customer. The *tekiya* followed the usual Yakuza organization: *oyabun,* underboss, officers, enlisted, and apprentices. The *oyabun* controlled the *kobun* and the allocation of stalls along with the availability of the goods. He also collected rents and protection money and would pocket the difference between the two. Everything they did was legal work. In the middle 1700s the feudal authorities recognized and therefore increased the power of the *tekiya. Oyabun* were given the authority of supervisor, now being able to have a surname and carry two swords similar to samurai, to reduce the threat of turf wars due to widespread fraud. However, the *tekiya* still embraced some criminal traits, such as protection rackets, the harboring of fugitives and known criminals, and brawling with other *tekiya* and gangs.

BAKUTO—THE GAMBLERS

The *bakuto* were first recognized during the Tokugawa era when the government hired them to gamble with construction and irrigation workers to regain a portion of the substantial wages the workers received.

The *bakuto* contributed to Japan's tradition for gambling, as well as the Yakuza's traditional "finger-cutting," and the origin of the word *yakuza.* The word comes from a hand in a card game called *hanafuda* (flower cards), similar to blackjack. Three cards are dealt per player, and the last digit of the total counts as the number of the hand. A hand of 20, the worst score, gives the score of zero. One such losing combination is 8-9-3, or ya-ku-sa, which began to be widely used to denote something useless. This term began to be used about *bakuto,* as they were, on the whole, useless to society.

Yubitsume, the custom of finger-cutting, was introduced by the *bakuto.* The top joint of the little finger is ceremoniously severed, signifying a weakening of the hand, which meant that the gambler could not hold his sword as firmly. *Yubitsume* was performed was usually performed as an act of apology to the oyabun. Further infractions would either mean the severing of the next joint or the top section of another finger. It is also used as a lasting punishment just before expulsion.

The use of tattoos also came from the criminal aspect of the *bakuto.* Criminals were usually tattooed with a black ring around an arm for each offense he had committed. However, the tattoos soon became a test of strength, as they were applied by undergoing 100 hours for a complete back tattoo. The tattoo also marked a misfit, always unwilling to adapt themselves to society.

MODERNIZATION OF THE YAKUZA

The Meiji Restoration, starting in 1867, gave Japan a rebirth and its first of many transformations into an industrial nation. Political parties and a parliament were created, as well as a powerful military.

The Yakuza also began to modernize, keeping in pace with a rapidly changing Japan. They recruited members from construction jobs and dockworkings. They even began to control the ricksha business. Gambling, however, had to be even more covert, as police were cracking down on bakuto gangs. The *tekiya,* unlike the *bakuto,* thrived and expanded, as their activites were not illegal, at least not on the surface.

The Yakuza began to dabble in politics, taking sides with certain politicians and officials. They cooperated with the government so they could get official sanction or at least some freedom from harassment.

The government did find a use for the Yakuza—as aid to ultranationalists, who took a militaristic role in Japan's adaption into democracy. Various secret societies were created and trained militarily in languages, assassination, blackmail, and so on. The ultranationalist reign of terror lasted into the 1930s, consisting of several coups d'etat, the assassination of two prime ministers and two finance ministers, and repeated attacks on politicians and industrialists. The Yakuza provided muscle and men to the cause and participated in "land-development" programs in occupied Manchuria or China.

Things changed, however, when Pearl Harbor was bombed. The government no longer needed the ultranationalists or the Yakuza. Members of these groups either worked with the government, put on a uniform, or were put into jail.

OCCUPATION YEARS

The American occupation forces in postwar Japan saw the Yakuza as a primary threat to their work. They began investigations into Yakuza activities. In 1948, their work stopped as the forces thought their investigation was over and the threat was at an end or at least diminished.

However, the forces had rationed food, thereby giving the black market business to keep the gangs in wealth and power. The gangs were able to act unhindered since the civil police was unarmed. Some occupation officials even aided the Yakuza.

The *gurentai* began to form during the occupation, as there was a power vacuum in the government, as the occupation swept away the topmost layer of control in government and business. The *gurentai* could be seen as Japan's version of the mob, its leader similar to what Al Capone was to the mob. They dealt in black marketeering, for the most part, but also they went so far as to use threat, extortion, and violence in their activities. Their members were the unemployed and the repatriated. The government used one *gurentai* as a controller of Korean labor, even though he was apprehended with criminal items.

The occupation forces soon saw that the Yakuza was well organized and continuing to operate under

two *oyabun* supported by unidentified high-level government officials. They admitted defeat in 1950, as they realized that they could not protect the Japanese people from the Yakuza.

In the postwar years, the Yakuza became more violent, both on the individual and collective scales. Swords had become a thing of the past, and guns were now becoming the new weapon of choice. They chose ordinary citizens, not just the other vendors or gamblers or specific group targets anymore, as their targets for shakedowns and robberies.

Their appearances also changed, taking American movie gangsters (a la *Guys and Dolls*) as their influence. They started wearing sunglasses, dark suits, and ties with white shirts and began to sport crewcuts.

Between the years of 1958 and 1963, the number of Yakuza members rose by more than 150 percent, to 184,000 members, more than the Japanese army. There were some 5,200 gangs operating throughout Japan. Yakuza gangs began to stake out their territories, and bloody and violent wars began to break out between them.

KODAMA

The man who brought peace between many of the Yakuza factions was named Yoshio Kodama.

Kodama was in jail for the early part of the occupation, placed in the same section as cabinet officers, military, and ultranationalists. He himself was part of the ultranationalist group *Kenkoku-kai* (Association of the Founding of the Nation). In the late 1930s and early 1940s he worked as an espionage agent for the Japanese government, touring East Asia. He worked on a major operation to obtain strategic material needed for the Japanese war effort.

By the end of the war, he had obtained the rank of rear admiral (an impressive feat at the age of 34), and was advisor to the prime minister. He was rounded up with other government officials in 1946 and placed in Sugamo Prison to await trial. The occupation forces saw Kodama as a high security risk, should he ever be released, due to his fanaticism with the ultranationalists.

Kodama had made a deal with the occupation forces G-2 section (intelligence corps), and upon his release, was working for the U.S. Army. He was the principal go-between for G-2 and the Yakuza by 1950.

In the early 60s, Kodama wanted the Yakuza gangs, who were now fighting one another, to join together into one giant coalition. He deplored the warfare, seeing it as a threat to anticommunist unity. He used many of his connections to secure a truce between the gangs. He made a fast alliance between Kazuo Taoka, *oyabun* of the Yamaguchi-gumi faction, and Hisayuki Machii, a Korean crimeboss in charge of Tosei-kai. The alliance broke the Kanto-kai faction for good. Kodama continued to use his influence to mediate the alliance between the Inagawa-kai and its Kanto allies and Yamaguchi-gumi. The truce that Kodama had envisioned was now at hand.

Yoshio Kodama was then referred to as the Japanese underworld's visionary godfather.

MODERN YAKUZA

The *oyabun* to the Yamaguchi-gumi from the mid 1940s until his death in 1981 was Kazuo Taoka. He was the third *oyabun* of the faction.

Taoka had survived many assassination attempts, including one in 1978, when he was shot in the neck by a member of the Matsuda (a rival Yakuza clan who had sworn vengeance on the Yamaguchi-gumi for the death of their *oyabun*) during a limbo dance exhibition at the Yamaguchi-gumi household.

The Yamaguchi-gumi is Japan's most powerful syndicate. Their symbol is a rhombus-shaped pin worn on the lapel of their suits. The combination of the pin plus the showing of their tattoos could get them anything they wanted.

However, the pin was not always as powerful as they seemed. In 1980, when the Yamaguchi-gumi attempted to expand their territory into Hokkaido, they were met at the Sapporo airport by 800 members of local gangs who united to keep the Yamaguchi-gumi out of their area. Nearly 2,000 police officers kept the two groups apart. The Yamaguchi-gumi were prevented from opening their headquarters in Sapporo.

In July 1981 Taoka suffered and died from a heart attack, ending his 35-year rule as *oyabun*. His death was celebrated by his Yakuza underlings in the finest Yakuza style. Police raided Yamaguchi-gumi homes and offices across Japan, arresting 900 members, and taking such contraband as firearms, swords, and amphetamines.

The funeral was grand indeed, bringing in members from nearly 200 gangs, singers, actors, musicians, and even the police (who attended dressed in riot gear).

Taoka's successor was to be his number-two man, Yakamen. However, he was in prison and was not due to be released until late 1982. During the absence of Yakamen, everyone (including the police) was surprised to see that the new temporary leader was Taoka's widow, Fumiko. However, Yakamen did not succeed Taoka, for he died of cirrhosis of the liver. The entire structure of Yamaguchi-gumi was now in chaos.

The Yamaguchi-gumi controlled more than 2,500 businesses, sophisticated gambling, and loan sharking and invested heavily in sports and other entertainment under Taoka's 35-year rule as *oyabun*. They operated under the same patterns that had existed for the Yakuza for more than 300 years, basically depending upon the *oyabun-kobun* relationship that controlled the day-to-day management of the syndicate. The syndicate was grossing much more than $460 million per year. Their management style was envied by such organizations as the Mafia and General Motors.

The Yamaguchi-gumi had 103 bosses of various rank from many more than 500 gangs. Each of these bosses fared well, making more than $130,000 annually. A syndicate head would make $43,000 per month ($360,000 annually after deducting $13,000 per month for entertainment and office expenses). Of course, this would depend on the number of soldiers the boss had under him.

The Yamaguchi-gumi began to deal in drugs now, primarily amphetamines. Other fields of choice brought in a high capital: moneylending, smuggling, and pornography (hard pornography is illegal in Japan). Rigging baseball games, horse races, and public-property auctions were commonplace for Yakuza. Seizing real estate, entertainment halls, hospitals, and English schools were also done by the Yakuza.

During Fumiko Taoka's rule, the membership of Yamaguchi-gumi rose to 13,346 members from 587 gangs by the end of 1983. Their control stretched to 36 of Japan's 47 prefectures. A council of eight high-ranking bosses took control, under the guidance of Fumiko Taoka, in 1983. However, the syndicate had to select a new godfather. Masahisa Takenaka became the new *oyabun*, as everyone preferred his militant style over Hiroshi Yamamoto's (his opponent) *interi* (intellectual) Yakuza.

Yamamoto, in a fit of anger after losing, took 13,000 men from the Yamaguchi-gumi and created the Ichiwa-kai, one of Japan's top three syndicates. In 1985, Ichiwa-kai assassins slaughtered Takenaka, creating a bloody gang war.

Kazuo Nakanishi became the new *oyabun* for Yamaguchi-gumi and declared war on the Ichiwa-kai. Police interfered and arrested nearly a thousand mobsters and confiscated many weapons. The Yamaguchi-gumi was desperate to win, so they turned to operations in the United States to fund their war. They had obtained many highly illegal weapons, including rocket launchers and machine guns, in exchange for narcotics; however, the conspirators were arrested, including Masashi Takenaka, Masahisa's brother, and Hideomi Oda, the syndicate's financial controller. The Yamaguchi-gumi was thrown back into chaos.

YAKUZA STRUCTURE

The structure of the Yakuza is easy to follow, once the *oyabun-kobun* relationship is understood. As an example to explain the structure of command of a Yakuza clan, the Yamaguchi-gumi (as of November 1991) will be used.

The *oyabun*, Yoshinori Watanabe, is the head of the clan, residing at the Yamaguchi-gumi headquarters in Kobe. He obtained the position of the fifth *oyabun* (or *kumicho*, supreme boss) in 1989. His original gang was the Kobe-based Yamaken-gumi.

Kazuo Nakanishi remains as a *saiko komon*, or a senior advisor. He resides in Osaka, with 15 sub-gangs under his control, giving him 439 members.

Saizo Kishimoto is the *so-honbucho*, the headquarters chief, with six gangs (108) members under his control in Kobe.

Masaru Takumi is the *wakagashira*, or number-two man. He controls 941 members in 41 gangs in Osaka.

Testuo Nogami is the *fuku-honbucho*, an assistant, with eight gangs (164 members) in Osaka.

Under the kumicho are various *komon* (advisors), *shingiin* (counselors), *kumicho hisho* (*kumicho's* secretaries), *kaikei* (accountants), and *wakagashira-hosa* (underlings of the second-in-command).

Keisuke Masuda is the number-three man (*shateigashira*), residing in Nagoya with four gangs consisting of 111 members under his care. He also has several *shateigashira-hosa* to aid him.

There are 102 senior bosses (*shatei*, "younger brothers") and numerous junior leaders (*wakashu*, "young men"), making up then 750 gangs with 31,000 members in the Yamaguchi-gumi.

THE YAKUZA AND TODAY'S JAPAN

Today's Japan does not appreciate the "noble" workings of the Yakuza. In fact, on March 1, 1992, the Japanese government passed the Act for Prevention of Unlawful Activities by Boryokudan (Yakuza or criminal gangs) Members.

This act designates the term *Boryokudan* as a group with more that a certain percentage of membership having a criminal record. It also identifies organizations with strong violent or criminal tendencies.

The act mainly prohibits the Boryokudans from realizing profits made from forms of extortion not covered in previous existing laws, that is, protection rackets.

The Yakuza is avoiding being called a Boryokudan, mostly by trying to hide behind actual businesses they use as fronts. They have also published a book entitled *How to Evade the Law,* which was distributed among the members of the Yamaguchi-gumi. In fact, 77 gangs affiliated with the Yamaguchi-gumi are registered as businesses or religious organizations.

In March 1992 wives and daughters of Yakuza members marched in protest of the new laws through the Ginza. The following month, high-ranking Yakuza argued that they are not truly evil; their code of chivalry (similar to *bushido*, the Way of the Warrior) and samurai values calls upon them to defend the interests of society's weaker members, and their conduct expresses their noble values, not violence.

However, these arguments were proven wrong in the public eye when members of the Yakuza ambushed and stabbed filmmaker Itami Juzo over an anti-Yakuza movie entitled *Minbo no Onna* (A Woman Yakuza Fighter). A Boryokudan defector commented on the attack and was later found shot in the leg.

Even outsiders of the Yakuza have protested the new laws against them. More than 130 lawyers, professors, and Christian ministers proclaimed that the Yakuza countermeasures were unconstitutional, basically on the grounds that they infringed basic rights, such as the freedom of assembly, the choice of occupation, and the ownership of property.

In fact, even ordinary citizens are against the Yakuza. Citizens of the neighborhood of Ebitsuka, a neighborhood of Hamamatsu, 130 miles southwest of Tokyo, did not want Yakuza activity in their backyard. The Yakuza were operating out of a green building, that the neighbors quickly termed as *burakku biru* ("black building"). The citizens video-taped everyone who went in and out of the building, noting specifically the ones wearing flashy suits, dark glasses, short hair, and hints of tattoos on their arms. The Yakuza retaliated against the citizens, smashing windows of the local garage mechanic, stabbing the town's lawyer in the lung, and slashing another activist in the throat.

However, after police arrested half of the gang, the Ichiri Ikka, led by Tetsuya Aono, abandoned the *burakku biru* in an out-of-court settlement, as they did not want to stir up trouble for gangsters elsewhere.

YAKUZA IN BUSINESS AND POLITICS

The Yakuza has been involved in politics and business right from the start. The groups are always hungry for more power and money, wherever they can find it.

In 1987 Noboru Takeshita was elected prime minister in Japan. There were always suspicions of gangster ties in the election. When questioned on the accusations in 1992, Takeshita denied knowing at the time that the Yakuza were involved. What happened was this: During one of his speeches, a group was blaring comments against Takeshita. Some other group of people had silenced the commentators.

The Liberal Democratic Party kingmaker was made to resign from politics in October 1992 when he admitted to receiving Y500 million ($4 million) from a delivery firm, Sagawa Kyubin. The owner of the firm, Hiroyasu Watanabe, paid the kingmaker for trying to help save his business. Watanabe admitted to asking Susumu Ishii, the late head of the Inagawa-kai, to silence the group. Susumu called in a gang from Kyoto, the Aizu Kotetsu, to do the job. Aizu Kotetsu had a grudge against Takeshita due to a confidence job (paying Y4 billion for a Y500 million gold screen). Takeshita denied the screen deal, although money from it was given to his secretary.

Shigeaki Isaka, who was very close to the leader of Aizu Kotetsu, would help Takeshita win the election to have a hold over him, possibly for future blackmail.

There is another Yakuza incident that hits closer to home. West Tsusho, a Tokyo-based real estate firm, bought two American companies with help from none other than Prescott Bush, Jr., President George Bush, Sr.'s, elder brother. What was not known at the time was that West Tsusho was an arm of a company run by the Inagawa-kai's leader, Ishii Susumu.

Tsusho purchased Quantum Access, a Houston-based software firm, and Asset Management International Financing and Settlement, a New York City–based company.

Bush received a $250,000 finder's fee for Asset Management, as was promised and another $250,000 per year for three years in consulting fees. Bush was unaware at the time that he was being a middleman for mob activity.

A BLEAK FUTURE?

With the anti-Yakuza countermeasure act in place, the future for the Yakuza seems bleak, at least in Japan. The North American expansion could do very well, as they channel nearly $10 billion into legitimate investments not only in the United States, but in Europe as well.

The Federal Bureau of Investigation is gearing up to handle the new threat from the Yakuza. However, their investigations will be difficult, as the Yakuza can operate though shell corporations without the close scrutiny that hampers crooks in other companies. Also, money laundering is not a crime in Japan, so the investigations into the money angles of the Yakuza will be extremely difficult.

However, Yakuza in Japan are already seeing their future weaken. Between April 21 and May 25, 1992, police stations in many prefectures received nearly 145 calls from gangsters and their families asking advice on how to leave the gangs and go legitimate. In response to this, more than 60 companies in Japan offered to take in reformed Yakuza as employees.

The future for the Yakuza as of right now is uncertain. Perhaps the gangs will still survive in Japan, moving back into the underground where they hid during the occupation. Perhaps they will just move their operations elsewhere, amongst the triads of southeast Asia, with whom they have had good relationships and business.

References

Janice Castro. "A Worrisome Brand of Japanese Investor." *Time.* Available online. URL: http://www.time.com/time/archive/preview/0,10987,1101920420-159441,00.html. Downloaded on July 15, 2004.

Howard G. Chua-Eoan. "Japan Thugs Beware: Citizens Rout the Yakuza." *Time.* Available online. URL: http://www.time.com/time/archive/preview/from_related/0,10

987,1101880314-148860,00.html. Downloaded on July 16, 2004.

Robert Delfs. "Feeding on the System: Gangsters Play Increasing Role in Business and Politics (Yakuza)." *Economic Review* 154 (November 1991).

David E. Kaplan and Alec Dubro. *Yakuza: Japan's Criminal Underworld, Expanded Edition.* Berkeley: University of California Press, 2003.

Eric Pooley, with S.C. Gwynne. "How George Got His Groove." *Time.* Available online. URL: http://www.time.com/time/archive/preview/0,10987,1101990621-26833,00.html. Downloaded on July 16, 2004.

Inami Shinnosuke. "Going after the Yakuza." *Japan Quarterly* 5, no. 4 (July–September 1992): 353–358.

YAMAGUCHI-GUMI

Yamaguchi-gumi is the largest gang or organized-crime syndicated classified under the Boryokudan, the modern version of the traditional Japanese Yakuza organization. Yamaguchi-gumi apparently reestablished part of its organization as the National League to Purify the Land, a nonprofit charity ostensibly dedicated to stamping out drug abuse.

See also: BORYOKUDAN; INAGAWA-KAI; SUMIYOSHI-KAI.

Reference

Parliamentary Joint Committee on the National Crime Authority. *Asian Organised Crime in Australia: A Discussion Paper by the Parliamentary Joint Committee on the National Crime Authority.* Available online. URL: http://www.aph.gov.au/senate/committee/acc_ctte/completed_inquiries/pre1996/ncaaoc/report/report5.htm. Accessed on November 24, 2004.

YAMAMOTO, Hiroshi

Hiroshi Yamamoto was a talented and well-respected, high-ranking member of the Yamaguchi-gumi. After the death of Kazuo Taoka, in 1981, Yamamoto and Masahisa Takenaka, who were bitter rivals, vied for the top spot, the *oyabun,* or godfather. Yamamoto was the smooth operator, more a clever businessman than aggressive street boss Takenaka. The old-timers picked Takenaka, and Yamamoto was enraged.

He then decided to start his own gang rather than follow Takenaka and took 13,000 men with him. A bloody civil war in the underworld was unleashed. Yamamoto called his gang the Ichiwa-kai, which the Yamaguchi-gumi hierarchy immediately saw as a rival group. Turf wars sprang up, and in an effort to bring the war to a quick end, Yamamoto planned and executed a daring assassination of Takenaka. It took place in Osaka at the home of Takenaka's mistress, but though it was successful, it brought no peace and no reunification. And it was a long time before these wounds and bloodshed were put behind both organizations, however. Today they coexist apparently with little bloodshed between them.

The Ichiwa-kai continue to operate as a separate and successful organized-crime organization, with some legitimate businesses.

See also: ICHIWA-KAI; YAKUZA; YAMAGUCHI-GUMI.

YARDIES

The term *Yardie* is a moniker given by the Jamaican people to someone recently arrived in the United Kingdom from Jamaica, which is referred to as the "back yard."

During the 1950s, while England was enjoying a postwar economic boom, the British government encouraged immigration to the country to fill existing job vacancies. As a result, many Afro-Caribbeans immigrated in search of a better standard of living. Most found unskilled employment and cheap housing in the run-down, inner-city areas. When the country's economic fortunes changed, many in this new workforce were among the first to feel the recession. Second-generation Caribbeans, in particular, found it difficult to match achievements with aspirations.

Within the low-income Afro-Caribbean communities of London, crime is not unlike that found in many major American cities. Living in poor housing—often public or "project" housing—the people comprise a disproportionately high ratio of the unemployed. Violence, usually drug related, continually plagues residents.

Over the years, police relations with residents of these communities have often been strained and, on occasion, violent. Policing ethnically sensitive and volatile areas is difficult and demanding, although considerable progress was made in developing the citizenry's trust in law enforcement.

However, the relationship between law enforcement and low-income, ethnic communities deteriorated rapidly when a new influx of immigrants arrived in the United Kingdom during the late 1970s. Unlike those who preceded them, these immigrants came as criminals, often fugitives, to earn money from crime. Gradually, these Yardies distinguished themselves from the local communities.

YARDIE PROFILE
Yardies are generally single males between the ages of 18 and 35. They are usually unemployed, often by choice, although some will claim to be involved in the music business as singers, musicians, record producers or promoters, or disc jockeys when challenged. Although determining the nationality of those who arrive is difficult, Jamaica is by far the predominant country of origin. Entering the country as tourists or to "visit relatives," Yardies usually assume false identities and carry forged credentials. Many have criminal convictions or are wanted by the police. Because they are known only by their street names to their associates, they are extremely difficult to identify. Some travel on false or fraudulently obtained British passports.

PATTERN OF IMMIGRATION
The United Kingdom became an attractive destination for Yardies because of its long-standing association with its former colonies in the Caribbean. Both share a common language and many cultural, social, sporting, and religious values—factors upon which legitimate immigration is built.

Unfortunately, with the immigration of convicted criminals and fugitives, a criminal infrastructure arose within the community that is hostile toward the police and provides a refuge for fugitives. Clubs, bars, and house parties that tend to imitate Jamaican street life provide the venues for crime.

Even though Yardies find support in these established ethnic communities, the United Kingdom is not the destination of choice for them; that honor is bestowed on the United States. However, as Jamaican violence and drug trafficking has grown, U.S. immigration authorities and other federal agencies have become aware of the dangers posed by Jamaican gangs. The United States has made it increasingly difficult for Jamaican criminals to gain entry into the country; consequently, they have been forced to look elsewhere, particularly to the United Kingdom. In many cases, though, Britain has simply become the staging point for entry into the United States on fraudulently obtained British passports.

YARDIES AND DRUGS
Once in the United Kingdom, the Yardies who assimilate into the community usually become involved in drug-related crime. Such crime is primarily introspective; that is, it is the community itself that is damaged the most. Drug sales are made predominantly to other residents; violence, usually drug related, is directed toward those who live there. Inevitably, and no doubt as a direct economic necessity, the crime spills over into other areas of the community, with burglary and robbery being committed outside the defined areas to fund drug abuse.

In many ways, the cultural strengths of the Afro-Caribbean communities are being debased and abused as vehicles for serious crime. Organized Jamaican reggae parties are used frequently to conduct drug transactions. International travel by couriers and traffickers is masked behind the "international culture of music." Nonauthorized radio stations are prolific advertisers of musical events where drugs are distributed.

The traditional use of marijuana has given way to cocaine and crack cocaine. Here, the methods of production and distribution of drugs emulates those of U.S. inner cities. Heavily armored doors, alarmed and protected by locks and grills, define the perimeters of drug houses. Pagers and mobile phones are common among the dealers, yet the greatest concern is the increasing use of firearms.

FIREARMS IN THE UNITED KINGDOM
For the most part, British police are unarmed. Also, access to firearms by the general public is strictly controlled. In comparison with the United States, shooting incidents are rare.

Unfortunately, there is a greater willingness among Jamaican drug dealers to settle disputes with a firearm. The fatal shooting of "Yardie Ron" on the streets of a busy London suburb during the course of dispute involving drugs evidences this fact. Eight shots were fired from three different weapons, an occurrence totally alien to the United Kingdom. In some areas where the unarmed British bobby has struggled to gain the confidence of the community, some Yardies routinely wear guns as macho displays.

YARDIE ORGANIZED CRIME
It is difficult to determine by the intelligence gathered whether Yardie or Jamaican crime is organized and comparable to other crime groups like La Cosa Nostra. Yet, one key element of organized crime—providing illegal goods or services—is clearly evident in Jamaican crime groups. Without question, these

groups are involved in supplying marijuana, cocaine, and to a certain extent, prostitutes. They also use force and violence, but here is where the analysis becomes more complex.

Traditionally, organized crime has been perceived to rely on corrupt public officials to maintain its monopoly. Yet, Jamaican crime groups do not have a monopoly or anything approaching it, nor is there any substantial evidence of them being involved in public corruption or the criminal infiltration of existing organizations, such as unions or businesses. There is also no evidence of any intent to establish quasi-legitimate corporations as fronts for criminal activities.

By far, the most vexing questions are those of leadership and group structure. Jamaican crime in the United Kingdom does not have a select group of senior figures controlling a complex, criminal pyramid. Rather, Jamaican crime groups have relatively small, flat organizational structures. The rise to the top is a relatively short step for anyone with access to drugs and the willingness to use force. In most cases, the top man not only imports the drugs but is also personally involved in street dealings.

Occasional conflicts between groups are manifested in street violence, but for the most part, groups support each other. In fact, it is not uncommon for members to belong to more than one group. Groups are not durable and frequently break up and reorganize. The dynamics of the groups are chaotic; the only common denominator is the ethnic origin of the members.

Reference

Roy A. Ramm. "The Yardies: England's Emerging Crime Problem." Gangland.net. Available online. URL: http://www.gangland.net/yardies.htm. Downloaded only July 16, 2004.

YOUNG Boys (a.k.a. YBI)

From the mid-1970s until 1982, the Young Boys was one of the most feared street gangs and organized-crime operations in the United States. Located in Detroit, Michigan, the Young Boys, Inc. as they liked to call themselves were responsible for 30 percent of all drug sales in Detroit. The law-enforcement officials estimated that the Young Boys were grossing $7.5 million a week.

Also known as the YBI, the organization was backed by drug supplier Sylvester "Seal" Murray, who was the middleman between the Young Boys and the Davis Family gang, who were the actual importers of the drug shipments. The main product was heroin. Murray and two other top YBI members were sentenced to jail in 1983. He was released in 1991 but was brought up on drug charges once again in 1993 and was sent back to prison.

YUNG-HO, Chen

Vicious leader of the Four Seas Gang, one of the most powerful gangs in Taiwan. Chen Yung-ho was shot to death in a Taipei restaurant in 1996. Many have suspected Yang Kuang-nan, a former trusted lieutenant.

See also: FOUR SEAS GANG; KUANG-NAN, YANG.

Reference

"Repatriated Gang Chief Sentenced to 22 Months." *Taipei Times.* Available online. URL: http://www.taiwanheadlines.gov.tw/20010718/2001071857.html. Posted on July 18, 2001.

ZAPINAKMINE, Oleg

Oleg Zapinakmine was the bodyguard of reputed Russian mob boss Monya Elson. On September 24, 1993, two months after the failed attempt on Monya Elson, bodyguard Oleg Zapinakmine was shot once in the back and killed by an unknown assailant. At the time he was shot, Zapinakmine was checking a flat tire on his car in front of his Brooklyn home.

See also: ELSON, MONYA; RUSSIAN MAFIYA.

Reference

New Jersey State Commission of Investigation, New York Organized Crime Task Force, New York State Commission of Investigation, Pennsylvania Crime Commission, with Rutgers University. "The Tri-State Joint Soviet-Émigré Organized Crime Project." 1992. Available online. URL: http://www.state.nj.us/sci/pdf/russian.pdf. Accessed on November 24, 2004.

ZILBERSTEYN, Vladimir

Vladimir Zilbersteyn was allegedly involved with criminal elements. Zilbersteyn was shot in the face and upper body by shotgun pellets fired from another vehicle while driving in Manhattan on November 20, 1992. The shooting was allegedly caused by a dispute with Italian mobsters involved in the bootleg motor-fuel tax scams.

See also: RUSSIAN MAFIYA.

Reference

New Jersey State Commission of Investigation, New York Organized Crime Task Force, New York State Commission of Investigation, Pennsylvania Crime Commission, with Rutgers University. "The Tri-State Joint Soviet-Émigré Organized Crime Project." 1992. Available online. URL: http://www.state.nj.us/sci/pdf/russian.pdf. Accessed on November 24, 2004.

Contributors

D.A.—David Amoruso, *Gangsters Incorporated*
(http://gangstersinc.tripod.com)

G.F.—Gary Francoeur, *Wiseguy Wally's Montreal Mafia.*
(http://www.geocities.com/wiseguywally)

M.G.—Mark Gribben, crime reporter

SEGAG—Southeastern Connecticut Gang Activities Group
(http://www.segag.org)

Index

Boldface page numbers refer to main entries. *Italic* page numbers refer to tables or illustrations.